Time Out
New York

Penguin Books

PENGUIN BOOKS

Published by the Penguin Group
Penguin Books Ltd, 27 Wrights Lane, London W8 5TZ, England
Penguin Books USA Inc., 375 Hudson Street, New York, New York 10014, USA
Penguin Books Australia Ltd, Ringwood, Victoria, Australia
Penguin Books Canada Ltd, 10 Alcorn Avenue, Toronto, Ontario, Canada M4V 3B2
Penguin Books (NZ) Ltd, 182-190 Wairau Road, Auckland 10, New Zealand

Penguin Books Ltd, Registered Offices: Harmondsworth, Middlesex, England

First published 1990
Second edition 1992
Third edition 1994
Fourth edition 1996
Fifth edition 1997
Sixth edition 1998
10 9 8 7 6 5 4 3 2 1

Colour reprographics by Precise Litho, 34–35 Great Sutton Street, London EC1
Mono reprographics printed and bound by William Clowes Ltd, Beccles, Suffolk NR34 9QE

Run, don't walk: Hoof it across the Brooklyn Bridge for a dramatic panorama of
downtown Manhattan, dominated by the twin towers of the World Trade Center.

Edited and designed by

Time Out New York
627 Broadway, seventh floor
New York, NY 10012
Tel: +1-212-539-4444
Fax:+1-212-673-8382
E-mail: letters@timeoutny.com
Internet: www.timeoutny.com

Editors Joe Angio, Cyndi Stivers **Managing Editors** Nancy E. Castro, Lisa Cindolo **Assigning Editor** Mary Jo Neuberger
Copy Editors Camille Cauti, Robert Green, Peter Keepnews, Winifred Ormond **Researchers** Kimberly Bradley,
Damien Cave, Billie Cohen, Nicole Keeter, Robin Rothman **Indexer** Winifred Ormond

Art Director Erin Wade **Designer** Bonnie Shelden **Photo Editors** Rossana Shokrian, Shana Sobel

Production Director Ayad Sinawi **Production Manager** Matthew Forrester **Systems Manager** Shambo Pfaff
Digital Operator Roopa Mascarenhas

Publisher Alison Tocci **Advertising Manager** Roger Gonzalez **Senior Advertising Sales Representative** Jim Lally
Advertising Sales Representatives Janine Brier, Dan Kenefick, Ridwana Lloyd-Bey, Lauren Miller, Tony Monteleone, Anne Perton,
Melanie B. Scherer **Junior Advertising Sales Representative** Caroline Klimerman **Advertising Production Manager** Caroline Jamieson
Advertising Production Coordinator Maria Raha

For

Time Out Guides Ltd
Universal House
251 Tottenham Court Road
London W1P OAB
Tel: +44(0)171 813 3000
Fax:+44(0)171 813 6001
E-mail: guides@timeout.co.uk
Internet: www.timeout.co.uk

Managing Editor Peter Fiennes **Series Editor** Caroline Taverne

Group Advertising Director Lesley Gill **Sales Director** Mark Phillips

Publisher Tony Elliott **Managing Director** Mike Hardwick **Financial Director** Kevin Ellis **Marketing Director** Gillian Auld
General Manager Nichola Coulthard **Production Manager** Mark Lamond

Features in this guide were written and researched by

History Frank Broughton, Robert W. Snyder, Mary Trewby **Welcome to New York** Steve Ellman, Robert Kolker, Mary Jo
Neuberger **New York by Season** Kimberly Bradley, Frank Broughton, Steve Ellman, Robert Kolker, Sue Stemp **Sightseeing**
Robert Kolker **Architecture** Frank Broughton, Steve Ellman **Museums** Robert Kolker, Sue Nelson, Linda Yablonsky **New York
by Neighborhood** Frank Broughton, Eve Claxton, Billie Cohen, Steve Ellman, Robert Kolker, Mary Jo Neuberger, Robin
Rothman **Accommodations** Kathy Passero **Eating & Drinking** Brandon Holley, Milena Damjanov, Adam Rapoport, Adam Sachs
Shopping & Services Gia Kourlas **Art Galleries** Howard Halle, Linda Yablonsky **Books & Poetry** Barbara Aria **Cabaret &
Comedy** Frank Broughton, Marisa Cohen, Elizabeth Goodman **Children** Barbara Aria **Clubs** Adam Goldstone **Dance** Gia Kourlas
Film Stephan Talty **Gay & Lesbian New York** Erik Jackson **Media** Frank Broughton, Daisy Chan, Steve Ellman, Michael
Friedson, Robert Kolker, John Sellers **Music** Matthew Dobkin, Smith Galtney, Robert Kemp, Gail O'Hara, Tom Samiljan, Ken
Smith, K. Leander Williams **Sports & Fitness** Frank Broughton, Brett Martin, Steve Ellman **Theater** Erik Jackson **Trips Out
of Town** Kimberly Bradley, Frank Broughton, Kathy McFarland **Directory** Frank Broughton, Steve Ellman, Kathy McFarland

Maps by JS Graphics, Hill View Cottage, 17 Beadles Lane, Old Oxted, Surrey RH8 9JG; maps on pages 345 and 346
reproduced by kind permission of the Metropolitan Transportation Authority.

Photography by Brian Finke, pages iii, 22, 46, 48, 50, 56, 73, 77, 86, 96, 97, 99, 102, 131, 168 (bottom), 170, 191,
212, 218, 219, 221, 237, 239, 240, 242, 245, 276, 280; Andrew Kist, pages v, 47, 80, 83, 89, 90, 113, 117, 119, 141,
144, 149, 152, 154, 158, 163, 168 (top), 179, 196, 225, 228, 243, 251, 253, 278; Jeremy Saladyga, pages 19, 21, 24,
26, 35, 37, 39, 42, 59, 84, 85, 87, 91, 101, 103, 104, 106, 111, 127, 133, 137, 143, 147, 151, 153, 160, 165, 167,
173, 181, 185, 255, 271, 283. **Additional photography by** Culver Pictures, pages 3, 4, 5, 6, 8, 11, 14; Public Theater,
page 9; New York Historical Society, page 12; Archive Photos, page 15; Berenice Abbott, page 16; Allen Ginsberg Trust
courtesy of Fahey/Klein Gallery, page 17; Diane Bondareff, page 18; The New York Yankees, pages 27, 275; Donal F.
Holway, page 29; courtesy of Macy's, page 30, 32; New York Road Runners Club, page 33; New York Convention and
Visitors Bureau, pages 38, 41, 54, 57, 65, 93, 95, 105, 307; Scott Jones, pages 45, 192; Casey Cronin, page 55; Peter
Aarons/ESTO, pages 60, 68; Museum of the City of New York, page 61; Fred George, page 62, 71; Mick Hales, page 63;
John Berens, page 68 (top); Leo Sorel, page 75; David Herald, page 79; Brian Rose, page 93; Joe Pineiro/Columbia
University, page 98; Steve Laise, page 100; Terry Deroy Gruber, page 109; Sharon Risedorph Photography, page 177; Joan
Marcus, page 201, 285, 287; Teri Slotkin, page 202; Pace Wildenstein, page 203; Michael Moran, page 206; Greene
Naftali Gallery, page 209; Nancy Crampton, page 211; Rahav Segev, page 215; Shannon Lee Parker, page 216; Christine
Wong, page 223; Josef Astor, page 232; Howard Schatz, page 234; Mira Armstrong, page 235; Muky Munkacsi, page 238;
Alida Montanez, page 249; Todd Plitt, page 257, 264; Robert Smith, page 266; Winnie Klotz/Metropolitan Opera, page 267;
David Atlas, page 262; Chris Lee, page 272; Fred George for Chelsea Piers, page 278; Mary Gearhart, page 290; Moses
Edwin Clay Berkson, page 291; Beverlie Leano, page 294; Steve Goodman, page 297; Atlantic City Convention and Visitors
Authority, page 299; Ted Speigel, page 300; Russ Clune, page 303; National Baseball Hall of Fame, page 305; New York
Racing Association, page 306; Charles Phillips, page 343.

Contents

*Do the Watusi: Young clubgoers get down and get funky at the **Tunnel** on the West Side.*

About the Guide

The *Time Out New York Guide* is one of an expanding series of city guides that includes London, Paris, Amsterdam, Rome, Prague, San Francisco, Los Angeles and Miami. They're published by the company responsible for *Time Out*, London's leading arts and entertainment magazine. This edition was a joint effort with sister weekly *Time Out New York*.

Our writers aim to provide you with all the information you'll need to take on the world's most exciting city—and win. The guide has been completely updated for this sixth edition: Some chapters have been rewritten from scratch, all have been thoroughly revised and new features have been added. A series of color maps of Manhattan and other areas has also been included.

CHECKED AND CORRECT

We've tried to make this book as useful as possible. Addresses, telephone numbers, transportation tips, opening times, admission prices and credit card information are all included in our listings. We've given up-to-date details on facilities, services and events, all checked and correct at press time. However, owners and managers can—and often do—change their policies. It's always best to call and check the when, where and how much.

PRICES

The prices we've given should be treated as guidelines, not gospel. Fluctuating exchange rates and inflation can cause prices, especially in stores and restaurants, to change overnight. If you find things altered beyond recognition, ask why—and then write to let us know. We aim to give the best and most up-to-date advice, so we always appreciate feedback.

CREDIT CARDS

The following abbreviations have been used for credit cards: **AmEx**: American Express; **DC**: Diners' Club; **Disc**: Discover; **JCB**: Japanese Credit Cards; **MC**: Mastercard (Access); **V**: Visa (Barclaycard). Nearly all shops, restaurants and attractions accept dollar traveler's checks issued by a major financial institution (such as American Express).

TELEPHONE NUMBERS

All telephone numbers in this guide are written as dialed from Manhattan. We have included the '1'

There's an online version of this guide, together with weekly events listings for New York and other international cities, at www.timeout.co.uk.

and the three-figure code you must dial if calling a location off the island. The code for Brooklyn, Queens, Staten Island and the Bronx is 718; for Long Island it's 516. To call a Manhattan number from anywhere off the island, preface the number listed with 1-212 (917 indicates a cellular phone or pager). Since there are too many phones and not enough 212 numbers to go around, a new 646 prefix is soon to be given to all new Manhattan numbers; all Manhattan calls will then require eleven digits (1 + prefix + local number). Numbers preceded by 1-800, 1-888 or 1-877 can be dialed free of charge from anywhere in the United States.

THINGS YOU SHOULD KNOW

While navigating through this guide and the city, there are a few facts you should know. Throughout the book, we have bold-faced information (place or restaurant names, for example) that is particularly important or referred to elsewhere in the guide.

New York City law requires that all facilities constructed after 1987 provide complete disabled access, including restrooms and entrances/exits. In 1990, the American Disabilities Act made the same requirements federal law. In the wake of this legislation, many owners of older buildings have voluntarily added disabled-access features. Due to the widespread compliance, we have not specifically noted the availability of disabled facilities in our listings. However, it's a good idea to call ahead and check. (For additional information on disabled access, *see chapter* **Directory**.)

The 1995 NYC Smoke-Free Air Act makes it illegal to smoke in virtually all public places, including subways, movie theaters and most restaurants—even if there isn't a NO SMOKING sign displayed. Exceptions are bars and restaurants with fewer than 35 indoor seats, although large restaurants can have separate regulated smoking areas. Smokers can be fined at least $100 for a violation, so be sure to ask before you light up.

RIGHT TO REPLY

The information we give is based on the editorial judgment of our writers. No organization has been included because it has advertised in our publications. We hope you enjoy the *Time Out New York Guide*, but please let us know if you don't. We welcome tips for places that you think we should include in future editions as well as criticism of our choices. There's a reader's report card at the back of this book.

Horsing around: The most romantic way to tour Central Park is in a horse-drawn carriage.

In Context

Key Events

1524 Giovanni da Verrazano is the first European to visit what is now Manhattan.

1570 Hiawatha's Five Nations alliance brings together the Iroquois tribes. They declare war on the Algonquin.

1600 The Algonquin are all but defeated.

1609 Henry Hudson sails into the bay.

1613 A trading post is established at Fort Nassau (now Albany).

1624 The colony of New Amsterdam is founded, and the first settlers arrive.

1626 Peter Minuit, the first governor, arrives and "buys" Manhattan from the Indians. New Amsterdam has a population of 300.

1637 William Kieft, the governor, antagonizes the native population, precipitating a war between the Dutch and the Indians.

1643 Peter Stuyvesant is made governor.

1644 Manuel de Gerrit is the first free black man to settle in New York, farming an area of what is now Soho.

1661 The Dutch colony is nearly bankrupt.

1662 John Bowne's struggle wins the people of New Amsterdam the right of religious freedom.

British rule and independence

1664 The British invade. New Amsterdam is renamed New York.

1700 New York's population is around 20,000.

1725 *The Gazette* is New York's first newspaper.

1733 The *New-York Weekly Journal*, a more independent paper, establishes the right to free speech.

1754 King's College (now Columbia University) is founded.

1774 Colonial delegates set up the Continental Congress and urge people to withhold taxes and arm themselves.

1776 The Declaration of Independence is adopted. The Revolutionary War rages; the British occupy New York.

1783 The defeated British army leaves New York.

1785–90 New York serves as the new nation's capital.

1789 George Washington is elected the United States' first president.

Birth of a city

1811 The Randel Plan envisages the geographical grid system that prescribes how the city ought to grow.

1812–14 America fights another war with Britain. New York is isolated from international trade.

1837 Financial panic ruins all but three city banks.

1843 Immigrants flood into the city.

1851 *The New York Times* is first published.

1858 Central Park is laid out.

1859 Cooper Union, the city's foremost political forum, is established.

1860 Abraham Lincoln is elected president.

1861 Civil war erupts over the issue of slavery.

1863 Conscription causes riots in New York.

1865 The Union (the North) wins, and slavery is ended.

1870 The Metropolitan Museum of Art is founded.

1872 Organized labor strikes for an eight-hour day.

1883 The Brooklyn Bridge is completed.

1886 The Statue of Liberty is unveiled.

1895 Photojournalist Jacob Riis publishes *How the Other Half Lives*, spurring new housing regulations. The New York Public Library is founded.

1898 New York City—comprising Manhattan, Brooklyn, Queens, Staten Island and the Bronx—is incorporated, creating the world's second-largest city.

Modern times

1902 The Flatiron, the world's first skyscraper, is built.

1907 Metered taxicabs are introduced.

1911 The Triangle Shirtwaist Factory fire sparks the introduction of workplace safety regulations.

1917 America enters WWI.

1920 Women win the right to vote. Prohibition bans alcohol.

1929 The Wall Street stock market crash on October 29 plunges the nation into the Great Depression. The Museum of Modern Art opens nine days later.

1930s Roosevelt's New Deal funds massive public works schemes. The Empire State Building, Chrysler Building and Rockefeller Center are built.

1939 Corona Park, Queens, hosts the World's Fair.

1941 America enters WWII.

1946 The United Nations is established in New York.

1947 The Brooklyn Dodgers' Jackie Robinson breaks the color barrier in major league baseball.

1959 The Guggenheim Museum opens.

1962 Lincoln Center opens.

1977 A 25-hour citywide power blackout causes a spike in the birth rate nine months later.

1968 A student sit-in shuts down Columbia University.

1970 The World Trade Center is built.

1975 The city goes bankrupt.

1978 Mayor Ed Koch presides over a short-lived economic turnaround.

1987 The other Wall Street crash.

1990 David Dinkins is the city's first black mayor.

1991 The city's budget deficit hits a record high.

1993 Terrorists attempt to blow up the World Trade Center. Rudolph Giuliani becomes the city's first Republican mayor in 28 years. Staten Islanders vote to secede from New York City—but don't.

1997 A new wave of immigration peaks. The Dow Jones average tops 7000. The murder rate hits a 30-year low. Disney arrives on 42nd Street.

1998 The Dow Jones average soars above 9000. New York City falls to 37th on the list of most dangerous urban centers; Bugs Bunny and Warner Bros. join Mickey Mouse and Disney in Times Square.

History

A short course in New York's milestones, as the city evolved from small Native American settlement to seething modern metropolis

The first New Yorkers

Two distinct groups of Native Americans lived and flourished in the area around New York long before Europeans arrived. The Algonquin and the Iroquois had established complex communities, along with their own languages and cultures, and occasionally fought each other. The arrival of Dutch and, later, British traders and settlers, who brought with them genocidal attitudes and foreign illnesses, swiftly decided the fate of these Native Americans. Apart from various Algonquin place names—such as Canarsie and Mannahatta, the original name for a certain 13-mile-long island—Europeans allowed little trace of New York's earlier inhabitants to remain.

The Native Americans of the New York region lived in longhouses covered in bark. They cultivated fields of corn, squash, potatoes, beans and peas; grew tobacco; planted fruit orchards; and raised domesticated animals and livestock. In the winter, they supplemented their diet by hunting. Clothes were made of cured skins, often fringed and decorated with complicated beadwork.

The women cooked, cleaned, grew crops and raised the children, while their men went out to fight and hunt. But the women were the center of the community. The tribes were organized into matrilineal family units, called *owachira,* with the eldest woman at the head. Husbands lived with their wives' families, the women owned all the marriage property—land, house and chattel—and name and property were inherited through the female line.

Dutch treaty: The settlers from Holland made a pact with the Indians at Fort Amsterdam.

So good they named it twice

The Big Apple? Fun City? There are lots of sobriquets for this town.

"The Naked City," "the City that never sleeps," "Babylon on the Hudson"—New York, New York (for city and state) has been named many more times than twice.

The first name, **Mannahatta,** or Manhattan, was given to the sheltered island by its original tenants, the Algonquin Indians. Centuries later, the Brooklyn-born poet Walt Whitman would praise the moniker: " 'Mannahatta, the place encircled by many swift tides and sparkling waters.' How fit a name for America's great democratic island city!"

When the Dutch moved, in the name became **New Amsterdam,** which gained currency after about 1624, when the first settlers began arriving. The settlement wasn't called **New York** until August 1664, when four British warships were welcomed into town and Captain Richard Nicolls signified British rule by honoring Charles II's brother, the Duke of York.

Besides its official appellations, New York has had many names in fact, fiction and fantasy. Gotham, its comic-book alter ego (the city Batman inhabits) is a name taken from a village near Nottingham famous for its insane residents (Gotham actually means "goat town"). It was coined in 1807 in a satirical story by Washington Irving, who noticed, as many have since, that New Yorkers work hard to preserve an impressive level of madness. The satire is subtle, since the original Gothamites were only feigning insanity in order to avoid King John's taxation.

The **Big Apple,** meaning "the pinnacle," was a phrase popularized around the 1920s. It was used by actors and musicians (especially jazz folk) to signify that performing in New York represented the height of success. In 1971, the nickname was given a boost when the city began using it to market itself to tourists, replacing the less successful 1960s campaign that christened New York **Fun City** (a moniker that was the subject of much derision).

Metropolis, alluding to the city of the future, was the title of Fritz Lang's 1926 film about a fascistic society that exploited its workers (against a backdrop of skyscrapers and flying cars). The same name was used for Superman's hometown, a thinly veiled version of New York.

In the real future, as suburban communities sprawl over the naked countryside and the notion of a city center is killed by telecommuting, New Yorkers could find themselves living in a gigantic conurbation extending from Boston to Washington, D.C. William Gibson, who coined the term "cyberspace," has written about this scenario, giving New York surely the last name it will need–**the Sprawl.**

Time flies: Old New Amsterdam (top) and Fritz Lang's movie Metropolis, *circa 1926.*

Leisure time was spent playing games like lacrosse (played with a solid-headed curved bat, and balls made of deer hide), and a type of football, both played on large fields without boundaries and with any number of players. Fierce competitions occasionally resulted in injuries. Teams would train hard before an important game, lots of bets would be placed, and the winners would be the heroes of the hour.

HIAWATHA AND THE FIVE NATIONS

The Iroquois enjoyed a powerful political structure, thanks to the Five Nations alliance, a confederacy of the Mohawk, Seneca, Onondaga, Cayuga and Oneida tribes. This was created around 1570, when Hiawatha, the warrior-turned-pacifist immortalized in verse by Henry Longfellow, united these previously feuding tribes. The resulting confederacy controlled a huge swath of the northern U.S., from the Mississippi River to New England.

Not long before the coming of the Europeans, the Iroquois engaged the Algonquin in a series of bloody wars. When the Dutch began trading firearms for fur, the Five Nations ensured their victory by arming themselves with guns.

The war was long and bloody, bringing great losses to both sides. The conflict lasted until the mid-1600s, when the Native Americans found themselves confronting a powerful new enemy—the colonizing Europeans.

MASSACRES AND LAND THEFT

In 1609, the explorer Henry Hudson described how the Indians welcomed him and his crew in the waters off Manhattan: "This day the people of the country came aboard of us, seeming very glad of our coming." Little could the Native Americans have dreamed that these friendly intruders would ultimately bring about their destruction.

The treatment of the Native American is a tragedy in both colonial and U.S. history. Native land was appropriated through treachery and gunpowder, and European diseases and alcohol wiped out whole tribes. The 19th century was probably the darkest period for the country as a whole, with massacres, forced relocations and the wholesale theft of Indian land. In New York, the devastation occurred much earlier, and few Indians remained alive after the 18th century.

Ironically, the U.S. Constitution mirrors the unique political structure that Hiawatha created for the Five Nations confederacy—with states, like the Iroquois tribes, being both independent and interdependent. But the fundamental rights of liberty and property later enshrined in America's defining document were not accorded the original Native American inhabitants.

Old man river: Henry Hudson sailed right in.

THE "DISCOVERERS"

Christopher Columbus never set eyes on what is now New York City. The first European to do so was Giovanni da Verrazano in 1524. A Florentine sailing under the French flag and searching for the fabled Northwest Passage to China, Verrazano took refuge from a storm in what is now New York Harbor and later took a small boat into the Upper Bay, where he was greeted by the local Indians.

It was a full 85 years later when the next European arrived. Henry Hudson was employed by the Dutch East India Company, a purely commercial concern involved in the romance of discovery only when it furthered the company's economic gains.

Hudson, too, was searching for the Northwest Passage. He sailed his ship, the *Half-Moon*, up the river that now bears his name, as far as Fort Nassau (today the state capital, Albany). The log book of the *Half-Moon* relates that Hudson and his crew found "friendly and polite people who had an abundance of provisions, skins, and furs of martens and foxes, and many other commodities, such as birds and fruit, even white and red grapes, and they traded amicably with the peoples."

DUTCH RULE

In 1611, Adriaen Block, an Amsterdam lawyer, heard of the riches of the newly discovered land, and tried his hand at trading with the Indians for fur. His first ship, the *Tiger*, was burned to the waterline with a full cargo. But using Indian labor, he built a new vessel, *Onrust* ("Restless"), with which he

Raw deal: Peter Minuit bought Manhattan from the Indians for a few measly trinkets.

charted much of the local coastline. In 1613, a trading post was established at Fort Nassau, the beginnings of the eventual Dutch settlement of the area.

In 1624, the Dutch West India Company was granted a long-term trade and governing monopoly by the Dutch government. It was authorized to make alliances with native rulers, to establish colonies, to appoint and discharge governors and other officers, and to administer justice.

Soon, the first Dutch settlers arrived—30 families, most of whom were Protestants fleeing a Belgian inquisition. Of these, eight families stayed on Nut Island (now Governors Island), while the others sailed upriver to Fort Nassau.

The company imposed tough conditions on the colonists: They were to stay put for six years, worship only through the Reformed Protestant Church, buy all their supplies from company stores and provide community labor to help build forts and public buildings. Trading outside the colony was forbidden, as was the sale of homemade goods for profit.

BUYING MANHATTAN FOR BEADS

By 1626, when the first governor, Peter Minuit, arrived, there were 300 Europeans living on the tip of Manhattan in a settlement named New Amster-

dam. In the honorable tradition of European colonizers, Minuit negotiated a land deal with the locals—that is, he gave an Indian chief a few trinkets and blankets, got him to sign an incomprehensible document and assumed that the Dutch had bought themselves all of Manhattan Island.

In fact, the Indians had very different ideas about the possession of property, and could not conceive of individuals—rather than groups—owning land, let alone in perpetuity; the trading goods that Minuit gave to the chief were probably considered to be no more than the traditional gifts exchanged between visitors and their hosts.

Once the Europeans had moved in, they refused to budge. Later governors enforced a deliberate policy of harassing Indian hunters, even though they were the main source of fur supplies and therefore crucial to the company's financial success. Attempts were made to tax them, they were forbidden firearms, and harsh penalties for petty crimes were imposed. As a result, a bloody war between the Dutch and the Indians broke out in the 1640s; it lasted two and a half years.

PEG-LEG PETE

The war drastically reduced the Dutch West India Company's profits. After the colonists massacred more than 100 Indians in 1643, the company decided calm and control were in its best interests. To restore peace, the firm hired Peter Stuyvesant, an experienced colonialist and staunch authoritarian. Stuyvesant's right leg had been shattered by a cannonball—hence his nickname, Peg-Leg Pete. He was sent in with explicit orders to restore peace and to consolidate the company's investment in New Amsterdam.

Stuyvesant saw how the strain of living under constant threat of attack had prevented the town's proper establishment. "The people have grown very wild and loose in their morals," he commented, and set about cleaning up the inhabitants, their town and their habits.

He ordered a fortified structure (a defensive ditch and wall) to be built along the northern end of New Amsterdam—today's Wall Street. The muddy streets were paved with cobblestones; gardens were planted; houses were built in Dutch style, with gables, checkered brickwork and brass door knockers. Most important, a commercial infrastructure was established—banks, brokers' offices, wharves—and the booming waterfront was soon lined with chandlers and taverns.

Stuyvesant founded the first municipal assembly, composed of members representing New Amsterdam and towns in the outlying areas, and he encouraged the education of the colony's children. In his 17 years as governor, trade prospered and the settlement doubled in size.

STUYVESANT'S INTOLERANCE

As it grew, New Amsterdam attracted and accepted a number of religious refugees, a challenge to the dominance of the Dutch Reformed Church. When a group of Jews arrived in 1653, Stuyvesant wrote to the directors of the Dutch West India Company, complaining that such immigrants jeopardized the cohesion of the colony. He didn't want to see it, "populated by the scrapings of all sorts of nationalities." However, Holland had a tradition of religious tolerance and, in any case, European Jews were important shareholders in the company. Stuyvesant was very firmly rebuked.

Despite this, he persisted in his intolerance, sparking a rebellion by the people of Flushing, led by John Bowne, a merchant and landowner. Bowne stood firm and invited members of another group, known as the Religious Society of Friends or Quakers, to worship in his kitchen.

Bowne was arrested and banished in 1662, only to be vindicated by the directors of the company, who once again scolded Governor Stuyvesant. The company allowed Bowne to return two years later, thus giving official approval to religious freedom in the colony.

THE BRITISH ARRIVE

In the end, Stuyvesant was a little too authoritarian for his own good. And the Dutch West India Company was a little too eager to exploit the colony. By 1661, New Amsterdam was bankrupt.

When four British warships sailed into the harbor one day in August 1664, the population abandoned the fortifications Stuyvesant had built and welcomed Captain Richard Nicolls and his crew. New Amsterdam was renamed after the British king's brother, the Duke of York. Apart from a brief period between 1673 and 1674 when the city again fell into Dutch hands, the British ruled uninterrupted until the American Revolution.

The British inherited a cosmopolitan settlement that was predominantly Dutch but included among its inhabitants English, French, Portuguese and Scandinavian settlers, and the first African slaves. Both English and Dutch were spoken. The administrative system Stuyvesant had put in place was retained, and the Dutch were allowed to continue their way of life. The settlement continued to grow.

Strategically, New York was important for the British. They had long claimed the entire East Coast stretch, from New England south to Virginia, and year by year their settlements crept toward New York. In English eyes, New York was first and foremost a port: the finest natural harbor in the eastern United States, well protected from the elements, and providing access along the Hudson to the agriculturally rich area to the west.

In 1683, while they squabbled with the Dutch in Europe, the British attempted to consolidate New York, New Jersey and New England into a single dominion to cut administrative costs. The colonies rebelled. A militia, led by an affluent German merchant named Jacob Leisler, took control of New York City and Long Island for 21 turbulent months. The town was divided, and Leisler and his supporters—Dutch and German artisans, retailers and farmers who were known as "the Black people"—alienated the rich merchants and landowners, the "Whites." When the British regained New York, Leisler and nine of his supporters were hanged for treason.

THE MELTING POT

By 1700, New York's population had reached about 20,000. It was, as it continues to be, a population of immigrants. Alongside the English and Dutch were sizable groups from France and Germany, as well as settlers from Ireland and Sweden and some from other American colonies. Perhaps as many as 15 percent were Africans, almost all of them slaves.

The mix of religions was just as complex. In 1687, Governor Thomas Dongan reported that there were "not many of the Church of England, few Roman Catholicks, but an abundance of Quakers, ranting Quakers, Sabbatarians, Anti-sabbatarians, some Anabaptists, some Independents, some Jews; in short, of all sorts of opinions there are some, and the most part of none at all."

New York's first newspaper, the *New-York Gazette,* was established in 1725, basically as a mouthpiece for the British. Eight years later, John Peter Zenger founded a rival, the *New-York Weekly Journal.* Zenger soon got himself into trouble when he attacked Governor William Cosby and his corrupt administration. Zenger's trial on libel charges brought a landmark decision: The newspaper publisher was acquitted because, as his lawyer argued, the truth cannot be libelous. The Zenger verdict sowed the seeds for the First Amendment to the Constitution, which established the principles of freedom of the press and the public's right to know. This was just the beginning of trouble for the British.

Independence and Civil War

In 18th-century Europe, the Age of Reason had arrived, and the concept of monarchy was hanging on by its fingernails. The radical European social philosophies were studied by such Americans as Benjamin Franklin, Thomas Jefferson and John Adams, who in turn spread the ideals of fair and democratic government. Meanwhile, the British were imposing more and higher taxes on their colonial possessions in order to pay off debts accumulated in colonial wars against

Backdraft: A Civil War riot, Lexington Avenue.

France. Bostonians rebelled by dumping British tea into Boston Harbor.

In 1774, the Americans set up the Continental Congress, made up of delegates from each of the colonies. Their interests were growing even further apart from those of the British government, and at a meeting in Philadelphia in September 1774, the colonial delegates urged citizens to withhold taxes and—importantly—to arm themselves. Revolution had become inevitable. The Continental Congress's most far-reaching decision was to accept the Declaration of Independence, drawn up in 1776 principally by Thomas Jefferson. The Declaration, proclaimed John Adams, was "the greatest single effort of national deliberation that the world has ever seen."

NEW YORK AT WAR
New York was in a key position during the Revolutionary War because of its dominant position on the Hudson River, which divided the New England colonies from their southern counterparts. The British commander Lord Howe sailed 200 ships into New York Harbor in the summer of 1776 and occupied the town. New Yorkers vented their fury by toppling a gilded equestrian statue of George III that stood on Bowling Green.

The American forces, led by George Washington, were initially defeated at the Battle of White Plains and were forced to regroup away from New York, in preparation for a long, drawn-out war.

On September 11, 1776, there was a peace initiative. Three colonists, led by Benjamin Franklin, met Lord Howe in Staten Island's Billop-Manor House (now known as the Conference House), only to refuse his conciliatory offer of rights and treatment equal to those of all other British subjects. "America cannot return to the domination of Great Britain," said Franklin, demanding independence.

Life in occupied New York was grim. The population swelled from 20,000 to 30,000 as the town was overrun with British soldiers and loyalists fleeing the American army. While war raged throughout the colonies, the besieged town succumbed to disease and a lack of essential supplies. Fires destroyed much of the city, and many of the inhabitants died slowly of starvation.

In 1783, the British surrendered; two years later they were driven out of the American colonies.

THE NEW REPUBLIC
New York won its freedom in November 1783. The last British act was to grease the flagpole in hopes of making it harder for the revolutionaries to raise the flag of the new republic.

But the war was won. On December 4, Washington joined his officers for an emotional farewell dinner, at Fraunces Tavern on Pearl Street, where the Virginian farmer and victorious general declared his retirement. However, he was not to fade from

Overdue books: John Jacob Astor's library, here in the 1880s, is now the Public Theater.

public life: On April 23, 1789, in the Old Federal Hall (on the same site as the present one), he took the oath of office as the first president of the United States of America. New York was the new nation's first capital.

Though the capital for barely a year, the city's business boomed, merchants grew richer and the port prospered. However, the streets remained narrow and dirty, and hygiene wasn't helped by the pigs, goats and horses that roamed free. Rents were high and demand was great. At the turn of the century, 60,000-plus people lived in what is now downtown New York. The authorities decided the city was getting untidy and came up with the famous "grid" street system as a solution.

In 1811, the commissioners presented their blueprint. It ignored all the existing roads—with the exception of Broadway, which ran the length of Manhattan Island, following an old Indian trail—and organized New York into a rectangular grid with wide, numbered avenues running north–south and streets river to river. Commenting on the vast area thus earmarked for the city, they observed: "It may be a subject of merriment that the Commissioners have provided space for a greater population than is collected at any spot on this side of China."

FORTUNES AND PHILANTHROPY

When the 362-mile Erie Canal opened in 1825, New York was linked, via the Hudson and the Great Lakes, to the Midwest. Along with the new railroads, this trade route facilitated the making of many fortunes, and New York's merchants and traders flourished. Summer estates and mansions were built, and by 1830 new villas had sprung up along Fifth Avenue as far as Madison Square. Joined with the democratic ideals of the Revolution, these new riches spawned a clutch of charitable organizations and philanthropic institutions.

Education was highly valued. The New York Society Library, established in 1754, painstakingly rebuilt its collection, which had been vandalized during the British occupation. The Astor Library, a mid-19th-century building opposite Colonnade Row on Lafayette Street (now the Public Theater), was built as the city's first free library, and Peter Cooper made plans for his Cooper Union for the Advancement of Science and Art.

POPULATION BOOM

Until the 1830s, most families lived in row houses. But the city was too successful, and growing too fast, to maintain that standard of housing. By 1840, 300,000 people lived here, and the flood of

Free for all: Brooklyn's Plymouth Church.

immigrants from Ireland and the rest of Europe had begun. The first grim tenement buildings, where whole families rented a bare room or two and shared washing facilities, were built.

By 1850, the mansions along Fifth Avenue had indoor plumbing, central heating and a reliable water supply—secured by the 1842 construction of the Croton Reservoir system (at what is now the site of the New York Public Library on 42nd Street). More than 100 miles of sewer pipes had been installed under the city streets.

Middle-class neighborhoods were also establishing themselves. In Brooklyn Heights and Park Slope, you can still see the rows of houses built in various styles—including Federal and Greek Revival—but all in brownstone, creating a unified, elegant whole.

CIVIL WAR

Throughout the first half of the 19th century, a bitter division was deepening between the Northern and Southern states. Slavery was at the center of the controversy. For the South, there seemed no other way; the region's economy and prosperity were based almost wholly on the plantation system and its unending need for manual labor. For many in the urban and increasingly egalitarian North, slavery had become impossible to accept. The numbers involved were staggering: In 1860, more than four million black people were considered the property of eight million whites.

Attempts by the Northern states to pass national legislation against slavery horrified white Southerners. While slavery had ended peacefully in the North, residents of the South were convinced that freed blacks would exact revenge. As new states joined the Union, upsetting the balance of power in Congress, violent conflict between North and South grew inevitable.

THE ABOLITIONISTS

"For revolting barbarity and shameless hypocrisy, America reigns without a rival," declared former slave Frederick Douglass, stoking the fires of the abolitionist cause.

In Boston, William Lloyd Garrison published an antislavery journal, *The Liberator*, starting in 1831. In New York, the cause was kept alive in the columns of Horace Greeley's *Tribune* newspaper and in the sermons of Henry Ward Beecher, pastor of the Plymouth Church of the Pilgrims on Orange Street in Brooklyn. The minister (brother of Harriet Beecher Stowe, who wrote *Uncle Tom's Cabin*) once shocked his congregation by auctioning a slave from his pulpit and using the proceeds to buy her freedom.

LINCOLN AND WAR

Abraham Lincoln was well-known as a vehement opponent of slavery. But in an attempt to preserve the Union, he proposed the return of runaway slaves to their "owners," and supported the idea of returning the black population to Africa. This prompted abolitionist orator Wendell Phillips to call him "that slavehound from Illinois."

Despite his complex position, Lincoln took a firm abolitionist stance when he addressed a meeting in the Great Hall of the Cooper Union in New York (the first American school open to all, regardless of race, religion or gender). Here he declared: "Neither let us be slandered from our duty by false accusations against us, nor frightened from it by menaces of destruction to the government nor of dungeons to ourselves. Let us have faith that right makes might, and in that faith let us, to the end, dare to do our duty as we understand it."

Following this famous speech, the newly formed Republican Party (a liberal alliance that had little in common with the party of today) moved to make Lincoln its presidential candidate. In 1860, with the announcement of his victory, the Southern states seceded from the Union and formed the Confederate States of America.

WARTIME NEW YORK

Although New York sided with the Union against the Confederacy, there was considerable sympathy for the South, particularly among poor Irish and German immigrants, who feared that freed slaves would compete with them for work.

When Lincoln introduced conscription in 1863, the streets of New York erupted in rioting. The protestors objected to the draft because it allowed the wealthy to avoid serving in the army, and left the poor to fight—in a battle for the freedom of people who, they feared, would take their jobs.

For three days, New York raged. Blacks were attacked in the streets; the homes and offices of abolitionists were gutted. The violence came to an end only when Union troops returning from victory at Gettysburg subdued the city. There were 100 fatalities and a thousand people injured. It was the worst riot in American history.

VICTORY

In 1865, the inevitable victory by the North was achieved by General Ulysses S. Grant, who had been made supreme commander of the Union armies two years earlier. He was helped by General Sherman's infamous "scorched earth" march through the South, during which the Union army burned mansions, wrecked railroads, freed slaves and gorged itself on the crops and livestock found en route. Robert E. Lee's Confederate troops surrendered in April 1865.

A week after victory was declared, Lincoln was assassinated. Following Andrew Johnson's disastrous presidency, the country chose General Grant as president and commander-in-chief.

The making of the metropolis

New York emerged from the Civil War virtually unscathed. It had not seen any actual fighting (only rioting) and instead had prospered as the financial center of the North and the most convenient port of entry from Europe. But as the city thrived, rich and poor grew further apart, and there was fierce economic competition among immigrant groups.

IMMIGRATION

"Give me your tired, your poor, your huddled masses yearning to breathe free," entreats Frédéric Auguste Bartholdi's 1886 Statue of Liberty, one of the first sights seen by newcomers to the U.S. as they approached by sea.

The first great waves of immigration to America started well before the Civil War; the twin ports of welcome were Boston and New York. German liberals were fleeing their failed 1848 revolution, and a huge influx of Irish had begun after the 1843 potato famine. In the 1880s, large numbers of immigrants from the old Russian empire— Ukrainians, Poles, Romanians and Lithuanians, many of them Jews—arrived, along with southern Italians. Many of the Chinese laborers who had been brought to America to do backbreaking work on the railroads in California moved east to New York.

From 1855 to 1890, the immigration center at Castle Clinton in Battery Park processed eight million newcomers. The Ellis Island center, built in 1892, served the same purpose for roughly the same length of time, and handled double that number. To the immigrants it was the "Isle of Tears," where they were herded like cattle, separated from loved ones, exam-

Rite of passage: Some 16 million immigrants entered the U.S. at Ellis Island after 1892.

ined for disease and physical defects, and sometimes sent all alone back to their homelands. With the introduction of a quota system in 1921, the flood of newcomers slowed, and Ellis Island was closed in 1932.

The new arrivals stuck together in communities of common origin. While they preserved their religion, customs, cuisine and language, they also relentlessly pursued the dream of bettering themselves and their children. The Jews, in particular, opened schools and libraries, published newspapers, and supported theaters and charitable institutions. By 1910, more than 1.5 million Jews were living in New York City.

At the same time, a quarter of New York's population was Irish. Although they were stuck in poverty, the Irish experienced a freedom denied them during three centuries of British occupation: the right of political action. They plunged into city government wholeheartedly, and within a few decades controlled it.

HOMES OF PAUPERS AND KINGS
New immigrants usually ended up in the grim, crowded tenements of the Lower East Side, which in 1894 filled six blocks. Whole families lived in one or two dark rooms, with no hot water or heat, sharing toilets with neighbors.

When Jacob Riis published his *How the Other Half Lives*, an exposé of life in the ghetto, the up-town populace was horrified. The employment of children in sweatshops and the squalid housing conditions of the Lower East Side were an affront to human dignity. (Riis's harrowing photographs are now in the Museum of the City of New York.) Stirred into action, in 1879 the city passed the first of a series of housing laws. The new laws laid down minimum water and toilet requirements, allowed for air shafts between buildings to let in light and air, and made fire escapes mandatory.

As the population of New York swelled, the established middle classes—the merchants and industrialists who were benefiting from the city's vigorous postwar economy—moved into brownstones like those in Park Slope, Brooklyn, or into row houses that sprang up in midtown.

The very wealthy were drawn farther north by the magnet of Central Park, which was built starting in 1857. Its Fifth Avenue side became the playground of the rich, with enormous mansions built for monied families such as the Vanderbilts, the Astors and the Whitneys. On the Upper West Side, street after street of row houses were constructed, attracting well-off European immigrants and intellectuals. Massive luxury apartment buildings, such as the stately Dakota on West 72nd Street at Central Park West, started to dominate the skyline, and the neighborhood gradually became desirable.

The new frontier: The Dakota building looms over Central Park ice-skaters in 1890.

ESTABLISHING AN INFRASTRUCTURE

Gradually, the city developed an infrastructure to sustain its crowded population. Supplies of clean water were provided by the Croton Reservoir, sewers were built throughout the island, and power was supplied by electricity—which had been harnessed by local genius Thomas Edison (even today, New Yorkers' electricity is delivered by his company, Consolidated Edison).

Railroads already connected the city to the rest of the country; now elevated railways cast shadows over the avenues, and subway lines were excavated under the streets. Trams rattled their way across town; the perilous, occasionally fatal turn at Broadway and 14th Street was dubbed "Dead Man's Curve" and drew crowds of morbid onlookers.

But all technological feats paled next to the extraordinary achievement of the Brooklyn Bridge (1869-1883). When it was built, it was the longest suspension bridge in the world and the first to use steel cable. Designed by John A. Roebling (who died in an on-site accident before construction began) and completed by his son Washington, the bridge opened up the independent city of Brooklyn and paved the way for its merger with New York in 1898.

THE SAD LOT OF LABOR

The frenetic growth of the city's industrial strength created appalling health and safety conditions. Combined with low wages—some women workers averaged only $2 or $3 for a 60-hour week—the squalid conditions spurred the labor force into action. In 1872, 100,000 workers went on strike for three months until they won the right to an eight-hour workday.

A year later, the country was plunged into a serious depression, and many of New York's workers were forced onto the streets: 90,000 hungry and unemployed people went homeless.

Enormous crowds attended labor and political meetings at the Cooper Union. The whole country was in disarray for nearly five years: The railroad strikes, in particular, turned very bloody, with the companies hiring private security forces and enlisting the often brutal support of the police.

The workers' resistance was eventually broken when the bosses took to employing newly arrived immigrants, whom they could pay even less. Child labor was also still common. "Nearly any hour on the East Side of New York City you can see them—pallid boy or spindling girl—their faces dulled, their backs bent under a heavy load of garments piled on head and shoulders, the muscles of the whole frame in a long strain," wrote Edwin Markham in 1907.

It took the horror of the 1911 fire at the Triangle Shirtwaist Factory on Washington Place in Greenwich Village, which killed 146 workers, to stir politicians into action. More than 50 health and

Derailed: Penn Station (1911) was torn down.

safety measures were passed by the state legislature within months of the fire. Today, a memorial gathering at the site on the northwestern corner of Washington Place and Greene Street is sponsored by the garment-workers union every March 25.

HIGH FINANCE

With the industrial revolution spurring the economy ever onward, New York's financiers, dominated by the Dutch since the early days of European settlement, made sure to carve themselves a substantial piece of the pie.

Market activity was frenzied. Swindles, panics and collapses were frequent but reached new heights in the late 19th century. Jay Gould made enormous profits during the Civil War by having the outcome of military engagements cabled to him secretly and trading on the results before they became public knowledge. Another master swindler was Jim Fisk, who, together with Gould, seduced Cornelius Vanderbilt into buying vast quantities of Erie Railroad bonds before the price dropped out of the market. Vanderbilt had the resources to sit out such a crisis, and the grace to call Gould "the smartest man in America." Vanderbilt, Andrew Carnegie and banker J.P. Morgan consolidated their fortunes by controlling the railroads. John D. Rockefeller made his in oil, owning, by 1879, 95 percent of the refineries in the United States. His company, Standard Oil, was finally broken up by an antimonopoly case brought by Theodore Roosevelt, who insisted "no amount of charities in spending such fortunes can compensate for the misconduct in acquiring them."

POLITICAL MACHINATIONS

Theodore Roosevelt became president in 1901 following the assassination of William McKinley, after having been governor of New York State and vice president of the U.S. He was an instinctive politician who was among the first world leaders to understand the importance of public image. Roosevelt was also an empire builder. He took America into the Philippines, leased a coast-to-coast stretch of Panama and stationed U.S. troops there, built up the navy fleet and increased the regulatory powers of his own federal government.

In New York, politics had become mired in corruption. William Marcy "Boss" Tweed, the young leader of a Democratic Party faction called Tammany Hall (named after a famous Indian chief), turned city government into a lucrative operation. As commissioner of public works he collected large payoffs from companies receiving city contracts. Tweed and his "ring" are estimated to have misappropriated $160 million, and they distributed enough of that money in political bribes to keep a lot of influential mouths shut.

But by 1871, Boss Tweed's number was up. A disgusted City Hall clerk passed damaging documents to *The New York Times,* whose publisher was reputed to have refused a half-million–dollar bribe. The crusade against Tammany Hall corruption continued in Thomas Nast's cartoons for

Depressed: Shantytown apple seller, 1932.

Harper's Weekly. Tweed said he didn't care what the newspapers wrote, because most of his supporters couldn't read, but they could understand "them damn pictures."

The most spectacular monument to Tweed's greed is the New York County Courthouse, known as the Tweed Courthouse. The city paid $14 million for it, $10 million to $12 million more than its true cost. Consequently, some of the work was very fine indeed: "If you pay a carpenter $360,747 for a month's work, they have to do something." In recent years, the Tweed Courthouse has been declared a landmark and again houses municipal offices.

MUSEUMS AND LIBRARIES

As the wealth of New York grew, the city's millionaires signaled their success by building concert halls, libraries and art museums, and donating entire collections to put in them.

Steel baron Andrew Carnegie, who, they say, never forgot his penniless immigrant origins, gave Carnegie Hall to New York. And when the New York Public Library was established in 1895, he offered $52 million to establish branch libraries. The nucleus of the library is the combined collections of John Jacob Astor, Samuel Jones Tilden and James Lenox.

The Metropolitan Museum of Art was founded in 1870 by members of the Union League Club and opened two years later with a modest collection of 174 Dutch and Flemish paintings, and some antiquities donated by General di Cesnola, a former U.S. consul to Cyprus. Now it is the largest art museum in the Western world.

NEW YORK STORIES

From the 19th century onward, New York sprouted its own artistic and literary movements. Following the first figures of New York letters—people like satirist Washington Irving and Gothic storyteller Edgar Allan Poe—were Brooklyn poet Walt Whitman and novelists Edith Wharton and Mark Twain.

Wharton became one of the most astute critics of old New York society; her most memorable novels, among them *The Age of Innocence,* are detailed renderings of New York life at the turn of the century. Mark Twain (whose real name was Samuel Clemens), one of the most widely read writers in 19th-century America, moved east to New York in 1870. *The Adventures of Tom Sawyer* was published six years later, followed by *Huckleberry Finn* in 1884. Twain was also a gifted satirist and a robust political commentator.

THE SUBWAY

New York's subway system, an unceasing network of civic arteries pumping 3.9 million passengers a day, was this century's largest single factor in the growth of the city. By offering a fast and inexpensive method of traveling between

Uptown pearl: Audiences took the A train to see Duke Ellington at Harlem's Cotton Club.

home and work, it finally allowed working people to leave the polluted congestion of lower Manhattan while retaining their stake in the life of New York. Not until the tracks had been laid would the city extend northward.

The ancestor of the subway system was an elevated line, opened in 1868, which ran along Greenwich Street, powered by a steam-driven cable. By the turn of the century it was electrified and had become part of an aerial network that extended into the Bronx, Queens and Brooklyn, darkening the streets above which it clattered and encouraging hookers to rent third-floor rooms (level with the trains) so they could sit in the windows and lure customers in. Outside Manhattan, much of the elevated track remains in use to this day, but in the central borough it was gradually dismantled, and the routes were sunk underground.

In 1900, building started on the first of three subterranean systems, which were eventually united to make up today's subway. The first was the IRT (Interborough Rapid Transit), running from City Hall to Grand Central Terminal to Times Square and then following Broadway to 145th Street. After digging a ceremonial hole to inaugurate construction, the mayor was so moved that he took away some soil in his hat.

New lines followed—the BMT (Brooklyn-Manhattan Transit Corporation) and the IND (Independent Subway System)—their names preserved in old signs, and in the confusing ways many New Yorkers still describe various routes. By the 1940s the system was very much as it is today.

The subways hold a unique place in the city's imagination, offering the perfect metaphor for New Yorkers' fast, crowded lives lived among strangers. Most famously, Duke Ellington's theme song, written by Billy Strayhorn, implored its listeners to "Take the A Train," noting "that's the quickest way to get to Harlem." Tin Pan Alley's songwriters composed such popular ditties as "Rapid Transit Gallop" and "The Subway Glide," and new words and phrases like "rush hour" entered the language. The most lyrical homage to the subway was New York wit O. Henry's observations on the opening of the first underground line. Capturing the city's delirious affection for its new way of getting around, he wrote: "The rapid transit is poetry and art; the moon but a tedious, dry body moving by rote."

There are now 714 miles (1142km) of subway routes, with 468 stations. The trains are new, the graffiti is gone, crime has been beaten back to a minimum, and—apart from the occasional flooding or derailment—it is the most convenient way to travel around the city during the day.

The 20th century

World War I thrust America onto center stage as a world power. Its pivotal role in the defeat of Germany boosted the nation's confidence, and New

Crossover hit: The young Triborough Bridge.

THE WALL STREET CRASH

On October 29, 1929, the party ended. New York was in a panic as the stock market collapsed, destroying most small investors and plunging thousands of people into poverty and unemployment. Central Park filled with the newly homeless, who built shantytowns called Hoovervilles, after President Herbert Hoover. By 1932, one in four New Yorkers was out of work. Banks failed every day—1,326 of them in 1930 alone—wiping out savings; bankers became one of the most despised groups in the country. The song of the day was Yip Harburg's "Brother, Can You Spare a Dime?"

LA GUARDIA AND THE NEW DEAL

With the country in turmoil, the search was on for new political ideas. New York became a bastion of socialism, as Trotskyites, anarchists and communists gained influence. In 1932, the city elected a stocky, short-tempered young congressman, Fiorello La Guardia, as mayor. He imposed austerity programs that, surprisingly, won wide support.

La Guardia was boosted by Franklin D. Roosevelt's election as president. Roosevelt's New Deal restored public confidence by re-employing the jobless on public works programs and allocating federal funds to roads, housing and parks. In what still stands as a unique period of generous federal support for the arts, the Works Progress Administration (WPA) also made money available to actors, writers, artists and musicians.

La Guardia served as mayor for 12 years, during which he reduced corruption within city government, waged war against organized crime and launched the most extensive public-housing program in the country. He is still regarded as the city's best-loved mayor.

ART AND ARCHITECTURE

Some of the great 20th-century New York buildings went up during this period: The Chrysler and Empire State Buildings and Rockefeller Center were all built in the 1930s. And as the Nazis terrorized the intelligentsia in Europe, New York became the favored refuge of artists, architects and designers. The architect Ludwig Mies van der Rohe and Walter Gropius, the former director of the influential Bauhaus school of design, were among those who moved to America from Germany.

When painters such as Arshile Gorky, Piet Mondrian, Hans Hofmann and Willem de Kooning arrived in New York, gradually the center of the art world began to shift. They were greeted by the fledgling Museum of Modern Art, founded in 1929 by three collectors—Abby Aldrich Rockefeller, Lillie P. Bliss and Mrs. Cornelius Sullivan—to document the Modern movement and represent the most important contemporary artists, a daring concept in its time.

York benefited from wartime trade and commerce. When Wall Street prospered, the nation prospered. As President Calvin Coolidge said in 1925: "The business of America is business."

THE JAZZ AGE

The Roaring Twenties were ushered in with two important legislative changes. The 19th Amendment, ratified in 1920, gave women the vote—and an independence that manifested itself in shorter hairstyles, shorter skirts and provocative dances like the Charleston. Prohibition had been ratified in 1919, and the bootleg liquor that flowed at illegal speakeasies fueled general Jazz Age wildness (and made many a gangster's fortune).

In Harlem's Cotton Club, Lena Horne, Josephine Baker and Duke Ellington played for exclusively white audiences, as New Yorkers enjoyed what poet Langston Hughes called "that Negro vogue." On Broadway, the Barrymore family—Ethel, John and Lionel (Drew's forebears)—were treading the boards between movies. Over at the New Amsterdam Theater on West 42nd Street, the high-kicking Ziegfeld Follies dancers were opening for such entertainers as W.C. Fields, Fanny Brice and Marion Davies. In 1926, hundreds of thousands of New Yorkers flooded the streets to mourn the death of matinee idol Rudolph Valentino. That same year, the city elected Jimmy Walker, a party-loving ex-songwriter, as mayor.

NEW YORK VOICES

The literary scene was dominated by Ernest Hemingway and his friend F. Scott Fitzgerald, whose *The Great Gatsby* turned a dark gaze on the 1920s. They worked with editor Maxwell Perkins at Scribner's publishing house, along with Thomas Wolfe, who constructed enormous semiautobiographical mosaics of small-town life, and Erskine Caldwell, author of *Tobacco Road*, the Depression novel set in the rural deep South.

Many of the city's other great chroniclers of the time gathered regularly at the famous Round Table at the Algonquin Hotel. These included such literary lights as Dorothy Parker, Robert Benchley, George S. Kaufman and Alexander Woollcott. The table was also frequently graced by visiting royals of stage and screen like Douglas Fairbanks, Tallulah Bankhead and various Marx brothers. Much of the modern concept of sophistication and wit took shape in the alcoholic banter of this glamorous clan.

THE COLD WAR

World War II jolted America out of the Depression. Government spending for war production revived the economy, and New York Harbor bustled with ships carrying soldiers, sailors and supplies to the battlefields of Europe.

After the victory, a long period of paranoia and distrust began, as the Cold War raged between the United States and the Soviet Union. With its long tradition of radical politics, New York saw bitter disputes between communists, anticommunists and civil libertarians. The crusading political spirit of the 1930s and 1940s gave way to enforced conformity and the conservative ideas of the 1950s.

Judging New York a world city, the United Nations established its headquarters overlooking the East River in Manhattan. Artists venturing into the new world of Abstract Expressionism also made the city their own, and a generation of Le Corbusier–inspired architects transformed the New York skyline with buildings that took the form of glass-and-steel boxes.

POPULATION GROWTH

The affluence of the '50s allowed many families to head for the suburbs: Towns sprang up around new highways, and about one million children and grandchildren of European immigrants—mostly Irish, Italian and Jewish—moved to live in them. Their places in the city were taken by a new wave of immigrants—one million Puerto Ricans and African-Americans from the South.

The better life sought by the new arrivals was not so easily obtained, however. Democratic politicians, who dominated the city, gave little more than

The Howling: *Beat poet Allen Ginsberg, a longtime East Villager, still had short hair in 1953.*

Meet the new boss: Mayor Rudolph Giuliani.

token recognition to the immigrants, and discrimination and the decline of the city's manufacturing base limited black and Latino prospects for economic success.

By the mid-'60s, New Yorkers could no longer ignore the large nonwhite communities who were systematically excluded from the city's power structure and prosperity. But despite some creative efforts to bring these newcomers into the city's mainstream—especially during the administration of Mayor John Lindsay—entrenched poverty and prejudice made for slow progress. Meanwhile, increases in street crime cast a shadow of fear across the entire city.

THE COUNTERCULTURE
New York remained a center for radical politics and the avant-garde. In the 1950s, as Columbia University dropouts Allen Ginsberg and Jack Kerouac met Times Square denizens like William Burroughs and Herbert ("the Junkie") Huncke, the East Coast faction of the Beat movement was born. The Beats, in turn, evolved into the hippie counterculture of the 1960s, and Manhattan provided the stage: from the folkie coffeehouses of Greenwich Village to the campus of Columbia University, where students protested against racism and the Vietnam War.

Meanwhile, in more conservative working- and middle-class neighborhoods, many white New Yorkers grew disenchanted with liberalism, seeing it as incapable of providing safe streets or effective schooling. To make matters worse, by 1975 the city was all but bankrupt. With a growing population on welfare and a declining tax base caused by middle-class flight to the suburbs, the city had resorted to heavy municipal borrowing.

BOOM AND BUST
To the rescue rode Mayor Edward I. Koch, a one-time liberal from Greenwich Village, who steered the city back to fiscal solvency with austerity measures and state and federal help. By shrewdly, if cynically, playing the city's ethnic politics and riding the 1980s boom in construction and finance, Koch won three successive four-year terms.

But there would not be a fourth. Amid the greed and conspicuous consumption of the 1980s, Koch was finally undone by a combination of corruption scandals, growing black activism and his inability to defuse the city's racial hostilities.

He was succeeded by David N. Dinkins, the city's first African-American mayor. An old-fashioned clubhouse politician with liberal instincts, Dinkins took office in 1990, inheriting a multitude of problems left over from the ugly underside of the Koch years: racial conflicts, poverty and large numbers of homeless people. Soon afterwards, the city was battered by a deep economic recession. Dinkins excelled at grand symbolic gestures, such as handsomely welcoming Nelson Mandela to the city. He made important inroads in the fight against crime by implementing new community-policing strategies. But he could not overcome global economic trends that drew manufacturing jobs away from the city. And many felt he lacked the saber-toothed ferocity necessary to run New York.

He was succeeded in 1994 by Rudolph Giuliani, a tough Italian-American lawyer, who entered the political limelight as a fearless federal prosecutor. Though initially welcomed as the antidote to the equivocal, often bumbling Dinkins, Giuliani's dictatorial style and the social implications of his policies have alienated many of his supporters.

TOWARD THE MILLENNIUM
The problems facing the mayor of New York are those of any other city, magnified: Racial tension, a depleted tax base, extremes of wealth and poverty, AIDS, homelessness and crime are part of urban life in the 1990s. The city is a modern invention struggling to survive, and New York remains a city of pioneers. Recent arrivals from Asia, Latin America, the Caribbean and the former Soviet Union make up a foreign-born population of more than two million. The flow of humanity gives the city energy. After all, if you can make it here, you'll make it anywhere.

Welcome to New York

Take a deep breath and get ready for an adventure of a lifetime. It's not called "the city that never sleeps" for nothing.

On a bright day, the towers of New York glisten in the distance like some lost city of legend. You catch glimpses of them as you pass through the boroughs on your way in from the airport; when you finally reach the river crossings and get your first close-up look at the island of Manhattan—a slender capsule of land and the inconceivable tons of steel and concrete that cover it—the sight is invariably breathtaking.

New York's tightly packed structure and frenzy of activity can seem overwhelming at times—to first-timers, it can feel like a pressure cooker. For most visitors, however, that density translates into accessibility. Because so many distinct and intriguing cultures, landmarks and neighborhoods stand side by side in a few square miles, your days here take on a kaleidoscopic quality.

Wend your way up from the glass-and-steel canyons of Wall Street (where the nearby Staten Island ferry and the World Trade Center offer stunning views) to Chinatown or Little Italy for lunch. Head west to soak up Soho chic or cross Houston Street to gather some East Village grunge. A few more blocks brings you to the classic bohemia of Greenwich Village and, farther up, the budding gallery district of Chelsea. From there, you're just minutes by public transportation to the midtown theater district, the great expanse of Central Park and the heart of black America, Harlem. All this can be done in one day (though, of course, one day in *each* of these locales is advisable). And that's only Manhattan; you still have four more boroughs to explore.

In addition to the countless sights to see, New York City offers more—and a wider range of—

*Snug harbor: Toast your beautiful surroundings at the Central Park **Loeb Boathouse** café.*

NEW YORK'S BEST
SIGHTSEEING & ENTERTAINMENT CRUISES

MORE CRUISES!
MORE OPTIONS!
MORE FUN!

Pier 83, West 42nd Street
3hr Full Island Cruise
90 min Semi-Circle Cruise
90 min Sunset/Harbor Lights Cruise

Pier 16, South Street Seaport
2hr Live Music Cruises
1hr Seaport Liberty Cruise
30 min. *BEAST* Speedboat Ride

212-563-3200

Silent partners: Tai chi enthusiasts practice all the right moves in a Chinatown Park.

entertainment and cultural activities than almost anywhere on earth. On any given day, you can start the morning by checking out the latest exhibit in one of the city's world-class museums or galleries. Follow that by hearing a renowned author reading from his or her latest work at a Barnes & Noble bookstore. After lunch, enjoy one of the numerous—especially in summer—free classical music recitals. Cinemaphiles will find a vast array of films—blockbusters, foreign classics or edgy indies—playing in the numerous theaters and film societies. Evening? Take your pick: The world's best in dance, rock, jazz, opera, cabaret and comedy occupy New York's stages every night of the week. And if you're *still* not tired, you can dance till dawn in the city's after-hours clubs.

A NEW YORK MINUTE

The phrase "New York minute" usually refers to the pace and intensity from which the natives suffer (and of which they boast). It shows most in the clarity of purpose New Yorkers demonstrate when they stride the avenues or dart through traffic, clutching their shopping bags, backpacks and briefcases. If time is money, the typical New Yorker has a miser's mentality. The tourist, by comparison, is graced with the one asset that is in chronically short supply here.

A New York holiday provides more information and stimulation per second than anywhere else. Don't be put off by that velocity, though. Underneath the surface toughness, New York excels at bringing people together—with the things of this world and with each other. The first Europeans arrived here 400 years ago to hunt and trade fur. In later centuries, the city became the great point of transfer for all the products of the New World. But New York's predominant commodity has always been people—the "tired, poor, huddled masses" beckoned by the Statue of Liberty.

WORLD GUMBO

In a city where half of the residents are either immigrants or the children of immigrants, ethnic communities thrive. What's different now is the wider spectrum of cultures in the mix; New York today is a world gumbo like never before. Whereas most of the immigration of the post-war decades came from the Caribbean islands and Latin America, current trends show increasing arrivals from the Far East, the Indian subcontinent and Eastern Europe. Relative newcomers from Korea have cornered the market on the corner-grocery business. South-Asian Americans (SAAs)—from India, Pakistan, and Bangladesh—are among the most visible and industrious immigrants. Pakistanis own and operate the city's newsstands, and SAAs make up nearly half of New York's cabbies. The city even has three distinct Indian sections: midtown in Murray Hill, along 6th Street in the East Village and, most recently, in Flushing, Queens (where an estimated 60,000 SAAs live). Similarly, New York's Chinese population long ago spilled over the boundaries of its traditional enclave in lower Manhattan and now includes satellite Chinatowns in Brooklyn and

Vapor trail

Nefarious brewings below? Nah, it's just the city blowing off steam.

You've seen it in a hundred movies: a dramatic Manhattan street scene where strange vapors seep from manholes and billow around busy pedestrians and speeding yellow cabs. It's not a special effect. In fact, few things are more quintessentially New York than steam creeping upward from the sidewalk.

Consolidated Edison (Con Ed), the world's first electrical utility company—founded by Thomas Edison himself—built the system in the 1890s. Today, it sells steam to more than 2,000 customers, and heats mostly large office and apartment buildings. The company generates 10.4 million pounds of steam per hour during winter, which hisses through a system of underground pipes at 500°F (260°C). Since many of the original pipes are still in use, the inevitable wear and tear on them causes the steam to rise to street level occasionally. In order to prevent injury to pedestrians and provide repair-site visibility, Con Ed workers make a hole and put up those striped Cat in the Hat–style plastic chimneys to funnel away the miasmic vapors.

New York's steam system is the largest on the planet. To some, it might seem like yet another example of the city's lurching toward the Third World. Actually, though, since the steam is a by-product of Con Ed's electricity generation, it's more ecologically sound than most other heating methods.

Boiling over: New York's steamy streets have puzzled New Yorkers and visitors alike.

Queens. And since the collapse of Communism, Russian immigrants have settled on Brooklyn's shore in Brighton Beach (bringing with them the city's newest branch of organized crime).

IF YOU CAN MAKE IT HERE...

Newcomers to the Big Apple don't just arrive from overseas, though. The city continues to attract a relentless stream of disaffected refugees from middle America: kids from the heartland blinded by the sheer excess and possibility of the place. Lower Manhattan, especially, teems with young hopefuls and trendoids. One prototypical success story is Beck Hanson, who hopped off a bus from sunny Southern California, made a beeline for the dark, dank Lower East Side, dropped his last name and emerged a short time later as *Rolling Stone*'s (and everyone else's) Artist of the Year. And all it took was two turntables and a microphone. Recently, more sophisticated technology has lured other would-be stars to New York's "Silicon Alley": young cutting-edge cyberheads who hope to make their mark on the digital frontier. And, as the longtime center of American banking, law, publishing, fashion, advertising and art, New York continues to draw the best and brightest from each of those fields, too.

FEAST OR FAMINE

In a town where so many are driven by bald ambition, the consequences can be exhilarating or disastrous. New Yorkers at the bottom rung of society keep grinding away just to survive. Those in the middle have to fight to hold on to what little they've acquired. And upper-class residents hoard it all or blow it with reckless indifference. This composite daily struggle for survival, at one extreme, and dominance, at the other, charges New York life with its do-or-die vigor.

In the upper reaches of the social strata, this energy rides the crest of the unprecedented bull stock market. With billions of dollars in bonus money paid out on Wall Street in recent years, developer Donald Trump was quoted as saying, "This makes the 1980s look like child's play." Condos and co-ops priced in six or even seven figures sell the same day they come on the market. Limousines line the blocks outside the various restaurants of the moment.

New York is reaping the benefits of the country's robust economy in other ways, too. As America nears the completion of its decades-long transition to a postindustrial economy, New York's heavy involvement in high technology and the "consciousness" industry—the information/entertainment axis—has paid off, big time. The city has also earned a fortune in tax dollars by catering to the economic winners, offering them unparalleled access to luxury services in fashion, food, design and the fine arts.

Four-season fun

Summer's most popular, but New York's a ball at any time of year

Unlike many other cities (*you* go to Chicago in the middle of winter), New York is great to visit 12 months a year. In fact, part of the city's charm is how it changes its face from season to season. Still, it's helpful to know what to expect at any given time.

The climate is at its sublime best in spring and early summer (April–June), when the Atlantic breezes are still fending off the sticky humidity that can make July and August insufferably hot, and in autumn (September–November), when the heat subsides before winter's chill sets in.

Summer temperatures will often reach the 90s (31°C), but even at lower temperatures, the humidity can make you feel much hotter. At the same time, air-conditioned buildings are cool to the point of being cold, so wear layers. The opposite problem may occur in the winter, when many large buildings are kept *too* warm by central heating.

New York is alive with things to do throughout the year, but during the summer the parks and plazas and other public places are especially busy with free entertainment. As a result, indoor diversions are few; museum, gallery and concert calendars are sparse. The American summer unofficially lasts from Memorial Day (end of May) to Labor Day (beginning of September), and most New Yorkers try to leave the heat of the city as often as possible. Springtime has the most parades and is when the shops are full of the newest bargains, while late summer and fall have the most festivals. Winter can get quite cold, but is the busiest time for cultural activities. Christmas is a very special time in the city, with enticing street decorations, ice-skating, roaming Santas and a wonderland in every store window. *See chapter* **New York by Season** *for more information.*

UNDERDOGS

If it is the best of times for some, it is the worst of times for others. For all the gravy at the top, New York still has more unemployed people than any other American city, an inflation rate among the nation's highest and one of the lowest overall job creation rates. Offices in lower Manhattan still sit vacant, despite efforts to convert skyscrapers into co-ops, condos and apartments. In the midst of the

Apple of his eye: The badge says it all for this satisfied visitor to New York.

boom, the income of middle-class New Yorkers who work outside banking and finance has barely kept pace with inflation. While the homeless are rarely seen on the streets of Manhattan these days, the city's public shelters are still overcrowded. Advocates place the current homeless population at 100,000 and estimate that 20 percent of that number are nomadic, camping under bridges and boardwalks in the outer boroughs.

For the city's working poor, *plus ça change*. Cutbacks in welfare spending nationwide have strained the social safety net severely in New York (and other major cities)—so much so that the Republican mayor, Rudolph Giuliani, came out against the 1996 federal welfare-law provisions denying aid to legal immigrants.

HIZZONER

In Giuliani, traditionally liberal New Yorkers have found their first Republican mayor since Fiorello La Guardia (1933–45) to inspire both huge levels of cross-party support and accusations of demagoguery. Democrat Ed Koch, the previous mayor to be re-elected to the post, made his catchphrase "How'm I doing?"; the current mayor prefers to preempt that question by augmenting his news conferences with charts and graphs. His relentless plugging of his own achievements and cheerleading on behalf of the city have often paid off: Tourism figures are higher than ever; crime is lower than anyone could have imagined (with the murder rate down to late-1960s numbers); high-profile

parts of town such as Soho and Times Square are noticeably cleaner; and increased film, theater and TV production have showcased New York's comeback to the nation and the world. But the reality is a little more complex.

The take-charge attitude that has helped Giuliani crack down on rude cabdrivers and padded bureaucracies is the same impulse that has caused him to try relentlessly to dismantle and sell off the city's public-hospital system and to prevent street artists and adult businesses from expressing their First Amendment rights. In his second term, which started in 1998, he has decided to focus on other "quality-of-life" concerns, such as the regulation of street vendors and newsstands. Bigger issues like homelessness and the city's crumbling infrastructure haven't seemed to make it onto his agenda.

While crime rates have indeed fallen, and there's no doubt that the city's overall vibe is less threatening, police relations with minority communities have soured in the wake of several highly publicized incidents of excessive force. Every year seems to bring a new high-profile accusation of brutality. In 1997, the alleged vicious attack on Haitian immigrant Abner Louima by officers in Brooklyn's 70th Precinct shocked the nation.

In schools, students' test scores are up, but so are class sizes, while spending per pupil is down. The Sanitation Department's claim that the streets are cleaner is seriously disputed by a *New York Times* study. The city's own figures indicate

---

Orientation express

To learn your way around, hit the road, Jack—on foot, that is

As New Yorkers will tell you, the best way to master Manhattan is on foot. The island is small, (13.4 miles [21.5 km] long by 2.3 miles [3.7 km] wide) and above 14th Street, logically laid out in a grid, which makes getting lost almost impossible. The avenues run north to south and are numbered from east to west (with Lexington, Park and Madison between Third and Fifth). Cross streets run perpendicular to the avenues, with Fifth Avenue acting as the dividing line between the East and West sides. The lower the building number, the closer it is to this equator. The major exception is Broadway, an old Indian trail that runs north to south, then cuts diagonally downtown from the West to the East Side. Downtown streets are more confusing, since they were built before the grid pattern was established. (*See* **Maps**, *page 331 for help*.) **Transportation**

Alternatives (628-3311), an organization that promotes city cycling and safe streets, is an excellent source of information.

Those seeking a faster pace can run, bike or in-line skate, assuming they have the confidence and experience needed. To rent or buy a set of wheels, *see chapters* **Shopping & Services** *and* **Sports & Fitness**.

If you *do* find yourself lost, don't be put off by New Yorkers' (often justified) reputation for gruffness; it's okay to ask for directions. The trick is to deliver your question within earshot of at least two people. One of them may be completely wrong, but the inevitable debate (sometimes involving the entire bus, subway car or street corner) will ensure that the issue is hammered out sufficiently for you to know where to go. The arguments sparked by your innocent inquiry may well continue long after you've left.

that the Fire Department response times are longer. All studies agree that AIDS deaths are down, but the number of new cases holds steady. The mayor routinely proposes budget cuts to parks, libraries and schools in a sort of tough-love approach meant to get these institutions to become more efficient, seek private funding or both.

On all matters large and small, Giuliani allows for no criticism. Since being elected in 1993, his circle of advisors has tightened to include only a few loyalists, and requests from the media and public service groups for routine information are regularly denied. While the city has been sued and lost repeatedly on Freedom of Information Act grounds, the official stance remains that they are, as the mayor put it, "actually working, rather than spending their time answering questions." City money that could go to library books instead goes to appeal these lawsuits.

GOOD-NATUREDLY GRUFF

Then again, maybe the mayor is just showing his true New York colors—after all, the natives can be notoriously brusque (as one stereotypical joke goes: Tourist to native: "Can you give me directions, or should I just tell myself to fuck off?"). Still, no one can live here happily without some curiosity about their fellow creatures. Witness the collective sangfroid after a major snowstorm shuts down the streets (as it did in 1996). Stroll through one of the vacant lots reclaimed as a community garden (an idea now under threat from Giuliani) and eavesdrop as a young green thumb instructs an elderly retiree on the subtleties of composting. Ride the subways and see Wall Street profiteers rubbing shoulders with welfare mothers. (As gallery owner Andrea Rosen points out, "New York is the only place you'll find a corporate-mergers specialist asking a 22-year-old artist about the meaning of life.")

Green day: Vendors plant their wares at the **Union Square Farmer's Market**.

At the end of the day, everyone's equal. Film director Spike Lee has a better view than most, but he cheers just as loudly as the folks in the (not so) cheap upper-deck seats at Knicks games. Stars of stage and screen wear sweatpants to the corner deli, just as your average schmo does, and no one seems to notice—or care.

PUT ON YOUR GAME FACE

You'll get the most out of New York if you can adopt the same hard, "seen-it-all," detached veneer the locals have. The richest experience of the city comes when you treat it as a round-the-clock assertiveness-training class. The natives respect directness. They may not cater to your every whim, but they won't delay your quest. They're on one of their own.

Some may feel that New York breeds a crushing anonymity, and it can do that—you're just one more face in the crowd. And yet, that cloak of invisibility is ultimately liberating. Because you're an unknown, you're free to reinvent yourself. New Yorkers do it all the time. It may be this monster city's greatest appeal.

I'm O.K., you're U.K.

A brief guide to the differences between U.K. and U.S. English

Forget **queuing** and **get in line**. Take the **elevator** and not the **lift**, and remember **fags** are only for smoking if you're a homophobic gunman. **WASPs** are White Anglo Saxon and Protestant, while **JAPs** are Jewish American Princesses. **Buppies** are black yuppies, and **guppies** are gay ones. **Jocks** are sporty types, named after their straps. A **hero** is a French bread sandwich, also a **sub** (after "submarine"). **Takeaway** food is **to go** or **delivered**. A **schmear** is the spreading of cream cheese that you ask for on your bagel. A **soda** is any flavor of fizzy drink, while soda is **seltzer**. **Malt liquor** is just strong beer. If someone's **pissed**, they're not necessarily drunk—they're angry. A **bum** is a tramp, and so your **bum** is your butt or your **tush** or **fanny**. And whatever you do, don't forget your euphemisms when asking for the toilet. **Bathroom**, **washroom**, **restroom** or (no lie) **comfort station** are sufficiently removed from reality for American ears. Get it wrong, of course, and you're a **schmuck**.

New York by Season

Gotham's lineup of parades, festivals and other events will keep you busy and entertained at any time of year

As each season turns, one of New York's multiple personalities emerges. Winter's holiday parties and slushy traffic jams melt into the flowers, in-line skates and miniskirts of spring. Summer is hot, sweaty and slower, with garden restaurants, outdoor concerts and neighborhood fairs (not to mention air-conditioning) providing welcome relief from the sizzling streets. The pace picks up again in the fall, when New Yorkers enjoy the last of the sun's long rays and the beginning of the opera, dance and music seasons.

The festivals, parades and events listed below are held regularly. For more information, including newer and smaller happenings that may not be included here, contact the **New York Convention & Visitors Bureau** (*see chapter* **Directory: Essential information**). For other sources of entertainment information, including websites, see chapter **Media**. Don't forget to confirm that an event is happening before you head off to it.

Spring

Whitney Biennial
Whitney Museum of American Art, 945 Madison Ave at 75th St (570-3600). Subway: 6 to 77th St. Late March–early June. Every two years, the Whitney showcases what it deems to be the most important American art, generating much controversy in the process. The next show is in 2000.

Athletic supporters: Spring means it's time to start living again for die-hard Yankees fans.

U.S. holidays

A roster of red-letter days

New Year's Day January 1

Martin Luther King Jr. Day third Monday in January

Presidents' Day third Monday in February

Memorial Day last Monday in May

Independence Day July 4

Labor Day first Monday in September

Columbus Day second Monday in October

Election Day first Tuesday in November

Veterans' Day November 11

Thanksgiving fourth Thursday in November

Christmas Day December 25

St. Patrick's Day Parade

Fifth Ave between 44th and 86th Sts (484-1222). Mar 17. Internet: www.nycvisit.com New York becomes a sea of green for the annual Irish-American day of days, starting at 11am with the parade up Fifth Avenue and extending late into the night in bars all over the city.

Ringling Bros. and Barnum & Bailey Circus

Madison Square Garden, Seventh Ave at 32nd St (465-6741). Subway: A, C, E, 1, 2, 3, 9 to 34th St–Penn Station. Late March–early May. The Barnum & Bailey half of this famous three-ring circus annexed the line "the Greatest Show on Earth" back in its early days in New York City. Don't miss the parade of animals through the Queens-Midtown Tunnel and along the streets that traditionally opens the show.

Baseball season

April–October. See chapter **Sports & Fitness**.

Easter Parade

Fifth Ave between 49th and 57th Sts (484-1222). Easter Sunday. Internet: www.nycvisit.com The annual Easter Parade kicks off at 11am. Try to get a spot around St. Patrick's Cathedral, which is the best viewing platform—but get there early.

New York City Ballet Spring Season

New York State Theater, 20 Lincoln Center Plaza, 65th St at Columbus Ave (870-5570). Subway: 1, 9 to 66th St–Lincoln Ctr. Late April–June. The NYCB's spring season usually features a new ballet in addition to repertory classics by Balanchine and Robbins, among others.

Bike New York: The Great Five Boro Bike Tour

Starts at Battery Park, finishes on Staten Island (932-0778). Early May. Every year, thousands of cyclists take over the city for a 42-mile (68km) bike ride through the five boroughs. You'll feel like you're in the Tour de France.

You Gotta Have Park

Throughout the city (360-3456). May. This is an annual celebration of New York's public spaces, with free events in the major parks of all five boroughs. It heralds the start of a busy schedule of concerts and other events.

Ninth Avenue International Food Festival

Ninth Ave between 37th and 57th Sts (581-7029). Subway: A, C, E, 1, 2, 3, 9 to 34th St–Penn Station. Mid-May. A glorious mile of gluttony. Hundreds of stalls serve every type of food. Fabulously fattening.

Fleet Week

Intrepid Sea, Air and Space Museum, Pier 86, 46th St at the Hudson River (245-2533/recorded info 245-0072). Subway: A, C, E to 42nd St. End of May. The U.S. Navy visits New York in force along with ships from other countries—with a sail past the Statue of Liberty, maneuvers, parachute drops, air displays and various ceremonies. During the week, you can visit some of the ships at Pier 86.

Lower East Side Festival of the Arts

Theater for the New City, 155 First Ave at 10th St (245-1109). Subway: L to First Ave, 6 to Astor Pl. Final weekend of May. This annual arts festival and outdoor carnival celebrates the neighborhood that helped spawn the Beats, Method acting and Pop Art. It draws performances by more than 20 theatrical troupes and appearances by local celebrities.

Summer

Toyota Comedy Festival

Various locations (1-800-798-6968). Early to mid-June. Hundreds of America's funniest men and women perform at 30 different venues around the city. The information line operates from May to mid-June only.

Puerto Rican Day Parade

Fifth Ave between 44th and 86th Sts (484-1222, 1-718-401-0404). First Sun in June. Internet: www.nycvisit.com Featuring colorful floats and marching bands, this parade has become one of the city's busiest street celebrations.

Central Park SummerStage

Rumsey Playfield, Central Park at 72nd St (360-2777). Subway: 6 to 77th St. June–August. Enjoy free weekend afternoon concerts featuring top international performers and a wide variety of music. There are also dance and spoken-word events on weekday-nights and a few benefit shows for which admission is charged.

Metropolitan Opera Parks Concerts

Various locations (362-6000). June. The Metropolitan Opera presents two different operas at open-air evening concerts in Central Park and other parks throughout the five boroughs and New Jersey. The performances are free. To get a good seat, you need to arrive hours early.

Museum Mile Festival

Fifth Ave between 82nd and 104th Sts (606-2296). Second Tue in June. Nine of New York's major museums hold an open-house festival. Crowds are attracted not only by the free admission but also by the highbrow street entertainment.

Gay and Lesbian Pride Parade

From Columbus Circle, along Fifth Ave to Christopher St (807-7433). Late June. Every year, New York's gay and lesbian community parades through the streets of midtown to Greenwich Village to commemorate the Stonewall uprising of 1969. The celebrations have expanded into a full week, and in addition to a packed club schedule, there is an open-air dance party on the West Side piers.

*Wait till next year: Bitter cold + drunken revelers = **New Year's Eve** fun in Times Square.*

The light fantastic: **Macy's fireworks** illuminate the sky over the East River every July 4.

New York Jazz Festival

Various locations (219-3006). Early June. More than 300 acts in ten different venues—including the Knitting Factory, one of the festival's sponsors—offer all kinds of jazz performances, from mainstream to acid, in this two-week festival. Note: The festival adopts the name of its major corporate sponsor each year (in 1998, it was the Texaco Jazz Festival), so call to find out what it is currently being called.

New York Shakespeare Festival

Delacorte Theater, Central Park at 81st St (539-8750, 539-8500). Subway: B, C to 81st St; 6 to 77th St. Late June–late August. The Shakespeare Festival is one of the highlights of a Manhattan summer, with big-name stars pulling on their tights for a whack at the Bard. There are two plays each year (one Shakespeare, one an American classic) and tickets are free. *See also chapter* **Theater**.

JVC Jazz Festival

Various locations (501-1390). Mid–late June. The direct descendant of the original Newport Jazz Festival, the first event of its kind ever held in the U.S., the JVC bash has become a New York institution, with concerts in most of the city's major venues and some smaller ones as well. Call the above number for information on programs, venues and tickets.

Bryant Park Free Summer Season

Sixth Ave at 42nd St (922-9393). Subway: N, R, S, 1, 2, 3, 9, 7 to 42nd St–Times Sq. June–August. This reclaimed park, a lunch-time oasis for midtown's office population, is the site of a packed season of free classical music, jazz, dance and film. Best of all are the Monday-night open-air movies.

Mermaid Parade

From Steeplechase Park to Boardwalk at 8th St, Coney Island, Brooklyn (1-718-372-5159). Subway: B, D, F to Stillwell Ave. Third weekend in June. If your tastes run left of center, don't miss Coney Island's annual showcase of bizarreness consisting of elaborate floats, paraders dressed as sea creatures, kiddie beauty contests and other *über*-kitschy celebrations.

Washington Square Music Festival

W 4th St at La Guardia Pl (431-1088). Subway: A, C, E, B, D, F, Q to W 4th St–Washington Sq. Tuesdays at 8pm in July and August. This open-air concert season, featuring mainly chamber music, has been running in Greenwich Village for years.

Macy's Fireworks Display

East River (494-4495). Jul 4 at 9:15pm. The highlight of Independence Day is this spectacular fireworks display. The FDR Drive between 14th and 51st Streets is the best viewing spot; it's closed to traffic for a few hours as $1 million worth of flashes light up the night. Another display is launched from the South Street Seaport.

New York Philharmonic Concerts

Various locations (875-5709). Late July–early August. The New York Philharmonic presents a varied program, from Mozart to Weber, in many of New York's larger parks. The bugs are just part of the deal.

Thursday Night Concert Series

Main Stage, South Street Seaport, South St at Fulton St (732-7678). Subway: J, M, R, 2, 3, 4, 5 to Fulton St. Memorial

Day–Labor Day. Free outdoor concerts—of all types of music—are held throughout the summer at the South Street Seaport. See chapters **Sightseeing and Downtown** for more information on the seaport.

Summergarden
Museum of Modern Art, 11 W 53rd St between Fifth and Sixth Aves (708-9400, 708-9480). Subway: E, F to Fifth Ave. July–August. Free classical concerts, organized with the Juilliard School, are presented in the museum's sculpture garden.

Celebrate Brooklyn!
Performing Arts Festival
Prospect Park Bandshell, 9th St at Prospect Park West, Park Slope, Brooklyn (1-718-855-7882). Subway: F to Seventh Ave. July–August. Nine weeks of free outdoor events—music, dance, theater and film—are presented in Brooklyn's answer to Central Park.

Mostly Mozart
Avery Fisher Hall, Lincoln Center, 65th St at Columbus Ave (875-5399). Subway: 1, 9 to 66 St–Lincoln Ctr. Late July–August. For more than a quarter-century, the Mostly Mozart festival has mounted an intensive four-week schedule of performances of Mozart's work. There are also lectures and other side attractions.

Harlem Week
Throughout Harlem (862-8477). Early–mid August. The largest black and Hispanic festival in the world features music, film, dance, fashion, exhibitions and sports. The highlight is the street festival on Fifth Avenue between 125th and 135th Streets, which includes an international carnival of arts, entertainment and great food. Don't miss the jazz, gospel and R&B performances.

U.S. Open
USTA National Tennis Center, Flushing, Queens (info and tickets 1-718-760-6200). Subway: 7 to Willets Point–Shea Stadium. Late August–early September. The final Grand Slam event of the year, the U.S. Open is also one of the most entertaining tournaments on the international tennis circuit. Tickets are hard to come by, however.

Greenwich Village Jazz Festival
Throughout Greenwich Village (929-5149). Late August. This ten-day festival brings together most of the Village's many jazz clubs and includes lectures and films. It culminates in a free concert in Washington Square Park.

West Indian Day Carnival
Eastern Pkwy from Utica Ave to Grand Army Plaza, Brooklyn (1-718-625-1515). Subway: 3, 4 to Utica Ave; 2, 3 to

Scary monsters and superfreaks
Halloween in the West Village is a costume psychodrama

Commemorated in song by downtown poet laureate Lou Reed, the **Halloween Parade** is a New York institution—but the city developed its Mardi Gras–like blowout only in the 1970s. What started out in 1973 as a neighborhood trick-or-treat walk for the children of a Greenwich Village puppeteer has expanded over the years into a wild, frenzied bacchanal that draws an estimated 25,000 participants and more than one and a half million spectators to the Village streets.

In the early days, elaborate masks and costumes set the tone for the event. By its third year, the Theater for the New City took it under its wing as part of its City in the Streets program. This alliance, and the parade's appeal to the deep theatricality of the Village's sizable gay community, resulted in exponential growth. By 1982, the crowd had swelled to 100,000 and the organizing committee included a range of municipal, business and civic groups.

The parade remains a populist forum for grassroots personal expression. Cuban *bamba* dancers share the limelight with drag queens and Scottish bagpipers; Christian groups dance alongside Hare Krishnas. Huge papier-mâché puppets dominate the march, created each year along themes that range from the whimsical to the political, sometimes combining both.

Several years devoted to environmental themes—endangered oceans, the rain forest, Antarctica—resulted in a giant ghost crab, spider-monkey puppets and a 60-foot whale skeleton. The theme "Great Snakes Alive" produced a Medusa so large that she had to limbo under the overhead cables; she remains a perennial crowd favorite. Carried by teams of volunteers, the puppets have rod-driven movable parts that reach out into the crowds and filch the occasional hat.

Spectators know that the weirder you look, the more you fit into the mayhem. Bizarre uniforms and blurred-gender eroticism are the norm. Ghosts and goblins are out in force, mixing with stilt-walkers and "creatures" encompassing animal, vegetable and mineral.

Dubbed a "rite of passage" by *Time* magazine, the parade has always been an example of New York cosmopolitanism at its finest. Revelers from some 40 different cultures, each with a distinct presence in the city, join in the Dionysian blowout. For one delirious night a year, hobnobbing hobgoblins come together to create the ultimate New York moment.

Halloween Parade
From Spring St to Broadway, up Sixth Ave to 23rd St (475-3333, ext. 7787). Oct. 31, around 7pm. Internet: info@halloween-nyc.com

Eastern Pkwy–Brooklyn Musuem. Labor Day weekend.
This loud and energetic festival of Caribbean culture, with
a parade of flamboyantly costumed marchers, offers a children's parade on Saturday and an even bigger celebration
on Labor Day.

Richmond County Fair

*Historic Richmond Town, 441 Clarke Ave between Rich-
mond and Arthur Kill Rds, Staten Island (1-718-351-
1611). Labor Day.* An authentic county fair, with crafts and
produce and strange agricultural competitions, just like in
rural America.

Wigstock

Pier 54 (1-800-494-8497). Labor Day weekend. This event
is a celebration of drag, glamour and artificial hair, when
anyone who can muster some foundation and lipstick dresses up as a woman. Real girls had better be extra fierce to
cope with the competition. Having outgrown its origins
in the East Village's Tompkins Square Park, Wigstock has
found a new home at Pier 54, on the Hudson River across
from the West Village.

Fall

Football season

August–December. See chapter **Sports & Fitness**.

Feast of San Gennaro

*Mulberry St to Worth St, Little Italy (484-1222). Subway: J,
M, N, R, Z, 6 to Canal St. Third week in September. Internet: www.nycvisit.com* Celebrations for the feast of the patron saint of Naples last ten days, from noon to midnight
daily, with fairground booths, stalls and plenty of Italian
food and wine.

Atlantic Antic

*Brooklyn Heights, Brooklyn (1-718-875-8993). Subway: N, R
to Court St; 2, 3, 4, 5 to Borough Hall. Last Sun in September.*
This multicultural street fair on Brooklyn's Atlantic Avenue
features live entertainment and waterfront art exhibitions.

New York Film Festival

*Alice Tully Hall, Lincoln Center, 65th St and Columbus Ave
(875-5135). Subway: 1, 9 to 66th St–Lincoln Ctr. Late September–early October.* One of the film world's most prestigious events, the festival is a showcase for major directors
from around the world. Many U.S. and world premieres are on
the schedule. *See also chapter* **Film**.

New York City Opera Season

*New York State Theater, Lincoln Center, 65th St and Colum-
bus Ave (870-5570). Subway: 1, 9 to 66th St–Lincoln Ctr.
September–November, February–April.* Popular and classical operas, more daring but lesser-known work and the occasional musical comedy all find a home here. *See also chapter*
Music (Houses of high culture).

Hockey season

October–June. See chapter **Sports & Fitness**.

Columbus Day Parade

*Fifth Ave between 44th and 86th Sts (484-1222). Columbus
Day. Internet: www.nycvisit.com* To celebrate the first recorded sighting of America by Europeans, the whole country gets a holiday with an Italian flavor—and the inevitable
parade up Fifth Avenue.

Basketball season

November–April. See chapter **Sports & Fitness**.

*Rising inflation: No, it's not some surreal horror film—it's just **Macy's Thanksgiving Parade**.*

Halloween Parade
See **Scary monsters and superfreaks**, *page 31*.

New York City Marathon
Starts at the Staten Island side of the Verrazano Narrows Bridge (860-4455). Last Sun in October, first Sun in November at 10:40am. A crowd of 35,000 runners covers all five boroughs over a 26.2-mile (42km) course. The race finishes at Tavern on the Green, in Central Park at West 67th Street.

Macy's Thanksgiving Day Parade
From Central Park West at 79th St to Macy's, Broadway at 34th St (494-4495). Thanksgiving Day at 9am. Bring the kids to this one: It features enormous inflated cartoon-character balloons, elaborate floats and Santa Claus, who makes his way to Macy's department store, where he'll spend the next month in Santaland.

Winter

The Nutcracker Suite
New York State Theater, Lincoln Center, 65th St at Columbus Ave (870-5570). Subway: 1, 9 to 66th St–Lincoln Ctr. November–December. The New York City Ballet's performance of this famous work, assisted by students from the School of American Ballet, has become a much-loved Christmas tradition. *See chapter* **Dance**.

Christmas Tree Lighting Ceremony
Rockefeller Center, Fifth Ave between 49th and 50th Sts (484-1222). Subway: B, D, F, Q to 47th–50th Sts–Rockefeller Ctr. Early December. Internet: www.nycvisit.com The giant tree in front of the GE Building is festooned with five miles of lights. The tree, the skaters on the rink in the sunken plaza and the shimmering statue of Prometheus make this the most enchanting Christmas spot in New York.

Messiah Sing-In
National Chorale Council (333-5333). Mid-December. Around Christmas—usually a week before—21 conductors lead huge audiences (sometimes 3,000-strong) in a rehearsal and a performance of Handel's *Messiah.* You don't need any experience, and you can buy the score on-site. Location changes from year to year, so call for date, time and place.

Christmas Spectacular
Radio City Music Hall, 1260 Sixth Ave at 50th St (632-4000). Subway: B, D, F, Q to 47th–50th Sts–Rockefeller Ctr. Mid-November–early January. This is the famous long-running show in which the fabulous high-kicking Rockettes top off an evening of tableaux and musical numbers that exhaust the thematic possibilities of Christmas.

New Year's Eve Fireworks
Central Park (360-3456). Dec 31. The best viewing points for a night of pyrotechnics are Central Park at 72nd Street, Tavern on the Green (Central Park West at 67th Street) and Fifth Avenue at 90th Street. The fun and festivities, including hot cider and food, start at 11:30pm.

New Year's Eve Ball Drop
Times Square (768-1560). Subway: N, R, S, 1, 2, 3, 9, 7 to 42nd St–Times Sq. Dec 31. A traditional New York year ends and begins in Times Square, where a ball encrusted with lights is hoisted above the crowd and dropped at midnight. A recent glitz-driven ball overhaul means the sphere now sports 180 75-watt bulbs and some 12,000 rhinestones. If teeming hordes of drunken revelers turns you on, by all means go. The surrounding streets are packed by 9pm.

Chinese New Year
Around Mott St, Chinatown (484-1222). Subway: J, M, Z, N, R, 6 to Canal St. First day of the full moon between Jan 21

Legwork: The **NYC Marathon** is a fall classic.

and Feb 19. Internet: www.nycvisit.com The Chinese population of New York celebrates the new year in style, with dragon parades, performers and delicious food throughout Chinatown. Private fireworks have now been banned, so the celebrations don't have the bang they used to.

Winter Antiques Show
Seventh Regiment Armory, Park Ave at 67th St (1-718-292-7392). Subway: 6 to 68th St. Mid-January. This is the most prestigious of New York's antique fairs, with an eclectic selection of items ranging from ancient to Art Nouveau. The show's vast American collections come from all over the country. Sales benefit the East Side House Settlement.

Outsider Art Fair
The Puck Building, 295 Lafayette St (777-5218). Subway: B, D, F, Q to Broadway–Lafayette St; 6 to Bleecker St. Late January. A highlight of the annual art calendar, this three-day extravaganza draws crowds of buyers and browsers from all over the world. Its 35 dealers exhibit outsider, self-taught or visionary art in all media, at prices that range from $500 to $350,000.

Black History Month
February. A variety of events to celebrate African-American history are held at venues around the city. The program changes each year; watch the media for details.

Empire State Building Run-Up
350 Fifth Ave at 34th St (860-4455). Subway: B, D, F, Q, N, R to 34th St. Early February. The race starts in the lobby; runners speed up the 1,575 steps to the 86th floor. The average winning time is an astonishing 12 minutes.

The Art Show
Seventh Regiment Armory, Park Ave at 67th St (715-1685). Subway: 6 to 68th St. Late February. Begun in 1988 and sponsored by the Art Dealers Association of America, this is the big daddy of New York art fairs. Exhibitors offer paintings, prints and sculpture dating from the 17th century to the present. Proceeds go to the Henry Street Settlement, a Lower East Side social-service agency.

(to Russia, with love)

Dialing **1 800 CALL ATT**® not only connects you to the U.S., it gets you

to the world. You can use your AT&T Calling Card or any of these credit cards.

Which makes it easy to reach Moscow from the Hudson.

It's all within your reach.

Magic bus: Get a great view of St. Patrick's Cathedral atop a New York Apple double-decker.

Sightseeing

CENTRAL Park SummerStage '98

Sightseeing

**It's the gateway to a continent and a universe unto itself:
New York, New York, it's a helluva town**

With no shortage of sights to see in New York, most visitors have trouble finding time for all the places on their list. This is a guide to some of the essential and most famous ones. We also include recommendations for guided tours and hints about finding more unusual perspectives on the city. Many of the places listed here are also covered in other chapters, notably **New York by Neighborhood**, **Architecture**, **Museums** and **History**.

The views

Flying into New York on a clear day or night provides one of the world's most unforgettable sights. It's impossible to know which approach your plane will take, but for any of the three area airports, your viewing odds are best if you sit on the left side of the plane. Other jaw-dropping vistas can be seen from the Promenade in Brooklyn Heights

(Subway: 2, 3 to Clark Street); from the New Jersey Turnpike and Liberty State Park across the Hudson River; from the elevated sections of the Brooklyn-Queens Expressway; from midspan on many bridges; from the tops of tall buildings; and from the Staten Island Ferry.

The Statue

The Statue of Liberty & Ellis Island Immigration Museum

Reached via the Circle Line–Statue of Liberty Ferry (269-5755), departing every half hour from Gangway 5 in Battery Park at the southern tip of Manhattan. Subway: 1, 9 to South Ferry; 4, 5 to Bowling Green. 9:30am–5:30pm; $7, seniors $6, ages 3–17 $3, under 3 free. No credit cards. "A big girl who is obviously going to have a baby. The Birth of a Nation, I suppose," wrote wartime wit James Agate about the Statue of Liberty. Get up close to this most symbolic New York structure by visiting the island it stands on. Frédéric Auguste

*Somewhere over **the Rainbow Room**: The view from this bar is an affair to remember.*

*Torch song: Lady **Liberty** is the crown jewel.*

Bartholdi's statue was a gift from the people of France (the framework was designed by Gustav Eiffel), but it took the Americans years to collect enough money to give Liberty her pedestal. The statue stands 111′6″ toe-to-crown; there's an excruciating wait to climb the 154 steps to the observation deck, and we recommend you don't bother. It's a tight squeeze, rarely takes less than two hours and, since you can no longer get up into the torch, not such a big deal, anyway. Better to spend your time on Ellis Island, walking through the restored buildings dedicated to the millions of immigrants who passed through here, and pondering the ghostly personal belongings that hundreds of people left behind in their hurry to become part of a new nation. It's an arresting and moving museum. A decades-long dispute between the states of New York and New Jersey over title to the island was recently settled in Solomonic fashion by the U.S. Supreme Court, with New York retaining the original acreage and the historic structures, and New Jersey getting the 20-odd acres created over the years by landfill. If you're on a tight budget, the way to see Lady Liberty and Ellis Island is to take a free round trip on the **Staten Island Ferry**, which passes close to the statue (*see* **Tours**, *page 43*). *See also chapter* **Museums**.

The districts

See chapter **New York by Neighborhood** for more information on the areas listed below, plus a roundup of the city's other unmissable areas.

Chinatown

Subway: J, M, N, R, Z, 6 to Canal St. New York's Chinatown is the closest you'll get to Hong Kong without actually going there. It's a colorful, noisy, smelly marketplace where traders will sell you anything from fresh fish to a fake Rolex. Tables and hand carts jam the sidewalks, and the shops are filled to overflowing with Chinese treasures and kitschy souvenirs. Chinatown has dozens of excellent inexpensive restaurants (everyone in New York has his/her favorite, usually impossible to find if you haven't been there). Additional attractions include the Mott Street Buddhist Temple (64B Mott Street), the statue of Confucius in Confucius Plaza, and an arcade (8 Mott Street) featuring a live chicken that plays tic tac toe—and usually wins.

South Street Seaport

Water St to the East River, between John St and Peck Slip (info 732-7678). Subway: A, C to Broadway–Nassau St; J, M, Z, 2, 3, 4, 5 to Fulton St. Museum: 12 Fulton St at South St on the East River (748-8600). Daily 10am–5pm. Admission $6, students $4, children under 12 $3, seniors $5. Credit: AmEx, MC, V. Despite being overly prettified, the Seaport is worth a visit if you want to get a feel for the maritime history of the city. Dine on fresh seafood and imbibe rum alongside the burly guys who work at the fish market (which is now supposedly free of Mafia connections). There's plenty of shopping—in fact, the Seaport is a rare Manhattan approximation of the all-American mall experience. Admission to the Seaport Museum includes entry to its interesting galleries and tours around the historic vessels docked here. There are also several boats on which to take a quick cruise around the harbor.

Times Square

Broadway at W 42nd St. Subway: N, R, S, 1, 2, 3, 9, 7 to 42nd St–Times Sq. Visit Times Square at night, and you'll find yourself with hordes of people weaving among hotels, restaurants and big Broadway shows. This is New York's tourist mecca, full of busloads of Iowans gasping at the profusion of neon overhead. Soak up the (relatively safe) sleaziness of the place—it's mostly gone now, since new zoning laws have closed up the old Times Square's notorious sex shops and peep shows. Even squeaky-clean Disney has put down roots here. Originally called Longacre Square, Times Square was renamed after *The New York Times* moved to the site in 1924, announcing its arrival with a spectacular New Year's Eve fireworks display. The *Times* erected the world's first moving sign, where it posted election returns in 1928. The paper has now moved to 43rd Street, but the New Year's celebrations and amazing signs remain. *See also* **Take a walk on the mild side**, *in chapter* **New York by Neighborhood: Midtown**.

The landmarks

See also chapter **Architecture**.

Brooklyn Bridge

Subway: 4, 5, 6 to City Hall–Brooklyn Bridge. New York has many bridges, but none are as beautiful or famous as the Brooklyn Bridge. The twin Gothic arches of its towers have offered a grand gateway, no matter which way you were heading, though the symbolism diminished somewhat after (thanks largely to the bridge) Brooklyn became part of New York City in 1898. The span took more than 600 men some 16 years to build; when completed in 1883, it was the world's largest suspension bridge and the first to be constructed of steel. Engineer John A. Roebling was one of 20 men who died on the project—before construction even started. His son stayed on the job until he was struck by caisson disease (the bends) and then supervised construction, with the help of his wife, from the window of his Brooklyn apartment. "All that trouble just to get to Brooklyn!" was the vaudevillian quip of the time. The walkway is great for an afternoon stroll; for some incredible views, take the A or C train to Brooklyn Bridge, and walk back to Manhattan.

*Hey, baby, what's your sign? Get a load of the ever-changing neon jungle in **Times Square**.*

Migratory patterns: **Ellis Island**, *the Supreme Court ruled, is now mostly New Jersey's.*

Empire State Building

350 Fifth Ave at 34th St (736-3100). Subway: B, D, F, Q, N, R to 34th St. Observatories open 9:30am–midnight; last tickets sold at 11:25pm. $6, seniors and children under 12 $3. No credit cards. In 1931, it was the champ—the world's tallest building at 1,250 feet (1,472 including the lightning rod, or 448 meters). It's still arguably the best of Manhattan's heights. Why? Location, location, location: The observatory in the dead center of midtown offers brilliant overviews in every direction, putting you right in the center of the world's most complex jigsaw puzzle. Visit it before seeing anything else to get the lay of the land. Expect to wait in line at the second stage (86th floor), where another elevator takes you to the giddy heights of floor 102. After a 1997 shooting incident, airport-style metal detectors have been installed, but the building is still impossibly romantic, so don't forget to pack a loved one for the ascent. If you're a fan of virtual-reality rides, the Empire State houses two amusing big-screen flight simulators (though both are useless as actual tours): New York Skyride (10am–10pm; $11.50, children and seniors $9.50) and Transporter: Movies You Ride (9am–11pm; $8.50–$14.50, children $6.50–$10.50).

Rockefeller Center

47th–51st Sts between Fifth and Sixth Aves (632-3975); self-guided tours available at the GE Building, 30 Rockefeller Plaza (the north-south street between Fifth and Sixth Aves). Subway: B, D, F, Q to 47th–50th Sts–Rockefeller Ctr. Free. Urban planners have been trying to emulate Rockefeller Center ever since it was built in the 1930s, but no one has come close. The scale is extraordinary: It originally covered three city blocks, and now stretches even farther across Sixth Avenue. People crowd the pedestrian spaces between the low-massed Maison Française and the British Empire Buildings, looking down on the **ice-skating rink** (a café in summer) and up at the slender apex of the RCA Building (now called the **GE Building**). If you go at sunset, the views accompanying the cocktails at the **Rainbow Room** can be spectacular. **Radio City Music Hall** (50th St and Sixth Ave, 632-4041; tours Mon–Sat 10am–5pm, Sun 11am–5pm; adults $12, children $6) is an Art Deco wonder. Tourists can also look through the *Today* show's studio window (49th St at Rockefeller Plaza, Mon–Fri 7–9am) and wander the halls of **NBC** itself (NBC Tours, lobby level of 30 Rockefeller Plaza, 664-7174; Mon–Sat 9:30am–4:30pm, $8.25). This is an excellent place to wrap up a Fifth Avenue shopping spree.

World Trade Center

West St between Liberty and Vesey Sts (323-2340, groups 323-2350). Subway: C, E to World Trade Ctr; N, R, 1, 9 to Cortlandt St. Observation deck open 9:30am–9:30pm, rooftop promenade open, weather permitting; $6, children ages 6–12 $3, seniors $3.50, under 6 free. MC, V. At 1,377 feet (420 meters), the WTC's Rooftop Promenade is the world's highest open-air observation platform. Even from the bottom looking up, the view is enough to make your head spin. Ascend to the 110th floor, and you'll really feel the vertigo, especially as the building sways slightly in the wind. The scariest thing is that there's another tower of equal size only a stone's throw away. First thing in the morning is the best time to avoid the line, which can take up to an hour. If you're in the mood to splurge, guzzle a few drinks at **the Greatest Bar on Earth** (*see chapter* **Cafés and Bars**) or dine at **Windows on the World** (*see chapter* **Restaurants**). If your wallet is more down-to-earth, the building's lower concourse is a fast foodie's paradise.

The height of ambition: Even the spires seem to aspire along the East River waterfront.

The museums

See also chapter **Museums**.

Metropolitan Museum of Art

1000 Fifth Ave at 82nd St (535-7710). Subway: 4, 5, 6 to 86th St. Tue–Thu, Sun 9:30am–5:15pm; Fri, Sat 9:30am–8:45pm. Suggested donation $8, students and seniors $4, members and under 12 free. No credit cards. Foreign-language tours (570-3711). Internet: www.metmuseum.org. This is the city's attic, containing all manner of objects from modern art and sculpture to Native American antiquities. Don't even think about trying to "do" the entire Met: It has two million square feet (186,000 square meters) of floor space. Visit one of the excellent themed exhibitions or lose yourself wandering through the centuries until it's time for a break in the fabulous rooftop garden overlooking Central Park (open May through October).

Museum of Modern Art

11 W 53rd St between Fifth and Sixth Aves (708-9480). Subway: E, F to Fifth Ave. Sat–Tue, Thu 10:30am–6pm; Fri 10:30am–8:30pm. $9.50, students and seniors $6.50, under 16 free if accompanied by adult; Fri 4:30–8:30pm suggested donation. No credit cards. Even the most oblivious visitor may recognize almost every work here. With room after room of 20th-century genius, arranged more or less chronologically, it's an unforgettable experience. Even though MoMA is not terribly large, the strength of the collection will soon exhaust you. Avoid the astronomical prices in the cafeteria, but have a look at the design gift shop across the street.

Solomon R. Guggenheim Museum

1071 Fifth Ave at 88th St (423-3500). Subway: 4, 5, 6 to 86th St. Sun–Wed 10am–6pm; Fri, Sat 10am–8pm. $12, students and seniors $7, under 12 free with adult, voluntary donation Fri 6–8pm. Credit: AmEx, MC, V. In 1943, when Frank Lloyd Wright drew a citrus press, labeled it Guggenheim and presented it to the New York building authorities, all hell broke loose. It was 16 years—and six months after Wright died—before work was completed on the building commissioned by Solomon R. Guggenheim to house his remarkable collection of works by modern artists. The museum itself is Wright's masterwork and his only New York building. The permanent collection of Impressionist and Post-Impressionist works is displayed in rotation; the grand spiral walkway inside the shell hosts intriguing temporary exhibitions. The Guggenheim also has a downtown branch in Soho that's well worth visiting and is open late.
Branch: Guggenheim Museum SoHo, *575 Broadway at Prince St (423-3500). Subway: N, R to Prince St. Wed–Fri, Sun 11am–6pm; Sat 11am–8pm. $8, students and seniors $5, under 12 free, voluntary donation Sat 6–8pm. AmEx, MC, V.*

All-day visits

Bronx Zoo/Wildlife Conservation Society

Bronx River Pkwy at Fordham Rd (1-718-367-1010). Subway: 2, 5 to Bronx Park East. Mon–Fri 10am–5pm; Sat–Sun 10am–5:30pm; $6.75 adults, $3 children under 12 and seniors. No credit cards. Internet: www.wcs.org. The pythons crawl around a lush, indoor tropical rain forest not far beneath your feet; the ponds are brimming with crocodiles; the elusive snow leopard wanders around the mountaintops of the Himalayan Highlands; more than 30 species of the Rodentia family coexist in the Mouse House; birds, giraffes, lions and reptiles abound; and apes mercilessly mimic anyone who catches their eye. This is the largest urban zoo in America, home to more than 4,000 creatures. Although it covers 265 acres, it's not too hard on the feet; there's a choice of trams, monorails and express trains.

Across the road is the New York Botanical Garden, where you'll find a complex of grand glass houses set among 250 acres of lush greenery, including a large section of virgin forest along the Bronx River.

Coney Island

Brooklyn. Subway: B, D, F to Coney Island. In the 1920s and '30s, a series of apocalyptic fires destroyed the original wooden structures of the various competing funfairs here. Nowadays, despite a thriving collection of rides, sideshows and other spangly things, the greatest attraction is the air of decayed grandeur. Grab a Nathan's Famous hot dog, get a gander at the gruesome sideshow (1208 Surf Ave at W 12th St, 1-718-372-5159), take a spin on the Cyclone at **Astroland** (*see chapter* **Children**), walk out to the beach and stroll along the boardwalk, perhaps as far as the **Aquarium for Wildlife Conservation** (Surf Ave at W 8th St, 1-718-265-FISH. 10am–6pm; $7.75, children and seniors $3.50). Marvel at its famous Beluga whales.

Corona Park, Flushing Meadows & Shea Stadium

Queens. Subway: 7 to Willets Pt–Shea Stadium. If you've ever wondered about those strange roadside structures on the way into the city from JFK, this is the answer. Corona Park contains the remnants of the 1939 and 1964 World's Fairs. A series of bizarre buildings, including the New York Hall of Science (*see chapter* **Children**) and dilapidated space junk (actual retrieved rocket fragments) are on display. Then there's the Unisphere, a huge stainless-steel globe that has been a backdrop for countless rap videos (and the climax of the hit movie *Men in Black*), and the Canadian Pavilion, a crown-of-thorns amphitheater with a huge map of New York State inlaid in the floor. The park itself contains barbecue pits, a boating lake and wide expanses of empty grass. Come here for a Mets baseball game at Shea Stadium or to the tennis center (home of the U.S. Open), and spend an afternoon wandering among the weirdness.

Historic Richmond Town

441 Clarke Ave between Arthur Kill and Richmond Rds, Richmond Town, Staten Island (1-718-351-1611). Travel: Staten Island Ferry from Battery Park, then S74 bus. Wed–Sun 1–5pm; $5, seniors and students $2.50, under 6 free. No credit cards. This collection of 29 restored historic buildings is the best place to get an idea of the history of New York. Fourteen of them are open to the public, including Lake-Tysen House, a wooden farmhouse built in about 1740 in Dutch Colonial style for a French Huguenot; and Voorlezer's House, the oldest surviving elementary school in America. Many of the buildings—which include a courthouse, general store, bakery and butcher, as well as private homes—have been moved here from elsewhere on the island. Actors in 18th-century garb lurk in the doorways; crafts workshops are never far away. It's as if you've left the city far behind.

Tours

Big Apple Greeter

1 Centre St at Chambers St, 20th floor (669-2896, fax 669-3685). Subway: 4, 5, 6 to Brooklyn Bridge–City Hall. Mon–Fri 9:30am–5pm; recorded information at other times. If you don't feel like letting one of the many tour companies herd you along the New-York–by–numbers trail, or if you'd simply prefer to have a knowledgeable and enthusiastic friend to accompany you as you discover the city, put in a call to Big Apple Greeter. This immensely successful program has been in operation since 1992, introducing visitors to one of 600 carefully chosen volunteer "greeters" and giving them a chance to see New York beyond the well-trodden tourist traps. Go visit Vinny's mom in Bensonhurst, have Renata show you around the hidden treasures of Polish Greenpoint, or let Carmine take you to the parks in the South Bronx where

Welcome to New York.

Now get out.

The obsessive guide to impulsive entertainment

On sale at newsstands in New York

Pick up a copy!

To get a copy of the current issue or to subscribe, call *Time Out New York* at 212-539-4444.

Sweet relief

Keep your pants on. Here's where to go when you really gotta go.

Visitors to New York—like New Yorkers themselves—are always on the go. But in between all that go, go go, sometimes you've really got to... *go*. Contrary to popular belief (and the general smell, especially in summer), the street is no place to drop trou. The real challenge lies in finding a (legal) public place to take care of your business.

Though they don't exactly have an open-door policy, the numerous **McDonald's** restaurants and **Barnes & Noble** bookstores all contain (usually clean) restrooms. Just don't announce that you're not a paying customer, and you should be all right. The same applies to most other fast-food joints (Au Bon Pain, Wendy's, etc.) that don't have a host or maître d' greeting you at the door. Here are some other options around town that can offer sweet relief (if you hold your breath).

Downtown

Kmart
770 Broadway at Astor Pl. Mon–Fri 9am–10pm; Sat, Sun 11am–8pm.

Tompkins Square Park
Ave A at 9th St, Mon–Thu 8am–7pm.

Wall City Toilet
Centre St at Chambers St, 6am–9pm.

Washington Square Park
Thompson St at Washington Sq South, 6am–midnight.

Midtown

Bryant Park
42nd St between Fifth and Sixth Aves, Mon–Sat 8am–7pm and until 1am in the summer.

Penn Station
Seventh Ave between 30th and 32nd Sts, 24 hours.

Port Authority
Eighth Ave at 41st St, 6am–1am.

St. Clement's Church
423 W 46th St between Ninth and Tenth Aves, Mon–Fri 10am–6pm; Sat, Sun 9–11am.

School of Visual Arts
209 E 23rd St between Second and Third Aves, Mon–Fri 8am–10pm.

United Nations
First Ave between 44th and 45th Sts, 9am–5pm.

U.S. Social Security Office
38 E 29th St between Madison Ave and Park Ave South, Mon–Fri 9am–4:30pm.

Uptown

Barneys New York
660 Madison Ave at 61st St; Mon–Sat 10am–8pm, Sun 10am–6pm.

Central Park
Midpark at 81st St, 7am–sundown.

Avery Fisher Hall at Lincoln Center
Amsterdam Ave at 65th St; Mon–Sat 10am–6pm, Sun noon–6pm.

*Porcelain gods: The staff at **Avery Fisher Hall** keeps its restrooms neat and clean.*

*Steerage class? The line for the **Ellis Island** ferry gives new meaning to "huddled masses."*

*I'm a Capricorn, too: Goats are among 4,000 beasts that inhabit the 265-acre **Bronx Zoo**.*

hip-hop was invented. The service is completely free, though donations are welcome, and it also can be tailored to visitors with disabilities. Write, call or fax the office to find yourself a New York friend.

By boat

Circle Line

Pier 83, W 42nd St at Twelfth Ave (563-3200). Subway: A, C, E to 42nd St. Three-hour trip $22, seniors $16, children under 12 $12; two-hour trip $18, seniors $14, children under 12 $10. Internet: www.seaportliberty.com From April to November, Circle Line operates a three-hour trip that circumnavigates Manhattan. From June to August, there's also a two-hour "harbor lights" cruise in the evening, one of the cheapest and best ways to see the city.

The *Petrel*

Battery Park (825-1976). Subway: 1, 9 to South Ferry. Call for charter rates. A 70-foot yawl designed by Sparkman & Stephens, the *Petrel* is built of teak and mahogany. It was launched in 1938 as a racing yacht, and the owners still pride themselves on using a sail as much as possible. This is a New York favorite, so you'll need to book two weeks in advance. The *Petrel* sails between May and November.

Seaport Liberty Cruises

Pier 16, South Street Seaport (630-8888). Subway: J, M, Z, 2, 3, 4, 5 to Fulton St. $12, seniors $10, children $6. Speedboat: $15, children $10. Internet: www.seaportliberty.com One-hour cruises and two-hour evening music cruises are offered on a large sightseeing boat. 30-minute trips on a speedboat called *The Beast* are also available.

Staten Island Ferry

Entrance at Battery Park (806-6940). Subway: 1, 9 to South Ferry; 4, 5 to Bowling Green. Free. The poor man's Circle Line is actually just as fun, provided you bring the one you love. Inspiring, no-cost panoramas of Manhattan and the Statue of Liberty turn this commuting barge into a romantic sojourn when the sun goes down. On the other side is Staten Island, which may not be as pretty but has a nice personality. Boats depart South Ferry at Battery Park every half hour, 24 hours a day, and provide views of New York's harbor and Manhattan.

By bus

Gray Line

Port Authority Bus Terminal, Eighth Ave at 42nd St (397-2600). Subway: A, C, E to 42nd St. 7:45am–8pm, $19–$49. AmEx, Disc, JCB, MC, V. Gray Line offers more than 20 bus tours around the city, from a basic two-hour ride to the monster nine-hour all-day "Manhattan Comprehensive," which includes lunch. The firm also runs Central Park trolley tours; call for info.

New York Apple Tours

1-800-876-9868. Tickets available at Rockefeller Center (Fifth Ave at 50th St), the Plaza Hotel (Fifth Ave at 59th St). Visitor's Information Center (Eighth Ave at 53rd St), and buses at Times Square (Seventh Ave at 42nd St). 65-stop tour runs

Green daze

When you need a bucolic break, veg out in Central Park

New Yorkers like their relaxation to be as intensive as possible, and for this there is Central Park: the condensed, urban version of Eden, and perhaps the only thing that keeps eight million New Yorkers from going crazy. This vast, 843-acre (340-hectare) expanse of greenery, set in the center of Manhattan, is home to a small city's worth of activities (some 15 million people visit the park every year) and has many distinct regions, each with its own atmosphere and purpose.

As natural as it may seem, the park is as prefab as Manhattan's street grid; everything except the prehistoric rock is man-made. Journalist and landscaper Frederick Law Olmsted and architect Calvert Vaux worked for 20 years to create their masterpiece. Although it was long believed that the land on which the park was built was nothing more than a swamp when construction began in 1840, it is now clear that a settlement of some 600 free blacks, Irish and German immigrants occupied an area known as Seneca Village, located in what is now the west 80s.

Anywhere you go in the park, watch out for joggers, cyclists and in-line skaters. The Byzantine **Bethesda Fountain and Terrace**, at the center of the 72nd Street Transverse Road, is the park's most popular meeting place. Just south is the **Mall**, site of weekend skating and volleyball.

To the east, on a mound behind the Naumburg Bandshell, is the site of the **Central Park SummerStage** and its impressive series of free concert and spoken-word performances (*see* **Fresh air guitars** *in chapter* **Music**). To the west is the **Sheep Meadow**—yes, sheep actually grazed here as recently as the 1930s. You may see kites, Frisbees or soccer balls zoom past, but most people are here to work on their tans. If you get hungry, repair to glitzy **Tavern on the Green** (*see chapter* **Restaurants**), or wolf down a hot dog.

West of Bethesda Terrace, near the 72nd Street entrance, is peaceful **Strawberry Fields**. This is where John Lennon, who lived and died nearby, is remembered. You can rent a boat or gondola at the **Loeb Boathouse** on the **Lake**, crossed by the elegant **Bow Bridge**. For sailing on a smaller scale, head east to the **Conservatory Water**, where model sailboats race. **The Ramble** is a wild area known for birdwatching by day and anonymous, mostly gay, rendezvous at night (not the safest place to be).

Farther uptown is **Belvedere Castle**, with its new **Henry Luce Nature Observatory**; the **Delacorte Theater**, where the New York Shakespeare Festival mounts plays by the Bard and others during the summer; and the recently restored **Great Lawn**, where classical concerts and other large events are held. The **Reservoir,**

*Om sweet om: The wheel world fades away in **Central Park**'s grassy **Sheep Meadow**.*

above 86th Street, was recently named in honor of Jacqueline Kennedy Onassis, who used to jog around it. North of the sports fields and tennis courts, the park is mostly wild and wooded. Highlights include the restored **Harlem Meer** at the northeastern corner and the beautiful formal **Conservatory Garden** (Fifth Avenue at 105th Street). *See also chapter* **Children**.

Henry Luce Nature Observatory

Belvedere Castle, Central Park, mid-park at 79th St (772-0210). Subway: B, C to 81st St; 6 to 77th St. October–February 11am–4pm, February–October Tue–Sun 10am–5pm. Free. Enjoy the hands-on "Woods and Water" exhibit, surveying the wide variety of plant and animal life in the park. Kits for birdwatching are also available.

Central Park Zoo/Wildlife Center

Fifth Ave and 64th St (861-6030). Subway: N, R to Fifth Ave. Mon–Fri 10am–5pm; Sat, Sun 10am–5:30pm. $3.50, children 50¢, under 3 free, seniors $1.25. No credit cards. This small zoo is one of the park's highlights. Seals, monkeys, penguins and the famous polar bear who swims laps are among the more than 130 species here—and there are 27 more in the new Tisch Children's Zoo.

Charles A. Dana Discovery Center

Enter at Fifth Ave at 110th St (860-1370). Subway: 6 to 110th St. Tue–Sun 10am–5pm. Free. Stop in for weekend family workshops, outdoor performances on the plaza and cultural exhibits in the gallery.

The Dairy

Central Park at 64th St (794-6565). Mid-April–mid-October Tue–Sun 11am–5pm, mid-October–mid-April Tue–Sun 11am–4pm. Free. This information center for Central Park contains an interactive exhibition and a six-minute video on the history of the park. The Dairy was built in 1870 to show city kids where milk came from. Nearby is the beautiful antique carousel (90¢ a ride) and Heckscher Playground.

Department of Parks & Recreation

Recorded info 360-3456. Recorded information is available on activities in all city parks.

Loeb Boathouse

Central Park, near Fifth Ave and E 74th St (517-4723). Subway: 6 to 77th St. Summer 11:30am–6pm; spring, autumn Sat, Sun 10:30am–6pm. $10 per hour plus $30 deposit; $30 per hour for chauffeured gondola. No credit cards. Rent a rowboat, ride a gondola or grab a picnic at the café.

Urban Park Rangers

360-2774. 9am–5pm. The Rangers, a division of the Parks Department, provide information and emergency services. Call about guided walks.

Wollman Memorial Rink

Mid-park at 62nd St (396-1010). Subway: B, Q to 57th St; N, R to Fifth Ave. Thu, Fri 10am–6pm; Sat 10am–8pm, Sun 10am–7pm. $4, children and seniors $3, skate and blade rental $6. MC, V (group rentals only). Donald Trump scored major points when he rescued this decaying rink. Bigger than the pricey spot at Rockefeller Center, this is the best open-air rink in Manhattan—and impossibly romantic at night, when the city lights tower over the park's leafy canopy.

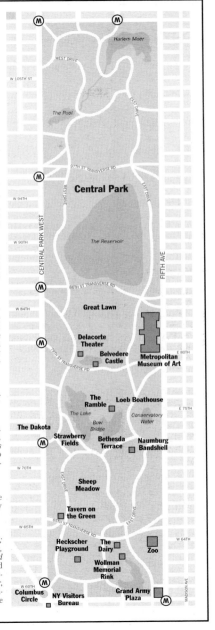

continuously starting at 9am. $21–$46. MC, V. Take a guided tour either uptown or downtown, or combine the two for a daylong ride around Manhattan in open-top, red-and-yellow double-deckers. Once you have a ticket, you can get on and off at any point on the route (on the combined tour you can spread this over two days). Buses are frequent enough to make this practical. The company also offers a "Harlem Gospel Express" itinerary, a tour that makes stops in Brooklyn, and tours by bus and helicopter.

By helicopter

Liberty Helicopter Tours

VIP Heliport, Twelfth Ave at W 30th St (967-6464, recorded info 465-8905). Subway: A, C, E to 34th St. 9am–9pm, $49–$129. MC, V. The Liberty copters are larger than most, which makes the ride fairly smooth. There are between 10 and 40 rides a day, depending on the weather. Reservations are unnecessary, and several tours are offered. Even the shortest ride is long enough to get a good close-up view of the Statue of Liberty, Ellis Island and the Twin Towers.

On foot

For more information on various walking tours of New York—covering historic neighborhoods, celebrity sites, ethnic cuisines, architectural themes and more—consult the Around Town section of *Time Out New York*.

Big Onion Walking Tours

Call 439-1090 for recorded schedules. Tours are scheduled every weekend and holiday. Most are $9, students and seniors $7. Internet: www.bigonion.com This business, started by Columbia University doctoral candidates in history, puts together astoundingly informative tours of New York's historic districts and ethnic neighborhoods. Private tours are also available.

Grand Central & 34th Street Partnerships

These neighborhood business organizations offer free tours of their districts, including a monthly tour of the remnants of the demolished Pennsylvania Station (call 868-0521 for info) and a grand tour of midtown, including Grand Central Terminal itself (call 818-1777 for info).

Harlem Spirituals

690 Eighth Ave between 43rd and 44th Sts (391-0900). Subway: A, C, E to 42nd St. Mon–Sat 9am–6pm; book at least one day ahead. $15–75. AmEx, MC, V. Sunday-morning gospel tours take in Sugar Hill, Hamilton Grange and the Morris-Jumel Mansion, as well as a service at a Baptist church. Gospel tours (Sun, Wed and Fri) pass by the Schomburg Institute for Research into Black Culture and visit a Baptist church choir. Visit cabarets on the evening "soul food and jazz" tours (Mon, Thu, Sat). The historical tour includes lunch and runs on Thursdays. Spanish-language tours are also available.

Heritage Trails New York

Federal Hall National Memorial, 26 Wall St between Broad and William Sts (888-4TRAILS). Subway: 4, 5 to Wall St. Mon–Fri 9am–5pm; guidebooks $5, guided tour fee varies (call for details). The red, blue, orange and green dots of paint that mark four and a half miles of lower Manhattan sidewalk make up this detailed self-guided tour, which highlights some of the neighborhood's tough-to-find tourist attractions, such as the Vietnam War Veterans Memorial and the Seamen's Church Institute. The necessary guidebook costs $5 and is available from the office. Heritage Trails also offers tours of the Federal Reserve and the Stock Exchange ($7–$11). Call for info on guided tours.

Free cable! The magnificent **Brooklyn Bridge**.

Kramer's Reality Tour

Pulse Theatre, 432 W 42nd St between Ninth and Tenth Aves (268-5525). Subway: A, C, E to 42nd St. Sat–Sun noon and 4pm; $37.50. This tour views America's greatest city through the lens of what some consider America's greatest sitcom. Kenny Kramer, the inspiration for *Seinfeld*'s Cosmo Kramer and now a tour guide, has put together this pricey ride past notable *Seinfeld* plot spots in Manhattan. Yes, the Soup Nazi is on the tour.

Municipal Art Society Tours

457 Madison Ave between 50th and 51st Sts (935-3960). Subway: 6 to 51st St. Mon–Wed, Fri, Sat 11am–5pm, $12–$15. The Society organizes some very informative tours, including hikes around Harlem, the Upper West Side, Greenwich Village, and Brooklyn Heights. They also offer a free tour of Grand Central Station Wednesdays at 12:30pm.

Talk-A-Walk

30 Waterside Plaza, NY, NY 10010 (686-0356). This mail-order service offers a choice of five 85-minute audiocassette tours ($9.95 each). Each contains directions and commentary for a walk lasting two to four hours. Fax the number above to receive a three-page catalog.

Tours with the 92nd Street Y

1395 Lexington Ave at 92nd St (996-1100). Subway: 4, 5, 6 to 86th St. Prices vary. Tours run May to September, mostly on Sundays, and cover Park Avenue, Irish New York, the Bowery, etc.

Urban Park Rangers

1234 Fifth Ave at 104th St (360-2774). Subway: 6 to 106th St. 9am–5pm. Free. A service of the Parks Department, the Rangers organize pleasant free walks and talks in all city parks. Subjects and activities covered include fishing, wildlife, bird watching and Native American history.

Architecture

When the expansion of a city is limited by its island location, the only way to go is up

O. Henry once said of New York, "It'll be a great place if they finish it." It is the constant construction of the city that has made it such an architectural wonderland (indeed, some buildings are torn down after only 20 years). The early European immigrants brought with them a wide range of architectural styles to be adopted, adapted or ignored, and the city's innate cockiness demanded nothing but the very finest, most impressive buildings.

Like few other cities, New York is truly three-dimensional. A map is useless in conjuring it; a model—or a helicopter ride—is more evocative. Space, rather than land, is what is valuable here, so a building plot is a mere footprint: Its true worth can be measured only when multiplied by height. And apart from Inwood Hill Park at Manhattan's northernmost tip, hardly a square inch of the island has escaped the attention of planners, builders and architects. Even the seemingly haphazard geography of Central Park is a deliberate architectural feat.

These are a few architectural highlights of New York, though there are hundreds of other buildings worth seeing. Most are accessible to the public in at least a limited way (especially the lobbies), and many of the more historic ones are now museums.

Anyone with a strong interest in the architecture of the city might want to get oriented with a visit to the **Urban Center** at 457 Madison Ave, home to both the Municipal Art Society and the Architectural League, where you'll find gallery space, lecture series and a wonderful bookstore devoted to architecture and urban design issues. The center's building—a Stanford White creation, the bulk of which is now the Palace Hotel—is quite appealing in its own right. Pick up some of the literature and plan your foray through the city while dining at the swanky Le Cirque 2000, which is in the same building, or at one of the tables in the charming courtyard.

*Art whorl: Come out of your shell and into Frank Lloyd Wright's at the **Guggenheim Museum**.*

Urban Center

457 Madison Ave between 50th and 51st Sts (bookstore 935-3592; Architectural League 753-1722; Municipal Art Society 935-3960). Subway: E, F to Fifth Ave; 6 to 51st St. Mon–Thu 10am–7pm, Fri 10am–6pm, Sat 10am–5pm.

Dutch beginnings

Under Dutch rule (1626–64) the city grew only as far north as Wall Street (the site of a defensive wall) and resembled a Dutch country town, even down to the odd windmill. The earliest buildings were built of fieldstone or were wood-framed with brick facing, and they had quirks brought from the Netherlands, such as tiled roofs, stepped gables, decorative brickwork and stone stoops (the word comes from the Dutch *stoep*, meaning step), which were originally designed to elevate the entrance from the wet Dutch landscape.

None of these buildings has survived in Manhattan, but in Brooklyn you can see the **Pieter Claesen Wyckoff House**, built in 1652, which is the oldest home in New York City. In Queens there is the **Bowne House** (1661), built by John Bowne, a Quaker who secured the rights of religious freedom for the colony. You'll also find the **Friends' Meeting House** (137-16 Northern Blvd between Main and Union Sts, Flushing) he built in 1694 in Queens. **Dyckman Farmhouse Museum**, the only remaining Dutch farmhouse in Manhattan, wasn't

built until 1785, though it retains the high-shouldered gambrel roof and flared eaves of the mature Dutch Colonial style. **Historic Richmond Town** on Staten Island (*see chapter* **Sightseeing**) contains several buildings in the Dutch style.

Bowne House

37-01 Bowne St between 37th and 38th Aves, Flushing, Queens (1-718-359-0528). Subway: 7 to Main St–Flushing. Tue, Sat, Sun 2:30–4:30pm. $2, $1 concessions. No credit cards.

Dyckman Farmhouse Museum

4881 Broadway at 204th St (304-9422). Subway: A to Dyckman St. Tue–Sun 11am–4pm. Free.

Pieter Claesen Wyckoff House Museum

5902 Clarendon Rd at Ralph Ave, East Flatbush, Brooklyn (1-718-629-5400). Subway: 2, 5 to Newkirk Ave, then B7, B8 or B78 bus to Clarendon Rd. Times vary; call for details. $2, $1 concessions. No credit cards.

British influence

The arrival of the British spurred growth, and there was much building during the 100 years of their rule. Landfill projects extended the island's shoreline, and commercial buildings were erected, driving the wealthier residents northward. New York grew to become the second largest city in the British Empire and expanded as far as the site of City Hall. The British were eager to make their mark, and many of the new structures were built in the Georgian style of the new colonists.

*Empire estate: You can still visit the colonial-era **Morris-Jumel Mansion**, built in 1765.*

The present **Trinity Church** is actually the third to stand on this site. The first was consecrated in 1698 but was destroyed by fire soon after the Revolutionary War. The second was completed in 1790 but demolished due to structural problems. The current structure, a square-towered Episcopal church designed by Richard Upjohn, was built in 1846. Its elegant Gothic Revival spire was the tallest structure in Manhattan until the 1860s.

In fact, very few buildings remain from the century of British rule. One exception is **St. Paul's Chapel** (1766) on Broadway at Fulton Street, a beautiful example of the style of church popularized in London by Christopher Wren. It is modeled on St. Martin-in-the-Fields, with an elegant temple portico and a steeple rising from the roof.

Fraunces Tavern (*see chapter* **Museums**) is actually a 20th-century reconstruction, but it gives a good idea of how the original structure, built in 1719 as a private residence, must have looked. This was where George Washington held a victory celebration in 1783. The **Van Cortlandt mansion** was built by Frederick Van Cortlandt in 1748 as the homestead of his wheat plantation in what is now the Bronx. Though it is simply constructed, with rugged fieldstone walls and hand-carved keystones, its traditional Georgian proportions are evident. The wooden **Morris-Jumel Mansion**, built in 1765, has the elegant low-pitched roof and colossal portico of the grand Georgian style. Apart from these selected buildings, the best place to see colonial New York is at Historic Richmond Town, where many buildings of the period have been gathered and restored (*see chapter* **Sightseeing**).

Morris-Jumel Mansion

1765 Jumel Terrace (which runs from Edgecombe Ave to St. Nicholas Ave) between 160th and 162nd Sts (923-8008). Subway: A, B to 163rd St. Wed–Sun 10am–4pm. $3, $2 concessions. No credit cards.

Trinity Church Museum

Broadway at Wall St (602-0872). Subway: 2, 3 to Wall St. Mon–Fri 7am–6pm; Sat, Sun 7am–4pm (closed during concerts). Free.

Van Cortlandt House Museum

Van Cortlandt Park, Broadway at 242nd St, Riverdale, Bronx (1-718-543-3344). Subway: 1, 9 to 242nd St–Van Cortlandt Park. Tue–Fri 10am–3pm; Sat, Sun 11am–4pm. $2, $1.50 concessions; under 12 free. No credit cards.

The Federal period

After the Revolution, architecture was used to express the city's new independence and its brief role as capital of the fledgling United States. The favored building style in the first half-century of the new republic was Federal, an Americanized version of English Georgian.

Pockets of Federal architecture can still be seen in lower Manhattan. The 1832 **Merchant's House Museum** is a lonely survivor of the period when

this area was fashionable (*see chapter* **Museums**). A row of nine red-brick houses dating from 1828 on Harrison Street in Tribeca has recently been restored as private homes. The largest group of Federal-style houses in New York City, dating from the 1820s, is the Charlton-King-Vandam Historic District on the southern boundary of Greenwich Village.

Many grand public buildings were erected in an area known as the Civic Center. The beautiful **City Hall** (1811), with its delicate columns and domed rotunda, combined the Federal style with French Renaissance influences.

The continuing vogue for neoclassicism led to an American version of Greek Revival architecture, exemplified by the massive colonnaded **Federal Hall** (1842) on Wall Street, built in the form of a Greek temple. Another fine surviving example of this fashion is the 1832 **Colonnade Row** (Lafayette St between 4th St and Astor Pl), which contained some of the most exclusive houses in the city. The less wealthy lived in brownstones, elegant middle-class row houses that were built by the thousands in the 19th century. At the same time, vast, overcrowded tenement buildings were built to house the poorest and most recent immigrants.

Charlton-King-Vandam Historic District

9–43 and 20–42 Charlton St, 11–49 and 16–54 King St, 9–29 Vandam St, 43–51 MacDougal St. Subway: 1, 9 to Houston St. In addition to having the largest concentration of Federal-style houses in New York, this area includes fine examples of Greek Revival, Italianate and late-19th-century domestic architecture.

City Hall

City Hall Park between Broadway and Park Row (Mayor's office: 788-3000). Subway: J, M, Z to Chambers St; 2, 3 to Park Pl; 4, 5, 6 to City Hall. Mon–Fri 10am–4pm. Free.

Federal Hall National Monument

26 Wall St at Nassau St (825-6888). Subway: 2, 3, 4, 5 to Wall St. 9am–5pm. Free. George Washington took the presidential oath in the Federal Hall that once stood on this site. The present building was erected between 1834 and 1842 as a customhouse. It is now a national monument, full of exhibits relating to the Constitution.

Beaux Arts

Another period of proud expansion occurred around the turn of the century, as the robber barons of the Gilded Age put their newfound wealth to work. The majority of the new landmarks employed the Beaux Arts style, a careful appropriation of European Renaissance forms. Richard Morris Hunt gave the city the **Metropolitan Museum** (1895, Fifth Ave between 80th and 84th Sts; *see chapter* **Museums**) and, under Andrew Carnegie's patronage, **Carnegie Hall** (1891, 156 W 57th St at Seventh Ave; *see chapter* **Music**). Cass Gilbert, later to design the Woolworth Building (*see page 57*), created the U.S. Custom House (1907, 1 Bowling Green between State and Whitehall Sts), a beautiful tribute to the city's role as a seaport, and which now houses the **National Museum of the American Indian** (*see chapter* **Museums**).

The firm of Carrère & Hastings provided a home for the **New York Public Library** (1911, Fifth Ave between 40th and 42nd Sts; *see chapter* **Museums**), a building that epitomizes the city's Beaux Arts architecture. Warren & Wetmore built the majestic soaring spaces of **Grand Central Terminal** (1913), still New York's grandest port of entry and recently restored to its full glory, as well as the **Helmsley Building** (1929, 230 Park Ave between 45th and 46th Sts).

The city's most important architectural firm, and easily the most famous, was McKim, Mead & White, which propounded the classical idioms of the Italian Renaissance. Its **Municipal Building** (1914, Centre St at Chambers St) echoes the City Hall it faces with a grand colonnaded tower. Charles McKim's **University Club** (1899, 1 W 54th St at Fifth Ave) is an elegant Renaissance-style palazzo, and White's grand **Metropolitan Club** (1894, 1 E 60th St at Fifth Ave) is more French than Italian, with a colonnaded gateway.

McKim was also responsible for what is now the **Pierpont Morgan Library** (1917, 33 E 36th St between Madison and Park Aves), one of New York's great buildings (*see chapter* **Museums**). It's a low classical temple built in the Greek manner, using marble blocks honed carefully so they could be laid without mortar. McKim's last work, Penn-

What goes up...

How NYC elevators became such an uplifting experience

All those skyscrapers that grace the New York skyline would be pretty empty if you had to take the stairs all the way up. There is a yearly footrace up the 86 flights of the Empire State Building, but fitness aside, who has the time? Tens of thousands of elevators are what make New York the great vertical city it is.

Mechanical hoists have been traced back at least to ancient Greece, and steam-driven and hydraulic freight elevators were developed in the early years of the Industrial Revolution. But passenger elevators came into wide use only after one Elisha Otis devised a mechanism that would automatically stop a cab's fall in the event of a broken rope. Otis caught the public eye with a demonstration of his invention at New York's Crystal Palace in 1857; that same year, he installed what is generally considered the first working passenger elevator in the five-story Haughwout Building at the corner of Broadway and Broome Street (*see page 56*).

New construction techniques and advances in elevator technology blossomed in tandem through the Gilded Age. The elevators of the day were opulently furnished, with fine chandeliers and richly upholstered benches. Marcel Duchamp was reportedly quite fond of those in the old Biltmore Hotel spending the occasional afternoon riding up and down in peaceful meditation. Almost all of those grand dowagers are now gone, replaced by prosaic stainless-steel boxes, but one classic cab of that time can still be found in the lobby at 34 Gramercy Park East, more than 100 years old and still in use, its ornate woodwork and inlaid floors carefully maintained.

New York's great elevators for speed and height today are, naturally, in the tallest buildings: the Empire State Building and the World Trade Center, where riders grab an express to a choice of "sky lobbies," then switch to a local for intermediary floors. While the world's fastest elevator is in Japan, these babies aren't far behind, topping out at 1,200 feet (366 meters) per second.

Elevator riding was undoubtedly a more human experience before automatic and computerized controls displaced the ubiquitous elevator operator, but certain buildings around town still have human beings at the controls.

Finally, two items of note, unsettling though they may be: Two thirds of the city's official elevator inspectors were fired in April 1997 for bribery and extortion, and that autumn, the union representing most of New York's elevator repairmen went on strike. City spokesmen insist there is no problem. Have a nice day.

*Get high: The **World Trade Center** towers.*

*By the book: The **New York Public Library** (1911) shows the city at its Beaux-Arts best.*

sylvania Station, is now, alas, destroyed (see photo, page 13); it lives on only in the firm's complementary design for the **General Post Office** (1913, Eighth Ave between 31st and 33rd Sts), which is across the street. Currently, there is a proposal to move Penn Station into this building, but nothing was definite at press time. White is probably best remembered for his **Washington Arch** (1895), which enriches the southern end of Fifth Avenue.

Grand Central Terminal

42nd St at Park Ave. Subway: S, 4, 5, 6, 7 to 42nd St–Grand Central. 24 hours. Free tours Wed at 12:30pm, meet in front of the information booth on the main level. Call the Municipal Art Society, 935-3960, for more information.

Cast iron

As thousands of immigrants arrived, so did new building techniques. Based on the British factories of the Industrial Revolution, large structures made of prefabricated cast-iron parts could be built quickly and cheaply. In fact, you could order numbered parts from a foundry catalog and then simply bolt them together. The resulting buildings consisted of layers of columns, and their gridded skeletons were clearly visible in their facades, which were often painted to resemble stone. Architects made Classical, Renaissance and Baroque forms with the cast-iron building blocks—you can see examples of the evolving styles throughout midtown and downtown Manhattan, especially around Soho, which has the highest concentration of cast-iron architecture in the world.

Since the medium lent itself to repetitive use of a single element, it was the Palazzo style, often with successive rows of slender columns, that dominated. The first cast-iron building to use this defining style was the **A.T. Stewart Dry Goods Store** (1846, 280 Broadway between Chambers and Reade Sts).

One of the finest examples is the **Haughwout Building** (1856, 488 Broadway at Broome St), which has been called "the Parthenon of cast-iron architecture" for its elegant proportions and beautiful detail. It is notable, too, as the site of the first Otis safety elevator, another development of this time, which allowed buildings to grow ever taller (see **What goes up...**, page 54).

Another early cast-iron masterpiece is the **Cary Building** (1857, 105–107 Chambers St at Church St), a five-story palazzo design of Corinthian columns topped with a triangular pediment. Other fine examples include 72–76 Greene Street, known as "the King of Greene Street," and 28–30 Greene Street, "the Queen," as well as a great many larger buildings in the district known as Ladies' Mile (Broadway between Union and Madison Squares).

Cast-Iron Tours

92nd Street Y, 1395 Lexington Ave at 92nd St (996-1100). Subway: 6 to 96th St. Joyce Mendelsohn, an expert on New York's cast-iron buildings, offers guided tours of Soho's Cast-Iron Historical District and Ladies' Mile.

Back on track: ***Grand Central****, built in 1913, recently unveiled its newly restored interior.*

Skyscrapers

The form of architecture that is most closely associated with New York is the assertively vertical skyscraper. With the development of steel-frame construction—an advancement of the techniques used for cast-iron buildings—the restrictions on height imposed by the need for load-bearing walls were eliminated. The first skyscrapers, such as the **Flatiron Building** (1902, 175 Fifth Ave between 22nd and 23rd Sts) and the **Woolworth Building** (1913, 233 Broadway between Park Pl and Barclay St), echoed traditional construction in their facades: The former is a restrained Renaissance palazzo, the latter a Gothic cathedral complete with gargoyles. By the 1920s and 1930s, the curtain wall had an expressive life of its own and was being used as a palette for many Art Deco designs.

The famous **Empire State Building** (1931, 350 Fifth Ave between 33rd and 34th Sts; *see chapter* **Sightseeing**), a perfectly massed 102-story tower of limestone and granite with thin vertical strips of nickel that glint when they catch the sun, was the work of William F. Lamb, who was given a brief to "make it big." It was built in only 18 months and quickly became the world's favorite building, as well as its tallest.

The Chrysler Building (1930, 405 Lexington Ave at 42nd St) was William van Alen's homage to the automobile. At the foot of the main tower are brickwork cars, complete with chrome hubcaps, and radiator caps enlarged to vast proportions and projected out over the edge as gargoyles. The needle-sharp stainless-steel spire, which is illuminated at night, was added to the original plans to add more height, and for a few months, the Chrysler was the world's tallest building.

A lesser-known but equally striking example of the Art Deco skyscraper is across the street: the **Chanin Building** (1929, 122 E 42nd St at Lexington Ave). The Chanin was designed with a network of public passageways connected to the nearby subway station. This, along with its ground-level storefronts accessible from inside the complex, made it the first building to be a "city within a city."

Rockefeller Center (1931, 47th–51st Sts between Fifth and Sixth Aves; *see chapters* **Sightseeing** *and* **New York by Neighborhood: Midtown**) was a far grander expression of this idea. Occupying three city blocks and comprising 21 buildings linked by open plazas and an extensive subterranean world of shops, restaurants and subway connections, it provides all the services its daytime occupants could ever need. Built by John D. Rockefeller and designed by a committee of architects led by Raymond Hood, it is an urban complex much admired for its masterful coordination of public space. The center was extended in the 1970s with the addition of four powerful towers on the west side of

Aglow: **Empire State** and **Chrysler Buildings**.

Sixth Avenue. Don't miss **Radio City Music Hall** (1932, Sixth Ave between 50th and 51st Sts).

Other important Art Deco works include the monochrome tower of the **Fuller Building** (1929, 45 E 57th St at Madison Ave); the twin copper crowns of the **Waldorf-Astoria Hotel** (1931, 301 Park Ave between 49th and 50th Sts); Raymond Hood's **News Building** (1930, 220 E 42nd St between Second and Third Aves), a soaring skyscraper of white brick piers with black and reddish-brown spandrels (as seen in the *Superman* films); and the **McGraw-Hill Building** (1931, 330 W 42nd St between Eighth and Ninth Aves), with shimmering blue-green bricks and ribbons of double-hung windows, once described as "proto jukebox modern."

Glass boxes

The Depression and World War II slowed New York's architectural pace, but by the 1950s designers were once again experimenting with the daring forms made possible by steel-frame construction. The main building of the **UN Secretariat** (1950, First Avenue between 42nd and 48th Sts), a perfectly proportioned single rectangle (its face is designed to the "golden ratio" of the Greeks), includes the first walls in New York made entirely of glass. It is attributed to Le Corbusier, but in fact he was just one member of an international committee of architects and was said to be unhappy with the final result.

Lever House (1952, 390 Park Ave between 53rd and 54th Sts) took glass curtain walls to the staid respectability of Park Avenue. Ludwig Mies van der Rohe's **Seagram Building** (1958, 375

Park Ave between 52nd and 53rd Sts) epitomized the new glass architecture, reflecting the world in its elegant bronze-framed surfaces.

The Seagram Building was also notable for its innovative atrium, a public space in a private building. The building laws were changed to encourage this concept. Frank Lloyd Wright's only New York building, the **Guggenheim Museum** (1959, Fifth Ave between 88th and 89th Sts; *see chapters* **Sightseeing** *and* **Museums**), caused a stir for its daring form. The upturned shell of its striking exterior conceals an interior spiral walkway.

The Pan Am Building, now the **Met Life Building** (1963, 200 Park Ave at 45th St), towers behind Grand Central Terminal. Park Avenue appears to rise up and hug the building's facade. Designed by Walter Gropius, it was the largest commercial building in the world and, with its famous heliport (now closed), symbolized the modern jet-set life of the 1960s in countless movies.

With a daytime population of around 50,000, the **World Trade Center** (1970, Church to West Sts and Liberty to Vesey Sts; *see chapter* **Sightseeing**) carries the city-within-a-city concept to its modern limits. The famous twin towers are just one element of a network of connected blocks, their colossal height further emphasized by the narrow stainless-steel detailing that rises vertically along the buildings' surface (actually a load-bearing structure rather than a decorative curtain wall). The World Trade Center's architecture has been widely criticized as banal, but it has come to be looked on with some affection, at least by New Yorkers—especially since it survived a terrorist bombing in 1993.

Hugh Stubbins & Associates' **Citicorp Center** (1977, Lexington Ave between 53rd and 54th Sts) is instantly recognizable for its smooth aluminum skin and sloping "sliced" roof. From street level, you can see the radical way the building's bulk is supported on huge stilts.

One of New York's most famous postmodernist buildings is Philip Johnson's AT&T Building, now the **Sony Building** (1983, 550 Madison Ave between 55th and 56th Sts), with its grand six-story entrance arch and instantly recognizable "Chippendale" top. Cesar Pelli's **World Financial Center** (1988) is the focal point of the landfill development of Battery Park City, at the southern tip of Manhattan. Its quirky yet elegant towers are topped by domes and pyramids with stepped cutbacks and walls whose proportion of reflective glass increases with their height.

United Nations Headquarters

First Ave at 46th St (recorded information 963-1234). Subway: S, 4, 5, 6, 7 to 42nd St–Grand Central. 9:15am–4:45pm. Free. Tours every half-hour. $7.50, $3.50–$5.50 concessions. The Modernist headquarters of the United Nations is very 1950s. You can visit the foyer and basement of the General Assembly Building, but to see any of the council rooms and the General Assembly itself, you must take a tour that lasts about an hour and is pretty dull. Free tickets are available

to General Assembly and council sessions on a first-come, first-served basis from the information desk (754-7539).

World Financial Center

West St to North End Ave between Cedar and Vesey Sts (945-0505). Subway: C, E to World Trade Ctr; 1, 9 to Cortlandt St. The WFC is a sleek public space in the tradition of Rockefeller Center, with restaurants, stores, great views of the Hudson and a pretty park. Its focal point is the Winter Garden, a frequent venue for concerts and recitals (*see chapter* **Music**).

Toward 2000

The cost and complexity of construction in New York guarantee a lengthy gestation for any project of real significance. Much of the interest in matters architectural now relates as much to preservation as to development. The major new action on the horizon centers on three prominent city locales that have suffered decline and look to innovative design for reinvigoration.

Downtown, Union Square is under renovation. The project's capstone, a building at the square's southern end that features an "artwall" 100 feet (30 meters) high by 60 feet (18 meters) wide, is nearing completion. The installation art team of Jones and Ginzel won the design competition by proposing a Zen-inspired vertical rock garden that will serve as a timepiece. With a steaming void at its center, the wall promises to be contemplative and vaguely apocalyptic.

Midtown's architectural focus is Columbus Circle, a confusing intersection born of the City Beautiful movement of the late 19th century. It houses the city's most prominent white elephant, the Coliseum, a large-scale exhibition hall whose architecture is undistinguished and whose function has been assumed by the Jacob Javits Convention Center. A design competition for the site is under way but is likely to drag on.

Elsewhere in midtown, Times Square's renovation has sparked several new development plans and drawn the interest of architects such as Frank Gehry, whose plan for the redesign of 1 Times Square (where the New Year's ball drops) features 25-story–high billowing mesh movable walls. It seems appropriately fantastical for the milieu, but unlikely to be realized in that form.

Even long-neglected Harlem is a target for developers now. A huge retail complex called Harlem USA is meant to anchor the revival of 125th Street, the commercial heart of the neighborhood; potential corporate investors include Disney and the Gap. High-profile participants such as actor Robert De Niro and restaurateur Drew Nieporent are working to renovate Minton's Playhouse, a jazz landmark on 118th Street. Further south, an ambitious proposal for a Harlem Arts Corridor (arts and music schools, clubs and artists' housing) is under consideration. These plans are still embryonic, so no designs are definite yet, but it will be interesting to see how and if planners respect Harlem's unique place in American society and culture.

Museums

From the vast treasure troves to the dozens of specialist collections, New York is a mecca for museum lovers

New York's museums are superb. More than 60 institutions hold collections of everything from art, antiquities and hands-on science to Ukrainian folk costumes and doll collections. The buildings themselves are equally impressive and eclectic. The spiral uptown Guggenheim is a real jaw-dropper, and the granite cube of the Whitney Museum, with its cyclops-eye window and concrete moat, is a striking contrast to the surrounding architecture.

It is usually self-defeating to try and cram several museum visits into a single day, or even to try to see every exhibit at a major museum such as the Metropolitan Museum of Art or the American Museum of Natural History. Pace yourself: Some museums have excellent cafés or restaurants, so you can break for coffee or a complete meal. Sarabeth's at the Whitney, Sette MoMA at the Museum of Modern Art, the Museum Café in the Pierpont Morgan Library and the Jewish Museum's Café Weissman all provide an excellent excuse to take a break from the collections.

Though entry usually costs no more than the price of a movie ticket, museum admission prices may still come as a shock to visitors. This is because most New York museums are funded privately and not by government money, a reason why the New York Historical Society, the city's oldest museum, had to close for two years (it has now reopened). However, most of the city's major museums, including the Metropolitan, the Whitney, the Museum of Modern Art and the **International Center for Photography** (*see chapter* **Art Galleries**), offer the public at least one evening a week when admission is free or by voluntary donation.

Many of New York's best-known museums—

*Skeleton key: Unlock mysteries of evolution in the **Museum of Natural History**'s dino halls.*

*Hebrew jewel: Cultural exhibits are housed in the Warburg Mansion, now the **Jewish Museum**.*

such as the Frick Collection, the Pierpont Morgan Library, the Schomburg Center for Research in Black Culture, the Whitney and the Guggenheim—started out as private collections. The Cloisters, at the northern tip of Manhattan in Fort Tryon Park, was John D. Rockefeller's gift. Its reconstructed Gothic monastery houses the Met's beautiful collection of medieval art. When the sun's shining and the sky's a deep blue, bring a picnic lunch, admire the red-tiled roof and inhale the delicate scents from the garden. It's a treat.

Also try not to miss the audio tour at the thought-provoking Ellis Island Museum, the eye-opening exhibitions at the Museum of Jewish Heritage and the tour at the Lower East Side Tenement Museum. All give visitors insight into NYC's multicultural melting pot. New Jersey's Liberty Science Center, with its hands-on exhibits and rooftop terrace overlooking Manhattan and the Statue of Liberty, is an unexpected pleasure. If you go on the weekend, when the ferry service is operating, it doubles as a sightseeing trip.

The prize for most neglected museum has to go to the Brooklyn Museum of Art. Its size and grandeur come as a pleasant surprise as you emerge from the subway station, just outside the Brooklyn Botanic Garden, but there's an even greater surprise inside: the excellent exhibits. Even though it's the second-largest museum in New York, it rarely draws the huge crowds that head for museums in Manhattan. And that's a shame, because its Egyptian collection rivals the Met's, and its recent temporary shows have been first-class.

It might be traditional to save museums for a rainy day, but since most are air-conditioned, they also offer a glorious respite from summer heat.

Most of New York's museums are closed on New Year's Day, Presidents' Day, Memorial Day, Independence Day, Labor Day, Columbus Day, Thanksgiving and Christmas Day. Some change their opening hours in the summer, so it's wise to check before setting out.

*Asp kisser: Fanny Davenport as Cleopatra in a **Museum of the City of New York** photo.*

shows bigger-than-life nature programs, and there are always innovative temporary exhibitions, in addition to an easily accessible research library with vast photo and print archives and a friendly, helpful staff.

Brooklyn Museum of Art

200 Eastern Pkwy at Washington Ave, Brooklyn (1-718-638-5000). Subway: 2, 3 to Eastern Pkwy. Wed–Fri 10am–5pm, Sat 11am–9pm, Sun 11am–6pm. Suggested donation $4, students $2, seniors $1.50; concessions $1–$10. AmEx, MC, V (gift shop only). The Brooklyn Museum, founded 175 years ago, recently appended the word "Art" to its name as part of a campaign to draw wider attention to the world-class collections inside this gorgeous 19th-century Beaux Arts building. The African art and pre-Columbian textile galleries are especially impressive, and the Native-American collection is outstanding. There are many works from the ancient Middle East and extensive holdings of American painting and sculpture by such masters as Winslow Homer, Thomas Eakins and John Singer Sargent. And don't miss the Egyptian galleries; the Rubin Gallery's gold-and-silver–gilded ibis coffin, for instance, is sublime. Two floors up, the Rodin sculpture court is surrounded by paintings by French contemporaries such as Monet and Degas. The 1998-99 season includes a 200-year survey of painting from the royal Persian courts; a show devoted to the final years of American photographer Lewis Hine; and a major exhibition detailing innovative America art 1941–62, including architecture, decorative arts, painting, photography and sculpture. There's also an informal café (it closes at 4pm) and a children's museum.

The Cloisters

Fort Tryon Park, Fort Washington Ave at Margaret Corbin Plaza, Washington Heights (923-3700). Subway: A to 190th St. March–October Tue–Sun 9:30am–5:15pm, November–February Tue–Sun. 9:30am–4:45pm. Suggested donation

Major institutions

American Museum of Natural History

Central Park West at 79th St (769-5000/recorded information 769-5100). Subway: B, C to 81st St. Mon–Thu, Sun 10am–5:45pm; Fri, Sat 10am–8:45pm. Suggested donation $7; concessions $4–$5. AmEx, MC, V (gift shop only). The fun begins right in the main rotunda, as a towering barosaur, rearing high on its hind legs, protects its young from an attacking allosaurus. It's an impressive window to the largest museum of its kind in the world, and a reminder to visit the dinosaur halls on the fourth floor. During their 1995–96 renovation (by the firm responsible for much of the excellent Ellis Island Museum), several specimens were remodeled in light of recent discoveries. The *Tyrannosaurus rex*, for instance, was once believed to have walked upright, Godzilla-style; now it stalks, head down, with tail parallel to the ground, and is altogether more menacing. The rest of the museum is equally dramatic. There's a particularly good Native-American section and an absolutely stunning collection of gems, including the obscenely large Star of India blue sapphire. An Imax theater

*Me, a pharoah? See who rules the Temple of Dendur at the **Metropolitan Museum of Art**.*

$8 (includes admission to the Metropolitan Museum of Art on the same day); concessions $4; under 12 free if accompanied by an adult. No credit cards. The Cloisters houses the Met's medieval art and architecture collections in an unexpectedly tranquil, rural setting. The museum was constructed 60 years ago in authentic Middle-Ages style; the result is a convincing, red-tiled Romanesque structure overlooking the Hudson River. Don't miss the famous unicorn tapestries or the *Annunciation Triptych* by Robert Campin.

Cooper-Hewitt National Design Museum

2 E 91st St at Fifth Ave (849-8400). Subway: 4, 5, 6 to 86th St. Tue 10am–9pm, Wed–Sat 10am–5pm, Sun noon–5pm. $3, under 12 free, no admission charge Tue 5–9pm; concessions $1.50. No credit cards. The Smithsonian's National Design Museum is worth a visit for both its content and its architecture—the turn-of-the-century building once belonged to Andrew Carnegie. Architects responded to his request for "the most modest, plainest and roomy house in New York" by designing a 64-room mansion in the style of a Georgian country house. This is the only museum in the U.S. devoted exclusively to historical and contemporary design; its changing exhibitions are always interesting. Sign language interpretation is available on request (849-8387).

Frick Collection

1 E 70th St at Fifth Ave (288-0700). Subway: 6 to 68th St. Tue–Sat 10am–6pm, Sun 1–6pm. $5, under 10 not admitted, ages 10–16 must be accompanied by an adult; concessions $3. No credit cards. This private, predominantly Renaissance collection, housed in an opulent residence once owned by industrialist Henry Clay Frick, is more like a stately home than a museum. American architect Thomas Hastings designed the 1914 building in 18th-century European style. The paintings, sculptures and furniture on display are consistently world-class, among them works by Gainsborough, Rembrandt,

Renoir, Vermeer, Whistler and the French cabinetmaker Jean-Henri Riesener. The indoor garden court and reflecting pool are especially lovely.

Solomon R. Guggenheim Museum

1071 Fifth Ave at 88th St (423-3500). Subway: 4, 5, 6 to 86th St. Mon–Wed, Sun 10am–6pm; Fri, Sat 10am–8pm. $12, students and seniors $7, under 12 free, voluntary donation Fri 6–8pm; concessions $4–$10. AmEx, MC, V. The Guggenheim itself is a stunning work of art. Designed by Frank Lloyd Wright, it's the youngest building to be designated a New York City landmark. In addition to works by Kandinsky, Picasso, Van Gogh, Degas and Manet, the museum owns Peggy Guggenheim's trove of Cubist, Surrealist and Abstract Expressionist works, and the Panza di Biumo collection of American Minimalist and Conceptual art from the 1960s and 1970s. The photography collection began after a donation of more than 200 works by the Robert Mapplethorpe Foundation. In 1992, the museum reopened after a two-year renovation; a new ten-story tower increased the museum's space to include a sculpture gallery (with great views of Central Park) and a cafe. Since then, the Guggenheim has made news with its ambitious global expansion, its penchant for sweeping historical presentations (such as its elegant overview of 5,000 years of Chinese art) and its in-depth retrospectives of such major American artists as Robert Rauschenberg. Admission prices are the highest of any museum's in the city; they do allow entry to the Guggenheim's Soho branch, but only for exhibitions being shown in both locations. Even if you don't want to pay to see the collection inside, visit the museum to admire the stunning white building coiled among the turn-of-the-century mansions on Fifth Avenue. *See also chapters* **Sightseeing** *and* **Architecture.**
Branch: Guggenheim Museum SoHo, *575 Broadway at Prince St (423-3500). Subway: N, R to Prince St. Wed–Fri, Sun 11am–6pm; Sat 11am–8pm.* The downtown Guggenheim opened in 1992 to showcase selections from the permanent collection, as well as temporary exhibitions. *See also chapter* **Architecture.**

Metropolitan Museum of Art

Fifth Ave at 82nd St (535-7710). Subway: 4, 5, 6 to 86th St. Tue–Thu, Sun 9:30am–5:15pm; Fri, Sat 9:30am–8:45pm. Suggested donation $8, under 12 free if accompanied by an adult; concessions $4. No credit cards. No strollers on Sun. Internet www.metmuseum.org It could take several days, even weeks, to cover the Met's 1.5 million square feet (139,354.5 square meters) of exhibition space, so try to be selective. Egyptology fans should head straight for the Temple of Dendur. There's also an excellent Islamic art collection and more than 3,000 European paintings, including major works by Rembrandt, Raphael, Tiepolo and Vermeer. The Greek and Roman halls have gotten a face-lift, and the museum has also been adding to its galleries of 20th-century painting. Each year, a selection of contemporary sculptures are installed in the open-air roof garden (open between May and October); have a sandwich there while taking in the panorama of Central Park. On weekend evenings, enjoy the classical quintet performing on the mezzanine overlooking the Great Hall. And don't forget the Costume Institute, or the new Howard Gilman photography gallery. Foreign-language tours are available (570-3711). *See also chapter* **Architecture.**

Museum of Modern Art

11 W 53rd St between Fifth and Sixth Aves (708-9400). Subway: E, F to Fifth Ave. Sat–Tue, Thu 10:30am–6pm; Fri 10:30am–8:30pm. $9.50, under 16 free if accompanied by an adult, voluntary donation Fri 4:30–8:30pm; concessions $6.50. No credit cards. Internet: www.moma.org The Museum of Modern Art, or MoMA for short, holds the finest and most comprehensive collection of 20th-century art in the world. The permanent collection is exceptionally strong on works by Matisse, Picasso, Miró and later Modernists. The photo collection has major holdings by just about every important figure in the medium. The film and video department is simply stupendous, with a collection of more than 14,000 films; it holds over 20 screenings per week in two plush theaters (advance ticket purchase recommended). The elegant Italian restaurant Sette MoMA (708-9710) overlooks the lovely Abby Aldrich Rockefeller Sculpture Garden; an informal café is on the ground floor. Free gallery talks begin at 1pm and 3pm daily (except Wednesday) and on Thursday and Friday evenings at 6pm and 7pm. A sculpture touch-tour is available to visually impaired visitors by appointment (708-9864). The museum recently acquired a neighboring site, on which it will build new galleries; it plans to remain open during construction.

National Museum of the American Indian

George Gustav Heye Center, U.S. Custom House, 1 Bowling Green between State and Whitehall Sts (668-6624). Subway: 1, 9 to South Ferry; N, R to Whitehall St. 10am–5pm. Free. The galleries, resource center and two workshop rooms of this museum, a branch of the Smithsonian Institution's sprawling organization of museums and research institutes, occupies two floors of the grand rotunda in the exquisite old U.S. Customs House. Located just around the corner from Battery Park and the Ellis Island ferry, it offers displays based on a permanent collection of documents and artifacts that offer valuable insights into the realities of Native American history. Exhibitions are thoughtfully explained, usually by Native Americans. Of special interest is All Roads Are Good, which reflects the personal choices of storytellers, weavers, anthropologists and tribal leaders. Only 500 of the collection's one million objects are on display; one reason that, despite the building's lofty proportions, the museum seems surprisingly small. A main branch, on the Mall in Washington, D.C., will open in 2002. *See also chapter* **Architecture**.

New Museum of Contemporary Art

583 Broadway between Houston and Prince Sts (219-1222). Subway: B, D, F, Q to Broadway–Lafayette St; N, R to Prince St; 6 to Bleecker St. Wed, Sun noon–6pm; Thu–Sat noon–8pm. $5, under 12 free, no admission charge Thu 6–8pm; concessions $3. AmEx, DC, Disc, MC, V. Internet: www. newmuseum.org Since its founding in 1977, this Soho institution has been the focus of controversy. With major group shows that gravitated toward the experimental, the conceptual and the latest in multimedia presentations, it quickly became a lightning rod for the fusion of art, technology and the politically correct. Even its window displays drew crowds. Now a $3 million renovation and expansion of its Victorian cast-iron building has given it a friendlier entrance, an airy second-floor exhibition space and an intimate downstairs bookshop and reading room visible from the street. Although it continues to mount important mid-career retrospectives for underrecognized artists, the museum has adopted a broader, more international outlook. Recent exhibitions have been devoted to Colombia's Doris Salcedo and Britain's Mona Hatoum; another involved an actual flea circus—projected on video. Through January '99, expect to see a retrospective of Faith Ringgold's amazing story-quilt paintings, an installation of German artist Marcel Odenbach's provocative videos and from Spain, Ana Prada's unconventional sculptures.

Pierpont Morgan Library

29 E 36th St between Madison and Park Aves (685-0008). Subway: 6 to 33rd St. Tue–Fri 10:30am–5pm, Sat 10:30am–6pm, Sun noon–6pm. $6, seniors and students $4, under 12 free. Concessions. No credit cards. This beautiful Italianate museum—also an extraordinary literary research facility—was once the private library of financier J.P. Morgan. Mostly gathered during Morgan's trips to Europe, the collection includes three Gutenberg Bibles, original Mahler manuscripts and gorgeous silver, copper and cloisonné 12th-century Stavelot

*Shh: If you want to see a unicorn, visit **the Cloisters**, at Manhattan's peaceful northern tip.*

Cubic feat

There are plenty of surprises inside the Whitney's granite box

Like the Guggenheim, the Whitney Museum of American Art sets itself apart first by its unique architecture. Some may find the building, a gray granite cube designed by Marcel Breuer, unprepossessing and even forbidding (it even has a cement moat in front of the entrance). But it is an appropriate setting for the uncompromising art inside. There, any comparison to other museums ends. The Whitney is a world unto itself, one whose often controversial exhibitions not only measure the historical importance of American art but mirror the culture of the moment as well.

When Gertrude Vanderbilt Whitney, a sculptor and art patron, opened the museum in 1931, she dedicated it to living American artists. Its first exhibition consisted of work by eight artists from her private collection, and its first space was three townhouses on East 8th Street (now the New York Studio School). Today the Whitney holds approximately 12,000 pieces, the work of nearly 2,000 artists. They include Edward Hopper (the museum owns his entire estate), Andrew Wyeth, Arshile Gorky, Georgia O'Keeffe, Jackson Pollock, Alexander Calder, Louise Nevelson, Jasper Johns, Andy Warhol, Agnes Martin and Jean-Michel Basquiat.

The museum is also perhaps the country's foremost showcase for American independent film and video artists. Over the past decade, it has vastly expanded its collection of contemporary photography as well.

The big—and very welcome—development at the Whitney this year is the creation of 11 new top-floor galleries, some with natural light, in what once were administrative offices. The intimate new exhibiton space allows for the permanent display of selected works from the Whitney archives (many pre-WWII and most recently seen on postcards in the lobby shop). Three of the galleries are reserved for photography, sculpture and works on paper. Calder's Circus, which disappeared from its place in the lobby years ago, has been restored and now has a permanent home in a mezzanine gallery devoted to the artist's signature mobiles; other rooms belong to O'Keeffe and Hopper.

Still, the Whitney's reputation rests mainly on its temporary shows, particularly the show everyone loves to hate: the **Biennial Exhibition.** Held every odd-numbered year, it remains the most prestigious assessment of contemporary American art in the U.S. The next Biennial has been postponed until 2000 to make way for "The American Century," a huge two-part exhibition set for 1999 that promises to be the Whitney's most comprehensive exploration of American art to date. Encompassing 20th-century painting, photography, sculpture and prints, the exhibition will assess the influence of the visual arts on America's cultural identity.

There are free guided tours daily; the expanded gift shop next door is now accessible through a lobby passage. **Sarabeth's** (570-3670), the museum café, is open every day till 4:30pm and offers a lively, up-from-under view of the street and food that is pricey but excellent.

Whitney Museum of American Art
945 Madison Ave at 75th St (570-3676). Subway: 6 to 77th St. Wed, Fri–Sun 11am–6pm; Thu 1–8pm. $8, under 12 free, no admission charge Thu 6–8pm; concessions $7. No credit cards. Internet: www.echonyc. com/~whitney

Whitney Museum of American Art at Philip Morris
120 Park Ave at 42nd St (878-2550). Subway: S, 4, 5, 6, 7 to 42nd St–Grand Central. Mon–Fri 11am–6pm, Thu 11am–7:30pm; sculpture court Mon–Sat 7:30am–9:30pm, Sun 11am–7pm. Free. The Whitney's midtown branch, located in a lobby gallery, is devoted to changing solo projects by contemporary artists.

Breuer's yeast: the **Whitney Museum.**

Whatever floats your boat: The good ship Intrepid *houses the **Sea, Air and Space Museum**.*

triptych. A subtly colorful marble rotunda with carved 16th-century Italian ceiling separates the three-tiered library from the rich red study. In fall '98, look for a show of master drawings from the Hermitage and Pushkin museums that date from the 15th to the 20th centuries, and a survey of American and European drawings from private New York collections in spring '99. Guided tours are available Tue–Fri at noon. There's also a modern conservatory attached to the museum, with a tranquil courtyard café.

Whitney Museum of American Art
See **Cubic Feat**, *opposite.*

Art and design

American Academy and Institute of Arts and Letters
Audubon Terrace, Broadway between 155th and 156th Sts (368-5900). Subway: 1, 9 to 157th St. Mon, Fri–Sun 10am–6pm; Thu 10am–8pm. Free. This organization honors 250 American writers, composers, painters, sculptors and architects. Edith Wharton, Mark Twain and Henry James were once members; today's list includes Terrence McNally, John Guare, Kurt Vonnegut and Alison Lurie. It's not actually a museum, but there are annual exhibitions open to the public and a magnificent library of original manuscripts and first editions, open to researchers by appointment only.

American Craft Museum
40 W 53rd St between Fifth and Sixth Aves (956-3535). Subway: E, F to Fifth Ave. Tue 10am–8pm, Wed–Sun 10am–5pm. $5; concessions $2.50. No credit cards. This is the country's leading art museum for 20th-century crafts in clay, fiber, glass, metal and wood. There are temporary shows on the four bright and spacious floors, and one or two exhibitions from the permanent collection each year, concentrating on a specific medium. The shop, though small, sells some unusually stylish jewelry and ceramics.

Dahesh Museum
601 Fifth Ave at 48th St (759-0606). Subway: B, D, F, Q to 47th–50th Sts–Rockefeller Ctr. Tue–Sat 11am–6pm. Free. This jewel-box museum houses the private collection of Sallim Moussa Achi, a Lebanese philosopher with a consuming passion for European Academic art. The collection focuses on Orientalism, landscapes, scenes of rural life, and historical or mythical images painted by 19th- and early 20th-century artists whose work you won't see in public collections anywhere else.

Forbes Magazine Galleries
62 Fifth Ave at 12th St (206-5548). Subway: L, N, R, 4, 5, 6 to 14th St–Union Sq. Tue, Wed, Fri, Sat 10am–4pm. Free; under 16 must be accompanied by an adult. The late magazine publisher Malcolm Forbes assembled this wonderful private collection of treasures. Besides toy boats and soldiers, the galleries showcase historic presidential letters and—best of all—a dozen Fabergé eggs and other superbly intricate pieces by the famous Russian jeweler and goldsmith Peter Carl Fabergé. Gallery hours are subject to change without warning, so call to check before visiting.

Museum of American Folk Art
2 Lincoln Sq, Columbus Ave between 65th and 66th Sts (977-7298). Subway: 1, 9 to 66th St–Lincoln Ctr. Tue–Sun 11:30am–7:30pm. Suggested donation $3. No credit cards.

Here's proof that beautiful things do come in small packages: The exhibits are exquisite. The range of decorative, practical and ceremonial folk art encompasses pottery, trade signs, delicately stitched log-cabin quilts and even windup toys. The craftsmanship is often breathtaking. There are occasional lectures, demonstrations and performances, and a museum shop next door.

National Academy of Design

1083 Fifth Ave at 89th St (369-4880). Subway: 4, 5, 6 to 86th St. Wed, Thu, Sat, Sun noon–5pm; Fri noon–8pm. $5, under 5 free, no admission charge Fri 5–8pm; concessions $3.50. No credit cards. Housed in an elegant Fifth Avenue townhouse, the Academy comprises the School of Fine Arts and a museum containing one of the world's foremost collections of 19th- and 20th-century American art (painting, sculpture, architecture and engraving). The permanent collection includes works by Mary Cassatt, John Singer Sargent and Frank Lloyd Wright. Temporary exhibitions are always impressive.

Isamu Noguchi Garden Museum

32-37 Vernon Blvd at 33rd Rd, Long Island City, Queens (recorded information 1-718-204-7088). Subway: N to Broadway. Shuttle bus from the Asia Society, 725 Park Ave at 70th St, every hour on the half-hour 11:30am–3:30pm. Apr–Oct Wed–Fri 10am–5pm; Sat, Sun 11am–6pm. Suggested donation $4; concessions $2. No credit cards. Sculptor Isamu Noguchi designed stage sets for Martha Graham and George Balanchine, as well as sculpture parks and immense works of great simplicity. Noguchi's studios are now a showcase for his pieces—in 12 small galleries and a sculpture garden. There's a guided tour at 2pm (call 1-718-721-1932), and films are shown throughout the day.

Queens Museum of Art

New York City Building, Flushing Meadows–Corona Park, Queens (1-718-592-9700). Subway: 7 to Willets Point–Shea Stadium. Wed–Fri 10am–5pm; Sat, Sun noon–5pm. Suggested donation $3; concessions $1.50. No credit cards. Located on the site of the 1964–65 World's Fair, the Queens Museum recently saw a thorough $15 million renovation. In addition to the art collections and its fine, site-specific temporary exhibitions, the museum offers a permanent miniature model of New York City. It's fun to try to find where you're staying—binoculars rent for $1 apiece. Dusk falls every 15 minutes, revealing tiny illuminated buildings and a fluorescent Central Park. The model is constantly updated; there had been some 60,000 changes at the last count. *See also chapter* **New York by Neighborhood: The Outer Boroughs.**

Nicholas Roerich Museum

319 W 107th St at Riverside Dr (864-7752). Subway: 1, 9 to 110th St. Tue–Sun 2–5pm. Free. Nicholas Roerich was a Russian-born philosopher, artist, architect, explorer, pacifist and scenery painter who collaborated with Nijinsky, Stravinsky and Diaghilev. The Roerich Peace Pact of 1935, an international agreement on the protection of cultural treasures, earned him a Nobel Peace Prize nomination. Roerich's wife bought this charming townhouse specifically as a museum to house her late husband's possessions. Paintings are mostly from his Tibetan travels and display his interest in mysticism. It's a fascinating place, but Roerich's intriguing life story tends to overshadow the museum.

Studio Museum in Harlem

144 W 125th St between Seventh Ave and Malcolm X Blvd (864-4500). Subway: 2, 3 to 125th St. Wed–Fri 10am–5pm; Sat, Sun 1–6pm. $5, no admission charge first Sat of each month; concessions $1–$3. No credit cards. The Studio Museum started out in 1967 as a rented loft space. In the next 20 years, it expanded onto two floors of a 60,000-square-foot (5,500-square-meter) building, a gift from a New York bank, and became the first black fine arts museum in the country.

Today, it shows changing exhibitions by African-American, African and Caribbean artists and continues its prestigious artists-in-residence program.

Urban Center

457 Madison Ave between 50th and 51st Sts (935-3960/tour information 439-1049). Subway: E, F to Fifth Ave; 6 to 51st St. Mon–Wed, Fri, Sat 11am–5pm. Voluntary donation. The Municipal Art Society founded this center for urban design in 1980. It functions as a gallery, bookshop, lecture forum and campaign office, with exhibitions on architecture, public art and community-based projects. The Urban Center is also headquarters of the Architectural League and the Parks Council. Its greatest attraction may be its location: inside the historic Villard Houses, opposite St. Patrick's Cathedral.

Arts and culture

Ethnic

Asia Society

725 Park Ave at 70th St (288-6400). Subway: 6 to 68th St. Tue, Wed, Fri, Sat 11am–6pm; Thu 11am–8pm; Sun noon–5pm. $3; concessions $1, under 12 free if accompanied by an adult; no admission charge Thu 6–8pm. No credit cards. The stalwart eight-story headquarters of the Asia Society reflects its importance in promoting Asian-American relations. It sponsors study missions and conferences, and promotes public programs on both continents. Galleries show major art exhibitions from public and private collections, including the permanent Mr. and Mrs. John D. Rockefeller III collection of Asian art. Asian musicians and performers often play here; call for a schedule.

China Institute in America

125 E 65th St between Park and Lexington Aves (744-8181). Subway: 6 to 68th St. Mon–Sat 10am–5pm, Sun 1–5pm. Suggested donation $5, children free; concessions $3. AmEx, MC, V. With just two small gallery rooms, the China Institute is somewhat overshadowed by the Asia Society. But its exhibitions, ranging from works by Chinese women artists to selections from the Beijing Palace Museum, are impressive. The society also offers lectures and courses on such subjects as cooking, calligraphy and Confucianism.

French Institute/Alliance Française

55 E 59th St between Madison and Park Aves (355-6160). Subway: 4, 5, 6 to 59th St. Tue–Fri 11am–7pm; Sat, Sun 11am–5pm. $7 non-members, students and seniors $5.50, members free. Membership $65 per year. Credit AmEx, MC, V. This is the New York home for all things French: The Institute, also known as the Alliance Française, holds the city's most extensive all-French library and offers numerous language classes and cultural seminars. There are also French film screenings and live dance, music and theater performances. *See also chapter* **Film.**

Garibaldi-Meucci Museum

420 Tompkins Ave, Staten Island (1-718-442-1608). Subway: 1, 9 to South Ferry, then Staten Island Ferry and S52 bus. Tue–Sun 1–5pm. Suggested donation $3. The 1840s Gothic revival home of Italian inventor Antonio Meucci, this museum is also the former refuge of Italian patriot Antonio Garibaldi.

Goethe-Institut/German Cultural Center

1014 Fifth Ave at 82nd St (439-8700). Subway: 4, 5, 6 to 86th St. Library Tue, Thu 10am–7pm; Wed, Fri 10am–5pm; Sat noon–6pm. Free. Goethe-Institut New York is just one branch of a German multinational cultural organization founded in 1951. Located across the street from the Metropolitan Museum in a landmark Fifth Avenue mansion, it mounts

*Water music: The **Frick Collection**'s Garden Court is a great spot to hear chamber concerts.*

*Between a rock and a nice place: the **Isamu Noguchi Garden Museum** in Long Island City.*

*What's that you say? Dub Bogie and Bacall at the **American Museum of the Moving Image**.*

shows featuring German-born contemporary artists, as well as concerts, film screenings and lectures. An extensive library offers books in German or English, German periodicals, videos and audiocassettes.

Hispanic Society of America

Audubon Terrace, Broadway between 155th and 156th Sts (926-2234). Subway: 1 to 157th St. Tue–Sat 10am–4:30pm, Sun 1–4pm; library Tue–Fri 1–4:30pm, Sat 10am–4:30pm. Free. Two limestone lions flank the entrance to this majestic building in Hamilton Heights, a gentrified area of Harlem. Outside, an equestrian statue of El Cid, Spain's medieval hero, stands on the Beaux Arts terrace between the society's two buildings. Inside, there's an ornate Spanish Renaissance court and an upper gallery lined with paintings by El Greco, Goya and Velázquez. The collection is dominated by religious artifacts, including a number of 16th-century tombs from the monastery of San Francisco in Cuéllar, Spain.

Japan Society

333 E 47th St between First and Second Aves (752-3015). Subway: E, F to Lexington–Third Aves; 6 to 51st St. Tue–Sun 11am–5pm (during exhibitions only). Suggested donation $3. No credit cards. The Japan Society promotes cultural exchange programs and special events plus exhibitions three or four times a year. The gallery shows both traditional and contemporary Japanese art. The society's film center is a major showcase for Japanese cinema in the U.S. There's also a library and language center in the lower lobby wing

Jewish Museum

1109 Fifth Ave at 92nd St (423-3230). Subway: 4, 5, 6 to 96th St. Mon, Wed, Thu, Sun 11am–5:45pm; Tue 11am–8pm. $7, under 12 free, no admission charge Tue 5–8pm; concessions $5. No credit cards. A fascinating collection of art, artifacts and media installations, the Jewish Museum is housed in the 1908 Warburg Mansion, which was renovated in 1993 to include the underground Café Weissman. The museum commissions a contemporary artist or group of artists to install a new show each year, and the results are always stellar. The permanent exhibition tracks the Jewish cultural experience through exhibits ranging from a 16th-century mosaic wall from a Persian synagogue and a filigree silver circumcision set to an interactive Talmud—there's even a Statue of Liberty Hanukkah lamp. Most of this eclectic collection was rescued from European synagogues before World War II. Look for an exhibition of paintings, sculpture, video and artists' books commemorating Israel's 50th anniversary and a major retrospective of Ben Shahn's "personal realism" period.

El Museo del Barrio

1230 Fifth Ave between 104th and 105th Sts (831-7272). Subway: 6 to 103rd St. Wed–Sun 11am–5pm. Donation $4, under 12 free; concessions $2. AmEx, MC, V. At the top of Museum Mile, not far from Spanish Harlem (the neighborhood from which it takes its name), El Museo del Barrio is dedicated to the art of Latinos in the United States as well as that of Latin America. Typical exhibitions are contemporary and consciousness-raising; El Museo also sponsors community events like the festive annual celebration of the Mexican Day of the Dead (Nov 1).

Museum for African Art

593 Broadway between Houston and Prince Sts (966-1313). Subway: B, D, F, Q to Broadway–Lafayette St; N, R to Prince St; 6 to Bleecker St. Tue–Fri 10:30am–5:30pm; Sat, Sun noon–6pm. $5, under 2 free; concessions $2.50. MC, V (over $10). This tranquil museum was designed by Maya Lin, who also created the stunningly simple Vietnam Veterans' Memorial in Washington, D.C. Exhibits change about twice a year; the quality of the works shown is high, and they often come from stunning private collections. There's an unusually good bookshop with a children's section.

Museum of Jewish Heritage: A Living Memorial to the Holocaust

18 First Pl at Battery Pl, Battery Park City (968-1800). Subway: 1, 9 to Rector St. Sun–Wed 9am–5pm; Thurs 9am–8pm; Fri and holiday eves 9am–2pm; closed Sat and Jewish holidays. $7, students and seniors $5, under 5 free. Advance ticket purchase recommended; call the museum or Ticketmaster (307-4007). You don't have to be Jewish to appreciate the contents of this institution, built in a symbolic six-sided shape (recalling the Star of David) under a tiered roof. Opened in 1997, it offers people of all backgrounds one of the most moving cultural experiences in the city. The well-thought-out exhibits feature 2,000 photographs, hundreds of surviving cultural artifacts, and plenty of archival films that vividly detail the crime against humanity that was the Holocaust. The exhibition continues beyond those dark times into days of renewal, ending in an upper gallery that is flooded with daylight and gives especially meaningful views of Lady Liberty in the harbor. It's an unforgettable experience. Closed-captioned video is available.

Tibetan Museum

338 Lighthouse Ave off Richmond Rd, Staten Island (recorded information 1-718-987-3500). Subway: 1, 9 to South Ferry, then Staten Island Ferry and S78 bus. April through November Wed–Sun 1–5pm; December through March by appointment only. $3; concessions $1–$2.50. No credit cards. This mock Tibetan temple stands on the highest hilltop on the Eastern seaboard. It contains a fascinating Buddhist altar and the largest collection of Tibetan art in the West, including religious objects, bronzes and paintings. There's a comprehensive English-language library containing books on Buddhism, as well as on Tibet and Asian art. The landscaped gardens house a zoo of stone animals (with birdhouses and wishing well) and offer good views.

Ukrainian Museum

203 Second Ave between 12th and 13th Sts (228-0110). Subway: L, N, R, 4, 5, 6 to 14th St–Union Sq. Wed–Sun 1–5pm. $1; concessions 50¢. No credit cards. The Ukrainian National Women's League of America provided most of the folk art here. It's a small, rather sorry-looking museum on two tiny floors, showing woven and embroidered textiles plus assorted crafts and objects from the 19th and early 20th centuries. Fund-raising for relocation is under way.

Yeshiva University Museum

2520 Amsterdam Ave at 185th Street (960-5390). Subway: 1 to 181st St. Tue–Thu 10:30am–5pm, Sun noon–6pm. $3; concessions $2. No credit cards. The museum usually hosts one major exhibition a year and several smaller ones, mainly on Jewish themes.

Fashion

The Museum at FIT

Seventh Ave at 27th St (760-7970). Subway: 1, 9 to 28th St. Tue–Fri noon–8pm, Sat 10am–5pm. Free. The Fashion Institute of Technology has the world's largest collection of costumes and textiles; only two galleries are open to the public. Recent exhibitions have been devoted to designers such as Cristobal Balenciaga and Norman Norell but have also included East Village streetwear and a history of lingerie.

Historical

American Numismatic Society

Audubon Terrace between 155th and 156th Sts (234-3130). Subway: 1 to 157th St. Tue–Sat 9am–4:30pm, Sun 1–4pm. Free. The collection covers 26 centuries of filthy lucre.

Brooklyn Historical Society

128 Pierrepont St at Clinton St, Brooklyn (1-718-624-0890). Subway: N , R to Court St; 2, 3, 4, 5 to Borough Hall. Mon, Thu–Sat noon–5pm. $2.50, no admission charge Mondays; concessions $1. No credit cards. What do Woody Allen, Mae West, Isaac Asimov, Mel Brooks and Walt Whitman have in common? Answer: They were all—along with Al Capone, Barry Manilow and Gypsy Rose Lee—born in Brooklyn. Thus they merit tributes in this tiny, recently refurbished museum dedicated to Brooklyn's past glories. There are displays on the borough's firefighters, its Navy Yard and its famous baseball team, the Dodgers, who won the World Series in 1955—only to break Brooklyn's heart by moving to Los Angeles two years later.

Fraunces Tavern Museum

54 Pearl St at Broad St, second and third floors (425-1778). Subway: 1, 9 to South Ferry. Mon–Fri 10am–4:45pm; Sat, Sun noon–4pm. $2.50, under 6 free; concessions $1. No credit cards. This tavern used to be George Washington's watering hole and was a prominent meeting place for anti-British groups before the Revolution. The 18th-century building, which has been partly reconstructed, is unexpectedly quaint, considering its setting on the fringes of the financial district. Most of its artifacts are displayed in period rooms. The changing exhibitions are often interesting.

Hall of Fame for Great Americans

Hall of Fame Terrace, 181st St and University Ave, Bronx (1-718 289 5161). Subway: 4 to Burnside Ave. 10am–5pm. Free. The Hall of Fame is a covered walkway lined with bronze busts of preeminent Americans, with sections devoted to scientists, authors, soldiers and statesmen. As the last two categories suggest, the tributees are mostly male, among them the Wright Brothers, Thomas Mann and Franklin D. Roosevelt. The Hall isn't very heavily visited—the subway ride is long, and then it's a 20-minute walk through the Bronx to its home behind Bronx Community College. On the other hand, it does sit on the highest natural summit of New York City—a getaway!

Lower East Side Tenement Museum

90 Orchard St at Broome St (431-0233). Subway: F, J, M, Z to Delancey St; B, D, Q to Grand St. Visitor Center Tue–Sun 11am–5pm. $7; concessions $6. AmEx, MC, V. For a fascinating look at the history of immigration, visit this 19th-century tenement. The building, in the heart of what was once Little Germany, contains two reconstructed apartments belonging to a German Jewish dressmaker and a Sicilian Catholic family. Tours are obligatory if you want to see the tenement itself; it's worth booking ahead, since they sell out. Tours are at 1pm, 2pm and 3pm Tue–Fri and every 45 minutes on weekends. The museum also has a gallery, shop and video room, and organizes local heritage walking tours.

Merchant's House Museum

29 E 4th St between Lafayette St and the Bowery (777-1089). Subway: 6 to Astor Pl. Mon–Thu, Sun 1–4pm. $3, under 12 free if accompanied by an adult; concessions $2. No credit cards. Seabury Tredwell was the merchant in question. He made his fortune selling hardware and bought this elegant Greek Revival house three years after it was built in 1832. The house has been virtually untouched since the 1860s; decoration is spare (except for the lavish canopied four-poster beds) and ornamentation tasteful. Guided tours are conducted on Sundays; call for details.

Museum of the City of New York

1220 Fifth Ave at 103rd St (534-1672). Subway: 6 to 103rd St. Wed–Sat 10am–5pm, Sun noon–5pm. Suggested donation $5; concessions $4. No credit cards. Internet: www .mcny.org In 1998–99, the city is celebrating the centennial of its five boroughs' merger, and several exhibitions have been timed to coincide with it. There's a vast archive of objects, prints and photographs that tell the Big Apple's story, and displays about its people (noted on its Wall of Fame). Among the 300,000 photos and prints and 2,000 paintings and sculptures, you'll find an unparalleled collection of Broadway memorabilia, and impressive historical collections of clothing and decorative household objects. There are temporary themed exhibitions; the Toy Gallery, with its justly famed dollhouses, is now on permanent display.

New York Historical Society

2 W 77th St at Central Park West (873-3400). Subway: B, C to 81st St. Tue–Sun 11am–5pm. Suggested donation $5; concessions $3. No credit cards. The society, which had been closed for several years after running out of money, is back in business. Founded in 1804, it was one of America's first cultural educational institutions and is New York's oldest museum. Exhibitions can include anything from Paul Robeson's diaries to a display about Pocahontas. The permanent collection includes such items as Tiffany lamps, lithographs and a lock of George Washington's hair.

Abigail Adams Smith Museum

421 E 61st St at First Ave (838-6878). Subway: N, R to Lexington Ave; 4, 5, 6 to 59th St. Tue–Sun 11am–4pm. $3, under 13 free; concessions $2. No credit cards. An 18th-century coach house once belonging to the daughter of John Adams, the second president of the U.S. The house is filled with period articles and furniture (Abigail died in 1813), and there's an adjoining formal garden.

South Street Seaport Museum

Herman Melville Gallery, 213 Water St at Beekman St (748-8600). Subway: A, C to Broadway–Nassau St; 2, 3, 4, 5 to Fulton St. 10am–5pm. Concessions $3–$6. AmEx, MC, V. The museum sprawls across 11 blocks along the East River—an amalgam of galleries, historic ships, 19th-century buildings and a visitors' center. The staff (mostly volunteers) is friendly, and it's fun to wander around the rebuilt streets, popping in to see an exhibition on tattooing before climbing aboard the four-masted 1911 *Peking*. The Seaport itself is pretty touristy, but still a charming place to spend an afternoon. Near the Fulton Fish Market building, there are plenty of cafés to choose from. *See also chapter* **Sightseeing**.

The Statue of Liberty and Ellis Island Immigration Museum

Subway: 4, 5 to Bowling Green, then ferry from Battery Park to Liberty Island and Ellis Island (363-3200/ferry information 269-5755). Ferries every half-hour daily 9:15am–3:30pm. $7; concessions $3–$5, including admission. Ticket sales at Castle Clinton, Battery Park, 8:30am–3:30pm. No credit cards. There's an interesting museum devoted to the statue's history contained in the pedestal itself. On the way back to Manhattan, the tour boat takes you to the Immigration Museum on Ellis Island, where more than 12 million people entered the country. The exhibitions are an evocative and moving tribute to anyone who headed for America with dreams of a better life. The audio tour (available in five languages; $3.50, concessions $2.50–$3) is excellent. *See also chapter* **Sightseeing**.

Media

American Museum of the Moving Image

35th Ave at 36th St, Astoria, Queens (1-718-784-0077). Subway: G, R to Steinway St. Tue–Fri noon–5pm; Sat, Sun 11am–6pm. $8; concessions $4–$5. No credit cards. Only a 15-minute subway ride from midtown Manhattan, AMMI is one of the city's most dynamic and entertaining institutions. Built within the restored complex that once housed the original Astoria studios (where commercial filmmaking got its start and continues today), it offers an extensive daily film and video program that should satisfy even the most demanding

*Sun spot: At the **Museum of Modern Art** garden, you can't see the trees for the sculpture.*

cinephile. If you're curious about the mechanics and history of movie and television production, the core exhibition, "Behind the Screen," will give you an intensely interactive insight into every aspect of it—storyboarding, directing, editing, sound-mixing and marketing. You can even make your own short at a digital animation stand. The museum has a café, but there are other restaurant options nearby; as the largest Greek community outside Greece, Astoria boasts some terrific Greek restaurants.

Museum of Television and Radio
25 W 52nd St between Fifth and Sixth Aves (621-6600). Subway: E, F to Fifth Ave; B, D, F, Q to 47th–50th Sts–Rockefeller Ctr. Tue, Wed, Sat, Sun noon–6pm; Thu noon–8pm; Fri noon–9pm. $6; concessions $3–$4. No credit cards. This is a living, working archive of more than 60,000 radio and TV programs. Just head to the fourth-floor library and use the computerized system to access a favorite *Star Trek* or *I Love Lucy* episode. The assigned console downstairs will play up to four of your choices within two hours. The radio listening room works the same way. There are also special public seminars and screenings. It's a must for TV and radio addicts.

Newseum/NY
580 Madison Ave between 56th and 57th Sts (317-7503/ recorded information 317-7596). Subway: E, F, N, R to Fifth Ave. Mon–Sat 10am–5:30 pm. Free. Internet: www. mediastudies.org The entrance to these branch galleries of a Washington, D.C., center for media studies—through the pleasant, glass-enclosed atrium of a midtown office tower—hardly prepares visitors for the intensity of what lies ahead. Newseum/NY presents topical photography exhibitions that illuminate, with no small emotional impact, the work of

prize-winning news photographers and correspondents the world over. Sponsored by the Freedom Forum, it also presents accompanying film and lecture series that encourage public discussion of First Amendment issues. Exhibitions change three or four times a year. Documentaries screen at 1pm every Monday and Friday and run about an hour; reservations are not necessary.

Military

Intrepid Sea, Air and Space Museum
USS Intrepid, Pier 86, 46th St at the Hudson River (245-2533/ recorded information 245-0072). Subway: A, C, E to 42nd St. Memorial Day–Labor Day Mon–Sat 10am–5pm, Sun 10am–6pm; Labor Day–Memorial Day Mon–Wed, Sun 10am–5pm. $10; concessions $5–$7.50. AmEx, MC, V. This museum is located on the World War II aircraft carrier *Intrepid*, whose decks are crammed with space capsules and various aircraft. There are plenty of audiovisual shows and hands-on exhibits to appeal to children.

Science and technology

The **Hayden Planetarium** is currently closed for major renovations and expansion; it is scheduled to reopen in 2000.

Liberty Science Center
Liberty State Park, 251 Phillip St, Jersey City, NJ (recorded information 1-201-200-1000). Travel: PATH train to Grove St, then connecting park bus; weekend ferry service (info 1-800-533-3779). Tue–Sun 9:30am–5:30pm. Exhibition halls $9.50, concessions $6.50–$8.50; halls and Omnimax cinema

$13.50, concessions $9.50–$11.50. AmEx, Disc, MC, V. This is an excellent museum with innovative exhibitions and America's largest and most spectacular Imax cinema. The observation tower provides great views of Manhattan and an unusual sideways look at the Statue of Liberty. The center's emphasis is on hands-on science, so get ready to elbow your way among the excited kids. It's pleasant to arrive by ferry on the weekend.

New York Hall of Science
47-01 111th St at 46th Ave, Flushing Meadows, Queens (1-718-699-0005). Subway: 7 to 111th St. Group bookings Mon, Tue 9am–2pm; Wed–Sun 10am–5pm. $4.50, no admission charge Wed, Thu 2–5pm; concessions $3. AmEx, MC, V. Internet: www.nyhallsci.org Since its opening during the 1964–65 World's Fair, the New York Hall of Science has built the largest collection of hands-on science exhibits in the city; it's now considered one of the top science museums in the country. The emphasis here is on education, and the place is usually filled with schoolchildren, for whom it successfully demystifies science with stimulating interactive exhibits. The museum includes a 48-foot-high entrance rotunda, a new dining pavilion and a 300-seat auditorium. (*See also chapter* **Children**.)

Urban services

Fire Museum
278 Spring St at Varick St (691-1303). Subway: 1, 9 to Houston St. Tue–Sun 10am–4pm, Thu 10am–9pm. Suggested donation $4; concessions $1–$2. AmEx, MC, V. This small but cheerful museum is located in an old three-story firehouse whose pole still gleams next to a few vintage fire engines and several displays of fireman ephemera dating back 100 years. Two tours a day allow groups of up to 30.

New York Transit Museum
Schermerhorn St at Boerum Pl, Brooklyn (1-718-243-3060). Subway: M, N, R to Court St; G to Hoyt/Schermerhorn Sts; 2, 3, 4, 5 to Borough Hall. Tue, Thu, Fri 10am–4pm; Wed 10am–6pm; Sat, Sun noon–5pm. $3; concessions $1.50. No credit cards. Don't look for a building—the Transit Museum is housed underground in an old 1930s subway station. Its entrance, down a flight of stairs, is beneath the Board of Education building, opposite the black-and-white-striped New York City Transit Authority building. Nose around vintage subways with wicker seats and canvas straps, a selection of antique turnstiles and plenty of ads—including one explaining that spitting "is a violation of the sanitary code." So there!

New York Public Library

The multitentacled New York Public Library, founded in 1895, comprises four major research libraries and 82 local and specialist branches, making it the largest and most comprehensive library system in the world. The library grew from the combined collections of John Jacob Astor, Samuel Jones Tilden and James Lenox. Today, it holds a total of 50 million items, including nearly 18 million books, with around a million items added to the collection each year. Unless you are interested in a specific subject, your best bet is to visit the system's flagship building, officially called the Center for the Humanities. The newest branch, the Science, Industry and Business Library, opened in 1996.

Center for the Humanities
Fifth Ave at 42nd St (recorded information 869-8089). Subway: B, D, F, Q to 42nd St; 7 to Fifth Ave. Mon, Thu–Sat 10am–6pm; Tue, Wed 11am–6pm. Free. Internet: www.nypl.org This landmark Beaux Arts building is what most people call the New York Public Library. The famous stone lions out front are wreathed with holly at Christmas; during the summer people sit on the steps or sip cool drinks at the outdoor tables beneath the arches. The free guided tours of the building at 11am and 2pm include the beautiful reading room (which will reopen on November 16, 1998, after a $15 million renovation); the first Gutenberg Bible brought to America; and a handwritten copy of George Washington's farewell address. The Bill Blass Public Catalogue Room was recently restored and renovated and now contains computers for surfing the Internet. Special exhibitions are frequent and always worthwhile, and lectures in the Celeste Bartos Forum are always well attended.

Donnell Library Center
20 W 53rd St between Fifth and Sixth Aves (621-0618). Subway: E, F to Fifth Ave. Mon, Wed, Fri noon–6pm; Tue, Thu 9:30am–8pm; Sat 10am–5:30pm. Free. This branch of the NYPL has an extensive collection of records, films and videotapes, with appropriate screening facilities. The Donnell specializes in foreign-language books—in more than 80 languages—and there's a children's section of more than 100,000 books, films, records and cassettes…and the original Winnie-the-Pooh dolls.

Library for the Performing Arts
Lincoln Center, 111 Amsterdam Ave between 65th and 66th Sts (870-1630). Subway: 1, 9 to 66th St–Lincoln Ctr. Mon, Thu noon–8pm; Tue, Wed, Fri, Sat noon–6pm. Free. Outstanding research and circulating collections cover music, drama, theater and dance.

Science, Industry and Business Library
Madison Ave between 34th and 35th Sts (930-0747). Subway: 6 to 33rd St. Mon, Fri, Sat 10am–6pm; Tue–Thu 11am–7pm. Free. Internet: www.nypl.org/research/sibl/index.html The world's largest public information center devoted to science, technology, economics and business occupies the first floor and lower level of the old B. Altman department store. Opened in 1996 after a $100 million renovation, the new Gwathmey Siegel–designed branch of the NYPL has a circulating collection of 50,000 books, an open-shelf reference collection of 60,000 volumes. Aiming to help people in small businesses, the library also specializes in digital technologies and the Internet.

Schomburg Center for Research in Black Culture
515 Malcolm X Blvd at 135th St (491-2200). Subway: 2, 3 to 135th St. Mon–Wed noon–8pm, Thu–Sat 10am–6pm, Sun 1pm–5pm. Free. Tours by appointment. Internet: www.nypl.org/research/sc/sc.html This extraordinary trove of vintage literature and historical memorabilia relating to black culture and the African diaspora was founded by its first curator, Puerto Rico–born bibliophile Arthur Schomburg, who established the collection in 1926. It now contains more then 5 million objects and artifacts, including rare books and manuscripts, periodicals, audio and video tapes, documentary and dramatic films, recordings, photographs and prints. Changing exhibitions display art dating back to the 17th century—masks, statuary, painting, sculpture and works on paper by African and African-American artists. The Schomburg also hosts live jazz concerts, films, lectures and tours. (*See also* **Black pride** *in chapter* **New York by Neighborhood: Northern Manhattan**.)

Rhythm method: East Village street musicians get down in Tompkins Square Park.

New York by Neighborhood

Downtown

Wall Street powerbrokers, Soho fashionistas, East Village punks and immigrants of every stripe make lower Manhattan come alive

Since New York City grew northward from Battery Park, the richest and most diverse concentration of places and people is located below 14th Street. Here, the crooked streets (most of which have names, not numbers) are made for walking. Lose yourself for hours wandering from the architectural wonderland of the financial district and Civic Center, through the trendy art-lined streets of Soho and the vivid ethnic enclaves of the Lower East Side, to the "punk's-not-dead" spirit of the East Village and the café society of Greenwich Village.

Battery Park

The southern tip of Manhattan is where you are most conscious of being on an island. The Atlantic breeze blows in from the bay, along the same route of the millions who arrived here by sea: past the golden torch of the **Statue of Liberty** (*see chapter* **Sightseeing**), over the immigration and quarantine center of **Ellis Island** (now a splendid museum) and on to the statue-lined promenade of Battery Park. The park often plays host to international touring events such as the Cirque du Soleil (*see chapter* **Children**). Free outdoor music is often a summer-evenings feature here as well.

Castle Clinton, inside the park, was originally built during the Napoleonic wars when New Yorkers felt threatened by the British they had just thrown out. The castle has been a theater and an aquarium, and now it's a National Parks visitors' center with historical displays. Buy your tickets for the Statue of Liberty and Ellis Island here.

Go around the shore to the east and you can catch the famous **Staten Island Ferry**, now free, and a great way to capture the wonder of arriving by sea (*see* **Tours** *in chapter* **Sightseeing**). The historic terminal was destroyed by fire in 1991, and its replacement has not yet been built, but next door is the beautiful **Battery Maritime Building**, terminal for the many ferry services that sailed between Manhattan and Brooklyn in the years before the Brooklyn Bridge was built.

North of Battery Park is the triangle of **Bowling Green**, the city's first park and home to the beautiful Beaux Arts **U.S. Custom House**, now the fascinating **National Museum of the American Indian**. Near here is Arturo DiModica's dynamic bronze bull sculpture that represents the snorting power of Wall Street, as well as the **Shrine of Elizabeth Ann Seton**, a strange curved building in the Federal style, dedicated to the first American-born saint. Also nearby is the **Fraunces Tavern Museum,** a restoration of the alehouse where Washington celebrated his victory against the British, now a museum of revolutionary New York and a restaurant (*see chapters* **Architecture** *and* **Museums**).

Wall Street

From New York's earliest days as a fur trading post to its place today at the hub of international finance, commerce has always been the backbone of the city's prosperity. Wall Street is the thoroughfare synonymous with the world's greatest capitalist gambling den.

Wall Street took its name from a defensive wall the Dutch settlers built. For a long time, it marked New York City's northern limits. In the days before telecommunications, financial institutions established their headquarters here to be near the action. This was where corporate America first asserted itself architecturally—there are many great buildings here built by grand old banks and businesses.

Notable ones include the Greek-colonnaded **Citibank Building**; the **Equitable Building**, whose greedy use of vertical space inspired the zoning laws governing skyscrapers; and the **Cunard Building**, the beautiful domed ticket office for the grand shipping company, now a post office.

At the western end of Wall Street is the Gothic spire of **Trinity Church**, once the island's tallest structure, but now dwarfed by skyscrapers. A block east is the **Federal Hall National Monument**, a Doric shrine to American constitutional history and the place where Washington became the country's first president.

Across the street is the **New York Stock Exchange**, though its grand frontage and public entrance are around the corner on Broad Street. The visitors' center here is excellent for educating the clueless about the workings of financial trading, and lets you look out over the trading floor in action. It's all computerized these days, so except for crashes and panics, it's not too exciting as a spectator sport (for the "buy! buy! buy!" action you've seen in the movies, you want the far more frenzied **Commodities Exchange,** *page 78*).

*Steeple chasing: The twin towers of the **World Trade Center** soar over **Trinity Church**.*

Today's catch: Anglers young and old fish from the pier at **Battery Park**.

The **Federal Reserve Bank**, a block north on Liberty Street, is the world's largest gold depository (you saw Jeremy Irons clean it out in *Die Hard 3*), holding bullion for half the countries of the world. This Florentine palazzo-fort is where they print money; it is the origin of any banknote with a big B next to its president. Take an empty canvas bag for the guided tour....

As you'd expect, the Wall Street area is fairly deserted after office hours, though the empty expanses of concrete and pavement make it a nighttime magnet for young daredevils on skateboards. The time to see it is around midday, when the suits emerge for their hurried lunches. Join them in stopping for a burger at the ultimate **McDonald's** (160 Broadway). By some quirk of individualism, it boasts liveried doormen, a special dessert menu and a Liberace-style pianist.

Federal Reserve Bank

33 Liberty St between William and Nassau Sts (720-6130). Subway: 2, 3, 4, 5 to Wall St. By appointment only. Free. The free one-hour tours through the bank must be arranged at least one week in advance; tickets are sent by mail.

New York Stock Exchange

20 Broad St at Wall St (656-5168). Subway: J, M, Z to Broad St; 2, 3, 4, 5 to Wall St. Mon–Fri 9am–4:30pm. Free. A gallery overlooks the trading floor, and there are lots of multimedia exhibits.

Trinity Church Museum

Broadway at Wall St (602-0872/0768). Subway: N, R to Rector St; 2, 3, 4, 5 to Wall St. Mon–Fri 9–11:45am, 1–3:45pm; Sat 10am–3:45pm; Sun 1–3:45pm; closed during concerts. Free. The small museum inside features exhibits on the history of the church and its place in New York history.

The Seaport

While New York's importance as a port has diminished, the city's fortune sailed in on the salt water that crashes around its natural harbor. The city was perfectly placed for trade with Europe—with goods from middle America arriving via the Erie Canal and Hudson River. And because New York was the point of entry for millions of immigrants, its character was formed primarily by the waves of humanity that arrived at its docks.

The **South Street Seaport**, an area of reclaimed and renovated buildings converted to shops, restaurants, bars and a museum, is where you'll best see this seafaring heritage. Though the shopping area of Pier 17 is little more than a picturesque mall of gift shops by day and an after-office yuppie watering hole by night, the other piers are crowded with antique vessels. The **Seaport Museum**—detailing New York's maritime history—is fascinating. The Seaport's public spaces are a favorite with street performers; there are outdoor concerts in the summer. The Fulton Market building (with gourmet food stalls and seafood restaurants that expand onto the cobbled streets in summer) is a great place for slurping oysters as you watch people stroll by.

There are fine views of the **Brooklyn Bridge** just to the north (*see chapter* **Sightseeing**) and plenty of restored 19th-century buildings, including Schermerhorn Row, constructed on landfill in 1812. **Fulton Fish Market**, America's largest, is here too, though the fish are delivered by land and the market lives under the constant threat of relocation. Organized crime has always had a presence here—and may have had something to do with the fire that damaged much of the area in 1996. Still, the district continues to thrive. If you wish to continue your day with a salt-water theme, Pier 16 is where to find the tour boats of **Seaport Liberty Cruises** (*see chapter* **Sightseeing**).

Fulton Fish Market

South St at Fulton St (669-9416). Subway: J, M, Z, 2, 3, 4, 5 to Fulton St. Midnight–9am. Tours April–October: first and third Thursday of the month at 6am. $10, reservations required. AmEx, MC, V.

Seaport Museum

See chapter **Museums** *for listings.*

South Street Seaport

Water St to the East River, between John St and Peck Slip (for info about shops and special events call SEA–PORT, 732-7678). Subway: J, M, Z, 2, 3, 4, 5 to Fulton St.

World Trade Center and Battery Park City

The area along lower Manhattan's "west coast" contains grand developments that combine vast amounts of office space with new public plazas, restaurants and shopping areas. There have been concerted efforts to inject a little cultural life into these spaces, and plenty of street performers work the area in summer months, though the general atmosphere is defined by the schedule of the working day.

The **World Trade Center** is actually seven buildings, though to most visitors it means the famous twin towers that dominate the downtown skyline (*see chapter* **Sightseeing**). Visit the observation deck—on good days you can walk outside—and spare a thought for the crazies who have suction-climbed the walls, parachuted off the top floor or walked a tightrope between the two towers. It's the city's tallest structure and, until Chicago's Sears Tower was completed, also held the world

height record. The great free floor show that is the Commodities Exchange is at 4 World Trade Center.

Across West Street is **Battery Park City**, built on land dug up when the World Trade Center's foundations were built. This partly residential complex houses, among others, wealthy Wall Streeters whose high rents go to subsidize public housing elsewhere in the city. The beautiful park links Battery Park with the piers to the north, which are slowly being claimed for public use, allowing you to spend a pleasant afternoon strolling along the riverside from Manhattan's southern tip right up to Christopher Street, in the company of bikers, 'bladers and cuddling couples.

The **World Financial Center**, the development's centerpiece, is the ultimate expression of the city-within-a-city concept. Crowned by Cesar Pelli's four elegant postmodern office towers, it contains an upscale retail area, a marina and a series of plazas with terraced restaurants. The stunning vaulted glass-roofed Winter Garden, with its indoor palm trees, has become a popular venue for

*Floor show: Traders get Dow and dirty at the computerized **New York Stock Exchange**.*

concerts and other entertainment, most of which are free (for more information, *see chapter* **Music**).

Commodities Exchange

4 World Trade Center, ninth floor (748-1006). Subway: N, R, 1, 9 to Cortlandt St. Mon–Fri 10:30am–3pm. Free. The Stock Exchange has lost much of its drama in these days of computerized trading; not so the Commodities Exchange. Here you can still see manic figures in color-coded blazers scream and shout at each other as they buy and sell gold, pork bellies and orange juice. There are three tours a day—at 11am, 1pm and 3pm; book two weeks in advance.

Lower Manhattan Cultural Council

432-0900. This group offers information on cultural events happening in and around this part of Manhattan.

World Financial Center

West St to the Hudson River, Vesey St to Albany St (945-0505). Subway: N, R, 1, 9 to Cortlandt St. Free. Phone for information about the many free arts events.

Civic Center

The business of running New York takes place among the many grand buildings of the **Civic Center**. Originally this was the city's focal point, and when **City Hall** was built in 1812, its architects were so confident the city would grow no farther north, they didn't bother to put any marble on its northern side (*see chapter* **Architecture**). The building, a beautiful blend of Georgian formality, Federal detailing and French Renaissance influences, sits in its own patch of green: **City Hall Park**. It was in this park, in 1776, that the Declaration of Independence was read to Washington's army. You're likely to see city officials giving press conferences here, and there are political protests and rallies of every sort.

The much larger **Municipal Building**, which faces City Hall and reflects it architecturally, is home to the overspill of civic offices, including the marriage bureau, which can churn out newlyweds at remarkable speed. **Park Row**, east of the park and now populated by an array of cafés and stereo shops, once held the offices of 19 daily papers and was known as "Newspaper Row." It was also the site of Phineas T. Barnum's sensationalist American Museum, which burnt down in 1865.

Facing the park from the west is Cass Gilbert's famous **Woolworth Building**, a vertically elongated Gothic cathedral of an office building that has been called "the Mozart of Skyscrapers." Its beautifully detailed lobby is open to the public during working hours. Two blocks down Broadway is **St. Paul's Chapel**, an oasis of peace, modeled on London's St. Martin-in-the-Fields in 1766, and one of the few buildings left from the century of British rule.

The houses of crime and punishment are also located in the Civic Center. Here you'll find the **New York County Courthouse**, a hexagonal building with a beautiful interior rotunda, and the **United States Courthouse**, a golden pyramid–topped tower above a Corinthian temple, both over-

looking Foley Square. Back next to City Hall is the old New York County Courthouse, more popularly known as the **Tweed Courthouse**, a symbol of the runaway corruption of mid-19th-century city government; Boss Tweed, leader of the political strong-arm faction Tammany Hall, pocketed $10 million of the building's soaring $14 million cost. You can't spend that much and fail to get a beautiful building, however. Its Italianate detailing may be symbolic of immense greed, but it is of the highest quality. The **Criminal Courts Building** is by far the most intimidating of them all. Great Babylonian slabs of granite give it an awesome presence, emphasized by the huge judgmental towers guarding the entrance. This Kafkaesque home of justice has been known since its creation as "the Tombs," a reference not only to its architecture but to the deathly conditions of the city jail it once contained.

All of these courts are open to the public (Mon–Fri 9am–5pm), though only some of the courtrooms will allow visitors. Your best bet for a little courtroom drama is the Criminal Courts, where if you can't slip into a trial, you can at least observe the hallways full of seedy-looking lawyers and the criminals they are representing.

Tribeca

Tribeca (for tri<u>a</u>ngle <u>be</u>low <u>Ca</u>nal Street) illustrates very nicely the process of gentrification in lower Manhattan. It's very much like Soho was 15 to 20 years ago, with some parts deserted and abandoned—the cobbles dusty and untrodden and the cast-iron architecture chipped and unpainted—and other pockets throbbing with arriviste energy. In particular, this is the hot spot for new restaurants, with the occasional bar or club also working hard to establish itself.

The buildings here are generally larger than in Soho and, especially towards the river, mostly warehouses. However, there is some fine smaller-scale cast-iron architecture along White Street and the parallel thoroughfares (*see chapter* **Architecture**), and Harrison Street is home to a row of well-preserved Federal-style townhouses.

As in Soho, art is the new industry here, and there are several galleries representing the more cutting-edge (read, hit or miss) side of things. The view from the balcony of the **Clocktower**—the gallery of the Institute for Art and Urban Resources in the tower rooms of the old **New York Life Insurance Building**—is as inspiring as the art inside is experimental (*see chapter* **Art Galleries**).

One famous Tribeca tenant is Robert De Niro, whose **Tribeca Film Center** at 375 Greenwich Street, the old Martinson Coffee Building, houses screening rooms and production offices and is home base to several prominent New York and visiting filmmakers. They dine, of course, at De Niro's **Tribeca Grill** on the ground floor.

Soho

Soho is designer New York, in every sense. Walk around its cobbled streets, among the elegant cast-iron architecture, the boutiques, art galleries and bistros, and you'll find yourself sharing the sidewalks with the beautiful people of young, monied, fashionable NYC. The chic bars and eateries are full of these trendsetters, while the shop windows display the work of the latest arrivals in the world of art and fashion.

Soho (south of Houston Street) was earmarked for destruction during the 1960s, but the area was saved by the many artists who inhabited its (then) low-rent ex-industrial spaces. They protested against the demolition of these beautiful buildings, whose cast-iron frames prefigured the technology of the skyscraper (*see chapter* **Architecture**).

As loft-living became fashionable and the buildings were renovated for residential use, the landlords were quick to sniff gentrification's increased profits. Surprisingly, plenty of sweatshops remain here—especially near Canal Street—though, increasingly, they house such businesses as graphics studios, magazines and record labels. There also has been a noticeable invasion over the last few years by a number of large chain stores: Starbucks, Staples, Pottery Barn, J. Crew and Banana Republic have all put down roots, leading locals to mutter darkly about the "malling of Soho."

(For an increasing number of more singular shops, head for the emerging area that borders Soho, Little Italy and the East Village dubbed Nolita [for north of Little Italy]. See **Meet ya in Nolita** in chapter **Shopping & Services**.)

Arch deluxe: Art gets institutionalized in the downtown **Guggenheim Museum**.

West Broadway is the main thoroughfare of Soho, lined with the chain stores, pricey shops and art galleries, including the famous **Leo Castelli**. Four blocks east, the **Guggenheim Museum** has a branch that exhibits both temporary collections and selections from the museum's permanent collection. In addition, Broadway has a collection of other galleries specializing in lesser-known artists. **The New Museum of Contemporary Art**, is the young cousin of MoMA, while the **Alternative Museum** and the neighboring **Museum for African Art** are both worth a look. Just off Broadway on Spring Street is the **Fire Museum**, a small building housing a collection of gleaming antique engines dating back to the 1700s (*see chapters* **Museums and Art Galleries** *for more details on these*).

Lower East Side

The Lower East Side tells the story of New York's immigrants: the cycle of one generation making good and moving to the suburbs, leaving space for the next wave of hopefuls. It is busy and densely populated, a patchwork of strong ethnic communities, great for dining and exploration. Today, outside **Chinatown** and **Little Italy** (which, strictly speaking, are part of this area), Lower East Side residents are largely Asian or Hispanic—Puerto Rican and Dominican—though the area is more famous for its earlier settlers, most notably Jews from Eastern Europe.

It was here that mass tenement housing was built to accommodate the 19th-century influx of immigrants. Unsanitary, overcrowded buildings forced the introduction of building codes. To appreciate the conditions in which the mass of immigrants lived, take a look at the reconstructions at the **Tenement Museum** (*see chapter* **Museums**).

Between 1870 and 1920, hundreds of synagogues and religious schools were established here, Yiddish newspapers were published and associations for social reform and cultural studies flourished. Now, however, only 10–15 percent of the population is Jewish: The **Eldridge Street Synagogue** finds it hard to round up the ten adult males required to conduct a service.

The area today is characterized by its large Hispanic population. *Bodegas*, or corner groceries, abound, with their brightly colored awnings, and there are many restaurants serving Puerto Rican dishes of rice and beans with fried plantains, pork chops and chicken. In the summer, the streets throb with the sounds of salsa and merengue as the residents hang out slurping ices, drinking beer and playing dominoes.

But these people are now being nudged aside by what could be described as the latest immigrants: the growing population of young artists, musicians and other rebels, attracted by the area's high drama and low rents. Most of the action is centered on Ludlow Street, an East Village extension that's home to an increasing number of interesting shops, small clubs and cool bars (see chapter **Cafés & Bars**).

Some remnants of the neighborhood's Jewish traditions remain. **Ratner's**, a kosher dairy restaurant, is a New York institution. The shabby **Sammy's Roumanian** is only for those with strong stomachs—hearty servings of East European fare are served with a jug of chicken fat—but it's one of the most famous of the Lower East Side eateries. If you prefer "lighter" food, **Katz's Deli** sells some of the best pastrami in New York, and the orgasms are pretty good, too, if Meg Ryan's performance in *When Harry Met Sally* is anything to go by—the scene was filmed there. For more on all three establishments, see chapter **Restaurants**.

Eldridge Street Synagogue

12 Eldridge St between Canal and Division Sts (219-0888). Subway: F to East Broadway. Tue, Wed, Sun 11am–4pm. This beautifully decorated (and now restored) building is the pride of the Jewish congregation that once filled it. Tours are at 11:30am and 2:30pm on Tuesdays and Thursdays.

First Shearith Israel Graveyard

55–57 St. James Pl between Oliver and James Sts. Subway: B, D to Grand St. The burial ground of the oldest Jewish community in the United States—Spanish and Portuguese

Jews who escaped the Inquisition—contains gravestones dating from 1683.

Israel Israelowitz Tours

1-718-951-7072. Call for details of guided tours of the Lower East Side, boat tours of Jewish New York and lecture programs.

Lower East Side Tenement Museum

See chapter **Museums** for listings.

Schapiro's Winery

126 Rivington St between Essex and Norfolk Sts (674-4404). Subway: F to Delancey; J, M, Z to Essex. Tours on the hour, Sun 11am–4pm. $1. Shapiro's has been making kosher wine ("so thick you can cut it with a knife") since 1899. The wine tours include tastings.

Chinatown

Chinatown spills out beyond Canal Street and the Bowery, but its focal point is Mott Street. The New York version is far removed from the sanitized ones in San Francisco or London. More than 150,000 Chinese live and work in this concentrated area, and it is a very self-sufficient community. The busy streets get even wilder during the Chinese New Year festivities in January or February, and around the 4th of July, when it is the city's source of (illegal) fireworks.

Food is everywhere. The markets on **Canal Street** sell some of the best fish, fruit and vegetables in the city. There are countless restaurants—Mott Street, from Worth Street right up to Kenmare Street, is lined with Cantonese and Sichuan places—and you can buy wonderful snacks from street stalls, such as bags of little sweet egg pancakes. Canal Street is also (in-)famous as a source of cheap imported trinkets and counterfeit designer items. From fake Rolexes to the cheapest "brand-name" running shoes, it's a bargain-hunter's paradise.

A statue of Confucius marks **Confucius Plaza**, near the Manhattan Bridge entrance. On Bayard Street is the **Wall of Democracy**, where political writings about events in Beijing are posted. Immediately upon entering the open doors of the **Eastern States Buddhist Temple of America**, you'll notice the glitter of hundreds of Buddhas and the smell of incense.

Then there's the noisy **Chinatown Fair**, at 8 Mott Street, which is really nothing more than an amusement arcade. However, doors at the back lead to the **Chinese Museum**, a place of such mystery that it is virtually impossible to gain entry—"only groups of eight," they say—but it is supposed to contain the dragon used in the New Year festival.

Eastern States Buddhist Temple of America

64B Mott St between Canal and Bayard Sts (966-6229). Subway: N, R, 4, 5, 6 to Canal St. 9am–7pm.

*Chinese checker-outers: Local residents shop for raw deals in **Chinatown**.*

Little Italy

Little Italy is a vivid pocket of ethnicity, with the sights and sounds of the mother country turned up full. It's getting smaller, though, as Chinatown encroaches and Italian families make an exodus to the suburbs. All that's really left of the Italian community that has lived here since the mid-19th century are the cafés and restaurants on Mulberry Street, between Canal and East Houston Streets, and short sections of cross streets. There remains, however, a strong ethnic pride, and limo-loads of Italians parade in from Queens and Brooklyn to show their love for the old neighborhood during the Feast of San Gennaro each September (*see chapter* **New York by Season**).

The restaurants here are mostly pricey, ostentatious grill and pasta houses that cater to tourists. Still, it's worth your while to enjoy an after-dinner dessert and coffee at one of the many small cafés lining the streets.

As you'd expect, there are great food stores (specializing in strong cheeses, excellent wines, spicy meats, freshly made pasta and the like). For that truly *unique* gift, **Forzano Italian Imports**, at 128 Mulberry Street, is the best (only?) place in New York for papal souvenirs, ghastly Italian pop music and soccer memorabilia.

Two buildings of note here are **Old St. Patrick's Cathedral**, which was once the premier Catholic church of New York but was demoted when the Fifth Avenue cathedral was consecrated, and the **Police Building**. Once the headquarters for the city's police, this has now been converted into much sought-after co-op apartments.

Greenwich Village

"The Village" has been the scene of some serious hanging-out its history. Stretching from 14th Street down to Houston Street, and from Broadway west to the river, these leafy streets with their townhouses, theaters, coffee houses and tiny bars and clubs have witnessed and inspired Bohemian lifestyles for almost a century.

It's a place for idle wandering, for people-watching from sidewalk cafés, for candlelit dining in secret restaurants, or for hopping between bars and cabaret venues. The Village gets overcrowded in summer, and has lost some of its charm as the retail center of lower Broadway has spread west, but much of what attracted creative types to New York still exists.

The jazz generation lives on in smoky clubs like the **Blue Note** and the **Village Vanguard** (*see chapter* **Music**). Sip a fresh roast in honor of the Beats—Jack Kerouac, Allen Ginsberg and their ilk—as you sit in the coffee shops they frequented. Kerouac's favorite was Le Figaro Café on the corner of MacDougal and Bleecker Streets.

The hippies, who tuned out in **Washington Square**, are still there in spirit, and often in person, as the park hums with pot dealers, musicians and street artists. Chess hustlers and students from **New York University** join in, along with today's new generation of hangers-out: the hip-hop kids who drive down in their booming jeeps and the Generation Y skaters/ravers who clatter around the fountain and the base of the arch (a miniature Arc de Triomphe built in 1892 in honor of George Washington).

The Village first became fashionable in the 1830s, when elegant townhouses were built around Washington Square. Literary figures including Henry James, Mark Twain and Edith Wharton lived on or near the square, and Herman Melville wrote *Moby-Dick* in a house at the northern reaches of the Village. In 1870, this growing artistic community founded the **Salmagundi Club**, America's oldest artists' club, which is still extant, just above Washington Square on Fifth Avenue.

The area continued to attract writers, and through Prohibition and beyond, people like John Steinbeck and John Dos Passos passed the time at **Chumley's**, a speakeasy, still unmarked at 86 Bedford Street (*see chapter* **Cafés & Bars**). And the **Cedar Tavern** on University Place was where the leading figures of Abstract Expressionism discussed how best to throw paint: Jackson Pollock, Franz Kline and Larry Rivers drank there in the 1950s. Eighth Street, now a long procession of punky boutiques, shoe shops, piercing parlors and cheap jewelry vendors, was the closest New York got to San Francisco's Haight Street; Jimi Hendrix's Electric Lady Sound Studios are still here at No. 52.

In the triangle formed by West 10th Street, Sixth Avenue and Greenwich Avenue you'll see the neo-Gothic Victorian **Jefferson Market Courthouse**, once voted America's fifth most beautiful building; it's now a library. Across the street is **Balducci's** (*see chapter* **Shopping & Services**), one of the finest food stores in the city, and down Sixth Avenue at 4th Street you stumble on "the Cage," the outdoor basketball courts where you can witness hot hoops action (*see chapter* **Sports & Fitness**).

The West Village, the area roughly between Seventh Avenue and the river, is filled with quaint tree-lined streets of historic houses. This famously gay area, centered on Christopher Street, was the scene of the 1969 Stonewall riots that marked the birth of the gay liberation movement. There are as many same-sex couples strolling along Christopher as straight ones, and plenty of shops, bars and restaurants that are out and proud (*see chapter* **Gay & Lesbian New York**).

Salmagundi Club

47 Fifth Ave at 12th St (255-7740) Subway: L, N, R, 4, 5, 6 to 14 St–Union Sq. Open for exhibitions only; phone for details. Free. Now the home of a series of artistic and historical societies, the club's fine 19th-century interior is worth a look.

The East Village is far scruffier than its western counterpart, housing today's young bohemians. East of Broadway between 14th and Houston Streets, and until recently considered part of the Lower East Side, it's where you'll find an amiable population of punks, hippies, homeboys, homeless and trustafarians—would-be bohos who live off their rich parents' trust funds. This motley crew coexists with older residents—mostly survivors from various waves of immigration—and provides the area with funky, cheap clothes stores (check for quality before forking over any cash), record shops, bargain restaurants, grungey bars and punky clubs.

St. Marks Place (another name for East 8th Street), with bars squeezed into tiny basements and restaurants overflowing onto the sidewalks, is the center of the action. It's packed until the wee hours with crowds browsing for bargains in boutiques, comic shops, record stores and bookshops. The more interesting places are to the east, and you'll find some great little shops and cafés on or around Avenue A between 6th and 10th Streets.

Astor Place, with its revolving cube sculpture, is where Peter Cooper's **Cooper Union**, the city's first free educational institute opened in 1859; it's now a design school. Astor Place marked the boundary between the ghettos to the east and some of the city's most fashionable homes, such as **Colonnade Row**, on Lafayette Street. Facing these was the distinguished Astor Public Library, now **Papp Public Theater**, a haven for first-run American plays and home of the **New York Shakespeare Festival** (*see chapter* **Theater**). In the '60s, Joseph Papp rescued the library from demolition and had it declared a landmark.

East of Lafayette Street on the Bowery is the famous **CBGB** club ("Country, Blue-Grass, Blues"), the birthplace of American punk. CB's still packs in guitar bands, both new and used (*see chapter* **Music**). Many other local bars and clubs successfully apply the formula of cheap beer and loud music, including **The Continental**, **Brownies** and **Under Acme**.

East 7th Street is a Ukrainian stronghold; the focal point is the Byzantine-looking **St. George's Ukrainian Catholic Church**, built in 1977 but looking at least a century older. Across the street is **McSorley's Old Ale House**, the oldest pub in the city (or so it claims) and still serving just one kind of beer, a frothy brew made in the basement (*see chapter* **Cafés & Bars**).

On East 6th Street, between First and Second Avenues, is **Little India** (one of several in New York). Here, roughly two dozen Indian restaurants sit side by side, the long-running rumor being that they all share a single kitchen. And if you're won-

C notes

Alphabet City cool hits Avenue C

Once a definite no-go street in the bowels of crack-vial–laden Alphabet City, Avenue C has become the latest frontier for edgy-but-fun nightlife. With Avenue A completely gentrified, Avenue B an established hipster's heaven and Avenue D still a clubber's wasteland, C is—for now, anyway—the adventurous option for late-night revelers.

In 1996, pioneers Ken Nye and Raff Ambron successfully ventured eastward to open their raucous country-rock juke joint, **9C**. Since then, other daring entrepreneurs have followed suit. Just around the corner is Stephan Gerville and Dmitri Vlahak's chic, loungy **Baraza**, where DJs have been spinning Latin, lounge and soul since early '98. Head out back to the garden and sample Baraza's featured cocktails—guava margaritas, Cuban mojitos and Brazilian caipirinhas—enough of which should give you ample time to check out the bathroom, which is covered entirely in pennies.

A little farther up the street, **C-Note** owners Jules Bailis and George Ganzle have brought a taste of old Greenwich Village to the East Side. Kick back under the soft lighting and groove to live jazz, a little Latin and the occasional poetry reading.

Trendsetters beware, though: Styles tend to change overnight around here. Enjoy funky Avenue C while you can. See you next year on Avenue D.

9C
700 E 9th St at Ave C (358-0048). Subway: L to First Ave. Mon–Thu 8pm–4am, Sun 3pm–4am.

Baraza
133 Ave C between 8th and 9th Sts (529-0811). Subway: L to First Ave. Sun–Thu 8pm–4am; Fri, Sat 6pm–4am.

C-Note
157 Ave C at 10th St (677-8142). Subway: L to First Ave. 8pm–4am.

dering about the inordinate number of fat men on Harleys on East 3rd Street between First and Second Avenues, it's because the New York chapter of Hell's Angels is headquartered here.

Toward the East River are Avenues A to D, an area sometimes known as **Alphabet City**, for obvious reasons. Its largely Hispanic population is slowly being overtaken by the influx of young

*Washington monument: A miniature Arc de Triomphe welcomes you to **Washington Square**.*

counterculture arrivals. The neighborhood has a long history with heroin; consequently, venturing much farther east than Avenue B can be dangerous at night. Alphabet City is not without its attractions, though: The **Nuyorican Poets Cafe** (*see chapter* **Books & Poetry**), a focus for the recent resurgence of espresso-drinking beatniks, is famous for its "slams," in which performance poets do battle before a score-keeping audience. **Tompkins Square Park** (7th to 10th Sts between Aves A and B), has been the focus for political dissent and rioting. The latest uprising was in 1991, after the controversial decision to evict the park's squatters and renovate it to suit the taste of the area's increasingly affluent residents.

North of Tompkins Square, around First Avenue and 11th Street, are remnants of earlier communities: good Italian cheese shops, Polish restaurants, discount fabric shops, empty theaters and two great Italian patisseries. Visit **De Roberti's** (176 First Avenue) for delicious cakes and **Veniero's** (342 East 11th Street) for wonderful mini-pastries and butter biscuits.

St. Mark's Church in-the Bowery

131 E 10th St at Second Ave (674-6377). Subway: 6 to Astor Pl. Mon–Fri 10am–6pm. St. Mark's was built in 1799 on the site of Peter Stuyvesant's farm. Stuyvesant, one of New York's first governors, is buried here, along with most of his descendants. The church is now home to several arts groups (it was the church in *The Group* where the wedding and funeral took place). Call for details of the performances here.

Midtown

Commuters and tourists crowd the gridlocked streets by day and come out to see the bright lights of Broadway at night

Midtown, 14th to 59th Streets, is the city's engine room, powered by the hundreds of thousands of commuters who pour in each day. By day, the area is all business: Garment manufacturers have long called the area on and around Seventh ("Fashion") Avenue home, while the rest is occupied by towering offices, many headquarters to huge interna-tional companies. It's also where you'll find most of the city's large hotels (and the hordes of tourists who occupy them), as well as the department stores and classy retailers of Fifth Avenue and Rockefeller Center. By night, life centers around the neon glitz of the newly rehabilitated Times Square. Locals and tourists converge here to see

*Rock solid: The Deco masterpiece **GE Building** is the heart and soul of **Rockefeller Center**.*

Broadway shows and movies, to eat in the numerous restaurants or to do some late-night shopping for home electronics.

Flatiron district

As Broadway cuts diagonally through the length of Manhattan, it inspires a public square wherever it intersects with an avenue. Two such places, Union Square at 14th Street, and Madison Square at 23rd, once marked the limits of a ritzy 19th-century shopping district known as **Ladies' Mile**. Extending along Broadway and west to Fifth Avenue, this collection of huge retail palaces attracted the "carriage trade" of wealthy ladies buying the latest fashions and household goods from all over the world. The ground levels of most of these buildings have changed completely, making way for today's shops and restaurants, but the rest of their proud cast-iron facades are intact. The Fifth Avenue section has been rejuvenated over the past decade, and is where designers like Matsuda, Paul Smith and Armani showcase their wares.

The **Flatiron Building**—originally named the Fuller Building after its first owners—is famous for its triangular shape and as the world's first steel-framed skyscraper (*see chapter* **Architecture**). It stands just south of Madison Square and gives its name to the surrounding streets, an area also known as the photo district for its preponderance of studios, photo labs and wandering models.

Madison Square itself is rich in history. It was the site of P.T. Barnum's Hippodrome and the original Madison Square Garden, the scene of prize fights, society duels and lavish entertainment. Today, these are gone, leaving a scruffy park surrounded by imposing buildings such as the **Metropolitan Life Insurance Company**, the **New York Life Insurance Company** and the **Appellate Court**.

Union Square is named not after the Union of the Civil War but simply for the union of Broadway and Bowery Lane (now Fourth Avenue). From the 1920s until the early 1960s, it had a reputation as a political hot spot, a favorite location for rabble-rousing oratory. These days, the gentrified square is home to a farmers' market on Wednesdays and Saturdays. It's also a popular meeting place: In the summer months, a large outdoor cafe (complete with open-air pool table) beckons alfresco diners while packs of skateboarders practice their wild-style stunts on the steps and railings of the square's southern edge. Across the street and extending west is the bargain bonanza of 14th Street's downmarket retail center, offering cheap clothes and electronics (*see chapter* **Shopping & Services**).

Union Square

Junction of Broadway, Park Ave South and Fourth Ave between 14th and 17th Sts. Subway: L, N, R, 4, 5, 6 to 14th St–Union Sq.

Gramercy Park

Gramercy Park, at the bottom of Lexington between Park and Third Avenues, must be entered with a key, something possessed only by those who live in the beautiful townhouses that surround it—or who stay at the **Gramercy Park Hotel** (*see chapter* **Accommodations**). Anyone, however, can enjoy the tranquillity of the neighboring district, squeezed between Third and Park Avenues. It was developed in the 1830s, copying the concept of a London square. **The Players**, at 16 Gramercy Park, was home to actor Edwin Booth, brother of Lincoln's assassin, John Wilkes Booth, and the foremost actor of his day. Booth had it remodeled as a club for theater professionals (it also claimed Winston Churchill and Mark Twain as members). Next door at 15 is the **National Arts Club**, whose members have often donated impressive works in lieu of their annual dues. Its bar houses perhaps the only original Tiffany stained-glass ceiling left in New York City.

Irving Place, leading south from the park to 14th Street, is named after Washington Irving, who didn't actually live here (his nephew did). It does have a literary past, though: **Pete's Tavern**, which insists that it (not McSorley's) is the oldest bar in town (*see chapter* **Cafés & Bars**), was where the New York wit O. Henry wrote *The Gift of the Magi*.

West of Gramercy Park is **Theodore Roosevelt's Birthplace**, now a small museum. To the east is the **Police Academy Museum**, where you can see hundreds of guns, including Al Capone's, and exhibitions describing famous cases and gruesome murders. The low, fortresslike **69th Regiment Armory** (Lexington Avenue at 25th Street), now used by the New York National Guard, was the site of the sensational Armory Show, held in 1913. This introduced modern art—in the form of Cubism, Fauvism, the precocious Marcel Duchamp and other outrages—to Americans.

Fashion runway: The **garment district** gives Seventh Avenue its other name.

National Arts Club

15 Gramercy Park South between Park Ave South and Irving Place (475-3424). Subway: 6 to 23rd St. Open for exhibitions only.

Police Academy Museum

235 E 20th St between Second and Third Aves (477-9753). Subway: 6 to 23rd St. Mon–Fri 9am–2pm. Free.

Theodore Roosevelt Birthplace

28 E 20th St between Broadway and Park Ave South (260-1616). Subway: 6 to 23rd St. Wed–Sun 9am–5pm. $2, children free. Concessions. No credit cards. The popular president's birthplace was demolished in 1916 but has since been fully reconstructed, complete with period furniture and a trophy room.

Chelsea

Chelsea is the region between 14th and 30th Streets west of Sixth Avenue. It is populated mostly by young professionals and has become a hub of New York gay life (*see chapter* **Gay & Lesbian New York**). You'll find all the trappings of an urban residential neighborhood on the upswing: (mostly) dull stores and a generous number of bars and fine restaurants. Its western warehouse district, currently housing some large dance clubs, is being developed for residential use. Pioneering galleries, like the **Dia Center for the Arts** at the west end of 22nd Street, have dragged the art crowd westward, and the whole area has become a thriving gallery district (with lower rents than Soho) (*see* **West Chelsea** *in chapter* **Art Galleries**).

Cushman Row (406–418 W 20th St) in the **Chelsea Historic District** is a good example of how Chelsea looked when it was developed in the mid-1800s—a grandeur that was destroyed 30 years later when the noisy elevated railways came to steal the sunlight and dominate the area. Just north is the **General Theological Seminary**; its garden is a sublime retreat. Over on Tenth Avenue, the flashing lights of the **Empire Diner** (a 1929 Art Deco beauty in chrome) attract pre- and post-clubbers (*see chapter* **Restaurants**).

Sixth Avenue around 27th Street can seem like a tropical forest at times, as the pavements overflow with the palm leaves, decorative grasses and colorful blooms of Chelsea's **flower district**. The garment industry has a presence here as well, as it spills down from its Seventh Avenue center farther north.

Around the corner on 23rd Street is the **Chelsea Hotel**, where many famous people checked in, and some checked out permanently—like Sid Vicious's girlfriend Nancy Spungen. It's worth a peek for its weird artwork and ghoulish guests (*see chapter* **Accommodations**). On Eighth Avenue, you'll find the **Joyce**, a stunning renovated Art Moderne cinema that's a mecca for dance lovers, and on 19th Street, the wonderful **Bessie Schönberg Theater**, where poets recite and mimes...well, do whatever mimes do. Farther out towards the river

*Eclectic Avenue: **Restaurant Row**, on West 46th Street, offers diverse cuisine to the theater crowd.*

on 19th Street is the **Kitchen**, the experimental arts center with a particular penchant for video (*see chapters* **Dance**, **Film** and **Theater**).

When you reach the Hudson River, you'll see the piers, derelict fingers raking out into the water. These were originally the terminals for the world's grand ocean liners (the *Titanic* was scheduled to dock here). Most are in a state of disrepair, though development has transformed the four between 17th and 23rd Streets into a dramatic sports center and TV studio complex, called **Chelsea Piers** (*see* **Fit to be tried** *in chapter* **Sports & Fitness**).

Chelsea Historic District

Between Ninth and Tenth Aves and 20th to 22nd Sts. Subway: A, C, E to 14th St; L to Eighth Ave.

General Theological Seminary

175 Ninth Ave between 20th and 21st Sts (243-5150). Subway: A, C, E, to 14th St; L to Eighth Ave. Mon–Fri noon–3pm, Sat 11am–3pm. Free. You can walk through the grounds of the seminary (when open) or take a guided tour in summer (call for details).

Herald Square and the garment district

Seventh Avenue around 34th Street has a second name: Fashion Avenue. Streets here are gridlocked permanently by delivery trucks. The surrounding area is the **garment district**, where midtown office blocks mingle with the buzzing activity of a huge manufacturing industry. Shabby clothing and fabric stores line the streets (especially 38th and 39th), and there are intriguing shops selling only lace, or buttons, or Lycra swimsuits. Most are wholesale only, but some sell to the public.

Macy's will most definitely sell things to you, though you can usually find the same items cheaper elsewhere. Macy's still impresses as the biggest department store in the world, however. **Manhattan Mall** across the street is a phenomenally ugly building, a kind of neon-and-chrome Jell-O mold. This is American mall shopping at its best, though, and most of the big chain stores have outlets here. This retail wonderland is located in Herald Square, named after a long-gone newspaper. The lower part is known as **Greeley Square** after the owner of the *Herald's* rival, the *Tribune*, a paper in which Karl Marx wrote a regular column. *Life* magazine was based around the corner on 31st Street, and its cherubic mascot can still be seen over the entrance of what is now the **Herald Square Hotel**.

The giant doughnut of a building one block west is the famous sports and entertainment arena, **Madison Square Garden** (*see chapter* **Sports & Fitness**). It occupies the site of the old **Pennsylvania Station**, McKim, Mead & White's architectural masterpiece that was destroyed by insane 1960s planners, an act that brought about creation of the Landmarks Preservation Commission. The

*Slice of NYC life: The **Flatiron Building** is the world's first steel-framed skyscraper.*

railroad terminal is now underground, its name shortened to Penn Station, as if in shame. Thankfully, the **General Post Office**, designed by the same prolific firm, still stands, an enormous colonnade occupying two city blocks along Eighth Avenue (*see chapter* **Architecture**).

Herald Square

Junction of Broadway and Sixth Ave at 34th St. Subway: B, D, F, Q, N, R to 34th St.

Broadway and Times Square

The night is illuminated not by the moon and stars but by acres of glaring neon. An enormous television broadcasting high above makes the place feel like some giant's brashly lit living room. Waves of people flood the streets as the blockbuster theaters disgorge their audiences. This bustling core of entertainment and tourism is often called "the crossroads of the world," and there are few places that represent the collected power and noisy optimism of New York quite as well as **Times Square**.

It's really just an elongated intersection, but Broadway is here—both the road and the idea—because this is the **theater district**. It's home to 30 or so grand stages used for dramatic productions, plus probably 30 more that are movie theaters, nightclubs or just empty—the latter due to the much ballyhooed clean-up of Times Square's once-famous sex trade. A major state development plan to attract hotels and family entertainment has virtually (some say regrettably) wiped out the cinematic lowlife that once dominated **42nd Street** west of Sixth Avenue. The sex industry is still here, but the few remaining video supermarkets and live peep shows now share space with theme restaurants and Hollywood studio stores—Mickey Mouse's squeaky-clean influence has gone a long way towards sanitizing the place. (*See* **A walk on the mild side**, *this page*).

The streets west of Seventh Avenue are home to dozens of eating establishments catering primarily to theatergoers. West 46th Street between Eighth and Ninth Avenues—**Restaurant Row**—has an almost unbroken string of them.

As you'd expect, the offices here are full of entertainment companies: recording studios, theatrical management, record labels, screening rooms and so on. The **Brill Building**, 1619 Broadway, at 49th Street, has the richest history, having long been the headquarters of music publishers and arrangers. It's known as **Tin Pan Alley** (though the original Tin Pan Alley was West 28th Street) and produced such luminaries as Cole Porter, George Gershwin, Rodgers and Hart, Lieber and Stoller, and Phil Spector.

Close by is the **Hearst Magazine Building** at 959 Eighth Avenue, headquarters of the publishing empire founded by William Randolph Hearst, on whom Orson Welles's *Citizen Kane* is based.

The great landmark on Broadway just south of Central Park is **Carnegie Hall** (*see chapter* **Music**). Nearby is the ever-popular **Carnegie Deli**, one of the city's most famous sandwich stops (*see chapter* **Restaurants**).

A walk on the mild side

For better or worse, Times Square just isn't as gamey as it used to be

Times Square—the emblematic "Crossroads of the World"—remains a center of tourism, full of theaters, restaurants, souvenir shops and dazzling billboards. Acres of neon still blaze nightly, and huge crowds still gather for the annual New Year's Eve ball drop (*see chapter* **New York by Season**). But a certain edginess is gone from the neighborhood. Internationally known as a locus of sleaze, Times Square is well on its way to being fully "sanitized for your protection": Peep shows, three-card monte dealers and other "undesirables" have been banished from "the Deuce," as 42nd Street between Seventh and Eighth Avenues is known.

The current transformation has been in the works since 1984 but only got under way when the State of New York condemned most 42nd Street property in 1990. Local businesses have joined with City Hall to provide new lighting and security guards in the district and to relocate the homeless. The private street-cleaning crew boasts of its 100-pound daily haul of cigarette butts. Most significantly, new zoning laws have been enacted to regulate "adult entertainment," specifically to drive the flesh peddlers from the area. While the legality of such measures is being argued in the courts, several sex-related enterprises have seen the writing on the (bathroom) wall and have moved to the outer boroughs.

While the center of vaudeville and legitimate theater at the turn of the century, Times Square has actually been cleaned up once before—when Mayor Fiorello La Guardia shut down the burlesque theaters in the '40s. Later, with the postwar flight of the middle class to the suburbs, Times Square emerged as the city's sexual supermarket. By the 1970s, it had become a tawdry bazaar enshrined in popular myth by movies like *Midnight Cowboy* and *Taxi Driver*. Its massage parlors, hardcore porn and streetwalkers of every sort both rankled and titillated the puritanical—and made it an irresistible target for civic-improvement types.

The Walt Disney Company has emerged as a major player on the new 42nd Street. With a massive merchandising outlet already dispensing trinkets at the end of the street, Mickey & Co. have completed the renovation of the historic New Amsterdam Theater (once home of the *Ziegfeld Follies*), where kids young and old can now take in the smash Broadway hit *The Lion King*. Other large corporations have joined Disney, some erecting brand-new skyscrapers just off the thoroughfare. Reuters news agency, ESPN Sports and the chi-chi publisher Condé Nast plan to occupy the once-seamy sector by the turn of the millennium.

Times Square will play host to one of the world's largest New Year's 2000 parties—but most of the performers will probably keep their clothes on.

*Study hall: You don't need to be a scholar to book the **Public Library**'s main reading room.*

Moving west from Times Square, past the curious steel spiral of the Port Authority Bus Terminal on Eighth Avenue, and the knotted entrance to the Lincoln Tunnel, is an area known as **Hell's Kitchen**. Formerly an impoverished Irish neighborhood, it has now been given the more real-estate–friendly name of Clinton and attracts the forces of gentrification. There's also a little Cuban district around Tenth Avenue in the mid-40s.

The main attraction here is the **Jacob K. Javits Convention Center** on Eleventh Avenue between 34th and 39th Streets; this enormous structure hosts conventions and trade shows. Finally, you reach the Hudson River piers. The **Circle Line** terminal is on Pier 83, at 42nd Street, and at the end of 46th Street you'll find the aircraft carrier *Intrepid* and the **Sea, Air and Space Museum** it contains (*see chapter* **Museums**).

Fifth Avenue

This majestic thoroughfare is New York's main street, the route of the city's many parades and marches. It slopes gently through a region of chic department stores and past some of the city's most famous buildings and public spaces.

The **Empire State Building** (*see chapters* **Sightseeing** *and* **Architecture**) is at 34th Street. Though it's visible across much of the city, only at

this corner can you marvel at its height from top to bottom. At 39th Street, **Lord & Taylor** is one of the Avenue's few remaining grand department stores. A block north, impassive stone lions guard the steps of the **New York Public Library**. This beautiful Beaux Arts building provides an astonishing escape from the noise and traffic outside. Behind the library is **Bryant Park**, an elegant lawn filled with lunching office workers and home to a dizzying schedule of free entertainment.

On the first block of West 44th Street is the famous **Algonquin Hotel**, where scathing wit Dorothy Parker held court at Alexander Woollcott's Round Table (*see chapter* **Accommodations**). The city's diamond trade is conducted along the 47th Street strip known as **Diamond Row**. In front of glittering window displays you'll see Orthodox Jewish traders, precious gems in their pockets, doing business in the street. Near here (231 East 47th Street, but since demolished) was where **Andy Warhol's Factory** enjoyed most of its 15 minutes of fame.

Walk off Fifth Avenue into **Rockefeller Center** (48th–51st Streets) and you will understand why this masterful use of public space is so lavishly praised. As you are drawn down the Channel Gardens, the stately Art Deco **GE Building** gradually rises over you. At its apex is the famous Rainbow Room restaurant and bar; gathered around it are the lower blocks of the **International Building** and its companions. Over on Sixth Avenue is **Radio City Music Hall**—the world's largest cinema when it was built—and the stark towers of Rockefeller Center's secondary phase.

Across Fifth Avenue from Rockefeller's sweeping lines is **St. Patrick's Cathedral**, a beautiful Gothic Revival structure and the largest Catholic cathedral in the U.S.

In the 1920s, 52nd Street was "Swing Street," a row of speakeasies and jazz clubs. All that remains is the "21" Club (at No. 21), now a power-lunching spot. This street also contains the **Museum of Television & Radio**. The **Museum of Modern Art** is on 53rd Street, as is the **American Craft Museum** (*see chapter* **Museums**).

The blocks of Fifth Avenue between Rockefeller Center and Central Park contain expensive retail palaces selling everything from Rolex watches to gourmet chocolate. Here, in the stretch between **Saks Fifth Avenue** (50th St) and **Bergdorf Goodman** (58th St), the rents are the highest in the world, and you'll find such names as Cartier, Chanel, Gucci and Tiffany. Recently, however, some upstart neighbors have joined them, including the big movie studio merchandising outlets of Warner Bros. and Disney. The pinnacle of this malling trend is **Trump Tower**, Donald's ostentatious, soaring chrome spire with its pink marble interior.

Fifth Avenue is crowned by **Grand Army Plaza**, at 59th Street. A statue of General Sherman presides over a public space with the elegant chateau of the **Plaza Hotel** to the west and the **General Motors Building**—with the famous FAO Schwarz toy store at ground level—to the east.

Grand Army Plaza
Fifth Ave at 59th Street. Subway: N, R to Fifth Ave.

Midtown East

Sometimes on New Year's Eve you can waltz in the great hall of **Grand Central Terminal**, just as the enchanted commuters did in *The Fisher King*. This beautiful Beaux Arts station (currently finishing renovation to the tune of $100 million), with the memories of muscular steam trains and lace-curtained carriages locked into its vaulted stone passageways, is surely the city's most spectacular point of arrival (though the constellations of the winter zodiac that adorn the ceiling of the main concourse are backward). The station stands at the junction of 42nd Street and Park Avenue, the latter rising on a cast-iron bridge and literally running around the terminal.

Rising behind it, the **Met Life** (formerly Pan Am) building was once the world's largest office building. Its most celebrated tenants are the peregrine falcons that nest on the roof, living on a diet of pigeons they kill in midair. On the other side of the Met Life tower is the **Helmsley Building**. Built by Warren & Wetmore, the architects responsible for Grand Central, its glittering gold detail presents a fitting punctuation to the vista south down Park Avenue.

Toy stories: FAO Schwarz, inside the **General Motors Building**, is home to serious fun.

Street walkers, beware

NYC pedestrians feel double-crossed by the city's new jaywalking laws

New York may be the best town in the world for visitors to explore by foot. But from now on, you'd better watch your step: New Yorkers' traditionally implied right to jaywalk (or, more accurately, city cops' reluctance to enforce existing jaywalking laws) is being put to the test.

In an effort to ease congestion in midtown's often gridlocked intersections, Mayor Giuliani raised the fine for jaywalking from $2 to $50 in early 1998. He also lobbied the state to make the fine as high as $100. Consequently, outside Rockefeller Center, on Fifth and Sixth Avenues, special crossing areas have been set up mid-block to prevent pedestrians from crossing at the corners. Also, a large swath between Lexington and Sixth Avenues has become a test area for pedestrian barricades that force people to cross *at* specific crosswalks.

While the barricades are being fought in the courts, many police officers are balking at issuing tickets for an act they're used to doing themselves. But jaywalking is no longer something New Yorkers can take for granted. As you make your own patrol of the streets, look both ways before doing anything rash.

*Sign of the times: Under new laws,
"don't walk" no longer means "run."*

On Park Avenue itself, amid the solid blocks of mansion-size apartments, is the **Waldorf-Astoria Hotel**, the sensation-causing glass **Lever House**, and the bronze and glass **Seagram Building**. On Madison is the **IBM Building** (at 56th St), which boasts one of the finest atrium lobbies. Across the street is the **Sony Building**, with its distinctive Chippendale crown. Inside are Sony's Public Arcade and Wonder Technology Lab, offering hands-on displays of innovative technology.

East 42nd Street also offers much of architectural distinction: Visit the spectacular hall of the **Bowery Savings Bank** (at No. 110); the Art Deco detail of the **Chanin Building** (No. 122); the sparkling chrome **Chrysler Building** (at Lexington Avenue); and the **News Building** (No. 220), which was immortalized in the *Superman* films and which still houses a giant globe in its lobby. (*See also chapter* **Architecture**.)

The street ends with **Tudor City**, a pioneering 1925 residential development that's a high-rise version of Hampton Court in London. North of here is an area called **Turtle Bay**, though you won't see too many turtles in the East River today. This is dominated by the **United Nations** and its famous glass-walled Secretariat building. Though you don't need your passport, you are leaving U.S. soil when you enter the UN complex—this is an international zone. Optimistic peacemongering sculptures dot the grounds, and the **Peace Gardens** along the East River bloom with delicate roses.

South of 42nd Street is **Murray Hill**. Townhouses of the rich and powerful were once clustered here around Park and Madison Avenues. While it's still a fashionable neighborhood, only a few streets retain the elegance that once made it such a tony address. **Sniffen Court**, at 150–158 East 36th Street, is an unspoiled row of carriage houses, within spitting distance of the Queens-Midtown Tunnel's ceaseless traffic.

The charming, Italianate **Pierpont Morgan Library** is the reason most visitors are drawn to the area. Two elegant buildings, linked by a glass cloister, house the silver and copper collections, manuscripts, books and prints owned by the famous banker, mostly gathered during his travels in Europe (*see chapter* **Museums**).

Grand Central Terminal

42nd St at Park Ave. Subway: S, 4, 5, 6, 7 to 42nd St–Grand Central.

Uptown

Downtown may have the fun and funk, but uptown has the cash and Culture—with a capital C. (And don't forget Central Park.)

At the end of the 1700s there wasn't much except farmland to be found this far north. It wasn't until Central Park was built in the mid-19th century that uptown became desirable, turning country estates into Fifth Avenue mansions and seducing New York society away from the crowded streets downtown. The park's glorious green space, which is bigger than Monaco, will always dominate Manhattan life between 59th and 110th Streets. The neighborhoods on either side are counterpoints: The east is rich and respectable, full of "establishment" fashion boutiques and museums; the west is more intellectual, revolving around the academia of Columbia University to the north and the music and performance of Lincoln Center to the south. For more information on many of the sites mentioned in this section, see chapters **Museums** and **Architecture**.

Upper East Side

The Upper East Side is all about money. The greed and gold of old New York high society reside in the mansions of Fifth and Park Avenues. Elderly ladies and young trust-funders spend their (ample) spare change in Madison Avenue's chi-chi boutiques; rich businessmen take advantage of tax write-offs to fund the area's cultural institutions (which their families probably founded), including the museums and societies of Museum Mile and beyond.

Once Frederick Law Olmstead and Calvert Vaux had wrenched the wondrous Central Park out of swampland (*see* **Green daze** *in chapter* **Sightseeing**), New York society felt ready to move north. In the mid-1800s the super rich had built mansions along Fifth Avenue. By the beginning of this century, the merely rich had warmed to the (at first outrageous) idea of living in apartment buildings, provided they were near the park. Many grand examples of these were built along Park Avenue and the streets joining it to Fifth. Amid the apartments sprang up the results of tycoons' philanthropic gestures—the many art collections, museums and cultural institutes that attract most visitors to the area.

Museum Mile is actually a promotional organization rather than a geographical description, but since most of the museums along Fifth Avenue are members, it is an apt name. The **Metropolitan Museum of Art**, set in Central Park between 80th and 84th Streets, is the grandest of them all. Walking

north from the steps of the Met, you reach the stunning spiral design of Frank Lloyd Wright's **Guggenheim Museum** at 88th Street; the **National Academy of Design** at 89th; the **Cooper-Hewitt Museum**—set in Andrew Carnegie's mansion—at 91st; the **Jewish Museum** at 92nd; and the **International Center of Photography** at 94th.

The brick fortress facade at 94th and Madison is what's left of the old **Squadron A Armory**. Just off Fifth Avenue at 97th Street are the onion domes and rich ornamentation of the **Russian Orthodox Cathedral of St. Nicholas**, and a little farther north are the **Museum of the City of New York** and **El Museo del Barrio**, at 103rd and 104th Streets, respectively.

There's another clump of museums farther south and east of Central Park. The **Frick Collection**, an art-filled mansion, faces the park at 70th Street. A few blocks south is the **Society of Illustrators**. At Madison and 75th Street is the **Whitney Museum of American Art**, home of the often controversial Whitney Biennial.

The wealth concentrated in this area has also been used to found societies promoting interest in the language and culture of foreign lands. Rockefeller's **Asia Society** is on Park Avenue at 70th Street. Nearby are the **China Institute in America** and the **Americas Society**, dedicated to the nations of South and Central America. On Fifth Avenue is the **Ukrainian Institute** (at 79th), the **German Cultural Center** (at 83rd) and the **YIVO Institute for Jewish Research** (at 86th).

Madison Avenue used to symbolize the advertising industry. Now it's also synonymous with ultra-expensive shopping: Don't even think about buying here unless you have serious loot. Established designers—Yves Saint Laurent, Givenchy, Missoni, Geoffrey Beene et al.—all have pricey boutiques here. (If you find the atmosphere of the Avenue too overbearing, you could always head to **Bloomingdale's**, that frantic, glitzy supermarket of high fashion.) Many commercial art galleries abound here too, including the Knoedler Gallery and Hirschl & Adler Modern. Established artists such as Robert Rauschenberg and Frank Stella prefer to show here rather than downtown in Soho's circus.

At 66th Street and Park Avenue is the **Seventh Regiment Armory**, whose interiors were designed and furnished by Louis Comfort Tiffany,

*Treasure chest: The **Metropolitan Museum of Art** crowns Fifth Avenue's Museum Mile.*

assisted by a young Stanford White. It now houses the Winter Antiques show, among other events.

From Lexington to the East River the aura is less grand. The **Abigail Adams Smith Museum** (421 E 61st St near First Ave) is a lovely old coach house dating from 1799 and now operated as a museum by the Colonial Dames of America. It was once part of a farm owned by the daughter and son-in-law of John Adams, the second American president.

Kim Novak, Montgomery Clift, Tallulah Bankhead and Eleanor Roosevelt all lived a little bit farther west, in the tree-lined streets of three- and four-story brownstones known as the **Treadwell Farm Historic District**, at 61st and 62nd Streets between Second and Third Avenues.

The central building of **Rockefeller University**—from 64th to 68th Streets, on a bluff overlooking FDR Drive—is listed as a national historic landmark. The Founders' Hall dates from 1903, the year the university was established as a medical research center. With the guard's permission, you may walk around the campus. Look out for the President's House and the domed Caspary Auditorium. Medical institutions, including the New York Hospital/Cornell Medical Center, into which the city's oldest hospital is incorporated, dominate the next few blocks of York Avenue.

Seventh Regiment Armory
643 Park Ave at 66th St (452-3067). Subway: 6 to 68th St. Open by appointment only.

Society of Illustrators
128 E 63rd St between Park and Lexington Aves (838-2560). Subway: B, Q to 63rd St. Tue 10am–8pm, Wed–Fri 10am–5pm, Sat noon–4pm. Free. Exhibitions featuring illustration are held regularly.

Yorkville

The east and northeast parts of the Upper East Side are residential, mostly yuppie-filled neighborhoods. There are endless restaurants and bars here (including the rip-roaring **Elaine's**, *see chapter* **Restaurants**), as well as gourmet food stores and, on streets like 86th, all the shops you could need.

Most of this area, extending from the 70s to 96th Street east of Lexington Avenue, is known historically as **Yorkville**. This predominantly German stronghold was once a quaint little hamlet on the banks of the river. In the last decades of the 19th century, East 86th Street became the Hauptstrasse, filled with German restaurants, beer gardens and pastry, grocery, butcher and clothing shops. When World War II broke out, tensions naturally developed. Nazis and anti-Nazis clashed in the streets, and a Nazi-American newspaper was published here. The European legacy includes **Schaller & Weber** (Second Ave between 85th and 86th Sts), a grocery that sells 75 different varieties of German sausages and cold cuts.

Although the famous comedy club **Catch a Rising Star**, where Robin Williams started out, has moved to West 28th Street, you can still have a good laugh at the **Comic Strip**—where Eddie Murphy kicked off his career—on Second Avenue near 81st Street (*see chapter* **Cabaret & Comedy**).

On East End Avenue at 86th Street is the **Henderson Place Historic District**, where 24 handsome Queen Anne row houses, commissioned by fur dealer John C. Henderson, still stand, their turrets, double stoops and slate roofs intact. Across the street is **Gracie Mansion**, New York's official mayoral residence and the only remaining Federal-style mansion in Manhattan still used as a home. The house is the focal point of **Carl Schurz Park**, named in honor of a German immigrant, senator and newspaper editor. The park is remarkable for its tranquility and offers spectacular views of the East River. Its long promenade, the John H. Finley Walk, is one of the most beautiful in the city (especially in the early morning or at dusk).

Gracie Mansion
Carl Schurz Park, 88th St at East End Ave (570-4751). Subway: 4, 5, 6 to 86th St. Open by appointment only. This house became the official mayoral residence in 1942. The tour (call for details) takes you through the mayor's living room, a guest suite and smaller bedrooms. One of the best things about it are the views down the river. Washington built a battery during the war on this strategic site.

Roosevelt Island

Roosevelt Island, the submarine-shaped island in the East River, was once called Welfare Island and housed a lunatic asylum, a smallpox hospital, prisons and workhouses. It now accommodates a largely residential community of 8,000 people and is accessible by road from Queens. The red cable cars ("trams") that cross the East River from Manhattan to Roosevelt Island offer some of the very best vistas of Manhattan (embark at Second Avenue at 60th Street).

The Indians called the land Minnahanonck ("island place"), then sold it to the Dutch, who made a vast creative leap and renamed it Hog's Island. The Dutch farmed it, as did Englishman Robert Blackwell, who moved here in 1686. His old clapboard farmhouse is in **Blackwell Park**, adjacent to Main Street (the one and only commercial street, on which you can find several restaurants).

A new pier faces Manhattan, and numerous picturesque picnic spots are scattered about. The recently opened **Octagon Park** has tennis courts, gardens and an ecological park. The riverfront promenades afford fabulous panoramas of the skyline and the East River, but the tram remains the biggest attraction: You've seen it in a host of films, including, most recently, *City Slickers*. Wander down the **Meditation Steps** for river views, or take one of the riverside walks around the

*Philharmonic convergence: Classical music, opera and ballet meet at **Lincoln Center**.*

island. The latest addition to the island's attractions is the **Sculpture Center**, at Motorgate Plaza, the island's unusual transportation complex. Here, large outdoor work is displayed, many of the pieces inspired by features of the island.

On the southern tip are the weathered neo-Gothic ruins of **Smallpox Hospital** and the burned-out shell of **City Hospital**. The **Octagon Tower** is the remaining core of the former New York City Lunatic Asylum. Charles Dickens once visited and was disturbed by its "lounging, listless, madhouse air." In an early feat of investigative journalism, reporter Nellie Bly feigned insanity and had herself committed to the asylum for 10 days in 1887, and then wrote a shocking exposé of the conditions in the "human rat trap." The decaying buildings tend to crop up in rock videos.

Roosevelt Island Operating Corporation
591 Main St (832-4540). Mon–Fri 9am–5pm. Call for details of events and free maps of the island.

Upper West Side

The Upper West Side is a fairly affluent residential area, rich in bookstores, movie theaters, bars and restaurants, and home to dozens of reclusive celebrities. Its residents have a reputation for being serious, intellectual and politically liberal. European immigrants were attracted here in the late 19th century by the building boom sparked by Central Park, as well as by Columbia University's new site to the north.

A rare rotary (where Broadway meets 59th Street and Central Park West) in a city of right angles, **Columbus Circle**—with its 700-ton statue of Columbus—can be confusing if you're behind the wheel. The curved white marble slab on stilts is New York City's **Department of Cultural Affairs**, home of the **New York Convention & Visitors Bureau**. West of the circle is the **New York Coliseum**. Apart from a few one-shot events, it has been largely out of business since the Javits Convention Center opened in 1986. Donald Trump and other real-estate moguls are in a heated contest to see who can grab the rights to new development in the area. On Broadway at 68th Street, the 12-screen (plus a huge 3-D–capable Imax facility) Sony Lincoln Square cinema is an example of a multiplex done right.

It's not unusual to see folks striding around here in evening dress; that's because they're going to **Lincoln Center**, a complex of concert halls and auditoriums that's the heart of classical music in the city (*see* **Houses of high culture** *in chapter* **Music**). The different buildings are linked by sweeping public plazas and populated by sensitive-looking musical types.

From the Lincoln Center Plaza you can see a small-scale replica of the Statue of Liberty on top of a building on West 64th Street. Across the street, at 2 Lincoln Square, is the small but fascinating **Museum of American Folk Art**.

It took longer for the West Side to become fashionable than it did for Fifth Avenue, but once the park was built, Central Park West soon filled up with luxury apartment buildings. Once well-off New Yorkers had adjusted themselves to living in "French flats," as they called them, apartment living became almost desirable.

The Art Deco building at 55 Central Park West is best remembered for its role in *Ghostbusters*. On 72nd Street is the **Dakota**, most famous these days as the building outside which John Lennon was murdered. It's one of New York's first great apartment buildings and the one that accelerated the drift to the west. Skeptical New Yorkers commented that it was so far away from the center of town that it might as well be in Dakota. Yoko Ono and other famous residents can be seen popping in and out. The massive twin-towered **San Remo** at 74th Street dates from 1930 and is such an exclusive address that even Madonna couldn't get an apartment here.

The **New York Historical Society**, the oldest museum in the city, is at 77th Street. Across the street, the **American Museum of Natural History** attracts visitors with its brand-new permanent rain-forest exhibit, along with such standbys as stuffed and mounted creatures, dinosaur skeletons and ethnological collections, not to mention the associated **Hayden Planetarium**, which is being completely rebuilt.

Columbus and Amsterdam, the avenues between Central Park West and Broadway, experienced a

Go Central Park West, young man: Urban pioneers settled in the stately **Dakota**.

renaissance when Lincoln Center was built. The neighborhood has long been gentrified and is now full of restaurants, shops, gourmet food outlets and fashion stores, though a few of the old inhabitants and shops remain.

On Broadway, the **72nd Street subway** is notable for its Art Nouveau entrance. It's on Sherman Square, named after the general. The opposite triangle, at the intersection of 73rd and Broadway, is **Verdi Square**; a fitting name since—along with Arturo Toscanini and Igor Stravinsky—Enrico Caruso lived in the Ansonia Hotel and kept the other inhabitants entertained/awake with renditions of his favorite arias. The **Ansonia**, a vast Beaux Arts apartment building with exquisite detailing, was also the location for *Single White Female*. Bette Midler got her break at the **Continental Baths**, a gay spa and cabaret that occupied the bottom few floors in the 1970s. This was also where star DJs Frankie Knuckles and Larry Levan first honed their skills.

The **Beacon Theater** on Broadway was once a fabulous movie palace and is now a concert venue. The phenomenal interior is a designated landmark. A few blocks north are the **Children's Museum of Manhattan**, the famous **Zabar's**, supplier of delicious delicacies (*see chapter* **Shopping & Services**), and some of Manhattan's best bookstores.

Just off Broadway, on the north side of 94th Street, is a quaint mews called **Pomander Walk**. Nearby is the **Claremont Riding Academy** (175 W 89th St), where you can rent horses to ride in Central Park. Back on Broadway, **Symphony Space** (*see chapter* **Music**) features repertory film series and eclectic musical programs, including the famous Wall-to-Wall concerts.

Riverside Park lies between Riverside Drive and the banks of the Hudson, from 72nd to 145th Streets. Once as fashionable an address as Fifth Avenue and similarly lined with opulent private houses, Riverside Drive was largely rebuilt in the 1930s with luxury apartment buildings. The park is a welcome stretch of undulating riverbank. You may see luxury yachts berthed at the little **79th Street Boat Basin**, along with a few houseboats. Further north, at 89th Street, the **Soldiers' and Sailors' Monument** is a memorial to the Civil War dead.

New York Historical Society

2 W 77th St at Central Park West (873-3400). Subway: B, C to 81st St. Wed, Thu, Fri noon–5pm and by appointment. $5, $3 concessions. No credit cards. The Society's library has an important architectural collection, including the archives of Cass Gilbert and McKim, Mead & White, plus a magnificent collection of Tiffany lamps.

Soldiers' & Sailors' Monument

Riverside Dr at 89th St. Subway: 1, 9 to 86th St. The 1902 monument was designed by French sculptor Paul DuBoy and architects Charles and Arthur Stoughton.

Northern Manhattan

Way uptown, find the soul of black America and be an eyewitness to the century-long construction of a glorious cathedral

Harlem

Harlem's reputation as a dangerous place is exaggerated. Certainly some parts are quite run-down, and if you're white you should be prepared to stand out in the crowd. But a daytime visit to the main attractions should pose no problems for anyone.

Harlem is probably the most African-American place in America. Its elegant stone buildings reverberate with the history of black America's struggle for equality. Its institutions and streets are christened with the names of great liberators,

teachers and orators, and there are constant reminders of proud Afrocentric culture, from the Francophone Africans selling their trinkets to the Jeeps booming out the latest hip-hop street politics.

Harlem was originally composed of country estates. But when the subways arrived at the turn of the century, the area was developed for middle-class New Yorkers. When the bourgeoisie failed to fill the grandiose townhouses, the speculators reluctantly rented them out to African-Americans. The area's population doubled during the 1920s and '30s, a growth that coincided with the cultural

*Can I get a witness? Worshipers gather in Harlem's famous **Abyssinian Baptist Church**.*

*Stepping stone: **Columbia University** students contemplate life in the real world.*

explosion known as the Harlem Renaissance. The poets, writers, artists and musicians living in this bohemian republic helped usher in the Jazz Age.

Harlem's soundtrack is now provided by the rap and reggae of the younger generation, as well as by the salsa and merengue of the Cubans and Dominicans who have moved in among the older black community. They have added to the Hispanic population of **Spanish Harlem**, or El Barrio ("the neighborhood"), the section east of Fifth Avenue and above 100th Street. Treat your senses to the colorful fruits and vegetables, spices and meats at **La Marqueta** on Park Avenue from 110th to 116th Streets, or smell the flowers in Central Park's **Conservatory Garden** at Fifth Avenue and 105th Street. **El Museo del Barrio**, Spanish Harlem's community museum, is on Fifth Avenue at 104th Street.

The **Graffiti Hall of Fame**, at 106th Street between Park and Madison Avenues, is actually just a schoolyard, but here you'll see the large-scale work of "old-school" graffiti writers—you may even bump into someone completing a piece. There are also several *casitas*, Puerto Rican "little houses" that function as communal hangouts and create a slice of island life amid the high-rises. Two of them can be found on the way from the 103rd Street subway station to El Museo del Barrio: one on a vacant lot at 103rd Street between Park and Lexington Avenues; the other around the corner on Lexington between 103rd and 104th Streets.

At 116th Street and Lenox Avenue is **Masjid Malcolm Shabazz**, the silver-domed mosque of Malcolm X's ministry. Opposite this is the market where the street vendors who once lined 125th Street now hawk T-shirts, tapes and purportedly African souvenirs. Just north is the **Lenox Lounge**, where Malcolm X's early career as a hustler began. Farther up Lenox is **Sylvia's**, the most famous of Harlem's soul-food restaurants, and even farther, at 138th Street, is the **Abyssinian Baptist Church**, containing a small museum dedicated to Adam Clayton Powell Jr., the first black member of New York's City Council and Harlem's Congressman from the 1940s through the 1960s. Just below 125th Street, on Fifth Avenue, lies **Marcus Garvey Park** (previously Mt. Morris Park), Harlem's only patch of green. It's located at the center of a historic district of elegant brownstones, and some of the more beautiful are open to the public several times a year. Call the Mt. Morris Park Community Association (369-4241) for details.

The **Studio Museum in Harlem** (*see chapter* **Museums**) presents exhibitions focusing on the area and its people, while the **Schomburg Center for Research in Black Culture** (*see* **Black pride**, *page 101*) is the largest research collection devoted to African-American culture.

Harlem's main drag is 125th Street, and the **Apollo Theatre** is its focus. For four decades after it began presenting live shows in the 1930s, the Apollo

*Heaven help them: After 106 years, the **Cathedral of St. John the Divine** is still unfinished.*

*When an ordinary headstone won't do: Guess who's buried in **Grant's Tomb**?*

was the world's most celebrated venue for black music. It's had its ups and downs since then, and its current owners have recently had to deal with allegations of financial mismanagement. But the Apollo continues to present live music, mostly hip-hop and R&B, as well as tapings of the television program *Showtime at the Apollo* (*see chapter* **Music**). The Theresa Towers office complex, at 125th Street and Seventh Avenue, was formerly the **Hotel Theresa**. Fidel Castro stayed here during a 1960 visit to the United Nations, and his visitors included Nikita Khrushchev and Gamal Abdel Nasser.

The area between 125th and 155th Streets west of St. Nicholas Avenue is known as **Hamilton Heights**, after Alexander Hamilton, who had a farm here at Hamilton Grange (Convent Avenue at 142nd Street). This is the gentrified part of Harlem, where you'll find City College, the northern outpost of the

City University of New York. It's also the location of **Audubon Terrace**, a double Beaux Arts row containing a group of museums: the **Hispanic Society of America**, the **American Numismatic Society** and the **American Academy of Arts and Letters** (*see chapter* **Museums**).

Harlem Spirituals
690 Eighth Ave between 43rd and 44th Sts (757-0425). Subway: A, C, E to 42nd St. Mon–Sat 9am–6pm. AmEx, MC, V. This organization offers a wide range of tours, including morning gospel tours, lunchtime historical tours and evening soul food and jazz tours. Prices range from $30 to $70.

Morningside Heights

The area sandwiched between Morningside Park and the Hudson River from 110th to 125th Streets is **Morningside Heights**, a region dominated by

Black pride

The rich history of Harlem lives on in the Schomburg Center

Those interested in the social and cultural history of African-Americans in New York should be sure to visit the Schomburg Center for Research in Black Culture. This modern brick structure is located in the heart of Harlem, at the corner of Lenox Avenue and 135th Street, on the site of one of the Speakers' Corners established by Marcus Garvey's Back to Africa movement.

The Center features an extensive research collection, and at least two exhibitions are mounted at all times, reflecting the range and depth of African-American achievement in the arts, literature and politics. Photographs and other archival materials chart the singular achievements of actors from Paul Robeson to Denzel Washington. Audio and visual recordings commemorate the outstanding talents of black musicians and singers from Bessie Smith to Tina Turner. Recorded speeches and publications explore the political messages and social impact of leaders like Marcus Garvey, the Black Panthers and Jesse Jackson.

Houston Cornwill's *Rivers*, an elaborate artwork of multicolored terrazzo with brass inlay, is on permanent display. The piece occupies the entire floor of the entrance to the Langston Hughes Auditorium. Based on Hughes's poem "The Negro Speaks of Rivers," the work traces the flow of the world's great rivers as if they were part of an astrological chart, with one ocean in the middle. The poet's words appear in brass.

The research collections are open to the public as part of the New York Public Library system. Beginning in the fall of 1998, the center is offering a series of exhibitions as part of the city's centennial celebration. The first one focuses on 100 black New Yorkers whose contributions in all fields have enriched the life of the city.

*Eyes on the prize: The **Schomburg Center** celebrates African-American achievement.*

*God's green earth: **Morningside Park** grows below the Cathedral of St. John the Divine.*

Columbia University. One of the oldest universities in the U.S., Columbia was chartered in 1754 as King's College (the name changed after U.S. independence). Thanks to its large student presence and that of its women's division, **Barnard College**, the surrounding area has an academic feel, with bookshops and cafés along Broadway and quiet, leafy streets toward the west overlooking Riverside Park.

The neighborhood has two immense houses of worship, the **Cathedral of St. John the Divine** and the **Riverside Church**, built with Rockefeller money and containing the world's largest carillon. You can ride to the top of the 21-story steel-framed tower for views across the Hudson and also of **Grant's Tomb** in Riverside Park (at 122nd Street), honoring the victorious Civil War General and U.S. President Ulysses S. Grant.

The hammering and chiseling at the Cathedral of St. John the Divine will continue well into the next century. Construction began in 1892 in Romanesque style, was stopped for a Gothic Revival redesign in 1911 and didn't begin again until 1941; after another pause for fund-raising purposes, the work resumed in earnest this last decade. When the towers and great crossing are completed, this will be one of the world's largest cathedrals. In addition to Sunday services, the cathedral also hosts concerts, tours and, on occasion, funerals of the rich and famous.

Cathedral of St. John the Divine

Amsterdam Ave at 112th St (662-2133). Subway: 1, 9 to 110th St. 7am–5pm.

Columbia University

Between Broadway and Amsterdam Ave and 114th to 120th Sts (854-1754). Enter Barnard College at Broadway, just north of 116th St (854-5262). Subway: 1, 9 to 116th St.

General Grant National Memorial

Riverside Dr at 122nd St (666-1640). Subway: 1, 9 to 125th St. 9am–5pm. Free. The classical temple that is more commonly known as Grant's Tomb dominates the upper reaches of Riverside Park. The architect of the Union victory, Ulysses S. Grant was elected president in 1868 and has remained a national hero despite what historians agree was an extremely unimpressive presidency. He is buried here with his wife, Julia, in twin black marble sarcophagi underneath a small white dome. The surrounding mosaic benches were designed in the 1960s by young community residents.

Riverside Church

Riverside Dr at 122nd St (870-6700). Subway: 1, 9 to 116th St. 9am–4pm.

Washington Heights

The area from 155th Street to the northern tip of Manhattan is called Washington Heights. Here the island shrinks in width, and the parks on either side culminate in the wilderness and forest of **Inwood Hill Park**, where in 1626 the Dutchman Peter Minuit "bought" Manhattan from the Indians for a handful of beads.

High Bridge (Amsterdam Ave at 177th St) gives an idea of how old New York got its water supply. This aqueduct carried water across the Harlem River from the Croton Reservoir in Westchester County to Manhattan. The central piers were replaced in the 1920s to allow large ships to pass underneath.

The main building of **Yeshiva University** (186th St at Amsterdam Ave) is one of the strangest in New York, a Byzantine orange-brick structure decorated with turrets and minarets.

Equally unlikely is **the Cloisters**, at the northern edge of flower-filled Fort Tryon Park. A reconstructed medieval monastery incorporating several original medieval cloisters shipped over from Europe, it might have been custom-designed for romantic picnics. The project, financed by the Rockefeller family, is in fact the Metropolitan Museum's medieval outpost, and contains illuminated manuscripts and priceless tapestries (*see chapter* **Museums**).

The neighborhood also has two significant historic sites. **Dyckman House**, a Dutch farmhouse built in 1748, is the oldest surviving home in Manhattan and something of a lonely sight on busy Broadway (at 204th St); inside it is filled with the Dyckman family's furniture.

Morris-Jumel Mansion (Edgecombe Ave at 160th St) was where George Washington planned for the battle of Harlem Heights in 1776 after the British colonel Roger Morris moved out (*see chapter* **Architecture**). The handsome 18th-century Palladian villa also has some fantastic views.

The Outer Boroughs

There's more to the metropolis than Manhattan. Anyone searching for the complete New York experience should beat it to the boroughs.

If you're surprised at how compact New York is, that's probably because you haven't left Manhattan yet. The city actually comprises five boroughs, each with its own character and its share of world-class museums, parks, restaurants and other attractions. Manhattan is the center of it all, but if you want to see where—and how—the majority of New Yorkers live, find time to visit Brooklyn, Queens, the Bronx and Staten Island.

Brooklyn

The most populous of the five boroughs, Brooklyn is far more than just an adjunct to Manhattan—as any Brooklynite will be glad to tell you. The grand spaces of its Civic Center, the scale of its public buildings and the beauty of its private houses all hint at a proud and independent history. In the language of hip-hop, it is a whole world— "the Planet"—and has been part of New York City for only a century.

In the middle of the 19th century, Brooklyn was a rich and powerful city, the third largest in the United States (today it would still be the fourth biggest). In 1861 Walt Whitman declared that its destiny was "to be among the most famed and choice of the half dozen cities of the world." Joining it to Manhattan required the construction of a bridge of unimaginable length.

Even more than Manhattan, Brooklyn is a collection of distinct ethnic neighborhoods. There is Jamaican Flatbush, African-American Bedford-Stuyvesant, Jewish Crown Heights, Polish Greenpoint, Italian Bensonhurst and the tripartite

*Not in Kansas anymore: Make tracks to **Coney Island** to ride the Cyclone roller coaster.*

House proud: a Brooklyn brownstone.

population of Williamsburg, with its Poles, Hispanics and Hasidim living alongside art-rebel loft-loungers (*see* **Boho on the waterfront**, *page 106*). This patchwork of communities has long made for a vivid cultural life. More famous Americans come from Brooklyn than anywhere else (or perhaps just those who make the most noise about it).

The **Civic Center**, a reminder of Brooklyn's earlier status, is dominated by the old City Hall, built in 1851 and now called Borough Hall (209 Joralemon St at Fulton St), and the massive General Post Office (271–301 Fulton St).

From here it's a short walk to **Brooklyn Heights**, with its well-preserved streets of Federal-style and Greek Revival brownstones. Middagh, Cranberry, Willow, Orange, Pineapple and Montague are some of the prettiest streets. Pierrepont Street, which is home to the **Brooklyn Historical Society** museum and library (*see chapter* **Museums**), takes you to the Promenade overlooking the river. This walkway, situated below glorious mansions, offers breathtaking views of the Brooklyn Bridge and Manhattan. Also in the Heights are the imposing **Plymouth Church of the Pilgrims**, on Orange Street, founded by the famous abolitionist Henry Ward Beecher.

Stroll through Cadman Plaza Park and you will reach the **Brooklyn Bridge** (*see chapter* **Sightseeing**). When the bridge was completed in 1883, it astounded residents on both sides of the East River and supplanted most of the 17 ferry companies that traversed it. It also led to Brooklyn's transformation from a separate city to a part of New York City. The bridge's anchorage space now houses the occasional rave (*see* **Fresh air guitars** *in chapter* **Music**).

The **Brooklyn Museum of Art** was originally planned to be the largest museum in the world. Though only a fifth of the projected construction was completed, it is still enormous and imposing, housing one and a half million artifacts, including one of the best Egyptian collections anywhere. Another museum worth visiting is the **New York Transit Museum**, which tells the intriguing story of New York's subways (*see chapter* **Museums** *for both*). Also nearby is the **Brooklyn Children's Museum** (*see chapter* **Children**).

The grand old opera house that is the **Brooklyn Academy of Music** (locals call it "BAM"), which puts on a fine range of musical and theatrical productions, is a further symbol of Brooklyn's independence (*see chapters* **Music** and **Theater**).

Nearby **Fort Greene** is Brooklyn's bohemian center, with an increasingly multiethnic population of successful creative types: Spike Lee, Chris Rock, Rosie Perez and Branford Marsalis have all called this neighborhood home.

At the **Concord Baptist Church of Christ** you can experience some old-time religion alongside the largest black congregation in the U.S. The fabulous gospel music here will convince you that the devil doesn't have dibs on all the best tunes.

Like Manhattan, Brooklyn has a heart of green. Built by the same architects who designed Central Park, **Prospect Park** is smaller but much calmer and more rural. On weekends, it fills with families enjoying barbecues and picnics, as well as with active types who play on its sports fields and skate, jog or bike around its closed-to-traffic road. The largely Caribbean community of Flatbush gathers on the eastern side—listen for the booming reggae and huge drumming circles. The park's many attractions include a children's zoo, opened in 1993; the restored Dutch Colonial–style **Lefferts Homestead,** one of the city's first buildings, which now houses a children's museum and a visitors' center; and a bandshell with a busy summer program of jazz, hip-hop, soul, gospel, classical and opera concerts (*see* **Fresh air guitars** *in chapter* **Music**).

At the park's main entrance is **Grand Army Plaza**, with the **Brooklyn Public Library** to the left and the **Soldiers' and Sailors' Memorial Arch** in the center. Designed, like the park itself, by Olmsted and Vaux, it commemorates the Brooklyn residents who were killed in the Civil War. The plaza is also the site of New York's only monument to John F. Kennedy.

Adjacent to the park and behind the museum is the peaceful **Brooklyn Botanic Garden**, famous for its Japanese cherry trees and the biggest bonsai collection in the U.S. Visit on the weekend and you're sure to see Catholic girls being photographed in their communion dresses, as well as the occasional freshly wedded couple enjoying their reception among the blossoms.

Park Slope, the area west of the park, is another enclave of elegant architecture—in this case, untouched 19th-century brownstone townhouses. This was the scene of Washington's 1776 retreat during the Revolutionary War.

Farther afield is the rusted wonder of **Coney Island** (*see chapter* **Sightseeing**). Given the crowds it attracts, the beach is surprisingly clean, and the amusement parks, boardwalk and piers that span its length are great fun. Walk along to the **Aquarium** (*see chapter* **Children**), where the collection of beluga whales, sharks and other sea dwellers has recently been augmented by a huge (60,000sq ft/5,600sq m) re-creation of the Pacific coastline. Neighboring **Brighton Beach** is known as Little Odessa because of its large population of Russian immigrants—you'll feel like you've landed somewhere in Eastern Europe. If you get an irresistible urge for caviar, vodka and smoked sausages, this is the place to come.

Brooklyn Botanic Garden

1000 Washington Ave between Eastern Pkwy and Empire Blvd (1-718-622-4433). Subway: 2, 3 to Eastern Pkwy. Tue–Fri 8am–6pm; Sat, Sun 10am–6pm (with seasonal variations). $3, $1 concessions. Travel from jungle to desert—and points in between—in the extensive conservatories here. There's also a beautiful rose garden, an outdoor café, a perfume garden for the blind and an area set aside for meditation.

Concord Baptist Church of Christ

833 Marcy Ave between Putnam and Madison Aves (1-718-622-1818). Subway: A, C to Nostrand Ave. Call for times of concerts and services.

Prospect Park

Flatbush Ave at Grand Army Plaza (events hotline 1-718-965-8999/Leffert's Homestead 1-718-965-6505/zoo 1-718-399-7333). Subway: 2, 3 to Grand Army Plaza.

Queens

A visit to Queens is like taking a world tour using some kind of twisted road map: Here's Bombay, Athens, Bogota; there's Quito, Seoul, Buenos Aires; down the road is Kilkenny, Manila, Milan. Thanks to the efforts of New York's master builder, Robert Moses, and his taste for superhighways, this borough's postwar development assumed a patchwork quality. Originally a handful of towns, Queens has evolved into an urban suburbia of foreign pockets. It is New York's new Lower East Side, today's destination for thousands of immigrants (a third of Queens residents are foreign-born).

Queens County was named after Queen Catherine, the wife of Charles II. It joined New York as a borough in 1898, the same year as Brooklyn and Staten Island. As means of transportation improved—the Queensboro Bridge (also known as the 59th Street Bridge) was built in 1909, and the first train tunnels were cut under the East River in 1910—Queens began to function as a residential satellite of Manhattan. Phenomenal building in the 1950s and 1960s merged the separate towns into a continuous sprawl, buffered only by parks, highways and enormous cemeteries. Chances are that you started your visit here: The city's two major airports, **LaGuardia** and **Kennedy**, are both in the borough. Should you return here, you'll find many attractions in the neighborhoods of Astoria, Long Island City, Jamaica, Flushing and Forest Hills.

Long Island City, closest to Manhattan, is the home of the recently renovated gallery-cum-museum **P.S. 1** (also known as the Institute for Contemporary Art), housed in an old city school

*Earth day: The **Unisphere** has been a **Flushing Meadows** landmark since the 1964 World's Fair.*

Boho on the waterfront

Brooklyn's artsy side emerges in Williamsburg

Since rents for Manhattan loft spaces are beyond the reach of all but a lucky few, the active machine of artistic creation has packed its paints and clay and moved across the river to the postindustrial neighborhood of Williamsburg in Brooklyn. While the artists' migration began well over a decade ago, only in recent years has gentrification followed: Cool restaurants, hipster cafés and trendy bars mostly clustered around Bedford Avenue's subway stop on the L line—all serve the new bohemian population.

The young artistic colonists are settling amid one of New York's more curious multi-culti amalgams. To the south, Broadway divides a noisy, vibrant Hispanic neighborhood from a quiet, ordered community of Hasidic Jews. Williamsburg's northern half is shared by Polish and Italian blue-collar residents who origi-

nally worked the East River docks. Manufacturing still occurs here, but the old factory buildings are increasingly being converted to artists' lofts and studios.

Not surprisingly, the neighborhood also houses several art galleries, and on some weekends, area artists hold group exhibitions in their studios or organize sprawling, almost carnival-style street fairs. Check the free neighborhood weekly, *Waterfront Week*, for details.

Food

Amarin Café
617 Manhattan Ave between Driggs and Nassau Aves (1-718-349-2788). Subway: G to Nassau Ave. Mon–Thu 11am–10:30pm; Fri, Sat 11am–11pm; Sun 11:30am–10:30pm. Cash only. The sign outside—MODERN THAI CUISINE—explains some of the more incongruous offerings on an otherwise traditional menu.

*Go to L: Williamsburg's young and restless while away the hours at the **L Café**.*

Kasia's

146 Bedford Ave at North 9th St (1-718-387-8780). Subway: L to Bedford Ave. Mon–Fri 6am–9pm. AmEx, MC, V. Greasy Polish diner food, including pierogi and apple sauce, are served amid '50s-era institutional decor.

L Café

189 Bedford Ave at North 7th St (1-718-388-6792). Subway: L to Bedford Ave. Daily 8:30am–midnight; kitchen closes at 11pm. Cash only. Schmooze with local artists and less motivated types in this smoky coffeehouse.

Napoli Bakery

619 Metropolitan Ave between Leonard and Lorimer Sts (1-718-384-6945). Subway: L to Lorimer St. Mon–Sat 7am–7pm. Cash only. This 60-year-old bakery designates its Italian-style breads only by size and shape (small or large rounds or loaves).

Oznot's Dish

79 Berry St at North 9th St (1-718-599-6596). Subway: L to Bedford Ave. Mon–Fri 11am–midnight; Sat, Sun 10am–midnight. Cash only. Eat your way through the Middle East and Mediterranean with dishes from North Africa, Greece, Italy, Turkey and more. Oznot's offers many vegetarian options and plenty of seafood.

Peter Luger

178 Broadway at Driggs Ave (1-718-387-7400). Subway: J, M, Z to Marcy Ave. Mon–Thu 11:45am–9:45pm, Fri–Sat 1–9:45pm, Sun 1–9:45pm. Cash only. Awaken your inner carnivore at this New York institution. Porterhouse is the only cut they serve in this old-school steakhouse. (*See also chapter* **Restaurants**.)

Plan-Eat Thailand

184 Bedford Ave between North 6th and 7th Sts (1-718-599-5758). Subway: L to Bedford Ave. Mon–Sat 11:30am–11:30pm, Sun 1–11pm. Cash only. One of the first neighborhood arrivals, this tiny Thai joint offers large (and tasty) portions for small money.

Seasons

556 Driggs Ave at North 7th St (1-718-384-9695). Subway: L to Bedford Ave. Sun, Tue–Thu 6–10:30pm; Fri, Sat 6pm–11:30pm. AmEx, MC, V. This charming little bistro serves American food influenced by Italian and French peasant fare at way-below-Manhattan prices.

Teddy's

96 Berry St at North 8th St (1-718-384-9787). Subway: L to Bedford Ave. Sun–Thu 11am–midnight; Fri, Sat 11am–2am. MC, V. Relax with a pint and enjoy simple pub fare alongside artists and firemen at this beautifully preserved bar/restaurant.

Vera Cruz

195 Bedford Ave between North 6th and 7th Sts (1-718-599-7914). Subway: L to Bedford Ave. Mon–Thu, Sun 4–11:30pm; Fri, Sat 4pm–midnight. AmEx, MC, V. Frosty margaritas are the perfect accompaniment to fine Mexican food at moderate prices.

Shopping

Beacon's Closet

110 Bedford Ave at North 11th St (1-718-486-0816). Subway: L to Bedford Ave. Mon–Fri noon–9pm; Sat, Sun 11am–8pm. AmEx, Disc, MC, V. Vintage clothes, books and music are the highlights here.

Domsey's Warehouse

431 Kent Ave between South 8th and 9th Sts (1-718-384-6000). Subway: J, M, Z to Marcy Ave. Mon–Fri 8am–5:30pm, Sat 8am–6:30pm, Sun 11am–5:30pm. Cash only. Ground zero of the New York thrift-store experience: The front part of the store sells new clothes, and in back you can buy unsorted clothes by the pound. Fight it out with the old ladies for the best bargains (*see also chapter* **Shopping & Services**).

Earwax Records and CDs

204 Bedford Ave between North 5th and 6th Sts (1-718-218-9608). Subway: L to Bedford Ave. Mon–Sat noon–8pm, Sun noon–6pm. AmEx, MC, V. A good thing about starving artists is that they usually have great used records and CDs to sell; here's where to buy them.

Main Drag Music

207 Bedford Ave between North 5th and 6th Sts (1-718-388-6365). Subway: L to Bedford Ave. Tue–Fri noon–9pm; Sat, Sun noon–6pm. MC, V. A good thing about struggling musicians is they often have vintage and used musical equipment to sell.…

Ugly Luggage

214 Bedford Ave between North 5th and 6th Sts (1-718-384-0724). Subway: L to Bedford Ave. Afternoons. Hours vary, call ahead. AmEx, MC, V. Used clothes, books, furniture and collectibles are available here.

Art

Flipside

84 Withers St between Leonard and Lorimer Sts, third floor (1-718-389-7108). Subway: L to Lorimer St. Sun 1–6pm. Visit this off-the-beaten-path gallery to sample homegrown Williamsburg art created by local, though not necessarily native, artists.

Momenta

72 Berry St between North 9th and 10th Sts (1-718-218-8058). Subway: L to Bedford Ave. Fri–Mon noon–6pm. The most professional and imaginative organization in the area, Momenta presents strong solo and group exhibitions by an exhilarating mix of emerging artists. Catch their work before it's snapped up by Manhattan dealers.

Pierogi 2000

167 North 9th St between Bedford and Driggs Aves (1-718-599-2144). Subway: L to Bedford Ave. Sat–Mon noon–6pm. Monthly openings at this artist-run gallery tend to attract the whole neighborhood—who show up as much for the free drinks and pierogi as for the art. The big draw is the Flatfile, which boasts an impressive collection of prints and photos by local artists that sell for less than $200 (*see also chapter* **Art Galleries**).

Williamsburg Art & Historical Center

135 Broadway at Bedford Ave (1-718-486-7372). Subway: L to Bedford Ave; J, M, Z to Marcy Ave. Sat, Sun noon–6pm; Mon by appointment. At the foot of the Williamsburg Bridge is this art center, built to acknowledge the presence of more than 3,000 artists and performers living in the neighborhood. Housed in a four-story 1867 building, it includes an art gallery and a theater.

(*see chapter* **Art Galleries**). A nonprofit studio space attracting artists from around the world, it has open workshops, multimedia galleries, several large permanent works and controversial, censor-taunting exhibitions. Nearby, in a striking riverside location, the **Socrates Sculpture Garden** contains large-scale sculptures by both well- and lesser-known artists, with occasional concerts and video presentations. Just down the road is the **Noguchi Museum**—Isamu Noguchi's great self-designed sculpture studios, where more than 300 of his works are displayed in 12 galleries (*see chapter* **Museums**).

In the primarily Greek community of **Astoria** is the **American Museum of the Moving Image**. The museum occupies part of the Kaufman Astoria movie studios, opened in 1917, where W.C. Fields, Rudolph Valentino, Gloria Swanson and the Marx Brothers all made films (*see chapter* **Museums**).

Farther east are **Flushing** and **Flushing Meadows–Corona Park**, a huge complex that contains Shea Stadium, home of the New York Mets, and the **National Tennis Center**, where the U.S. Open championships are held every August. The 1939 and 1964 World's Fairs were held in Corona Park (then known as Flushing Meadow Park), leaving some incredible half-derelict structures and the huge stainless steel **Unisphere** globe in their wake. Preservationists are working to make sure that the remaining structures are spared from the wrecker's ball. Outside the curved concrete structure of the **New York Hall of Science**, you can marvel at cast-off pieces of space rockets. Have a look too at the ghostly amphitheater overlooking the boating lake. A leftover 1939 World's Fair pavilion is the home of the **Queens Museum**, where the main attraction is a 1:12,000 scale model of New York City made for the 1964 fair. Today, Corona Park is the scene of weekend picnics and some hotly contested soccer matches between teams of European- and South American–born locals. You can rent bikes in the summer.

You can visit several noteworthy historical buildings in Queens. East of Flushing Meadows is the **Friends' Meeting House**. Built in 1694 by religious protester John Bowne, it is still used as a Quaker meeting place, making it the oldest house of worship in continuous use in the United States. Next door is **Kingsland House**, a mid-18th-century farmhouse that is also the headquarters of the **Queens Historical Society**. You can also visit John Bowne's residence, **Bowne House**, which dates back to 1661 (*see chapter* **Architecture**).

The **Queens County Farm Museum**, in the edge-of-borough Floral Park neigoborhood, has a farm dating back to 1772 containing exhibits on the city's agricultural history. Near Kennedy Airport are the tidal wetlands of the **Jamaica Bay Wildlife Refuge**, home to a large population of birds, plants and animals. Waterfowl flock here during the autumn. Bring your binoculars and spot both birds and planes.

Friends' Meeting House
137-16 Northern Blvd between Main and Union Sts, Flushing (1-718-358-9636). Subway: 7 to Main St–Flushing. By appointment only. Voluntary donation.

Institute for Contemporary Art/P.S. 1
46-01 21st St, Long Island City (1-718-784-2084). Subway: E, F to 23rd St. Wed–Sun noon–6pm. $2 suggested donation.

Jamaica Bay Wildlife Refuge
Cross Bay Blvd at Broad Channel (1-718-318-4340). Subway: A to Broad Channel. 8:30am–5pm. Free. The wildlife refuge is part of a local network of important ecological sites, administered by the National Parks Service. Guided walks, lectures and all sorts of nature-centered activities are offered.

Kingsland House/ Queens Historical Society
Weeping Beech Park, 143-35 37th Ave at Parsons Blvd, Flushing (1-718-939-0647). Subway: 7 to Main St–Flushing. Tue, Sat, Sun 2:30–4:30pm. $2, $1 concessions. No credit cards. Built in 1785 by a wealthy Quaker, the house was moved to a site beside Bowne House. The Queens Historical Society now uses it for exhibitions detailing local history. Staffers can give you more information about the borough's historical sites.

Queens Council on the Arts
79-01 Park Lane South, Woodhaven (1-718-647-3377/info 718-291-ARTS). Mon–Fri 9am–4:30pm. This organization provides exhaustive details of all cultural events in the borough, updated daily.

Queens County Farm Museum
73-50 Little Neck Pkwy, Floral Park (1-718-347-3276). Subway: E, F to Kew Gardens, then Q46 bus to Little Neck Pkwy. 9am–5pm (farmhouse and museum galleries Sat, Sun noon–5pm). Voluntary donation.

Socrates Sculpture Park
Broadway at Vernon Blvd, Long Island City (1-718-956-1819). Subway: N to Broadway. 10am–sunset. Free. The setting, a vacant postindustrial lot by the river, is inspiring. Some of the pieces, like the Sound Observatory, are engagingly interactive.

The Bronx

For years, the plight of this borough's southern section overshadowed the entire area. The mere words "South Bronx" conjured up images of run-down housing projects looming from the charred rubble of what looked like bomb sites—a whole community left for dead. However, thanks to federally funded programs and a newly created Empowerment Zone, this erstwhile urban hell is being reborn: New communities are emerging from the ashes of burned-out neighborhoods. As a tourist destination, it should appeal only to hardcore urban archaeologists and rap fans—it was here, in parks and social clubs, that DJs like Kool Herc and Afrika Bambaata first experimented with the boom-boom-bap of cut-up records and rhyming accompaniment. For less intrepid travelers, the subway lines—elevated here—rattle over

*Love in bloom: The **Brooklyn Botanic Garden** really does promise you a rose garden.*

the battle grounds, allowing you a safe glimpse while taking you to the more friendly territory of the northern parts.

The Bronx is so named because it once belonged to the family of Jonas Bronck, a Swede from the Netherlands who built his farm here in 1636. (It is, therefore, "the Bronck's.") As Manhattan's rich were moving into baronial apartment palaces up Fifth Avenue alongside Central Park, a similar metamorphosis took place here. The **Grand Concourse**, a continuation of Madison Avenue, is the Bronx's main thoroughfare. It was built up in the 1920s and is now lined with grand Art Deco apartment buildings.

Yankee Stadium, the fabled home of the equally fabled baseball team, dominates the Concourse at 161st Street. But maybe not for long. Team owner George Steinbrenner has threatened to move to New Jersey, while Mayor Giuliani is making a pitch to relocate the Bronx Bombers to Manhattan. Halfway up Grand Concourse, just south of Fordham Road, the rotunda of the **Hall of Fame of Great Americans** comes into view. This wonderful early 20th-century institution honors scholars, politicians and others deemed worthy of the accolade "great" (*see chapter **Museums***). Several blocks north is the small clapboard house where Edgar Allan Poe lived out the last sad years of his life. Fordham Road itself leads past **Fordham University**, a Jesuit institution founded in 1841.

Watching a game of cricket in Van Cortlandt Park will do a lot to dispel the standard image of the Bronx. The **Van Cortlandt Mansion**, a fine example of prerevolutionary Georgian architecture, sits amid this vast expanse of green and has been open to the public since 1897 (*see chapter **Architecture***).

Wave Hill, in upscale Riverdale, is a small, idyllic park overlooking the Hudson River. Originally a Victorian country estate where exotic plants were cultivated, it has been occupied by such illustrious tenants as William Thackeray, Theodore Roosevelt, Arturo Toscanini and Mark Twain.

The borough's main attraction is probably the **Bronx Zoo**, on the banks of the Bronx River. The largest urban zoo in the U.S., it allows an unusual degree of space and freedom to its animals. Alas, it's still a zoo, and many of the creatures here exhibit the boredom and listlessness caused by years in captivity (*see chapter **Sightseeing***).

Across from the zoo's main gate in **Bronx Park**, you'll find the vast **New York Botanical Garden** (*see chapter **Children***). The area near the zoo is **Belmont**, the Bronx's answer to Little Italy and a far more expansive neighborhood of restaurants, food markets and coffee shops than its tiny counterpart in Manhattan.

Much farther to the northeast, facing Long Island Sound, is **Pelham Bay Park**, which offers all sorts of diversions, including the man-made shoreline of Orchard Beach (rumored to be the city's favorite dumping ground for dead bodies). Inside the park is **Bartow-Pell Mansion**, a Federal manor set amid romantic formal gardens.

Perhaps the most uncharacteristic part of the Bronx is **City Island**, on Long Island Sound. Settled in 1685 and only a mile and a half long and half a mile wide, it was originally a prosperous shipbuilding center with a busy fishing industry. Back when New York was first being developed, this tiny piece of real estate was a serious competitor for Manhattan's prestige. Now, it offers New Yorkers a slice of New England–style maritime recreation—it's packed with marinas, seafood restaurants and nautically themed bars.

Bartow-Pell Mansion

895 Shore Rd at Pelham Bay Park (1-718-885-1461). Subway: 6 to Pelham Bay Park, then one-mile walk or cab ride.

Accommodations

Where to catch some ZZZs in the city that never sleeps

With the plummeting crime rates and the Cinderella-like transformation of Times Square from peep-show paradise into Disneyfied family-entertainment capital, New York is back on the map as a safe and vibrant city to visit. If you're planning a trip, however, all the Big Apple polishing can be a mixed blessing. It seems everybody's heading to Gotham these days, which means hotels are full to overflowing and, unless you plan far enough ahead, you may find no room at the inn. Hotel occupancy hit an all-time high of 85.5 percent in 1997, and average room rates topped $200 for the first time ever, according to recent statistics. And with the U.S. economy going strong, there's no end in sight to the domestic travel boom. Not surprisingly, the biggest push is for hotels under $100 a night—a rare commodity in NYC. Although about 30 new hotels are scheduled to open by the millennium, they won't ease the room crunch any time soon.

So what's a traveler to do? If you're not one of the fortunate few to have a friend with a hide-a-bed, book well ahead. And always ask about special deals, weekend rates, family discounts and other bargains. It usually pays to shop around.

Consider checking with the reservation agencies listed in this section; many book blocks of rooms in advance and can offer deals even when everyone else swears the city is completely sold out. Another option: Bed-and-breakfasts, once the domain of quaint New England villages, are now catching on in New York. Several services listed here offer thousands of hosted and unhosted apartments.

One more caveat: Even though room taxes were rolled back to 15.25 percent a few years ago, they can still cause sticker shock for the uninitiated. Brace yourself for a $2-per-night occupancy tax, and ask in advance about unadvertised costs—like phone charges, minibars and faxes—or you might not find out about them till you check out.

For more information, contact the Hotel Association of New York City, 437 Madison Avenue, New York, NY 10022 (754-6700; Internet: www.hanyc.org), or write to the New York Convention & Visitors Bureau at 2 Columbus Circle, New York, NY 10019, to ask for a copy of its accommodations booklet.

Telephone tip: 800- numbers can be called toll-free from within the U.S., but you must dial 1 first.

*Lobbyists: Pop Art brightens the walls of the midtown bohemian **Gershwin Hotel**.*

HOTEL RESERVATION AGENCIES

These companies book blocks of reservations in advance and thus can offer reduced rates. Discounts cover most price ranges, from economy upward; some agencies claim savings of up to 65 percent, although around 20 percent is more likely. If you already know where you'd like to stay, it's worth calling a few agencies before booking, in case the hotel is on their list. If you're simply looking for the best deal, mention the part of town you'd like to stay in and the approximate rate you're willing to pay, and see what's available. The following agencies work with selected hotels in New York and are free of charge. A few require payment by credit card or personal check ahead of time, but most let you pay directly at the hotel.

Accommodations Express
801 Asbury Ave, sixth floor, Ocean City, NJ 08226 (1-609-391-2100, 1-800-444-7666). Internet: www.accommodationsxpress.com.

Central Reservations Service
9010 SW 137th Ave, #116, Miami, FL 33186 (1-305-408-6100, 1-800-950-0232; fax 1-305-408-6111). Internet: www.reservation-services.com.

Hotel Reservations Network
8140 Walnut Hill Lane, suite 203, Dallas, TX 75231 (1-800-964-6835). Internet: www.180096hotel.

Express Reservations
3825 Iris Ave, Boulder, CO 80301 (1-303-440-8481, 1-800-356-1123). Internet: www.express-res.com.

Quikbook
381 Park Ave South, New York, NY 10016 (779-ROOM, 1-800-789-988; fax 212-779-6120). Internet: www.quikbook.com.

Deluxe

The Carlyle Hotel
35 E 76th St between Park and Madison Aves (744-1600, 1-800-227-573; fax 717-4682). Subway: 6 to 77th St. Single/double $350–$595, suite $600–$2,500. AmEx, DC, MC, V.
The sumptuous Carlyle is one of the Big Apple's most luxurious hotels, featuring whirlpools in almost every bathroom. Since it opened in 1930, the hotel has attracted numerous famous guests—especially those who want privacy. Service is so discreet that two members of the Beatles stayed here after the group split, without either knowing the other was there. The Cafe Carlyle, a cozy cabaret with low lighting, rose-velvet banquettes and pastel murals, is a perpetual draw for its live musical acts, including Eartha Kitt, Dixie Carter, Woody Allen on Mondays, and the gravel-voiced Bobby Short, a perpetual crowd pleaser now in his 30th year there. Across the hall is Bemelmans Bar, named for Ludwig Bemelmans, the children's author who created Madeline; it's lined with charming murals he painted in 1947, when he lived at the hotel.
Hotel services Air-conditioning. Baby-sitting. Bar. Beauty salon. Cable TV. Conference facilities. Currency exchange. Fax. Fitness center. Laundry. Multilingual staff. Restaurant. **Room services** Cable TV. Fax. Hair dryer. Minibar. Radio. Refrigerator. Room service. Safe. VCR.

Four Seasons Hotel
57 E 57th St between Park and Madison Aves (758-5700, 1-800-332-3442; fax 758-5711). Subway: N, R to Lexington
Ave; 4, 5, 6 to 59th St. Single from $495, double from $545, suite from $975. AmEx, DC, JCB, MC, V. Renowned architect I.M. Pei's sharp geometric design combines with neutral cream and honey tones for a sleek and elegant ultramodern lobby befitting this favorite haven of media moguls and entertainment execs. The Art Deco–style rooms are among the largest in the city, with bathrooms made from Florentine marble and tubs that fill in just 60 seconds. Views of Manhattan from the higher floors are superb. Guests can get utterly wasted on martinis at Fifty Seven Fifty Seven, the hotel's ultrachic piano bar, where power brokers and gossipmongers gather nightly.
Hotel services Air-conditioning. Baby-sitting. Bar. Conference facilities. Currency exchange. Disabled: access, rooms. Fax. Laundry. Multilingual staff. Parking. Restaurants. Fitness center and spa. **Room services** Cable TV. Fax. Hair dryer. Minibar. Radio. Refrigerator. Room service. Safe. VCR.

Millennium Hilton
55 Church St between Fulton and Dey Sts (693-2001, 1-800-HILTON; fax 571-2316). Subway: N, R, 1, 9 to Cortlandt St. Single $455, double $505, suite $550–$2,000. AmEx, DC, Disc, JCB, MC, V. This 58-story black-glass skyscraper, located next to the World Trade Center and a stone's throw from Wall Street, draws a large corporate clientele. Lower Manhattan's only four-star hotel features fax machines in each room and high-tech facilities, including a rooftop swimming pool and solarium overlooking historic St. Paul's Church. The upper floors have splendid views of New York Harbor and the Brooklyn Bridge.
Hotel services Air-conditioning. Bar. Conference facilities. Currency exchange. Disabled: rooms. Fax. Fitness center. Laundry. Multilingual staff. Parking. Restaurant. **Room services** Cable TV. Fax. Hair dryer. Minibar. Radio. Refrigerator. Room service. Safe. VCR.

The New York Palace
455 Madison Ave at 50th St (888-7000, 1-800-697-2522; fax 303-6000). Subway: E, F to Fifth Ave. Single/double from $425, tower room from $550, suite from $900. AmEx, DC, Disc, JCB, MC, V. Every inch of the luxurious New York Palace was renovated last year. It now has an elegantly refurbished lobby and new room decor, ranging from traditional to Art Deco, as well as new fitness and meeting centers. The main hotel—once the Villard Houses, a cluster of mansions designed by Stanford White—is the new home of Sirio Maccioni's acclaimed Le Cirque 2000, and the decor is something to see: Pre-Raphaelite murals combined with whimsical details that conjure images of life under the big top; it's nearly impossible to get into, but worth the effort.
Hotel services Air-conditioning. Baby-sitting. Bar. Conference facilities. Disabled: access, rooms. Fax. Laundry. Parking. Restaurant. **Room services** Cable TV. Hair dryer. Minibar. Radio. Refrigerator. Room service. VCR.

The Pierre Hotel
795 Fifth Ave at 61st St (838-8000, 1-800-PIERRE4; fax 940-8109). Subway: N, R to Fifth Ave. Single from $425, double from $475, suite from $695. AmEx, DC, JCB, MC, V. Once Salvador Dali's favorite hotel, the Pierre has been seducing guests since 1929 with its superb service and discreet, elegant atmosphere. The rooms may be out of your price range, but you can always take afternoon tea in the magnificent rotunda. Front rooms overlook Central Park, and some of Madison Avenue's most famous designer stores are a block away.
Hotel services Air-conditioning. Baby-sitting. Bar. Beauty salon. Conference facilities. Currency exchange. Fax. Fitness center. Laundry. Parking. Restaurant. Theater desk. Valet packing/unpacking. **Room services** Cable TV. Hair dryer. Minibar. Radio. Refrigerator on request. Room service. Safe. VCR and fax on request.

The Plaza Hotel
768 Fifth Ave at 59th St (759-3000, 1-800-228-3000; fax 759-3167). Subway: N, R to Fifth Ave. Single/double

$265–$575, suite $450–$15,000. AmEx, Disc, DC, JCB, MC, V. Perfectly located for a shopping spree, the famous Plaza Hotel is just a few minutes' walk from Fifth Avenue's most exclusive stores. It's also across the street from Central Park, with breathtaking views from the high-floor rooms facing 59th Street. Although Ivana Trump no longer runs the place, her signature touches remain. The rooms and suites, renowned for their baroque splendor, have been freshly renovated. The famous Palm Court has a delightful Tiffany ceiling, but the Edwardian Room is currently closed for a makeover by designer du jour Adam Tihany. In the meantime, stop in at Istana, a new Mediterranean restaurant featuring more than 30 types of olives, a sherry menu and a tapas afternoon tea. A Plaza spa is also in the works.
Hotel services Air-conditioning. Bar. Beauty salon. Conference facilities. Fax. Fitness center. Laundry. Multilingual staff. Parking. Restaurant. **Room services** Cable TV. Dual-line phones. Hair dryer. Minibar. Radio. Room service. Safe. VCR on request. Voice mail.

Trump International Hotel & Tower
1 Central Park West at Columbus Circle (299-1000; fax 299-1150). Subway: A, C, B, D, 1, 9 to 59th St–Columbus Circle. Suite $395–$1,350 ($325–$900 on weekends). AmEx, DC, MC, V. The Donald's striking glass-and-steel skyscraper towers over Columbus Circle, just steps from Central Park. Inside the year-old hotel, all is subdued elegance—from the small marble lobby to the 168 suites equipped with fax machines, Jacuzzis and floor-to-ceiling windows. Each guest is assigned a personal assistant to cater to his or her whims, and a chef will come to your room to cook on request. Better yet, head downstairs to Jean Georges, the newest restaurant from four-star chef Jean-Georges Vongerichten, of Jo Jo and Vong fame.
Hotel services Air-conditioning. Bar. Cellular phones. Conference facilities. Fitness Center. Restaurant. **Room services** Cable TV. CD player. Computer on request. Fax. Hair Dryer. Minibar. Refrigerator. Room service . VCR.

The Waldorf-Astoria
301 Park Ave at 50th St (355-3000, 1-800-924-3673; fax 872-7272). Subway: E, F to Lexington Ave; 6 to 51st St. Single $295–$390, double $335–$430, suite $335–$1,075. AmEx, DC, Disc, JCB, MC, V. The famous Waldorf salad made its debut in 1931 at the grand opening of what was then the world's largest hotel. Ever since, the Waldorf has been associated with New York's high society (former guests include Princess Grace, Cary Grant, Sophia Loren and a long list of U.S. presidents). This year, the *grande dame* of New York hotels wraps up a $60 million renovation that will restore the main lobby to its original Art Deco grandeur. Peacock Alley restaurant has drawn rave reviews for its new French chef, and the erstwhile coffee shop, Oscar's, is now a stylish American bistro.
Hotel services Air-conditioning. Baby-sitting. Bar. Beauty salon. Conference facilities. Fax. Fitness center with steam rooms. Laundry. Multilingual staff. Parking. Restaurant. **Room services** Cable TV. Fax in tower rooms. Hair dryer. Minibar. Radio. Room service.

Stylish

The Mercer
99 Prince St at Mercer St (966-6060). Subway: N, R to Prince St. Single from $325, double from $350, suite from $850. AmEx, DC, MC, V. Five years ago, entrepreneur Andre Balazs bought the site for the Mercer hotel. Since then, scenesters have watched and waited for its doors to open. Balazs finally unveiled his 75-room gem this past spring. Its location in the dead center of Soho gives it a leg up on its closest competitor, the two-year-old SoHo Grand. The lobby offers a hint of the understated chic you'll find in the rooms: Each features oversized bathrooms, furniture made of exotic African woods and techno amenities such as Web TV.

Square deal: **Washington Square Hotel** *is a budget-minded gem on the park.*

Hotel services Air-conditioning. Lobby book and magazine library. Bar. Private meeting rooms. Private business cards and stationery. Video and CD library. Complimentary sessions at David Barton Gym. **Room services** Cable TV. VCR. Cassette and CD player. Modem/fax. Three two-line telephones. Direct-dial number. Minibar. Safe. Fireplace. Room service.

Morgans
237 Madison Ave between 37th and 38th Sts (686-0300, 1-800-334-3408; fax 779-8352). Subway: S, 4, 5, 6, 7 to 42nd St–Grand Central. Single $240–$305, double $245–$335, suite $425–$525. AmEx, Disc, DC, JCB, MC, V. This cozy, understated hotel was the first non-nightclub venture by Studio 54 impresarios Ian Schrager and Steve Rubell. It's named in honor of J.P. Morgan, whose nearby library was converted to a museum (the Pierpont Morgan Library) in 1924. The cavelike Morgans Bar remains a favorite late-night haunt of models and other trendy types. New on the scene is Asia de Cuba, a restaurant that serves spicy Chino-Latino cuisine.
Hotel services Air-conditioning. Baby-sitting. Bar and café. Conference facilities. Fax. Fitness center and spa. Laundry. Multilingual staff. Restaurant. **Room services** Cable TV. Hair dryer. Minibar. Refrigerator. Room service. VCR on request.

Paramount
235 W 46th St between Broadway and Eighth Ave (764-5500, 1-800-225-7474; fax 575-4892). Subway: N, R to 49th St. Single $135–$260, double $220–$550, suite $395–$550. AmEx, DC, Disc, JCB, MC, V. Ian Schrager's Philippe Starck–designed Paramount, like the Royalton (see below), is chic almost beyond belief. The cavernous, windowless lobby was inspired by the great transatlantic liners. (There's also a Dean & DeLuca shop and espresso bar.) A "weather mirror" near the elevator on each floor gives the daily forecast, and Vermeer's *Lacemaker* is silk-screened on the headboard of each bed. The hotel has just been renovated, but one thing hasn't changed: The Whiskey Bar is still a good place for model spotting.

Hotel services Air-conditioning. Bar. Business center. Conference facilities. Currency exchange. Fax. Fitness center. Laundry. Multilingual staff. Nonsmoking floors. Restaurants. **Room services** Cable TV. Room service. VCR.

Royalton

44 W 44th St between Fifth and Sixth Aves (869-4400, 1-800-635-9013; fax 869-8965). Subway: B, D, F, Q to 42nd St; 7 to Fifth Ave. Single $325–$400, double $340–$425, suite from $500. AmEx, DC, JCB, MC, V. Like the Paramount (see above), Ian Schrager's Royalton was designed by Philippe Starck. Waitresses in satin minidresses serve fashionable young things in the vaultlike lobby, and the restaurant (called 44) has some of the most sought-after lunch tables in town (keep an eye out for Condé Nast editors). The rooms feature sleek slate fireplaces and marvelous round bathtubs. Discounted weekend rates are often available.
Hotel services Air-conditioning. Bar. Conference facilities. Currency exchange. Fax. Fitness center. Laundry. Multilin-

gual staff. Parking. Restaurant. **Room services** Cable TV. Minibar. Radio. Room service. VCR.

SoHo Grand Hotel

310 West Broadway between Grand and Canal Sts (965-3000, 1-800-637-7200; fax 965-3200). Subway: C, E to Canal St. Single $319–$359, double $339–$379, suite from $1,200. AmEx, DC, MC, V. When it opened in 1996, this was Soho's first hotel to open since the 1800s. The unusual design pays homage both to Soho's contemporary artistic community and to the area's past, when many of the lofts were working factories. Architecturally, it's one of the city's most striking hotels. A dramatic bottle-glass–and–cast-iron stairway leads up from street level to the elegant lobby and reception desk, which is presided over by a monumental clock. Rooms are decorated in soothing grays and beiges, with nonfat munchies in the minibar and photos from local galleries on the walls. Both the Grand Bar and the Canal House

---

Dive right in!

If you prefer quirks to consistency, consider these oddball oases

These colorful classics are really off the beaten track. What you won't find: complimentary shoe shines or chocolate mints on the pillow. What you will find: loads of atmosphere, interesting characters and a one-of-a-kind experience. Just keep an open mind, and think of the stories you'll have to tell the folks back home.

Carlton Arms Hotel

160 E 25th St at Third Ave (684-8337). Subway: 6 to 23rd St. Single $52 with shared bath, $62 with private bath; double $66 with shared bath, $76 with private bath; triples $82–$92; quads $86–$96. MC, V. The Carlton Arms is a cheerful and basic budget hotel popular with Europeans. The corridors are brightly decorated with murals of the city; each room has been painted by a different artist. The artwork is hit-and-miss, but fun. Check out the

*Up in arms: Crash in one of the **Carlton Arms**' uniquely painted rooms.*

funky new top-floor bathroom with walls covered in toys, tickets, sunglasses and other tchotchkes. Discounts are offered for students and overseas guests.
Hotel services Multilingual staff. Café. Telephone in lobby. **Room services** Hair dryer on request.

Chelsea Hotel

222 W 23rd St between Seventh and Eighth Aves (243-3700). Subway: A, C, E, 1, 2, 3, 9 to 23rd St. Single $135, double $165, studio $175, suite from $300. AmEx, DC, JCB, MC, V. The Chelsea has a reputation to uphold. Built in 1884, the famous red-brick building oozes history. In 1912, Titanic survivors stayed here for a few days; other former residents include the likes of Dylan Thomas, Mark Twain, Thomas Wolfe, O. Henry and Brendan Behan. No evidence remains of the hotel's most infamous association: the murder of Nancy Spungen by Sid Vicious of the Sex Pistols. Although there's a decided air of seediness, the Chelsea has atmosphere. The lobby doubles as an art gallery, showing work by past and present guests, and rooms are large, with high ceilings. Most, but not all, have a private bathroom. A basement café is in the works.
Hotel services Air-conditioning. Fax. Multilingual staff. Valet parking. **Room services** Kitchenettes and refrigerators in some rooms. Safe. TV.

Hotel 17

225 E 17th St between Second and Third Aves (475-2845; fax 677-8178). Subway: 4, 5, 6, L, N, R to 14th St–Union Sq. Single $75, double $109–$130, weekly rates from $303. No credit cards. This is the ultimate dive hotel and one of the hippest places to stay if you're an artist, musician or model. Everyone on the underground circuit knows the place. Madonna posed here for a magazine shoot, and Woody Allen used the hotel in *Manhattan Murder Mystery*. The decor is classic shabby chic, with labyrinthine hallways leading to high-ceilinged rooms filled with a hodgepodge of discarded dressers, gorgeous old fireplaces, velvet curtains and 1950s wallpaper. Don't be put off by the permanent "no vacancy" sign.
Hotel services Air-conditioning in some rooms. Fax. Laundry. Roof terrace. **Room services** Cable TV in some rooms. Hair dryer on request.

restaurant are worth a visit. If you're feeling lonely, request a pet goldfish to keep in your room during your stay. **Hotel services** Air-conditioning. Bar. Conference facilities. Fax. Fitness center. Laundry. Restaurant. **Room services** Cable TV. Minibar. PC port. Room service. Voice mail.

First-class

Algonquin

59 W 44th St between Fifth and Sixth Aves (840-6800, 1-800-555-8000; fax 944-1419). Subway: B, D, F, Q to 42nd St; 7 to Fifth Ave. Single/double from $329, suite from $429. AmEx, DC, Disc, JCB, MC, V. Arguably New York's most famous literary landmark, this was the place where Dorothy Parker, James Thurber and other literary lights of the 1920s and '30s gathered at the Oak Room's legendary Round Table to gossip and match wits. The newly refurbished rooms are on the small side but cheerful and charming, and the hallways now feature *New Yorker*–cartoon wallpaper. Don't miss Hamlet, the house cat, who has his own miniature suite and four-poster bed in a corner of the redone lobby. On Sunday and Monday evenings, there are readings by local playwrights and authors—or you may prefer to head straight to the cozy Blue Bar.
Hotel services Air-conditioning. Baby-sitting. Bar. Conference facilities. Currency exchange. Disabled: rooms. Fax. Laundry. Multilingual staff. Nonsmoking floors. Restaurant. **Room services** Cable TV. Hair dryer. Radio. Refrigerator in suites and on request. Room service. Safe. VCR on request. Voice mail.

Barbizon Hotel

140 E 63rd St at Lexington Ave (838-5700, 1-800-223-1020; fax 888-4271). Subway: N, R to Lexington Ave; 4, 5, 6 to 59th St. Single $210–$280, double $230–$300, suite from $425. AmEx, DC, Disc, MC, V. The Barbizon was originally a hotel for emancipated women (whose parents could feel confident that their daughters were safe in its care). During its years as a women-only residence, guests included Grace Kelly, Ali McGraw and Candice Bergen, and the rules stated that men could be entertained only in the lounge. The hotel recently completed a $40 million renovation, which included adding a branch of the local Equinox health club (free for guests) with an Olympic-size pool and full spa. Children under 12 stay free if sharing a room with their parents.
Hotel services Air-conditioning. Currency exchange. Disabled: rooms. Fax. Laundry. Multilingual staff. **Room services** Cable TV. CD player. Hair dryer on request. In-room safes. Minibar. Refrigerator.

The Doral Tuscany Hotel

120 E 39th St between Lexington and Park Aves (686-1600, 1-800-22DORAL; fax 779-0148). Subway: S, 4, 5, 6, 7 to 42nd St–Grand Central. Single $179–$299, double $199–$319, suite from $450. AmEx, DC, Disc, MC, V. Nestled among brownstones in historic Murray Hill, the Doral Tuscany has such a residential feel that it's hard to believe Grand Central Terminal is just around the corner. Standard rooms are absolutely enormous, and each has an entrance hallway with separate dressing room and Italian-marble bath. Suites go one step further, with tiny portable TV sets in the bathrooms.
Hotel services Air-conditioning. Bar. Conference facilities. Disabled: rooms. Fax. Laundry. Multilingual staff. Restaurant. **Room services** Cable TV. Hair dryer. Minibar. Radio. Refrigerator. Room service. VCR on request.

Hotel Elysee

60 E 54th St between Park and Madison Aves (753-1066; fax 980-9278). Subway: E, F to Lexington Ave; 6 to 51st St. Single/double $265–$295, suite $375–$425. AmEx, DC, JCB, MC, V. This a charming and discreet hotel with friendly service, antique furniture and Italian-marble bathrooms. Some of the rooms also have colored-glass conservatories and roof terraces. It's popular with publishers, so don't be surprised if you see a famous author enjoying the complimentary afternoon tea in the club room. You can also eat in the whimsically decorated Monkey Bar next door. Rates include continental breakfast and evening wine and hors d'oeuvres. The Elysee has been restored to its original 1930s look and displays photographs showing the likes of Joan Crawford and Marlene Dietrich gathered around the piano.
Hotel services Air-conditioning. Baby-sitting. Bar. Conference facilities. Disabled: rooms. Fax. Laundry. Library. Multilingual staff. Valet parking. **Room services** Cable TV. Hair dryer. Minibar. Radio. Refrigerator. Room service. TV. VCR. Voice mail.

The Mark

25 E 77th St between Fifth and Madison Aves (744-4300, 1-800-843-6275; fax 744-2749). Subway: 6 to 77th St. Single $370–$435, double $400–$465, suite $600–$2,500. AmEx, DC, MC, V. Towering potted palms and arched mirrors line the entranceway to this cheerful European-style Upper East Sider. The marble lobby, decorated with 18th-century Piranesi prints and magnums of Veuve-Clicquot, is usually bustling with dressy international guests and white-gloved bellmen. Especially popular are Mark's Bar, a clubby hideaway with lots of dark green and polished wood, and the more elegant Mark's Restaurant.
Hotel services Air-conditioning. Bar. Conference facilities. Fax. Fitness center. Laundry. Multilingual staff. Restaurant. **Room services** Cable TV. Hair dryer. Room service.

The Michelangelo

152 W 51st St at Seventh Ave (765-1900, 1-800-237-0990; fax 581-7618). Subway: B, D, E to Seventh Ave; N, R to 49th St; 1, 9 to 50th St. Single/double $295–$395, suite $425–$950. AmEx, DC, Disc, JCB, MC, V. Posh and very European, this charming little haven in the theater district welcomes guests with a cozy lobby full of peach marble, oil paintings, giant potted palms, and overstuffed couches in rose and salmon tones. The 178 sizable rooms are decorated in styles ranging from French country to Art Deco; each room includes two TVs (one in the bathroom), fax machines, terry-cloth robes and oversized tubs. Complimentary breakfast includes espresso, cappuccino and Italian pastries.
Hotel services Air-conditioning. Bar. Business center. Conference facilities. 24-hour fitness center. Multilingual staff. Free limo to Wall Street. Laundry. **Room services** Cable TV. Complimentary shoe shine and newspaper. Fax, printer, copier. Minibar. PC port. Radio. Room service.

Roger Smith

501 Lexington Ave between 47th and 48th Sts (755-1400, 1-800-445-0277; fax 319-9130). Subway: 6 to 51st St. Single/double $225, suite from $275. AmEx, DC, JCB, MC, V. The hotel is owned by sculptor and painter James Knowles, and some of his work decorates the lobby. The large rooms are individually furnished, the staff is friendly, and there's a library of videocassettes for those who want to stay in for the night. It's popular with touring bands, and there's often live jazz in the restaurant.
Hotel services Air-conditioning. Baby-sitting. Bar. Conference facilities. Disabled: rooms. Fax. Laundry. Multilingual staff. Restaurant. Valet parking. **Room services** Cable TV. Hair dryer on request. Refrigerator. Room service. VCR.

The Warwick

65 W 54th St at Sixth Ave (247-2700; fax 957-8915). Subway: B, Q to 57th St. Single $230–$275, double $255–$295, suites $280–$600. AmEx, DC, JCB, MC, V. Built by William Randolph Hearst and patronized by Elvis and the Beatles in the 1950s and 1960s, the Warwick is still polished and gleaming. It was once an apartment building, and the rooms are exceptionally large by midtown standards. Ask for a view of

Sixth Avenue (double glazing keeps out the noise). The top-floor suite was once the home of Cary Grant.
Hotel services Air-conditioning. Baby-sitting. Bar. Conference facilities. Currency exchange. Disabled: rooms and access. Drug store. Fax. Fitness center. Laundry. Men's clothing store. Multilingual staff. Parking. Restaurant. Theater desk. **Room services** Cable TV. Hair dryer. Minibar. Radio. Refrigerator. Room service. Safe. VCR.

Comfortable

Ameritania Hotel

1701 Broadway at 54th St (247-5000, 1-800-922-0330; fax 247-3316). Subway: B, D, E to Seventh Ave; N, R to 57th St; 1, 9 to 50th St. Single/double $195, suite $265–$285. AmEx, DC, Disc, JCB, MC, V. The lobby of this theater district standby is futuristic, but the rooms are more traditional. The hotel is next door to the Ed Sullivan Theater, home of *Late Show With David Letterman*, so be prepared for the occasional appearance of cameras—Dave likes to pop in unannounced.
Hotel services Air-conditioning. Bagel shop (24 hours). Bar. Fax. Fitness center. Laundry. Multilingual staff. Restaurant. Theater/excursion desk. **Room services** Cable TV. Hair dryer in suites, on request in rooms. Radio. Refrigerator on request. Room service.

Comfort Inn Manhattan

42 W 35th St between Fifth and Sixth Aves (947-0200, 1-800-228-5150; fax 594-3047). Subway B, D, F, Q, N, R to 34th St. Single/double $169–$229. AmEx, CB, DC, Disc, MC, V. This small, family-oriented hotel, around the corner from Macy's and the Empire State Building, underwent a $4.5 million renovation several years ago. Alex at the front desk is a hoot. A hotel fixture for more than a decade, he loves collecting bizarre English place names, so come prepared if you can. Rates include free continental breakfast and a newspaper.
Hotel services Air-conditioning. Fax. Multilingual staff. **Room services** Cable TV. Hair dryer on request. Radio.

Excelsior Hotel

45 W 81st St between Columbus Ave and Central Park West (362-9200, 1-800-368-4575; fax 721-2994). Subway: B, C to 81st St; 1, 9 to 79th St. Single/double $149–$169, suite $179–$199. AmEx, MC, V. On the Upper West Side, where hotels are scarce, the Excelsior offers a prime location just steps from Central Park and across the street from the American Museum of Natural History. Some say the rooms are a bit faded and cold, but they're comfortable and affordable.
Hotel services Air-conditioning. Coffee shop. Fax. **Room services** Radio. Room service from coffee shop. TV.

Gramercy Park Hotel

2 Lexington Ave at 21st St (475-4320, 1-800-221-4083; fax 505-0535). Subway: 6 to 23rd St. Single $145–$150, double $160, suite from $190. AmEx, DC, Disc, JCB, MC, V. This hotel is in a surprisingly quiet location adjoining the small green oasis of Gramercy Park. Guests vary from business travelers to rock stars. There are no nonsmoking rooms.
Hotel services Air-conditioning. Bar. Beauty salon. Conference facilities. Disabled: rooms. Fax. Laundry. Multilingual staff. Newsstand/theater-ticket office. Parking. Restaurant. **Room services** Cable TV. Refrigerator. Radio. Room service.

Hotel Beacon

2130 Broadway between 75th and 76th Sts (787-1100, 1-800-572-4969; fax 787-8119). Subway: 1, 2, 3, 9 to 72nd St. Single $135, double $155–$165, suite $195–$450. AmEx, DC, MC, V. If you're looking for a break from the throngs of tourists clogging Times Square—or if you want to see how Gothamites really live—consider the Beacon. It's in a desirable residential neighborhood and only a short walk from Central Park, Lincoln Center and the famous Zabar's food market. The hotel has a cheerful black-and-white marble

lobby and friendly staff. Halls are a bit drab, and rooms vary in decor, but they are all clean and spacious. Since the Beacon is the tallest building around, its windows let in light and offer views of the neighborhood (unlike many other hotels).
Hotel services Air-conditioning. Coffee shop. Fax. Laundry (self-service). Nonsmoking rooms. Valet dry cleaning (24 hours). **Room services** Cable TV. Coffeemaker. Hair dryer. Kitchenette. Radio. Refrigerator. Voice mail.

Hotel Metro

45 W 35th St between Fifth and Sixth Aves (947-2500, 1-800-356-3870; fax 279-1310). Subway: B, D, F, Q, N, R to 34th St. Single/double $165–$250, suite $200–$325. AmEx, DC, MC, V. It's not posh by any stretch of the imagination, but the Metro has good service and a convenient location near the Empire State Building. The lobby has a charming retro feel, though the halls are army chic, with olive-drab doors and greenish-gray carpets. Rooms are small but neat and clean, and the roof terrace offers splendid views. The new Metro Grill in the lobby specializes in Mediterranean and Italian food.
Hotel services Air-conditioning. Fax. Fitness center. Laundry. Multilingual staff. Rooftop terrace. **Room services** Cable TV. Hair dryer. Radio.

Hotel Wellington

871 Seventh Ave at 55th St (247-3900, 1-800-652-1212; fax 581-1719). Subway: B, D, E to Seventh Ave; N, R to 57th St. Single/double $155, suite from $185, triple $170. AmEx, DC, Disc, JCB, MC, V. This hotel has some charming old-fashioned touches, like a gold-domed ceiling with a chandelier, though it's a tad frayed around the edges. Still, it's close to Central Park, Broadway and the Museum of Modern Art. There's a diner, a steakhouse and a new Greek restaurant next door.
Hotel services Air-conditioning. Bar. Beauty salon. Conference facilities. Access for the disabled. Fax. Laundry. Multilingual staff. Parking. Restaurant. Ticket service. **Room services** Cable TV. Refrigerator in some rooms. Room service.

Lexington Hotel

511 Lexington Ave at 48th St (755-4400; fax 751-4091). Subway: 6 to 51st St. Single $185, double $205, suite $375. AmEx, Disc, DC, MC, V. The Lexington, which is close to both Grand Central Terminal and the United Nations, is popular with business travelers. The lobby has a marble floor and rosewood pillars; 20 of the 27 floors have been renovated. There are two restaurants: Vuli, serving Italian cuisine, and the Chinese J Sung Dynasty.
Hotel services Air-conditioning. Baby-sitting on request. Bar. Coffee shop. Conference facilities. Currency exchange. Disabled: rooms. Exercise room. Fax. Laundry. Multilingual staff. Restaurants. **Room services** Cable TV. Hair dryer. Radio on request. Refrigerator. Room service. Safe.

The Mayflower Hotel

15 Central Park West at 61st St (265-0060, 1-800-223-4164; fax 265-0227). Subway: A, C, B, D, 1, 9 to 59th St–Columbus Circle. Single $165–$205, double $180–$220, suite $215–$295. AmEx, DC, Disc, MC, V. This haven for musicians faces Central Park and is just a few blocks from Lincoln Center. You can't argue with the spectacular park views from the front rooms, though the decor is getting a bit drab, and the hotel now has stiff competition from its new neighbor, the Trump International. The Conservatory, on the first floor, is still a nice spot for a light breakfast.
Hotel services Air-conditioning. Baby-sitting. Bar. Conference facilities. Fax. Fitness center. Laundry. Multilingual staff. Parking. Restaurant. **Room services** Cable TV. Hair dryer on request. PC ports. Radio. Refrigerator. Room service. VCR on request.

Quality Hotel Fifth Avenue

3 E 40th St between Fifth and Madison Aves (447-1500, 1-800-228-5151; fax 213-0972). Subway: B, D, F, Q to 42nd St; 7 to Fifth Ave. Single/double $149–$225. AmEx, DC, Disc,

Pedestrians

Possibilities

TimeOut | London's Living Guide.

http://www.timeout.co.uk

JCB, MC, V. The rooms here are basic but clean, neat and well-lit, with paisley furnishings and sizable bathrooms. Ask for room numbers three to six (the higher the floor, the better) for a street view with more light; back rooms are darker and look directly into offices. The Quality offers good value a stone's throw from the New York Public Library, Bryant Park and Lord & Taylor. Ask about corporate and weekend rates.
Hotel services Air-conditioning. Business services. Complimentary newspaper. Disabled: rooms. Fax. Restaurant. **Room services** Cable TV. Coffeemaker. Iron and ironing board. PC port. Radio. Room service.

Quality Hotel & Suites Midtown

59 W 46th St between Fifth and Sixth Aves (719-2300, 1-800-848-0020; fax 768-3477). Subway B, D, F, Q to 47th–50th Sts–Rockefeller Ctr. Single $149, double from $159, suite from $179. AmEx, CB, DC, MC, V. Somehow this convenient theater district hotel, built in 1902 and recently refurbished, has hung onto its old-time prices.
Hotel services Air-conditioning. Barber shop. Beauty salon. Fax. Multilingual staff. 24-hour business center. 24-hour fitness center. **Room services** Cable TV. Coffeemaker. Hair dryer. In-room safe. Iron and ironing board. Radio.

Radisson Empire

44 W 63rd St at Broadway (265-7400, 1-800-333-3333; fax 245-3382). Subway A, C, B, D, 1, 9 to 59th St–Columbus Circle. Single/double $180–$300, suite $300–$650. AmEx, DC, Disc, JCB, MC, V. This hotel is perfectly located opposite Lincoln Center and next door to the eccentrically stylish Iridium bar. The lobby is surprisingly baronial, with wood paneling and velvet drapes. The rooms are small—some almost closet-size—but tasteful, with plenty of chintz and floral prints.
Hotel services Air-conditioning. Bar. Conference facilities. Currency exchange. Disabled: rooms. Fax. Laundry (self-service). Multilingual staff. Restaurant. Theater/tour ticket desk. Valet parking. **Room services** Cable TV. Hair dryer. Minibar. Radio. Refrigerator on request. Room service. VCR, CD and cassette player.

The Roosevelt Hotel

45 E 45th St at Madison Ave (661-9600, 1-888-TEDDY-NY, 1-800-223-0888). Internet: www.theroosevelthotel.com. Subway: S, 4, 5, 6, 7 to 42nd St–Grand Central. Single/double $169–$289, suite $350–$1,800. AmEx, DC, MC, V. After a two-year, $65 million makeover, this historic charmer is back and better than ever. Built in 1924, the 1,033-room hotel was a haven for celebs and socialites in the Golden Age (it's where Guy Lombardo first broadcast "Auld Lang Syne" on New Year's Eve). Nostalgic grandeur lives on in the bustling lobby, with 27-foot fluted columns, lots of marble, huge sprays of fresh flowers—and, often, large groups of teen tourists on class trips. The Palm Room serves afternoon tea under a brilliant blue sky mural; the Madison Club Cigar Bar serves cocktails in a clubby setting with stained-glass windows.
Hotel services Air-conditioning. Bar. Business services. Conference facilities. Concierge. Fax. Health club. Laundry. Valet. Valet parking. **Room services** Cable TV. PC ports. Room service. Voice mail.

Shelburne Murray Hill

303 Lexington Ave between 37th and 38th Sts (689-5200; fax 779-7068). Subway: S, 4, 5, 6, 7 to 42nd St–Grand Central. Suite from $259–$499. AmEx, MC, V. The Shelburne is an elegantly furnished all-suite hotel with an attractive lobby and pleasant decor. Suites have a full kitchen with microwave, iron and filter coffee machine. The hotel's a good value, especially considering the facilities, which include a restaurant and health club with sauna.
Hotel services Air-conditioning. Bar. Conference facilities. Rooms for the disabled. Fax. Fitness club. Laundry. Multilingual staff. Parking. Restaurant. Safe. **Room services** Cable TV. Hair dryer on request. Iron. Microwave. Radio. Refrigerator. Room service. VCR on request.

Less than $150

Best Western Manhattan

17 W 32nd St between Broadway and Fifth Ave (736-1600, 1-800-551-2303; fax 563-4007). Subway: B, D, F, Q, N, R to 34th St. Single/double $119–$189, suites from $159–$209. AmEx, DC, Disc, JCB, MC, V. This is a good-value hotel with a stylish Beaux Arts facade, a black-and-grey marble lobby and rooms inspired by different neighborhoods—choose between a floral Central Park room and a trendy Soho motif. The hotel is just a few blocks from Macy's and the Empire State Building, but the block is a bit seedy. Intrepid travelers will enjoy exploring the eclectic Korean shops lining 32nd Street; first-timers might want to opt for a more mainstream locale. Tullio's, an Italian restaurant next door, is open 24 hours and provides room service for guests.
Hotel services Air-conditioning. Beauty salon. Business center. Conference facilities. Disabled: rooms. Fax. Fitness center. Multilingual staff. Restaurant. Valet parking. **Room services** Cable TV. Hair dryer and minibar in most rooms.

Cosmopolitan

95 West Broadway at Chambers St (566-1900, 1-888-895-9400; fax 566-6909) Subway: 1, 9, A, C, E to Chambers St. Single $89, double $119. AmEx, MC, V. It's not luxurious by anyone's standards, but after years as a down-at-the-heels rooming house, this recently renovated little hotel does have rock-bottom rates and a primo location in the trendy Tribeca area, an easy walk to Chinatown, Little Italy, the South Street Seaport and the art galleries of Soho.
Hotel services Air-conditioning. Discounted parking. **Room services** Modem line. Cable TV.

Hotel Edison

228 W 47th St at Broadway (840-5000, 1-800-637-7070; fax 596-6850). Subway: N, R to 49th St; 1, 9 to 50th St. Single $115, double $125 ($10 for each extra person up to four in a room), suite $130–$200. AmEx, DC, Disc, JCB, MC, V. After its full renovation, the Edison looks decidedly spruced up. The large, high-ceilinged Art Deco lobby is particularly colorful, and even the green marble-lined corridors look good. Rooms are standard, but theater lovers won't find a more convenient location. The Edison coffee shop just off the lobby is a longtime favorite of Broadway gypsies.
Hotel services Air-conditioning. Baby-sitting. Bar. Beauty salon. Currency exchange. Disabled: rooms. Dry cleaning. Guest fax (596-6868). Laundry. Multilingual staff. Parking. Restaurants. Travel/tour desk. **Room services** Cable TV. Hair dryer on request.

Howard Johnson

429 Park Ave South between 29th and 30th Sts (532-4860, 1-800-258-4290; fax 545-9727). Subway: N, R, 6 to 28th St. Single $105–$199, double $115–$249, suite $149–$449. AmEx, DC, Disc, JCB, MC, V. Popular with Europeans, this recently renovated hotel has good-value suites and friendly staff. There's a small breakfast bar that doubles as a cocktail lounge in the evenings. It's enough to make you forget you're at the less fashionable end of Park Avenue.
Hotel services Air-conditioning. Baby-sitting. Bar. Disabled: rooms. Fax. Laundry. Multilingual staff. **Room services** Cable TV. Hair dryer. Minibar. Radio. Room service for breakfast.

Pickwick Arms

230 E 51st St between Second and Third Aves (355-0300; fax 755-5029). Subway E, F to Lexington Ave; 6 to 51st St. Single $60 with shared bath, $70 with semiprivate bath, $90 with private bath; double from $110. AmEx, DC, MC, V. Although rooms are small, the Pickwick Arms is clean, and it's located in a reasonably quiet district. It's near restaurants, movie theaters, Radio City Music Hall and the United Nations. Most of the rooms have private bathrooms.

Boutique chic

When size does matter, check into one of these intimate inns

For a small-town feel in the big city, check out (or rather, check into) one of Manhattan's growing number of boutique hotels. Generally speaking, boutiques are small (150 rooms or less), independently owned inns with a unique atmosphere. You'll find several worthwhile options in the theater district; others are tucked away in unusual, renovated historic buildings all over the city. Ambience ranges from quaint Victorian to ultrachic contemporary.

Broadway Inn

264 W 46th St at Eighth Ave (921-1824, 1-800-826-6300; fax 768-2807). Subway: A, C, E to 42nd St. Single $85, double $95–$160, suite $185. AmEx, DC, Disc, MC, V. In contrast to Times Square's megahotels (many of which have prices to match), this inn (a renovated single-room-occupancy) feels small and personal—think Off Broadway rather than Broadway. The lobby, though small, has exposed-brick walls, ceiling fans, shelves loaded with books you can borrow, and a hospitable front-desk staff. The 40 guest rooms are a bit spartan but are new, clean and fairly priced for the district. Be warned: The stairs are steep, and the inn has no elevator. Rates include continental breakfast.
Hotel services Air-conditioning. Multilingual staff. **Room services** Cable TV.

Fitzpatrick Manhattan Hotel

687 Lexington Ave between 55th and 56th Sts (355-0100, 1-800-367-7701; fax 308-5166). Subway: E, F, N, R to Lexington Ave; 6 to 59th St. Single $165–$265, double $165–$295, suite $195–$380. AmEx, DC, Disc, MC, V. Lest you miss the fact that this cheerful, family-run East Sider is New York's only Irish-owned hotel, there's a kelly-green carpet with a Book of Kells pattern in the lobby and a mat spelling out the day of the week in Gaelic in the elevator. The 92 rooms are decorated with matching floral bedspreads and curtains. Fitzer's, the hotel restaurant, serves rashers, bangers and soda bread (what else?) daily from 7am until 10:30pm, and high tea from 3pm to 5pm. Just don't plan to go on St. Patrick's Day; you'll never get in.
Hotel services Air-conditioning. Bar. Fax. Laundry. Restaurant. **Room services** Cable TV. Room service. Trouser press/ironing board.

Franklin Hotel

164 E 87th St between Third and Lexington Aves (369-1000, 1-800-600-8787; fax 369-8000). Subway: 4, 5, 6 to 86th St. $199–$219. AmEx, MC, V. Though nowhere near Seventh Avenue's garment district, the Franklin is a perpetual favorite of the fashion industry. The minimalist decor makes for a somewhat somber atmosphere, but the rates are reasonable, and there are amenities—free cappuccino and espresso, and cedar-lined closets. Rates include continental breakfast, a nightly dessert buffet and free on-site parking.
Hotel services Air-conditioning. Parking. CD and video library. Multilingual staff. **Room services** Cable TV. CD player. Hair dryer. VCR.

The Gorham New York

136 W 55th St between Sixth and Seventh Aves (245-1800, 1-800-735-0710; fax 582-8332). Subway: B, Q, N, R to 57th St; B, D, E to Seventh Ave. Single/double $195–$360, suite $225–$400. AmEx, DC, JCB, MC, V. The 120-room Gorham, opposite the City Center theater, has clocks over the front desk showing the hour everywhere from Paris to Tokyo. The lobby's marble floors, maple walls and slightly worn oriental carpets contribute to the rather European ambience. Rooms, though not luxurious, have been recently redecorated in a contemporary style. The kitchenettes in each are a definite plus for families.
Hotel services Air-conditioning. Baby-sitting. Bar. Parking. Conference facilities. Fax. Disabled: rooms. Fitness center. Laundry. Multilingual staff. Restaurant. **Room services** Cable TV. Hair dryer. Kitchenette with coffeemaker, tea and coffee. Mini-bar. Radio. Refrigerator. Room service. Safe. VCR on request.

Hotel Casablanca

147 W 43rd St between Sixth Ave and Broadway (869-1212, 1-888-9-CASABLANCA; fax 944-6223). Subway: N, R, S, 1, 2, 3, 9, 7 to 42nd St–Times Sq; B, D, F, Q to 42nd St. Single from $225, double from $245, suite from $325. AmEx, MC, V. A lovely little 48-room hotel in the theater district with a cheerful and welcoming Moroccan-style lobby. Rick's Café (get it?) is on the second floor, serving free wine and cheese on weeknights. A rooftop bar is set to open in fall 1998. The only major drawback is heavy construction on the massive new Condé Nast building across the street.
Hotel services Air-conditioning. Conference facilities. Disabled: rooms. Fax. Laundry. Multilingual staff. Restaurant. **Room services** Cable TV. Radio.

Hotel Wales

1295 Madison Ave at 92nd St (876-6000, 1-800-428-5252; fax 860-7000). Subway: 4, 5, 6 to 96th St. Single/double from $195, suite $245–$265. AmEx, MC, V. The Wales is a charming turn-of-the-century hotel in the attractive Carnegie Hill area, a few blocks from Museum Mile. The rooms aren't luxurious, but they're comfortable and quite spacious, with oak details and large windows. Complimentary afternoon tea is served in the Pied Piper Room, a Victorian parlor. Some suites overlook the Central Park reservoir.
Hotel services Air-conditioning. Parking. Disabled: access, rooms. Fax. Laundry. Multilingual staff. Restaurant. Video library. Also see Mansfield (below). **Room services** Cable TV. Hair dryer. Radio. Refrigerator in some rooms. Room service. Safe. VCR.

The Inn at Irving Place

56 Irving Pl between 17th and 18th Sts (533-4600, 1-800-685-1447; fax 533-4611). Subway: L, N, R, 4, 5, 6 to 14th St–Union Sq. Rates $275–$395. AmEx, DC, MC, V. For a bit of Victorian charm, book a room at this 19th-century townhouse near Gramercy Park. With only a dozen rooms, it's one of Manhattan's smallest inns and one of its most romantic. Instead of a front desk, there's a parlor with a blazing fireplace and an antique cart serving punch and sherry. Some rooms are quite small, but each has a fireplace and a four-poster bed. The Madame Wollenska suite has a pretty window seat. Rates include continental breakfast.

Hotel services Air-conditioning. **Room service.** Safe. Room services Cable TV. CD player. Hair dryer. Mini-bar. VCR.

Larchmont Hotel

27 W 11th St between Fifth and Sixth Aves (989-9333; fax 989-9496). Subway: 1, 9 to Christopher St–Sheridan Sq. Single $60–$70, double $85–$99. AmEx, DC, Disc, MC, V. This attractive, affordable newcomer is housed in a renovated 1910 Beaux Arts building on a quiet side street. Guests enter through a hallway adjacent to the lobby, making the place feel more like a private apartment. Some rooms are small, but all are cheerful and clean. Each is equipped with a washbasin, robe and slippers, although none has a private bath. Rates include continental breakfast.

Hotel services Air-conditioning. Fax. **Room services** Cable TV. Hair dryer.

The Lowell Hotel

28 E 63rd St between Park and Madison Aves (838-1400; fax 319-4230). Subway: N, R to Lexington Ave; 4, 5, 6 to 59th St. Single $325, double from $425, suite from $525–$1,800. AmEx, DC, Disc, MC, V. Renovated in 1997, the Lowell is a small, charming hotel in a landmark Art Deco building. Rooms boast Scandinavian comforters, Chinese porcelain and marble baths—there are even wood-burning fireplaces in the suites. The gym suite has lodged the likes of Madonna, Arnold Schwarzenegger and Michelle Pfeiffer.

Hotel services Air-conditioning. Baby-sitting. Bar. Cable TV. Currency exchange. Fitness center. Laundry. Multilingual staff. Restaurant. **Room services** Fax. Hair dryer. Mini-bar. PC ports. Radio. Refrigerator. Room service. VCR.

Mansfield

12 W 44th St between Fifth and Sixth Aves (944-6050, 1-800-255-5167; fax 764-4477). Subway: B, D, F, Q to 42nd St; 7 to Fifth Ave. Standard $209, deluxe $229, double $249, one-bedroom suite $279. AmEx, MC, V. Once a fashionable bachelors' residence, the Mansfield fell upon hard times until a boutique-hotel company rescued it a few years ago, uncovering the lobby's original white marble and spectacular ceilings. Halls are narrow, rooms are tiny, and there's enough silver mesh and ebony for a film noir. But many find the minimalist decor intriguing, and the suites are elegant. A cozy first-floor library hosts piano and harp recitals. (The other Gotham Hospitality Group inns—the Roger Williams, Shoreham and Wales hotels—also present live music and offer a free nightly dessert buffet.) Rates include continental breakfast.

Hotel services Air-conditioning. Parking. CD and video library. Multilingual staff. **Room services** Cable TV. CD player. Hair dryer. VCR.

The Roger Williams Hotel

131 Madison Ave at 31st St (448-7000, 1-888-448-7788; fax 448-7007). Subway: N, R, 6 to 28th St. Single/double $225–$245, suite from $375. AmEx, DC, MC, V. Striking 30-foot windows and fluted zinc columns soaring to the ceiling make for a striking use of light and space in this newly renovated hotel. The stylish lobby features a restored Steinway grand piano as well as unusual oil paintings and statues. Rooms have Shoji-style window screens, brushed stainless-steel lamps and maplewood headboards. Rate includes continental breakfast.

Hotel services Air-conditioning. CD and video library. Multilingual staff. Also see Mansfield (above). **Room services** Cable TV. CD player. Hair dryer. PC port. VCR.

Shoreham Hotel

33 W 55th St between Fifth and Sixth Aves (247-6700, 1-800-553-3347; fax 765-9741). Subway: B, Q to 57th St; E, F to Fifth Ave. Standard $245–$275, suite $295–$335. AmEx, DC, MC, V. The look is Deco moderne at this midtowner, with retro 1930s decor, marble floors, curvilinear ceilings, aluminum furniture in the Frank Lloyd Wright vein and alcoves of artfully arranged flowers. In fact, the whole place feels a bit like a wing of the Museum of Modern Art. Rooms are a decent size. Rates include continental breakfast.

Hotel services Air-conditioning. Complimentary passes to nearby health club. Multilingual staff. Valet parking. Also see Mansfield (above). **Room services** Cable TV. CD player. Hair dryer. Refrigerator. VCR.

Washington Square Hotel

103 Waverly Pl between Fifth and Sixth Aves (777-9515, 1-800-222-0418; fax 979-8373). Subway: A, C, E, B, D, F, Q to W 4th St–Washington Sq. Single $110, double $129, quad $159. Location, not luxury, is the key here. Both Bob Dylan and Joan Baez lived in this Greenwich Village hotel when they were street musicians singing for change just steps away in Washington Square Park. Rooms are no-frills, and hallways are so narrow that you practically open your door into the room opposite. Rates include breakfast at C3 (the bistro next door).

Hotel services Air-conditioning. Baby-sitting. Bar. Coffee shop. Conference facilities. Fax. Fitness center. Multilingual staff. Restaurant. **Room services** Hair dryer on request.

*Steel and magnolias: Fresh flowers enliven the Deco moderne lobby of the **Shoreham**.*

Name your fantasy

Some say you are where you sleep. These are the best hotels for...

ASPIRING WRITERS

History practically seeps from the walls of the **Algonquin**, a literary landmark where Dorothy Parker, James Thurber and other famous wits once gathered. Even the wallpaper is peppered with *New Yorker* cartoons. Or try the **Chelsea Hotel**, where Mark Twain, Thomas Wolfe and other novelists spent their more down-at-the-heels years. If you end up with writer's block, at least you can follow in Dylan Thomas's footsteps and stumble down to a nearby watering hole in the West Village to drown your sorrows.

BUDGET-MINDED BROADWAY FANS

Broadway Inn and the **Hotel Casablanca**, just off Broadway, are two of the theater district's few truly affordable options.

FOOD FANATICS

Who says hotel dining can't be fabulous? **The New York Palace**'s Le Cirque 2000 and **Trump International Hotel and Tower**'s Jean Georges rank among the top restaurants on every gourmet's list. **The Waldorf-Astoria**'s new Peacock Alley chef has also been drawing praise.

HISTORY LOVERS

The recently reopened **Roosevelt Hotel** is where Guy Lombardo broadcast "Auld Lang Syne" on many a New Year's Eve. Another good bet: **the Waldorf-Astoria**, a society favorite for decades, where the lost-and-found department has turned up items like Sophia Loren's eyeglasses, Cary Grant's X rays and Matt Dillon's barbells.

KILLER VIEWS

The **Millennium Hilton** offers unparalleled vistas of New York Harbor and the Brooklyn Bridge from the upper floors. If you're not lucky enough to land a room with a view, just head to the rooftop pool. The elegant **Four Seasons Hotel** on 57th Street also offers breathtaking views.

ART BUFFS

The restored **Hotel Wales** is a historic charmer and an easy stroll from Museum Mile on upper Fifth Avenue. **The Mark** is also popular, thanks to its proximity to major museums like the Met, the Whitney and the Guggenheim. If you'd rather stay downtown, try the **SoHo Grand Hotel**, a stone's throw from New York's trendiest art galleries.

MUSIC AFICIONADOS

The Carlyle's Cafe Carlyle is where Woody Allen plays jazz on Monday nights, Eartha Kitt and Dixie Carter are frequent performers, and gravel-voiced crooner Bobby Short is in his 30th year. You can also hang out in Bemelmans Bar across the lobby and enjoy live piano music for free. Classical-music fans won't want to miss the **Radisson Empire**, across the street from the operas and symphonies of Lincoln Center.

ROCK & ROLLERS

The eccentric **Hotel 17**, where Madonna and David Bowie have done photo shoots, is home to many up-and-coming rockers. At the **Washington Square Hotel** you can retrace the steps of Bob Dylan and Joan Baez, both of whom stayed here and played for pennies in nearby Washington Square Park before hitting the big time.

SHOPAHOLICS

Strategically placed for a visit to Fifth and Madison Avenues' finest stores, **the Plaza Hotel** is perfect for a shopping spree. And if you're a generous parent, F.A.O. Schwarz is just across the street.

SPORTS FANS

The **Southgate Tower Hotel** is nothing special, but it's directly across the street from Madison Square Garden and close to all the bars offering pregame drink and dinner specials.

Hotel services Air-conditioning. Coffee shop. Fax. Multilingual staff. **Room services** Radio. Room service. TV. Voice mail.

Ramada Milford Plaza Hotel

270 W 45th St at Eighth Ave (869-3600, 1-800-2RAMADA; fax 944-8357). Subway: A, C, E to 42nd St; N, R, S, 1, 2, 3, 9, 7 to 42nd St–Times Sq. Single $109–$179, double $124–$195. AmEx, Disc, JCB, MC, V. The dismal shopping-mall lobby, with its fluorescent lighting and lack of decor, makes this enormous theater-district hotel anything but welcoming. Still, as the ads used to say, it *is* in the center of it all, close to the Broadway shows and Restaurant Row. There's very visible 24-hour security and, thanks to an influx of new upscale coffeehouses and shops, this stretch of Eighth Avenue is much more visitor-friendly than it was in past years. Recently added: an international-telephone room.
Hotel services Air-conditioning. Bar. Beauty salon. Conference facilities. Disabled: access. Fax. Fitness center. Laundry. Multilingual staff. Parking. Restaurant. Tour/transportation desk. **Room services** Cable TV. Radio.

Southgate Tower Hotel

371 Seventh Ave at 31st St (563-1800, 1-800-637-8483; fax 643-8028). Subway A, C, E, 1, 2, 3, 9 to 34th St–Penn Sta-

tion. *Studio suite $139, one-bedroom suite $399. AmEx, DC, Disc, JCB, MC, V.* Popular with conference-goers headed for the Javits Convention Center nearby, the Southgate Tower has been completely renovated. Some of the suites are positively enormous. Kitchens contain toasters, filter coffee machines and microwaves, and there's also room service until midnight. Although not in the most scenic part of town, the hotel is conveniently located directly across the street from Madison Square Garden and just a few blocks from Macy's.
Hotel services Air-conditioning. Bar. Conference facilities. Currency exchange. Parking. Disabled: rooms. Drugstore. Fax. Fitness center. Laundry. Multilingual staff. Restaurants. **Room services** Cable TV. Hair dryer on request. Microwave. Radio. Refrigerator. Room service. Toasters. VCR on request.

The Wolcott Hotel

4 W 31st St between Broadway and Fifth Ave (268-2900; fax 563-0096). Internet: www.wolcott.com. Subway: B, D, F, Q, N, R to 34th St. Single/double $65 with shared bath, $120 with private bath; suite $150. AmEx, JCB, MC, V. The ornate gilded lobby comes as a surprise in this garment-district hotel. Rooms are small but inexpensive .
Hotel services Air-conditioning. Bar. Fax. Laundry. Multilingual staff. **Room services** Cable TV.

Wyndham Hotel

42 W 58th St between Fifth and Sixth Aves (753-3500, 1-800-257-111; fax 754-5638). Subway: N, R to Fifth Ave; B, Q to 57th St. Single $125–$140, double $140–$155, suite $180–$225. AmEx, CB, DC, MC, V. Popular with actors and directors, the Wyndham has generous rooms and suites with walk-in closets. The decor is a little worn, but homey. This is a good midtown location—you can walk to the Museum of Modern Art, Fifth Avenue shopping and many of the Broadway theaters—and it's well priced, so book well ahead.
Hotel services Air-conditioning. Bar. Disabled: rooms. Fax. Multilingual staff. Restaurant. **Room services** Cable TV. Hair dryer on request. Radio.

Budget

The Gershwin Hotel

7 E 27th St between Fifth and Madison Aves (545-8000; fax 684-5546). Internet: www.homenet.com/gershwin. Subway: N, R, 6 to 28th St. $25 per person in four- to eight-bed dorms, $89–$129 for one to three people in private rooms. MC, V. The colorful, bohemian Gershwin offers extremely reasonable accommodation just off Fifth Avenue. It pays homage to Pop Art with Roy Lichtenstein posters, a signed Andy Warhol Campbell's Soup can, and gigantic, colorful sculptures on the walls. The rooms are spartan but clean; the bathrooms are decorated with Mondrianesque tile. The ambience is definitely no-frills, with lots of student types playing pool beneath the enormous carved 1908 fireplace in the TV room. Check out the pseudo-psychedelic bar across from the lobby.
Hotel services Bars. Fax. Lockers. Multilingual staff. Public telephones. Restaurant. Roof garden. Transportation desk. **Room services** TV in private rooms.

The Herald Square Hotel

19 W 31st St between Fifth Ave and Broadway (279-4017, 1-800-727-1888; fax 643-9208). Subway: B, D, F, Q, N, R to 34th St; 1, 2, 3, 9 to 34th St–Penn Station. Single $50 with shared bath, $95 with private bath; double $105; triple $115; quad $125. AmEx, Disc, JCB, MC, V. Herald Square was the original *Life* magazine building, and it retains its charming cherub-adorned entrance. All rooms were recently renovated and most have private bathrooms; corridors are filled with framed *Life* illustrations. It's near Macy's and the Empire State Building, and it's a good deal, so book well in advance. There are discounts for students.

Hotel services Air-conditioning. Fax. Multilingual staff. **Room services** Cable TV. Radio. Safe.

Malibu Studios Hotel

2688 Broadway at 103rd St (222-2954, 1-800-647-2227; fax 678-6842). Subway: 1, 9 to 103rd St. Single with private bath from $79, with shared bath $45; double with private bath from $89, with shared bath $59. Cash or traveler's checks only. Rooms are neat and clean, and Malibu has some surprising amenities—even chocolates on check-in. Free passes to local nightclubs are often available. Far from the traditional tourist sights around Times Square, this Upper West Side offers visitors a chance to live like a local in a primarily residential neighborhood near Riverside Park and not far from Columbia University. The neighborhood is generally safe, but it can get a bit dicey after dark.
Hotel services Air-conditioning. Concierge. Fax. Nonsmoking rooms. Agreements with local gyms. **Room services** Cable TV. CD player. Clock radio. Iron and ironing board.

Murray Hill Inn

143 E 30th St between Third and Lexington Aves (683-6900, 1-888-996-6376; fax 545-0103). Subway: 6 to 28th St. Single from $65, double from $85. Cash or traveler's checks only. Tucked away on a quiet, tree-lined street in midtown within walking distance of the Empire State Building and Grand Central Terminal, this recently opened 50-room inn offers good value for the price. Rooms are basic, but neat and clean. All have sinks, though baths are shared.
Hotel services Air-conditioning. Concierge. Fax. Message center. Multilingual staff. **Room service** TV.

Off-Soho Suites Hotel

11 Rivington St between Christie St and the Bowery (979-9808, 1-800-633-7646; fax 979-9801). Subway: B, D, Q to Grand St. Single suite $97.50, suite for two $169. AmEx, MC, V. Off-Soho is an excellent value for suite accommodation, but the Lower East Side location might not suit everyone. If you're into clubbing, bars and the Soho scene, this spot is perfect—but take a cab back at night. All suites are well sized, clean and bright, with a fully equipped kitchen and polished wooden floors. There's a café on the ground floor by the lobby.
Hotel services Air-conditioning. Café. Disabled: rooms. Fax. Fitness room. Laundry. Multilingual staff. Parking. **Room services** Hair dryer. Microwave. Refrigerator. Room service. TV.

Riverside Towers Hotel

80 Riverside Dr at 80th St (877-5200, 1-800-724-3136; fax 873-1400). Subway: 1, 9 to 79th St. Single $75, double $80, suite $90–$115. AmEx, MC, V. The Riverside has a good price for the Upper West Side and is the only hotel in Manhattan located on the Hudson River. The views are fine, but accommodation is basic: This is strictly a place to sleep. The wonderful Zabar's deli is around the corner on Broadway.
Hotel services Air-conditioning. Fax. Laundry. Multilingual staff. **Room services** Hair dryer on request. Refrigerator. TV.

Hostels

Chelsea Center

313 W 29th St between Eighth and Ninth Aves (643-0214; fax 473-3945). Subway: A, C, E to 34th St–Penn Station. $23 per person in dorm, including linen. No credit cards. This is a small, friendly hostel with clean bathrooms and a patio garden at the back. It has the feel of a shared house. Since there's a limited number of beds in each dorm, book at least a week in advance. There's no curfew, and the price includes continental breakfast.
Hotel services All rooms nonsmoking. Fax. Garden patio. Kitchen facilities. Multilingual staff. TV room.

Hosteling International New York

*891 Amsterdam Ave at 103rd St (932-2300; fax 932-2574).
Internet: www.hostelling.com. Subway: 1, 9 to 103rd St. $24 per
person in dorm sleeping 10–12 people; $25 in dorm sleeping
6–8; $27 in room sleeping 4; $3 extra for nonmembers; $75
family room; $100 private room with bath. MC, V.* This 500-bed
hostel was formerly a residence for elderly women. It was recently renovated to include a new coffee bar with CD jukebox.
Rooms are basic but clean, the staff is friendly, and there's a garden in the back. Off-season rates (November to April) are lower.
Hotel services Air-conditioning. All rooms nonsmoking.
Café. Conference facilities. Fax. Garden. Laundry. Lockers.
Multilingual staff. Travel bureau. TV lounge and game room.

International House

*500 Riverside Dr at 125th St (316-6300; fax 316-8415). Sub-
way: 1, 9 to 125th St. Single $95, double/suite $115. MC, V.*
This hostel is in a peaceful location, surrounded by college
buildings and overlooking the small but well-tended Sakura
Park. There's a subsidized cafeteria with main dishes at
around $3 and a delightful living room and terrace overlook-
ing the park. Only the suites have a private bathroom. Summer is by far the best time to book, since during the academic
year International House is filled with foreign graduate students and visiting scholars. Summer single rates drop as low
as $40. Be warned that though the area immediately around
Columbia University is generally safe, you might not want to
stroll far after dark if you don't know the neighborhood.
Hotel services Air-conditioning in suites. Bar. Cafeteria.
Conference facilities. Fax. Game room. Gymnasium. Laundry. Multilingual staff. TV room.

YMCA (Vanderbilt)

*224 E 47th St between Second and Third Aves (756-9600;
fax 752-0210). Subway: S, 4, 5, 6, 7 to Grand Central. Single $55, double $68, suite $110. MC, V.* This cheerful,
standard YMCA was completely renovated in 1992. The
more expensive rooms have sinks, but they're not very large;
the beds can barely fit in some rooms. Book well in advance
by writing to the reservations department and including a
deposit for one night's rent. There are about 377 rooms, but
only the executive suites have private baths.
Hotel services Air-conditioning. Conference facilities. Fax.
Disabled: rooms. Gift shop. Laundry. Left luggage room. Multilingual staff. Restaurant. Sports and fitness facilities.
Room services All rooms nonsmoking. Cable TV. Radio.
Refrigerator on request. Room service.

YMCA (West Side)

*5 W 63rd St between Central Park West and Broadway (787-
4400; fax 875-1334). Subway: A, C, B, D, 1, 9 to 59th St–
Columbus Circle. Single $59, $85 with bath; double $69, $95
with bath. MC, V.* A large, echoing building close to Central
Park and Lincoln Center, this Y has rooms that are simple and
clean. Book well in advance. A deposit is required to hold a
reservation. Most of the 540 rooms have shared bathrooms.
Hotel services Air-conditioning. Cafeteria. Disabled:
rooms. Fax. Laundry. Multilingual staff. Sports and fitness
facilities. **Room services** Cable TV.

YMHA (de Hirsch Residence at the 92nd St Y)

*1395 Lexington Ave at 92nd St (415-5650, 1-800-858-
4692; fax 415-5578). Subway: 4, 5, 6 to 96th St. For stays less
than two months $53 nightly, single occupancy; $38 nightly,
double occupancy; for stays greater than two months $575 a
month with shared bath, $715 a month for private rooms.
AmEx, MC, V.* The Young Men's Hebrew Association is
rather like its Christian counterpart, the YMCA, in that to stay
there you don't have to be young, male or—in this case—Jewish. The dorm-style rooms are spacious and clean, with two
desks and plenty of closet space. There are kitchen and dining
facilities on each floor. The YMHA is good for tours, lectures
and classes, and the Upper East Side location is a bonus.

Hotel services Air-conditioning (extra charge). Disabled:
rooms. Fitness center. Laundry. Library. Multilingual staff.
TV lounge. **Room services** Refrigerator on request.

Bed and breakfast

New York's bed-and-breakfast scene is deceptively
large. There are thousands of beds available, but
since there isn't a central B&B organization, rooms
may be hard to find. Many of the rooms are unhosted, and breakfast is usually continental (if it exists
at all). The main difference from a hotel is in the
more personal ambiance. Prices are not necessarily
low, but B&Bs are a good way to feel less like a
tourist and more like a New Yorker. Sales tax of 8.25
percent is payable on hosted bed-and-breakfast
rooms, but not on unhosted apartments if you're
staying for more than seven days. It's always a good
idea to ask about decor, location and amenities
when booking and, if safety is a concern, whether
the building has a 24-hour doorman. One caveat:
Last-minute changes can be costly; some agencies
charge guests for a night's stay if they cancel reservations less than 10 days before arriving.

At Home in New York

*P.O. Box 407, New York, NY 10185 (956-3125, 1-800-692-
4262; fax 247-3294; private number, please call Mon–Fri
10am-5pm; e-mail: athomeny@starpass.net). Hosted single from $60, hosted double from $85, unhosted studio
from $100. AmEx, MC, V.* This agency has reasonably
priced accommodations in about 300 properties; most of
them are in Manhattan, a few in Brooklyn. The minimum
stay is two nights.

Bed & Breakfast (& Books)

*35 W 92nd St, apartment 2C, New York, NY 10025 (865-
8740 phone and fax; please call Mon–Fri 10am–5pm). Hosted single $60–$100, hosted double $80–$110, unhosted
studio $110–$140. No credit cards (though AmEx, DC, Disc,
MC, V, can be used to guarantee room).* Several of the hosts in
this organization are literary types, hence the bookish title.
There are 40 hosted and unhosted rooms; two-bedroom
apartments cost $200 and up.

Bed and Breakfast in Manhattan

*P.O. Box 533, New York, NY 10150 (472-2528; fax 988-9818).
Hosted $95–$105, unhosted from $100. No credit cards.* Each
of this organization's 100 or so properties has been personal-
ly inspected by the owner, who also helps travelers select a
B&B in the neighborhood best suited to their interests.

City Lights Bed & Breakfast

*P.O. Box 20355, Cherokee Station, New York, NY 10021 (737-
7049; fax 535-2755). Hosted single $85–$95 with private bathroom, $75–$85 with shared bath; hosted double $85–$115 with
private bathroom, $75–$95 with shared bath; unhosted apartments $115–$300. DC, MC, V.* This helpful agency lists 300 to
400 properties in Manhattan and Brooklyn. A two-night minimum stay and a 25-percent deposit are required.

New World Bed & Breakfast

*150 Fifth Ave, suite 711, New York, NY 10011 (675-5600;
fax 675-6366). Hosted single $75, hosted double $90, unhosted studio from $110, unhosted one-bedroom apartment from
$130. AmEx, DC, MC, V.* Accommodations can be arranged
in most Manhattan neighborhoods. Hosted apartments include continental breakfast. There are reduced rates for
monthly stays. Larger apartments are also available.

You want fries with that? Les Deux Gamins offers French bistro food, Village-style.

Eating & Drinking

Restaurants

Chow, Manhattan: When you savor New York, you taste the whole world

Listen to New Yorkers talk about the restaurants they love. You'll hear something more than just individual taste and habit, or civic pride. Like everything else in this city, dining out is part spectacle and sport, part protected solace. More so than in most cities, restaurants are central to everyday life here. New Yorkers wear a good deal on their sleeves—mainly because they don't have room in their closets at home— and where you eat has a lot to do with how you like, or can afford, to live. Everyone eats out occasionally; some people do it all the time. To satisfy this voracity there is, famously, all manner of eating to be done in New York: The renowned hot dog competes for attention with the rarefied talents of the best chefs on the planet. Papaya King for lunch, Daniel for dinner.

Newcomers immediately adopt restaurants as their own, and even born-and-bred New Yorkers are forever updating their lists as tastes and neighborhoods change. The one rule to enjoyment is to embrace the vastness: the authentic Greek grill in Astoria; the intensely hip downtown spot, whose star will burn out before you have time to tell friends about it; and the midtown joint that somehow escaped the wrecking ball and is still serving meat to old men who ate there when they were young. New York is a city of unparalleled contrasts, and the best way to experience it is to eat out.

It can be as hard as ever to get a table in a place that's hot, but it's also a good idea to call ahead and check if the place that was sizzling last week is still in business. To snare a table at one of the city's premier eateries, you'll often need to reserve weeks in advance. Many smaller restaurants and bistros prefer to operate on a first-come, first-served basis, and you may have to wait at the bar. Book ahead,

Happy campers: The garden tent at **Rialto** is a hot spot for fashionable Nolita diners.

when possible, at all the restaurants listed in the **Celebrated chefs, Landmark restaurants** and **Contemporary American** sections below. Check the handy pocket Zagat Survey ($11.95) for a comprehensive yearly overview of the best places, and peruse the food columns of *The New York Times* and *New York*. The listings in the Eat Out section of *Time Out New York* are more up-to-date than any annual guide to such a frenetic and constantly changing scene could hope to be; also keep an eye out for the *Time Out New York Eating & Drinking Guide*.

During the first weeks of July, the city proclaims Restaurant Week, when some of its finest establishments offer a prix-fixe lunch, which in 1999 will cost $19.99 (most restaurants run the special throughout the summer). It's a great way to sample the talents of chefs who are otherwise unaffordable. Needless to say, you should make reservations well in advance.

Few New York restaurants add a service charge to your bill, but it is customary to double the 8.25-percent local sales tax as a tip. Many small places accept cash only, and some cards—AmEx, Visa and Mastercard—are more welcome than others. Ask before you sit down.

As in every other financial transaction in the Big Apple, restaurant customers complain vociferously if they feel that they're not getting a fair deal. Don't be afraid of offending your waiter by moaning, but never withhold a tip.

Prices indicate the average cost of a main course at dinner, unless specified.

Celebrated chefs

An American Place

2 *Park Ave at 32nd St (684-2122). Subway: 6 to 33rd St. Mon–Fri 11:45am–3pm (lunch). Mon–Sat 5:30–10pm (dinner). Average main course $30. AmEx, CB, DC, Disc, MC, V.* Larry Forgione has expanded his business into a line of jams and a downtown restaurant, **the Grill Room** (945-9400), but the Place is still the spot to taste the talents of the godfather of new American cuisine. The patriotic premise at this grand, Deco-style Park Avenue institution is that produce, wine and inspiration need not come from anywhere but home.

Arcadia

21 *E 62nd St between Madison and Fifth Aves (223-2900). Subway: 4, 5, 6 to 59th St; N, R to Lexington Ave. Mon–Sat noon–2:30pm (lunch). Mon–Thu 6–10pm; Fri, Sat 6– 10:30pm (dinner). Three-course prix-fixe $58. AmEx, DC, MC, V.* Recognized as one of the country's finest woman chefs, Anne Rosenzweig turns out American haute cuisine in a lovely townhouse setting. For a slightly more relaxed vibe, try her **Lobster Club** restaurant (249-6500) and its sublime namesake dish.

Aureole

34 *E 61st St between Madison and Park Aves (319-1660). Subway: 4, 5, 6 to 59th St; N, R to Lexington Ave. Mon–Fri noon–2:30pm (lunch). Mon–Sat 5:30–11pm (dinner). Four-course prix-fixe $65. AmEx, Disc, MC, V.* Charles Palmer has created a small but formidable gastronomic empire that in-cludes four restaurants—Aureole, **Lenox Room** (772-0404), **Alva** (228-4399) and **Astra** (644-9394)—and a partnership in the rustic Egg Farm Dairy. The smooth and sedate Aureole and Lenox Room feature elegant contemporary American cuisine; Astra is a midtown lunch oasis; and the more afford-able Alva specializes in sophisticated home-style American cooking in a noirish bar setting.

Bouley Bakery

120 *West Broadway at Duane St (964-2525). Subway: 1, 9 to Franklin St. 11am–3pm (lunch). Mon–Sat 5–11pm, Sun 5–11pm (dinner). Average main course $32. AmEx, Disc, MC, V.* One of *People* magazine's "50 Sexiest People," uber-chef David Bouley is biding his time with this charming, 12-table bakery-restaurant while preparing to unveil a cooking school, an Austrian eatery and his flagship French restau-rant. As for the bakery, don't let the name fool you: Both the food and the prices are very upscale.

Chanterelle

2 *Harrison St at Hudson St (966-6960). Subway: 1, 9 to Franklin St. Tue–Sat noon–2:30pm (lunch). Mon–Sat 5:30–11pm (dinner). Prix-fixe lunch $35. Prix-fixe dinners $75, $89. AmEx, Disc, MC, V.* Karen and David Waltuck's elegant but spare space in Tribeca's landmark Mercantile Exchange Building mirrors the restaurant's refined cuisine. If you want architectural fusion creations, go elsewhere, but if you want immaculately prepared modern takes on classic French dishes, such as grilled sea bass or tender rack of lamb, come to Chanterelle.

Felidia

243 *E 58th St between Second and Third Aves (758-1479). Subway: N, R to Lexington Ave; 4, 5, 6 to 59th St. Mon–Fri noon–3pm (lunch). Mon–Thu 5–11pm; Fri, Sat 5–11:30pm (dinner). Average main course $28. AmEx, Disc, MC, V.* Lidia Bastianich is considered the mother of authentic Ital-ian restaurant cuisine in New York. At her flagship restau-rant— and her more affordable projects, **Becco** (397-7597) and **Frico Bar** (564-7272)—the menu of hearty dishes is pre-dominantly northern Italian; the recipes were handed down by her Istrian grandmother.

Gotham Bar and Grill

12 *E 12th St between University Pl and Fifth Ave (620-4020). Subway: L, N, R, 4, 5, 6 to 14th St–Union Sq. Mon–Fri 11:30am–2:30pm (lunch). Sun–Thu 5:30–10pm; Fri, Sat 5:30–11pm (dinner). Average main course $29. AmEx, Disc, MC, V.* Crispy sweetbreads, towering seafood salad, deadly choco-late bread pudding—Gotham's acclaimed take on the Ameri-can oeuvre is neither meek nor limited to steak and potatoes. Alfred Portale's tall concoctions have been imitated all over town, but nothing tastes as good as the real thing.

Jean Georges

Trump International Hotel, 1 Central Park West between 59th and 60th Sts (299-3900). Subway: A, C, B, D, 1, 9 to 59th St–Columbus Circle. Mon–Fri 6:30–10am, Sat 6:30am–noon, Sun 8am–3pm (breakfast). Mon–Fri noon–2:30pm (lunch). Mon–Sat 5:30–11pm, Sun 5:30–9:30pm (dinner). Average main course $35. AmEx, MC, V. Alsace-born Jean-Georges Vongerichten pulls out all the stops in his immaculate self-named restaurant. He strikes a star-tling contrast with the sleek, spare setting by serving emi-nently creative food in traditional French fashion, complete with tableside trolleys and silver dish hoods. To appreciate the breadth of his skills, also try his Asian fu-sion fare at **Vong** (486-9592) and his sophisticated bistro cuisine at **Jo Jo** (223-5656).

Mesa Grill

102 *Fifth Ave between 15th and 16th Sts (807-7400). Subway: F to 14th St. Mon–Fri noon–2:30pm; Sat, Sun 11:30am–3pm (lunch). 5:30–10:30pm (dinner). Average*

main course $25. AmEx, Disc, MC, V. Thanks to his imaginative use of traditional Southwestern ingredients (such as blue corn and jalapeños), chef Bobby Flay continues to keep Mesa Grill—and the newer **Mesa City** (207-1919) on the short list of perennially popular Manhattan restaurants. Large parties and couples alike will find this high-ceilinged, colorful restaurant inviting and memorable.

Nobu

105 Hudson St at Franklin St (219-0500). Subway: 1, 9 to Franklin St. Mon–Fri 11:45am–2:15pm (lunch). 5:45–10:15pm (dinner). Average main course $18. AmEx, Disc, MC, V. The original Nobu is still packed nightly with high-powered New Yorkers and Hollywood honchos (friends of partner Robert De Niro's). Welcome the chance to pay through the nose for one of Nobu Matsuhisa's masterful tasting menus, and forget about being satisfied by any lesser sushi ever again.

Patria

250 Park Ave South at 20th St (777-6211). Subway: 6 to 23rd St. Mon–Fri noon–2:45pm (lunch). Mon–Thu 6–11pm; Fri, Sat 5:30pm–midnight; Sun 5:30–10:30pm (dinner). Average main course $24. AmEx, DC, MC, V. Park Avenue South's restaurant canyon keeps expanding, but the crowds haven't diminished at Patria. They come for the wild nuevo-Latino inventions of chef Douglas Rodriguez: fish and fruit fusion, assorted seafood *ceviches*, chocolate "cigars"—all in swinging, split-level surroundings.

Daniel

60 E 65th St between Madison and Park Aves (288-0033). Subway: 6 to 68th St. Due to open in December 1998. Average main course $35. AmEx, DC, MC, V. A native of Lyon, chef Daniel Boulud has won critical acclaim for his virtuoso's ability to elevate classic peasant dishes to haute cuisine. Because of his skill, Daniel is revered as one of the country's finest French restaurants, and that made reservations difficult to come by in his 76th Street space, which closed in August. Happily, the restaurant is due to reopen soon in larger quarters (actually, the renovated former site of Le Cirque, where Boulud used to work). Call to check hours.

Landmark restaurants

'21'

21 W 52nd St between Fifth and Sixth Aves (582-7200). Subway: B, D, F, Q to 47th–50th Sts–Rockefeller Ctr. Mon–Fri noon–2:30pm (lunch). Mon–Thu 5:30–10pm; Fri, Sat 5:30–11:15pm (dinner). Average main course $35. AmEx, MC, V. The unofficial mess hall of capitalism and hallowed haunt of old-boydom has a new chef and a few nouveau infiltrators, like Hawaiian snapper tartare with papaya and mango. But toys still hang from the low ceiling, and you can still order chicken hash and the famous burger, which is the size and weight of a newborn. The other traditions of this former speakeasy—the money chatter, swank and cheer—remain as present as the smell of well-prepared sirloin.

Café des Artistes

1 W 67th St between Columbus Ave and Central Park West (877-3500). Subway: 1, 9 to 66th St–Lincoln Ctr. Sat 11am–2:45pm, Sun 10am–2:45pm (brunch). Mon–Fri noon–3pm (lunch). Mon–Sat 5:30–11:45pm, Sun 5:30–10:45pm (dinner). Average main course $21. Prix-fixe lunch $19.50, prix-fixe dinner $39.95. AmEx, DC, MC, V. Jackets are mandatory at this Upper West Side holdout, where you'll eat amid murals of frolicking naked nymphs and couples who have come to dine at what's considered one of the most romantic restaurants in New York. Prices are high, but you'll find plenty of pleasant choices on the continental menu, including roast duckling and sturgeon schnitzel.

Four Seasons

99 E 52nd St between Park and Lexington Aves (754-9494). Subway: 6 to 51st St. Mon–Fri noon–2:30pm (lunch). Mon–Fri 5–9:30pm, Sat 5–11pm (dinner). Average main course $39. AmEx, DC, Disc, JCB, MC, V. The only restaurant in Manhattan to have been granted official landmark status, the 39-year-old, Philip Johnson–designed Four Seasons plays host to power-lunching publishing execs by day and free-spending tourists at night. The tycoons gather in the manly Grill Room amid plenty of leather and steel, while civilians repair to the Pool Room, home to an impressive modern art collection and a large illuminated pool.

The Oyster Bar

Grand Central Station lower level, 42nd St and Park Ave (490-6650). Subway: S, 4, 5, 6, 7 to 42nd St–Grand Central. Mon–Fri 11:30am–9:30pm. Average main course $25. AmEx, Disc, DC, MC, V. Back to its original splendor after suffering a fire in 1997, this Grand Central Station institution serves fine, straightforward seafood under sloping vaulted ceilings. The Oyster Bar can be noisy and pricey (oysters Rockefeller, $14.95), but no experience is more placid and dignified than stopping here after the early dinner rush to be alone with a plate of perfect half shells on ice.

Rainbow Room

30 Rockefeller Plaza, 49th St between Fifth and Sixth Aves (632-5000). Subway: B, D, F, Q to 47th–50th Sts–Rockefeller Ctr. Tue–Thu 5–11pm; Fri, Sat 6–11:30pm; Sun 6–9pm. Average main course $35. AmEx, MC, V. Chef Waldy Malouf has reinvigorated this timeless jewel at the top of 30 Rock by adding contemporary dishes and bringing back favorites such as lobster thermidor and baked Alaska. Dress to kill and dance to big bands and mambo music while enjoying the restaurant's breathtaking view and Art Deco trappings.

Tavern on the Green

W 67th St at Central Park West (873-3200). Subway: 1, 9 to 66th St–Lincoln Ctr. Sat, Sun 10:30am–3:30pm (brunch). Mon–Fri 11:30am–3:30pm (lunch). 5:30–10:45pm (dinner). Average main course $28. AmEx, Disc, MC, V. Tavern on the Green is one of the prettiest places in the city—think Christmas lights year-round and chandeliers dripping with crystal. The food is notoriously average, no doubt due to the restaurant's enormous size (1,500 meals are served here per night), but the fairy-tale setting is enchanting and romantic. To complete the effect, take a horse-drawn carriage home through the park.

Windows on the World

1 World Trade Center, West St between Liberty and Vesey Sts, 107th floor (938-1111). Subway: C, E to World Trade Ctr. Sun 11am–3pm (brunch). Mon–Fri noon–2pm (lunch at bar). Mon–Thu 5–9pm; Fri, Sat 5–10:30pm (dinner). Average main course $30. AmEx, DC, Disc, MC, V. Thanks to former '21' chef Michael Lomonaco, Windows finally has food to match its spectacular view. Not that most New Yorkers would know. Perched atop the World Trade Center, the restaurant caters mostly to European tourists who don't mind the bill vertigo and hotel–dining-room decor. Still, there's no knocking the heavenly panorama.

Contemporary American

First

87 First Ave between 5th and 6th Sts (674-3823). Subway: 6 to Astor Pl. Sun 4pm–1am, Mon–Thu 6pm–2am; Fri, Sat 6pm–3am (dinner). Average main course $15. AmEx, MC, V. You can be fairly certain of two things after dining at First: You will be both drunk and full. Order a round of teeny-weeny martinis (served on a mound of ice in glass beakers) and then indulge in Sammy DeMarco's creative, stick-to-

Triple play: Chef Jean-Georges Vongerichten works his magic at **Jean Georges**, **Vong** *and* **Jo Jo**.

your-ribs food. Hang around the mod-Gothic dining room long enough, and you'll spot many of the city's best chefs stopping by for a late-night snack.

Gramercy Tavern

42 E 20th St between Broadway and Park Ave South (477-0777). Subway: 6 to 23rd St. Restaurant: noon–2pm (lunch). Sun–Thu 5–10pm; Fri, Sat 5:30–11pm (dinner). Three-course prix-fixe dinner $58. Tavern: Sun–Thu noon–11pm; Fri, Sat noon–midnight. AmEx, DC, MC, V. Visitors have several inviting options at this Flatiron mecca, a younger sibling of the ever-popular **Union Square Café** (243-4020). The innovative prix-fixe menu is offered only in the elegant dining room. If you're more budget-minded or want to show up on impulse, grab a table or a seat at the bar in the front tavern area, where delightful dishes are also served.

Indigo

142 W 10th St between Greenwich Ave and Waverly Pl (691-7757). Subway: 1, 2, 3, 9 to 14th St. Mon–Thu 6–11pm; Fri, Sat 6–11:30pm, Sun 6–10:30pm (dinner). Average main course $14. AmEx. Indigo serves delicious French-American cuisine by Scott Bryan, the chef at **Luma** (633-8033). West Villagers love the bold dishes—like wild mushroom strudel and roast pork loin—and the affordable prices.

Liam

170 Thompson St between Bleecker and Houston Sts (387-0666). Subway: 1, 9 to Houston St. Tue–Thu 6–11pm; Fri, Sat 6–11:30pm, Sun 5:30–10pm. Average main course $15.

AmEx. You will not find better cooking at mid-level prices than at this year-old bistro. Chef William Prunty (formerly of Jean Claude and Soho Steak) prepares intensely flavored food that is as attractive as it is delicious. With such dishes as pureed potato–and–mascarpone ravioli in a foie-gras broth, Liam attracts both middle-aged parents and downtown hipsters.

Max & Moritz

426A Seventh Ave between 14th and 15th Sts, Park Slope, Brooklyn (1-718-499-5557). Subway: F to Seventh Ave–Park Slope. Mon–Fri 5:30–11pm; Sat, Sun 11am–11pm. Average main course $13. AmEx, MC, V. The pride of Park Slope, this stylish yet relaxed bistro has won a devoted clientele with its exceptional comfort fare, from warm goat-cheese cake to roasted monkfish with spinach puree. In Manhattan, such choices would run $30 an entrée—and you wouldn't be able to get in anyway.

Restaurant Boughalem

14 Bedford St between Sixth Ave and Downing St (414-4764). Subway: 1, 9 to Houston St. Tue–Sun 6pm–midnight. Average main course $16. Cash only. If Martha Stewart were to open a bistro, it might look something like Boughalem: glossy white walls, candlelit tables and bouquets of narcissus, and a location on one of the West Village's most precious streets. The menu won't throw you many curves (filet mignon, seared sea scallops, etc.), but Boughalem's charm is undeniable.

Rialto

265 Elizabeth St between Houston and Prince Sts (334-7900). Subway: B, D, F, Q to Broadway–Lafayette St. 11am–1am. Average main course $14. AmEx, DC, MC, V. With curvy red banquettes that look like they spun off a Tilt-a-Whirl, a magnificent back garden and a sardonic staff, Rialto is a bistro with some bite. Expect a beautiful (and noisy) clientele, but don't expect food for waifs: Rialto's chicken-fried pork chops and creamy garlic soup will help you fill out your leather pants.

The River Café

1 Water St at Cadman Plaza West, Brooklyn (1-718-522-5200). Subway: A, C to High St. Mon–Fri noon–2:30pm (lunch), Mon–Sun 6–11pm (dinner), Sun 11:30am–2:30pm (brunch). Three-course prix-fixe dinner $68. AmEx, DC, MC, V. The irony of Manhattan's awe-inspiring skyline is that you have to leave it in order to enjoy it. Hop across the Brooklyn Bridge to this romantic restaurant abutting the East River. In winter, ask for a window table; in summer, enjoy American cuisine in open air, with the lights of the Brooklyn Bridge and of the looming metropolis shining on your table.

Verbena

54 Irving Pl between 17th and 18th Sts (260-5454). Subway: L, N, R, 4, 5, 6 to 14th St–Union Sq. Sat, Sun noon–2:45pm (lunch). Mon 5:30–10pm, Tue–Thu 5:30–10:30pm; Fri, Sat 5:30–11pm, Sun 5:30–9:30pm (dinner). Average main course $25. AmEx, DC, MC, V. The theme here is flora, from the flowers pressed in glass on the walls to the back courtyard herb garden. Chef Diane Forley's menu relies on the creative use of her homegrown herbs for such dishes as a rolled herb soufflé and butternut squash ravioli flavored with sage.

Chic

147

147 W 15th St between Sixth and Seventh Aves (929-5000). Subway: F, 1, 2, 3, 9 to 14th St. Sun noon–4pm (brunch). Sun, Mon 6–11pm, Tue–Thu 6pm–midnight; Fri, Sat 6pm–1am (dinner). Average main course $20. AmEx, MC, V. Located in a former firehouse, this cavernous restaurant features live jazz, a menu of modern New York staples (seared tuna, grilled hanger steak, etc.) and big tables full of fashion industry types who look like they're having more fun than you ever will. After dinner, check out 147's downstairs lounge.

Asia de Cuba

Morgans Hotel, 237 Madison Ave between 37th and 38th Sts (726-7755) Subway: 6 to 33rd St. 5:30pm–midnight (dinner). Average main course $20. AmEx, MC, V. Never mind that Asia de Cuba's Chino-Latino cuisine sometimes misses more than it hits. What matters is that this restaurant is flat-out fun. The kinetic bar scene, the long, lit-from-beneath family-style table and the hologram waterfall make the bilevel, Philippe Starck–designed space as electric as the sparklers poking out of the Guava Dynamite dessert.

Balthazar

80 Spring St between Crosby St and Broadway (965-1414). Subway: C, E, 6 to Spring St. Mon–Thu noon–2am, Fri noon–3am; Sat, Sun 11:30–2am. Average main course $20. AmEx, MC, V. Still a magnet for celebutantes and models, Balthazar remains one of the city's most alluring restaurants. Its Parisian brasserie decor (red leather banquettes, patinated mirrors) is irresistible; its roasted meats and raw-bar platters are always dependable. Remember to wear your elbow pads: You'll need them while waiting at the bar.

Clementine

1 Fifth Ave at 8th St (253-0003). Subway: N, R 8th St–NYU. Mon–Fri noon–4am; Sat, Sun 5pm–4am. Average main course $21. AmEx, DC, Disc, MC, V. If you can stand the mad crush at the bar and the beeping cell phones, Clementine will award you with some of the more interesting cooking in the city. Ask to sit in the Deco dining room (the front lounge is crowded and smoky) and enjoy John Shenk's boldly flavored creations, such as spicy tuna sashimi and barbecued sparerib salad. Save room for dessert: Pastry chef Heather Ho's souped-up versions of American classics are delectable.

Elaine's

1703 Second Ave between 88th and 89th Sts (534-8103). Subway: 4, 5, 6 to 86th St. 6pm–2am (dinner). Average main course $22. AmEx, Disc, MC, V. Elaine's is the dinosaur of high-society restaurants, and even after all these years, it still pulls in an A-list crowd. The food, though respectable, isn't what counts. What does is the outspoken proprietress, Elaine Kaufman, and a stellar cast of characters that on any given night might include Woody Allen, Barbra Streisand or George Plimpton.

Moomba

See **Pour nutrition**, page 162.

Odeon

145 West Broadway between Thomas and Duane Sts (233-0507). Subway: 1, 2, 3, 9 to Chambers St. Mon–Thu noon–2am, Fri noon–3am, Sat 11:30am–3am, Sun 11:30am–2am. Average main course $15. AmEx, DC, MC, V. More than a decade after appearing on the cover of *Bright Lights, Big City*, the Odeon remains one of Tribeca's biggest draws: The large, Deco dining room is always energizing, and the bistro food is always reliable. Jay McInerney might be a relic of the '80s, but the Odeon, thankfully, is not.

Raoul's

180 Prince St between Sullivan and Thompson Sts (966-3518). Subway: C, E to Spring St. 6pm–2am. Average main course $22. AmEx, DC, MC, V. The Elaine's of downtown, Raoul's is a time-tested favorite that is constantly packed for dinner. Quirky as only an established joint can be, it has a good bar scene for after-work gallery types and late-night club crawlers. Then there's the dark, romantic dining room, which serves excellent French bistro food—and there's a tarot-card reader upstairs.

Restaurant Florent

69 Gansevoort St between Greenwich and Washington Sts (989-5779). Subway: A, C, E to 14th St; L to Eighth Ave. 24 hours. Average main course $10. No credit cards. After a night of club hopping in west Chelsea or drinking in the lounges that line the cobblestoned streets of the hip meat-packing district, stop by Florent—it opened long before the recent rash of trendy night spots. It's open 24 hours, and the omelettes and *frites* on its French-bistro menu will help absorb all that beer sloshing around in your gut.

Torch

See **Pour nutrition**, page 162.

Waterloo

145 Charles St at Washington St (352-1119). Subway: 1, 9 to Christopher St. Tue–Sun 6pm–2am (dinner). Average main course $15. AmEx, DC, MC, V. Located on a serene corner in the far West Village, this minimalist Belgian brasserie is at once soothing and maddening. Because reservations are accepted only for parties of six or more, expect a long wait at the bar. But when you've got a big pot of mussels (the best item on the menu) and a cannister of *frites* on the table, and the retractable facade is rolled up to let in a warm breeze, you won't want to be anywhere else.

Cheap eats

Ecco-La

1660 Third Ave at 93rd St (860-5609). Subway: 6 to 96th St. 11:30am–3:45pm (lunch). Sun–Thu 4–11:30pm; Fri, Sat 4pm–midnight (dinner). Average main course $11. AmEx. The first room at Ecco-La is cheerful, noisy and boldly colorful; the second is quiet, with gilt-framed pictures and upholstered chairs. Choose your room according to your mood and enjoy the simple menu, which offers endless variations of pastas and sauces.

Eisenberg's Sandwich Shop

174 Fifth Ave between 22nd and 23rd Sts (675-5096). Subway: N, R to 23rd St. Mon–Fri 6am–5pm, Sat 7am–4pm. Average main course $5. No credit cards. You've got two reasons to stop by this time warp of a restaurant: its chicken and tuna salads. You won't find a better version of either anywhere in the city. The narrow, cramped space looks as though it hasn't changed in 50 years, and so does the staff.

Elvie's Turo-Turo

214 First Ave between 12th and 13th Sts (473-7785). Subway: L to First Ave. Mon–Sat 11am–9pm, Sun 11am–8pm. Average main course $5. No credit cards. This Filipino buffet-style diner caters to hungry New Yorkers from all walks of life. They come for Elvira Samora Cinco's stews, grills, barbecued pork and seafood—a choice of two served on a mountain of rice costs under $5. A New York delight.

La Taza de Oro

96 Eighth Ave between 14th and 15th Sts (243-9946). Subway: C, E to 14th St; L to Eighth Ave. Mon–Sat 6am–11:30pm. Average main course $8. No credit cards. You don't need to be able to speak Spanish to get by at this Puerto Rican lunch counter. Just remember three words in English: *rice*

Morning glories

Want to feel like a real New Yorker? Here's how to join the brunch bunch.

New Yorkers have an odd, almost schizophrenic relationship with breakfast. During the work week, the first meal of the day is given perfunctory attention: usually a doughnut or muffin and a cup of coffee bought from a street vendor on the way to the office. Come Saturday, however, breakfast is suddenly called brunch. Manhattanites often spend the morning making rounds of phone calls to set a time and a place to meet and eat.

Yes, weekend brunch is serious business. On Saturdays and Sundays, the breakfast period doesn't start before ten o'clock and often ends late in the afternoon. Some brunchers make the extended meal a gossipy social occasion; others ritualistically read the Sunday edition of *The New York Times* from first page to last. Menus vary from down-home to refined, but typically include omelettes, bacon, pancakes, oatmeal, bagels and lox, fresh fruit and champagne or a Bloody Mary.

Certain eateries are as famous for their brunch hordes as they are for their food. It's almost impossible not to end up waiting in line for weekend brunch at any of the following establishments, even though they have three branches each. **EJ's Luncheonette** (447 Amsterdam Ave between 81st and 82nd Sts, 873-3444; 432 Sixth Ave between 9th and 10th Sts, 473-5555; 1271 Third Ave at 73rd St, 472-0600) serves diner-with-a-twist fare, such as French toast coated with cornflakes and almonds, to a twentysomething contingent. **Royal Canadian Pancake House** (2286 Broadway between 82nd and 83rd Sts, 873-6052; 1004 Second Ave at 53rd St, 980-4131; 180 Third Ave at 17th St, 777-

9288) offers mattress-size pancakes and eggs that defeat even the most monstrous appetite. **Sarabeth's** (1295 Madison Ave between 92nd and 93rd Sts, 410-7335; Whitney Museum, 945 Madison Ave at 75th St, 570-3670; 423 Amsterdam Ave between 80th and 81st Sts, 496-6280) is the upscale brunch experience, where yuppies come for their "Goldilocks" fix: scrambled eggs with lox and cream cheese.

More common are restaurants with only one branch to satisfy the hordes of hungry weekenders. In the Flatiron district, two popular joints serve yummy comfort food (macaroni and cheese, enormous omelettes, etc.): the hip **Mayrose** diner (920 Broadway at 21st St, 533-3663) and **Chat 'n Chew** (10 E 16th St between Fifth Ave and Union Square West, 243-1616). Farther downtown, **Aggie's** (146 Houston St at MacDougal St, 673-8994) has a wall-board menu that lists simple breakfast food in large portions. And **Bubby's** (120 Hudson St at North Moore St, 219-0666) serves brunch to the ever-growing numbers who have decided to make Tribeca their home.

For a breakfast that's off the beaten track, visit **Ninth Street Market** (337 E 9th St between First and Second Aves, 473-0242), **Café Mogador** (101 St. Marks Pl between First Ave and Ave A, 677-2226) or Flea Market (*see French, page 145*).

Finally, for the most cosmopolitan of all morning meals, head for **Fifty Seven Fifty Seven** (57 E 57th St between Madison and Park Aves, 758-5757), in the I.M. Pei–designed Four Seasons Hotel.

and beans. They simply don't get any better than this. Don't miss the vinegary avocado salad, either.

Mama's Food Shop

200 E 3rd St between Aves A and B (777-4425). Subway: F to Second Ave. Mon–Sat 11am–11pm. Average main course $6. No credit cards. An instant institution in the East Village, this pint-size, casual eatery offers a taste of the South, cafeteria-style. Maybe it's the mother-size portions of mashed potatoes, macaroni, fried chicken and meatloaf, or the portraits of various moms on the walls, but the regulars keep coming back for a dose of comfort.

Margon

136 W 46th St between Sixth and Seventh Aves (354-5013). Subway: N, R to 49th St. Mon–Fri 6am–4:45pm, Sat 7am–2:30pm. Average main course $7. No credit cards. Margon is a packed Cuban joint that offers a blessed deliverance from the usual midtown lunch hustle. Line up for Cuban sandwiches, octopus salad, tripe and pig's feet, or soft beef pot roast—all of it served with great amounts of beans (black or red) and rice. Sharing tables with strangers is encouraged, so don't hog the hot sauce.

Panna II

93 First Ave between 5th and 6th Sts (598-4610). Subway: F to Second Ave. Noon–midnight. Average main course $5. No credit cards. An Indian restaurant American-style, with riotous paper decorations, loud, piped-in sitars and a typically East Village mix of customers. Panna II serves North Indian specialities (most of which cost less than $5) at a rapid clip.

Plan-Eat Thailand

184 Bedford Ave between N 6th and N 7th Sts, Brooklyn (1-718-599-5758). Subway: L to Bedford Ave. Mon–Sat 11:30am–11:30pm; Sun 1–11pm. Average main course $7. No credit cards. Sit at the bar and watch the cooks concoct extra-spicy peanut or coconut curries, or grab a table and take a gander at art created by some homegrown Williamsburg talent, while sampling the delicious vegetable pad Thai. Portions are large enough to warrant a doggie bag.

Pommes Frites

123 Second Ave between 7th and 8th Sts (674-1234). Subway: 6 to Astor Pl. Sun–Thu 11:30–midnight; Fri, Sat 11:30am–1am. Regular fries: $2.50. It's midnight. You're drunk, and you need fried food: Welcome to Nirvana. Pommes Frites' Belgian-style fries are so good—hot, crispy and salty—that this storefront doesn't sell anything else, except a selection of 28 mostly mayo-based toppings.

American

Cajun

Acadia Parish

148 Atlantic Ave between Clinton and Henry Sts, Brooklyn (1-718-624-5154). Subway: N, R to Court St; 2, 3, 4 to Borough Hall. Mon, Wed, Thu 5–9:45pm; Fri, Sat 5–10:45pm, Sun 4–8:45pm. Average main course $14. AmEx, DC, Disc, MC, V. In the best Southern style, the good folks at Acadia Parish will feed you, or try to, till there's hot sauce coming out of your ears. Dishes such as crawfish étouffée and blackened chicken breast are scrumptious, fortifying and served, as the menu puts it, "with one starch and one vegetable."

Chantale's Cajun Kitchen

510 Ninth Ave between 38th and 39th Sts (967-2623). Subway: A, C, E to 42nd St–Times Sq. Mon–Thu 11:30am–7:30pm; Fri, Sat 11:30am–8:30pm. Average main course $7. No credit cards. Chantale's does thriving business at lunchtime, both eat-in and delivery, but it's also a great and

inexpensive choice for a pretheater dinner. The menu includes meaty curries, gumbos and creoles, plus a good selection of vegetarian options.

Great Jones Café

54 Great Jones St between the Bowery and Lafayette St (674-9304). Subway: 6 to Bleecker St. Sat, Sun 11:30am–4pm (brunch). Mon–Thu 5pm–midnight; Fri, Sat 5pm–1am (dinner). Average main course $8. No credit cards. Minute but easy to spot by its bright-orange exterior and a bust of Elvis in the front window, Great Jones is one of the best Cajun restaurants in the city. The basic menu is small and painted on the wall; the changing specials almost always include some kind of catfish and a po'boy (French bread sandwich) or two.

Delis

Carnegie Deli

854 Seventh Ave between 54th and 55th Sts (757-2245). Subway: N, R to 57th St. 6:30am–4am. Average main course $10. No credit cards. The decor is unprepossessing and the waiters are infamously rude at this deli in the theater district, but the supersize sandwiches, piled high with corned beef and other typical New York deli meats, are worth any visual or emotional distress you may suffer.

Ess-a-Bagel

359 First Ave at 21st St (260-2252). Subway: 6 to 23rd St. Mon–Sat 6:30am–10pm; Sun 6:30am–5pm. Plain bagel 60¢. ● 831 Third Ave between 86th and 87th Sts (call 980-1010 for hours). Let's talk about what a bagel should be: huge, with a crust that's a little chewy but breaks. There should be no—or almost no—space in the hole. At Ess-a-Bagel's original downtown location, the ideal bagel is served by fat-fingered guys who touch everything and make dumb jokes. Perfection at 60¢ a pop.

Katz's Deli

205 E Houston St at Ludlow St (254-2246). Subway: F to Second Ave. Sun–Tue 8am–10pm; Wed, Thu 8am–11pm; Fri, Sat 8am–3am. Average main course $8. AmEx, MC, V. This venerable New York deli, famous for its old-style cafeteria decor and superb salamis and hot dogs, stands at the invisible portals of the Lower East Side. Order a sandwich piled high with thick slabs of pastrami or corned beef, a platter of salami and eggs, or an egg cream, an old-fashioned drink with a misleading name.

Pastrami King

124-24 Queens Blvd at 82nd Ave, Queens (1-718-263-1717). Subway: E, F to Union Tpke–Kew Gardens. 9am–10pm. Average main course $10. AmEx, MC, V. Although it's under new ownership (and some claim the change is not for the better), you can still head to this famous old Art Deco deli for the ultimate pastrami sandwich.

Second Avenue Deli

156 Second Ave at 10th St (677-0606). Subway: 6 to Astor Pl. Mon–Thu, Sun 7am–midnight; Fri, Sat 7am–2am. Average main course $14. AmEx, Disc, MC, V. The dwindling number of authentic Jewish delicatessens in town makes this one a mandatory East Village stop; it's been serving since 1954 (but was recently renovated, so it looks brand new). Soothe your soul with a matzo ball soup, and then embark on a trip down heartburn lane with a hot corned beef sandwich, some knishes and a serving of chopped liver. Prices are a bit steep, but most customers will find the large portions easy to share.

Stage Deli

834 Seventh Ave between 53rd and 54th Sts (245-7850). Subway: N, R to 57th St. 6am–2am. Average main course $15. AmEx, Disc, MC, V. Famous for its monolithic sandwiches and top-quality deli food, Stage Deli serves much the same food as nearby rival Carnegie at the same high prices. Visit both and decide which is better. Expect to see many tourists.

Diners

Cheyenne Diner

411 Ninth Ave at 33rd St (465-8750). Subway: A, C, E to 34th St. 24 hours. Average main course $7. AmEx, DC, MC, V. Cheyenne is the kind of place that cigarette ad location scouts would give a lung for; it's also a rare piece of the heartland in NYC: a silver-sided, pink-neon–signed breadbox of a diner. Brunch specials ($6.95) include juice, fruit salad, coffee and megacaloric helpings of eggs and meat. Indulge, and enjoy the delightfully crappy mise-en-scène of Ninth Avenue.

Comfort Diner

214 E 45th St between Second and Third Aves (867-4555). Subway: S, 4, 5, 6, 7 to 42nd St–Grand Central. Mon–Fri 7:30am–11pm; Sat, Sun 9am–11pm. Average main course $15. AmEx, Disc, MC, V. This retro diner is inspired by, rather than torn from, the pages of history. The red lights along the wall look like they were swiped from a Cadillac's fin and the terrazzo tabletops resemble old diner floors. All you really need to know is that this is one of the friendliest spots in east midtown. It's perfect for a cup of joe–and–waffle breakfast, or a memory-jogging bite of grilled s'mores.

Empire Diner

210 Tenth Ave at 22nd St (243-2736). Subway: C, E to 23rd St. 24 hours; closed Mon 4am–Tue 8am. Average main course $10. AmEx, Disc, MC, V. This west Chelsea all-nighter is the essence of preserved Americana. Come at night when the place glows, and sample some above-average diner fare. At 3am everything tastes fine and a little illicit. It's a shame the rest of the city isn't like this—shiny and as edgily smooth as early Tom Waits.

Jones Diner

371 Lafayette St at Great Jones St (673-3577). Subway: 6 to Astor Pl. Mon–Sat 6am–6pm. Average main course $6. No credit cards. This corner has been on this corner for 80 years and, fortunately, shows every bit of it. Though the dingy facade keeps newcomers away, the craggy regulars are devoted to the basic and ultracheap sandwiches, breakfast specials and burgers.

M&G Soul Food Diner

383 W 125th St at Morningside Ave (864-7326). Subway: B, C to 116th St. 24 hours. Average main course $9. No credit cards. Who doesn't order fried chicken just for the crispy coating? At this Harlem diner, the chicken pieces are almost more deeply seasoned crust than meat—which is a good thing. Sit at the Formica-topped counter, and soon you'll be swaying to the jukebox tunes of Marvin Gaye and Curtis Mayfield.

Moondance

80 Sixth Ave between Grand and Canal Sts (226-1191). Subway: A, C, E to Canal St. Mon–Fri 8:30am–11pm; Sat, Sun 24 hours. Average main course $9. AmEx, Disc, MC, V. Here,

*Bright spot: A ray of light amid Soho's snootier establishments is **Jerry's** (101 Prince Street, 966-9464), a favorite stop for gallery-hoppers, supermodels and regular folks.*

the good, cheap diner specials come with a retro New Wave vibe. The best deal in the house is the appetizer for two: a cholesterol jackpot of fried onion rings, chicken fingers, mozzarella sticks and potato pancakes ($6.75). Look for the young things on rock & roll budgets who gather here, droopy-eyed, on Saturday mornings.

Tom's Restaurant

2880 Broadway at 112th St (864-6137). Subway: 1, 9 to 110th St–Cathedral Pkwy. Mon–Wed, Sun 6am–1:30am; Thu–Sat 24 hours. Average main course $7. No credit cards. Columbia University students come to this diner on a weekly, if not daily, basis for the grilled cheese sandwiches, hamburgers, fries and milk shakes. Suzanne Vega sang about it, and the characters on the ever-popular *Seinfeld* used it as the seat for all their neurotic get-togethers (an exterior shot of Tom's precedes all diner scenes).

Southern

Charles' Southern Style Kitchen

2841 Frederick Douglass Blvd between 151st and 152nd Sts (926-4313). Subway: C, D to 155th St. Mon 6pm–midnight, Tue–Sat 4am–4am, Sun 1–8pm. Average main course $7. AmEx, MC, V. Perhaps no place does fried chicken as well as the fluorescent-lit Charles' Southern Style Kitchen. Owner Charles Gabriel tosses his chickens in a secret blend of seasonings before dunking the parts in a massive oil-filled cast-iron skillet. The best accompaniments to the crunchy chicken are the custardy macaroni and cheese, and collard greens emboldened with shreds of smoked turkey.

The Hog Pit

22 Ninth Ave at 13th St (604-0092). Subway: A, C, E to 14th St. Tue–Sun 5–11pm. Average main course $12. AmEx, MC, V. This honky-tonk eatery in the meatpacking district feels like a sleepy roadside bar in the middle of the South: Cow skulls adorn the walls, Hank Williams Jr. plays on the juke and an American flag hangs over a window. The belt-loosening soul food—including golden-brown hush puppies and excellent chicken-fried steak—is just as down-home.

Justin's

31 W 21st St between Fifth and Sixth Aves (352-0599). Subway: F to 23rd St. Mon–Sat 5:30pm–midnight, Sun 5:30–11pm. Average main course $23. AmEx, Disc, MC, V. These days, it seems that anything Sean "Puffy" Combs touches turns to gold. Recently, the rap impresario helped open this slick, new Southern-style hot spot (he's a managing partner), and so far, so good. The food—such as smothered chicken livers and fried chicken with waffles—is surprisingly good, but the real reason to come is to rub shoulders with Puff Daddy and other rap-world players.

Mekka

14 Ave A between Houston and 2nd Sts (475-8500). Subway: F to Second Ave. Sun noon–3:30pm (brunch). Mon–Thu, Sun 5:30–11pm; Fri, Sat 5:30pm–2am (dinner). Average main course $13. AmEx, DC, MC, V. Mekka's got a chic clientele, a nightclub vibe and a DJ who starts at 10pm on weekends. The hip-hop and Caribbean music go perfectly with the food—a combo of traditional soul food and island references. Sit in the back garden and wash down your barbecued pork and po'boys with a Mambo beer.

Pink Tea Cup

42 Grove St between Bedford and Bleecker Sts (807-6755). Subway: 1, 9 to Christopher St–Sheridan Sq. Mon–Thu, Sun 8am–midnight; Fri, Sat 8am–1am. Average main course $12. No credit cards. Within these pink West Village walls is a charmingly intimate restaurant that's a hot spot for brunch. There will most certainly be a line on weekends; use the wait as an opportunity to decide whether you want grilled pork chops or fried chicken with your pancakes.

Sylvia's

328 Lenox Ave between 126th and 127th Sts (996-0660). Subway: 2, 3 to 125th St. Mon–Sat 7:30am–10:30pm; Sun 12:30–7pm. Average main course $11. AmEx, Disc, MC, V. Harlem's most famous dining spot has become a bit touristy (tour buses wait patiently outside the place). But no matter; the ribs are still tender, sweet and way ahead of any downtown contenders, and the collard greens would sate any Southerner.

Virgil's Real BBQ

152 W 45th St between Broadway and Sixth Ave (921-9494). Subway: N, R, S, 1, 2, 3, 9, 7 to 42nd St–Times Sq. Sun 11:30am–10pm, Mon 11:30am–11pm, Tue–Sat 11:30am–midnight. Average main course $15. AmEx, MC, V. A two-story barbecue emporium, this always-mobbed Times Square restaurant serves the best smoked spareribs, brisket and pulled pork in Manhattan. Bring a monstrous appetite and Virgil's will take care of the rest.

Seafood

Aquagrill

210 Spring St at Sixth Ave (274-0505). Subway: C, E to Spring St. Sat, Sun noon–4pm (brunch). Mon–Fri noon–3pm (lunch). Mon–Thu 6–10:30pm; Fri, Sat 6–11:45pm; Sun 6–10:30pm (dinner). Average main course $22. AmEx, MC, V. A relative newcomer to Soho's world of the raw and the booked, Aquagrill is distinguished by location and extremely fresh aquatic fare. A briny to creamy range of oysters is shipped in every day, from locations as far away as Chile and Japan.

Blue Water Grill

31 Union Sq West at 16th St (675-9500). Subway: L, N, R, 4, 5, 6 to 14th St–Union Sq. Mon–Thu 11am–12:30am; Fri, Sat 11am–1am; Sun 11am–11pm. Average main course $20. AmEx, MC, V. This cool, high-ceilinged Union Square building was once the Bank of the Metropolis, but if you listen closely you can hear the sea. The space is elegant, all marble and blue banquettes, and the soft lights are like beacons. The menu has an oyster lexicon, but it's not too fishcentric to be fun. Try the "Coffee and Donuts" dessert: dewy cinnamon sweets with a mug of coffee-flavored *pot de crème*.

Johnny's Reef

2 City Island Ave at Belden's Point, City Island, Bronx (1-718-885-2086). Subway: 6 to Pelham Bay Park, then Bx29 bus to City Island. Mon–Thu, Sun 11am–midnight; Fri, Sat 11am–1am. Average main course $10. No credit cards. This cheapo fry-fest is one of the best ways to take part in a central ritual of city life—complaining about never leaving and then never going very far. City Island feels like a sleepy shoreside vacation spot, but it's accessible by mass transit. The main drag is lined with clam shacks, but go to the end, to Johnny's, for all manner of fried sea life, which you eat outside among the throng of locals and low-circling seagulls.

Le Bernardin

155 W 51st St between Sixth and Seventh Aves (489-1515). Subway: B, D, F, Q to 47th–50th Sts–Rockefeller Ctr. Mon–Fri noon–2:30pm (lunch). Mon 6–10:30pm; Tue–Thu 5:30–10:30pm; Sat, Sun 5:30–11pm (dinner). Average main course $42 lunch, $70 dinner. AmEx, Disc, MC, V. The unimpressive corporate decor matters little at this midtowner—especially once you've sat down and had some of the best fish you've ever tasted. Chef Eric Ripert dazzles with appetizers such as *escabèche* of chilled baby oysters and entrées like the whole red snapper baked in a rosemary-and-thyme salt crust (which you must order 24 hours in advance, *s'il-vous plaît*).

Mazel tov! *The recently renovated **Second Avenue Deli** is worth celebrating.*

Lundy Bros.

1901 Emmons Ave at Ocean Ave, Sheepshead Bay, Brooklyn (1-718-743 0022). Subway: D, Q to Sheepshead Bay. Sun 11am–2pm (brunch). Mon–Sat noon–3:15pm (lunch). Mon–Thu 5–10pm; Fri, Sat 5pm–midnight; Sun 3–9pm (dinner). Average main course $16. AmEx, MC, V. After a 17-year absence, more than just the Lundy name has been revived. This Sheepshead Bay waterfront institution is throbbing with customers—families at big tables, couples at the raw bar, and a good time being had by all. The combination dinners of chowder, lobster and chicken satisfy, as does the reconstructed spirit of a time when Brooklyn was the world.

Milos

125 W 55th St between Sixth and Seventh Aves (245-7400). Subway: B, D, E to Seventh Ave. Mon–Fri noon–3:15pm (lunch). Mon–Sat 5:30pm–midnight, Sun 5–10:45pm (dinner). Average main course $27. AmEx, MC, V. At this new seafood restaurant in musty midtown, fish is not ordered; it is chosen, market-style, from the mountains of ice in the back of this soaring space and then paid for by the pound. The easygoing, attentive staff and big round tables of happy Greek-Americans make for a boisterous evening. Go with a group and share a red snapper, some delicate pompano and exotic Mediterranean sea bass.

Pearl

18 Cornelia St between W 4th and Bleecker Sts (691-8211). Subway: A, C, E, B, D, F, Q to West 4th St–Washington Sq. Mon–Fri noon–2:30pm (lunch). Mon–Sat 6–11pm (dinner). Average main course $17. MC, V. Pearl is just what the name suggests: miniature (a long bar with stools and one solitary table), gleaming (simple shades of white and silver, the dewy sheen of oysters) and a rare find (straightforward, not too

pricey). The sea bass is perfectly charred on the outside, moist and laced with herbs on the inside. And how's this for simple pleasures: a plate of littlenecks on ice, a bowl of scallop chowder and a cold German pilsner.

Steak houses

Ben Benson's Steak House

123 W 52nd St between Sixth and Seventh Aves (581-8888). Subway: N, R to 49th St. Mon–Thu 11:45am–11pm, Fri 11:45am–midnight, Sat 5pm–midnight, Sun 5–10pm. Average main course $30. AmEx, MC, V. Teeming with men in pinstripes, this traditional steak house features a menu of luscious classics, including shimmery oysters on the half shell and hearts of romaine served in a tangy Caesar dressing. When it's time for steak, get the juicy porterhouse for two, and don't forget mashed potatoes with horseradish and the superb creamed spinach. The career waiters in tan smocks will be sure to keep things moving.

Old Homestead

56 Ninth Ave between 14th and 15th Sts (242-9040). Subway: A, C, E to 14th St; L to Eighth Ave. Mon–Fri noon–4pm (lunch). Sat 1–11:45pm; Sun 1–9:45pm (dinner). Average main course $30. AmEx, CB, DC, MC, V. There are plenty of pleasures at the oldest steak house in the city (founded 1868), but many come for the Kobe—that coddled, beer-fed Japanese bovine of mythological softness. A Kobe steak is $110, but it's so finely marbled and tender, it's the Grail for carnivores. Still, you'll be forgiven if you opt instead for a more classic porterhouse for two ($58) and soak in the meaty history of the room.

Upper crust: The brick-oven pies at **John's Pizzeria** are a New York institution.

Palm

837 Second Ave between 44th and 45th Sts (687-2953). Subway: S, 4, 5, 6, 7 to 42nd St–Grand Central. Mon–Fri noon–11:30pm, Sat 5–11:30pm. Average main course $29. AmEx, MC, V. A total of 15 other Palms have appeared around the USA, but this 70-year-old speakeasy is the original. **Palm Too** (697-5198) opened across the street in 1973, and the two are basically identical: no frills, with stern Italian waiters in flesh-colored jackets and yellowed walls bearing the cartoons and caricatures of such past regulars as Jackie Gleason and J. Edgar Hoover. Palm Too, however, is open on Sundays (2–10pm). Go supple (filet mignon, $29) or savory (New York strip, $29), but either way have the cheesecake.

Peter Luger

178 Broadway between Driggs and Bedford Aves, Williamsburg, Brooklyn (1-718-387-7400). Subway: J to Marcy Ave. Mon–Thu, Sun 11:45am–9:45pm; Fri, Sat 11:45am–10:45pm; Sun 1–9:45pm. Steak for two $58. No credit cards. Is the hike to this Williamsburg institution worth it? Without question. Pulled from a bank of infernal broilers, the massive porterhouses (the only cut the 110-year-old restaurant serves) emerge a crunchy dark brown, still tender pink on the inside. Dripping with fat and melted butter, this huge cut of beef ($59.95 for two) awakens bone-gnawing urges you thought mankind had abandoned in the Paleolithic era.

Smith & Wollensky

797 Third Ave at 49th St (753-1530). Subway: E, F to Lexington–Third Aves; 6 to 51st St. Mon–Fri 11:30am–11pm; Sat, Sun 5–11pm. Average main course $55. AmEx, Disc, MC, V. Smith & Wollensky, one of the most enduringly pop-

ular midtown steak houses, refuses to catch up with the times. The ratio of men to women is still grossly uneven, and the decor is still defiantly conservative. Thankfully, though, the steaks are still unmanageably large and available in a great choice of cuts, from sirloin to filet mignon.

Sparks

210 E 46th St between Second and Third Aves (687-4855). Subway: S, 4, 5, 6, 7 to 42nd St–Grand Central. Mon–Fri noon–3pm (lunch). Mon–Thu 5–11pm; Fri, Sat 5–11:30pm (dinner). Average main course $25. AmEx, CB, DC, MC, V. So maybe Big Paul Castellano did ingest his last saturated fats here before being unceremoniously gunned down. But there's really no dark mystery at Sparks, with its bulging jeroboams, gargantuan family dinners and long lines. What's here is a 30-year history of good steaks in a setting of comfortably familiar swank. Waiters are happy to improvise lavish, off-the-menu chopped salads—and what better warm-up for a black and blue (charred outside, rare inside) sirloin than a salad thick with bacon and blue cheese?

Chinese

20 Mott Street

20 Mott St between Pell St and the Bowery (964-0380). Subway: J, N, R, 6 to Canal St. 9am–11pm. Average main course $9. AmEx, Disc, MC, V. Come early to this three-story dim sum emporium—one of the most popular in Chinatown. The mouthwatering appetizer-like dumplings, rolls and buns are served from carts that stop periodically at each table. The menus are in Chinese and the waiters can be unhelpful, but the dim sum selection, including duck feet and jellyfish, is extensive, guaranteeing a full stomach and a good time.

Broadway Cottage

2690 Broadway at 103rd St (316-2600,2601).Subway: 1, 9 to 103rd St. Mon–Thu 11:30am–11:30pm; Fri, Sat 11:30am–midnight; Sun noon–11:30pm. Average main course $7. AmEx, MC, V. Innumerable "Cottage" Chinese restaurants dot the city, but they aren't all created equal. While many of these restaurants for the free, cheap-tasting, all-you-can-drink white wine, Broadway Cottage is worth a visit for the attentive and polite service and for such satisfying dishes as pan-fried scallion pancakes and crispy sweet-and-sour prawns with walnuts.

Home's Kitchen

222 E 21st St between Broadway and Park Ave South (475-5049). Subway: 6 to 23rd St. 11am–11pm. Average main course $7. AmEx, MC, V. It's hard to find good Peking duck—the kind that's crispy on the outside, meaty and juicy on the inside. But Home's Kitchen serves the real thing. Start with dumplings (steamed or fried), and get the Peking duck to share. The dumplings are filled to the dough with well-seasoned meat (a rarity), and the crispy, rich duck comes with all the fixings.

Joe's Shanghai

9 Pell St between Mott St and the Bowery (233-8888). Subway: J, N, R, 6 to Canal St. 11am–11:15pm. Average main course $12. No credit cards. Although you'll find dishes such as fried pork dumplings and cold chicken in wine, the main attractions at Joe's are the steamed buns, which hold inside them a mouthful of hot soup and morsels of pork or crabmeat. Don't shove the whole dumpling into your mouth or you'll burn yourself; hold it on the spoon, take a tiny bite and then drink the liquid that collects in the utensil's well.

New Chao Chow Restaurant

111 Mott St between Canal and Hester Sts (226-2590/8222). Subway: J, N, R, 6 to Canal St. 8:30am–10pm. Average main course $5. No credit cards. Ignore the unimpressive decor at this cheap noodle shop, where no dish tops $9, and focus instead on the soups, which are the true draw. Try the Chao Chow fishball, a combo of noodles in chicken broth, topped with more than enough fishballs to satiate any seafood lover's craving.

Red Hot Szechuan

347 Seventh Ave at 10th St, Park Slope, Brooklyn (1-718-369-0700). Subway: F to Seventh Ave–Park Slope. Mon–Thu 11:30am–10:30pm; Fri, Sat 11:30am–11pm; Sun 2–10:30pm. Average main course $8. AmEx, MC, V. This Park Slope restaurant does Chinese right—and it's a good value, too. Red Hot offers a full selection of vegetarian dishes (including some Buddhist cuisine) and a brunch that can't be beat: You'll get your choice of various main dishes, plus egg drop or wonton soup, and vegetable, plain or brown rice for $4.15! Be sure to try the steamed celery–with–sesame sauce appetizer; in summer, there's lobster, served as you like it.

Shun Lee Palace

155 E 55th St between Lexington and Third Aves (371-8844). Subway: 4, 5, 6 to 59th St; N, R to Lexington Ave. Noon–11:30pm. Average main course $20. AmEx, DC, MC, V. In this city of a thousand cheap, accessible Chinese food joints, it might seem silly to venture to this place on the posh Upper East Side, where main courses can cost as much as $30. But you'll see why when you try the food, such as the crab seasoned with ginger and scallion or the roast squab. And if Shun Lee's elegance doesn't surprise you, maybe the courteous and friendly service will.

Eastern European

FireBird

365 W 46th St between Eighth and Ninth Aves (586-0244). Subway: A, C, E to 42nd St–Times Sq. Tue–Sat 11:45am–2:15pm (lunch). Mon–Thu, Sun 5–10:15pm; Fri, Sat 5–11:15pm (dinner). Average main course $24. AmEx, Disc, MC, V. Located on Restaurant Row in the theater district, FireBird dedicates itself to old-style Russian extravagance. If you're not up to trying some of the grander main courses (such as marinated lamb), order from the *zakuska* menu (a sort of Russian tapas), which changes daily.

Rasputin

2670 Coney Island Ave at Ave X, Brighton Beach, Brooklyn (1-718-332-8333). Subway: F to Ave X; D to Neck Rd. Mon–Thu 11am–midnight, Fri–Sun 11am–3am. Average $50. AmEx, MC, V. Come to this restaurant in Brooklyn's Little Odessa for an authentic Russian evening—some dining and dancing and much smoking and drinking. Order typical Russian dishes such as boiled tongue, radish salad and caviar before heading to the crowded dance floor. Arrive early if you want to catch the Vegas-style floor show.

Russian Samovar

256 W 52nd St between Broadway and Eighth Ave (757-0168). Subway: C, E to 50th St. Tue–Sat noon–3pm (lunch). Mon 5–11:30pm; Tue–Thu, Sun 5pm–midnight; Fri, Sat 5pm–12:30am (dinner). Average main course $18. AmEx, MC, V. You may not recognize them, but this mid-price theater district restaurant is where Russia's beautiful people go when they are in town. Mikhail Baryshnikov is an investor.

Ukrainian East Village Restaurant

140 Second Ave between 8th and 9th Sts (529-5024). Subway: 6 to Astor Pl. Noon–11pm. Average main course $7. No credit cards. Experience true Ukrainian dining and service at this plain-looking restaurant tucked away behind the Ukrainian National Home. Order the combo platter and stuff yourself with stuffed cabbage, kielbasa, four types of pierogi and a choice of potatoes or kasha (buckwheat). And if you're full, don't let the grandmotherlike waitresses convince you otherwise.

Veselka

144 Second Ave at 9th St (228-9682). Subway: 6 to Astor Pl. 24 hours. Average main course $10. AmEx, MC, V. This bohemian Ukrainian coffee shop, open around the clock, was recently renovated, so it might not seem like the old East Village hangout it actually is. After a tour of the small shops in the vicinity, stop here for a cheap bowl of chicken soup and a slab of challah bread.

French

Alison on Dominick

38 Dominick St between Varick and Hudson Sts (727-1188). Subway: 1, 9 to Canal St. Mon–Thu 5:30–9:30pm; Fri, Sat 5:15–10:30pm; Sun 5:15–9:30pm (dinner). Average main course $27. AmEx, DC, MC, V. This French country restaurant is one of the most romantic hideaways in the city, with light—almost healthy—versions of southwestern French cuisine and a quiet, jazz-tinged atmosphere.

Flea Market

131 Ave A between 8th and 9th Sts (358-9280). Subway: 6 to Astor Pl. Sat, Sun 10am–4pm (brunch). Mon–Fri 9am–4:30pm (lunch). Mon–Fri 5:30pm–midnight; Sat, Sun 5pm–midnight (dinner). Average main course $13. AmEx. Named after the vintage bric-a-brac scattered about, Flea Market whips up traditional French bistro fare with authenticity and plenty of rich sauces. No matter what you choose—the steak au poivre and sautéed skate with roasted-garlic mashed potatoes are delicious—your fork will inevitably trespass onto your companion's plate. In summer, choose a table near the doors and watch motley East Villagers traipse by.

Jean Claude
137 Sullivan St between Houston and Prince Sts (475-9232). Subway: C, E to Prince St; 1, 9 to Houston St. Mon–Thu 6:30–11pm; Fri, Sat 6:30–11:30pm; Sun 6–10:30pm. Average main course $18. No credit cards. Perpetually mobbed, Jean-Claude Iacovelli's bustling restaurant is a Soho favorite, thanks to its imaginative mix of continental and nouvelle cuisine, offered at bistro prices.

Jules
65 St. Marks Pl between First and Second Aves (477-5560). Subway: 6 to Astor Pl. 11am–2am. Average main course $16. AmEx. Jules may be at its best at Sunday brunch-time, when the sun shines through the lace curtains and an accordionist wanders around the room. Regulars favor the goat-cheese omelette, steak frites and the salad *frisée aux lardons.*

Le Cirque 2000
New York Palace Hotel, 455 Madison Ave between 50th and 51st Sts (303-7788). Subway: 6 to 51st St. Mon–Sat 11:45am–2:45pm, Sun 11:30am–2:30pm (lunch). Mon–Sat 5:45–11pm, Sun 5:30–10:30pm (dinner). Average main course $35. AmEx, MC, V. Step into Sirio Maccioni's revamped Le Cirque and you'll be surprised by the loony, futuristic redesign of Stanford White's decor. But then chef Sottha Khunn's menu will grab your attention, from the exquisite sautéed foie gras and lobster salad to the "juggler's ball" of pink meringue filled with lemon curd and vanilla ice cream.

Les Deux Gamins
170 Waverly Pl at Grove St (807-7047). Subway: 1, 9 to Christopher St–Sheridan Sq. 8am–midnight. Average main course $14. AmEx. Watch the Village go by as you soak up an atmosphere that's *très* Parisian and bistro food that's almost as authentic.

Patois
255 Smith St between Douglass and DeGraw Sts, Carroll Gardens, Brooklyn (1-718-855-1535). Subway: F to Carroll St. 11am–3pm (brunch). Tue–Thu 6–10:30pm; Fri, Sat 6–11:30pm (dinner). Average main course $23. AmEx, MC, V. With its fashionably worn vintage furniture and fair prices, Patois, a new Carroll Gardens bistro, feels like it's been a part of the neighborhood for years. The tables are filled by 8pm for the superb French fare, which includes a crustless tart with layers of thinly sliced leek and potato blended with melted Roquefort, and duck ravioli with diced pumpkin.

Payard Patisserie & Bistro
1032 Lexington Ave between 73rd and 74th Sts (717-5252). Subway: 6 to 77th St. Mon–Sat 7am–11pm. Average main course $40. AmEx, Diners, MC, V. Opened in 1997 by François Payard, the pastry chef at Daniel, this hybrid restaurant is a sugar wonderland that would make Willy Wonka jealous. The stunning confections in the polished glass display cases include myriad handmade chocolates, moonpie-size macaroons and lush homemade sorbets and ice creams. The bistro also serves top-notch provincial French cooking, but the huge assortment of traditional pastries and crisp fruit tarts remind you that you were right as a kid: Dessert *should* come first.

Provence
38 MacDougal St between Houston and Prince Sts (475-7500). Subway: C, E to Spring St. Noon–3pm (lunch). Mon–Sat 6–11pm; Sun 5:30–10:30pm (dinner). Average

main course $20. AmEx. Provence has been a Soho institution since 1986, thanks to its informal, flirtatious staff and superb Provençal food. During the warm months, try to sit in the garden out back.

Savann
414 Amsterdam Ave between 79th and 80th Sts (580-0202). Subway: 1, 9 to 79th St. Mon–Thu, Sun 6–11pm; Fri, Sat 6pm–midnight. Average main course $20. DC, MC, V. This Upper West Side bistro offers an inexpensive and innovative menu that mixes French basics and Asian flavors, emphasizing whatever is light and fresh.

Greek

S'Agapo
34-21 34th Ave at 35th St, Astoria, Queens (1-718-626-0303). Subway: N to Broadway; R to Steinway St. Tue–Fri 3pm–midnight; Sat, Sun noon–midnight. Average main course $16. AmEx, DC, Disc, MC, V. Servicing Astoria's Greek population, S'Agapo produces the real stuff in its undiluted form. The grilled octopus is among the tenderest on earth, while *pastitsio* is a satisfying rendition of Greek lasagna. On weekends, a singer and accordionist add to the fun, and the owner has been known to dim the lights and dance a little.

Agrotikon
322 E 14th St between First and Second Aves (473-2602). Subway: L to First Ave. Tue–Sun 5pm–midnight. Average main course $16. AmEx, MC, V. Cheaper and more adventurous than an haute Greek like Periyali (*see below*), Agrotikon is a happy and relatively recent addition to 14th Street. The grilled octopus is wonderful here, as is the sheep's milk cheese Saganaki. For fish, choose grilled over baked. Or try the fisherman's pie—a stew with chunks of fish and squid baked under garlic-cod mashed potatoes. The chocolate baklava is a true original.

Elias Corner for Fish
24-02 31st St at 24th Ave Astoria, Queens (1-718-932-1510). Subway: N to Astoria Blvd. 4pm–midnight. Average main course $15. No credit cards. This newly expanded but still simple Greek seafood restaurant doesn't take reservations, so there may be a wait. That's fine, since you can use the time in the lobby to select the right fish from the glass case. There's no menu, but no matter: Everything comes in extremely fresh and leaves the grill perfectly charred and full of flavor. The crowds come for swordfish kebabs and whole red mullet, snapper and striped bass. Treat the waitresses nicely and perhaps they'll bring a platter of fried dough with honey, a free dessert that's as sweet as the mood here.

Meltemi
905 First Ave at 51st St (355-4040). Subway: 6 to 51st St; E, F to Lexington–Third Aves. Noon–11pm. Average main course $20. AmEx, MC, V. Meltemi's airy look befits its Sutton Place location, but the atmosphere here comes from its Greek customers and authentic food. The exacting chef really knows his way around a grill, and the squid are perfect: Cooked over charcoal until just moist, they're sweet and tender to the point of indecency.

Molyvos
871 Seventh Ave between 55th and 56th Sts (582-7500). Subway: N, R to 57th St; B, D, E to Seventh Ave. Mon–Fri noon–3pm (lunch), 5:30–11:30pm (dinner). Average main course $20. All major cards accepted. This midtown taverna offers superior Greek home cooking refined for Manhattan taste buds. Instead of bread and butter, expect a basket of warm, chewy pita and a ramekin of pungent feta–and–roasted red pepper spread. Homey entrées include baby chicken bathed in a tangy lemon-dill cream sauce; desserts are irre-

*Bar food: Beat the dinner rush during **Takahachi**'s supercheap early-bird specials.*

sistibly sweet. Like everything at Molyvos, they're not fancy—just plain delicious.

Periyali

35 W 20th St between Fifth and Sixth Aves (463-7890). Subway: N, R to 23rd St. Mon–Fri noon–3pm (lunch). Mon–Fri 5:30–11pm; Sat 5:30pm–midnight (dinner). Average main course $20. AmEx, DC, MC, V. Periyali was one of the first restaurants in Manhattan to elevate Greek cuisine above the level of coffee-shop *spanikopita*. And though the best Greek cooking is now available more cheaply in Astoria, this traditional coal-grill place is still a good upscale spot for *moussaka*, *taramasalata*, grilled meat and vegetable appetizers.

Indian

Dawat

210 E 58th St between Second and Third Aves (355-7555). Subway: 4, 5, 6 to 59th St; N, R to Lexington Ave. 11:30am–2.45pm (lunch). Mon–Thu, Sun 5:30–10.45pm; Fri, Sat 5:30–11:15pm (dinner). Average lunch $12.95; dinner $35. AmEx, DC, MC, V. Perhaps the city's best Indian, Dawat offers a long, diverse, pricey menu within its pretty peach walls. East midtown is an unlikely place for midday bargains, and Dawat's prix-fixe lunches qualify ($12.95–$13.95). Standbys such as chicken *keema masala* are transformed here into subtle dishes that float on the tongue.

Haveli

100 Second Ave between 5th and 6th Sts (982-0533). Subway: 6 to Astor Pl. Noon–midnight. Average main course $9. AmEx, MC, V. The best thing about 6th Street's Little Delhi isn't even on 6th; it's just around the corner. In fact, Haveli is better than the neighborhood deserves. Behind the shattered-on-purpose wall of glass, all the standards are a notch above average with only a moderate price hike.

Jackson Diner

37-03 74th St at 37th Ave, Jackson Heights, Queens (1-718-672-1232). Subway: E, F to 74th St–Broadway. 11am–10pm. Average main course $9. No credit cards. Word has got out about this Queens diner; people now line up for its huge portions of Indian food. There's also the added attraction of leaving the East Village to dine in a place that serves a large Indian community. The *murg lajawab* (chicken in a ginger and chili sauce) has real kick. Jackson also has a small choice of mostly vegetarian, southern Indian food.

Nirvana

30 W 59th St between Fifth and Sixth Aves (486-5700). Subway: N, R to Fifth Ave. Noon–1am. Average main course $18. AmEx, DC, Disc, MC, V. The high-rent panorama of Central Park is the real attraction here; the menu is virtually identical to every place on 6th Street—despite the elephantine prices. If you're determined to have your curry with a view, go for the "theater dinner," which is served all day. For $5 more than a main course, you'll also receive an appetizer sampler, dessert and coffee.

*American revolution: Tasteful turns on classic American fare are served at **Gramercy Tavern**.*

Anar Bagh

338 E 6th St between Second and Third Aves (529-1937). Subway: 6 to Astor Pl. 6pm–midnight. Average main course $6. AmEx. At most Indian restaurants on Sixth Street, there are a few things you can count on: The decorations will be kooky, the service will be rushed and the dinners will be the cheapest in town. At Anar Bagh, the service is more relaxed, the food doesn't taste as if it's stewed too long and the decor is less than gaudy. The vindaloos and curries cost a few dimes more, but it buys you a more sophisticated dining experience—and you won't regret it in the middle of the night.

Thali

28 Greenwich Ave between 10th and Charles Sts (367-7411). Subway: A, C, E, B, D, F, Q to W 4th St–Washington Sq. Mon–Sat noon–3pm (lunch); Mon–Sat 6–9:30pm, Sun 5–10pm (dinner). Average main course $10. No credit cards. There is no menu at the sparsely decorated, closet-size vegetarian restaurant. Just sit down and order tea, and within minutes, a server brings a large silver tray of *thali*, a traditional Indian meal consisting of vegetable curries, a lentil dish, chutney, pickles, bread, a pile of rice and dessert. You can be sure the food is fresh—the place has no storage area, so the food is bought and prepared on the same day.

Italian

Andy's Colonial

2257 First Ave at 116th St (410-9175). Subway: 6 to 116th St. Mon–Fri 11am–9pm; Sat 5–10pm. Average main course $15. No credit cards. At this eight-table wood-paneled bar-restaurant, there are no printed menus: Co-owner Joe Medici (your bartender and waiter) will hand you a short list of Italian specials. If those don't interest you, Joe will offer you any kind of chicken or veal—cooked by his 81-year-old father.

Il Bagatto

192 E 2nd St between Aves A and B (228-0977). Subway: F to Second Ave. Tue–Thu 7pm–midnight; Fri, Sat 7pm–1am; Sun 6–11pm. Average main course $12. No credit cards. There are few convincing reasons to send anyone unfamiliar with Alphabet City into its bowels. Count the spinach gnocchi at the dark and cozy Il Bagatto as one of them. These plump morsels are made fresh at least four times a week and are served in a ripe, creamy Gorgonzola sauce. Other dishes worth the inconvenience of dodging prone junkies: the antipasto Il Bagatto, a sampler of the house antipasti; and the *stracceti al rosmarino*, a round of beef sliced paper thin.

Barolo

398 West Broadway, between Spring and Broome Sts (226-1102). Subway: C, E to Spring St. Mon–Fri 10am–midnight; Sat, Sun 10am–1am. Average main course $20. AmEx, Disc, MC, V. This Soho attraction draws a swanky crowd that's heavily into money and looks. Barolo is a place where you can comfortably chat on your cell phone while digging into penne with lamb and artichokes. It's a perfect summer choice, due to the enormous garden in the back, complete with lush trees lit with tiny lights.

Bona Fides

60 Second Ave between 3rd and 4th Sts (777-2840). Subway: 6 to Astor Pl. Mon–Thu, Sun 5–11pm; Fri, Sat 5pm–midnight (dinner). Average main course $9. AmEx, DC, MC, V. A mellow and unremarkably pretty place with a long dining room and a partially tented garden area, this East Village Italian restaurant serves meals that never exceed the $10 mark and include free bruschetta. Even regu-

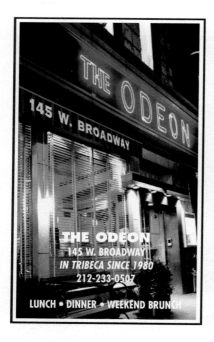

Dog day afternoon: For a quick lunch fix, grab a hot dog (don't forget the sauerkraut) and go.

lar diners still regard Bona Fides as a place they have just stumbled upon, wondering at their luck.

Carmine's

2450 Broadway between 90th and 91st Sts (362-2200). Subway: 1, 2, 3, 9 to 96th St. Mon–Thu 5–11pm; Fri 5pm–midnight; Sat 5pm–1am; Sun 2–10pm. ● *200 W 44th St between Broadway and Eighth Ave (221-3800). Subway: N, R, S, 1, 2, 3, 9, 7 to 42nd St–Times Sq. Tue–Sat 11:30–midnight; Sun, Mon 11:30am–11pm. Average main course $20. AmEx, MC, V.* Plenty of pasta and garlic are the hallmarks of Manhattan's two Carmine's, both southern Italian eateries that serve gargantuan portions of noodles in a warm, raucous setting. The reservation policy can be tricky; call ahead, and if you can't get a table, be ready to wait.

La Focacceria

128 First Ave between 7th St and St. Marks Pl (254-4946). Subway: 6 to Astor Pl. Mon–Thu 10am–10pm; Fri, Sat 10am–11pm. Average main course $7. No credit cards. First, order a half carafe of the delicious house chianti, fill your tumbler and drink to the abolition of long-stemmed glasses and overpriced wine lists. Now, scan the food choices on the wall. (This brightly lit pasta factory has been here since 1914 and still hasn't got around to printing a menu.) Everything's so cheap you can probably afford to order appetizers, pasta and a main course, but portions are big enough that you don't have to.

Le Madri

168 W 18th St between Sixth and Seventh Aves (727-8022). Subway: 1, 9 to 18th St. Noon–3pm (lunch), 5:30–11pm (dinner). Average main course $25. AmEx, DC, MC, V.

You'll be hungry after an arduous day of shopping at Loehmann's. Just a step away is this spotless, classy Tuscan restaurant serving exciting pastas, pizzas, bread salads and grilled vegetables. The garden patio opens with the arrival of warm weather.

La Mela

137 Mulberry St between Grand and Broome Sts (431-9493). Subway: B, D to Grand St. Noon–11pm. Average main course $13. AmEx, DC, MC, V. Located on the main strip in Little Italy, La Mela looks a bit touristy, but you'll still find many old-timers ordering wine by the color (white or red) to go with mounds of traditional Italian antipasti, heaps of pasta (lasagna, tortellini, ravioli and spaghetti) and large plates of desserts.

Orologio

162 Ave A between 10th and 11th Sts (228-6900). Subway: 6 to Astor Pl, L to First Ave. Mon–Thu, Sun 5:30pm–midnight; Fri, Sat 5:30pm–1am. Average main course $10. No credit cards. Orologio is one of the many restaurants that have sprouted in the past five years on the formerly desolate and now gentrified Avenue A. There's little elbow room at this trattoria, which offers a modestly priced wine list and cheap pasta that's always properly al dente and never swimming in sauce.

Piadina

57 W 10th St between Sixth and Seventh Aves (460-8017). Subway: C, E to 14th St. 5:30–11:30pm. Average main course $12. No credit cards. At times, Piadina feels less like a restaurant and more like a commissary for the fashion industry. Even if you're wearing chinos instead of Helmut Lang, you'll love this eatery's worn-in Euro-bohemian vibe, candlelit glow and impressive Tuscan food. Start off with warm polenta bathed in Gorgonzola cream sauce, move on to spinach gnocchi and try not to stare too much at that model sitting at the next table.

Pó

31 Cornelia St between Bleecker and W 4th Sts (645-2189). Subway: A, C, E, B, D, F, Q to W 4th St–Washington Sq. 11:30am–2pm Wed–Sun (lunch). Tue–Thu 5:30–11pm; Fri, Sat 5:30–11:30pm; Sun 5–10pm (dinner). Average main course $23. AmEx. Chef Mario Battali, who has his own show on cable's TV Food Network, makes this tiny West Village restaurant an unforgettable treat. The complimentary rosemary-laced white bean bruschetta that's brought to the table as you're seated is a harbinger of the simple masterpieces to come.

Trattoria Dell'Arte

900 Seventh Ave between 56th and 57th Sts (245-9800). Subway: N, R to 57th St. Sat, Sun 11:45am–3:30pm (brunch). Mon–Fri 11:30am–2:30pm (lunch). Mon–Sat 5–11:30pm (dinner). Average main course $25. AmEx, Disc, MC, V. Decorated with artwork of body parts, including a huge nose near the bar, this trilevel pretheater spot is popular with celebrities. Hope to get seated downstairs, though the contemporary Italian food will taste great no matter where you are.

Pizza

John's Pizzeria

278 Bleecker St between Sixth and Seventh Aves (243-1680). Subway: A, C, E, B, D, F, Q to W 4th St–Washington Sq; 1, 9 to Christopher St. Mon–Sat 11:30am–midnight; Sun noon–midnight. Medium pizza $10. No credit cards. The brick-oven pizza at John's has long been a contender for annu-

al best pizza awards. Although there are two newer uptown branches, head to the original in the Village, which has been expanded. Find the oldest part of the restaurant and sit in a scratched wooden booth. Someone will inevitably play Sinatra on the jukebox, and your thin-crusted pizza, which can easily be shared by two, will arrive within minutes.
Branches: *408 E 64th St (935-2895); 48 W 65th St (721-7001). Call for hours.*

Lombardi's

32 Spring St between Mott and Mulberry Sts (941-7994). Subway: 6 to Spring St. Mon–Thu 11:30am–11pm; Fri, Sat 11am–midnight; Sun 11:30am–10pm. Large pizza $12.50. No credit cards. This narrow pizzeria in Little Italy first opened at the turn of the century as a pasta restaurant. Closed in the late 1980s, Lombardi's reopened four years ago to sell only pizza and quickly became a hit with the locals. The pizza, made with fresh ingredients, is baked in a coal oven and has a thin but chewy crust.

Patsy Grimaldi's

19 Old Fulton St between Front and Water Sts, Brooklyn Heights, Brooklyn (1-718-858-4300). Subway: A, C to High St. Mon–Thu 11:30am–11pm; Fri 11:30am–midnight; Sat 2pm–midnight; Sun 2–11pm. Large pizza $12. No credit cards. Make a detour to this bustling sit-down pizzeria near the stunning waterfront facing downtown Manhattan. The thin, brick-oven pizza, piled with fresh mozzarella and tomatoes, has a delicious, slightly oily crust that could be eaten on its own.

Totonno's

1524 Neptune Ave between 15th and 16th Sts (1-718-372-8606). Subway: B, D, F, N to Stillwell Ave–Coney Island. Thu–Sun noon–8:30pm. Large pizza $14.50 AmEx, DC, MC, V. Pizza lovers in search of the best New York pie no longer need to make the pilgrimage to Coney Island. After almost 75 years at the beach, the Pero family brought their deli-

*Take your time: Get in line for the popular weekend brunch at **Time Café** (380 Lafayette Street, 533-7000), especially in summer, when this East Village fave serves alfresco.*

*Steak out: The pound-and-a-half porterhouse at **Peter Luger** is a vegetarian's nightmare.*

*Culture clash: Italy meets Louisiana at **Two Boots** (37 Ave A, 505-2276). Favorites at this kid-friendly restaurant include the Cajun pizza—shrimp, crawfish and jalapeños. Hot stuff!*

cious pies to Manhattan in 1997. The tomatoes are just as fresh and the mozzarella just as creamy, but the dining experience is more memorable in funky Luna Park.
Branch: *1544 Second Ave between 80th and 81st Sts. Subway: 6 to 79th St (327-2800). Call for hours.*

Patsy's Pizzeria
2287 First Ave between 117th and 118th Sts (534-9783). Subway: 6 to 116th St. 11am–midnight. Large pizza $10. No credit cards. No matter how hard you try, you'll never find coal-oven pizza in Manhattan that can measure up to a pie at Patsy's. Not only is each ingredient perfect on its own, but they're even better blended together on a blackened, blistered crust (which somehow is still moist and chewy). But the purity of the design evident in the pizza is less apparent in the decor. Expect a crude wood counter, a hulking oven, random oil paintings and a few pictures of the late, great Frank Sinatra.

Japanese

Honmura An
170 Mercer St between Prince and Houston Sts (334-5253). Subway: N, R to Prince St. Tue–Thu 6:30–10pm; Fri, Sat 6–10:30pm; Sun 6–9:30pm (dinner). Average main course $20. AmEx, DC, MC, V. There's quiet, Zenlike harmony just off Houston—for a price. Start with *edamame* pea pods, then get into buckwheat noodles like you've never tasted, including hearty *nabeyaki udon* with chicken and shrimp.

Sandobe Sushi
330 E 11th St between First and Second Aves (780-0328). Subway: L to First Ave, 6 to Astor Pl. 5:30pm–1am. Average main course $11. No credit cards. When you leave this three-room restaurant, you will feel foolish for ever having eaten mediocre sushi. Chef Kirjin Kim's menu is incredibly delicious, especially considering his fish is some of the cheapest in the city. There are lush, generous slabs of tuna and salmon, but the real stars here are the rolls, in all the colors of the sushi rainbow.

Oikawa
805 Third Ave at 50th St (980-1400). Subway: 6 to 51st St; E, F to Lexington–Third Aves. Mon–Fri 11:30am–2:30pm (lunch). Mon–Sat 5:30pm–12:30am; Sun 5:30–11pm (dinner). Average meal $18.50. AmEx, DC, MC, V. Located in a glassy, mall-like midtown building, Oikawa may look sterile, but the food is thrilling. Sample the shredded jellyfish, chopped shark fin with plum sauce, or squid with spicy cod roe. Even the sushi is pretty creative; try the salmon-and-eel roll, gently fried tempura-style.

Omen
113 Thompson St between Prince and Spring Sts (925-8923). Subway: C, E to Spring St. 5:30–10:30pm. Average main course $18. AmEx. Not even the salads are bad omens at this calm Soho eatery. The house salad is enlivened with seaweed and baby scallops, a perfect accompaniment to an assortment of sashimi. Order the herby *chiso* rice on the side.

Takahachi
85 Ave A between 5th and 6th Sts (505-6524). Subway: F to Second Ave. 5:30pm–12:45am. Average main course $14. AmEx, MC, V. Fresh slivers of fish and waiters in matching T-shirts are about the only consistent elements here; everything else is Avenue-A eclectic. Early-bird specials ($13, until 7pm) are a good value and and a smart way to beat the dinner rush.

Tomoe Sushi
172 Thompson St between Houston and Bleecker Sts (777-9346). Subway: A, C, E, D, F Q to W 4th St–Washington Sq;

1, 9 to Houston St. Wed–Sat 1–3pm (lunch). Mon, Wed–Sat 5–11pm (dinner). Average main course $18. AmEx. The fussy folks here take only American Express and expect you to wait outside in the cold for a table. Everyone puts up with it, though, because the bargain sushi is always as big as your fist, and sometimes, it's among the silkiest and tastiest in the city.

Yama

122 E 17th St at Irving Pl (475-0969). Subway: L, N, R, 4, 5, 6 to 14th St–Union Sq. Mon–Fri noon–2:20pm (lunch). Mon–Thu 5:30–10:20pm; Fri, Sat 5:30–11:20pm (dinner). Average main course $16. AmEx, MC, V. Good, fresh sushi and big bento-box dinner deals keep this place packed. (It's the former home of writer Washington Irving.) If you have to line up outside, you couldn't pick a prettier block.

tive Mexican restaurant has two floors, the upper being quieter. Owner Zarela Martinez is serious about the food she offers and has even penned a cookbook, *Food From My Heart.*

Zócalo

174 E 82nd St between Lexington and Third Aves (717-7772). Subway: 4, 5, 6 to 86th St. 6pm–midnight. Average main course $20. AmEx, MC, V. At this candlelit spot (with orange-colored walls and a green ceiling), you can expect the kind of food that Mexicans eat in their homes. Empanadas are filled with such ingredients as oysters or zucchini, and the *pozole* (pork and hominy stew) is a great choice after too many margaritas.

South American / Caribbean

848). Subain course f the best theater or arnations a coconut Brazilian

lve (586-on–midrse $20. able theinhattan way's fao with a to sweet

Deegan 07th St. n. Patio: course: and the Taking t mecca t nightis with s of the ction of

6412). verage A failwhere nen sit mptuunnyway to

E to , Sun st Sts n. Avmeal h exboth ed to nt to

OSPREY
h o l i d a y s

NEW YORK
HELPFUL HINTS

• • • CONTENTS • • •

order more—say, the *menudencias fritas*, a melange of chicken hearts, liver, gizzards and necks gently sauteed. Portions are large, so choose carefully or be prepared to cart around your leftovers.

Chimichurri Grill

606 Ninth Ave between 43rd and 44th Sts (586-8655). Subway: A, C, E to 42nd St. Mon–Thu noon–11pm; Fri, Sat noon–11:30pm. Average main course $18. Amex, V, MC. The warm atmosphere in this compact, neatly appointed dining room is reason enough to squeeze into one of Chimichurri's 30 seats, but the simple, rich Argentinean cuisine cinches the deal. Main courses revolve around imported Argentinean beef, best accented with *chimichurri*, a pesto-like mixture of garlic, olive oil, oregano, parsley and roasted red peppers.

Southeast Asian

Dok Suni

119 First Ave between 7th St and St. Marks Pl (477-9506). Subway: 6 to Astor Pl. 4:30–11:30pm. Average main course $12. No credit cards. Korean "home cooking" might not resemble anything you've ever cooked at home. But this woody East Villager is downtown-homey, featuring an ample menu of stir-fried kimchi with rice, braised short ribs, grilled squid and other straightforward alternatives to Chinese takeout.

Kelley and Ping

127 Greene St between Houston and Prince Sts (228-1212). Subway: N, R to Prince St. 11:30am–5pm (lunch), 6-11:30pm (dinner). Average main course $13. AmEx, MC, V. This cool spot is part Saigon corner deli, part pan-Asian noodle bar. Nothing beats the cold weather like an oversize bowl of steaming soup with chow fun noodles and shredded pork. K and P is narrow and packed at lunchtime, but you and your credit card will feel far away from the area's shopping traps.

Penang

109 Spring St between Greene and Mercer Sts (274-8883). Subway: N, R to Prince St. Mon–Thu 11:30am–midnight; Fri, Sat 11:30am–1am; Sun 1pm–midnight. ●*38-04 Prince St at Main St, Flushing, Queens (call 1-718-321-2078 for hours). Subway: 7 to Main St–Flushing.* ●*240 Columbus Ave at 71st St (call 769-3988 for hours). Subway: A, C, B, D to 72nd St.* ●*1596 Second Ave between 82nd and 83rd Sts (call 585-3838 for hours). Subway: 4,5,6 to 86th St. Average main course $13. AmEx, MC, V.* The Penangs are variously owned but share a transporting, slightly silly decor and menu of serious Malaysian intrigue. Ask for traditional fish-head soup, or stick to more approachable fare, such as spring rolls with jicama or a whole striped bass in banana leaves.

Pho Bang

117 Mott St at Hester St (966-3797). Subway: J, N, R, 6 to Canal St. 10am–10pm. Average main course $8. No credit cards. The AOR background music and the dapper wait staff in vests and bowties add to the charm of this Vietnamese diner. The Bang family has six restaurants in the metropolitan area, but this is where to get the greatest Bang for your buck: For $5.95, you get logs of beef stuffed with onions, which you roll up with squares of vermicelli rice noodles and crisp greens, and then dunk in a sweet fish sauce. But think twice before ordering the salty lemonade.

Spanish

El Faro

823 Greenwich St at Horatio St (929-8210). Subway: A, C to 14th St; L to Eigth Ave. Mon–Thu 11:30am–midnight; Fri, Sat 11:30am–1am. Average main course $19. AmEx, Disc, MC, V. Ancient and constant, this West Villager is widely regarded as having some of the best Spanish food in the borough of Manhattan.

Ñ

33 Crosby St between Broome and Grand Sts (219-8856). Subway: 6 to Spring St. 5pm–midnight. Average main course $15. No credit cards. Straight out of an Almodóvar movie, Ñ (pronounced en-yay) has yellow and red polka-dotted walls and copper-penny sculptures. It's a narrow, cool, dark spot, great for beating the heat of a Soho summer with a pitcher of sangria, or for cozying up in cooler seasons with copious tapas. Tuck yourself into a table and try the *pan con tomate*, and marinated anchovies called *boquerones*.

El Quixote

226 W 23rd St between Seventh and Eighth Aves (929-1855). Subway: 1, 9 to 23rd St. Mon–Thu, Sun noon–midnight; Fri, Sat noon–1am. Average main course $19. AmEx, DC, Disc, MC, V. It's in the eternally quirky Chelsea Hotel, but El Quixote is straight-faced, old-school Spanish. With its endearingly serious uniformed waiters, murals starring the ubiquitous Mr. La Mancha, and its huge platters of paella and cut-rate lobster specials, El Quixote proves it's hip to be square.

Rio Mar

7 Ninth Ave at Little West 12th St (243-9015). Subway: A, C, E to 14th St. Noon–3am. Average main course $14. AmEx. On a desolate, ragged stretch of the meat packing district sits Rio Mar, partying all by itself. It's an unexpected home of sangria by the pitcher, fantastically oily and garlicky tapas, a nearly all-Spanish jukebox, and a hell of a lot of up-late fun.

Tapas Lounge

1078 First Ave between 58th and 59th Sts (421-8282). Subway: N, R to Lexington Ave; 4, 5, 6 to 59th St. Mon, Tue, Sun 5:30pm–midnight; Wed–Sat 5:30pm–3am. Average main course $12. AmEx. Little Spanish snacks are the familiar premise around which the guys at Tapas Lounge have built an ongoing party. Music, chatter, low lighting, low seating and a higher than expected pretty-people quotient for this residential Siberia all add to the good time. The look is midway between a fetishist's dark chamber and a theme-park lounge, but the paella is moist and huge. Where else in the neighborhood can you stay up all night smoking Turkish tobacco in a hookah?

Vegetarian

Angelica Kitchen

300 E 12th St between First and Second Aves (228-2909). Subway: L to First Ave; N, R, 4, 5, 6 to 14th St–Union Sq. 11:30am–10:30pm. Average main course $10. No credit cards. The best vegan restaurant in the city, this soothing oblong fishbowl serves up tasty dishes such as the velvety sesame-noodle dish soba sensation, the (huge) Wee Dragon bowl and an array of cheesy cheeseless specials. If you are a vegan, vegetarian or health-food enthusiast, you must pay Angelica's a visit.

B&H Dairy

127 Second Ave between 7th St and St. Marks Pl (505-8065). Subway: 6 to Astor Pl. Mon–Sat 6:30am–10pm; Sun 7am–10pm. Average main course $8. No credit cards. B&H looks just like a standard ham'n'eggs American diner but serves an astonishing range of hearty vegetarian soups, juices, great homemade challah bread and veggie burgers. It's the antidote to prissy, self-righteous vegetarian dining.

Kate's Joint

58 Ave B between 4th and 5th Sts (777-7059). Subway: F to Second Ave. Mon–Wed 8:30am–11pm; Thu–Sun 8:30am–midnight. Average main course $9. AmEx, DC, MC, V. Kate's is a lazy, laid-back Alphabet City family business, with a comfy living-room area at the front. Kate, the chef, is a master at faux meat. Try her mock popcorn shrimp with Abijah's Secret Sauce and her faux Jamaican patties. Watch out for her kids.

Strictly Roots

2058 Adam Clayton Powell Blvd between 122nd and 123rd Sts (864-8699). Subway: 2, 3 to 125th St. Mon–Sat 11am–11pm; Sun noon–7pm. Average main course $8. No credit cards. This Harlem diner serves "nothing that crawls, swims, walks or flies." Delicious food such as the mock-beef stew

make it worth a visit, but don't miss the frothy shakes with names like Bad Man, served by friendly Rasta dudes.

Zen Palate

34 Union Sq East at 16th St (614-9291). Subway: L, N, R, 4, 5, 6 to 14th St–Union Sq. Mon–Sat 11:30am–3pm (lunch). Mon–Sat 5:30–11pm, Sun 5–10:30pm (dinner). ● 663 Ninth Ave at 46th St (call 582-1669 for hours). Subway: A, C, E, to 42nd St. ● 2170 Broadway between 76th and 77th Sts (call 501-7768 for hours). Subway: 1, 2, 3, 9 to 79th St. Average main course $13. AmEx, DC, MC, V. Decorated like delicate Japanese bistros, these restaurants have quickly become favorites among many New Yorkers, vegetarian or not. Despite selections with names such as Shredded Melody, the food is good, and each branch is perennially packed.

Amazing grazing

These storefronts and food carts help you feed your constant craving

Quintessential New York grub can be eaten anywhere—standing up, sitting down, even running. The classic meals are pizza, hot dogs, falafel, bagels, sandwiches and soup. But like the city itself, the list is constantly expanding to include new immigrant foods and new ideas. Whatever your taste, you'll never have to go too far to find a cart, a shallow storefront or a kiosk where cheap but delicious food is sold. Just follow your nose.

Here are some perennial favorites, as well as some noteworthy newcomers.

Ask any midtown drone for the most popular food stand and you'll be directed to **Soup Kitchen International** (259A W 55th St between Eighth and Ninth Aves, 757-7730). The owner, commonly known as the "Soup Nazi" (a reference to his cantankerous personality, made famous by the *Seinfeld* show), offers deliciously thick soups with innovative ingredients. If you want to see New Yorkers standing in line like Soviet-era grandmothers, head to **Moshe's Falafel** stand (Sixth Ave at 46th St). Here the pita is stuffed with falafel, salad and a sweet pickle and then drenched in tahini; Israeli hot sauce is optional. If you're still in the nabe the next day, stop by the treasure trove of carts on 45th St between Vanderbilt and Lexington Avenues. Choose from baked potatoes, soup and salad, Philly cheese-steak sandwiches or Egyptian chicken and rice.

Though midtown is cart central, other areas have their gems too. In Harlem, swing by the small taco stand in front of the restaurant **Hecho en Mexico** (234 E 116th St between Second and Third Aves). Chunks of roasted pork are spooned into doubled-up tortillas, along with pickled onion, tomato and fresh cilantro—all for $1.

The Upper West Side boasts two great bageleries: **Columbia Bagels** (2836 Broadway between 110th and 111th Sts, 222-3200) has unforgettable, and very oniony, tuna salad; **H&H Bagels** (2239 Broadway at 80th St, 595-8003; or 639 W 46th St at Twelfth Ave, 595-8000) serves bagels that are large, chewy and always fresh.

Downtown, it's much harder to find a cheap snack. **Le Gamin Buvette** (410 West Broadway between Prince and Spring Sts), a new crepe stand, now fills the fast-food void in Soho. If you're passing through Greenwich Village, **Joe's Pizza** (233 Bleecker St at Carmine St, 366-1182) serves up pies with a thin, chewy crust, topped by a tangy sauce and fresh mozzarella. Heading east, you'll find one of the most popular new snack stands, Pommes Frites (*see* **Cheap eats**, *page 140*). This storefront can make a meal out of fresh, hot and salty Belgian fries, authentically served in a large paper cone.

The ethnic neighborhoods to the south have their own culinary charms. **The Italian Food Center** (186 Grand St at Mulberry St, 925-2954) is Little Italy's finest takeout spot. Order a house-baked roll stuffed with Genoa salami, mortadella, fresh mozzarella and roasted peppers. And in Chinatown you'll find carts offering huge portions of chow fun, egg rolls and scallion pancakes at the confluence of Walker, Canal and Lafayette streets.

Finally, don't forget to stop by **Gray's Papaya** for a couple of cheap and tasty hot dogs (2090 Broadway at 72nd St, 799-9243; Sixth Ave at 8th St, 260-3532). With a perfect dog in hand, you're ready to start hunting for your next snack.

Cafés & Bars

Of all the gin joints in the world, you have to walk into these. Here's where to drink your fill, with a heady slug of New York life as a chaser.

Bookish prize: Catch up on some reading over a pot at the Anglophilic **Tea & Sympathy**.

Cafés

For a while there, it seemed as if New Yorkers were trying to classify coffee bars as more of a trend than a habit. But with Starbucks and other chains still gobbling up retail space, the citywide addiction is out in the open, and it's safe to say that New Yorkers are permanently hooked on joe. The question is how you want to get your fix: The trendy crowd likes its lattes in laid-back lounges that offer a profusion of sofas and magazines. Foodies want a bite to eat while they're sipping their brew, and many cafés offer delectable home-made desserts and sandwiches. Those on the run can stop into a coffee bar and get a double cappuccino to go. And traditionalists can still find a string of old-fashioned cafés on Bleecker Street in the West Village; there you can sit with your espresso and watch the crowds go by.

Big Cup

228 Eighth Ave between 21st and 22nd Sts (206-0059). Subway: C, E to 23rd St. Mon–Thu 7am–1am; Fri 7am–2am; *Sat, Sun 8am–2am. No credit cards.* This Chelsea coffee shop is a popular morning hangout for the local gay population. The café has a comfortable mix of living-room furniture that makes it an ideal place to skim the newspaper while inhaling a muffin and some coffee.

Cafe Gitane

242 Mott St between Houston and Prince Sts (334-9552). Subway: N, R to Prince St; B, D, F, Q to Broadway–Lafayette St. 9am–midnight. No credit cards. Walk by this Frenchy café on a sunny day, and you'll feel as if you've discovered the source of downtown cool. Hipsters lounge outside on small benches; inside, they sip café au lait, smoke and read the many fashion glossies the café offers as reading material. Don't be afraid to join the scene—these pretty young things don't bite (and you might get some swell fashion ideas).

Café Lalo

201 W 83rd St between Amsterdam Ave and Broadway (496-6031). Subway: 1, 9 to 86th St. Mon–Thu, Sun 9am–2am; Fri, Sat 9am–4am. No credit cards. This perennially popular Upper West Side café has one of the city's largest dessert selections—all sorts of chocolate and fruit cakes, plus all-American pies, such as pecan and apple. In summer, the long windows open onto the tree-lined street, European-style. Classical melodies are the music of choice here.

Caffe Reggio

119 MacDougal St between W 3rd and Bleecker Sts (475-9557). Subway: A, C, E, B, D, F, Q to West 4th St–Washington Sq. Mon–Thu, Sun 10am–2am; Fri, Sat 10am–4am. No credit cards. A favorite spot with tourists and New Yorkers who don't live downtown (if they did, they'd know of more chic and less crowded places to go), Caffe Reggio is a great spot for people watching and coffee drinking.

Ceci-Cela

55 Spring St between Lafayette and Mulberry Sts (274-9179). Subway: 6 to Spring St. Mon–Sat 7am–7pm, Sun 8am–7pm. MC, V. Tucked in a narrow space away from the weekend throngs of Soho, Ceci-Cela offers its own French pastries and crispy croissants in a cozy and relaxed setting. Get some dessert to go, or walk to the back room, where there are a few rattan tables and waitress service.

City Bakery

22 E 17th St between Fifth Ave and Broadway (366-1414). Subway: L, N, R, 4, 5, 6 to 14th St–Union Sq. Mon–Sat 7:30am–6pm. AmEx, MC, V. Don't be fooled by the drafty, industrial decor of this Flatiron bakery. The rich tarts found here are some of the best in the city, scoring high marks for taste, originality and design. Make a detour on Saturday morning before heading to the Union Square's outdoor farmer's market and order a coffee and a tart. Before you know it, you'll be craving chef/owner Maury Rubin's pastry cookbook, available in the store.

Cupcake Café

522 Ninth Ave at 39th St (465-1530). Subway: A, C, E to 42nd St. Mon–Fri 7am–7pm, Sat 8am–7pm; Sun 9am–5pm. No credit cards. There's little room for loungers at this off-the-beaten-track bakery in Hell's Kitchen; it only has a few shabby tables. Cupcakes and cakes are exquisitely decorated with rich, buttery frosting swirled into colorful flowers. If you can't stomach so much fat, try a freshly made doughnut or muffin.

DeRoberti's

176 First Ave at 11th St (674-7137). Subway: L to First Ave. Tue–Thu, Sun 9am–11pm; Fri, Sat 9am–midnight. MC, V. Located in a pocket of the East Village that closely resembles Little Italy, DeRoberti's is a decades-old patisserie where espresso, cappuccino and Italian desserts such as cannoli and hazelnut meringues are served in a beautiful old-fashioned setting.

Drip

489 Amsterdam Ave between 83rd and 84th Sts (875-1032). Subway: 1, 9 to 86th St. Mon–Thu 7am–1am; Fri, Sat 7am–3am; Sun 7am–midnight. MC, V. Brightly colored mock-leather couches fill this coffee lounge and bar. Its walls display junk food props, such as Cap'n Crunch cereal and Orangina soda. The list of coffees—espresso, cappuccino, au lait, mochaccino—is short, but sufficient. At the back is a "love life" notice board, where you can fill out a questionnaire about the mate of your dreams.

DT/UT

1626 Second Ave at 84th St (327-1327). Subway: 4, 5, 6 to 86th St. Mon–Thu, Sun 7:30am–midnight; Fri, Sat 8:30am–2am. No credit cards. The name of this brick-walled space, decorated with Gothic candles and primitive art, is an abbreviation for downtown/uptown. Plop into a couch or easy chair and choose from a tantalizing array of baked goods—perfect accompaniments for the many different types of coffee listed on the blackboard.

Felissimo

10 W 56th St between Fifth and Sixth Aves (956-0082). Subway: N, R to Fifth Ave. Mon–Sat 10:30am–6pm. AmEx, DC, Disc, MC, V. The newly renovated Felissimo is a chic bazaar occupying a narrow townhouse off the deluxe shopping extravaganza that is Fifth Avenue. The simple Japanese-inspired decor is wonderfully soothing; this is a great place to rest your tired feet. On the top floor, you'll find a tranquil café serving sandwiches, cakes and tea. Sometimes a tarot-card reader takes up residence in one corner, selling a glimpse of the future to the forever hopeful.

Hungarian Pastry Shop

1030 Amsterdam Ave at 111th St (866–4230). Subway: B, C, 1, 9 to 110th St. Mon–Fri 8am–11:30pm, Sat 8:30am–11:30pm, Sun 8:30am–10pm. No credit cards. A Morningside Heights original, this plain-looking coffee shop offers coffee, tea and many pastries (made in-house) to Columbia University students and teachers. Ignore the pretentious students around you reading Kant and pull out that Jackie Collins novel you've been meaning to read.

Limbo

47 Ave A between 3rd and 4th Sts (477-5271). Subway: F to Second Ave. Mon–Fri 7am–midnight; Sat, Sun 8am–midnight. No credit cards. To get a real sense of the East Village, come to this stylish self-service coffee hangout. Freelance writers, actors and artists sit for hours, drinking large cups of tea or coffee, reading scripts and typing manuscripts on their portable computers. A continuous stream of book, poetry and tarot-card readings attracts crowds in the evenings.

Once Upon a Tart

135 Sullivan St between Houston and Prince Sts (387-8869). Subway: N, R to Prince St; C, E to Spring St. Mon–Fri 8am–8pm, Sat 9am–8pm, Sun 9am–6pm. AmEx, MC, V. Waiting for the shops in Soho to open, which many do notoriously late? Stop by this small, tin-ceilinged café first for a steaming cup of café au lait or cappuccino. At breakfast, try one of the café's excellent muffins or scones. Or order a sandwich, packed with fresh ingredients on fresh bread or focaccia.

Tea & Sympathy

108 Greenwich Ave at 13th St (807-8329). Subway: L, 1, 2, 3, 9 to 14th St. Mon–Fri 11:30am–10:30pm, Sat 11:30am–10:30pm, Sun 11:30am–10pm. No credit cards. Visit this cramped English nook during the week—on weekends the wait is annoyingly long—and order delights from Blighty, including beans on toast and cucumber sandwiches. Afternoon tea consists of an assortment of finger sandwiches, two cakes, two scones, clotted cream, jam and a pot of tea. Here, Britannia rules.

Bars

Whether your taste runs to dingy gin mill, fabulous lounge or ale house, New York is a damn fine drinking town. This year's hottest openings are bar-restaurants (*see* **Pour nutrition,** *page 162*) that are swarming with fashionistas and European expats. Leonardo DiCaprio sightings are also not uncommon. The brewhouse and cigar bar fads are fading, and the cosmopolitan—the early-'90s libation of choice—is now officially tired (for a list of the city's best and most dangerous cocktails, *see* **Name your poison,** *page 161*). The rest of the bars here should quench the thirst of any type of drinker, from the polite sipper to the perenially pickled hooch hound.

288

288 Elizabeth St between Houston and Bleecker Sts (260-5045). Subway: B, D, F, Q to Broadway–Lafayette St; 6 to Bleecker St.

*Good for what ales ya: Serving double-fisted fun at **McSorley's**, Manhattan's oldest pub.*

Noon–4am. No credit cards. Also called Tom & Jerry's, this is a cavernous drinking hall that gets smoky and loud. It also serves a great Guinness to an arty, slightly slackerish crowd.

Baby Jupiter
170 Orchard St at Stanton St (982-2229). Subway: F to Second Ave. 11am–4am. MC, V, Transmedia, IGT. Good barbecue and a raucous back room featuring local unsigned bands have made Baby Jupiter an excellent addition to the batch of no-cover music venues on the Lower East Side.

Barmacy
538 E 14th St between Aves A and B (228-2240). Subway: L to First Ave. Mon–Fri 5:30pm–4am; Sat, Sun 7:30pm–4am. No credit cards. Formerly (you guessed it) a pharmacy, Barmacy is American-kitsch queen Deb Parker's latest project. Packed to the hilt with 1950s Rx paraphernalia, it remains a fun and trendy spot (when taken in the right dosage). The decor includes ads for prosthetics, adult diapers, beakers instead of glasses and, thankfully, good DJs on the weekends.

Botanica
47 E Houston St between Mott and Mulberry Sts (343-7251). Subway: B, D, F, Q to Broadway–Lafayette St. 5pm–4am. No credit cards. It's easy to choke on the bohemian atmosphere here, but besides a few modern beatniks and a lot of Gitanes smoke, Botanica is a fine neighborhood gin mill with good DJs most nights.

Bubble Lounge
228 West Broadway between Franklin and White Sts (431-3433). Subway: 1, 9 to Franklin St; A, C, E to Canal St. Mon–Thu 5:30pm–4am; Fri, Sat 4:30pm–4am; Sun 4:30pm–1am. AmEx, DC, MC, V. Tribeca's very own cigar-and-champagne bar has the requisite sofas, wing-back chairs, Persian rugs and chandeliers, and it's made more bearable by the live jazz and good, caviar-heavy bar menu.

Chumley's
86 Bedford St between Barrow and Grove Sts (675-4449). Subway: A, C, E, B, D, F, Q to West 4th St–Washington Sq. Mon–Fri 5pm–midnight; Sat, Sun 5pm–2am. No credit cards. Someone needs to tell Chumley's that the days of prohibition are over. This ex-speakeasy still doesn't have a sign over the door, so it's easy to walk straight past it. Inside is a pub-restaurant with book-lined walls and a cozy atmosphere. The food is passable and well priced.

P. J. Clarke's
915 Third Ave at 55th St (355-8857). Subway: 6 to 51st St; E, F to Lexington Ave. 10am–4am. AmEx, DC, MC, V. A classic mahogany and cut-glass saloon dates from the days when Third Avenue was darkened by an elevated train and every corner had a watering hole. It survived prohibition; it also served as the location for The Lost Weekend. The whiskey's still good, and even the urinals should be a landmark.

Fanelli's
94 Prince St at Mercer St (226-9412). Subway: B, D, F, Q to Broadway–Lafayette St; N, R to Prince St; 6 to Bleecker St. Mon–Thu 10am–2am; Sat 11am–3am. AmEx, DC, Disc, MC, V. Fanelli's is the oldest and one of the best bars in Soho. It has a great wooden bar, wonderful barmen, tiled floors, framed pictures of boxers on the walls and local beers. It's decidedly unpretentious and a favorite with art-gallery owners. The food is good, but many use it as ballast for shots of Jack.

Fez
at Time Café, 380 Lafayette St at Great Jones St (533-7000). Subway: 6 to Astor Pl. Mon–Thu, Sun 6pm–2am; Fri, Sat

6pm–4am. AmEx, MC, V. Downstairs you'll find music and readings, but the bar is perfect for a good old lounge. Deep sofas, low tables, good low lighting and a slight Moroccan theme (just copper tables and paintings of Magreb mamas) all conspire to keep you reclining long into the night.

Global 33

93 Second Ave between 5th and 6th Sts (477-8427). Subway: 6 to Astor Pl. Mon–Thu 6pm–1am; Fri, Sat 6pm–2am. AmEx. The big modernist clocks in Global 33's back room tell you the time in Monte Carlo, Shanghai, Tangier, Istanbul and Havana—helpful if you're on an international espionage mission. But even if you're not, the sleek 1960s design practically forces you to drink something sophisticated, and the bar staff won't disappoint.

The Greatest Bar on Earth

Windows on the World, 1 World Trade Center, West St between Liberty and Vesey Sts, 107th floor (524-7011). Subway: C, E to World Trade Ctr; 1, 9 to Cortlandt St. Mon–Thu 4pm–midnight; Fri 4pm–2am; Sat noon–2am; Sun 11am–11pm. AmEx, DC, Disc, MC, V. No, this postmodern saloon in the sky certainly doesn't live up to the hyperbolic name, but it's nicely unearthly and brings an unlikely hip crowd to the Wall Street area. Get high among the odd spiky sculptures in the sky, and the whole city below appears festive.

Joe's

520 E 6th St between Aves A and B (473-9093). Subway: F to Second Ave. Noon–4am. No credit cards. Joe's is an East Village refuge for barflies young and old, with Hank Williams

Name your poison

When any old beer just won't do, swill these killer cocktails

There's a lot more to the cocktail culture than the garden-variety martini. Here is a guide to the city's most lethal and ludicrous concoctions.

THE ASILAH
Chez Es Saada

42 E 1st St between First and Second Aves (777-5617). Subway: F to Second Ave. Sun–Thu 6pm–2am; Fri, Sat 6pm–4am. $8. If you didn't make reservations two weeks ago, forget about eating in the Morrocan-inspired caverns of this downtown hotspot. Taste the best the upstairs bar has to offer—the delicate periwinkle blue Asilah, made with Stoli *oranj*, Parfait Amour, lemon juice and tonic—and cut the kick with the free hard-boiled eggs.

THE BIBLE BELT
Cowgirl Hall of Fame

519 Hudson St at W 10th St (633-1133). Subway: 1, 9 to Christopher St–Sheridan Sq. Sun–Thu noon–1am; Fri, Sat noon–3am. $5. You'll be praising the Lord after you commune with this margarita, made with Jack Daniels on the rocks and sugar on the rim. It's best enjoyed next to the big fireplace in the American Baroque backroom.

THE BONGWATER
Burrito Bar

305 Church St at Walker St (219-9200). Subway: 1, 9 to Canal St. Mon–Fri 11am–1am; Sat, Sun 11am–2am. $2 a shot. The bartenders here aren't too sure what's in this drink, but vodka, rum, peach and pineapple are involved. Sometimes it comes out green, sometimes black or blue, but it's a crowd pleaser at this Wall Street clubhouse.

THE CAJUN MARTINI
Great Jones Cafe

54 Great Jones St between Lafayette St and the Bowery (674-9304). Subway: 6 to Bleecker St. Mon–Thu 5pm–midnight, Fri 5pm–1am, Sat 11:30am–1am, Sun 11:30am–midnight. $3. You can keep your freaking cosmopolitan; the Cajun martini is the best enhanced-vodka drink in town. Its beauty is in its simplicity: jalepeños and

house vodka. It'll get you jumping to the excellent R&B and rockabilly jukebox in no time.

THE CANNIBAL CONCOCTION
Jekyll and Hyde

91 Seventh Ave South between Grove and Barrow Sts (989-7701). Subway: 1, 9 to Christopher St–Sheridan Sq. Mon–Thu 11:30am–4am; Sat, Sun noon–4am. $4.50 a shot. So what if this place is extremely Disneyfied? If you can squeeze past the tourists in this haunted house of spirits, sample the "deadly mixture" of rum, vodka and triple sec. After a couple, it will be hard to decide which is scarier, the crowd or the Bela Lugosi–era decorations.

THE LYCHEE DAIQUIRI
Angel's Share

8 Stuyvesant St between Third Ave and Ninth St (598-3041). Subway: 6 to Astor Pl. 9pm–2am. $8. The bartenders here make drinks with the grave caution of doctors handling test tubes of Ebola virus. They don't like publicity, and they won't share ingredients. But as you've gathered from the name, this delicious frozen confection does contain sweet lychee nut.

THE MOLOTOV COCKTAIL
KGB

85 E 4th St between Second and Third Aves (505-3360). Subway: F to Second Ave. 8pm–3am. $4 a shot. This former speakeasy was for many years the Ukranian communist headquarters in New York. Those days are gone, but after a few shots of Cuban rum and 100-proof Stoli, you'll definitely be seeing red.

THE PURPLE MONKEY
Monkey Bar

Hotel Elysee, 60 E 54th St between Park and Madison Aves (838-2600). Subway: E, F to Fifth Ave. Mon–Sat 4:30pm–2am. $8. No, there's no Brass Monkey in this fabulous purple sipper. Its delicately tart personality comes from vodka, Chambord and sweet-and-sour—perfect for the exotic, insouciant Monkey Bar.

and Dolly Parton on the jukebox, stingy bartenders and a pool table in the back.

Landmark Tavern
626 Eleventh Ave at 40th St (757-8595). Subway A, C, E to 42nd Street. Mon–Thu, Sun, noon–11pm; Fri, Sat noon–midnight. No credit cards. One of the most beautiful and tranquil of the town's old saloons, the Landmark has tin ceilings, wood-burning potbelly stoves and about five dozen single-malt Scotches on hand.

Lansky Lounge
104 Norfolk St between Delancey and Rivington Sts (677-9489). Subway: F to Delancey St; J, M, Z to Essex St. Sun–Thu 8pm–4am, Sat 10pm–4am. No credit cards. Named after Meyer Lansky, the legendary Jewish gangster who used to eat next door at the adjoining Ratner's deli, Lansky has a hidden entrance and a 1930s back room feel. It also has steep drink prices and an intermittent cover charge, suggesting that the owners think this place is cooler than it actually is. And remember—don't go on Friday nights: The club is kosher and closed for the Jewish sabbath.

McSorley's Old Ale House
15 E 7th St between Second and Third Aves (473-9148). Subway: 6 to Astor Place; N, R to 8th St. Mon–Sat 11–1am, Sun

1pm–1am. No credit cards. The oldest pub in Manhattan now admits women—and to judge by the usual clientele, these are mainly women who like their men in baseball caps and slobbery stages of inebriation. Still, it's a classic place for a mug of warm ale and a whiff of times gone by.

Max Fish
178 Ludlow St between Houston and Stanton Sts (529-3959). Subway: F to Second Ave. 5:30pm–4am. No credit cards. Before stumbling on to the Lower East Side's newest bars on Ludlow and Orchard Streets, enjoy a cheap beer at this nine-year-old institution, which caters to a cool bunch of musicians and artists who have remained loyal regulars.

Milano's
51 E Houston St between Mott and Mulberry Sts (226-8632). Subway: N, R to Prince St; B, D, F, Q to Broadway–Lafayette St. Mon–Sat 8–4am, Sun noon–4am. No credit cards. Have yourself a New York moment and a great pint of Guinness at this Irish/Italian dive bar on the cusp of Little Italy. Frank Sinatra's on the walls and on the jukebox, and the die-hard barflies are always ready for boozy conversation, should you be in the mood.

North Star Pub
93 South St at Fulton St (509-6757). Subway: A, C to Broadway–Nassau St; 2, 3, 4, 5, J, M, Z to Fulton St.

Pour nutrition

It ain't the eats, it's the potions at these swanky restaurant bars

Yes, they're restaurants—but most people don't go there for the food. They're really places to drink—but don't say that to the chef. During the past year, there has been a curious proliferation of high-profile, high-concept eateries equipped with spacious (often subterranean) cocktail areas, which is where the fabulosi gather. No reservations are required to enjoy the bar scenes, though you may need some pull with the doormen—yes, there are now doormen at restaurants. Best of all, if you get hungry, you won't have to go far.

Astor
316 Bleecker St at the Bowery (253-8644). Subway: 6 to Bleecker St. 6pm–3am. MC, V. Buried beneath Astor's 100-seat brasserie is a 1,500-square-foot lounge studded with seductive Moroccan tiles. Affordable contemporary American food is served on both floors until 4am on weekends, but when you're hanging out on a street that was once home to nearly every wino in New York, you're not here to eat.

Bond Street
6 Bond St between Broadway and Lafayette St (777-2500). Subway: 6 to Astor Pl. 5:30pm–2am. AmEx, MC, V. Perhaps the only thing more attractive than Bond Street's Gucci-wearing staff is the space itself: three floors of Japanese-inspired design, complete with a candlelit basement-level lounge. In addition to a full bar and a wide array of sake, the cocktail den also offers impeccable sushi.

Lot 61
550 W 21st St between Tenth and Eleventh Aves (243-6555). Subway: A, C, E to 23rd St. Mon–Sat 6pm–3am

AmEx, MC, V. Feeding on West Chelsea's thriving art scene, this former truck garage not only attracts a gallery-going clientele, it *looks* like a gallery, right down to its collection of commissioned works from big-name artists. Sliding scrims and funky furniture subdivide the warehouse-size space, and the eclectic menu of appetizers gives you something to talk about besides art.

Moomba
133 Seventh Ave South between W 10th and Charles Sts (989-1414) Subway: 1, 9 to Christopher St. 6pm–4am AmEx, MC, V. If you can get by the velvet rope, Moomba's attentive staff will actually make you feel as though you belong in this swank, triv-level celebrity superconducter. And in case you care, chef Frank Falcinelli's food is as interesting as the clientele.

Tonic
107 Norfolk St between Delancey and Rivington Sts (358-7503). Subway F to Delancey Street. 8–4am. AmEx, MC, V. Housed in a former Lower East Side kosher winery, Tonic is equal parts hair salon, café and bar. Most intriguing is the downstairs cocktail lounge, which utilizes remnants of the Kedem winery, including circular booths built within 2,500-gallon hardwood wine casks.

Torch
137 Ludlow St between Rivington and Stanton Sts (228-5151). Subway: F to Delancey Street. Sun–Thu 6pm–2am; Fri, Sat 6pm–4am. AmEx, MC, V. Combining elements of pre-Castro Havana and post-Hitler Paris, this sexy supper club is the first high-style eatery to touch down on bar-laden Ludlow Street. Sip a martini and enjoy the chanteuses performing nightly, or slip into one of the half-moon booths and savor the superb shrimp *ceviche* made with popcorn.

11:30am–midnight. AmEx, CB, DC, MC, V. Popular with homesick Brits and local Anglophiles, this waterfront pub is the genuine article (imported Brit beer *and* HP sauce to drench your pub grub with).

Oak Room
Algonquin Hotel, 59 W 44th St between Fifth and Sixth Aves (840-6800). Subway: B, D, F, Q to 42nd St; 7 to Fifth Ave. 11:30–1am. AmEx, CB, DC, Disc, MC, V. Once home to Dorothy Parker's legendary literary Round Table, the Oak Room recently underwent a major renovation. The patina of cigar smoke and spilled highballs has been removed, but the clubby atmosphere of one of New York's finest hotel bars remains.

Old Town Bar
45 E 18th St between Broadway and Park Ave South (529-6732). Subway: N, R, L, 4, 5, 6 to 14th St–Union Square. Mon–Sat 11:30am–midnight, Sun 1–10pm. AmEx, MC, V. Having aged like a fine whiskey, this wood-paneled bar is still going strong after more than a century. The two floors fill up with regulars and after-work mobs, but make your way to the long bar, order some stiff drinks and a top-notch burger, and you'll feel welcome.

Rudy's
627 Ninth Ave between 44th and 45th Sts (974-9169). Subway: A, C, E to 42nd St. 10–4am. No credit cards. Ninth Avenue may finally be getting its share of hip lounges, but the best place to be is parked at the bar at this unchanging institution. The red banquettes are full of customers because the beer is cheap, the hot dogs are free and the jukebox is full of great jazz. Then there's the human jazz of Rudy's dedicated regulars, young and old.

Sophie's
507 E 5th St between Aves A and B (no phone). Subway: F to Second Ave. 11–4am. No credit cards. Expect to find a young crowd here on weekends, when this seasoned East Village dive bar is packed with coeds looking for cheap draft beer and a turn at the pool table.

Spy
101 Greene St between Prince and Spring Sts (343-9000). Subway: N, R to Prince St; 6 to Spring St. 8pm–4am. AmEx, DC, MC, V. Spy is appropriately decadent, with dripping chandeliers and overstuffed seating. Even with the proliferation of sofas, this is really no place to relax—you've got far too much posing to do. Drop by any evening, and you're sure to spy a model or two.

Temple Bar
332 Lafayette St between Bleecker and Houston Sts (925-4242). Subway: 6 to Bleecker St. Mon–Thu 5pm–1am; Fri, Sat 5pm–2am, Sun 7pm–1am. AmEx, DC, MC, V. Temple's bartenders are dedicated masters of their trade, and the decor is sophisticated and opulent, lending an otherworldly air to what could become a long, dark night of expensive drinking.

Vasac
108 Ave B at 7th St (473-8840). Subway: L to First Ave. Noon–4am. AmEx, DC, Disc, MC, V. Also called 7B and the Horseshoe Bar, Vasac, with its spit and sawdust atmosphere, has been featured in countless films. The formerly edgy crowd has been replaced by a younger, bridge-and-tunnel set that likes to rock out to Dinosaur Junior and Superchunk on the alterna-heavy jukebox.

White Horse
567 Hudson St at 11th St (243-9260). Subway A, C, E to 14th St; L to Eighth Ave. Mon–Wed 11am–2am, Thu–Sat 11am–4am, Sun noon–2am. No credit cards. The White Horse is best visited on weekdays—in the evenings and on weekends the crowd becomes cheesy and noisy. It is one of New York's oldest pubs and is famous for being the site where Dylan Thomas had his final whiskey before he died in 1953. Don't expect anything special from the food.

*Drink like a fish: The Lower East Side's **Max Fish** is popular with musicians and artists.*

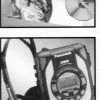

It's in the bag: Hit the streets of Manhattan if you need some hard-core retail therapy.

Shopping & Services

Shopping & Services

If you can't find it here, it probably never existed

Successful shopping in New York requires speed, tenacity and, above all, manners. There's an unspoken etiquette that separates the novices from the experienced; without being too gushy (New Yorkers don't trust anyone), remember that a smile goes an awfully long way. Some helpful tips: If an object strikes your fancy, grab it! You won't have to buy it—you've simply put it *on hold,* in a manner of speaking. In a midtown electronics shop or at a flea market, by all means haggle your heart out, but it's not appropriate behavior in even the smallest East Village boutique.

TACTICAL SPENDING

It's best to arrange your shopping trips by neighborhood. Starting at the southern tip of Man-

hattan, the skyscrapers of the **World Financial Center** are crammed with restaurants and shops. The Winter Garden, located in the central courtyard, contains tall palm trees and is flanked by a wide variety of boutiques and cafés.

Shopping becomes more serious as you head uptown, to the fashion haven of **Soho.** Lately, a herd of big-name designers have joined the likes of Comme des Garçons and agnès b. Also look for bookshops, art galleries, good-quality vintage clothes, modern furniture and shoe stores. **Lower Broadway below Houston,** bordering on Soho, is starting to resemble a pedestrian mall, with chain stores galore: Banana Republic, J. Crew and Victoria's Secret are all represented here. **Canal Street** is the place to find fake

*One shirt makes you larger...: Searching for buried treasure at **Alice's Underground**.*

*Market improvement: **Dean & DeLuca** sells some of the city's finest fruits and vegetables.*

*Click here: **Willoughby's** camera store brings your film and photo needs into sharp focus.*

Rolexes and Prada bags, as well as the best DJ mix tapes, at market stalls selling endless piles of counterfeit designer wares, electronics, sports shoes and T-shirts. And in **Chinatown**, along Mott and Mulberry Streets, you can pick up slippers, parasols and lanterns.

The **Lower East Side** is bargain-hunting territory. Many of the shops close early on Fridays and all day on Saturdays for the Jewish Sabbath. Don't miss **Orchard Street** from Houston to Delancey Streets, where you'll find leather goods, luggage, designer clothes, belts, shoes and yards of fabric. Another strip, on **Ludlow Street**, showcases a different side of the neighborhood: Here there are plenty of hip bars and boutiques filled with clothes by up-and-coming designers. The **East Village** has plenty of the latter, along with an abundance of secondhand shops. Check **9th Street** for clothes and furnishings, and **7th Street** for young designers.

As you wander west through **Greenwich Village**, the streets become progressively more deserted and winding. As in the East Village, shops here stay open late and are especially good for jazz records, rare books and vintage clothing—and don't forget the unmissable food shop Balducci's.

Fifth Avenue between 14th and 23rd Streets shelters quite a few designer boutiques, and the famous department stores—with their fantastic window displays—are ranged along the upper stretch of the avenue. **Madison Avenue** is the place for expensive top designers: Prada, Valentino, Versace et al. It's also great for window shopping and celebrity spotting, especially on weekends. On the **Upper West Side**, Columbus Avenue boasts another mall-like stretch of stores. It's much more interesting to proceed north to **125th Street in Harlem**, where you can lunch in Mart 125 or at Sylvia's and shop for hip-hop clothing.

EVERYTHING MUST GO!

Don't be fooled by hysterical signs in shop windows. Permanent closing sales are actually the norm in certain stretches of midtown, on lower Broadway and along 14th Street. Department stores usually hold sales at the end of major seasons—August and March seem to be the best months. The post-Christmas reductions tend to occur earlier in December than they used to, but most shopkeepers think all holidays (Fourth of July, Easter, Labor Day, etc.) are a good enough reason for a sale. For the latest information, see *Time Out New York's* Check Out section, the weekly "Sales & Bargains" column in *New York* magazine and the ads in *The New York Times*.

Designers' sample sales are good sources of low-priced chic clothes. For information about what's on where, either pick up a copy of the *S&B Report* (available from 108 E 38th St, suite 2000, New York, NY 10016, 683-7612); or call the **Bargain Hotline** (540-0123). These are also sources for details of appliance, furniture and other sales. *Time Out New York* lists sample sales every week.

Many shops are open late, especially downtown (those tend to open later in the morning, too). At some of the larger and more tourist-oriented places you can avoid paying the 8.25-percent city sales tax if you arrange to have your purchase shipped outside New York State. Although the governor of New York is considering a law that would drop the city sales tax on clothing and shoes, it's otherwise added at the time of purchase.

Department stores

Barneys

660 Madison Ave at 61st St (826-8900). Subway: N, R to Fifth Ave; 4, 5, 6 to 59th St. Mon–Fri 10am–8pm, Sat 10am–7pm, Sun noon–6pm. AmEx, MC, V. All the top designers, as well as a decent selection of lesser-known labels, are represented at this haven for New York style. There are also hip home furnishings and fancy children's clothes, and the Christmas windows are usually the best in town. Every August and March, the store hosts the Barneys Warehouse Sale (call for locations), which is highly recommended if you're in town. Alterations are free.

Bergdorf Goodman

754 Fifth Ave at 58th St (753-7300). Subway: E, F to Fifth Ave. Mon–Wed 10am–6pm, Thu 10am–8pm, Fri, Sat 10am–7pm. AmEx, JCB, MC, V. While Barneys shoots for a young, trendy crowd, Bergdorf is dedicated to the elegant, understated one—check out the hat department for proof. As department stores go, it's one of the best for clothes and accessory shopping, being neither too big nor too cavernous. In addition to selling all the major American and European designers, Bergdorf has a number of exclusive lines. The men's store is across the street.

Bloomingdale's

1000 Third Ave at 59th St (355-5900). Subway: N, R to Lexington Ave; 4, 5, 6 to 59th St. Mon–Fri 10am–8:30pm, Sat 10am–7pm, Sun 11am–7pm. AmEx, MC, V. This gigantic, glitzy department store has everything you could ever want to buy. The ground floor features designer handbags, scarves, hosiery, makeup and jewelry, and upstairs you'll find linens, and two floors of shoes, designer names and a variety of cheaper goods. The sale racks are always worth a look.

Henri Bendel

715 Fifth Ave at 56th St (247-1100). Subway: E, F to Fifth Ave; N, R to Lexington Ave; 4, 5, 6 to 59th St. Mon–Wed, Fri, Sat 10am–7pm; Thu 10am–8pm, Sun noon–6pm. AmEx, DC, Disc, JCB, MC, V. Bendel is a sweet-smelling sliver of heaven. Its lavish quarters resemble a plush townhouse—there are elevators, but it's nicer to mount the elegant, winding staircase, created by Marie-Paule Pellé. Designer James Mansour kept the original boutiques and has added several eye-grabbing extras, including those reserved for the designs of Claude Montana and Todd Oldham. The first floor features travel kits, makeup and all sorts of gift items. Prices are comparable with those in other upscale stores, but somehow things look more desirable here. It must be those darling brown-and-white-striped bags.

Lord & Taylor

424 Fifth Ave between 38th and 39th Sts (391-3344). Subway: B, D, F, Q to 42nd St. Mon, Tue 10am–7pm; Wed–Fri 10am–8:30pm, Sat 9am–7pm; Sun 11am–6pm. AmEx, Disc, MC, V. Lord & Taylor is a conservative, rather

Miles of aisles: The **Strand** claims to be the world's biggest secondhand bookstore.

old-fashioned department store, the only one left in New York that stocks Germaine Monteil cosmetics. American designers are well represented, and there are often good sales. It was here that the Fifth Avenue tradition of dramatic Christmas window displays began.

Macy's

Herald Square, 151 W 34th St between Broadway and Seventh Ave (695-4400/customer service 494-5151). Subway: B, D, F, Q, N, R, 1, 2, 3, 9 to 34th St. Mon–Sat 10am–8:30pm, Sun 11am–7pm. AmEx, MC, V. Being lost in Macy's isn't a pleasant feeling, but it's worth the trip for nostalgia alone. Macy's still calls itself the biggest department store in the world—it occupies an entire city block. This colossal store has faced certain financial difficulties over the years, so the huge bargains of its famous sales have been somewhat reduced. Nevertheless, you'll still find everything from designer labels to cheap, colorful knockoffs, a pet shop, a fish market, the Metropolitan Museum gift shop and a juice bar. Beware the aggressive perfume sprayers, and resign yourself to getting hopelessly lost. The store has its own concierge service (560-3827) to help you maximize your shopping potential.

Saks Fifth Avenue

611 Fifth Ave between 49th and 50th Sts (753-4000). Subway: B, D, F, Q to 47th–50th Sts–Rockefeller Ctr; E, F to 53rd St. Mon–Wed, Fri, Sat 10am–6:30pm; Sun 10am–8pm; Sun noon–6pm. AmEx, CB, DC, Disc, JCB, MC, V. Saks is a classic department store that features all the big names, an excellent menswear department, a fine household linens, a newly expanded kids' section and good service. The ground floor is packed with accessories and has a stylish beauty area where personal consultations and makeovers are available. Upstairs, you'll find a well-chosen selection of designer labels.

Shanghai Tang

655 Madison Ave at 61st St (888-0111). Subway: N, R to Fifth Ave; 4, 5, 6 to 59th St. Mon–Fri 10am–8pm, Sat 11am–7pm, Sun noon–6pm. AmEx, Disc, MC, V. This is the first Hong Kong department store to grace New York. Owner David Tang worships color, so expect lots of it. Along with silk Chinese dresses and jackets, there are housewares, watches and lamps constructed from Chinese lanterns.

Takashimaya

693 Fifth Ave between 54th and 55th Sts (350-0100). Subway: E, F to Fifth Ave. Mon–Wed, Fri, Sat 10am–6pm; Thu 10am–8pm. AmEx, DC, Disc, JCB, MC, V. The New York branch of this Japanese department store opened in April 1993 and has been giving Bergdorf a run for its money ever since. The five-story palace mixes Eastern and Western aesthetics and extravagance. The first two floors offer 4,500 square feet (419 square

meters) of art gallery space and a men's and women's signature collection, as well as Japanese makeup and exotic plants; the top floor is dedicated to designer accessories.

Beauty shops

Most drugstores stock a range of good, cheap makeup and general beauty products (*see* **Pharmacists**, *page 195*). Department stores are a good source for the major names—as well as personal attention—but you will probably pay more than you would at some of the discount stores. *See also* **Eco-friendly**, *page 189*.

Aveda

509 Madison Ave between 52nd and 53rd Sts (832-2416). Subway: E, F to Fifth Ave; 6 to 51st St. Mon–Fri 10am–7pm, Sat noon–6pm, Sun noon–5pm. ●*233 Spring St between Sixth Ave and Varick St (call 807-1492 for hours). Subway: C, E to Spring St.* ●*456 West Broadway between Houston and Prince Sts (call 473-0280 for hours). Subway: C, E to Spring St; N, R to Prince St.* ●*140 Fifth Ave at 19th St (call 645-4797 for hours). Subway: N, R to 23rd St. AmEx, JCB, MC, V.* This is a small but tranquil boutique filled with an exclusive line of hair- and skin-care products, makeup, massage oils and cleansers, all made from flower and plant extracts.

Face Stockholm

110 Prince St at Greene St (334-3900). Subway: N, R to Prince St. Mon–Wed 11am–7pm, Thu–Sat 11am–8pm, Sun noon–7pm. ●*224 Columbus Ave between 70th and 71st Sts (call 769-1420 for hours). Subway: 1, 2, 3, 9 to 72nd St. AmEx, MC, V.* Along with a full line of shadows, lipsticks, tools and blushes (at very reasonable prices), Face offers two services: makeup applications ($40) and lessons ($75). Phone for an appointment or just stop by and check it out yourself.

I Natural

430 West Broadway between Prince and Spring Sts (965-1002). Subway: N, R to Prince St. Mon–Sat 11am–7pm, Sun noon–6pm. AmEx, MC, V. This self-proclaimed beauty sanctuary features makeup that starts at $6. Customers are encouraged to experiment with any of the cosmetics, displayed on the "Great Wall of Color."

MAC

14 Christopher St between Sixth and Seventh Aves (243-4150). Subway: 1, 9 to Christopher St–Sheridan Sq. Mon–Sat 11am–7pm, Sun noon–6pm. ●*MAC Soho, 113 Spring St between Greene and Mercer Sts (call 334-4641 for hours). Subway: C, E to Spring St. AmEx, MC, V.* Makeup Art Cosmetics, a Canadian company, is committed to the development of cruelty-free products and is famous for its line of matte and frosted lipsticks in otherwise unobtainable colors. The Queen of New York, drag star Lady Bunny, gives consultations here; current spokespersons are RuPaul and k.d. lang. The enormous Soho branch is a bit like an art gallery and features nine makeover counters.

Make Up Forever

409 West Broadway between Prince and Spring Sts (941-9337). Subway: N, R to Prince St; C, E to Spring St. Mon–Sat 11am–7pm, Sun noon–6pm. AmEx, Disc, MC, V. Make Up Forever, a French line introduced to the U.S. a few years ago, is popular with women and drag queens alike. Colors range from theatrical, bold purples and fuschias to muted browns and soft pinks. Although the line is sold at Barneys and the Pierre Michel Salon, this is the only New York boutique of its kind.

Manic Panic

64 White St between Broadway and Church St (254-5517). Subway: 1, 9 to Franklin St; A, C, E to Canal St. Mon–Fri

9am–5pm; Sat, Sun noon–8pm. MC, V. It's all about being noticed at Manic Panic. For those seeking a quick transformation, the store offers semipermanent hair color (including Electric Sunshine, Hot Hot Pink or Infra Red), nail polish, lipsticks, false eyelashes and, of course, hair pieces.

L'Occitane

1046 Madison Ave at 80th St (396-9097). Subway: 6 to 77th St. Mon–Sat 10am–7pm, Sun noon–6pm. ●146 Spring St at Wooster St (call 343-0109 for hours). Subway: C, E to Spring St. ●198 Columbus Ave at 69th St (call 362-5146 for hours). Subway: 1, 9 to 66th St–Lincoln Ctr. AmEx, MC, V. Fans of L'Occitane, a 20-year-old line of bath and beauty products made in Provence, flock to this shop to pick up their fix of brick-size soaps, massage balm and hand cream.

Shu Uemura

121 Greene St between Prince and Spring Sts (979-5500). Subway: N, R to Prince St. Mon–Sat 11am–7pm, Sun noon–6pm. AmEx, MC, V. The entire rapturous line of Shu Uemura Japanese cosmetics is on hand at this stark Soho boutique. Choose from hundreds of brushes, lipsticks, blushes and eye shadows.

Books

There's no shortage of sources for books—both new and used. Many shops have no problem mailing your selections overseas (if the books are shipped out of state, you don't pay sales tax, which usually works out about the same as mailing charges). The Barnes & Noble chain has expanded considerably in the past few years, and its new outlets offer massive discounts on recent hardcover releases and best sellers as well as readings by prominent authors (check the Book listings in *Time Out New York* for weekly schedules). Don't overlook the smaller landmark stores, however, which continue to provide meticulous service. For A Different Light Bookstore & Café and the Oscar Wilde Memorial Bookshop, see chapter **Gay & Lesbian New York**.

General

Barnes & Noble

105 Fifth Ave at 18th St (675-5500). Subway: L, N, R, 4, 5, 6 to 14th St–Union Sq. Mon–Fri 9:30am–7:45pm, Sat 9:30am–6:15pm, Sun 11am–5:45pm. AmEx, DC, Disc, MC, V. The world's largest bookstore and the flagship of this bustling chain is a good source of recent hardcovers and discount prices. The record, tape and CD department has one of the largest classical music selections in the city, as well as videos, and there are also children's books, toys and an enormous number of secondhand paperbacks, including play scripts. One of B&N's many branches, the megastore at 2289 Broadway (at 82nd St, 362-8835), carries some 1,500 magazines and newspapers and features a children's theater, a reading area and gift-wrapping service. Check the phone book for other locations.

Blackout Books

50 Ave B between 3rd and 4th Sts (777-1967). Subway: F to Second Ave. 11am–10pm. AmEx, MC, V. The spirit of '68 lives. Anarchist, enviro-feminist, situationist and left-wing texts of every description are found here.

Borders Books & Music

461 Park Ave at 57th St (980-6785). Subway: N, R to Lexington Ave; 4, 5, 6 to 59th St. Mon–Fri 9am–10pm, Sat 10am–8pm, Sun 11am–8pm. ●5 World Trade Center between Church and Vesey Sts (call 839-8049 for hours). Subway: A, C to Chambers St; J, M, Z, 2, 3, 4, 5 to Fulton St; N, R, 1, 9 to Cortlandt St. AmEx, Disc, MC, V. Borders seems folksier than Barnes & Noble; there's an extensive selection of music and videos, and even if you're searching for an obscure book, a staff member is usually able to come across a copy.

Gotham Book Mart

41 W 47th St at Sixth Ave (719-4448). Subway: B, D, F, Q to 47th–50th Sts–Rockefeller Ctr. Mon–Fri 9:30am–6:30pm, Sat 9:30am–6pm. AmEx, MC, V. "Wise men fish here" is Gotham's motto—and they most certainly do. This is a delightful haven for out-of-print titles, first editions and rare books. Opened by Frances Steloff in the '20s, Gotham was one of the leaders in the fight against censorship, stocking banned books by James Joyce, D.H. Lawrence and Henry Miller. Upstairs is a gallery showing works on literary themes. It's dusty and wonderful.

Gryphon Book Shop

2246 Broadway between 80th and 81st Sts (362-0706). Subway: 1, 9 to 79th St. 10am–midnight. MC, V. Gryphon specializes in poetry and fiction and also stocks rock records. A good source for secondhand and rare books on theater, film, music and drama.

Shakespeare & Co.

716 Broadway at Washington Pl (529-1330). Subway: N, R to 8th St; 6 to Astor Pl. Mon–Thu, Sun 10am–11pm; Fri, Sat 10am–midnight. ●939 Lexington Ave between 68th and 69th Sts (call 570-5148 for hours). Subway: 6 to 68th St. AmEx, MC, V. This bookshop has no real connection to the famous Hemingway haunt in Paris, except in spirit. Real service is the raison d'être here; the major qualification for staff is that they must be college graduates—i.e., readers. Not only will they order anything you covet, they'll probably have heard of it, too.

St. Mark's Bookshop

31 Third Ave between 8th and 9th Sts (260-7853). Subway: 6 to Astor Pl. Mon–Sat 10am–midnight, Sun 11am–midnight. AmEx, Disc, MC, V. This late-night East Village literary and political bookshop stocks works on cultural criticism and feminism as well as university and small-press publications. Newspapers and more than 800 periodicals are available; it's also a good source for magazines and literary journals.

Strand Book Store

828 Broadway at 12th St (473-1489). Subway: L, N, R, 4, 5, 6 to 14th St–Union Sq. Mon–Sat 9:30am–9:30pm, Sun 11am–9:30pm. AmEx, Disc, MC, V. In the '50s there were 40 or 50 antiquarian booksellers along Broadway between Astor Place and 14th Street. The Strand is the only one left; it is also reputedly the largest secondhand bookshop in the U.S. More than two million books on all subjects are stocked. Most are sold at half the published price or less.

Tompkins Square Books & Records

111 E 7th St between Ave A and First Ave (979-8958). Subway: F to Second Ave, L to First Ave, 6 to Astor Pl. Mon–Sun noon–11pm. No credit cards. It's hard to leave this cozy secondhand book and record shop without a paperback or two. There's also a vintage record collection complete with a record player—you're always welcome to audition your selections in the shop.

Tower Books

383 Lafayette St at 4th St (288-5100). Subway: B, D, F, Q to Broadway–Lafayette St; 6 to Bleecker St. 11am–11pm. AmEx, Disc, MC, V. Tower isn't just about movies and CDs. Tower Books is a decent stop for literature, travel books, photography titles and paperbacks. It's also turned into the best

Meet ya in Nolita

A vibrant new shopping strip of specialty boutiques sprouts next to Soho

Perhaps the most exciting shopping in the city is in the tiny boutiques and eateries clustered in the area bordered by Soho, Chinatown, Little Italy and the Lower East Side called Nolita. Hunt for clothing, shoes, glasswear, stationery and hats along Lafayette, Mulberry, Mott and Elizabeth Streets, from Houston down to Spring Street. On weekends, when Soho is cluttered and the East Village is crammed, this friendly neighborhood is an oasis of calm.

Calypso (280 Mott St, 965-0990) sells gorgeous slip dresses, suits, sweaters and scarves, many from unknown French designers. The shoes at **Sigerson Morrison** (242 Mott St, 219-3893) come in the prettiest colors, among them ruby red, shiny pearl, crocodile olive and burnt orange. **Kazuyo Nakano** (223 Mott St, 941-7093) specializes in mesh, silk organza, leather and linen handbags. A couple of doors down is **p.a.k.** (229 Mott St, 226-5167), where minimalist women's clothing is designed by owner Corey Pak (hence the name). **Wang** (219 Mott St, 941-6134), a boutique owned by sisters Sally and Jennifer Wang, carries simple, chic clothes; **Resurrection** (217 Mott St, 625-1374) is a vintage gold mine.

For treasures from Tibet and the Himalayas, visit **Dö Kham** (51 Prince St, 996-2404). Next door is the **Dressing Room** (49 Prince St, 431-6658), a violet-painted boutique with a small but stylish selection of new young designer labels. **Ina** (21 Prince St, 334- 9048) recycles high fashion: Here you'll find slightly worn Chanel, Ann Demeulemeester and John Galliano, plus tons of Manolo Blahnik shoes. Another shop for antique couture and vintagewear is **About Time** (13 Prince St, 941-0966), on the corner of Prince and Elizabeth Streets. Owner Beverly Wilburn, who worked at Barneys and Bergdorf before opening her beautiful boutique, stocks only the best: early Geoffrey Beene, Courrèges, Dries Van Noten, Yohji Yamamoto and Commes des Garçons. Also on Prince Street is **Scarlet and Sage** (7 Prince St, 219-1290), cluttered with artifacts collected from all over the world—including India, Turkey, Spain and Portugal.

Elizabeth Street is the most crowded Nolita block. For gorgeous hats, try **Kelly Christy** (*see* Hats, *page 190*). At **Daily 2-3-5** (235 Elizabeth St, 334-9728), a general store of sorts, you'll find a variety of necessary and not-so-necessary objects like soap, newspapers, magazines, condoms, rubber bugs, cigarettes and voodoo dolls. **Shi** (the name means *is* in Chinese) sells hanging glass vases and beautiful lamps (233 Elizabeth St, 334-4330). The eclectic furniture of **Ace** (269 Elizabeth St, 226-5123) is just below antique quality. Cashmere sweaters and fragrance may seem like an odd pairing, but somehow it works at **Lucien Pellat-Finet** (226 Elizabeth St, 343-7033). At **Phare** (252 Elizabeth St, 625-0406), stock up on women's and men's clothing designed by ex-model Jane Mayle and her boyfriend and partner, Chris Jarvis.

On Mulberry Street, explore your Eastern side at **Jade** (284 Mulberry St, 965-8910), which carries silk Chinese pajamas and dresses. Don't miss the **Tracy Feith** boutique (280 Mulberry St, 925-6544), stocked with the designer's lovely women's clothing. Down the block, **Push** (240 Mulberry St, 965-9699) specializes in handmade jewelry—gorgeous engagement rings, necklaces and bracelets for men and women, made from sterling silver, 14-carat gold and platinum. **Language** (238 Mulberry St, 431-5566) is a mini–department store, housed in a former ceramics studio; here you'll find clothing, furniture, *objets* and housewares.

Lafayette Street is by far the noisiest street of them all, but it's not to be missed. There's ravewear galore at **Liquid Sky** (241 Lafayette St, 343-0532). While you're there, walk down the stairs in the back of the store to **Temple**

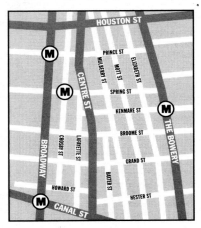

*Playing footsie: **Sigerson Morrison**.*

Records, a haven for domestic and imported techno, trance and jungle (343-3595). **Supreme** (274 Lafayette St, 966-7799) is a skater's dream, stocking the latest decks, trucks and wheels, along with the requisite fashions. At **Smylonylon** (222B Lafayette St, 431-0342), you will be sure to smile on nylon. The stock includes the the greatest (and sometimes strangest) '60s and '70s styles. The very cool **X-Large** (267 Lafayette St, 334-4480), part-owned by Mike D of the Beastie Boys, sells oversized heavy cotton work jackets, cords and polo shirts. Among the many great items in **Pop Shop** (292 Lafayette St, 219 2784), a store devoted to the designs of the late Keith Haring, are posters, patches and T-shirts, along with inflatable babies and groovy fridge magnets.

The huge **Urban Archaeology Company** (285 Lafayette St, 431-6969) specializes in the discarded everyday items of the past. Here you'll find architectural and household treasures, from a bookshelf to a pair of wrought-iron gates complete with stone pillars. And don't forget to poke your head into **Label** (265 Lafayette St, 966-7736), for clothes inspired by female revolutionaries (think Patty Hearst), and **555 Soul** (290 Lafayette St, 431-2404), for Camelia Ehike's line of sportswear that has evolved from its rap roots (it was a favorite label of De La Soul and LL Cool J) into a line of sophisticated separates for men and women.

spot for obscure newspapers, the strangest of fanzines and international magazines. Browsing isn't deterred.
For **Tower Records**, *see page 195.*

Specialist

A Photographers Place
133 Mercer St between Prince and Spring Sts (431-9358). Subway: C, E to Spring St; N, R to Prince St. Mon–Sat 11am–8pm, Sun noon–6pm. AmEx, Disc, MC, V. Books on all subjects by the world's best photographers.

Biography Bookshop
400 Bleecker St at 11th St (807-8655). Subway: A, C, E to 14th St; L to Eighth Ave. Mon–Thu noon–8pm, Fri noon–10pm, Sat 11am–11pm, Sun 11am–7pm. AmEx, MC, V. Proof, if proof were needed, that biography is of wide interest: This whole store is devoted to it. (New titles only.)

Complete Traveler Bookstore
199 Madison Ave at 35th St (685-9007). Subway: 6 to 33rd St. Mon–Fri 9am–7pm, Sat 10am–6pm, Sun 11am–5pm. AmEx, DC, Disc, MC, V. Travel books and maps of all descriptions, covering New York City, the U.S. and the world.

Drama Bookshop
723 Seventh Ave at 48th St (944-0595). Subway: C, E, 1, 9 to 50th St; N, R to 49th St. Mon, Tue, Thu, Fri 9:30am–7pm; Wed 9:30am–8pm; Sat 10:30am–5:30pm; Sun noon–5pm. AmEx, MC, V. Everything a theater lover desires, including plays and biographies.

Forbidden Planet
840 Broadway at 13th St (473-1576). Subway: L, N, R, 4, 5, 6 to 14th St–Union Sq. 10am–8:30pm. AmEx, Disc, MC, V. Devotees of science fiction and fantasy won't be able to resist Forbidden Planet's vast selection of comics, featuring vintage and new titles from around the world. There are also stacks of classic books and magazines, and even a pricey toy section.

Murder Ink
2486 Broadway between 92nd and 93rd Sts (362-8905). Subway: 1, 2, 3, 9 to 96th St. Mon–Sat 10am–7:30pm, Sun 11am–6pm. • 1465 Second Ave between 76th and 77th Sts (call 517-3222 for hours). Subway: 6 to 77th St. AmEx, MC, V. If you're in need of a killer title, this is your best bet. Murder Ink's enormous stock ranges from William Faulkner's *The Unvanquished* to the complete works of Jim Thompson, along with books on how to write mysteries and *The Mystery Reader's Walking Guide: New York.*

Mysterious Book Shop
129 W 56th St between Sixth and Seventh Aves (765-0900). Subway: B, D, E to Seventh Ave; N, R to 57th St. Mon–Sat 11am–7pm. AmEx, DC, MC, V. More than 20,000 new and secondhand mystery and murder titles. There's a free rare-book finding service.

See Hear
59 E 7th St between First and Second Aves (505-9781). Subway: F to Second Ave; L to First Ave; 6 to Astor Pl. Mon–Sun noon–8pm. MC, V. This shop has moved back to its original nook on 7th Street. A haven for fanzines, music books, comics and assorted subcultural texts, See Hear is an ideal place to lose an afternoon.

Village Comics
214 Sullivan St between 3rd and Bleecker Sts (777-2770). Subway: A, C, E, B, D, F, Q to W 4th St–Washington Sq. Mon–Wed 9:30am–8:30pm; Thu–Sat 10am–9:30pm; Sun 11:30am–7:30pm. AmEx, DC, MC, V. Comics are big business: Shop here for complete sets, missing back issues of Marvel or underground comics, and new releases. There's a

free mail-order service. The **Science Fiction Shop** (940 Third Ave at 56th St, 759-6255) is run by the same company.

Cameras and electronics

The midtown electronics area (14th–23rd Streets between Broadway and Sixth Avenue) offers some great bargains. Rapid turnover (we hope) is what allows shopkeepers to price items such as Walkmans, CD players and computers at low prices. Know exactly what you want before venturing inside: If you look lost, you will certainly be given a hard sell. When buying a major item, check newspaper ads for price guidelines (the Science section in Tuesday's *New York Times* is good). If you're brave, you can get small pieces such as Walkmans even cheaper in the questionable establishments along Canal Street, but don't expect a warranty. Another reason to go to a more reputable place is to get reliable (and essential) advice about compatibility with whatever country you want to use the equipment in. For video and TV rental, *see* **Television and video**, *page 200*.

J & R Music World

33 Park Row at Centre St (732-8600). Subway: 4, 5, 6 to City Hall; J, M, Z to Chambers St. Mon–Sat 9am–6:30pm, Sun 11am–6pm. AmEx, Disc, MC, V. Everything for home entertainment is here at discount prices: CD players, hi-fi, Walkmans and tapes. See the weekly ads in the *New York Post* and *The Village Voice* for the latest deals.

Nobody Beats the Wiz

726 Broadway between Washington and Waverly Pls (677-4111). Subway: N, R to 8th St; 6 to Astor Pl. Mon–Sat 10am–9pm, Sun 11am–6pm. AmEx, Disc, MC, V. With the Wiz's claim to match or beat any advertised price on electronic equipment, even the illegal importers on Canal Street have a hard time keeping up. Check the ads in the *Voice* and load up on gear and gadgets at unbelievable prices. Check the phone book for other locations.

Willoughby's

136 W 32nd St between Sixth and Seventh Aves (564-1600). Subway: B, D, F, Q, N, R to 34th St. Mon–Fri 8:30am–8pm; Sat, Sun 10am–7pm. AmEx, DC, Disc, MC, V. Willoughby's claims to be the world's largest camera and audio store—and it does seem to stock everything. Know what you are looking for, and expect long lines, slow service and heavy security.

Photo processing

Photo-developing services can be found on just about any busy city block. Pharmacies and most department stores offer this service, although the best results should be expected from those who develop on the premises.

Harvey's One Hour Photo

698 Third Ave between 43rd and 44th Sts (682-5045). Subway: 4, 5, 6, 7 to 42nd St–Grand Central. Mon–Fri 8am–6pm. AmEx, MC, V. Color film can be developed in 60 minutes; slides and black-and-white film require 24 hours.

Showbran Photo

1347 Broadway at 36th St (947-9151). Subway: B, D, F, Q, N, R to 34th St. Mon–Fri 7am–6pm. ●*512 Seventh Ave between*

37th and 38th Sts (call 575-9580 for hours). Subway: 1, 2, 3, 9 to 34th St–Penn Station. ●*Lobby of the Empire State Building, 350 Fifth Ave at 33rd St (call 868-5888 for hours). Subway: 6 to 33rd St. AmEx, Disc, MC, V.* Passport and visa photos are taken and developed while you wait. Showbran also offers other developing and printing services as well as photocopying.

Clothing rental

Just Once

292 Fifth Ave between 30th and 31st Sts (465-0960). Subway: 6 to 28th St. By appointment only. AmEx, MC, V. This bridal service stocks a wide selection of expensive gowns (Vera Wang and Carolina Herrera are among the labels) for sale or rental. The rentals range from $300 to $800.

Zeller Tuxedos

201 E 56th St at Third Ave, second floor (355-0707). Subway: 4, 5, 6 to 59th St; N, R to Lexington Ave. Mon–Fri 9am–6:30pm, Sat 10am–5pm. AmEx, MC, V. Armani, Ungaro and Valentino tuxes are available for (horrors!) those who didn't think to pack theirs.

Cross-dressing

Miss Vera's Finishing School for Boys Who Want to Be Girls

85 Eighth Ave between 14th and 15th Sts (242-6449). Subway: A, C, E to 14th St; L to Eighth Ave. No credit cards. Feeling feminine? Private classes begin at $550 and are taught by Veronica Vera and her faculty. All-day sessions begin at $1,125; a weekend on the town with Vera and the girls starts at $3,250. Consult the back pages of *The Village Voice* and the *New York Press* for similar services. There are even "telephone classes" available, via Miss Vera's 900 line.

Dry cleaners

Midnight Express Cleaners

Call 921-0111 or 1-800-999-8985. Mon–Fri 8am–10pm, Sat 9am–3pm. AmEx, MC, V. Telephone Midnight Express and your laundry will be picked up anywhere below 96th Street within 10 to 15 minutes. It costs $6.95 for a man's suit to be cleaned, including pick-up and delivery. There are various minimum charges, depending on your location.

Sutton Cleaners

1060 First Ave between 57th and 58th Sts (755-1617). Subway: 4, 5, 6 to 59th St; N, R to Lexington Ave. Mon–Fri 7am–6:30pm, Sat 8am–4pm. AmEx, MC, V. Sutton does one-hour jobs as well as normal, nonurgent service. Same-day alterations on garments brought in before 10am. Collection and delivery is free up to ten blocks from the store.

Fashion

The designers

agnès b.

116 Prince St between Wooster and Greene Sts (925-4649). Subway: N, R to Prince St. Mon–Sat 11am–7pm, Sun noon–6pm. ●*1063 Madison Ave between 80th and 81st Sts (call 570-9333 for hours). Subway: 6 to 77th St.* ●*Men's store: 79 Greene St between Spring and Broome Sts (call 431-4339 for hours). Subway: C, E to Spring St. AmEx, MC, V.* Simple designs for women, men and children— though the men's lines are available only at the branch on Greene Street. If only the timeless styles could withstand wear and tear a bit longer.

Giorgio Armani

760 Madison Ave at 65th St (988-9191). Subway: 6 to 68th St. Mon–Wed, Fri, Sat 10am–6pm; Thu 10am–7pm. AmEx, MC, V. This enormous boutique features all three Armani collections, including the signature Borgonuovo—tailored suits, evening wear and a bridal line—as well as the Classico and Le Collezioni. Keep an eye out for Jodie Foster.

Chanel

15 E. 57th St between Fifth and Madison Aves (355-5050). Subway: E, F, N, R to Fifth Ave; 4, 5, 6 to 59th St. Mon–Wed, Fri 10am–6:30pm; Thu 10am–7pm; Sat 10am–6pm. AmEx, DC, MC, JCB, V. The spirit of Mademoiselle Chanel lives on at this opulent flagship store. There's even the Chanel Suite, a Baroque salon modeled after the divine Coco's private apartment on the Rue Cambon in Paris.

Christian Dior

703 Fifth Ave at 55th St (223-4646). Subway: E, F to Fifth Ave. Mon–Wed, Fri, Sat 10am–6pm; Thu 10am–7pm; Sun 11am–5pm. AmEx, JCB, MC, V. Like Alexander McQueen at Givenchy, John Galliano has breathed new life into formerly predictable designs. This elegant boutique carries the famous French line.

Comme des Garçons

116 Wooster St between Spring and Prince Sts (219-0660). Subway: C, E to Spring St; N, R to Prince St. Mon–Sat 11am–7pm, Sun noon–6:30pm. AmEx, DC, MC, V. This minimalist store is devoted to Rei Kawakubo's architecturally constructed, quintessentially Japanese designs for men and women. It's no surprise that the boutique is found in Soho—Kawakubo's clothing is hung like art.

Costume National

108 Wooster St between Prince and Spring Sts (431-1530). Subway: C, E to Spring St; N, R to Prince St. Mon–Sat 11am–7pm, Sun noon–6pm. AmEx, MC, V. This sleek collection features Italian fashions designed by Ennio Capasa, who collaborated with architect Cosimo Antoci for the look of this 3,000-square-foot space. Very minimal.

D&G

434 West Broadway between Prince and Spring Sts (965-8000). Subway: N, R to Prince St. Mon–Sat 11am–7pm, Sun noon–6pm. ●*825 Madison Ave between 68th and 69th Sts (call 249-4100 for hours). Subway: 6 to 68th St–Hunter College. AmEx, JCB, MC, V.* The Italian design team of Domenico Dolce and Stefano Gabbana opened two posh shops in a single week last fall. Custom-mixed music—house, disco and opera—plays as you shop for jeans, collection dresses, suits and signature black bags.

Emporio Armani

601 Madison Ave between 67th and 68th Sts (317-0800). Subway: 6 to 68th St. Mon–Fri 10am–8pm, Sat 10am–6pm, Sun noon–6pm. ●*110 Fifth Ave at 16th St (call 727-3240 for hours). Subway: L, N, R, 4, 5, 6 to 14th St–Union Sq. AmEx, DC, JCB, MC, V.* The postmodern decor serves as a stark backdrop for top Armani designs. The store also houses the chic Armani Café.

Romeo Gigli & Spazio

21 E 69th St between Madison and Park Aves. (744-9121). Subway: 6 to 68th St. Mon–Sat 10:30am–6:30pm. AmEx, MC, V. This three-story former townhouse is worth visiting for the interior alone, with its Fornasetti screens and Murano light fittings. And then of course there's Romeo Gigli.

Givenchy

954 Madison Ave at 75th St (772-1040). Subway: 6 to 77th St. Mon–Sat 10am–6pm. AmEx, DC, MC, V. With the talented English designer Alexander McQueen holding the scissors, the styles are no longer quite as discreet as when Hubert de Givenchy created Audrey Hepburn's to-die-for ensembles. Although McQueen's imagination is wild, his clothes aren't unwearable.

Gucci

685 Fifth Ave at 54th St (826-2600). Subway: E, F to Fifth Ave. Mon–Wed, Fri, Sat 9:30am–6pm; Thu 9:30am–7pm; Sun noon–6pm. AmEx, DC, JCB, MC, V. When Tom Ford revitalized Gucci a few years back, he made the old-lady label hip again. Its slinky, Halston-inspired duds are still extremely popular. Pants start at $400, and there are always plenty of logo belts, key chains and sunglasses to choose from.

Marc Jacobs

163 Mercer St between Houston and Prince Sts (343-1490). Subway: N, R to Prince St. Mon–Sat 11am–7pm, Sun noon–6pm. AmEx, MC, V. Marc Jacobs's first Manhattan boutique, housed in a former art gallery, is long and narrow, with white walls and endless ceilings. Jacobs's impeccable designs are all on display here, including collections of both men's and women's ready-to-wear, accessories and shoes.

Betsey Johnson

130 Thompson St between Prince and Houston Sts (420-0169). Subway: N, R to Prince St. Mon–Sat 11am–7pm, Sun noon–7pm. ●*248 Columbus Ave at 72nd St (call 362-3364 for hours). Subway: 1, 2, 3, 9 to 72nd St.* ●*251 E 60th St between Second and Third Aves (call 319-7699 for hours). Subway: N, R to Lexington Ave; 4, 5, 6 to 60th St.* ●*1060 Madison Ave at 80th St (call 734-1257 for hours). Subway: 6 to 77th St.* ●*138 Wooster St between Houston and Prince Sts (call 995-5048 for hours). Subway: B, D, F, Q to Broadway–Lafayette St. AmEx, MC, V.* Johnson's funky, flamboyant clothes have been on the market since the '70s. Fortunately, they never look out-of-date. The prices are relatively reasonable.

Jussara

125 Greene St between Houston and Prince Sts (353-5050). Subway: N, R to Prince St. Mon–Sat 11am–7:30pm, Sun noon–7pm. AmEx, MC, V. Jussara Lee, of Korean descent, was raised in Brazil, which explains a lot about this shop's decor as well as her style—romantic modernism. One side is decorated with slanted roofs constructed from terra-cotta shingles, a tall balcony, a stone fountain and benches; the other side features tweed and velvet jackets, coats and dresses.

Omo Norma Kamali

11 W 56th St between Fifth and Sixth Aves (957-9797). Subway: B, Q to 57th St.; N, R to Fifth Ave. Mon–Sat 10am–6pm. AmEx, MC, V. Classic-cut clothes with a slightly offbeat touch. Suits and dresses are shapely, with perhaps an oddly pleated skirt, a strangely shaped collar or an unusual cutout. Relatively inexpensive knits are sold alongside great daywear, provocative swimsuits and some spectacular evening designs.

Calvin Klein

654 Madison Ave at 60th St (292-9000). Subway: N, R to Lexington Ave; 4, 5, 6 to 59th St. Mon–Wed, Fri, Sat 10am–6pm; Thu 10am–8pm; Sun noon–6pm. AmEx, Disc, MC, V. Here's where to come if you're after an understated silhouette. This flagship store opened in 1995 and is *tout* CK, from the couture lines to footwear and housewares.

Helmut Lang

80 Greene St between Spring and Broome Sts (925-7214). Subway: C, E to Spring St; N, R to Prince St. Mon–Sat 11am–7pm; Sun noon–6pm. AmEx, MC, V. This 3,000-square-foot store houses Austrian designer Helmut Lang's sexy suits and dresses. The casual Helmut Lang Jeans line, which features denim pants and sweaters, is also available.

Les Copains

807 Madison Ave between 67th and 68th Sts (327-3014). Subway: 6 to 68th St. Mon–Sat 10am–6pm. AmEx, DC, JCB, MC, V. This clothier specializes in Italian knits. It's very expensive, though; check out the more aggressive Trend line for better prices and the jeans collection.

René Lezard

417 West Broadway between Prince and Spring Sts (274-0700). Subway: N, R to Prince St; C, E to Spring St. Mon–Sat 11am–7pm, Sun noon–6pm. AmEx, JCB, MC, V. This space, the former home of Mary Boone's Soho gallery, is now filled with Lezard's luxurious Italian designs.

Luca Luca

690 Madison Ave at 62nd St (755-2444). Subway: N, R to Lexington Ave; 4, 5, 6 to 59th St. Mon–Wed, Fri, Sat 10am–6:30pm; Thu 10am–8pm; Sun noon–5pm. AmEx, MC, V. The young Italian designer Luca Orlandi finds black a bore. As long as you're all right with color, you'll do just fine here.

Missoni

836 Madison Ave at 69th St (517-9339). Subway: 6 to 68th St. Mon–Sat 10am–6pm. AmEx, MC, V. Italian polychromatic fine knits made of wildly beautiful fabric; the designs sometimes don't quite match up.

Miu Miu

100 Prince St between Mercer and Greene Sts (334-5156). Subway: N, R to Prince St. Mon–Sat 11am–7pm; Sun noon–6pm. AmEx, MC, V. This is the first home for Prada's secondary line, Miu Miu. The clothes are tiny and expensive—you won't find much for less than $100.

Issey Miyake

992 Madison Ave between 77th and 78th Sts (439-7822). Subway: 6 to 77th St. Mon–Fri 10am–6pm, Sat 11am–6pm. AmEx, MC, V. This minimalist store houses Issey Miyake's breathtaking women's and men's collections and accessories.

Moschino

803 Madison Ave between 67th and 68th Sts (639-9600). Subway: 6 to 68th St. Mon–Wed, Fri, Sat 9am–6pm; Thur 10am–7pm. AmEx, MC, V. Expensive and irreverent clothes for men and women. And you can always pick up a pencil kit for $5. Really.

Polo/Ralph Lauren

867 Madison Ave at 72nd St (606-2100). Subway: 6 to 68th St. Mon–Wed, Fri, Sat 10am–6pm; Thu 10am–8pm. AmEx, DC, Disc, JCB, MC, V. Ralph Lauren spent $14 million turning the old Rhinelander mansion into an Ivy League superstore, filled with Oriental rugs, English paintings, riding whips, leather chairs, old mahogany and fresh flowers. The homeboys, skaters and other young blades who've adopted Ralphie's togs for a season or two head straight to Polo Sport across the street at 888 Madison Ave (434 -8000).

Todd Oldham

123 Wooster St between Spring and Prince Sts (219-3531). Subway: C, E to Spring St; N, R to Prince St. Mon–Sat 11am–7pm, Sun noon–6pm. AmEx, MC, V. This colorful boutique, which houses Todd Oldham's imaginative and attractive fashions, has been open for three years.

Prada

841 Madison Ave at 70th St (327-4200). Subway: 6 to 68th St. Mon–Wed, Fri, Sat 10am–6pm; Thu 10am–7pm. ●45 E 57th St between Park and Madison Aves (call 308-2332 for hours). Subway: N, R to Lexington Ave; 4, 5, 6 to 59th St. AmEx, MC, V. Miuccia Prada has created quite a sensation with her '60s-inspired suits (for men and women), coats and dresses. The Madison Avenue location is the largest Prada shop in the world

and features high-tech computer-sensored windows with polarized glass that changes according to the light.

Cynthia Rowley

112 Wooster St between Prince and Spring Sts (334-1144). Subway: C, E to Spring St; N, R to Prince St. Mon–Sat 11am–7pm, Sun noon–6pm. AmEx, MC, V. Rowley's signature dresses, pouches, pants and shirts are all housed in this bright, youthful boutique.

Yves Saint Laurent

855-859 Madison Ave between 70th and 71st Sts (988-3821). Subway: 6 to 68th St. Mon–Sat 10am–6pm. AmEx, DC, JCB, MC, V. Saint Laurent's fashions are a bit old-lady chic, but his clothes are still glamorous enough to be sought after.

Sean

132 Thompson St between Houston and Prince Sts (598-5980). Subway: C, E to Spring St; N, R to Prince St. Mon–Sat noon–7pm, Sun noon–6pm. AmEx, MC, V. A former director of marketing at Scholastic, Sean Cassidy (don't laugh) discovered French designer Pierre Emile Lafaurie during visits to Paris; he fell in love with Lafaurie's men's suits, cotton shirts and corduroy jackets. Now Sean carries Lafaurie's designs exclusively.

Paul Smith

108 Fifth Ave between 15th and 16th Sts (627-9770). Subway: L, N, R, 4, 5, 6 to 14th Street–Union Sq. Mon–Wed, Fri, Sat 11am–7pm; Thu 11am–8pm; Sun noon–6pm. AmEx, Disc, MC, V. For the relaxed English gentleman look. These designs are exemplary in their combination of elegance, style and quality. Accessories are also available.

Anna Sui

113 Greene St between Spring and Prince Sts (941-8406). Subway: C, E to Spring St. Mon–Sat noon–7pm, Sun noon–6pm. AmEx, MC, V. Judging from her frequent sweeps of thrift stores in the East Village and flea markets throughout the city, Anna Sui's ideas come directly from the past. Her clothes, displayed in a lilac-and-black–decorated boutique, are popular with wealthy kids.

Vivienne Tam

99 Greene St between Prince and Spring Sts (966-2398). Subway: N, R to Prince St; C, E to Spring St. Mon–Fri 11am–7pm, Sat–Sun 11:30–7:30pm. AmEx, MC, V. Vivienne Tam's first U.S. boutique, with its oxblood walls and massive Chinese character cut out of a partition (it means "double happiness"), is decidedly exotic. Offering long, transparent dresses with mandarin collars, flowy skirts and sheer knit sweaters, the Canton-born Tam has that special something for your feminine side.

Atsuro Tayama

120 Wooster St between Prince and Spring Sts (334-6002). Subway: N, R to Prince St; C, E to Spring St. Mon–Sat 11am–7pm, Sun noon–6pm. AmEx, MC, V. Former Yohji Yamamoto assistant designer Atsuro Tayama has been creating his own looks since 1982. Choose from asymmetrical modern dresses, sheer shirts and billowy skirts.

Tocca

161 Mercer St between Prince and Houston Sts (343-3912). Subway: C, E to Spring St; N, R to Prince St. Mon–Sat 11am–7pm, Sun noon–6pm. AmEx, MC, V. What girl doesn't melt at the sight of Tocca's window? Colorful dresses and suits are housed in this gorgeous cerulean-blue boutique. There are children's and home lines, previously only available in the Tokyo store.

Valentino

747 Madison Ave at 65th St (772-6969). Subway: 6 to 68th St. Mon–Sat 10am–6pm. AmEx, MC, V. Celebrities and New

*No hands on deck: At **J.Crew**, you can try on designs you've admired in the catalog.*

York ladies who lunch just adore Valentino. Can you be as elegant as Sharon Stone? Only if you have enough money, honey.

Gianni Versace

647 Fifth Ave between 51st and 52nd Sts (759-3822). Subway: E, F to Fifth Ave. Mon–Wed, Fri, Sat 10am–6pm; Thu 10am–7pm. AmEx, DC, MC, V. Housed in the former Vanderbilt mansion, this is one of the largest (28,000 square feet) boutiques in the city. Go and stare longingly at the mosaics, even if you can't afford to buy the clothes.

Yohji Yamamoto

103 Grand St at Broadway (966-9066). Subway: J, M, Z, N, R, 6 to Canal St. Mon–Sat 11am–7pm, Sun noon–6pm. AmEx, DC, MC, V. The designer's flagship store is a huge, lofty space filled with well-cut designs.

Emerging designers

Mary Adams The Dress

159 Ludlow St at Stanton St (473-0237). Subway: F to Second Ave. Thu–Sun 1–6pm and by appointment. No credit cards. For frocks' sake: Mary Adams makes beautifully girly new versions of the old-fashioned party dress, favoring silks, satins, velvets and cottons.

Steven Alan

330 E 11th St between First and Second Aves (982-2881). Subway: L to First Ave, 6 to Astor Pl. Mon–Sun 1–8pm. ● 60 Wooster St between Spring and Broome Sts (call 334-6354 for hours). Subway: C, E to Spring St. AmEx, MC, V. Steven Alan's stock is coveted by hip girls in all neighborhoods. This East Village branch is filled with clothing by names like Built by Wendy, Pixie Yates and Rebecca Dannenberg.

Jill Anderson

331 E 9th St between First and Second Aves (253-1747). Subway: 6 to Astor Pl. Mon noon–7pm, Tue–Sun noon–8pm. AmEx, MC, V. Jill Anderson's classic, stylish silhouettes reflect the time the designer spent in Greece. Choose from coats, wrap dresses, pants and suits, which are always elegant but not always conventional.

Blue

125 St. Marks Pl between First Ave and Ave A (228-7744). Subway: F to Second Ave, L to First Ave, 6 to Astor Pl. Mon–Sat noon–8pm, Sun noon–6pm. AmEx, MC, V. This is a must stop if you're in the market for a wedding or cocktail dress, a fancy suit or just a pick-me-up. And if your size isn't available, owner Christina Karas will custom-make whatever style you fancy.

Veronica Bond

171 Sullivan St between Houston and Bleecker Sts (254-5676). Subway: 1, 9 to Houston St. Tue–Sun 2–7pm. AmEx, MC, V. American-born German Veronica Bond's couture and ready-to-wear line is inspired by stints working in the costume department at the Munich Opera and for Karl Lagerfeld. Along with drama-queen silk gowns, the shop features Bond's lovely, wearable separates.

Shin Choi Coleridge

199 Mercer St between Prince and Spring Sts (625-9202). Subway: B, D, F, Q, to Broadway–Lafayette St; N, R to Prince St; 6 to Bleecker St. Mon–Sat 11am–7pm. AmEx, MC, V. Shin Choi likes to mix her fine fabrics with a touch of Lycra; that way, the Korean-born designer explains, the clothes are not only more comfortable, but they travel well. You'll find sleek dresses, suits, pants and shirts in sexy, classic styles.

Daryl K

*208 E 6th St between Bowery and Second Ave (475-1255).
Subway: 6 to Astor Pl. Mon–Sun noon–7pm.* ●*21 Bond St at
Lafayette St (call 777-0713 for hours). Subway: B, D, F, Q to
Broadway–Lafayette St. AmEx, MC, V.* Daryl Kerrigan's cloth-
ing attracts rock & rollers, with vinyl pants, colored cords, hip-
hugger bootlegs and Latin-inspired dresses.

Patricia Field

*10 E 8th St at Fifth Ave (254-1699). Subway: N, R to 8th St.
Mon–Sat noon–8pm, Sun 1–7pm. AmEx, Disc, MC, V.* Field
is brilliant at working club and street fashion. Her store, with
its ambisexual staff, has an eclectic mix of original jewelry,
makeup, on-the-edge club gear and East Village design.
There's always something new, the clothing is gorgeous and
durable, and the wigs are the best in town. *See also* **Hotel
Venus** *below.*

Garb

*328 E 9th St between First and Second Aves (254-9073). Sub-
way: F to Second Ave, L to First Ave, 6 to Astor Pl. Tue–Fri
1–8pm, Sat–Sun noon–6pm. AmEx, MC, V.* Owner Selia
Yang designs delicate dresses and skirts in limited quantities, so clothes are practically one of a kind. Prices generally
range from $100 to $400.

Pierre Garroudi

*530 W 25th St between Tenth and Eleventh Aves (243-5166).
Subway: C, E to 23rd St. Mon–Sun 10am–6pm.* ●*139
Thompson St between Houston and Prince Sts (call 475-2333
for hours). Subway: C, E to Spring St. AmEx, MC, V.* This remote area of Chelsea has become a choice neighborhood for
designers who want to leave Soho. Garroudi spent five years
there, before signing the lease for a new store—15 times larger
than his previous boutique. For the Iranian-born designer, the
space means gads more room for his signature slinky, low-cut
gowns ($1,200 and up) and men's suits ($1,500 and up).

Harwood

*110 Stanton St between Essex and Ludlow Sts (677-4067).
Subway: F to Second Ave. Tue–Sat noon–7pm, Sun noon–
6pm. MC, V.* Texan Harwood Coleman Lee V displays his
lean creations in his tiny Lower East Side boutique. He's
heavily influenced by Halston and Kate Moss, although his
designs (for men and women) aren't at all androgynous.

Hotel Venus

*382 West Broadway between Broome and Spring Sts (966-
4066). Subway: C, E to Spring St. Mon–Sun noon–8pm.
AmEx, JCB, MC, V.* Patricia Field's new store features a
Japanese-animation influence; the decor is more mod and the
staff more serious and dressed-up than at her 8th Street boutique (see above). Along with clothing, Hotel Venus stocks
platforms, stationery, barrettes, wallets, blow-up furniture
and lots of bags.

Living Doll

*49 Prince St at Mulberry St (966-5494). Subway: B, D, F, Q to
Broadway–Lafayette St; 6 to Bleecker St. Mon–Wed noon–
6:30pm, Thu–Sun noon–7pm. AmEx, MC, V.* Amanda Up-
richard's highly coveted women's clothing is sold in stores
from TG-170 to Barneys, but if you don't want to sift through
racks to find it, head straight to her store. The tiny shop is a
launching pad for future pieces; expect to find more experimental items here.

Mark Montano

*434 E 9th St between First Ave and Ave A (505-0325). Sub-
way: F to Second Ave, L to First Ave, 6 to Astor Pl. Tue–Fri
1–8pm, Sat noon–8pm, Sun 1–6pm. MC, V.* A mixture of
classic glamorous suits and siren satin dresses from a terrific
emerging designer. If you have to go to a wedding and want
to look better than the bride, look no further.

Janet Promesso Atelier New York

*161 Lafayette St at Grand St, second floor (343-1956, 802-
7143). Subway: 6 to Spring St. By appointment only. No
credit cards.* Janet Promesso designs custom-made shirts
for women in her small atelier—a former Chinese massage
parlor. She has a loyal following; her made-to-order shirts
($180) come in several categories, including "classic-prep-
py" and "princess line," although mixing and matching is
perfectly acceptable. Promesso also designs women's suits
and shirtdresses.

TG-170

*170 Ludlow St between Houston and Stanton Sts (995-
8660). Subway: F to Second Ave. Mon–Sun noon–8pm.
AmEx, MC, V.* Terry Gillis has an eye for emerging designers: Her boutique was the first to carry the clothes of Rebecca
Dannenberg, Pixie Yates and Built by Wendy. Gillis also has
her own line—called TG-170, of course—consisting of simple separates in unusual fabrics.

Xuly Bët

*189 Orchard St between Houston and Stanton Sts (982-
5437). Subway: F to Second Ave. Tue–Sun 1–8pm. AmEx,
DC, MC, V.* In the past year, Orchard Street has become
home to at least a dozen businesses—including this store,
which sells the eponymous Parisian clothing line Xuly Bët.
Groovy French deconstructionist designs are housed
here—not for the meek.

All-Americans

APC

*131 Mercer St between Prince and Spring Sts (966-9685).
Subway N, R to Prince St. Mon–Sat 11am–7pm; Sun noon–
6pm. AmEx, JCB, MC, V.* Okay, so it's French. But really, APC
is France's answer to the Gap: Here, you'll find basic essentials in muted colors and minimal styling in a stunning store
designed by Julian Schnabel. The French part is evident in
the prices, which tend to be on the high side.

Banana Republic

*552 Broadway between Spring and Prince Sts (925-0308).
Subway N, R to Prince St; C, E to Prince St. Mon–Sat 10am–
8pm, Sun noon–6pm. AmEx, Disc, JCB, MC, V.* This reputable chain doesn't mass-produce everything quite like
some of its rivals. Prices are often slashed during sales, but
original prices are higher than the Gap's. Kind of classy.
Check the phone book for other locations.

Brooks Brothers

*346 Madison Ave at 44th St (682-8800). Subway: S, 4, 5, 6, 7
to 42nd St–Grand Central. Mon–Wed, Fri, Sat 9am–7pm;
Thu 9am–8pm; Sun noon–6pm.* ● *1 Liberty Plaza at Church
St (call 267-2400 for hours). Subway: N, R, 1, 9 to Cortlandt
St. AmEx, DC, JCB, MC, V.* The classic men's store, now
owned by Marks & Spencer, is still the place for high-quality
preppy clothing—button-down shirts, madras jackets, chi-
nos and wonderful striped dressing gowns.

Canal Jeans

*504 Broadway between Spring and Broome Sts (226-1130).
Subway: N, R to Prince St; 6 to Spring St. Mon–Thu, Sun
10am–8pm; Fri, Sat 10:30am–9pm; Sun 11am–9pm.
AmEx, DC, MC, V.* Browse among a vast acreage of jeans, T-
shirts and other basics, plus new (like French Connection) and
vintage clothing and accessories, socks, bags and fun jewelry.
Canal's prices are definitely worth the trip.

Charivari 57

*18 W 57th St between Fifth and Sixth Aves (333-4040). Sub-
way: E, F, N, R to Fifth Ave. Mon–Wed, Fri 10:30am–7pm;
Thu 10:30am–8pm; Sat 10:30am–6:30pm; Sun 12:30–
6pm. AmEx, MC, V.* Stylish working clothes for men and

Searching for lost treasures

Scavenging the city's flea markets will bring out the Sherlock Holmes in you

For bargain-hungry New Yorkers, rummaging through flea markets qualifies as a religious experience. There's no better way to walk off that two Bloody Mary weekend brunch than by wandering through aisles of vinyl records, 8-track tapes, clothes, books and furniture.

Although Mayor Giuliani has clamped down on the number of illegal street vendors working in the city, you might still get lucky: East Village vendors are persistent, if unreliable. Try along Second Avenue and Avenue A at night or lower Broadway on weekend afternoons for used clothes, records and magazines. And when the weather's nice, there are sidewalk or stoop sales. Although not as common in Manhattan, stoop sales are held on Saturdays in parts of Brooklyn (Park Slope especially) and Queens. If you have a car, you'll quickly spot the signs attached to trees and posts; if not, local papers provide the hours, dates and addresses. Sidewalk shopping is popular with the natives and they're serious, so head out early.

Annex Antiques & Flea Market
Sixth Ave between 25th and 27th Sts (243-5343). Subway: F to 23rd St. Sat, Sun 9am–5pm. Designer Todd Oldham hunts regularly here, as do plenty of models and the occasional dolled-down celebrity. This market is divided into two sections: One is free, the other charges $1. Both sections feature heaps of secondhand clothing (some of it actually antique quality), old-fashioned bicycles, platform shoes, bird cages, funky tools and those always-necessary accessories—hats, purses, gloves and compacts. Don't forget to stop by the vintage–eyeglass-frame stand.

Antique Flea & Farmer's Market
P.S. 183, 67th St between First and York Aves (721-0900). Subway: 6 to 68th Street. Sat 6am–6pm. A small market , but one that's good for antique lace, silverware and tapestries. Fresh eggs, fish and vegetables are also often available.

The Garage
112 W 25th St between Sixth and Seventh Aves. Subway: F to 23rd St; 1, 9 to 28th St. This indoor market is a gold mine for the same type of merchandise sold across the street in the outdoor market, along with the unusual: A pristine '60s map clock was unearthed here not too long ago at a deep, deep discount. It's heaven, especially on a cold day.

I.S. 44 Flea Market
Columbus Ave between 76th and 77th Sts (721-0900). Subway: B, C to 72nd St. Sun 10am–6pm. Sadly, this flea isn't what it used to be. New merchandise, like dried flowers, T-shirts and tube socks, has slowly pushed out the secondhand wonders. But with more than 300 stalls, you're still likely to find *something*.

Park Slope Flea Market
Seventh Ave between 1st and 2nd Sts, Park Slope, Brooklyn (1-718-330-9395). Subway: 2, 3, to Grand Army Plaza. Sat 9am–6pm. Keep in mind that the outer boroughs are where the best deals are. If you don't mind the trip to this picturesque neighborhood, this is quite a good market; some of the same vendors who work out of the Soho Antique Fair (see below) hawk their merchandise here—at substantially lower prices.

Soho Antique Fair & Collectibles Market
Grand St at Broadway (682-2000). Subway: J, M, Z, N, R, 6 to Canal St. Sat, Sun 9am–5pm. This flea market opened in 1992, and although it's smaller than the sprawling Sixth Avenue market, you just might walk away with more. Vintagewear, collectible radios, linens and all manner of kitsch cover a parking lot. There isn't a huge selection (when the weather's bad, the choice is hit-and-miss), but prices are fair. Sunday is always best.

At last, poor Yorick: A flea market find.

Jeans: From left, Keetar vintage dirty denim 736, Fellow vintage dirty denim 736.
Jacket: Drake vintage dirty denim 736.

The DIESEL Store • 60th Street and Lexington Avenue

women are carefully selected from a variety of designers: Gaultier, Ghost, Yamamoto. Pricey.

Club Monaco

160 Fifth Ave at 21st St (352-0936). Subway: N, R to 23rd St. Mon–Fri 10am–8pm, Sat 10am–7pm, Sun noon–6pm. ●*2376 Broadway at 87th St (call 579-2587 for hours). Subway: 1, 9 to 86th St.* ●*1111 Third Ave at 65th St (call 355-2949 for hours) Subway: 6 to 68th St–Hunter College. AmEx, DC, JCB, MC, V.* This Canadian-owned chain has acquired quite a following (there are 38 stores in Korea alone). In this one you'll find an impressive array of men's and women's sportswear, cosmetics and jewelry.

Diesel

770 Lexington Ave at 60th St (308-0055). Subway: N, R to Lexington Ave; 4, 5, 6 to 59th St. Mon–Sat 10am–8pm, Sun noon–6pm. AmEx, DC, Disc, JCB, MC, V. This 14,000-square-foot emporium will quench any denim craving you might have. In addition to jeans and stylish vinyl clothing and accessories, there are also shoes, under and outerwear, and refreshments of the coffee variety.

Eileen Fisher

395 West Broadway between Spring and Broome Sts (431-4567). Subway: C, E to Spring St. Mon–Thu 11am–7pm, Fri and Sat 11am–8pm, Sun noon–6pm. ●*521 Madison Ave between 53rd and 54th Sts (call 759-9888 for hours). Subway: E, F to Fifth Ave.* ●*341 Columbus Ave between 76th and 77th Sts (call 362-3000 for hours). Subway: 1, 9 to 79th St.* ●*103 Fifth Ave at 17th St (call 924-4777 for hours). Subway: L, N, R, 4, 5, 6 to 14th St–Union Sq.* ●*1039 Madison Ave between 79th and 80th Sts (call 879-7799 for hours). Subway: 6 to 77th St. AmEx, Disc, MC, V.* Fisher's timeless fashions—now modeled by the timeless beauty Isabella Rossellini—are available throughout the city. The Soho location is by far the largest. Customers must pass through an outdoor garden (complete with a crab-apple tree) in order to enter the store. Sift through racks of simple separates in soft cotton, wool crepes and plush velvet.

Gap

AmEx, Disc, JCB, MC, V. The Gap is the original outlet for affordable staples like T-shirts, jackets, blue jeans and chic dresses. Luckily, with more than 20 stores in Manhattan, there's always a branch nearby. Check the phone book for the nearest location and store hours.

Guess?

537 Broadway between Prince and Spring Sts (226-9545). Subway: N, R to Prince St; C, E to Spring St. Mon–Sat 10am–8pm, Sun 11am–7pm. AmEx, Disc, MC, V. This is Guess?'s first clothing store in New York. Shop here, learn how to pout, and boom—you're Lolita! Along with women's clothing, Guess? carries a line of accessories and shoes.

J. Crew

99 Prince St between Mercer and Greene Sts (966-2739). Subway: B, D, F, Q to Broadway–Lafayette St; N, R to Prince St; 6 to Bleecker St. Mon–Sat 10am–8pm, Sun 11am–6pm. AmEx, MC, V. J. Crew's enormous two-floor store carries both men's and women's lines, shoes, accessories and the women's "collection," which is on display in its own swanky room. The clothes are far from middle-American cheese, and there's plenty of Soho black.

Old Navy

610 Sixth Ave at 18th St (645-0663). Subway: F to 14th St, L to Sixth Ave. Mon–Sat 9:30am–9pm, Sun 11am–6pm. AmEx, Disc, JCB, MC, V. Owned by the Gap, this chain features unisex clothing at inexpensive prices. Some of it's funky; some is classic. Call the store and listen to a recorded message regarding what the deals of the week are. Check the phone book for other locations.

*Just browsing: your own big **MAC** attack.*

Phat Farm

129 Prince St between West Broadway and Wooster St (533-7428). Subway: C, E to Spring St. Mon–Sat 11am–7pm, Sun noon–6pm. AmEx, MC, V. Def Jam records impressario Russell Simmons's classy and conservative take on hip-hop couture. Phunky-phresh oversized and baggy clothing.

Product

71 Mercer St between Broome and Spring Sts (274-1494). Subway: N, R to Prince St; C, E to Spring St. Mon–Sat 11am–7pm, Sun noon–6pm. AmEx, MC, V. A hip clothier for women that features wonderful stretchy fabrics, sleek lines and frivolous accessories. Very good-looking clothes, and not as expensive as APC, which is just up the block. Sales are fast and frequent.

Saba

468 West Broadway between Houston and Prince Sts (614-8889). Subway: N, R to Prince St; C, E to Spring St. Mon–Wed 11am–7pm, Thu–Sat 11am–8pm, Sun noon–7pm. AmEx, MC, V. This Australian chain features men's and women's business and weekend separates in Aussie wool gabardine and sharkskin.

Stüssy Store

104 Prince St between Mercer and Greene Sts (274-8855). Subway: N, R to Prince St. Mon–Sat 11am–7pm, Sun noon–6pm. AmEx, MC, V. All the fine hats, T-shirts and other skatesome/surfy West Coast gear that Mr. Stüssy is famous for.

Trash & Vaudeville

4 St. Marks Pl between Second and Third Aves (982-3590). Subway: 6 to Astor Pl. Mon–Fri noon–8pm, Sat 11:30am–9pm, Sun 1–7:30pm. AmEx, MC, V. This punk staple has two floors of fashion, accessories and shoes: Stretchy tube dresses, leathers, snakeskin boots, collar tips and jewelry are *yours.*

Urban Outfitters

628 Broadway between Houston and Bleecker Sts (475-0009). Subway: B, D, F, Q to Broadway–Lafayette St; 6 to Bleecker St. Mon–Sat 10am–10pm, Sun noon–8pm. ●374 Sixth Ave at Waverly Pl (call 677-9350 for hours). Subway: A, C, E, B, D, F, Q to W 4th St–Washington Sq. ●127 E 59th St between Park and Lexington Aves (call 688-1200 for hours). Subway: N, R to Lexington Ave; 4, 5, 6 to 59th St. AmEx, MC, V. Clothes for urban survival. Basics include jeans and T-shirts for men and women, but there is also a good deal of trendy, inexpensive clothing. Labels include Girbaud, Anthopologie, Free People and Esprit. The store also stocks vintage "urban renewal" clothing, candles, bean bags and postcards.

Yellow Rat Bastard

487 Broadway between Broome and Grand Sts (334-2150). Subway: J, M, Z, N, R, 6 to Canal St. Mon–Sat 10am–9pm, Sun noon–8pm. AmEx, Disc, MC, V. Who can resist this name? Yellow Rat Bastard features reasonably priced hip-hop gear. In addition to clothing, customers are encouraged to gape at the store's six TV screens, which replay hip-hop performances and New York–themed films.

Discount fashion

Century 21 Department Store

22 Cortlandt St at Broadway (227-9092). Subway: N, R, 1, 9 to Cortlandt St. Mon–Thu 7:45am–7pm; Fri, Sat 11am–9pm. AmEx, Disc, MC, V. Some discerning shoppers report finding clothes by Romeo Gigli and Donna Karan here, but you have to visit every ten days or so to get these kinds of bargains. Rack upon rack is heavy with discounted designer and name-brand fashions. Housewares and appliances are also sold cheap, plus underwear, accessories, cosmetics, fragrances and women's shoes. Service is good, but with the exception of the designer section, there are no fitting rooms. Dress accordingly.

Daffy's

111 Fifth Ave at 18th St (529-4477). Subway: L, N, R, 4, 5, 6 to 14th St–Union Sq. Mon–Sat 10am–9pm, Sun noon–7pm. ●335 Madison Ave at 44th St (call 557-4422 for hours). Subway: S, 4, 5, 6, 7 to 42nd St–Grand Central. Disc, MC, V. Some swear by Daffy's ability to knock off designer wear in no time flat. There are three floors of current mainstream fashions: silk blouses, leather jackets and bags, Calvin Klein and French lingerie, men's suits and shirts. Prices are much lower than retail stores', and there are often remarkable bargains. The kids' clothes are fabulous.

Dollar Bill's

32 E 42nd St between Madison and Fifth Aves (867-0212). Subway: 4, 5, 6, 7, S to 42nd St–Grand Central. Mon–Fri 10am–8pm, Sat 10am–6pm, Sun noon–5pm. AmEx, DC, MC, V. Two floors of designer heaven—Versace, Montana, Byblos, Gigli and many more labels for men and women. Also discounted accessories and underwear, belts and ties.

Loehmann's

101 Seventh Ave between 16th and 17th Sts (352-0856). Subway: 1, 9 to 18th St. Mon–Sat 9am–9pm, Sun 11am–7pm. ●5740 Broadway between 235th and 236th Sts, Riverdale, Bronx (Call 1-718-543-6420 for hours). Disc, MC, V. After 75 years of waiting, bargain-happy Manhattanites finally got a branch of the Bronx original. The fantastic prices and designer merchandise are the same as ever, as is the enormous turnover of stock. The basement of the five-story building is reserved solely for menswear and accessories.

TJ Maxx

620 Sixth Ave at 18th St (229-0875). Subway: F to 14th St; L to Sixth Ave. Mon–Sat 9:30am–9pm, Sun 10am–6pm. *AmEx, DC, MC, V.* This new discount designer clothes store, with its brightly lit Woolworth's-like appearance, is less of an obvious treasure trove than Century 21 (see above), but if you're prepared to sift through the junk, you will undoubtedly find some fabulous purchases. Maxx also stocks household goods, luggage and shoes.

Syms

42 Trinity St at Rector St (797-1199). Subway: N, R to Rector St. Mon–Wed 9am–8:30pm; Thu, Fri 9am–8pm; Sat 10am–6:30pm; Sun noon–5:30pm. AmEx, Disc, MC, V. Syms has seven floors of designer discount fashions for men, women and children, with labels still intact. The store also sells shoes and luggage.

Vintage and secondhand clothes

The pyramid rule of secondhand clothes means the less you browse, the more you have to pay. Although we've included them in our listings, the shops along lower Broadway tend to ask inflated prices for anything except the most mundane '70s disco shirts. The alternatives, too numerous and ever-changing to list here, are the many small shops in the East Village and on the Lower East Side. These nooks (along with the now-famous Domsey's in Brooklyn) are where real bargains can be found. Salvation Army and Goodwill stores are also worth checking out—as is anyplace with the word *Thrift* in its name.

Alice Underground

481 Broadway at Broome St (431-9067). Subway: B, D, F, Q to Broadway–Lafayette St; 6 to Bleecker St. 11am–7:30pm. AmEx, MC, V. A good selection of '40s–'60s gear in all sorts of fabrics and in varied condition. Prices are high, but the bins at the front and in the back are always worth rummaging through. There's also a nice selection of bedding.

Allan & Suzi

416 Amsterdam Ave at 80th St (724-7445). Subway: 1, 9 to 79th St. Mon, Tue, Sat noon–7pm; Wed–Fri noon–8pm; Sun noon–6pm. AmEx, JCB, MC, V. Models drop off their once-worn Comme des Garçons, Muglers and Gaultiers here. The platform-shoe collection is unmatched. A great store, but not cheap.

Andy's Chee-Pees

691 Broadway between 3rd and 4th Sts (420-5980). Subway: B, D, F, Q to Broadway–Lafayette St; 6 to Bleecker St. Mon–Sat 11am–9pm, Sun noon–8pm. ●16 W 8th St between Fifth and Sixth Aves (Call 460-8488 for hours). Subway: N, R to 8th St. AmEx, MC, V. Pricey, but good for jeans and shirts.

Anna

150 E 3rd St between Aves A and B (358-0195). Subway: F to Second Ave. Mon–Sun noon–8pm. No credit cards. Anna is Kathy Kemp's middle name. Her shop, a haven for uptown fashion stylists and thrifters alike, usually stocks whatever is Kemp's current rage. Most recently, the racks were filled with clothes from the '50s and the '80s, and with things Japanese.

Antique Boutique

712–714 Broadway at Washington Pl (460-8830). Subway: N, R to 8th St; 6 to Astor Pl. Mon–Sat 11am–10pm, Sun noon–8pm. ●227 E 59th St (call 752-1680 for hours). AmEx, DC, Disc, JCB, MC, V. This used to be one of the largest shops for vintage gear; now the collection has been banished to the basement. The good news is that much of it (generally in the '60s–'70s timeline) is sold by the pound.

*Life of brine: Pick a peck of **Guss Pickles**.*

Cheap Jack's

841 Broadway between 13th and 14th Sts (777-9564). Subway: L, N, R, 4, 5, 6 to 14th Street–Union Sq. Mon–Sat 11am–8pm, Sun noon–7pm. AmEx, MC, V. A great vintage selection, but prices are exorbitant for anything nice. With army surplus gear that runs into the high hundreds, cheap is the last thing Jack's is.

Cherry

185 Orchard St between Houston and Stanton Sts (358-7131). Subway: F to Second Ave. Mon, Wed, Thu, Sun noon–9pm; Fri–Sat noon–10pm. AmEx, Disc, MC, V. Owners Racquel Honore, Cesar Padilla and Radford Brown specialize in vintage clothing from the '20s through the '80s; much of the clothing is dead stock, complete with original tags.

Domsey's Warehouse

431 Kent Ave at S 9th St, Williamsburg, Brooklyn (1-718-384-6000). Subway: J, M, Z to Marcy Ave. Mon–Fri 8am–5:30pm, Sat 8am–6:30pm, Sun 11am–5:30pm. No credit cards. The quality here has gone way down recently—there's too much competition. Still, it's usually easy to turn up something worthwhile. Choose from a huge selection of used jeans, jackets, military and industrial wear, ball gowns, shoes and hats. Especially notable are the Hawaiian shirts, the sportsgear windbreakers and the unreal prices on cowboy boots.

FAB 208

77 E 7th St between First and Second Aves (673-7581). Subway: F to Second Ave, 6 to Astor Pl. Mon, Wed–Sun noon–7:45pm. JCB, MC, V. This East Village staple attracts club kids and the fashion conscious, and both would agree: It's so much cheaper than Patricia Field. There are two stores side by side. One features top-of-the-line new and vintage items, the other is the sale store.

Resurrection

123 E 7th St between First Ave and Ave A (228-0063). Subway: F to Second Ave, L to First Ave, 6 to Astor Pl. Mon–Sat 1–9pm, Sun 1–8pm. ●217 Mott St between Prince and Spring Sts (call 625-1374 for hours). Subway: B, D, F, Q to Broadway–Lafayette St; 6 to Bleeker st. AmEx, MC, V. This vintage boutique is a Pucci wonderland—Kate Moss and Anna Sui are regulars. Owner Katy Rodriguez rents the space from the Theodore Wolinnin Funeral Home next door. Two dressing rooms take the place of the altar, and as you walk along the racks of leopard coats, 1940s dresses and beaded cardigans, you'll find yourself stepping on the metal outline of a coffin lifter. But don't worry: Rodriguez's shop looks more like a jewel box than a haunted house.

Screaming Mimi's

382 Lafayette St at 4th St (677-6464). Subway: N, R to 8th St; 6 to Astor Pl. Mon–Fri 11am–8pm, Sat noon–8pm, Sun 1–7pm. AmEx, DC, Disc, MC, V. This was where Cyndi Lauper shopped in the '80s. The prices are more reasonable and the selection more carefully chosen than at the Broadway stores around the block, and the window displays are always worth a look.

Transfer International

594 Broadway between Prince and Houston Sts, suite 1002 (941-5472). Subway: B, D, F, Q to Broadway–Lafayette St; N, R to Prince St; 6 to Spring St. Tue–Sun 1–7pm. AmEx. Well-connected Manhattanites Roberto Mitrotti and Linda Stein have collected celebrity castoffs from Ivana Trump, Christie Brinkley, Trudie Styler and a host of others. This is a good bet for designer clothes, from Azzedine Alaïa to Zang Toi.

Children's clothes

Baby Gap and Gap Kids

Baby Gap, 1037 Lexington Ave at 74th St (327-2614). Subway: 6 to 68th St. Mon–Sat 10am–7:30pm, Sun 11am–6pm. AmEx, Disc, MC, V. Gap sure knows how to hit a nerve. Even those repulsed by the mass-produced Gapwear swoon at the sight of a pair of tiny blue jeans or a miniature V-neck sweater. Gap Kids also features adult clothing. Check the phone book for other locations. *See also **Gap**, page 181.*

Julian & Sara

103 Mercer St between Spring and Prince Sts (226-1989). Subway: N, R to Prince St; C, E to Spring St. Tue–Fri 11:30am–7pm; Sat, Sun noon–6pm. AmEx, MC, V. Choose from ingenious hats, dresses and fancy outfits for boys and girls. It's all very French.

Lilliput

265 Lafayette St between Prince and Spring Sts (965-9567). Subway: B, D, F, Q to Broadway–Lafayette St; N, R to Prince St; 6 to Bleecker St. Mon, Sun noon–6pm; Tue–Sat 11am–7pm. AmEx, DC, MC, V. This hip staple for kids and babies sells secondhand as well as new clothing.

Me-Ki Kids

149 Ave A between 9th and 10th Sts (995-2884). Subway: 6 to Astor Pl. Mon–Fri 1–7pm; Sat, Sun 1–6pm. MC, V. Seriously trendy clothes for kids. Some accessories, too.

Oh Baby

153 Ludlow St between Stanton and Rivington Sts (673-5524). Subway: F to Second Ave. Mon–Sun 1–6pm. No credit cards. A baby haven, and it's smack on the ever-cool Ludlow Street. Stock includes funky velvet hats, pantsuits and hilarious aprons.

Shoofly Q

465 Amsterdam Ave at 83rd St (580-4390). Subway: B, C, 1, 9 to 86th St. Mon–Sat 11am–7pm, Sun noon–6pm. ●42 Hudson St between Duane and Thomas Sts (call 406-3270 for hours). Subway: 1, 2, 3, 9 to Chambers St. AmEx, MC, V. Boaters, caps, fleece-lined boots, suspenders, gloves and shoes are to be found among the *Flintstones*-style furniture, tree trunks and animal-footprint decor.

Space Kiddets

46 E 21st St between Park Ave and Broadway (420-9878). Subway: 6 to 23rd St. Mon, Tue, Fri 10:30am–6pm; Wed, Thu 10:30am–7pm; Sat 10:30am–5:30pm. AmEx, MC, V. A shop that specializes in that unique combination: clothing that is hip, practical, comfortable and fun for kids. There's always a range of one-of-a-kind items (including some furniture and toys) created by tiny, artsy companies, as well as secondhand clothes (it's *the* place for 1950s cowboy outfits).

Florists

For Interflora deliveries worldwide, phone City Floral at 410-0303 or 1-800-248-4692.

Blue Ivy

206 Fifth Ave between 25th and 26th Sts, fifth floor (448-0006). Subway: N, R to 28th St. Mon–Sat 8am–6pm, Sun 10am–6pm. AmEx, MC, V. Simon Naut, a former chief floral designer for the Ritz-Carlton Hotel, joined forces with graphic artist Michael Jackson to open this upscale floral shop. Arrangements start at $50.

Elizabeth Ryan Floral Designs

411 E 9th St between Ave A and First Ave (995-1111). Subway: L to First Ave, 6 to Astor Pl. Mon–Fri 9:30am–7pm, Sat 10am–6pm. AmEx, MC, V. Elizabeth Ryan has arranged her shop like one of her gorgeous bouquets, and the results are simply magical. Fork out $25 (or whatever you can afford) for an original bouquet and request whatever you're interested in.

Perriwater Ltd.

960 First Ave at 53rd St (759-9313). Subway: E, F to Lexington Ave; 6 to 51st St. Mon–Fri 9am–6pm, Sat 10am–6pm. AmEx, MC, V. Patricia Grimley doesn't believe that white flowers should be reserved for weddings; she loves the pure effect of an all-white arrangement for any occasion.

Renny

505 Park Ave at 59th St (288-7000). Subway: N, R to Lexington Ave; 4, 5, 6 to 59th St. Mon–Fri 9am–6pm. AmEx, DC, MC, V. "Exquisite flowers for the discriminating" is the slogan. Customers include David Letterman, Calvin Klein and myriad party-givers.

Very Special Flowers

204 W 10th St between Bleecker and W 4th Sts (206-7236). Subway: A, C, E, B, D, F, Q to W 4th St–Washington Sq. Mon 10am–5pm, Tue–Fri 10am–7pm, Sat 11am–5pm. AmEx, MC, V. And very special they are indeed. Dried flower arrangements, exotic bonsai, miniature topiary and extravagant bouquets are the specialities.

Food and drink

Balducci's

424 Sixth Ave at 9th St (673-2600). Subway: A, C, E, B, D, F, Q to W 4th St–Washington Sq. 7am–8:30pm. AmEx, MC, V. The Balducci family's grocery store has grown over three generations into a gourmet emporium that offers every luxurious foodstuff imaginable, from exotic fruit and freshly picked funghi to edible flowers and properly hung game. It also sells its own brand of pasta and sauces, preserves and salamis.

Dean & DeLuca

560 Broadway at Prince St (431-1691). Subway: N, R to Prince St. Mon–Sat 10am–8pm, Sun 10am–7pm. AmEx, MC, V. Dean & DeLuca is consolidating its position as *the* designer deli. The uninitiated will be amazed by the range and quality of the stock. The cheese counter is almost legendary, but this is the place to come for every kind of gourmet delicacy from raspberry vinegar to pâté de foie gras. Check the phone book for other locations.

Erotic Baker

Telephone orders only (721-3217). Tue–Fri 10am–6pm. AmEx, MC, V. They go through a lot of flesh-toned icing here. Need we say more? At least you'll be practicing safe sex.

Gourmet Garage

453 Broome St at Mercer St (941-5850). Subway: N, R to Prince St. Mon–Sun 7:30am–8:30pm. ●*301 E 64th St between First and Second Aves (call 535-6271 for hours). Subway: 6 to 68th St–Hunter College. AmEx, Disc, MC, V.* A converted garage full of gourmet goodies, this was the first store in Manhattan to sell fresh food at wholesale prices and in retail quantities. The Starving Artist sandwiches are delish, as is the vast assortment of olives.

Grace's Marketplace

1237 Third Ave at 71st St (737-0600). Subway: 4, 5, 6 to 68th St. Mon–Sat 7am–8:30pm, Sun 8am–7pm. AmEx, DC, MC, V. A schism in the Balducci family (see above) caused Grace to move to the Upper East Side, where she has established an admirable food store with a selection of all sorts of fabulous foods comparable to that in the Village store. Her Marketplace is the best bet for one-stop gourmet shopping in the neighborhood, but it is expensive.

Greenmarket

Information 477-3220, Mon–Fri 9am–5pm. There are more than 20 open-air markets, sponsored by city authorities, in various locations and on different days. The most famous is at Union Square, on East 14th Street (Mon, Wed, Fri 8am–6pm), where small producers of organic cheeses, honey, vegetables, herbs and flowers sell their wares from the backs of their flat-bed trucks. Arrive early, before the good stuff sells out.

Guss Pickles

35 Essex St between Grand and Hester Sts (254-4477). Subway: F to East Broadway. Mon–Thu, Sun 9am–6pm; Fri 9am–3pm. MC, V. Once upon a time there was a notorious rivalry between two pickle merchants, Guss and Hollander, but eventually it was settled. Guss put his name over the door of the old Hollander store and became the undisputed Pickle King, selling them sour or half-sour and in several sizes. Also excellent are the sauerkraut, pickled peppers and watermelon rinds.

Kam Man Food Products

200 Canal St at Mott St (571-0330). Subway: J, M, Z, N, R, 6 to Canal St. Mon–Sun 9am–9pm. MC, V. A selection of fresh and preserved Chinese, Thai and other Asian foods, as well as utensils and kitchenware.

Li-Lac

120 Christopher St between Bleecker and Hudson Sts (242-7374). Subway: 1, 9 to Christopher St–Sheridan Sq. Summer Tue–Sat noon–8pm, Sun noon–5pm; winter Mon–Sat 10am–8pm, Sun noon–5pm. AmEx, Disc, MC, V. Handmade chocolates par excellence are the specialty here.

Lung Fong Bakery

41 Mott St at Pell St (233-7447). Subway: J, M, Z, N, R, 6 to Canal St. Mon–Sun 7:30am–9pm. No credit cards. Lung Fong Bakery sells fortune cookies, plus delicious breads and biscuits.

McNulty's Tea and Coffee

109 Christopher St between Bleecker and Hudson Sts (242-5351). Subway: 1, 9 to Christopher St–Sheridan Sq. Mon–Sat 10am–9pm, Sun 1–7pm. AmEx, Disc, MC, V. The original McNulty began selling tea here in 1895; in 1980, the shop was taken over by the Wong family. Of course, coffee is included in the bevy of stimulants, but the real draw is the tea. From the rarest, the White Flower Pekoe (it's harvested once a year in China and costs $25 per pound), to a simple Darjeeling or a box from Fortnum & Mason, this is a tea haven.

Meyer & Thompson Fish Co.

146 Beekman St (233-5427). Subway J, M, Z to Fulton St. Fishmongers Mon–Fri 3–11am; art gallery Fri–Sun noon–6pm and by appointment. AmEx in gallery only. In the afternoons the fish shop, famous for its smoked cod, turns into a gallery displaying paintings by Naima Rauam.

Myers of Keswick

634 Hudson St between Horatio and Jane Sts (691-4194). Subway: A, C, E to 14th St; L to Eighth Ave. Mon–Fri 10am–7pm, Sat 10am–6pm, Sun noon–5pm. AmEx, V. Can't live without Heinz beans, treacle sponge or rice pudding? Hungry for Bovril, Bird's custard or Ribena? Sate yourself at Myers of Keswick, popularly known as the English Shop, a little corner of Coronation Street in the Big Apple.

Once Upon a Tart...

135 Sullivan St between Prince and Houston Sts (387-8869). Subway: C, E to Spring St; N, R to Prince St. Mon–Fri 8am–8pm, Sat 9am–8pm, Sun 9am–6pm. AmEx, MC, V. Along with fresh sandwiches, vegetable tarts and soup, this delectable bakery carries brownies, biscotti, a range of madeleines and fresh bread.

Raffeto's Corporation

144 Houston St at MacDougal St (777-1261). Subway: A, C, E, B, D, F, Q to W 4th St–Washington Sq. Tue–Fri 9am–6:30pm, Sat 8am–6pm. No credit cards. In business since 1906, Raffeto's is the source of much of the designer pasta that is sold in gourmet shops all over town. But the staff will serve special ravioli, tortellini, fettucine, gnocchi and manicotti in any quantity to anyone who calls in, with no minimum order.

Russ & Daughters

179 Houston St between Allen and Orchard Sts (475-4880). Subway: F to Second Ave. Mon–Wed 9am–6pm, Thu–Sat 9am–7pm, Sun 8am–6pm. MC, V. This New York institution, founded in 1914, still boasts Sunday morning lines of loyal customers waiting patiently for the most delicious smoked fish, gefilte fish, herring and whitefish salad in the city. A treasure.

Zabar's

2245 Broadway at 80th St (787-2000). Subway: 1, 9 to 79th St. Mon–Fri 8am–7:30pm, Sat 8am–8pm, Sun 9am–6pm. AmEx, MC, V. By common consent the best food store in the city and, naturally therefore, the world. Zabar's is not only an excellent delicatessen but a great grocer and a first-class fish shop. The variety and quality of the coffee and cookies, cheeses and croissants is breathtaking: Sniff the air and you'll understand why Zabar's is heaven.

A. Zito & Sons Bakery

259 Bleecker St at Seventh Ave (929-6139). Subway: A, C, E, B, D, F, Q to W 4th St–Washington Sq. Mon–Sat 6am–6pm, Sun 6am–3pm. No credit cards. Customers of this Bleecker Street bakery have included Frank Sinatra, who stopped by for a Sicilian loaf, and Bob Dylan, whose preference is for whole wheat. Tony Zito makes the best Italian bread in the Village, so if you're planning a picnic, this is the place to begin.

Liquor stores

Most supermarkets and corner delis sell beer and aren't too fussy about ID, although they may ask for proof that you are over 21. To buy wine and spirits, though, you need to go to a liquor store. And, to further confuse you, most liquor stores don't sell beer, nor are they open on Sundays.

Astor Wines & Spirits

12 Astor Pl at Lafayette St (674-7500). Subway: N, R to 8th St; 6 to Astor Pl. Mon–Sat 9am–9pm. AmEx, JCB, MC, V. This is a modern wine supermarket that would serve as the perfect blueprint for a chain, were it not for a law preventing liquor stores from branching out. There's a wide range of wines and spirits.

Best Cellars

1291 Lexington Ave between 86th and 87th Sts (426-4200). Subway: 4, 5, 6 to 86th St. Mon–Thu 10am–9pm; Fri, Sat 10am–10pm. AmEx, MC, V. This wine shop stocks only 100 selections, but each one is delicious and has been tasted by the owners (who tested more than 1,500 bottles). The best part is that they're all under $10.

Maxwell Wine & Spirits

1657 First Ave at 86th St (289-9595). Subway: 4, 5, 6 to 86th St. Mon–Wed 9am–11pm, Thu–Sat 10am–midnight. AmEx, MC, V. Maxwell stocks popularly priced French, Italian and Californian wines.

Park Avenue Liquor Shop

292 Madison Ave between 40th and 41st Sts (685-2442). Subway: 4, 5, 6, 7 to 42nd St–Grand Central. Mon–Fri 8am–7pm; Sat 8am–5pm. AmEx, MC, V. An impressive range of more than 400 Californian wines is complemented by an excellent selection of spirits and fine European bottles. Buy by the case to qualify for a 16-percent discount.

Schumer's Wine & Liquor

59 E 54th St between Park and Madison Aves (355-0940). Subway: E, F to Lexington Ave; 6 to 51st St. Mon–Sat 9am–midnight. AmEx, DC, MC, V. Schumer's has a large selection of French, Californian and Italian wines as well as champagnes, and a wide range of spirits, including cognacs, armagnacs and single-malt Scotches. They deliver.

Sherry-Lehmann

679 Madison Ave at 61st St (838-7500). Subway: N, R to Lexington Ave; 4, 5, 6 to 59th St. Mon–Sat 9am–7pm. AmEx, MC, V. Perhaps the most famous of New York's numerous liquor stores, Sherry-Lehmann has a vast selection of Scotches, brandies and ports, as well as a superb range of French, American and Italian wines.

Warehouse Wines & Spirits

735 Broadway between 8th St and Waverly Pl (982-7770). Subway: N, R to 8th St; 6 to Astor Pl. Mon–Thu 9am–8:50pm; Fri, Sat 9am–9:50pm. AmEx, MC, V. For the best prices in town for wine and liquor, look no further. Grab a cart, because you'll need it.

Gifts

Alphabets

115 Ave A between St. Marks Pl and 7th St (475-7250). Subway: L to First Ave. Mon–Thu noon–10pm; Fri, Sat noon–midnight; Sun noon–8pm. ●47 Greenwich Ave between Charles and Perry Sts (call 229-2966 for hours). Subway: 1, 9 to Christopher St–Sheridan Sq. ●2284 Broadway at 82nd St (call 579-5702 for hours). Subway: 4, 5, 6 to 86th St. AmEx, MC, V. Hilarious postcards, wrapping paper and tiny treasures fill the packed shelves here, together with a range of Josie and the Pussycats T-shirts and offbeat souvenirs of New York. The Sanrio line is extensive—new items arrive weekly.

Cobblestones

314 E 9th St between First and Second Aves (673-5372). Subway: 6 to Astor Pl, L to First Ave. Tue–Sat noon–7pm, Sun noon–6pm. AmEx, MC, V. A thrift store of sorts, this wonderful place stocks everything from elegant cigarette holders to antique lingerie and shoes. Gazing into the glass cases filled with bejeweled chokers can take the better part of a day.

Disney Store

711 Fifth Ave at 55th St (702-0702). Subway: E, F to Fifth Ave. Mon–Sat 10am–8pm, Sun 11am–7pm. ●141 Columbus

Ave at 66th St (call 362-2386 for hours). Subway: 1, 9 to 66th St–Lincoln Ctr. ● *39 W 34th St between Fifth and Sixth Aves (call 279-9890 for hours). Subway: B, D, F, Q, N, R to 34th St.* ● *210 W 42nd at Seventh Ave (call 221-0430 for hours). Subway: N, R, S, 1, 2, 3, 7, 9 to 42nd St–Times Sq. AmEx, Disc, Disney, MC, V.* This is where all your favorite Disney characters come to life (in great quantity)—Mickey, Minnie, Goofy, etc. At the Fifth Ave store, the largest of them all, merchandise previously available only by catalogue is for sale.

Eclectiques

55 Wooster St at Broome St (966-0650). Subway: C, E to Spring St. Mon–Sun 1–5:30pm. AmEx, MC, V. A peculiar mix of old Vuitton luggage, Lalique and other beautiful, covetable objects.

Hammacher Schlemmer

147 E 57th St between Third and Lexington Aves (421-9000). Subway: E, F to Lexington Ave; 4, 5, 6 to 59th St. Mon–Sat 10am–6pm. AmEx, JCB, DC, Disc, MC, V. Six floors of bizarre toys for home, car, sports and leisure, each one supposedly the best of its kind. The perfect place to buy a gift that will permanently attach a smile to anyone's face—especially the electric nose-hair remover.

Little Rickie

492 First Ave at 3rd St (505-6467). Subway: F to Second Ave. Mon–Sat 11am–8pm, Sun noon–7pm. AmEx, DC, MC, V. A bizarre collection of ludicrous, eye-popping, mirth-making toys, cards and trinkets gathered from around the world. Visit the photo booth and have your face added to the window display.

Love Saves the Day

119 Second Ave at 7th St (228-3802). Subway: 6 to Astor Pl. Mon–Thu noon–8pm, Fri–Sun 11am–11pm. AmEx, MC, V. More kitsch toys and tacky novelties than you can shake an Elvis doll at. There are Elvis lamps with pink shades, Elvis statuettes, ant farms, lurid machine-made tapestries of Madonna, glow-in-the-dark crucifixes and Mexican Day of the Dead statues.

Mxyplyzyk

125 Greenwich Ave at 13th St (989-4300). Subway: 1, 9 to Christopher St–Sheridan Sq. Mon–Sat 11am–7pm, Sun noon–5pm. ● *123 Greenwich Ave at 13th St (call 647-0777 for hours). Subway: 1, 9 to Christopher St–Sheridan Sq. AmEx, MC, V.* This West Village store (its name doesn't mean anything, although it's similar to the name of a character from *Superman* comics) offers a hodgepodge of lighting, furniture, toys, stationery, housewares and gardening items.

Serendipity

225 E 60th St between Second and Third Aves (838-3531). Subway: N, R to Lexington Ave; 4, 5, 6 to 59th St. Mon–Thu 11:30am–12:30am, Fri 11:30am–1am, Sat 11:30am–2am, Sun 11:30am–midnight. AmEx, DC, MC, V. Serendipity has been in business for over 35 years as both a restaurant and a general store selling clothing and gifts. The restaurant is famous for its frozen hot chocolate.

Warner Bros. Studio Store

1 E 57th St at Fifth Ave (754-0300). Subway: E, F, N, R to Fifth Ave; 4, 5, 6 to 59th St. Mon–Sat 10am–8pm; Sun noon–8pm. ● *1 Times Square between Broadway and Seventh Ave (call 840-4040 for hours). Subway: N, R, S, 1, 2, 3, 9, 7 to 42nd St–Times Sq.* ● *330 World Trade Center at Cortlandt St. (call 775-1442 for hours). Subway: N, R to Cortlandt St. AmEx, DC, JCB, MC, V.* The outlet for anything and everything that has a Warner Bros. character slapped on it features baseball hats, T-shirts and a few surprises.

Gift deliveries

Baskets by Wire

Call 724-6900 or 1-718-746-1200. Mon–Sat 8am–7pm, Sun 8am–3pm. AmEx, DC, Disc, MC, V. Fruit, gourmet food, flowers and mylar or helium balloon bouquets are delivered nationwide.

Select-a-Gram

Call 1-800-292-156 or 874-4464. Mon–Sat 9am–6pm. AmEx, DC, MC, V. Create your own gift basket with anything from champagne and caviar to jelly beans, T-shirts and stuffed animals. Nationwide delivery.

Children's toys

Enchanted Forest

85 Mercer St between Spring and Broome Sts (925-6677). Subway: 6 to Prince St. Mon–Sat 11am–7pm, Sun noon–6pm. AmEx, DC, Disc, JCB, MC, V. Browse through this gallery of beasts, books and handmade toys in a magical forest setting.

FAO Schwarz

767 Fifth Ave at 58th St (644-9400). Subway: E, F, N, R to Fifth Ave; 4, 5, 6 to 59th St. Mon–Wed 10am–6pm, Thu–Sat 10am–7pm, Sun 11am–6pm. AmEx, DC, Disc, JCB, MC, V. This famous toy store, which has been supplying New York kids with toys and games since 1862, stocks more stuffed animals than you could imagine in your worst nightmare. There are also kites, dolls, games, miniature cars, toy soldiers, bath toys and so on.

B. Shackman & Co.

85 Fifth Ave at 16th St (989-5162). Subway: B, D, F, Q, L, N, R, 4, 5, 6 to 14th St–Union Sq. Mon–Fri 9am–5pm, Sat 10am–4pm. AmEx, MC, V. Old-fashioned toys, miniatures, dollhouse furniture, wind-up toys and china dolls make this a nostalgic visit for adults and a fascinating one for kids.

Tiny Doll House

1146 Lexington Ave between 79th and 80th Sts (744-3719). Subway: 6 to 77th St. Mon–Fri 11am–5:30pm; Sat 11am–5pm. AmEx, MC, V. Everything in this shop is tiny: miniature furniture and furnishings for dollhouses, including chests, beds, kitchen fittings and cutlery. Even adults will love it.

The Body Shop

773 Lexington Ave at 61st St (755-7851). Subway: N, R to Lexington Ave; 4, 5, 6 to 59th St. Mon–Wed, Fri 10am–7pm; Thu 9:30am–7:30pm; Sun 10am–6pm. AmEx, Disc, MC, V. The Body Shop, as most everyone knows, is the premier place for natural beauty products in no-nonsense, biodegradable plastic bottles. Grab a basket and start filling. Check the phone book for other locations.

Felissimo

10 W 56th St at Fifth Ave (956-4438). Subway: N, R, B, Q to 57th St. Mon–Wed, Fri, Sat 10am–6pm; Thu 10am–8pm. AmEx, JCB, MC, V. This five-story townhouse is a Japanese-owned, eco-hip speciality store that stocks a collection of covetable items for the heart and home. Choose from jewelry, furnishings, clothing and collectibles. Assistance is available in nine languages.

Planet Hemp

423 Broome St between Crosby and Lafayette Sts (965-0500, 1-800-681-HEMP). Subway: 6 to Spring St. Mon–Sun noon–6pm. AmEx, Disc, MC, V. The hemp rage lives on at this shop that sells men's and women's sportswear, bed linens, paper goods and body products. There are even shoes made from hemp and "terra-gard," a leather substitute.

Terra Verde

120 Wooster St between Prince and Spring Sts (925-4533). Subway: N, R to Prince St. Mon–Sat 11am–7pm, Sun noon–6pm. AmEx, MC, V. Manhattan's first eco-market, combining art and activism. Architect William McDonough renovated this Soho space using non-toxic building materials and formaldehyde-free paint. Get your chemical-free linens, natural soaps and solar radios here.

Hats

Amy Downs Hats

103 Stanton St at Ludlow St (598-4189). Subway: F to Second Ave. Wed–Sun 1–6pm. No credit cards. Downs's soft wool and felt hats are neither fragile nor prissy. In fact, feel free to crumple them up and shove them in your bag (after purchasing them, of course)—they just won't die. Check out her trademark Twister: cone-shaped with tassels.

Casa de Rodriguez

150 Spring St between Wooster and West Broadway (965-1927). Subway: C, E to Spring St. Mon–Sun noon–8pm. MC, V. Jody Rodriguez, who collaborates on her whimsical creations with her husband, David, has no millinery training; perhaps that's why she focuses more on the fabric of her hats than the design. With that in mind, prepare to have fun.

Kelly Christy

235 Elizabeth St between Houston and Prince Sts (965-0686). Subway: N, R to Prince St. Tue–Sat noon–7pm, Sun noon–6pm. AmEx, MC, V. The selection, for both men and women, is lovely, and the atmosphere relaxed. Try on anything you like—Christy is more than happy to help and give the honest truth.

The Hat Shop

120 Thompson St between Prince and Spring Sts (219-1445). Subway: C, E to Spring St; N, R to Prince St. Tue–Sat noon–7pm; Sun 1–5pm. AmEx, JCB, MC, V. Linda Pagan isn't a hat designer herself, merely a hat junkie, and her delightful boutique is a cross between a millinery shop and a department store. Not only are customers able to choose among 40 different designers, they receive scads of personal attention too.

Lola Millinery

2 E 17th St between Fifth Ave and Broadway (366-5708). Subway: L, N, R, 4, 5, 6 to 14th St–Union Sq. Mon–Fri 11am–7pm, Sat 11am–6pm. AmEx, MC, V. Probably the best-known hat designer in the city, Lola designs classical and modern shapes for men and women. Prices range from $175 for feather clips and fancy combs to $275 for an animal-print fedora. Hats can be bought off the rack, customized or made to order.

van der Linde Designs

Lombardy Hotel, 111 E 56th St between Park and Lexington Aves, second floor (758-1686). Subway: N, R to Lexington Ave; 4, 5, 6 to 59th St. By appointment only. AmEx, MC, V. Susan van der Linde is the protégée of designer Don Marshall (whose creations graced the heads of Joan Crawford and Grace Kelly, among others). Her small boutique is akin to an elegant '30s parlor. There are stunning cocktail hats, rain wear and polar-fleece wrap hats —alternately very diva and ski bunny.

Worth & Worth

331 Madison Ave at 43rd St (867-6058). Subway: 4, 5, 6, 7, S to 42nd St–Grand Central. Mon–Fri 9am–6pm, Sat 10am–5pm. AmEx, DC, MC, V. This is the grandest men's

hat shop in the city, where you'll find the finest Panama hats under the sun and a vast assortment of fedoras.

Hairdressers
Model discounts

Swank salons free up their $200 chairs one night a week for those willing to become a guinea pig for trainees. Not to worry—there's much supervision, and the results are usually wonderful. Best of all, it costs a fraction of the usual price. All of the following have model nights, with prices ranging between $25 and $45 (often payable in cash only). Phone for details of their next model night; you may well have to get yourself on a waiting list.

Peter Coppola Salon (988-9404)
Frédéric Fekkai (753-9500)
Louis Licari (517-8084/327-0639)
Pierre Michel Salon (759-3000)
Vidal Sassoon (223-9177)

Cheap cuts
Astor Place Hair Designers

2 Astor Pl at Broadway (475-9854). Subway: N, R to 8th St; 6 to Astor Pl. Mon–Sat 8am–8pm, Sun 9am–6pm. No credit cards. The classic New York hair experience. An army of barbers does anything from neat trims to shaved designs, all to pounding music, usually hip-hop. You can't make an appointment; just take a number and wait with the crowd outside. Sunday mornings are quiet. Cuts cost from $11.

Ginger Rose 2

37 E 8th St between University Pl and Greene St (677-6511). Subway: N, R to 8th St. Mon–Wed 9:30am–8pm, Thu–Sat 9:30am–10pm, Sun noon–7pm. Similar to the Astor, haircuts here start at $10.

Heads & Tails Haircutting

22 St. Marks Pl between Second and Third Aves (677-9125). Subway: 6 to Astor Pl. Tue–Fri 1pm–midnight, Sat 11:30am–7pm. No credit cards. A basic hairdressing service—wash and cut, styling and blow-drying. Just walk in; no appointment is necessary.

Salon Seven

110 E 7th St between Ave A and First Ave (677-7399). Subway: F to Second Ave, L to First Ave, 6 to Astor Pl. Mon–Fri 10am–8pm, Sat 10am–6pm. Mark D, an East Village staple, and his wife, Lori Goldstein, run this tiny salon that offers men's and women's haircuts for $35.

Stylists
Robert Stuart Salon

510 Amsterdam Ave between 84th and 85th Sts (496–1530). Subway: 1, 9 to 86th St. Tue–Fri 10:30am–6:30pm, Sat 9am–5pm. AmEx, MC, V. The ever-friendly Stuart, who worked at Henri Bendel and Vidal Sassoon, has been cutting hair in his own salon for the past 15 years. Haircuts cost $70, coloring starts at $55.

Studio 303

Chelsea Hotel, 222 W 23rd St between Seventh and Eighth Aves (633-1011). Subway: C, E, 1, 9 to 23rd St. Tue–Fri 11am–8pm, Sat 10am–6pm. No credit cards. Owned by three ex-Racine stylists, Studio 303 is located in the wonderfully spooky Chelsea Hotel. Haircuts start at $65.

Wardwell Salon

200 W 80th St between Amsterdam Ave and Broadway (362-7617). Subway: 1, 9 to 79th St. Tue–Sat 11am–8pm. No credit cards. Deborah Wardwell gave up a career in magazines to open her own salon. She reserves an hour for each haircut and does color as well; the results are breathtaking. Haircuts start at $70; highlights cost $125 and up.

Home furnishings

Bed, Bath & Beyond

620 Sixth Ave at 18th St (255-3550). Subway: L to Sixth Ave; F to 14th St. Mon–Fri 9:30am–9pm, Sat 9:30am–8pm, Sun 10am–8pm. AmEx, Disc, MC, V. As the name suggests, everything you need for your house, with particular emphasis on sheets and towels. Low prices and generally good quality.

Bennison Fabrics

76 Greene St between Spring and Broome Sts (941-1212). Subway: C, E to Spring St. Mon–Fri 10am–6pm. MC, V. An unusual downtown shop with a classic but innovative range of fabrics silkscreened in England. Prices are steep, but the fabrics—usually 70 percent linen, 30 percent cotton—end up in some of the best-dressed homes in town.

Crate & Barrel

650 Madison Ave at 59th St (308-0011). Subway: N, R to Lexington Ave; 4, 5, 6 to 59th St. Mon–Fri 10am–8pm, Sat 10am–7pm, Sun noon–6pm. AmEx, Disc, MC, V. Crate & Barrel combines mid-range antique furniture and *objets* with the very best and latest in household goods.

Gracious Home

1217 and 1220 Third Ave between 70th and 71st Sts (988-8990). Subway: 6 to 68th St. Mon–Fri 8am–7pm, Sat 9am–7pm, Sun 10am–6pm. AmEx, DC, MC, V. If you need a new curtain rod, place mat or drawer pull, give them a call. They deliver all over Manhattan, and there's no minimum charge.

Pottery Barn

117 E 59th St between Lexington and Park Aves (753-5424). Subway: N, R to Lexington Ave; 4, 5, 6 to 59th St. Mon–Wed, Fri 10:30am–7pm; Thu, Sat 10am–8pm; Sun noon–6pm. AmEx, Disc, MC, V. Candlesticks, candlesticks, candlesticks! The 1990s answer to every decoration dilemma is melting wax, and Pottery Barn helps out in that department. You'll find plain ceramics, glassware and furniture (as in lamps and tables), tortoise-shell glass bowls, rattan chairs and picture frames. The designs are stripped down, stark and quite appealing. Check the phone book for other locations.

Rhubarb Home

26 Bond St between Lafayette St and Bowery (533-1817). Subway: B, D, F, Q to Broadway–Lafayette St; 6 to Bleecker St. Noon–7pm. AmEx, DC, MC, V. Stacy Sindlinger scouts flea markets and yard sales in Ohio for impeccably battered furniture. Chipped work tables, French Deco mirrors, even a baker's table have all been in her ingenious shop at one time or another.

White Trash

304 E 5th St between First and Second Aves (598-5956). Subway: F to Second Ave; 6 to Astor Pl. Wed–Sat 2–9pm, Sun 1–8pm. MC, V. After holding a monthly yard-sale event at First Avenue and 4th Street for a while, "white trash" connoisseurs Kim Wurster and Stuart Zamksy opened this popular store to the delight of those in dire need of Jesus night lights, Noguchi lamps and 1950s kitchen tables. Great prices.

Williams-Sonoma

20 E 60th St at Madison Ave (980-5155). Subway: N, R to Lexington Ave; 4, 5, 6 to 59th St. Mon–Fri 10am–7pm, Sat 10am–6pm, Sun noon–5pm. AmEx, Disc, MC, V. Even if you don't know how to cook, once you enter this store you'll

*Clip and shave: To make a short statement, let **Astor Place** haircutters go to your head.*

feel the urge to start. A branch of the famous San Francisco kitchen store, Williams-Sonoma stocks all the best kinds of kitchen equipment: KitchenAid food mixers, Gaggia ice cream machines, professional slicers, great copper and stainless-steel pots, grills, fine glassware, maple salad bowls, Sabatier knives and so on. The outlet store sells end-of-line and sale items. Check the phone book for other locations.

Personal home shopper

Design Find

1-516-365-4321. By appointment only. Interior designer Lauren Rosenberg-Moffit claims to know Manhattan like the back of her hand and will escort you on a memorable shopping tour of the city's showrooms, antiques markets and back-alley stores, bringing you discounts of up to 20 percent. Her fee varies according to your needs.

Jewelry

Cartier

653 Fifth Ave at 52nd St (753-0111). Subway: N, R to Fifth Ave; 6 to 51st St. Mon–Sat 10am–5:30pm. AmEx, DC, JCB, MC, V. Cartier bought its Italianate building, one of the few survivors of this neighborhood's previous life as a classy residential area, for two strands of Oriental pearls. All the usual Cartier items—jewelry, silver, porcelain—are sold within.

Clear Metals

72 Thompson St between Spring and Broome Sts (941-1800). Subway: 6 to Spring St. Mon 12:30–6pm, Tue–Sat 12:30–7pm, Sun 1–6pm. AmEx, MC, V. Metalsmith Barbara Klar creates modernist silver forms that are engraved with signs and symbols. Her wedding rings are contemporary and lovely.

David Webb

445 Park Ave at 57th St (421-3030). Subway: N, R to Lexington Ave; 4, 5, 6 to 59th St. Mon–Fri 10am–5:15pm, Sat 10am–5pm. AmEx, DC, Disc, JCB, MC, V. David Webb is best known for distinctive, and much imitated, gem-studded 18-carat gold jewelry. The pieces are expensive, often figurative; the quality is impeccable and the prices appropriately high.

Ilias Lalaounis

733 Madison Ave at 64th St (439-9400). Subway: N, R to Lexington Ave; 4, 5, 6 to 59th St. Mon–Sat 10am–5:30pm. AmEx, DC, Disc, JCB, MC, V. This Greek jewelry designer's

Stress-free zones

Feeling frazzled? Pamper your weary body with a visit to a spa.

After long days of battling vicious city crowds and being always on the go, you may soon find yourself feeling like a hardened New Yorker. So treat yourself as they do—by plunking your sore, stressed-out body onto a masseuse's table. Or you can opt for an alternative treatment, like a soothing seaweed wrap or an acupuncture face-lift. Maybe a glycolic fruit peel is more your speed? Just choose the spa that best suits your personality and think of it as a little present to yourself. Most treatments start at $60, but no matter how ridiculously relaxed you feel afterwards, don't forget to leave a tip (15 to 20 percent).

To get rid of holiday cellulite, go to a specialist: The experts at the **Anushka Day Spa** will reveal more than you ever wanted to know about the horror of cottage-cheese thighs.

For some good, old-fashioned New Age aromatherapy, head to **Aveda Salon and Spa**, where the scents of eucalyptus and chamomile fill the air. The trendy, luxurious **Bliss Spa** is popular for more than just its mighty massages and beautifying facials—the Bliss lounge boasts a famous buffet loaded with fresh cucumbers, chilled water with lemon slices, chocolates and cheese and crackers. **Carapan,** which means "a beautiful place of tranquility where one comes to restore one's spirit" in the language of the Pueblo Indians, offers reiki, craniosacral therapy and manual lymphatic drainage. At **Susan Ciminelli**, the lighting is dim and the scent is sandalwood: a perfect setting for reiki sessions or a lymphatic drainage massage.

Frédéric Fekkai Beauté de Provence isn't exactly like a trip to France, but the salon is modeled after Fekkai's hometown of Aix-en-Provence. Fekkai is known for its hair services,

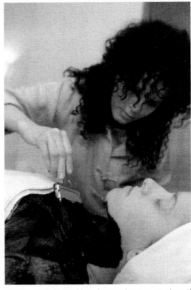

Down and dirty: Here's mud on your chest!

like the shea-butter mask. Two uptown mainstays, **Elizabeth Arden Red Door Salon** and **Georgette Klinger,** specialize in skin care, offering exquisite aromatherapy facials with plenty of pampering. Find some Zen peace at **Kozué Aesthetic Spa,** where there are seven kinds of body treatments to wrap yourself in.

---

work is inspired by his native country's ancient symbols as well as American Indian and Arab designs. Expensive.

Manny Winick & Son

19 W 47th St at Fifth Ave (302-9555). Subway: B, D, F, Q to 47th–50th Sts–Rockefeller Ctr. Mon–Fri 10am–5pm; Sat 10am–4:30pm. AmEx, Disc, MC, V. Fine jewelry made from precious metals is sold alongside more sculptural contemporary pieces.

Piaget

730 Fifth Ave at 57th St (246-5555). Subway: E, F, N, R to Fifth Ave; 4, 5, 6 to 59th St. Mon–Sat 10am–6pm. AmEx, MC, V. This giant boutique full of glittering jewels would surely make Holly Golightly swoon. Piaget has a diamond (or an emerald) for every girl.

Robert Lee Morris

400 West Broadway between Spring and Broome Sts (431-9405). Subway: C, E to Spring St; N, R to Prince St. Mon–Fri 11am–6pm, Sat 11am–7pm, Sun noon–6pm. AmEx, MC, V. Robert Lee Morris is one of the foremost contemporary designers; his bright Soho gallery is filled with strong, striking pieces.

Ted Muehling

47 Greene St between Broome and Grand Sts (431-3825). Subway: N, R to Prince St. Tue–Fri, Sat noon–6pm. AmEx, MC, V. Ted Muehling creates beautiful organic shapes in the studio behind the store, which sells the work of other artists, too.

Tiffany & Co.

727 Fifth Ave between 56th and 57th Sts (755-8000). Subway: E, F, N, R to Fifth Ave; 4, 5, 6 to 59th St. Mon–Wed, Fri, Sat 10am–6pm; Thu 10am–7pm. AmEx, DC, JCB, MC, V.

La Casa de Vida Natural New York Day Spa, a cross between a pediatrician's office and a tropical bordello, specializes in flotation. Don't miss the mini-waterfall. **The Peninsula Spa**, situated in the grand Peninsula Hotel, prides itself on its heated seaweed body wraps.

If you're brave, venture to the **Russian & Turkish Baths** in the East Village, where the massage tables and rustic steam room aren't very pretty, but do score well on authenticity. For a more esoteric experience, **Soho Sanctuary** is a healthy alternative. At least it will feel that way—the Moor-Life Body Wrap consists of heated moor-life mud (taken from a remote moor in Upper Austria), applied with a paintbrush. And if you still feel the urge to have "thread" pins stuck into your facial meridians, try an acupuncture face-lift at the **Spa at Equinox**. Happy melting.

Anushka Day Spa
241 E 60th St between Second and Third Aves (355-6404). Subway: N, R to Lexington Ave; 4, 5, 6 to 59th St. Mon 9am–6pm; Tue, Thu 9am–8pm; Wed, Fri 9am–7pm; Sat 9am–6pm. Closed Mondays in July and August. AmEx, MC, V.

Aveda Salon and Spa
The Aveda Institute, 233 Spring St between Sixth Ave and Varick St (807-1492). Subway: C, E to Spring St; 1, 9 to Houston St. Mon–Fri 10am–7pm, Sat 10am–6pm, Sun noon–6pm. AmEx, MC, V.
Branch: 456 West Broadway (473-0280).

Bliss Spa
568 Broadway at Prince St, second floor (219-8970). Subway: N, R to Prince St. Mon, Wed 12:30–10pm; Tue, Thu, Fri 11am–8pm. AmEx, MC, V.

Carapan
5 W 16th St between Fifth and Sixth Aves (633-6220). Subway: F to 14th St; L to Sixth Ave. Daily 10am–9:30pm. AmEx, MC, V.

Susan Ciminelli Day Spa
Bergdorf Goodman, 754 Fifth Ave between 57th and 58th Sts (872-2650). Subway: N, R to Fifth Ave; 4, 5, 6 to 59th St. Mon–Fri 8am–8pm, Sat 8am–7pm. AmEx, MC, V.

Frédéric Fekkai Beauté de Provence
Chanel, 15 E 57th St between Fifth and Madison Aves (753-9500). Subway: N, R to Fifth Ave; 4, 5, 6 to 59th St. Mon–Wed, Fri, Sat 9am–6pm; Thu 9am–8pm. AmEx, MC, V.

Elizabeth Arden Red Door Salon
691 Fifth Ave between 54th and 55th Sts (546-0200). Subway: E, F to Fifth Ave. Mon, Tue, Fri, Sat 8am–6pm; Wed 8am–7:30pm; Thu 8am–8pm; Sun 9am–5pm. AmEx, MC, V.

Georgette Klinger
501 Madison Ave at 53rd St (838-3200). Subway: E, F to Fifth Ave. Mon, Wed 9am–8pm; Tue, Thu, Fri 9am–6pm; Sat 9am–4pm; Sun 9am–3pm. AmEx, MC, V.
Branch: 978 Madison Ave (744-900).

Kozué Aesthetic Spa
795 Madison Ave between 67th and 68th Sts, second floor (734-8600). Subway: 6 to 68th St. Mon–Tue 10am–4pm; Wed–Fri 10am–8pm; Sat, Sun 10am–6pm. AmEx, MC, V.

La Casa de Vida Natural New York Day Spa
41 E 20th St between Park Ave South and Broadway (673-2272). Subway: 6 to 23rd St. Mon–Tue 10am–8pm; Wed–Fri 10am–6pm; Sat, Sun 9am–6pm. AmEx, MC, V.

The Peninsula Spa
Peninsula Hotel, 700 Fifth Ave at 55th St, 21st floor (903-3910). Subway: E, F to Fifth Ave. Mon–Fri 8:30am–8:30pm; Sat, Sun 8:45am–6:45pm. AmEx, MC, V.

Russian & Turkish Baths
268 E 10th St between First Ave and Ave A (473-8806). Subway: 6 to Astor Pl. 7:30am–10pm; Wed women only; Thu, Sun men only. AmEx, Disc, MC, V.

Soho Sanctuary
119 Mercer St between Prince and Spring Sts (334-5550). Subway: N, R to Prince St; C, E to Spring St. Tue–Fri 9am–9pm, Sat 10am–6pm, Sun noon–6pm. AmEx, MC, V.

The Spa at Equinox
205 E 85th St between Second and Third Aves (439-8500). Subway: 4, 5, 6 to 86th St. Mon–Thu 9am–10pm; Fri 9am–9pm; Sat, Sun 9am–8pm. AmEx, MC, V.

Tiffany's heyday was around the turn of the century, when Louis Comfort Tiffany was designing his famous lamps and sensational Art Nouveau jewelry. Today, the big star is Paloma Picasso, who designs big pieces at bigger prices. Three stories are stacked with precious jewels, silver accessories, chic watches and porcelain. Don't forget your credit cards.

Laundry

Most neighborhoods have coin-operated laundromats, but in New York it costs about the same amount to drop off your wash and let someone else do the work. On the Upper West Side, we recommend **Ecomat** (362-2300) on 72nd Street: It's one of the city's only laundries to use ecologically sound detergents. Check the phone book for other establishments and locations.

Leather goods and luggage

Bag House
797 Broadway at 11th St (260-0940). Subway: L, N, R, 4, 5, 6 to 14th St–Union Sq. Mon–Sat 11am–6:45pm, Sun 1–5:45pm. AmEx, MC, V. All manner of bags from the tiniest tote to something you could stow a small family away in are available here.

Behrle
89 Franklin St between Church St and Broadway (334-5522). Subway: 1, 9 to Franklin St. Tue–Sat noon–7pm. AmEx, MC, V. Carla Dawn Behrle's Tribeca shop fea-

tures leather skirts, dresses, camisoles and pants that can be best described as duds for that modern Bond girl in your life. Among the celebs who have donned Behrle's designs are the Spice Girls, Bono and the Edge.

Coach

710 Madison Ave at 63rd St (319-1772). Subway: N, R to Lexington Ave; 4, 5, 6 to 59th St. Mon–Wed 10am–7pm; Thu, Fri 10am–8pm; Sat 10am–7pm; Sun noon–6pm. AmEx, MC, V. The buttery-soft leather briefcases, wallets and handbags found here are exceptional. This is the only Coach store in Manhattan to stock the complete clothing collection for men. Check the phone book for other Coach locations.

Il Bisonte

72 Thompson St between Spring and Broome Sts (966-8773). Subway: C, E to Spring St. Tue–Sat noon–6:30pm; Mon, Sun noon–6pm. AmEx, MC, V. Stylish, tough basics—bags, belts and saddlebags—from the famous Florentine company are sold here.

Jutta Neumann

317 E 9th St between First and Second Aves (982-7048). Subway: L to First Ave, 6 to Astor Pl. Tue–Sat noon–8pm and by appointment. AmEx, MC, V. Neumann designs leather sandals ($130–$325) and bags ($100–$500) as well as belts and jewelry. Haven't you always wanted a leather choker?

Louis Vuitton

49 E 57th St between Park and Madison Aves (371-6111). Subway: N, R to Lexington Ave; 4, 5, 6 to 59th St. Mon–Fri 10am–6pm, Sat 10am–5pm, Sun noon–5pm. AmEx, DC, Disc, JCB, MC, V. The luggage and handbags are expensive, but beautiful.

Lingerie

Between the Sheets

241 E 10th St between First and Second Aves (677-7586). Subway: L to First Ave, 6 to Astor Pl. Mon–Sat noon–8pm, Sun noon–6pm. AmEx, MC, V. Sylvia Shum stocks American and European brands of bras and panties, along with silk slips, lacy cotton camisoles and teddies. Everything's extra pretty—she knows that many of her clients wear their underthings on the outside.

Enelra

485 E 7th St between First and Second Aves (473-2454). Subway: F to Second Ave; 6 to Astor Pl. Mon–Sat noon–9pm, Sun noon–8pm. AmEx, MC, V. During the 1980s, Madonna was a regular. Plenty of corsets, bras and slinky slips, as well as fluffy marabou mules.

Lingerie & Co.

1217 Third Ave between 70th and 71st Sts (737-7700, 1-800-737-1217). Subway: 6 to 68th St. Mon–Sat 9:30am–7pm, Sun noon–5pm. AmEx, Disc, MC, V. Owners Mark Peress and Tamara Watkins take a look at your body (and ask a few questions) before they announce their lingerie recommendations.

La Petite Coquette

51 University Pl between 9th and 10th Sts (473-2478). Subway: N, R to 8th St; 6 to Astor Pl. Mon–Sat 11am–7pm, Sun noon–6pm. AmEx, MC, V. There are too many goodies for the eye to take in at Rebecca Apsan's tiny lingerie boudoir. Customers can flip through panels of pinned-up bras and underpants before making a selection. Once you know what you like, she'll order it for you.

Victoria's Secret

565 Broadway at Prince St (274-9519). Subway: N, R to Prince St. Mon–Sat 10am–8pm, Sun noon–7pm. AmEx,

Disc, MC, V. There's lots of colored satin and plenty of sales at this lingerie chain. Phone for details of your nearest branch. Check the phone book for other locations.

Magic

Prediction

110 W Houston St between Sullivan and Thompson Sts (677-9588). Subway: C, E to Spring St; 1, 9 to Christopher St–Sheridan Sq. Tue–Sun noon–8pm. AmEx, MC, V. Roger Pratt and Billy Barbanes, co-owners of this pagan shop (formerly Altar Egos), stock statues, candles, books and, of course, good advice. Custom work is done on the premises.

Other Worldly Waxes

131 E 7th St between Ave A and First Ave (260-9188). Subway: F to Second Ave, L to First Ave, 6 to Astor Pl. Mon–Fri 2–10pm; Sat, Sun 1–10pm. ● *213 W 80th St between Amsterdam Ave and Broadway (call 799-3000 for hours). Subway: 1, 9 to 79th St. AmEx, MC, V.* Witchery by a psychologist? Dr. Catherine Riggs-Bergesen blends both crafts and will do her damnedest to straighten out your life. Her book *Candle Therapy,* a must for amateurs, is sold here.

Mail order

It isn't instant gratification, but shopping from the comfort of your hotel room or apartment beats fighting the crowds in the mean stores of Manhattan. Simply pick up your phone, and boom! You're the proud owner of a power drill, contact lenses, a personal computer or a string of pearls. Most services are open 24 hours a day and deliver within 48 hours, and there's always the possibility of having merchandise shipped back home. All you need is a phone and a credit card. Most of the major stores—Tiffany, Saks, Barnes & Noble—produce catalogs (see above for their listings); some of the major catalog companies—Victoria's Secret, Sharper Image, J. Crew—also have stores. If you have a favorite shop, try calling the toll-free directory (1-800-555-1212) to see if it has a listing. Otherwise, try one of the following:

Austads (1-800-759-4653). Essential for golfers, Austads' novelty items are dead funny.

L.L. Bean (1-800-221-4221). One of the top ten catalog companies, Bean specializes in country clothing (denim, khaki, etc.) and home accessories.

Lillian Vernon (1-800-285-5555). Call here to order pencils with your name engraved on them, hats with built-in fans, or anything else that you don't need. But they make great gifts.

Mac Warehouse (1-800-255-6227). Software for your Apple Macintosh—plus other Mac accessories—is just a phone call away.

Nature's Bounty (1-800-645-5412). A hypochondriac's dream—page after page of every dietary supplement you could possibly ingest.

Orvis (1-800-815-5900). Hunters and anglers love this established and reliable source of sporting goods and clothing.

Pottery Barn (1-800-922-5507). This store has a mail-order service that features the same cheap and fashionable home furnishings with a vaguely ethnic or country flavor.

Opticians

Alain Mikli Optique
880 Madison Ave at 71st St (472-6085). Subway: 6 to 68th St. Mon–Fri 10am–6pm, Thu 9:30am–7pm, Sat 10:30am–6pm. AmEx, Disc, MC, V. French frames and eyeglasses for the bold and beautiful are available from this Madison Avenue outlet.

Cohen's Optical
117 Orchard St at Delancey St (674-1986). Subway: F to Delancey St; J,M, Z to Essex St. Daily 9am–6pm. AmEx, DC, MC, V. The main branch of a large Manhattan company (phone for the location of their other branches). There are thousands of frames in stock, and most prescriptions (glasses or contact lenses) can be filled within the hour.

Myoptics
42 St. Marks Pl at Second Ave (533-1577). Subway: 6 to Astor Pl. Mon–Fri 11am–7pm, Sat 11am–6pm, Sun noon–5pm. ●*82 Christopher St between Seventh Ave South and Bleecker St (call 741-9550 for hours). Subway: 1, 9 to Christopher St–Sheridan Sq.* ●*96 Seventh Ave between 15th and 16th Sts (call 633-6014 for hours). Subway: 1, 9 to 18th St.* AmEx, Disc, MC, V. A full optician's service and frames by Matsuda, Oliver Peoples, L.A. Eyeworks and Paul Smith.

Pharmacists

Boyd's Chemists
655 Madison Ave between 60th and 61st Sts (838-6558). Subway: N, R to Lexington Ave; 4, 5, 6 to 59th St. Mon–Fri 8:30am–7:30pm, Sat 9:30am–7pm, Sun noon–6pm. AmEx, DC, Disc, JCB, MC, V. This 50-year-old pharmacy, boutique and salon stocks the largest selection of hair accessories and eye shadow ever assembled under one roof. It also offers facials, makeovers, manicures and so on. Boyd's has its own cosmetics line, Renoir, which includes all the hot matte shades from the 1960s that are so hard to find.

Caswell-Massey
518 Lexington Ave at 48th St (755-2254). Subway: E, F to Lexington Ave; 6 to 51st St. Mon–Fri 9am–7pm, Sat 10am–6pm. AmEx, Disc, MC, V. America's oldest pharmacy was established in 1752 and still supplies items such as soaps made of almond cream, seaweed, lettuce or coconut oil; extracts of roses; fragrant oils; cucumber creams; huge sponges and loofahs.

Duane Reade Drug Stores
AmEx, Disc, MC, V. This chain of stores offers good discounts on cosmetics, vitamins, soaps, shampoos and other essentials. There are branches everywhere. Check the phone book for the location of the one nearest you.

Kiehl's
109 Third Ave between 13th and 14th Sts (677-3171). Subway: L, N, R, 4, 5, 6 to 14th St–Union Sq. Mon–Fri 10am–6:30pm, Sat 10am–6pm. AmEx, DC, MC, V. Kiehl's is practically a New York institution; once you stop by for a sample of the company's luxurious face cream, body lotion or silk groom for hair, you'll be hooked for life. The staff is knowledgeable and friendly.

Kaufman Pharmacy
Beverly Hotel, 557 Lexington Ave at 50th St (755-2266). Subway: E, F to Lexington Ave; 6 to 51st St. 24 hours. AmEx, MC, V. New York's only all-night full-service pharmacy. You can get prescriptions filled here.

Records, tapes and CDs

HMV
1280 Lexington Ave at 86th Street (348-0800). Subway: 4, 5, 6 to 86th St. Mon–Sat 9am–11pm, Sun 10am–10pm. ●*2081 Broadway at 72nd St (call 721-5900 for hours). Subway: 1, 2, 3, 9 to 72nd St.* ●*57 W 34th St at Sixth Ave (call 629-0900 for hours). Subway: 1, 2, 3, 9 to 34th St–Penn Station.* AmEx, Disc, MC, V. The biggest record store in North America, with a jaw-dropping selection of vinyl, cassettes, CDs and videos.

J&R Music World
23 Park Row between Beekman and Ann Sts (238-9000, 1-800-221-8180). Subway: J, M, Z to Chambers St; 4, 5, 6 to Brooklyn Bridge–City Hall. Mon–Sat 9am–6:30pm, Sun 11am–6pm. AmEx, Disc, MC, V. Part of the massive, block-long home electronics emporium, here you'll find box sets, jazz, Latin and popular titles by all the big names.

Tower Records
692 Broadway at 4th St (505-1500). Subway: N, R to 8th St. 9am–midnight. ●*66th Broadway at 66th St (call 799-2500 for hours). Subway: 1, 9 to 66th St–Lincoln Ctr.* AmEx, Disc, MC, V. All the current sounds on CD and tape. Visit the clearance store around the block on Lafayette Street for knockdown stuff in all formats, including vinyl (especially classical).

Virgin Megastore
1540 Broadway between 45th and 46th Sts (921-1020). Subway: N, R, S, 1, 2, 3, 9, 7 to 42nd St–Times Sq. Mon–Thu, Sun 9am–1am; Fri, Sat 9am–2am. AmEx, Disc, MC, V. As enormous record stores go, this one is pretty good. Check out the Virgin soda machine and keep an eye out for dates of in-store performances. Vinyl is available.

Dance

8-Ball Records
105 E 9th St between Third and Fourth Aves (473-6343). Subway: 6 to Astor Pl. Mon–Sat noon–9pm, Sun 1–7pm. AmEx, MC, V. Since the label owns the store, this is where you'll get those 8-Ball faves first. It's also a great house resource, with a broad range of imports and a fruitful bargain bin.

Dance Tracks
91 E 3rd St at First Ave (260-8729). Subway: F to Second Ave. Mon–Thu noon–9pm, Fri noon–10pm, Sat noon–8pm, Sun 1–6:30pm. AmEx, Disc, MC, V. Stocked with Euro imports hot off the plane (nearly as cheap to buy here) and with fast-flowing racks of domestic house, dangerously enticing bins of Loft/Paradise Garage classics and private decks to listen on, Dance Tracks is a must.

Fat Beats
406 Sixth Ave between 8th and 9th Sts, second floor (673-3883). Subway: A, C, E, B, D, F, Q to W 4th St–Washington Sq. Mon–Thu noon–9pm; Fri, Sat noon–10pm; Sun noon–8pm. MC, V. Hip-hop central: This small store carries a large selection of the latest in hip-hop, acid jazz and reggae.

Specialist

Bleecker Bob's Golden Oldies
118 W 3rd St between Sixth Ave and MacDougal St (475-9677). Subway: A, C, E, B, D, F, Q to W 4th St–Washington Sq. Mon–Thu, Sun noon–1am; Fri, Sat noon–3am. AmEx, MC, V. Imports, independents, deleted records, tapes and CDs, and all sorts of rarities are sold here. It's the place to go when you really can't find what you want anywhere else.

Footlight Records

113 E 12th St between Third and Fourth Aves (533-1572). Subway: N, R, 4, 5, 6 to 14th St–Union Sq. Mon–Fri 11am–7pm, Sat 10am–6pm, Sun noon–5pm. AmEx, DC, MC, V. This spectacular store specializes in vocalists, Broadway cast recordings and film soundtracks.

Gryphon Record Shop

251 W 72nd St between Broadway and West End Ave (874-1588). Subway: 1, 2, 3, 9 to 72nd St. Mon–Sat 11am–7pm, Sun noon–6pm. MC, V. This solidly classical store, with a sprinkling of jazz and show music, sells vinyl only.

Jazz Record Center

236 W 26th St between Seventh and Eighth Aves, eighth floor (675-4480). Subway: C, E to 23rd St; 1, 9 to 28th St. Tue–Sat 10am–6pm. AmEx, MC, V. Quite simply, it's the best jazz store in the city, selling current and out-of-print records. You can have your purchases shipped worldwide.

Kim's Underground

6 St. Marks Pl between Second and Third Aves (598-9985). Subway: 6 to Astor Pl. 9am–midnight. ● 144 Bleecker St between Laguardia and Thompson Sts (call 387-8250 for hours). Subway: A, C, E, B, D, F, Q to W 4th St–Washington Sq. ● 350 Bleecker St at 10th St (call 675-8996 for hours). Subway: 6 to Bleecker St. AmEx, MC, V. Located in the old St. Marks Baths, this gigantic music store carries more vinyl and CDs than you'd think possible.

Midnight Records

263 W 23rd St between Seventh and Eighth Aves (675-2768). Subway: C, E, 1, 9 to 23rd St. Tue–Sat 10am–6pm. AmEx, MC, V ($15 minimum). A great place for rarities and hard-to-find rock records. The 1960s and 1970s are the eras Midnight does best.

Other Music

15 E 4th St between Broadway and Lafayette St (477-8150). Subway: N, R to 8th St; 6 to Astor Pl. Mon–Sat noon–9pm; Sun noon–7pm. AmEx, MC, V. This music store is a gem. Owned by three former Kim's slaves (see above), it stocks a full selection of indie, ambient, kraut rock, psychedelia, noise and French pop. There's also a fine used section.

Record Mart

Times Square subway station, near the N and R platform (840-0580). Subway: N, R, S, 1, 2, 3, 9 to 42nd St–Times Sq. Mon–Thu 9am–9pm, Fri 9am–11pm, Sat 10am–10pm, Sun noon–8pm. MC, V. It costs the price of a subway token to get in, but Record Mart stocks the largest selection of Caribbean and Latin American music in the city, much of it on vinyl.

Rocks in Your Head

157 Prince St between Thompson St and West Broadway (475-6729). Subway: A, C, E, B, D, F, Q to W 4th St–Washington Sq; C, E to Spring St. Noon–9pm. MC, V. If you like vinyl browsing, you'll find plenty of indie and alt-rock LPs here, as well as singles and ten-inches.

*Bin there: **Bleecker Bob's Golden Oldies** is a trove of hard-to-find vinyl, CDs and tapes.*

St. Mark's Sounds

16 and 20 St. Marks Pl between Second and Third Aves (677-3444). Subway: N, R to 8th St; 6 to Astor Pl. Mon–Thu noon–10:30pm; Fri, Sat noon–11:30pm. No credit cards. Two stores situated side by side; one is smaller and features new releases, the other focuses more on budget vinyl.

Subterranean Records

5 Cornelia St between W 4th and Bleecker Sts (463-8900). Subway: A, C, E, B, D, F, Q to W 4th St–Washington Sq. Mon–Thu, Sun noon–7pm; Fri, Sat noon–8pm. AmEx, MC, V. It's an indie world at Subterranean, which focuses its attention on that genre as well as alt rock and its predecessors.

Venus Records

13 St. Marks Pl between Second and Third Aves (598-4459). Subway: N, R to 8th St; 6 to Astor Pl. Mon–Thu, Sun noon–8pm; Fri, Sat noon–11pm. AmEx, Disc, MC, V. The basement is filled with excellent vinyl—hardcore, country, rock, jazz—and the main floor stocks secondhand CDs. Prices are usually good. It gets crowded on weekends.

Repairs

Cameras and camcorders

B&S Camera Repair

110 W 30th St between Sixth and Seventh Aves (563-1651). Subway: N, R to 28th St. Mon–Fri 9am–6:30pm, Sat 11am–4pm. AmEx, MC, V. All kinds of camera and camcorder problems can be solved here, with an eye to speed if necessary.

Computers

Emergency Computer Repairs

250 W 57th St between Eighth and Ninth Aves (586-9319, 1-800-586-9319). Subway: A, C, B, D, 1, 9 to 59th St–Columbus Circle; N, R to 57th St. Mon–Sun noon–midnight. AmEx, Disc, MC, V. Specialists in Apples, IBMs and all related peripherals, ECR's staffers can recover your lost data and soothe you through all manner of computer disasters. They perform on-site repairs.

Leather

R&S Cleaners

176 Second Ave at 11th St (674-6651). Subway: L, N, R, 4, 5, 6 to 14th St–Union Sq. Sept–Jul Mon–Fri 7:30am–6:30pm, Sat 7:30am–5pm; Aug Mon–Fri 7:30am–6:30pm, Sat 7:30am–noon. No credit cards. R&S specializes in cleaning, repairing and tailoring leather jackets. Prices start at $30, and cleaning generally takes three to five business days (24-hour service available).

Clothes

Raymond's Tailor Shop

306 Mott St between Houston and Bleecker Sts (226-0747). Subway: B, D, F, Q to Broadway–Lafayette St; 6 to Bleecker St. Mon–Fri 7:30am–7:30pm, Sat 9am–6:30pm. No credit cards. Raymond's can alter or repair "anything that can be worn on the body." There's also an emergency service; delivery and collection is free in much of Manhattan.

Shoes

European Shoe Repair

124 Fulton St at Nassau St (227-5818). Subway: 2, 3, 4 to Fulton St. Mon–Fri 7:30am–6:30pm. ●113 E 31st St between Lexington and Park Aves (call 889-7258 for hours). Subway: 6 to 33rd St. No credit cards. Not only will they repair goods, from shoes to jackets, they'll pick up and deliver, too.

Watches

Fait Watch Company

Grand Central Terminal, 42nd St at Park Ave, third floor (697-6380). Subway: 4, 5, 6, 7 to 42nd St–Grand Central. Tue–Fri 10am–5pm. No credit cards. The staff will repair just about any watch.

Shoes

West 8th Street has shoe stores lining either side of the block between Broadway and Sixth Avenue. Here you'll find sneakers, boots and designer knockoffs. For shoe repairs, *see* **Repairs** *above.*

Aldo

700 Broadway at 4th Street (982-0958). Subway: N, R to 8th St; 6 to Astor Pl. Mon–Sat 10am–8pm, Sun noon–7pm. AmEx, MC, V. This Montreal-based company sells trademark shoes, boots and handbags.

Anbar Shoes

60 Reade St between Church St and Broadway (227-0253). Subway: 1, 2, 3, 9 to Chambers St. Mon–Fri 9am–6:30pm, Sat 11am–6pm. AmEx, Disc, MC, V. You can save up to 70 per cent on Jourdan, Ferragamo and other high-priced footwear at this two-floor emporium.

Athlete's Foot

AmEx, Disc, MC, V. The best of the sneaker-driven chain stores, with the widest selection and the newest models, plus minimal amounts of casual sports gear. Check the phone book for the location of your nearest branch.

Billy Martin's

810 Madison St at 68th St (861-3100). Subway: 4, 5, 6 to 68th St. Mon–Fri 10am–7pm, Sat 10am–6pm, Sun noon–5pm. AmEx, MC, V. Founded in 1978 by many-time Yankee manager Billy Martin and ex-Yankee slugger Mickey Mantle, this Western superstore features heaps of cowboy boots in all colors and sizes.

John Fluevog

104 Prince St between Mercer and Greene Sts (431-4484). Subway: N, R to Prince St. Mon–Sat 11am–7pm, Sun noon–6pm. AmEx, JCB, MC, V. Fluevog is unique, stylish, often outrageous and definitely unmissable.

McCreedy & Schreiber

37 W 46th St between Fifth and Sixth Aves (719-1552). Subway: B, D, F, Q to 47th–50th Sts–Rockefeller Ctr; 7 to Fifth Ave. Mon–Sat 9am–7pm. ●213 E 59th St between Second and Third Aves (call 759-9241 for hours). Subway: N, R to Lexington Ave; 4, 5, 6 to 59th St. AmEx, DC, Disc, MC, V. This well-known quality men's shoe store is good for all traditional American styles: Bass Weejuns, Sperry Topsiders, Frye boots and the famous Lucchese boots, in everything from goatskin to crocodile.

Manolo Blahnik

15 W 55th St between Fifth and Sixth Aves (582-3007). Subway: B, D, F, Q to 47th–50th Sts–Rockefeller Ctr; E, F to Fifth Ave. Mon–Sat 10:30am–6pm, Sat 10:30am–5:30pm. AmEx, MC, V. From the high priest of style, timeless shoes in innovative designs and maximum taste will put style in your step.

Martinez Valero

1029 Third Ave at 61st St (753-1822). Subway: N, R to Lex-ington Ave; 4, 5, 6 to 59th St. Mon–Fri 10am–8pm, Sat 11am–7pm, Sun noon–6pm. AmEx, DC, MC, V. These beautiful Spanish shoes are made in combinations of colored suede and leather. Styles range from elegant but practical flats to sleek heels. The men's shoes are just as well made, al-though a bit less vibrant.

Steve Madden

540 Broadway between Prince and Spring Sts (343-1800). Subway: N, R to Prince St; 6 to Spring St. Mon–Sat 10:45am–8:30pm, Sun 11:30am–7:30pm. AmEx, MC, V. Funky styles for all seasons at deeply reasonable prices make this a certain Soho stop. There's almost always a decent sale.

Timberland

709 Madison Ave at 63rd St (754-0434). Subway: N, R to Fifth Ave; 4, 5, 6 to 59th St. Mon–Fri 10am–6:30pm, Sat 10am–6pm, Sun noon–5pm. AmEx, MC, V. The complete American line of Timberland shoes and boots for men and women is sold here. The company's ruggedly elegant apparel is also available.

Tootsi Plohound

413 West Broadway between Prince and Spring Sts (925-8931). Subway: N, R to Prince St; C, E to Spring St. Mon–Fri 11:30am–7:30pm, Sat 11am–8pm, Sun noon–7pm. ●137 Fifth Ave between 20th and 21st Sts (call 460-8650 for hours). Subway: N, R to 23rd St. AmEx, MC, V. One of the best places for shoes, Tootsi carries a good range of stylish imports, especially flats and lace-ups, at tolerable prices. Note the wide and witty selection of socks for women.

V.I.M.

686 Broadway between 3rd and 4th Sts (677-8364). Sub-way: N, R to 8th St; B, D, F, Q to Broadway–Lafayette St; 6 to Bleecker St. Mon–Sat 10am–8pm, Sun 11am–7pm. ●15 W 34th St between Fifth and Sixth Aves (call 736-4989 for hours). Subway: B, D, F, Q, N, R to 34th St. ●16 W 14th St between Fifth and Sixth Aves (call 255-2262 for hours). Subway: L, N, R, 4, 5, 6 to 14th St–Union Sq. AmEx, MC, V. Sneakers are treated like hit singles here, with a "latest release" display. One of the largest selections of athletic footwear in the city, complete with overhead monorail delivery system.

J.M. Weston

812 Madison Ave at 68th St (535-2100). Subway: 6 to 68th St. Mon–Wed, Fri, Sat 10am–6pm; Thu 10am–7pm. AmEx, MC, V. J.M. Weston shoes appeal to such diverse men as Woody Allen, Yves Saint Laurent and the King of Morocco. The beautiful handmade shoes are available in 34 styles: "We-stons don't fit you; you fit them," notes Robert Deslauriers, the man who established the Manhattan store. The shop also stocks women's shoes—and they're also expensive.

Speciality shops and services

Arthur Brown & Brothers

2 W 46th St between Fifth and Sixth Aves (575-5555). Sub-way: B, D, F, Q to 47th–50th Sts–Rockefeller Ctr; 7 to Fifth Ave. Mon–Fri 9am–6:30pm, Sat 10am–6pm. AmEx, DC, Disc, MC, V. Pens of the world unite at Arthur Brown, which has one of the largest selections anywhere, including Mont Blanc, Cartier, Dupont, Porsche and Schaeffer.

Big City Kite Company

1210 Lexington Ave at 82nd St (472-2623). Subway: 4, 5, 6 to 86th St. Mon–Wed, Fri 11am–6:30pm; Sat 10am–6pm; Thu 11am–7:30pm; Sun noon–5pm. AmEx, Disc, JCB, MC, V. Act like a kid again and fly a kite—there are over 150 to choose from.

Collectors' Stadium

17 Warren St between Church St and Broadway (353-1531). Subway: 1, 2, 3, 9 to Chambers St. Mon–Fri 10am–6pm, Sat 10am–5pm. AmEx, MC, V. Here's where to find that elusive baseball card to complete your set of the 1938 Yankees.

Condomania

351 Bleecker St at 10th St (691-9442). Subway: 1, 9 to Christopher St–Sheridan Sq. Sun–Thu 11am–10:45pm; Fri, Sat 11am–11:45pm. AmEx, DC, Disc, JCB, MC, V. Con-doms in all shapes, sizes, flavors and colors are sold in this West Village store.

Evolution

120 Spring St between Greene and Mercer Sts (343-1114). Subway: C, E to Spring St. Mon–Sun 11am–7pm. AmEx, Disc, JCB, MC, V. If natural history is an obsession, look no further. Insects in Plexiglas, giraffe skulls, seashells and wild boar tusks are among the items for sale in this relatively polit-ically correct store—the animals died of natural causes or were culled.

Game Show

1240 Lexington Ave at 83rd St (472-8011). Subway: 4, 5, 6 to 86th St. Mon–Wed, Fri, Sat 11am–6pm; Thu 11am–7pm; Sun noon–5pm. AmEx, MC, V. Every board game imaginable is here, guaranteed to leave you alternative-ly intrigued and offended.

Goldberg's Marine Distributors

12 W 37th St between Fifth and Sixth Aves (594-6065). Sub-way: B, D, F, Q to 34th St. Mon–Sat 9am–6pm, Sun 10am–6pm. AmEx, Disc, MC, V. "Where thousands of boaters save millions of dollars" is Goldberg's intriguing slo-gan. Get your marine supplies, fishing gear, nautical fashion and deck shoes here.

Jerry Ohlinger's Movie Material Store

242 W 14th St between Seventh and Eighth Aves (989-0869). Subway: A, C, E, 1, 2, 3, 9 to 14th St; L to Eighth Ave. 1–7:45pm. AmEx, Disc, MC, V. Ohlinger has an extensive stock of "paper material" from movies past and present—includ-ing photos, programs, posters and fascinating lists of infor-mation on the stars.

Karen's for People & Pets

1195 Lexington Ave between 81st and 82nd Sts (628-2312). Subway: 4, 5, 6 to 86th St. Mon–Fri 8am–6pm, Sat 9am–6pm. AmEx, MC, V. Karen designs and manufactures witty clothing, accessories and even fitted sheets for the dog, cat or canary in your life.

Kate Spade

59 Thompson St between Broome and Spring Sts (965-0301). Subway: C, E to Spring St. Mon–Sat 11am–7pm, Sun noon–6pm. AmEx, MC, V. Cult handbag designer Kate Spade sells affordable, chic bags ($80–$400) from her stylish store.

Lucky Wang

100 Stanton St between Orchard and Ludlow Sts (353-2850). Subway: F to Second Ave. Mon–Fri noon–7pm, Sat–Sun noon–6pm AmEx, MC, V. Emily Wang and Kit Lee, the funky duo behind the recent rage for Astroturf-like bags, opened their first showroom and retail space last Feb-ruary (their zany accessories have been sold for years at FAB208, Patricia Field and TG-170). Along with the fuzzy purses and pouches, the stock includes plushy vests, pil-lows, hats and lamps.

Metropolitan Opera Shop

136 W 65th St at Broadway (580-4090). Subway: 1, 9 to 66th St–Lincoln Ctr. Mon–Sat 10am–9:30pm. AmEx, Disc, MC, V. Located in the Metropolitan Opera, this shop sells CDs, cassettes and laser discs of every opera imaginable. There's also a wealth of opera memorabilia.

Nat Sherman

500 Fifth Ave at 42nd St (246-5500). Subway: 4, 5, 6 to 42nd St–Grand Central; 7 to Fifth Ave. Mon–Fri 9am–7pm, Sat 10am–5:30pm, Sun 11am–5pm. AmEx, DC, MC, V. Just across the street from the glorious New York Public Library, Nat Sherman specializes in slow-burning cigarettes, cigars and smoking accoutrements from a cigar hostler to a smoking chair. Upstairs is the famous smoking room, where you can test out your tobacco.

Paramount Vending

1158 Second Ave at 61st St (279-1095). Subway: N, R to Lexington Ave; 4, 5, 6 to 59th St. Mon–Fri 10am–6pm. AmEx, Disc, MC, V. Looking for a secondhand jukebox, pinball machine or bowling machine? Here's the place.

Pearl Paint Co.

308 Canal St between Church St and Broadway (431-7932). Subway: J, M, Z, N, R, 6 to Canal St. Mon–Wed, Fri, Sat 9am–6pm; Sun 9am–7pm; Sun 9am–5:30pm. AmEx, Disc, MC, V. This artist's mainstay is as big as a supermarket and features everything you could possibly need to create your masterpiece—even if it's just in your hotel room.

Pearl River Chinese Products Emporium

277 Canal St at Broadway (431-4770). Subway J, M, Z, N, R, 6 to Canal St. 10am–7:30pm. AmEx, MC, V. In this downtown emporium you can find all things Chinese, from clothing to pots, woks, teapots, groceries, bonsai, medicinal herbs, bedroom slippers and traditional stationery.

Poster America Gallery

138 W 18th St between Sixth and Seventh Aves (206-0499). Subway: 1, 9 to 18th St. Tue–Sat 11am–6pm. AmEx, MC, V. This gallery stocks original advertising posters from both sides of the Atlantic, dating as far back as 1880.

Quark Spy Center

537 Third Ave at 35th St (889-1808). Subway: 6 to 33rd St. Mon–Fri 9am–6pm, Sat by appointment only. AmEx, MC, V. A little creepy, but worth a visit if you're curious or interested in donning some body armor or bugging your ex-spouse's house. For those with elaborate James Bond fantasies.

Rand McNally Map & Travel Center

150 E 52nd St between Lexington and Third Aves (758-7488). Subway: E, F to Lexington Ave; 6 to 51st St. Mon–Fri 9am–6pm, Sat 11am–5pm, Sun noon–5pm. AmEx, Disc, JCB, MC, V. Rand McNally stocks maps, atlases and globes, even those from rival publishers.

Stack's Coin Company

123 W 57th St between Sixth and Seventh Aves (582-2580). Subway: B, Q, N, R to 57th St. Mon–Fri 10am–5pm. No credit cards. The largest and oldest coin dealer in the United States, Stack's deals in rare and ancient coins from around the world.

Sports

Blades Downtown

659 Broadway between Bleecker and Bond Sts (477-7350). Subway: B, D, F, Q to Broadway–Lafayette St; 6 to Bleecker St. Mon–Sat 11am–9pm, Sun noon–7pm. AmEx, MC, V. This is where to come for those pesky in-line skates, as well as a wide range of skateboard and snowboard equipment and clothing. Phone for the location of other branches.

Gerry Cosby

3 Pennsylvania Plaza, inside Madison Square Garden (563-6464). Subway: A, C, E, 1, 2, 3, 9 to 34th St–Penn Station. Mon–Fri 9:30am–6:30pm, Sat 9:30am–6pm, Sun noon–5pm. AmEx, Disc, MC, V. Cosby features a huge selection of official team wear and other sporting necessities.

Modell's

AmEx, DC, MC, V. A comprehensive range of sporting equipment and clothing at competitive prices can be found in its various locations. Check the phone book for the branch nearest you.

Niketown

6 E 57th St between Fifth and Madison Aves (891-6453). Subway: E, F, N, R to Fifth Ave; 4, 5, 6 to 59th St. Mon–Fri 10am–8pm, Sat 10am–7pm, Sun 11am–6pm. AmEx, Disc, JCB, MC, V. Every 20 minutes a huge screen drops down and plays a Nike ad. There are interactive CD-ROMs to help you make an informed shoe choice. Don't scoff: There are 1,200 kinds of footwear to choose from.

Paragon Sporting Goods

867 Broadway at 18th St (255-8036). Subway: L, N, R, 4, 5, 6 to 14th St–Union Sq. Mon–Sat 10am–8pm, Sun 11am–6.30pm. AmEx, Disc, MC, V. A full line of sports equipment and sportswear is available at this store. There's a good range of swimwear, surfwear, tennis rackets, climbing gear and shoes.

Tattoos and piercing

Tattooing was made legal in New York only last year. Check the advertisements on the back page of *The Village Voice* for information. Piercing is completely unregulated, so be discriminating.

Fun City

94 St Marks Pl between First and Second Aves (353-8282). Subway: F to Second Ave. Mon–Sun noon–midnight. • 124 MacDougal St between Bleecker and W 3rd Sts (call 674-0754 for hours). Subway: A, C, E, B, D, Q, F to W 4th St–Washington Sq. No credit cards. The setting isn't that of a doctor's office, but the folks at Fun City can be trusted. While both locations service tattoos, piercing is offered at the MacDougal Street location only.

Gauntlet

144 Fifth Ave at 19th St (229-0180). Subway: F, N, R to 23rd St. Mon–Sat 12:30–7:30pm. AmEx, MC, V. A place with unrivaled experience, Gauntlet is where to go if you aren't satisfied with the holes you were born with. A Prince Albert costs $35, though navels, nipples and noses remain the more popular perforations.

NY Adorned

47 Second Ave at 3rd St (473-0007). Subway: F to Second Ave. Wed, Thu 1–8pm; Fri, Sat 2–10pm; Sun 1–8pm. AmEx, MC, V. The waiting area of this beautiful store seems more like the lobby of a clean, hipster hotel. Along with piercing, Adorned offers tattooing and henna designs.

Temptu

26 W 17th St between Fifth and Sixth Aves, fifth floor (675-4000). Subway: L, N, R, 4, 5, 6 to 14th St–Union Sq; F to 14th St. Mon–Fri 9am–5pm. MC, V. For those who can't take the needle, this is the home of the temporary tattoo. It has every design imaginable in paint-on, water-based and rubbing-alcohol formats. Prices start at $1.25 a sheet. Temptu gave Robert De Niro those nasty tats for *Cape Fear.*

Village Tattoos & Piercings

2 St. Marks Pl between Second and Third Aves, booth four (677-6028). Subway: 6 to Astor Pl. Mon–Thu 11am–10pm;

Fri, Sat 11am–midnight. AmEx, Disc, MC, V. This claustrophobic booth—there isn't much in the way of privacy—offers both tattooing and piercing for the spontaneous at heart.

Television and video

Current ID (such as a passport) plus a credit card, and sometimes proof of address, are needed if you want to rent a video from any of the following outlets. American videos are NTSC format and don't work in British or Australian VCR machines, which are PAL.

Columbus TV & Video Center

552 Columbus Ave at 86th St (496-2626). Subway: B, C, 1, 9 to 86th St. Mon–Fri 9am–7pm, Sat 9am–6pm. AmEx, Disc, MC, V. All types of VCRs and TVs are available for rent.

Couch Potato Video

9 E 8th St at University Pl (260-4260). Subway: N, R to 8th St. Mon–Sat 10am–10pm, Sun noon–10pm. AmEx, MC, V. No membership is required at this video store, which delivers within a ten-mile radius.

Evergreen Video

37 Carmine St between Bleecker and Bedford Sts (691-7362). Subway: A, C, E, B, D, F, Q to W 4th St–Washington Sq. Mon–Thu 10am–10pm, Fri–Sun noon–10pm. AmEx, MC, V. Steve Feltes launched Evergreen as a mail-order company, renting and selling videos of independent and foreign films. It grew into a rental business, due to the popularity of its owner and local demand for offbeat titles. Evergreen remains the best place to purchase hard-to-find laser discs and videos, and the staff can order whatever you can't find.

Kim's Video

6 St. Marks Pl between Second and Third Aves (505-0311). Subway: 6 to Astor Pl. 8am–midnight. ●85 Ave A between 5th and 6th Sts (call 529-3410 for hours). Subway: F to Second Ave. ●144 Bleecker St between Laguardia and Thompson Sts (call 387-8250 for hours). Subway: A, C, E, B, D, F, Q to W 4th St–Washington Sq. ●350 Bleecker St at 10th St (call 675-8996 for hours). Subway: 6 to Bleecker St. AmEx, MC, V ($20 minimum). If Kim's doesn't have it, no one else will. Kim's stocks more than 7,000 titles and specializes in cult, classic and foreign films.

Tower Video

1961 Broadway at 66th St (496-2500). Subway: 1, 9 to 66th St. 9am–midnight. ●1721 Fifth Ave between 56th and 57th Sts (call 838-8110 for hours). Subway: E, F to Fifth Ave. ●383 Lafayette St at 4th St (call 505-1500 for hours). Subway: 6 to Bleecker St. AmEx, MC, V. Tower sells and rents every type of video—cultural, exercise, theatrical, special interest, music, the lot.

Visas

Visa Express

421 Seventh Ave at 33rd St (629-4541). Subway: A, C, E, 1, 2, 3, 9 to 34th St–Penn Station. Mon–Fri 10:30am–6pm. MC, V. Visas for all countries can be obtained here, for individual or business use, though not extensions of tourist visas.

Weddings

So you want to get hitched in Manhattan? Whether it's a complicated affair or just a laid-back trip to

City Hall, look no further. For rings, see **Jewelry** *page 191;* most bridal shops stock veils, but if you're in the mood for something different, see Hats *page 190.*

Bridal wear

See also **Blue** and **Mary Adams,** *page 177;* **Zeller Tuxedos** *and* **Just Once** *page 174.*

Ghost Tailor

80 Fifth Ave at 14th St (645-1930). Subway: F to 14th St; L to Sixth Ave. By appointment only. AmEx, MC, V. Ghost sells gorgeous, custom-made dresses for brides who are anything but conventional.

Here Comes the Bridesmaid

326 E 11th St between First and Second Aves (674-3231). Subway: L, N, R, 4, 5, 6 to 14th St–Union Sq. By appointment only. MC, V. Stephanie Harper has traveled down the aisle 13 times (12 of those times as a bridesmaid). She carries sophisticated, sleek choices for bridesmaids; designers include Vera Wang, Watters and Watters, Dessy, Galina and Bari Jay.

Kleinfeld

82nd St and Fifth Ave, Bay Ridge, Brooklyn (1-718-833-1100). Subway: R to 86th St. Tue, Thu 11am–9pm; Wed, Fri 10am–6pm; Sat, Sun 9am–6pm. AmEx, MC, V. Kleinfeld, which opened in 1940 as a fur store, is one of the biggest names in the wedding business, carrying everything from veils and pumps to gowns. Appointments are necessary.

Legacy

109 Thompson St between Spring and Prince Sts (966-4827). Subway: N, R to Prince St; C, E to Spring St. Noon–7pm. AmEx, MC, V. Rita Brookoff carries a number of low-priced dresses by little-known designers, including Heather Scott and Colleen MacCallum.

Vera Wang Bridal House

991 Madison Ave at 77th St (628-3400). Subway: 6 to 77th St. By appointment only. AmEx, MC, V. Bridal creations are sold at Wang's famous wedding boutique.

Groom wear

D/L Cerney

13 E 7th St between Second and Third Aves (673-7033). Subway: 6 to Astor Pl. Noon–8pm. AmEx, MC, V. This vintage shop specializes in menswear from the 1930s to the 1960s, plus new, timeless original designs—for the swanky groom.

Ceremonies

Civil Marriage Ceremony

City Hall (669-2400). To get married in NYC, find your nearest municipal wedding chapel by calling the number above. (In Manhattan, it's the Municipal Building on Centre Street.) You'll need a $30 money order to cover the marriage license. You can get married after 24 hours. The ceremony costs $25, and you don't need a blood test.

Judges

You can reach the Honorable Howard Goldfluss, who's appeared on the Gordon Elliot and Geraldo Rivera shows, at 421-5300. If the waiting list is too long, phone 417-4911 for a list of former judges willing to perform wedding ceremonies.

Marcy Blum & Associates

688-3057. This international wedding consultant will arrange every last detail for people who want a romantic experience without the traditional complications.

Raise the Rent: *After a successful Off Broadway run,* Rent *became a Broadway smash.*

Arts & Entertainment

Art Galleries

From Picassos off Park Avenue to budding Braques below the Brooklyn Bridge, art sprouts everywhere in New York

With an abundance of galleries that exhibit everything from Old and Modern Masters to contemporary experiments in new media, New York is an art lover's dream. You'll find galleries not just amid the refined residences of upper Madison Avenue and the glossy boutiques of 57th Street but in areas you might not expect: in postindustrial West Chelsea, on the scruffy Lower East Side, by the meat-packing hinterlands of Greenwich Village, even under the ramps across the Brooklyn Bridge. Real-estate values have forced relocations and forged a few new partnerships. While uptown galleries remain stable and sedate, occasionally taking on new artists, gallerists in the cast-iron district of Soho—until recently the world capital of the contemporary art market—have had to compete with an increasing number of retail shops, restaurants and hotels moving into their Dickensian streets. Consequently, dozens of Soho galleries have defected to more spacious (and quieter) quarters in West Chelsea, the former warehouse district now almost entirely dedicated to the exhibition and sale of contemporary art. There are still notable holdouts in Soho, though, and on weekends, the neighborhood fills with a colorful mix of shoppers, tourists and art enthusiasts— often the same people.

Tribeca has its own odd assortment of small galleries and fine, art-friendly restaurants, and with more artists priced out of Manhattan studios, the areas of Brooklyn known as Williamsburg and DUMBO (Down Under the Manhattan and Brooklyn Bridge Overpass) have begun to offer free-wheeling, often festive delights in quirky new artist-run spaces. In fact, the art world's current structure resembles that of the film industry: uptown corporate studios bearing the names Gagosian, PaceWildenstein and Marlborough; major independent productions in Chelsea and Soho; with smaller art-house upstarts and satellite productions on the fringes.

There has also been a curatorial shift in many galleries, which have reduced their emphasis on American (particularly New York) artists to take

*Art attack: The opening-night crowd gathers at Tribeca's **Art in General**.*

on a more global perspective. Photography is enjoying a renaissance, along with so-called "outsider art" (*see chapter* **New York by Season**). And traditional, object-oriented exhibitions are sharing equal billing with multidisciplinary, often site-specific artworks that incorporate several media at once (especially video), adding quite a theatrical flavor to viewing and collecting.

Gallerygoers should check the weekly reviews and listings in *Time Out New York,* the reviews in the Weekend section of *The New York Times* each Friday and the monthly notices in such glossies as *Artforum* ($7), *Flash Art* ($7) and *Art in America* ($4.95). The *Art Now Gallery Guide,* free for the asking at most galleries (or $1.50 at museum bookstores), dependably lists current exhibitions and gallery hours each month and includes helpful neighborhood maps. For an overview of the market itself, look to the monthlies *Art and Antiques* ($3.95), *Art & Auction* ($6) and *ArtNews* ($6).

Opening times listed are for September to May or June. Summer visitors should keep in mind that most galleries are open Monday to Friday from late June to early September; some close at the end of August. Call before visiting.

*Heavy metal: John Chaimberlain's art-from-scrap at **PaceWildenstein** gallery.*

Upper East Side

Most galleries on the Upper East Side are well established and sell masterworks priced for millionaires. Still, anyone can look for free, and many works are treasures that could swiftly vanish into someone's private collection. Check the auction-house ads for viewing schedules of important collections before they go on the block.

DC Moore Gallery

724 Fifth Ave between 55th and 56th Sts (247-2111). Subway: E, F, N, R to Fifth Ave. Tue–Sat 10am–5:30pm. This airy gallery overlooking Fifth Avenue shows prominent 20th-century and contemporary artists such as Milton Avery, Paul Cadmus, Robert Kushner, Jacob Lawrence and George Platt Lynes.

Dintenfass/Salander-O'Reilly

20 E 79th St at Madison Ave (581-2268). Subway: 6 to 77th St. Winter Tue–Sat 10am–5:30pm. A merger of two notable galleries has expanded their combined artist base to include important European and American realists.

Gagosian

980 Madison Ave at 76th St (744-2313). Subway: 6 to 77th St. Sept–Jun Tue–Sat 10am–6pm. The prince of 1980s success, Larry Gagosian is still one of New York's major players in contemporary art, showing new work by such artists as Francesco Clemente and David Salle; he has also been hugely successful in the resale market.

M. Knoedler & Co. Inc.

19 E 70th St between Madison and Fifth Aves (794-0550). Subway: 6 to 68th St. Sept–May Tue–Fri 9:30am–5:30pm, Sat 10am–5:30pm. Knoedler shows name abstractionists and Pop artists and a selection of new contemporaries, including Frank Stella, Nancy Graves, Robert Rauschenberg, Richard Diebenkorn, Howard Hodgkin and Caio Fonseca.

Michael Werner

21 E 67th St between Madison and Fifth Aves (988-1623). Subway: 6 to 68th St. Sept–May Mon–Sat 10am–6pm. The genteel Werner's Manhattan addition to his successful operation in Germany is a small but elegant space with finely curated exhibitions of work by such protean European art stars as Marcel Broodthaers, Sigmar Polke and Per Kirkeby.

57th Street

The home of Carnegie Hall, exclusive boutiques and numerous art galleries, 57th Street is a beehive of cultural and commercial activity—ostentatious and expensive but fun.

Mary Boone

745 Fifth Ave between 57th and 58th Sts, fourth floor (752-2929). Subway: E, F, N, R to Fifth Ave. Tue–Fri 10am–6pm, Sat 10am–5pm. This former Soho celeb continues to attract major attention. Boone's list of contemporaries currently includes Eric Fischl, Ross Bleckner and Barbara Kruger; she has also begun showcasing the ideas of independent curators. They organize stellar group shows that include new photography and sculpture as well as painting.

André Emmerich

41 E 57th St between Madison and Fifth Aves (752-0124). Subway: 4, 5, 6 to 59th St; N, R to Fifth Ave. Sept–May Tue–Sat 10am–5:30pm. Now a division of Sotheby's, this establishment gallery's interest is divided between important modern painting, particularly from the Surrealist school, and contemporary sculpture. Various works by Man Ray and David Hockney are on display, as well as pieces by Anthony Caro, Dorothea Rockurne and Judy Pfaff, among others.

Marian Goodman

24 W 57th St between Fifth and Sixth Aves (977-7160). Subway: B, N, R to 57th St. Mon–Sat 10am–6pm. Work by acclaimed European contemporary painters, sculptors and conceptualists predominates here, usually in striking installations. The impressive roster of gallery artists includes

*Cracking the code: An Ellsworth Kelly captivates visitors at **Matthew Marks**.*

Anselm Kiefer, Christian Boltanski and Rebecca Horn, as well as Jeff Wall, Juan Muñoz and Gabriel Orozco.

Marlborough
40 W 57th St between Fifth and Sixth Aves, second floor (541-4900). Subway: B, N, R to 57th St. Sept–May Mon–Sat 10am–5:30pm. This monolithic international gallery shows work by modernist bigwigs Larry Rivers, Red Grooms, Marisol, Alex Katz, Francis Bacon, R.B. Kitaj, Kurt Schwitters, Magdalena Abakanowicz and more—much more. Marlborough Graphics is just as splendiferous; a branch for new sculpture and painting is in Chelsea.
Branch: Marlborough Chelsea *211 W 19th St between Seventh and Eighth Aves (463-8634). Subway: 1, 9 to 18th St. Tue–Sat 10am–5:30pm.*

Robert Miller
41 E 57th St at Madison Ave, second floor (980-5454). Subway: 4, 5, 6 to 59th St; N, R to Fifth Ave. Sept–May Tue–Sat 10am–6pm. No trip to 57th Street would be complete without a visit here, where you'll see work by artists as familiar to museums as to private collections: Lee Krasner, Al Held, Alice Neel and Philip Pearlstein, as well as popular contemporaries such as Diane Arbus, Robert Mapplethorpe and Bruce Weber.

PaceWildenstein
32 E 57th St between Park and Madison Aves (421-3292). Subway: 4, 5, 6 to 59th St; N, R to Fifth Ave. Sept–May Tue–Fri 9:30am–6pm, Sat 10am–6pm. Internet: www.pacewildenstein.com. The heavyweight of dealerships, this corporate giant offers work by some of the most significant artists of the century: Picasso, Mark Rothko, Alexander Calder, Ad Reinhardt, Lucas Samaras, Alice Martin and Chuck Close, along with Julian Schnabel, Kiki Smith and Elizabeth Murray. Pace Prints and Primitives, at the same address, publishes prints from Old Masters to big-name contemporaries, and has a fine collection of African art. *See also pages 207 and 210.*

Yoshii
20 W 57th St between Sixth and Seventh Aves (265-8876). Subway: B, N, R to 57th St. Tue–Sat 10am–6pm. This smallish gallery presents lively shows by contemporaries in painting, photography, sculpture and installation, as well as terrific historical surveys featuring work by such important modernists as Picasso and Giacometti.

Chelsea
The growth of the West Chelsea art district has been nothing short of phenomenal. Until 1993, the 10-year-old nonprofit Dia Art Center was the area's only major claim to art. Now new galleries seem to open every month. All this activity has inevitably attracted trendy restaurants and shops such as Comme des Garçons; despite the gentrification, the area retains its frontier feeling. Some galleries have such distinctive architecture that it's worth a trip just to see them—and to catch the light from the nearby Hudson River. Take the C or E trains on the Eighth Avenue line, although a taxi or the 23rd Street crosstown bus will bring you closer—the blocks between avenues are long.

West 15th Street

Gavin Brown's enterprise Corp.
436 W 15th St between Ninth and Tenth Aves (627-5258). Subway: A, C, E to 14th St. Wed–Sat 10am–6pm. Londoner Gavin Brown champions young hopefuls in an admirably anti-establishment gallery that has managed to establish such artists as Rirkrit Tiravanija and Elizabeth Peyton, while showcasing more established talents such as Stephen Pippin and Peter Doig.

Tenth Avenue

Alexander and Bonin
132 Tenth Ave between 18th and 19th Sts (367-7474). Subway: A, C, E to 14th St. Tue–Sat 10am–6pm. This is a long, cool drink of an exhibition space featuring contemporary painting, sculpture, photography and work on paper by an interesting group of international artists including Doris Salcedo, Willie Doherty, Ree Morton and Paul Thek.

West 20th Street

Cristinerose Gallery
529 W 20th St between Tenth and Eleventh Aves, second floor (206-8494). Subway: C, E to 23rd St. Tue–Fri 10am–6pm, Sat 11am–7pm. A quirky newcomer from Soho, this gallery consistently mounts engaging shows, spotlighting high-IQ artists whose focus is on materials or the media, thankfully not both at once.

Bill Maynes
529 W 20th St between Tenth and Eleventh Aves, eighth floor (741-3318). Subway: C, E to 23rd St. Wed–Sun 11am–6pm. Maynes is a bright, energetic fellow whose lovely gallery offers a great downtown view toward New York Harbor. He shows youngish American painters and sculptors who take traditional media to quirky, emotionally affecting new heights.

John Weber
529 W 20th St between Tenth and Eleventh Aves, second floor (691-5711). Subway: C, E to 23rd St. Sept–May Tue–Sat 10am–6pm. Weber shows strong conceptual and

minimalist work, with the emphasis on sculpture. Artists include Sol LeWitt, Hans Haacke, Daniel Buren, Alice Aycock and Allan McCollum.

West 21st Street

Bonakdar Jancou Gallery
521 W 21st St between Tenth and Eleventh Aves (414-4414). Subway: C, E to 23rd St. Mon–Sat 10am–6pm. In her dreamy new skylighted Chelsea gallery, British-born Bonakdar presents odd, often rather disturbing—and just as often quite distinguished—installations by such vanguard artists as Damien Hirst, Charles Long, Uta Barth and Matt Collishaw.

Paula Cooper Gallery
534 W 21st St between Tenth and Eleventh Aves (255-1105). Subway: C, E to 23rd St. Tue–Sat 11am–6pm, summer Mon–Fri 10am–6pm. Cooper opened the first art gallery in Soho and, as an early settler in West Chelsea, built one of the grander temples for the predominantly minimalist, largely conceptual work of artists whose careers have flourished under her administration. They include Donald Judd, Carl Andre, Tony Smith, Jonathan Borofsky, Dan Walsh and Robert Gober, as well as photographers Andres Serrano and Zoe Leonard.

West 22nd Street

Jessica Fredericks
504 W 22nd St between Tenth and Eleventh Aves (633-6555). Subway: C, E to 23rd St. Tue–Sat 11am–6pm. Fredericks and partner/spouse Andrew Freiser live and work out of this small gallery on the ground floor of an art-dedicated townhouse. They have been effective in developing a new generation of collectors for work by both midcareer and emerging artists from New York and Los Angeles, with a roster that includes Brenda Zlamany, Robert Overby and John Wesley.

Tom Healy
530 W 22nd St between Tenth and Eleventh Aves (243-3753). Subway: C, E to 23rd St. Tue–Sat 11am–6pm. Healy recently broke with partner Paul Morris but retained most of the gallery's resident artists. Several, including Helen Marden, Tom Sachs, George Stoll and Meg Webster, have become Chelsea favorites.

Pat Hearn Gallery
530 W 22nd St between Tenth and Eleventh Aves (727-7366). Subway: C, E to 23rd St. Wed–Sun 11am–6pm. This vanguard gallerist helped establish the East Village and Soho art scenes before moving up to Chelsea to continue presenting her roster of rigorous abstractionists and conceptualists. Hearn represents Mary Heilmann, Jutta Koettker, Joan Jonas, Renee Green and Lincoln Tobier.

Linda Kirkland
504 W 22nd St between Tenth and Eleventh Aves (627-3930). Subway: C, E to 23rd Street. Wed–Sun 11am–6pm. The brains behind the conversion of this 1860 town house, Kirkland runs a nifty operation on the third floor, which she gives over to the work of the most emerging artists on the street, as well as to joyous group shows in all media.

Matthew Marks
522 W 22nd St between Tenth and Eleventh Aves (243-1650). Subway: C, E to 23rd St. Tue–Sat noon–6pm. ● 523 W 24th St between Tenth and Eleventh Aves (243-0200). Tue–Sat 10am–6pm, summer Mon–Fri 10am–6pm. The driving force behind Chelsea's rebirth as an art center, the ambitious Marks has two galleries. The first is a beautifully lit, glass-fronted converted garage devoted to large-scale work by such blue-chip modernist heroes as Willem de Koon-

ing, Ellsworth Kelly, Brice Marden, Terry Winters and Richard Serra. The second is a 9,000-square-foot, two-story space featuring new work by contemporary painters, photographers and sculptors including Lucian Freud, Nan Goldin, Roni Horn, Gary Hume, Andreas Gursky, Katharina Fritsch and Tracey Moffat.

Max Protetch Gallery
511 W 22nd St between Tenth and Eleventh Aves (633-6999). Subway: C, E to 23rd St. Tue–Sat 10am–6pm. Protetch, relocated from Soho, has been hosting marvelous group shows of contemporary work imported from China and elsewhere; he also shows important new painting, sculpture and ceramics. This is also one of the few galleries that leaves room for architectural drawings and installations.

303 Gallery
525 W 22nd St between Tenth and Eleventh Aves (255-1121). Subway: C, E to 23rd St. Tue–Sat 11am–6pm. Lisa Spellman's cutting-edge gallery features international artists working in several media who have all garnered critical acclaim. They include photographers Thomas Ruff and Collier Schorr, sculptor Daniel Oates and painters Sue Williams and Karen Kilimnik.

West 23rd Street

Cheim & Read
521 W 23rd St between Tenth and Eleventh Aves (242-7727). Subway: C, E to 23rd St. Tue–Sat 10am–6pm. Louise Bourgeois, Alice Neel and Joan Mitchell are examples of the high-profile artists these expatriates from West 57th Street's Robert Miller Gallery have put on view in their cool and sensibly human-scale gallery. Look for a high concentration of photographers such as Jack Pierson, Adam Fuss and August Sander, along with such contemporary sculptors and painters as Lynda Benglis and Louise Fishman.

Paul Morris Gallery
465 W 23rd St between Ninth and Tenth Aves (727-2752). Subway: C, E to 23rd St. Tue–Sat 10am–6pm. Morris's new gallery in Chelsea's London Terrace complex is a shoebox compared to his former digs on West 20th Street, but his roster of emerging talents makes the traditional art exhibited in larger surrounding galleries look terribly stuffy and old-hat.

West 24th Street

Barbara Gladstone
515 W 24th St between Tenth and Eleventh Aves (206-9300). Subway: C, E to 23rd St. Sept–Jun Tue–Sat 10am–6pm, after Jun 20 Mon–Fri 10am–6pm, closed August. Gladstone is strictly blue-chip and presents often spectacular shows of high-quality painting, sculpture, photography and video by established artists including Richard Prince, Matthew Barney, Rosemarie Trockel, Anish Kapoor, Ilya Kabokov and Vito Acconci.

Luhring Augustine
531 W 24th St between Tenth and Eleventh Aves (206-9100). Subway: C, E to 23rd St. Sept–May Tue–Sat 10am–6pm, summer Mon–Fri 10am–6pm. Luhring Augustine's gracious, skylighted new Chelsea gallery (designed by the area's architect of choice, Richard Gluckman) features work from an impressive stable of artists that includes the Germans Albert Oehlen, Gerhard Richter and Günther Förg, Britons Rachel Whiteread, Fiona Rae and Richard Billingham, and Americans Janine Antoni, Christopher Wool, Larry Clark and Paul McCarthy.

Metro Pictures
519 W 24th St between Tenth and Eleventh Aves (206-7100). Subway: C, E to 23rd St. Sept–May Tue–Sat 10am–

A report card on the avant-garde

In an old school, contemporary art goes to the head of the class

Perhaps nowhere in New York can viewers obtain a more immediate grasp of what's new in the art world than at the P.S. 1 Contemporary Art Center. Located just across the East River from midtown Manhattan—in Long Island City, Queens, just across the Queensboro Bridge—this sprawling, somewhat seedy facility, housed in a four-story Romanesque Revival building that was once a public school, offers visitors a veritable funhouse of new art in action. During its 28-year history, the 30,000- square-foot P.S. 1 has continually defied Manhattanites' usual resistance to traveling outside their borough for anything but a vacation. No fewer than 10,000 people showed up for the Center's reopening (after a three-year renovation) in the fall of 1997. Though the pace of pedestrian traffic has since slowed, weekends are still busy and the art still communicates the expansive energy and ingenuity of the contemporary scene.

Entry is through a wide courtyard whose surrounding walls introduce the flavor of what's inside with large-scale graphics by conceptualists Lawrence Weiner and John Baldessari. (In the summer there are concerts, films and musical performances here.) Open the building's glass doors and look up; there, in what was once a chimney, you'll see Keith Sonnier's neon "Tunnel of Tears." Within the building proper, two or three sprawling group exhibitions are simultaneously on view at any given moment, along with a couple of single-artist surveys and several site-specific pro-

jects by other contemporaries. Art of all kinds—painting, sculpture, video, photography, installation—pops up everywhere, sometimes quite unexpectedly, from the darkest corners of the basement to the upper reaches of the stairwells. In other words, roaming the old school's large galleries and musty halls is like going to a 1960s-style Happening in the '90s. It's an event.

P.S. 1 curators favor avant-garde, experimental work that falls outside mainstream currents but doesn't exclude prevailing international art trends. In fact, such shows as "New York, New Wave" in 1981 actually established what would become the decade's significant direction in art, while recent exhibitions, like 1997's "Jack Smith: Flaming Creature," put local audiences in touch with artists whose recognition has long been overdue. P.S. 1 also imports major shows from other parts of the world, as it does with "Inside-Out/Chinese Contemporary Art" (Sept 13, 1998 through Jan 3, 1999), which gives Western viewers perhaps their first comprehensive look at contemporary art from mainland China, Taiwan and Hong Kong. A permanent sky piece by that master of light, James Turrell, is accessible at dusk, weather permitting.

Institute for Contemporary Art/ P.S. 1 Museum

22–25 Jackson Ave at 45th St, Long Island City (1-718-784-2084). Subway: E, F to 23rd St–Ely Ave; 7 to Courthouse Square. Wed–Sun., noon–6pm. Suggested donation $4.

*Grade A: You never know where you'll bump into art at the surprising **P.S. 1**.*

6pm, summer Tue–Fri 10am–6pm. This great playground for artists features the hip, keenly critical, cutting-edge work of Cindy Sherman, Fred Wilson and Laurie Simmons, along with Carroll Dunham's wildly polymorphous paintings, Mike Kelley's sublime conflation of pathos and perversity, Jim Shaw's California kitsch, and Tony Oursler's eerie and eye-popping video projections.

Andrea Rosen Gallery
525 W 24th St between Tenth and Eleventh Aves (627-6000). Subway: C, E to 23rd St. Sept–May Tue–Sat 10am–6pm, Summer Mon–Fri 10am–6pm. Count on this place to show you the young heroes of the decade, where Rita Ackermann's endearing but disturbing waifs, John Currin's equally disturbing young babes and Wolfgang Tillman's unsettling fashion photos all found their way into the limelight.

West 26th Street

Greene/Naftali
526 W 26th St between Tenth and Eleventh Aves, eighth floor, (463-7770). Subway: C, E to 23rd St. Wed–Sat 10am–6pm, Sun noon–6pm. Carol Greene's airy aerie has wonderful light, a spectacular view, and a history of knock-'em-sock-'em group shows of a somewhat conceptualist nature, as well as fine solo work by American painters and installation specialists.

Soho

Despite its "mallification," you can find something of interest and import on every street in Soho, along with such solid institutions as the downtown branch of the Guggenheim, the Museum of African Art and the New Museum for Contemporary Art. What follows is a selection of the most consistently rewarding galleries in the community.

Broadway

Anton Kern
558 Broadway between Prince and Spring Sts (965-1706). Subway: N, R to Prince St. Sept–Jun Tue–Sat 10am–6pm. The son of artist Georg Baselitz, this Gladstone gallery protégé presents installations by young American and European artists whose futuristic, site-specific installations have provided the New York art world with some of its most visionary shows.

Curt Marcus Gallery
578 Broadway between Houston and Prince Sts (226-3200). Subway: 6 to Bleecker St; B, D, F, Q to Broadway–Lafayette St; N, R to Prince St. Sept–May Tue–Sat 10am–6pm. This is a place for the peculiar but appealing, from Richard Pettibone's Shakerish objects to the mysterious pinhole photography of Barbara Ess.

Nolan/Eckman
560 Broadway at Prince St, sixth floor (925-6190). Subway: 6 to Spring St; N, R to Prince St. Sept–May Tue–Sat 10am–6pm. This small but high-level gallery primarily shows work on paper by established contemporary artists from the U.S. and Europe.

Grand Street

CRG Art
93 Grand St between Mercer and Greene Sts (966-4360). Subway: N, R, 6 to Canal St. Sept–May Tue–Sat 11am–6pm. Carla Chammas, Richard Desroche and Glenn McMillan's premises represent such eminent risk-takers as Cathleen Lewis, Mona Hatoum and Sam Reveles.

Deitch Projects
76 Grand St between Wooster and Greene Sts (343-7300). Subway: A, C, E, N, R to Canal St. Tue–Sat noon–6pm. Though Deitch, a former Saatchi Gallery curator, is now director of 57th Street's Emmerich Gallery, his temporary-project space still attracts stellar crowds to its openings and continues to focus on emerging artists who create elaborate, often outrageously provocative multimedia installations.

Paul Kasmin
74 Grand St between Wooster and Greene Sts (219-3219). Subway: A, C, E, N, R to Canal St. Sept–May Tue–Fri 10am–6pm, Sat 11am–6pm. Among well-chosen group shows of gallery artists who include such established names as Donald Sultan and Donald Baechler are solos by Alessandro Twombly, Suzanne McClelland, Nancy Rubins and Elliott Puckette, whose reputations—and prices—increase with every new appearance. Catch them now.

Greene Street

Casey M. Kaplan
48 Greene St between Broome and Grand Sts, fourth floor (226-6131). Subway: C, E, 6 to Spring St; N, R to Canal St. Sept–Jun Tue–Sat 10am–6pm. In only three years, twentysomething Kaplan has made his gallery one of the brightest spots on the Soho art map, introducing work by artists based primarily in New York and Los Angeles. Among the most notable: Amy Sillman, Amy Adler and Anna Gaskell.

Lehmann Maupin
39 Greene St between Broome and Grand Sts (965-0753). Subway: A, C, E, N, R to Canal St; 6 to Spring St. Tue–Sat 10am–6pm. This flexible project space designed by famed architect Rem Koolhaas features epic group shows of hip Americans and Europeans. Possibly the most eclectic of the high-end galleries in Soho.

PaceWildenstein
142 Greene St between Prince and Houston Sts (431-9224). Subway: 6 to Bleecker St; B, D, F, Q to Broadway–Lafayette St; N, R to Prince St. Sept–May Mon–Sat 10am–6pm. This luxurious downtown branch of the famous 57th Street gallery is where you'll find grand-scale installations by such big-time contemporaries as Robert Irwin, Sol Lewitt, Joel Shapiro, Julian Schnabel, George Condo, John Chamberlain and Robert Whitman.

Postmasters
80 Greene St between Spring and Broome Sts, second floor (941-5711). Subway: C, E, 6 to Spring St. Sept–Jul Tue–Sat 11am–6pm. This intriguing international gallery presents cutting-edge art in a wide variety of media, most having insistent conceptual leanings. A downtown art-tour requirement.

Sperone Westwater
142 Greene St between Houston and Prince Sts (431-3685). Subway: 6 to Bleecker St; B, D, F, Q to Broadway–Lafayette St; N, R to Prince St. Sept–mid-Jun Tue–Sat 10am–6pm, summer Mon–Fri 10am–6pm. A stronghold of painting, and one of the best places to see work by the Italian neo-Expressionists Francesco Clemente, Sandro Chia, Luigi Ontani and Mimmo Paladino. Among the gallery's other illustrious contemporaries are Frank Moore, Jonathan Lasker, Susan Rothenberg and Richard Tuttle.

David Zwirner
43 Greene St between Broome and Grand Sts (966-9074). Subway: A, C, E, N, R, 6 to Canal St. Sept–May Tue–Sat 10am–6pm, summer's shop. This maverick German expatriate's shop has been the hot spot on Greene Street since it opened five years ago, offering shows that easi-

ly serve as a barometer of what's important in art, not just in New York but internationally. The stable of cutting-edge talent includes Raymond Pettibon, Jason Rhoades, Toba Khedoori and Stan Douglas.

Mercer Street

Ronald Feldman Fine Arts
31 Mercer St between Grand and Canal Sts (226-3232). Subway: N, R, 6 to Canal St. Sept–Jun Tue–Sat 10am–6pm, summer Mon–Fri 10am–6pm. Feldman's history in Soho is marked by landmark shows by such artists as Komar & Melamid, Ida Applebroog, Leon Golub and Hannah Wilke, but also includes more avant-garde installations by Eleanor Antin, Roxy Paine, Nancy Chunn and newcomer Carl Fudge.

Sean Kelly
43 Mercer St between Broome and Grand Sts (343-2405). Subway: N, R, 6 to Canal St. Sept–Jun Tue–Sat 10am–6pm, summer Mon–Fri 10am–6pm. This ex-Brit's exhibited gallery offers exhibitions by established conceptualists including Ann Hamilton, Lorna Simpson and Marina Abramovic and also showcases emerging talents such as Cathy de Monchaux and James Casebere.

Holly Solomon Gallery
172 Mercer St at Houston St (941-5777). Subway: 6 to Bleecker St; B, D, F, Q to Broadway–Lafayette St; N, R to Prince St. Sept–May Tue–Fri 10am–5pm. Solomon's dramatic space shouldn't be missed. The reigning doyenne of the Soho scene shows distinctive work in all media, by a quirky selection of artists including Nam June Paik, Izhar Patkin and Nick Waplington.

Crosby Street

Bronwyn Keenan
3 Crosby St at Howard St (431-5083). Subway: N, R, 6 to Canal St. Tue–Sat 10 am–6pm. Among the younger dealers in New York, Keenan may have the sharpest eye of all for new talent. While work can be inconsistent, shows tend to be bigger than the sum of their parts, making this gallery a very worthwhile stop more often than not.

West Broadway

Leo Castelli
420 West Broadway between Spring and Prince Sts, second floor (431-5160). Subway: C, E, 6 to Spring St; N, R to Prince St. Sept–Jun Tue–Sat 10am–6pm. With the revered Castelli past 90, there has been much speculation about the future of his world-famous gallery, known for representing such seminal Pop figures as Jasper Johns, Roy Lichtenstein and James Rosenquist, as well as the rigorous conceptual art of Lawrence Weiner and Joseph Kosuth. The place now seems more like a museum than a contemporary gallery; of late, it has been showcasing only its stunning inventory.

Charles Cowles
420 West Broadway between Prince and Spring Sts, fifth floor (925-3500). Subway: C, E, 6 to Spring St; N, R to Prince St. Tue–Sat 10am–6pm. This gallery shows modern and contemporary paintings, sculpture and installations, including the paintings of David Bates, Manny Farber, Patrick Ireland and Beverly Pepper, and fantabulous blown-glass works by Dale Chiluly.

Sonnabend Gallery
420 West Broadway between Spring and Prince Sts, third floor (966-6160). Subway: C, E, 6 to Spring St; N, R to Prince St. Sept–Jun Tue–Sat 10am–6pm. Do visit this elegant old

standby for strong new work from artists such as Haim Steinbach, Ashley Bickerton, Gilbert & George, John Baldessari and Matthew Weinstein.

Wooster Street

American Fine Arts, Colin deLand
22 Wooster St at Grand St (941-0401). Subway: A, C, E to Canal St. Tue–Sat 11am–6pm. Dealer Colin deLand mounts what are arguably the most unusual exhibitions in Soho. His shows retain a refreshingly ad-hoc feeling that belies the consistently strong quality of the work. Artists include filmmaker John Waters and the subversive collective Art Club 2000.

Basilico Fine Arts
26 Wooster St at Grand St (966-1831). Subway: A, C, E to Canal St. Sept–Jun Tue–Sat 11am–6pm. Stefano Basilico's high-concept gallery has a group of strong contenders for future art stardom in his stable, most of them artists working in various media who turn 1960s conceptualism into visual pleasure for the millennium. Expect the unexpected—maybe the unheard-of.

Friedrich Petzel
26 Wooster St between Grand and Canal Sts (334-9466). Subway: A, C, E to Canal St. Sept–Jun Tue–Sat 11am–6pm. Locals have nicknamed this "the morphing gallery" for its emphasis on the conceptually based art of mutating forms seen in work by Victor Estrada and Jorge Pardo, but Petzel has now taken on painter Richard Phillips and up-and-coming photographers Sharon Lockhart and Dana Hoewy, putting him on the leading edge of his generation of dealers.

Gagosian
136 Wooster St between Houston and Prince Sts (228-2828). Subway: C, E to Spring St; N, R to Prince St. Sept–Jun Tue–Sat 10am–6pm. A branch of Larry Gagosian's bluechip uptown gallery, this dazzling ground-floor space provides a perfect setting for the imposing (at times, mammoth) pieces it houses—by such names as Damien Hirst, Richard Serra and Andy Warhol as well as newcomers Ellen Gallagher and Britain's Jake and Dinos Chapman.

Downtown Beyond Soho

AC Project Room
15 Renwick St between Spring and Hudson Sts, second floor (219-8275). Subway: C, E to Spring St. Tue–Sat 11am–6pm. The somewhat remote location of this consistently innovative artist-run space doesn't keep it from hooking up with a cross-generational mix of New York-based artists working in diverse forms.

Apex Art
291 Church St at Walker St (431-5270). Subway: 1, 9 to Franklin St. Wed–Sat 11am–6pm. This is an interesting gallery, where the impulse comes from independent critics who experiment with cleverly themed shows in all media.

Nonprofit spaces

New York may have more commercial galleries than you can count, but they haven't overwhelmed either the significance or the mission of the city's best not-for-profit spaces. Museumlike alternatives that are supported by a combination of public and private funds, these highly valued organizations showcase avant-garde work of both past and present, in expertly curated, sometimes eventful contexts.

Alternative Museum

594 Broadway near Prince St, suite 402 (966-4444). Subway: 6 to Spring St; N, R to Prince St. Tue–Sat 11am–6pm. The Alternative Museum has a reputation for exhibitions with humanitarian and sociopolitical concerns, especially from artists who are well beyond the mainstream.

Art in General

79 Walker St between Broadway and Lafayette St (219-0473). Subway: N, R, 6 to Canal St. Sept–Jun Tue–Sat noon–6pm. Internet: www.artingeneral.org. On its fourth and sixth floors, this venerable Tribeca institution holds exhibitions of contemporary work in development by emerging and under-recognized artists, with an emphasis on cultural diversity. It also sponsors eye-catching window installations at street level all year 'round.

Artists Space

38 Greene St between Grand and Broome Sts (226-3970). Subway: A, C, E, N, R to Canal St. Sept–Jun Tue–Sat 10am–6pm. Laurie Anderson, Jonathan Borofsky, Cindy Sherman, Robert Longo and David Salle all had exhibitions here early in their careers. The emphasis is on innovative work in all forms, so expect performance art, installations and video art, and some terrific curatorial adventures.

Dia Center for the Arts

548 W 22nd St between Tenth and Eleventh Aves (989-5912). Subway: C, E to 23rd St. Mid-Sept–mid-Jun Thu–Sun noon–6pm. $4, $2 Concessions. Internet: www.diacenter.org. Dia presents commissioned work by major contemporaries. Shows remain on view throughout a season; there's a program that includes poetry readings, panels and long-term temporary installations in its new annex across the street. The 1998–99 schedule includes a new two-part installation by that wizard of perception Robert Irwin. And don't miss

*Air space: Art can breathe at Chelsea's wide-open **Greene/Naftali** gallery.*

the wondrous glass house by Dan Graham, permanently installed on the roof.

The Drawing Center

35 Wooster St between Broome and Grand Sts (219-2166). Subway: C, E, 6 to Spring St; A, C, E, N, R to Canal St. Tue, Thu, Fri 10am–6pm, Wed 10am–8pm, Sat 11am–6pm. Exhibitions here are devoted to work on paper by emerging international talent, which the Center promotes in its group shows. It also holds important historical exhibitions; this year's fall show is devoted to Willem de Kooning. The Drawing Room, a project space at 40 Wooster St, features site-specific solo shows by both emerging and established artists of all stripes. Look for work by Raymond Pettibon and a show of contemporary drawings from Ireland.

Exit Art: The First World

548 Broadway between Prince and Spring Sts, second floor (966-7745). Subway: 6 to Bleecker St; B, D, F, Q to Broadway–Lafayette St. Tue–Thu 10am–6pm, Fri 10am–8pm, Sat 11am–8pm. Expect the best in multimedia cross-pollinations and culture clashes at this sprawling alternative space. Shows have big themes (and sometimes living organisms) and include dozens of artists. Exit Art is noisy and colorful and fun—and it can easily overwhelm. There's also a charming tapas bar and a shop that sells artists' work.

Grey Art Gallery and Study Center at New York University

100 Washington Square East between Waverly and Washington Pls (998-6780). Subway: A, C, E, B, D, F, Q to W 4th St–Washington Sq; N, R to 8th St. Tue, Thu, Fri 11am–6pm; Wed 11am–8pm; Sat 11am–5pm. Closed mid-Jul–Aug. Suggested donation $2.50. Internet: www.nyu.edu/greyart. NYU's recently renovated museum-laboratory has a collection comprising nearly 6,000 works that cover all the visual arts. During the 1998–99 season, look for an installation of blown-glass works by sculptor Maya Lin, a witty survey of the Parisian avant-garde from 1875–1905, and a comparative study of work by three masters of self-invention: artist Cindy Sherman, filmmaker Maya Deren and surrealist Claude Cahun.

International Center of Photography

1130 Fifth Ave at 94th St (860-1777). Subway: 6 to 96th St. Tue 11am–8pm, Wed–Sun 11am–6pm. $5.50, $4; voluntary contribution Tue 6–8pm. ● *ICP Midtown, 1133 Sixth Ave at 43rd St (768-4680). Subway: B, D, F, Q to 42nd St; 7 to Fifth Ave. Tue 11am–8pm, Wed–Sun 11am–6pm. $5.50, $4, $1.* The collection, which began in the 1960s as the International Fund for Concerned Photography, contains work by photojournalists Robert Capa, Werner Bischof, David Seymour and Dan Weiner, who were all killed on assignment. Their work was preserved and exhibited by Cornell Capa, brother of Robert, who went on to found the ICP in 1974. Given this history, it's no surprise that exhibitions are particularly strong on news and documentary photography. The library houses thousands of biographical and photographic files, as well as back issues of photography magazines. There's also a charming bookshop, space for video installations and a small screening room. ICP's branch gallery in midtown has two floors of exhibition space for retrospectives devoted to single artists such as the ever-popular Weegee, as well as a screening room and its own, equally pleasant bookshop. Exhibitions change throughout the year.

Sculpture Center

167 E 69th St between Third and Lexington Aves (879-3500). Subway: 6 to 68th St. Tue–Sat 11am–5pm. This is one of the best places to see contemporary work by emerging and midcareer sculptors. The Sculpture Center also runs an ongoing project on Roosevelt Island.

Thread Waxing Space

476 Broadway between Grand and Broome Sts, second floor (966-9520). Subway: 6 to Spring St; R to Canal St. Tue–Sat 10am–6pm. A block-long, truly dynamic multimedia space for contemporary art that also hosts video, performance, poetry and lecture series as well as the occasional musical evening.

White Columns

320 W 13th St between 4th and Hudson Sts (924-4212). Subway: A, C, E to 14th St. Sept–Jun Wed–Sun noon–6pm. Group shows organized by up-and-coming curators and presented by this venerable alternative organization, which recently acquired this location, have helped launch the careers of a number of important artists. Always a lively scene.

Photography

In the past decade, there has been a renewal of interest in art photography in New York, along with notable strides forward in the medium. For an overview, look for the bimonthly directory *Photography in New York International* ($2.95). *See also chapter* **Museums** *for public collections.*

Janet Borden

560 Broadway at Prince St (431-0166). Subway: 6 to Bleecker St; N, R to Prince St; B, D, F, Q to Broadway–Lafayette St. Sept–May Tue–Sat 11am–5pm. No tour of contemporary photography can be complete without a visit to this Soho stalwart, where the latest work by Oliver Wassow, Jan Groover, Tina Barney, Sandy Skoglund and David Levinthal, among others, is regularly on view.

James Danziger

851 Madison Ave between 70th and 71st Sts (734-5300). Subway: 6 to 68th St–Hunter College. Wed–Sat 11am–6pm and by appointment. With a vast collection of photographs that belong as comfortably to the classic as to the trendy, this uptown gallery shows such photographers as Ansel Adams, Andre Kertesz, Walker Evans, Annie Liebovitz and Richard Avedon.

Edwynn Houk Gallery

745 Fifth Ave between 57th and 58th Sts, fourth floor (750-7070). Subway: N, R to Fifth Ave. Sept 7–Jul 3 Tue–Sat 11am–6pm; Jul 6–Aug 14 Mon–Fri 11am–6pm. This highly respected specialist in 20th-century vintage and contemporary photography has two professional-looking new rooms in which to show such artists as Sally Mann, Dorothea Lange, Man Ray, Alfred Stieglitz, Brassaï, Cartier-Bresson, Danny Lyon and Elliott Erwitt, all of whom command over-the-top dollar.

Howard Greenberg & 292 Gallery

120 Wooster St between Prince and Spring Sts, second floor (334-0010). Subway: N, R to Prince St; C, E to Spring St. Tue–Sat 11am–6pm. These connecting galleries exhibit one enticing show after another of name 20th-century photographers, including Berenice Abbot, William Klein, Robert Frank, Ralph Eugene Meatyard and Imogen Cunningham.

Julie Saul Gallery

560 Broadway at Prince St (431-0747). Subway: 6 to Bleecker St; N, R to Prince St; B, D, F, Q to Broadway–Lafayette St. Tue–Sat 11am–6pm. Contemporary photography with a noticeable edge on ideas and an obvious visual intelligence.

PaceWildensteinMacGill

32 E 57th St between Park and Madison Aves (759-7999). Subway: 4, 5, 6 to 59th St; N, R to Lexington Ave. Sept–May Tue–Fri 9:30am–5:30pm, Sat 10am–6pm. A gallery that never misses. Look for such well-known names as Weegee, William Wegman, Lisette Model, Joel-Peter Witkin and Walker Evans, in addition to important contemporaries Harry Callahan, Philip-Lorca DiCorcia and William Christenberry.

Yancey Richardson Gallery

560 Broadway at Prince St (343-1255). Subway: 6 to Bleecker St; N, R to Prince St; B, D, F, Q to Broadway–Lafayette St. Tue–Sat 10am–6pm. An intimate gallery showing contemporary, often experimental American, European and Japanese photographers, each with a solid following.

Brooklyn

Artists living and/or working in these postindustrial blue-collar neighborhoods have generated several art galleries as well as singularly art-friendly bars and restaurants (*see chapter* **Outer Boroughs**). Some summer weekends, area artists sponsored by the Dumbo Arts Center hold group exhibitions in their studios or big, carnival-style art fairs. You might also want to check out Arena, an art salon in Cobble Hill (for an appointment, call 1-718-624-1307).

Flipside

84 Withers St between Leonard and Lorimer Sts, Williamsburg, second floor (1-718-389-7108). Subway: L to Lorimer St. Sun 1–6pm. This intimate, artist-run gallery features work in all media by accomplished home-grown talents.

GAle GAtes et. al.

37 Main St between Front and Water Sts, DUMBO (1-718-522-4596). Subway: F to York St. Wed–Sun 12:30–6pm, Fri 12:30–10pm. The first and most energetic gallery to open in DUMBO, this huge nonprofit complex on the Brooklyn waterfront hosts group exhibitions and performances of all sorts by a wide variety of local artists.

Momenta

72 Berry St between N 9th and 10th Sts, Williamsburg (1-718-218-8058). Subway: L to Bedford Ave. Mon, Fri–Sun noon–6pm. The most professional and imaginative organization in Williamsburg, Momenta presents strong solo and group exhibitions by an exhilarating mix of emerging artists. Catch their work here, before it's snapped up by Manhattan dealers.

Pierogi 2000

167 N 9th St between Bedford and Driggs Aves, Williamsburg (1-718-599-2144). Subway: L to Bedford Ave. Sept–Jun Mon, Sat, Sun noon–6pm and by appointment. Monthly openings at this artist-run gallery feature work by emerging and midcareer Brooklyn artists and tend to attract the whole neighborhood, which shows up as much for the free drinks and pierogi as for the art. At the Flat File, you can peruse an impressive collection of drawings, prints and photos by local artists that sell for under $200.

The Rotunda Gallery

33 Clinton St between Pierrepont St and Cadman Plaza West, Brooklyn Heights (1-718-875-4047). Subway: 2, 3, 4, 5 to Court St–Borough Hall. Tue–Fri noon–5pm, Sat 11am–4pm. Internet: www.brooklynx.org/rotunda. This beautiful Brooklyn Heights gallery is the borough's oldest and easily its foremost nonprofit exhibition space. Shows here change each month and feature innovative sculpture, painting, site-specific installation, photography and video by Brooklyn-based artists, always in top-quality presentations.

Books & Poetry

From world-class authors to hip-hop poetry slammers, literary New York covers every page in the book

"I have taken a liking to this abominable place," confessed Mark Twain about the city in which he married, made his fortune and died. His conversion was probably helped by the fact that New Yorkers took such a liking to him. Known as "the belle of New York," Twain was wined and dined and frequently quoted in the press. Far from the old Mississippi, the author was a bona fide celebrity.

New York has always been a literary town, a place where the published few are sought-after guests at dinner parties, and where both best-selling authors and up-and-comers gather at a writers' haunt like Elaine's to exchange gossip and be seen. Why, Norman Mailer once even ran for mayor. As the publishing capital of the USA, New York creates literary stars the way L.A. creates movie stars. Million-dollar advances and Hollywood options bring fame and gossip-column coverage to authors (and, in some cases, to their editors). The literary crème de la crème mingles in the fashion world; even the lavish literary breakfasts hosted from 1994–97 by Harry Evans, then Random House president and publisher, were held not within the book-lined walls of some dusty scholarly establishment but at the ultrachic department store, Barneys.

Still, you don't have to be part of the literati to get literary satisfaction in New York. Whether you want to hear Walter Mosley or Dorothy Allison reading from their latest novels, poets trying out their new work or speakers dazzling audiences

*It's fun to say at the YMCA: Norman Mailer reaches out to the audience at the **92nd Street Y**.*

*Making a point: A reader shoots for a perfect score at a **Nuyorican** poetry slam.*

with intellectual pyrotechnics, there's always a place to do so, often for free—it's one of the best entertainment deals in the city.

"Spoken word," formerly known as performance poetry, has become a popular New York pastime. Not since the Beats reinvented the American aural tradition have poets attracted this kind of media attention or been as fashionable. Walk in the Nuyorican Poets Cafe on any Friday night and it's standing-room only; poetry has even invaded clubland.

Spoken word's mainstays are the often-raucous slams (in which selected audience members award points to competing poets) and open-mike nights (when unknowns get five minutes to do their thing before the crowd). Reg E. Gaines, who made a big name for himself and for the downtown spoken-word world with his rap-inspired poetry for the smash-hit musical *Bring in 'da Noise, Bring in 'da Funk*, is a graduate of this scene. You'll find the most innovative performance poetry in the ongoing reading series and festivals; in these, poets cross-pollinate their verses with performance art, theater, dance and music, particularly rap and jazz.

Dead poets (and novelists) are getting an airing, too, in the form of marathon readings, a truly New York event. Some annual readings star a stream of big-name personalities. Past readers at Symphony Space's Joycean Bloomsday event have included Jason Robards and Claire Bloom. You can also celebrate Good Friday with *Dante's Inferno* at the Cathedral of St. John the Divine, complete with devils' food cake, or ring in the New Year with *Finnegan's Wake* or some other hefty modernist tome at the Paula Cooper Gallery. Also watch out for one-time-only marathons, usually in celebration of a literary anniversary.

New York's bookstores—especially the superstores—have become meccas for anyone seeking a good read, a cappuccino and a comfortable lounge chair, or a café table around which to spend a literate evening with like-minded friends. Some of

these stores have become known among bookishly inclined lonely hearts as hot pick-up spots (Barnes & Noble stores stay open until midnight). Many feature literary events, including author readings, talks and signings, and discussions on arcane matters, such as setting and location in fiction.

For the most comprehensive listings of book and poetry events, get the monthly *Poetry Calendar*, free at poetry venues and in many bookstores, or find it online in the Academy of American Poets site (www.poets.org). For more selective listings, check the Books and Around Town sections of *Time Out New York* and the Spoken Word section in *The New York Times*. Some reading series take long summer breaks, so call to check events before setting out. Also, the New York Public Library hosts poetry and author readings, listed in *Events for Adults*, available free at all branches.

April is National Poetry Month: Poets can be found reading all over the city. The last Sunday in September, the New York is Book Country publishers' festival takes over midtown Fifth Avenue. All the major houses exhibit their latest wares and authors as they prove that literacy can be lots of fun.

Author readings

In today's cutthroat publishing climate, where books either make the best-seller lists or die an early death, authors are clamoring for the chance to promote their latest titles at bookstores, some of which schedule almost daily events. These are always free, usually in the early evening and well-attended; arrive early if you want a seat. At the superstores, events range from lowbrow to highbrow: You're as likely to catch a supermodel promoting her new exercise book as you are one of your favorite novelists. The following offer frequent author readings, talks and signings.

Barnes & Noble superstores

Check phone directory for locations. Calendars of events for each branch are available in-store.

Borders Books and Music

5 World Trade Center at the corner of Church and Vesey Sts (839-8049). Subway: C, E to World Trade Center. ● *461 Park Ave at 57th St (980-6785). Subway: 4, 5, 6 to 59th Street; E, F to 53rd St–Lexington Ave.*

A Different Light

151 W 19th St between Sixth and Seventh Aves (989-4850). Subway: 1, 9 to 18th St. This gay and lesbian bookstore hosts frequent readings.

Posman Books

1 University Pl between Waverly Pl and 8th St (533-2665). Subway: N, R to 8th St. A haunt of New York University students, Posman presents lesser-known novelists and poets.

Rizzoli Bookstore

454 West Broadway between Prince and Houston Sts (674-1616). Subway: N, R to Prince St; B, D, F, Q to Broadway–Lafayette St. ● *31 W 57th St between Fifth and Sixth Aves (759-2424). Subway: B, Q to 57th St.* Soho's arty bookstore and its midtown sister are on the author-tour map of big-name novelists, photographers and artists.

Science Fiction, Mysteries & More!
140 Chambers St between Hudson and Greenwich Sts (385-8798). Subway: 1, 2, 3, 9 to Chambers St. Sci-fi and mystery authors frequently read here.

Three Lives & Co.
154 W 10 St at Waverly St (741-2069). Subway: 1, 9 to Christopher St–Sheridan Sq; A, C, E to 14th St. Hear established novelists read in this cozy West Village bookstore.

Reading series

The following host fiction and poetry readings; some also offer lectures. For spoken-word poetry, see **Spoken word**.

ABC No Rio
156 Rivington St between Suffolk and Clinton Sts (674-3585). Subway: F to Delancey St. Sundays at 3pm, $2 contribution. The Unorganicized Reading series, unorganized years ago by a pioneer Lower East Side arts collaborative, is an anything-goes event where anyone can read for as long as they like and whenever they like.

Brooklyn Museum of Art
Free with museum admission. See chapter **Museums** *for listings.* The museum's Saturday-afternoon fiction and poetry series, A Spoken Word, is followed by music performances and films from around the world.

The Drawing Center
35 Wooster St between Broome and Grand Sts (219-2166). Subway N, R to Prince St. Free. Nightlight is a dynamic monthly series in a pristine gallery, in which guest curator Linda Yablonsky blends readings with a visual element. Phone for dates. *See also chapter* **Art Galleries**.

Chuck Levitan Gallery
42 Grand St between West Broadway and Thompson St (836-2789). Subway: A, C, E, 1, 9 to Canal St. Wed 6:30pm. $3 contribution. The Phoenix Reading Series is followed by an open mike.

New School for Social Research
66 W 12th St between Fifth and Sixth Aves (229-5488). Subway: A, C, E, B, D, F, Q to 4th St–Washington Sq. Admission varies. This occasional, short spoken-word series is sometimes organized by one of New York's slickest and most venerable spoken-word-and-music artists, Sekou Sundiata, a New School faculty member. The school also holds lecture series. The Academy of American Poets also schedules occasional readings here (at the Tishman Auditorium) by some of the country's best-known poets.

92nd Street Y Unterberg Poetry Center
1385 Lexington Ave at 92nd St (996-1100). Subway: 6 to 96th St. The Academy of American Poets and the 'Y' co-sponsor regular readings, with the 1998–99 season featuring such luminaries as Edward Albee, Athol Fugard, David Mamet and Alice Walker. Panel discussions and lectures by high-profile academics are also held.

The Urban Center
457 Madison Ave at 51st St (935-3960). Subway: E, F to Lexington–Third Ave. $5. This occasional series features well-known literary names.

Writer's Voice/West Side YMCA
5 W 63rd St between Central Park West and Columbus Ave (875-4128). Subway: A, C, B, D, 1, 9 to 59th St–Columbus

Circle. $5. Regular events include readings by poets, playwrights and novelists. The Y also offers highly-regarded writers' workshops.

Spoken word

Dia Center for the Arts
548 W 22nd St between Tenth and Eleventh Aves (989-5566). Subway: C, E to 23rd St. Monthly on a Friday at 7pm. $5, $2.50 students & seniors. Dia's Readings in Contemporary Poetry series features established American poets. Past readers have included Adrienne Rich, Amiri Baraka and Jayne Cortez.

Dixon Place
258 Bowery between Houston and Prince Sts (219-3088). Subway: 6 to Spring St. Ellie Covan hosts a performance salon in her loft, with open-performance night on the first Tuesday of each month. Poets mix with storytellers, fiction writers and performance artists, but not stand-up comics.

A Gathering of Tribes
285 E 3rd St between Aves B and C (674-3778). Subway: F to Second Ave. Regular poetry readings and poetry parties. A Gathering of Tribes publishes its own poetry magazine.

Total New York

The city reveals its many faces in the following works of literature

New York at its...

most degenerate
Last Exit to Brooklyn by Hubert Selby Jr.

most Anglophilic
The Age of Innocence by Edith Wharton

most cartographic
City of Glass by Paul Auster

most transcendent
Jazz by Toni Morrison

most delirious
The Waterworks by E. L. Doctorow

most subterranean
Table Money by Jimmy Breslin

most satanic
Rosemary's Baby by Ira Levin

most raw
The Basketball Diaries by Jim Carroll

most neurotic
The Catcher in the Rye by J.D. Salinger

most didactic
The Alienist by Caleb Carr

most hedonistic
Bright Lights, Big City by Jay McInerney

KGB

85 E 4th St between Second Ave and the Bowery (505-3360). Subway: 6 to Bleecker St; B, D, F, Q to Broadway–Lafayette St. Free. This weekly reading series (Mondays at 7:30pm) located in a funky East Village bar features luminaries of the downtown poetry scene.

Knitting Factory/AlterKnit Theater

74 Leonard St between Broadway and Church St (219-3055). Subway: A, C, E to Canal St; 1, 9 to Franklin St. A weekly open-mike session (Fridays, in the bar) and an invitational (The Last Word, on Mondays), plus occasional spoken-word specials, are held in one of downtown's most happening music venues. *See also chapters* **Music** *and* **Dance**.

Mother

432 W 14th St at Washington St (366-5680). Subway: A, C, E, L to 14th St. Verbal Abuse first Sunday of the month 9:30pm–1am. $10, free before 10pm. Verbal Abuse, one of the city's most interesting poetry series at one of New York's most interesting clubland spots, starts with an open mike sprinkled with invited readers, and then settles into an hour-long lineup of top spoken-word poets. Performance is the key here; shock value is secondary. A words-and-music segment finishes up the night. For the *Verbal Abuse* magazine, log on to its website (www.echonyc.com/interjackie).

Nuyorican Poets Cafe

236 E 3rd St between Aves B and C (505-8183). Subway: F to Second Ave. Admission varies. The now-famous Nuyorican goes beyond open mikes and slams (open slam Wednesdays, "slam invitational" Fridays) with multi-media events, staged readings, hip-hop poetry nights and more. Elbow your way past slumming media execs on the hunt for new talent.

Poetry Project

St. Mark's Church in-the-Bowery, 131 E 10th St at Second Ave (674-0910). Subway: 6 to Astor Place. Admission varies. The legendary Poetry Project, whose hallowed walls first

The etiquette of spoken word

Never heard poetry performed before? Here are some important tips to help you fit right in.

Spoken word may have been beyond the purview of Emily Post, but as with any social event, attending a poetry performance has its do's and don'ts. Ignore the following at your own risk:

• At readings, don't clap until the program is over.

• At slams, it's considered good manners to express your enthusiasm or disgust whenever you feel the urge, preferably mid-poem and at full volume.

• Don't forget to wear black.

heard the likes of Allen Ginsberg and Anne Waldman, is still a thriving center for whatever's new and worth hearing. Living legends like Jim Carroll and Patti Smith still read here.

Strictly Roots

Strictly Roots, 2058 Adam Clayton Powell Blvd at 123rd St (864-8699). Subway: A to 125th St. First and third Thursdays of the month at 8pm. Admission Contribution. This Harlem bookstore's Word Thursdays feature spoken word, sometimes with music.

Talks and lectures

Though nowhere near as trendy as the city's poetry scene, the lecture world is still thriving, with people-in-the-know talking about everything from post-structuralism to the Inner Smile. If you're into Self-Help/New Age, pick up a copy of the Open Center's catalog, available free in book and health-food stores. The following venues offer lectures of a more or less literary nature.

Brecht Forum

122 W 27th St between Sixth and Seventh Aves, tenth floor (242-4201). Subway: 1, 9 to 28th St. The old-style leftist institution offers lectures, forums, discussions and bilingual poetry readings.

Museum of the City of New York

Admission $9. See chapter **Museums** *for listings.* Gotham Readers is a monthly discussion series designed to feed Gen Xers' passions for New York and the literature it has inspired. Authors discussing their books include novelists, cultural commentators and documentarists.

New School for Social Research

See **Reading series** *for listings.* Esoteric lectures by visiting savants.

92nd Street Y

Admission varies. Regular lectures by and dialogues between top-notch speakers on subjects ranging from literature and the arts to feminism, politics and international scandals. People like Susan Sontag and Wole Soyinka have appeared. *See also* **Reading Series**.

New York Public Library, Celeste Bartos Forum

Fifth Ave at 42nd St (930-0855). Subway: B, D, F, Q to 42nd St; 7 to Fifth Ave. Several annual lecture series feature renowned writers and thinkers, including quite a few Guggenheim fellows, speaking on issues of contemporary culture, science and the humanities.

Literary tours

Mark Twain Annual Birthday Tour

The tour starts from the southwest corner of Broadway and Spring St (873-1944 for information). Subway: N, R to Prince St. Last Saturday in November, rain date Sunday. $15. The tour, led by Peter Salwen, a Twain aficionado, ends with a birthday toast at one of Twain's New York City homes.

Greenwich Village Past and Present

Sundays at 2pm, meet at Washington Square Arch, Washington Square Park, Fifth Ave at Waverly Place. Call Street Smarts at 969-8262 for more information. Subway: A, C, E, B, D, F, Q to W 4th St–Washington Sq. A walk past homes and hangout spots of Village writers past and present.

Cabaret
& Comedy

In New York's most intimate spots, you can sway and swoon to Gershwin or laugh till your belly aches

New York is the cabaret capital of the U.S., and quite possibly of the world. No other city supports a cabaret industry where you can take your pick from a dozen different shows on any given night.

In the strict New York sense, the term cabaret covers both a venue and an art form. It's an intimate club where songs are sung, usually by one person, but sometimes by a small ensemble of performers. The songs are usually drawn from what's known as the Great American Songbook—the vast repertoire of the American musical theater—and are supplemented with the occasional new number by a contemporary composer. More than anything, a cabaret is an act of intimacy: The best

singers are able to draw the audience in until each member feels that he or she is being sung to directly in the most private of concerts.

The Golden Age of cabaret in New York was the 1950s and early 1960s. The advent of rock music and changing tastes eventually made cabaret an art form for the connoisseur, but today there are still plenty of fans and performers who keep it alive. Today's rooms basically fall into two groups: classic, elegant, expensive boîtes like Rainbow & Stars, the Oak Room and Cafe Carlyle, where you'll spend $30 to $50 just to get in and hear the likes of Bobby Short, Rosemary Clooney and Andrea Marcovicci; and less formal neighborhood clubs like

*Sky high: Michael Feinstein shines at the swank 65th-floor **Rainbow & Stars**.*

Don't Tell Mama, Eighty Eight's and Danny's Skylight Room, where up-and-coming singers—many of them enormously talented—perform for enthusiastic fans who pay much lower cover charges.

Classic cabaret

Cafe Carlyle
Carlyle Hotel, 35 E 76th St at Madison Ave (744-1600/ 1-800-227-5737). Subway 6 to 77th St. Tue–Sat 8:45pm, 10:45pm. Closed Jul–mid Sept. Cover $50. AmEx, DC, MC, V. The epitome of chic New York, especially when Bobby Short or Eartha Kitt do their thing (or Woody Allen, who's become a regular at the early show on Monday nights with his Dixieland band). Don't dress down; this is about plunking down some cash and remembering it's the Naughty Nineties. If you want to rub up against some atmosphere more cheaply, **Bemelmans Bar** across the hall always has a fine pianist, like Barbara Carroll or Peter Mintun, Tuesday to Saturday from 9:30pm to 1:30am with a $10 cover. *See also chapter* **Accommodations.**

Delmonico Lounge
Hotel Delmonico, 502 Park Ave at 59th St (355-2500). Subway: N, R, 4, 5, 6 to 59th St. Show times vary. Cover $15–$25, no minimum. AmEx, DC, MC, V. It doesn't get much more intimate than this tiny East Side hotel lounge, with its lush decor and cozy seating. Sit on one of the half-dozen bar stools, sip a martini and listen to one of the elegant chanteuses who sing here regularly.

The FireBird Cafe
363 W 46th St between Eighth and Ninth Aves (586-0244). Subway: A, C, E to 42nd St; N, R, S, 1, 2, 3, 9, 7 to 42nd St–Times Sq. Tue–Thu 9pm; Fri–Sat 9, 11pm. Cover $30, two-drink minimum. AmEx, DC, MC, V. This classy joint, opened in early 1998, is next door to the regal-looking Russian restaurant of the same name. If the caviar and the mosaic reproduction of Klimt's *The Kiss* don't ignite your passions, the first-rate performers, such as Phillip Officer and the outrageous British trio Fascinating Aida, will.

Michael's Pub at Bill's Gay Nineties
57 E 54th St between Park and Madison Aves (758-2272). Subway: E, F, 6 to 51st St. Tue–Sat 9, 11pm. Cover $20–$25, $15 minimum. AmEx, DC, Disc, MC, V. Julie Wilson, the glamorous sylph with the gardenia in her hair, is widely considered one of cabaret's greatest interpreters, and she has made Michael's Pub her new home (though it's always a good idea to call first and make sure she's playing). After having spent decades a few blocks east, Michael's has moved into Bill's, a former speakeasy. Go see the inimitable Ms. Wilson for a glimpse of cabaret the way it's meant to be.

The Oak Room
Algonquin Hotel, 59 W 44th St between Fifth and Sixth Aves (840-6800/1-800-555-8000). Subway: B, D, F, Q to 42nd St. Tue–Thu 9:30pm; Fri, Sat 9:30pm, 11:30pm. Cover $35, $15 drink minimum. AmEx, DC, Disc, MC, V. This resonant banquette-lined room was recently renovated and it is the place to savor the cream of cabaret performers, including names like Andrea Marcovicci and Steve Ross. *See also chapter* **Accommodations.**

Rainbow & Stars
30 Rockefeller Plaza, 49th St between Fifth and Sixth Aves, 65th floor (632-5000). Subway: B, D, F, Q to 47th–50th Sts-Rockefeller Center. Tue–Sat 8:30pm, 11:30pm. Cover $40, dinner compulsory at first show. AmEx, DC, MC, V. On the same floor as the famous Rainbow Room, in the GE Building, Rainbow & Stars is suffused with elegance, giving it the kind of Manhattan glamour you've seen in old movies. Sixty-five

stories up, you get a delirious view of the Hudson. The singers are big names like Rosemary Clooney and Michael Feinstein. And the food is good.

The Supper Club
240 W 47th St between Eighth Ave and Broadway (921-1940). Subway: C, E, 1, 9 to 50th St; N, R to 49th St. Show times vary. Cover $15. AmEx, DC, Disc, MC, V. This beautifully restored ballroom is the setting for dining and dancing to a 12-piece big band. The decor and better-than-average food attract a glamorous crowd of pre-theater dahlings. It also serves as a concert venue, hosting such performers as Ute Lemper and Marianne Faithfull, not to mention the occasional rock show. The strikingly azure Blue Room has recently reopened for more intimate sets by performers such as the talented pianist-singer Eric Comstock.

Emerging talents

Danny's Skylight Room
346 W 46th St between Eighth and Ninth Aves (265-8133). Subway: A, C, E to 42nd St. Show times vary. Cover $8–$15. AmEx, DC, MC, V. A pastel nook of the Grand Sea Palace restaurant, "where Bangkok meets Broadway" on touristy Restaurant Row, Danny's features pop-jazz, pop and cabaret, with the accent on the smooth. In addition to up-and-comers, this is a good place to catch a few mature cabaret standbys like Blossom Dearie and Barbara Lea.

Don't Tell Mama
343 W 46th St between Eighth and Ninth Aves (757-0788). Subway: A, C, E to 42nd St. Show times vary. No cover for piano bar; $6–$15 in cabaret room, two-drink minimum at tables (no food served). AmEx, V. Showbiz pros like to visit this Theater District venue. The acts range from strictly amateurish to potential stars of tomorrow. The nightly lineup can include pop, jazz or Broadway singers, female impersonators, magicians, revues or comedians.

Eighty Eight's
228 W 10th St between Bleecker and Hudson Sts (924-0088). Subway: 1, 9 to Christopher St–Sheridan Sq. Show times vary. Cover $10–$15, two-drink minimum (no food except Sunday brunch). No credit cards. Downtown's classy high-tech venue. Local favorites like Baby Jane Dexter and Charles Cermele perform upstairs, while downstairs in the piano bar, owner Karen Miller tickles a cultish crowd until closing time. Sunday brunch ($22.50) draws a crowd, too. This is one of the West Village's most convivial spots, where chorus boys and cabaret singers make up much of the clientele.

Village people: Yuks at **55 Grove Street.**

55 Grove Street
Upstairs at Rose's Turn

55 Grove St between Seventh Ave and Bleecker St (366-5438). Subway: 1, 9 to Christopher St–Sheridan Square. Show times vary. Cover $6–$15, two-drink minimum. No credit cards. This is the oldest cabaret showroom in Greenwich Village and where the Duplex started 40 years ago, before it moved to new quarters across Seventh Avenue (see below). It's a dark room with zero atmosphere. The emphasis tends to be on comedy, as well as pocket-sized one-act musicals like *Our Lives & Times*, a hilarious spoof of current events, with only the occasional vocalist.

The Oaks

49 Grove St between Bleecker St and Seventh Ave South (243-8885). Subway: 1, 9 to Christopher St–Sheridan Sq. Dinner seating at 7pm, shows at 8pm. Cover $5–$15, $10 food and drink minimum. No cover or minimum at piano bar. AmEx, DC, MC, V. Nestled on the same Greenwich Village block as Rose's Turn, this inviting space has been building a steady cabaret following, with a mix of unknowns and cool cats (director/writer/musician Melvin Van Peebles has dropped by to rock the house with his band, Roadkill), a popular piano bar, and food that's so good you don't mind the minimum charge.

Triad

58 W 72nd St between Broadway and Columbus Ave (799-4599). Subway: B, C, 1, 2, 3, 9 to 72nd St. Mon, Wed, Thu, Fri 8pm; Sat, Sun 3pm, 7:30pm. Cover $42.50–$47.50 for musical, varies for other acts. AmEx, DC, MC, V. The only cabaret on the Upper West Side has been the launching pad for many successful revues over the years, several of which (*Forever Plaid, Forbidden Broadway*) have moved to larger spaces Off Broadway. Dinner is available, and, in a smaller spot downstairs, there's an occasional singer or benefit show.

Alternative venues

Bar d'O

29 Bedford St at Downing St (627-2580). Subway: 1, 9 to Houston St. Show times vary. Cover varies. No credit cards. Bar d'O is a busy little mixed/gay bar packed with a bubbly crowd that comes here to catch the very best acts on the drag circuit. A regular performer here is scene stalwart Joey Arias, who is guaranteed to astound with his breathtaking re-creations of Billie Holiday numbers. *See also chapter* **Clubs**.

Brandy's

235 E 84th St between Second and Third Aves (650-1944). Subway: 4, 5, 6 to 86th St. Show times vary. No cover, two-drink minimum. No credit cards. An old, local good-time piano bar where singing bartenders meet shower singers. On weekends it draws a yuppie crowd, but after 2am, Brandy's evolves into a people's bar for a few hours.

The Duplex

61 Christopher St at Seventh Ave South (255-5438). Subway: 1, 9 to Christopher St–Sheridan Square. Show times vary. Piano bar 9pm–4am daily. Cover $6–$12, two-drink minimum. No credit cards. New York's oldest cabaret has been going for 40-plus years, and sets the pace for good-natured fun. It attracts a mix of regulars and tourists, laughing and singing along with classy drag performances, comedians and rising stars.

Jazz

Almost all the established jazz clubs adhere to a cabaret format. For information on some of the larger venues, including Birdland, Iridium and others, *see chapter* **Music.**

Arthur's Tavern

57 Grove St between Bleecker St and Seventh Ave South (675-6879). Subway: 1, 9 to Christopher St–Sheridan Square. 9:30pm daily. No cover, two-drink minimum at tables. No credit cards. A funky, divey-looking joint in the Village, where the schedule includes Dixieland bands and pianists Johnny Parker and Al Bundy.

Five and Ten No Exaggeration

77 Greene St between Spring and Broome Sts (925-7414). Subway: N, R to Prince St. Tue–Sun 8pm. Cover $5, $10 food or drink minimum. AmEx, DC, MC, V. A warm, 1940s-style supper club where even the lamps wear beaded fringes and the jiving swing survivors share their pink-draped stage with an old Esso gas pump. Various artifacts in the club are for sale, including rhinestone earrings, vintage radios and Coke signs.

Tavern on the Green

67th St at Central Park West (873-3200). Subway: B, C to 72nd St; 1, 9 to 66th St. Tue, Thu, Sun 8, 9:30pm; Fri, Sat 8:30, 10pm. Cover varies. AmEx, Disc, MC, V. You can dance in the oh-so-romantic garden throughout the week, preceded most nights by jazz performances in the Chestnut Room, ranging from trad to pop. The expensive dinner menu is the same as in the main restaurant. *See also chapter* **Restaurants**.

Comedy clubs

Comedy, particularly in New York City, has experienced a renaissance over the past few years. Small, out-of-the-way clubs and bars have been nurturing a new generation of performers with an avant-garde approach to comedy. Many of the talented fringe performers are gradually making their way into bigger clubs and mainstream outlets. Marc Maron, who does edgier stand-up, frequently appears on such talk shows as *Late Show with David Letterman* and the Upright Citizens Brigade has been tapped to do a weekly half-hour show on Comedy Central. Nonetheless, you can still catch the cutting edge at some smaller venues.

If the avant-garde isn't your comedic cup of tea, New York City's comedy clubs are never short of traditionalists. In the following clubs you can check out a wide range of comedians—from dark and bitter to light and sweet.

Show times vary at the stand-up clubs listed below; it's always best to call ahead.

Boston Comedy Club

82 W 3rd St between Thompson and Sullivan Sts (477-1000). Subway: A, C, E, B, D, F, Q to W 4th St–Washington Sq. $5 Mon–Thu, Sun; $10 Fri, Sat, two-drink minimum. AmEx, MC, V. This rowdy basement-level room is a late-night option where the bill can include as many as ten different acts. The first show on Saturdays is a new talent showcase.

Caroline's Comedy Club

1626 Broadway between 49th and 50th Sts (757-4100). Subway: C, E, 1, 9 to 50th St; N, R to 49th St. $12.50–$17.50, two-drink minimum. AmEx, DC, MC, V. A few blocks north of Times Square's Disneyfied madness, Caroline's colorful lounge is the place for up-and-coming TV faces such as MTV's Bill Bellamy or comics with broad appeal such as Wendy Liebman. Billy Crystal and Jay Leno honed their craft at the original Caroline's in Chelsea.

*Funny business: The next Seinfeld? You might find him at **Catch a Rising Star.***

Catch a Rising Star

253 W 28th St between Seventh and Eighth Aves (244-3005). Subway: 1, 9 to 28th St. $8–$15, two-drink minimum. AmEx, V. This 200-seat club and restaurant was the place that launched the career of Jerry Seinfeld. Now jazz and rock bands share the bill with stand-ups, cabaret acts and sketch improv groups. On Tuesday nights, Catch features an amateur night called *Freshly Squeezed Talent.* Rick Newman, the club's owner, has been in the comedy business for more than 25 years, so it's a good place to check out bright newcomers.

Comedy Cellar

117 MacDougal St between 3rd and Bleecker Sts (254-3480). Subway: A, C, E, B, D, F, Q to W 4th St. $5 Mon–Thu, Sun; $10 Fri, Sat, two-drink minimum. AmEx, MC, V. Amid the coffeehouses of MacDougal Street, this well-worn underground lair recalls the counterculture vibe of another era, before the neighborhood became besieged by out-of-towners every weekend. Still, the Comedy Cellar regularly provides an excellent roster of popular local talent.

Comic Strip

1568 Second Ave between 81st and 82nd Sts (861-9386). Subway: 4, 5, 6 to 86th St. $8 Mon–Thu, Sun; $12 Fri, Sat, $9 drink minimum. AmEx, DC, Disc, MC, V. This saloonlike stand-up club is known for separating the wheat from the chaff, a blessing in a city with its share of comics high on ambition and short on talent. Monday is amateur night—comic hopefuls should sign up the Friday before.

Dangerfield's

1118 First Ave between 61st and 62nd Sts (593-1650). Subway: 4, 5, 6 to 59th St. $12.50 Mon–Thu, Sun; $15 Fri, Sat. *AmEx, DC, MC, V.* Opened by comedian Rodney Dangerfield of *Caddyshack* fame over 20 years ago, this glitzy lounge is now one of New York's oldest and most formidable clubs.

Gotham Comedy Club

34 W 22nd St between Fifth and Sixth Aves (367-9000). Subway: F, N, R, 1, 9 to 23rd St. $8, two-drink minimum. AmEx, V. The Gotham Comedy Club, located in Chelsea, books a lineup of top comedians from all over the country, including stand-ups such as Todd Barry and Louis CK, who perform here regularly.

New York Comedy Club

241 E 24th St between Second and Third Aves (696-5233). Subway: 6 to 23rd St. $5 Mon–Thu, Sun; $10 Fri, Sat, two-drink minimum. AmEx, D, MC, V. A relative newcomer, the New York Comedy Club combines a democratic approach with a packed lineup and a bargain cover price.

The Original Improv

433 W 34th St between Ninth and Tenth Aves (279-3446). Subway: A, C, E to 34th St–Penn Station. $10, $9 minimum. AmEx, DC, Disc, MC, V. This venerable comedy club books big names and up-and-comers. As you'd expect, most performances are improvisational.

Stand-Up NY

236 W 78th St at Broadway (595-0850). Subway: 1, 9 to 79th St. $7 Mon–Thu, Sun; $12 Fri, Sat, two-drink minimum. AmEx, MC, V. A clinically decorated but small and intimate place, Stand-Up NY always features a good mix of club-circuit regulars and new faces.

Children

**Growing up with cool parents amid oodles of culture,
New York City kids are more than all right**

New York is a noisy, nonstop, loudmouthed, horn-honking, in-your-face city where anything goes and everything seems possible—which could be why so many kids think it was made for them. It's the perfect environment for short attention spans and experience-hungry spirits: It's possibly the only city in the world where a child can wake up in the morning and make breakfast for animals in a zoo kitchen, practice an obscure Indian dance form in the afternoon and go to a pajama-party storytime before bed. Kids don't get bored in New York. They get "overscheduled."

Since parents here scramble to get their tots into a good nursery school, even play should be enriching. From September through May, museums and other institutions offer lots of hands-on learning. In summer, the emphasis shifts to unmitigated fun, though there's still plenty to inspire: free outdoor theater in parks and parking lots, Lincoln Center's wonderful Out-of-Doors festival, Central Park's SummerStage and much more.

There are also the unscheduled pleasures of the street. If you let them, kids will have a ball scaling industrial loading bays, ogling street performers, swinging on subway poles or just wandering around taking it all in. Especially during the warm months, street life feeds all of a child's senses and will provide yours with endless stories to take home.

The weekly *Time Out New York* magazine and Friday's *New York Times* have good listings of children's activities. Also read the monthly *Parentguide Magazine* distributed free in libraries, toy stores, play centers and other child-intensive places. Pick up a copy of *Events for Children* from any branch of the New York Public Library for extensive listings of free storytellings, puppet shows, films and workshops in libraries. The Donnell Library, home of the Central Children's Room, is the best place for events; it also houses the original Winnie the Pooh and other toys that belonged to Christopher Robin (*see chapter* **Museums**).

All Barnes & Noble and Borders bookstores

The circle game: A family frolics in Tompkins Square Park, heart of the artsy East Village.

have regular free story-reading hours and events; pick up a calendar in any branch. You might also want to invest in a copy of Alfred Gingold and Helen Rogan's slim paperback, *The Cool Parents' Guide to All of New York* (City Books). For a complete guide to child-friendly eateries, check out Sam Freund and Elizabeth Carpenter's *Kids Eat New York* (The Little Bookroom). Sam was nine when he compiled this book with his mom. The New York CitySearch website (www.citysearchnyc.com) has well-organized family listings and you can search by child's age, location or date.

Though there's no end of events and activities designed specifically for kids, don't pass by some of the cutting-edge stuff for adults; some of the zany Off Broadway shows are sure hits with children, as are most "new media" art shows.

For more ideas, *see also chapters* **Sightseeing, New York by Season, Trips Out of Town** and **Sports & Fitness**.

Amusement parks

Astroland

1000 Surf Ave at W 8th St, Coney Island, Brooklyn (1-718-372-0275). Subway: B, D, F, N to Stillwell Ave–Coney Island. Winter, phone for details; Summer, noon–late daily (weather permitting). $1.75 single kiddie rides. No credit cards. Coney Island's amusement park is rather run-down and tacky now, but a delight to children nonetheless. In summer, you can ride the frightening Cyclone roller coaster (younger kids like the Tilt-a-Whirl), watch a snake charmer, get sticky cotton-candy fingers, bite into a Nathan's Famous hot dog and, if you navigate around the boom boxes, enjoy the sun and sand.

Circuses

Check the press for details of when the artsy, animal-free, French-Canadian **Cirque du Soleil** is in town (usually April). The music, costumes and staging are pure fantasy, though younger children might find the stylish clowns a little grotesque. Tickets are snapped up fast.

Big Apple Circus

Information 268-0055/offices 268-2500/Ticketmaster 307-4100. Prices vary. New York's own traveling circus was founded 12 years ago as a traditional, one-act-at-a-time alternative to the Ringling Bros. three-things-at-once extravaganza. Big Apple prides itself on being a true family affair, with acts by the founder's two children and his equestrienne wife. The circus has a regular winter season (Oct–Jan) in Damrosch Park at Lincoln Center and, budget permitting, travels to other city parks in early spring.

Ringling Bros. and Barnum & Bailey Circus

Madison Square Garden, Seventh Ave at 32nd St (465-6741). Subway: A, C, E, 1, 2, 3, 9 to 34th St–Penn Station. Apr. $10.50–$22.50. AmEx, DC, Disc, MC, V. The original (and most famous) American circus, this has three rings, lots of glitz and plenty to keep you glued to your seat, as well as Barnum's famous sideshow of freaks, which was revived last year. It's extremely popular, so reserve seats well in advance.

UniverSoul Big Top Circus

Downing Stadium, Randalls Island (307-7171). Subway: 4, 5, 6 to 125th St, then take the M35 bus to Randalls Island–Downing Stadium. Late Apr–mid-May. Tue–Fri 10:30am, 7:30pm; Sat noon, 4:30, 8pm; Sun noon, 3:30, 6:30pm. $8–$40. This African-American circus has all the requisite clowns, animal acts and hoopla. Owned and operated by the man who promoted the Commodores, UniverSoul is the result of a two-year nationwide search for black circus performers.

Museums and exhibitions

Check the **By Neighborhood** and **Museums** chapters for plenty more museum options, including the revamped dinosaur halls at the American Museum of Natural History, the Liberty Science Center (don't miss the touch tunnel), the New York Transit Museum and the Sea, Air & Space Museum, a collection of military and maritime paraphernalia housed on an aircraft carrier. Most of these museums offer weekend workshops for children (*see* **Bring us your budding Picassos**).

Brooklyn Children's Museum

145 Brooklyn Ave at St. Mark's Ave, Brooklyn (recorded information 1-718-735-4400). Subway: 3 to Kingston Ave; B43, B45, B47, B65 bus. Winter Wed–Fri 2–5pm; Sat, Sun 10am–5pm; summer Mon, Wed, Fri, Sat, Sun 10am–5pm. Winter and spring school vacations 10am–5pm. Suggested donation $4. No credit cards. Founded in 1899, this was the world's first museum designed specifically for children. You reach the exhibits via a walkway through a long, water-filled tunnel. In the music studio, children can play synthesizers and dance on the keys of a walk-on piano. A new gallery houses exhibitions from museums around the country. There are weekend performances and special workshops daily.

Brooklyn Museum of Art

See **Bring us your budding Picassos**.

Children's Museum of the Arts

182 Lafayette St between Broome and Grand Sts (274-0986). Subway: N, R to Prince St; B, D, F, Q to Broadway–Lafayette St; 6 to Spring St. Daily, call for hours and admission. AmEx, MC, V. A favorite hangout for the under-sevens, this is less a museum than an art playground, with a floor-to-ceiling chalkboard, art computers and vast stores of art supplies—perfect for young travelers pining for their crayons. Visual and performing arts workshops are scheduled regularly. Children must be accompanied by an adult.

Children's Museum of Manhattan

212 W 83rd St between Broadway and Amsterdam Ave (721-1234). Subway: 1, 9 to 86th St. Tue–Sun 10am–5pm. $5. AmEx, Disc, MC, V. The Children's Museum of Manhattan promotes literacy of every kind through its dynamic and playful hands-on exhibits. Currently, WordPlay lets toddlers discover the pleasures of language in a 1,900-square-foot play environment. Bigger kids can head to the sound studio, equipped with keyboards and digital sound-editing equipment. Then there's the state-of-the-art media lab, where they operate the cameras, edit tape, play talk-show host and make their own TV shows. Workshops are scheduled on weekends and during school vacations. There are no eating facilities, but you may leave for lunch and return on the same ticket.

Lower East Side Tenement Museum

See chapter **Museums** *for listings. Children's tours Sat, Sun noon, 1, 3pm. $8, children $6.* Housed in an old tenement building that was home to successive families of new immigrants, this museum offers a weekly interactive children's

*Giddyap: a spin on **Central Park's carousel**.*

tour of the Sephardic Confino family's former home. The tour is led by 13-year-old Victoria Confino (actually a staff member posing as her), who teaches visitors about the New York of the early 1900s by dancing the fox-trot, playing games and answering questions—like "Where does everyone sleep?" Recommended for ages seven to 14.

Metropolitan Museum of Art
See chapter **Museums** *for listings. See also* **Bring us your budding Picassos**.

Museum of Modern Art
See chapter **Museums** *for listings. See also* **Bring us your budding Picassos**.

New York Hall of Science
47-01 111th St at 46th Ave, Flushing Meadows, Queens (1-718-699-0005). Subway: 7 to 111th St. Summer Mon, Tue 10am–2pm; Wed–Sun 10am–5pm. Fall–spring Tue, Wed 9:30am–2pm; Thu, Fri 9:30am–5pm; weekends 11am–5pm. $6, children 15 and under $4, under 4 free. Summer Wed, Thu 2–5pm free, fall–spring Thu, Fri 2–5pm free. AmEx, MC, V. Located on the site of the 1964 World's Fair, flanked by prehistoric-looking rocket ships and housed in the mysterious former Space Pavilion, the Hall of Science offers curious minds some terrific adventures. In the most popular of its interactive exhibits, the immense outdoor Science Playground (open late spring through fall; ages six and up), youngsters engage in whole-body science exploration, discovering principles of balance, gravity, energy and sound as they play.

Socrates Sculpture Park
Broadway at the East River, Long Island City, Queens (1-718-956-1819). Subway: N to Broadway–Long Island City. 10am–sunset daily. Free. Unlike most art exhibitions, this outdoor city-owned spread of large-scale contemporary sculpture is utterly devoid of snarling guards and "don't touch" signs. Without even risking an adult's glare, children climb on, run through, sit astride and generally interact with the works that seem to have been plopped haphazardly around the five-acre park.

Sony Wonder Technology Lab
550 Madison Ave between 55th and 56th Sts (833-8100). Subway: 4, 5, 6 to 51st St; E, F to Fifth Ave. Tue, Wed, Fri, Sat 10am–6pm, Thu 10am–9pm, Sun noon–6pm (school groups have priority Tue–Fri 10am–noon). Free. Most chil-

dren think this is the coolest place on earth. At six digital workstations, visitors can play at being medical diagnosticians, remix a Celine Dion song, design computer games, edit a music video or crisis-manage an earthquake. Best of all is the High Definition Interactive Theater, where the audience directs the action in an exciting video adventure. Get here early—by 2:30pm on weekends—or you might not get in.

Music

Growing Up With Opera
John Jay Theater, 899 Tenth Ave at 59th St (769-7008). Subway: A, C, B, D, 1, 9 to 59th St–Columbus Circle. $15-$25. AmEx, MC, V. Short operas, some especially for young audiences, sung in English by the Metropolitan Opera Guild.

Jazz for Young People
Alice Tully Hall, Lincoln Center, Broadway at 65th St (information 875-5299/tickets 721-6500). Subway: 1, 9 to 66th St. $8–$12. AmEx, MC, V. These interactive concerts, led by trumpeter and jazz educator Wynton Marsalis, help children figure out answers to such questions as "What is jazz?"

Little Orchestra Society
Florence Gould Hall, 55 E 59th St between Park and Madison Aves (704-2100). Subway: 4, 5, 6 to 59th St; N, R to Lexington Ave. $15–$32. AmEx, MC, V. "Lollipop" presents participatory orchestral concerts for children ages three to five, combining classical music with dance, puppetry, theater and mime. *Amahl and the Night Visitors* is done every Christmas. "Happy Concerts" are presented at Avery Fisher Hall.

New York Philharmonic Young People's Concerts
Avery Fisher Hall, Lincoln Center, Broadway at 65th Street (875-5030). Subway: 1, 9 to 66th St. $6–$20. AmEx, MC, V. Musicians address the audience directly in these educational concerts, initiated by Leonard Bernstein. They're preceded by hour-long "Children's Promenades," during which kids can meet orchestra members and try out their instruments.

Puppets

International Festival of Puppet Theater
Information 439-7529, ext 1998. Sept 2000. This biennial festival of puppet theater from several continents is produced by the Jim Henson Foundation. Although its central component is cutting-edge productions for adults, children will also enjoy the rich blend of offerings. Watch for other puppet activity piggybacking on the festival.

Los Kabayitos Puppet Theater
CSV Cultural Center, 107 Suffolk St between Delancey and Rivington Sts (260-4080, ext 14). Subway: F to Delancey St; J, M, Z to Essex St. $10, children $6. No credit cards. While some of the productions at New York's only year-round puppet theater are for adults only, others are spectacular and fantastical enough to engage kids. Don't miss Bread and Puppet Theater's winter season.

Puppet Company
31 Union Square West at 16th St, loft 2B (741-1646). Subway: F, L, N, R, 4, 5, 6 to 14th St. Oct–Apr. Sat, Sun 1, 3pm. $7.50. No credit cards. Three- to seven-year-olds cram onto benches in this intimate loft space, as the company's handpuppet host, the debonair Al E. Gator, introduces the play. Each show includes a humorous, inventive puppet revue and a short puppet-making demonstration. Performances last about 50 minutes; reservations are essential.

Puppetworks

338 Sixth Ave at 4th St, Brooklyn (1-718-965-3391). Subway: M, N, R to Union St. Sat, Sun 12:30, 2:30pm. $7, ages 2–18 $5. No credit cards. This company, established in 1938, offers two plays a season, alternating weekly. Usually performed with marionettes, the lavish productions are based on classic tales, such as *Beauty and the Beast* or *Alice in Wonderland*, and always accompanied by classical music.

Swedish Cottage Marionette Theater

Central Park at 81st St (988-9093). Subway: B, C to 81st St. Sept–May, Tue–Fri 10:30am, noon; Sat 11am, 1, 3pm; Jun–Aug Mon–Fri 10:30am, noon. $5, ages 2–12 $4. No credit cards. Run by New York's Department of Parks and Recreation, this intimate theater has just completed a $1.5-million renovation. Reservations are essential.

Theaters

Several small theaters and repertory companies offer weekend matinee family performances. Most of these are musical productions of questionable value. Check magazine listings for details. The following are the best of New York's family theaters.

West End Kids' Productions

West End Children's Theatre, West End Cafe, 2911 Broadway at 113th St (877-6115). Subway: 1, 9 to 110th St. Caroline's Kids' Klub, Caroline's Comedy Club, 1626 Broadway between 49th and 50th Sts (757-4100). Subway: C, E, 1, 9 to 50th St; N, R to 49th St. Sept–Apr Sat, Sun 1 pm. $8.50.

AmEx, MC, V. West End Kids' Productions programs a variety of acts at two locations, both of which offer pre- or post-theater dining and performances that include puppetry, magic, variety and some acts that defy description. Caroline's, a famous comedy venue, schedules monthly stand-up comedy by kids, as well as auditions. Most performances are geared to kids ages three to nine. Phone for a schedule.

New Amsterdam Theater

See chapter **Theater** *for listings.* Disney laid claim to 42nd Street by renovating this splendid theater, an Art Deco masterpiece. Its inaugural show: *The Lion King*, directed by wizardly puppeteer Julie Taymor.

New Victory Theater

209 W 42nd St between Broadway and Eighth Ave (382-4020/tickets, Telecharge 239-6200). Subway: A, C, E, N, R, S, 1, 2, 3, 9 to 42nd St. $10–$30. AmEx, MC, V. New York's only year-round, full-scale children's theater (and the first of the New 42nd Street theaters to be reclaimed from porndom when it opened, fully renovated, in 1995), the New Victory is a gem that shows the very best in international theater and dance, mostly for the over-ten set. During the summer, Theatreworks USA presents a season of free musical theater for kids.

TADA! Youth Ensemble

120 W 28th St between Sixth and Seventh Aves (627-1732). Subway: 1, 9 to 28th St. Dec, Jan, Mar, Jul, Aug; call for times. $12, under 17 $6. No credit cards. This group presents musicals performed by and for children. The cast, ages eight and up, is drawn from auditions in city schools. The shows are usually musical comedies—extremely well presented, high-spirited and very popular. Reservations are advised; phone for details of school-year and vacation workshops.

Bring us your budding Picassos

At the city's best grown-up museums, art can often be child's play

With "arts in education" a buzz word around the city these days (and a powerful magnet for government and corporate support), museum education departments have been busily beefing up and expanding both school time and family programming. Sure, you could be your own child's tour guide; but wouldn't you rather someone else get to say, "Don't touch, don't run…"? Besides, museum educators are experts in how to engage children in the art, how to encourage discussion and how to keep youngsters at the center of the museum-going experience. Best of all, from a kid's point of view, is that all of this happens in the company of other kids: It's a social experience. Yo, Picasso, wassup?

Brooklyn Museum of Art

See chapter **Museums** *for listings. Sat and weekdays during some school vacations 11am, 2pm. Tour free with museum ticket.* With its famous Egyptian collection, totem poles and the masks and chairs of its African collection, the Brooklyn Museum of Art is naturally child-friendly. "Arty facts" is the museum's lively drop-in program for four- to seven-year-olds, focusing on a different theme each month—for example, legs (teapot

legs, chair legs, human legs). Children and parents examine in depth three or four works in the museum's galleries, learn about the people who made them and the materials used, and then go make their own related art in a real art studio. Afterward, there's storytelling in the galleries (at 4pm).

Metropolitan Museum of Art

See chapter **Museums** *for listings. Tours Oct–May Sat 11am–12:30pm, 2–4:30pm, Sun 11am–12:30pm. Call for summer schedule. Tour free with museum ticket.* Most kids will want to head straight for the Egyptian galleries for a look at mummies and the awesome Temple of Dendur. And then what? The Met's education department has it all planned out. Every week, groups of children ages six to 12 and their accompanying grown-ups are led to a specific area of the museum, where they go hunting for whatever relates to the theme of the day—it could be flowers in the arms-and-armor galleries or serpents in Medieval art. There's plenty of discussion, and kids are encouraged to sketch what they see using the materials provided. Independent types can use the museum's self-guided children's tours ("art hunts"), designed with an unusually acute sense of what makes kids tick; themes range from "Mummies" to "Colonial Children." Instructions are in large type with very cool graphics, a simple floor map, step-by-step directions and playful questions and tidbits of information. A tour takes about an hour to complete.

Outdoor activities

Brooklyn Botanic Gardens

1000 Washington Ave, Brooklyn (1-718-622-4544). Subway: 2, 3 to Eastern Pkwy–Brooklyn Museum. Winter Tue–Fri 8am–4:30pm; Sat, Sun, holidays 10am–4:30pm. Summer Tue–Fri 8am–6pm; Sat, Sun, 10am–6pm. $3; $1 concessions; Tue free. No credit cards. In the indoor Discovery Center, children learn about plants and nature through some inventive exhibits. The garden's highlight, a 13,000-square-foot (1,200-square-meter) "Discovery Garden," lets children play botanist, make toys out of natural materials, weave a wall and get their hands dirty.

New York Botanical Garden

Southern Blvd at 200th St, Bronx (1-718-817-8705). Subway: C, D, 4 to Bedford Pk, then BX26 bus. Apr–Oct Tue–Sun 10am–6pm; Nov–Mar Tue–Sun 10am–4pm. Summer $3, under 6 free; $1 concessions. Winter $1.50, children and seniors 50¢, under 6 free. Wed 10am–6pm, Sat 10am–noon free. No credit cards. The immense Children's Adventure Garden, opened in spring 1998, is an interactive "museum of the natural world" with "galleries" both indoors and out. Children can also run under "Munchy," a giant topiary; poke around in a touch tank; and plant, weed, water and harvest in the Family Garden. Ask for a kid's guide to the Enid A. Haupt Conservatory (admission $3.50), the spectacular glass house.

Nelson Rockefeller Park

Hudson River at Chambers St (information 267-9700). Subway: C, E to World Trade Center. 10am–sunset daily. Free. River breezes always keep this park several degrees cooler than most of the city, a big plus in the summer. There's plenty

for kids to do here besides watch the boats (Saturday's a good day for ocean liners). They can play on Tom Otterness's quirky sculptures in the picnic area (near the Chambers Street entrance); enjoy one of New York's best playgrounds; and participate in art, sports or street-game activities (Mon–Thu afternoons, May–Oct; call for locations). Special events such as kite flying or fishing are planned throughout the summer. Two blocks north on Pier 25 is a mini-golf course as well as a sand-and-sprinkler area for overheated tots. The River Project (941-5901) on Pier 26 admits children on weekends; they can help set river traps, examine small creatures under microscopes and feed the aquarium fish.

Central Park

Manhattanites don't have gardens; they have Central Park, which like the rest of the city is overpopulated with people doing all sorts of things, some of which are fun to watch. There are plenty of places and programs specially for children; call 360-8236 for details. **Arts in the Park** (988-9093) organizes an extensive program of children's summer arts events here and in other parks throughout the city. The **Urban Park Rangers** (360-2774) arrange guided walks, nature-related activities and school vacation programs. The **Parks Department** events hotline (360-3456) provides a huge menu of citywide events and activities. Don't miss the beautiful **antique carousel** (90¢ a ride) and the **Heckscher Playground,** which has

*Mummy's the word: Kids visit ancient Egypt at the **Metropolitan Museum of Art**.*

Museum of Modern Art

*See chapter **Museums** for listings.* Tours Sat 10–11am (sign-in at 9:45am). Tour free with museum ticket. Tours for Tots selected Saturdays 10–10:45am. $5 per family includes admission. Art Safari tours selected Saturdays 10am–noon. $20 per family includes admission and copy of Art Safari book. A melting clock, a sleeping gypsy, bright drips and splashes, tiny buildings with tinier cars, not to mention escalators—MoMA has it all. Guided "One-at-a-Time" family tours, with a different slant each week, introduce children ages five to ten to the highlights of MoMA (before the museum opens to the public). A film series follows at noon, with screenings of artful shorts that relate to the day's theme (often a single artist or medium). Four-year-olds get their own whimsical tours. The museum's *Art Safari* (available from its bookshop), by the education department's Joyce Raimondo, helps kids look carefully at

eight animal-related artworks in the collection (*is* the gypsy sleeping?). Also see if Raimondo is leading one of her Art Safaris in person. The entrance for all tours is at the John Noble Education Center, 18 W 54th St.

Solomon R. Guggenheim Museum/ Guggenheim Museum Soho

*See chapter **Museums** for listings.* Tours some Sundays 2-4pm. $10 per child plus adult museum admission. Soho Tots some Fridays 11am–noon. $10 per child, adults free. The cool museum with the spiral ramp you're not allowed to run down offers occasional tours of special exhibitions for children ages five to ten. Each tour is followed by an artist-led workshop—not your typical artsy-crafty affair. The Guggenheim's Soho branch, which houses the museum's galleries of technological art, offers the city's only museum program for very young children. Three- to five-year-olds get a cursory introduction to the work on view before launching into simple activities—art making, storytelling, game playing—that might or might not illuminate their art-viewing experience. Preregistration is essential for all Guggenheim programs.

Whitney Museum of American Art

*See chapter **Museums** for listings.* Tours Sat 1pm; workshops Oct–May selected Saturdays 9–11am. Tour free with museum ticket, workshop $6 per family. The Whitney's Look Out! tours include discussion and sketching. Specially trained teenage docents lead the tours, telling young visitors about the artists and their work; as you might expect, young children listen in rapt attention to their slightly older peers. Family Fun! art-making workshops, for which you must register in advance, are truly imaginative and interactive events: You look at the work of a single American artist and then try to get a sense of what went into the making of it—so kids might, for example, end up posing for and drawing one another.

handball courts, horseshoes, several softball diamonds, a puppet theater, a wading pool and a crèche. *See also chapter* **Sightseeing**.

Charles A. Dana Discovery Center
Central Park at 110th St near Fifth Ave (860-1370). Subway: 2, 3 to 110th St. Apr–mid-Oct Tue–Sun 10am–5pm, mid-Oct–Mar Tue–Sun 11am–4pm. Free. Now that Harlem Meer has been restored and stocked, you can take the kids fishing here. Poles and bait are given out (with a parent's ID) to children over five until 90 minutes before closing; staff is available to help. Other activities: bird watching and workshops such as kite making or sun printing (1–3pm weekends).

Conservatory Water
Central Park at 77th near Fifth Ave. Subway: 6 to 77th St. Known as Stuart Little's Pond after E.B. White's storybook mouse, this ornamental pond is the place to watch model yacht races. When the boatmaster is around, you can rent one of the remote-controlled vessels ($7–$10/hour). Be warned—it's not as speedy as Nintendo. The large bronze statue of *Alice in Wonderland* nearby is excellent for climbing.

Henry Luce Nature Observatory
Belvedere Castle, Central Park at 79th St (772-0210). Subway: B, C to 81st St. Oct–Mar Tue–Sun 11am–4pm; Apr–Oct Tue–Sun 10am–5pm. Free. This is the newest children's hot spot in Central Park, with telescopes, microscopes and simple hands-on exhibits that teach about the plants and animals living (or hiding) in the surrounding area. Workshops are held on weekend afternoons (1–3pm), and kids (with a parent's ID) can borrow a "discovery kit"—a backpack containing binoculars, a bird-watching guide and various cool tools.

North Meadow Recreation Center
Central Park at 79th St (348-4867). Borrow (with ID) a fun-in-the-park kit bag containing a Frisbee, hula hoop, whiffle ball and bat, jump rope, kickball and other diversions.

Stories at the Hans Christian Andersen Statue
Central Park at Conservatory Water (929-6871, 340-0906). Jun–Sept Sat 11am, Jul Wed 11am. Free. For generations, children have gathered at the foot of the statue for Saturday stories read by master storytellers from all over America—a real New York tradition, not to be missed.

Wildman's Edible Park Tours
Various city parks, including Central and Prospect Parks. Phone for meeting place and instructions (1-718-291-6925). $10, children $5. No credit cards. Irrepressible urban forager and naturalist "Wildman" Steve Brill was once arrested for munching Central Park's dandelions; now his eat-as-you-go foraging tours are sanctioned by the parks commissioner. His tours aren't meant specifically for kids, but he pays them special attention, and they delight in his joke-laden banter.

NY Skateout
For free social skate meet at Fifth Ave and 72nd St, Apr–Oct Sat 3pm. Skate lessons Apr–Oct Sat 9am. $25. Call to reserve (486-1919). Kids who already know how to in-line skate can swish around the park's loop with other children. Novices (ages three and up) can take lessons. NY Skateout is dedicated to skating safety: Don't even think of showing up without all the gear. Call for information on equipment rental.

Zoos

Central Park Wildlife Conservation Center
See chapter **Sightseeing** *for listings.* This small zoo is one of the highlights of the park. You can watch seals frolic above and below the waterline, crocodiles snap at swinging monkeys, and huge polar bears swim endless laps like true neurotic New Yorkers. The chilly penguin house is a favorite summer retreat for overheated kids.

International Wildlife Conservation Park (Bronx Zoo)
See chapter **Sightseeing** *for listings.* Some 4,000 animals and 543 species live in reconstructed natural habitats here—one of the world's largest and most magnificent zoos. Inside is the Bronx Children's Zoo, scaled down for the very young, with lots of domestic animals to pet, plus exhibits that show you the world from an animal's point of view. Camel and elephant rides are available from April to October. Don't miss the sea-lion feeding (daily at 3pm).

New York Aquarium for Wildlife Conservation
Surf Ave at W 8th St, Brooklyn (1-718-265-3405). Subway: D, F to W 8th St. Summer 10am–6pm daily, Winter 10am–5pm daily. $8.75, children and seniors $4.50. No credit cards. Although the aquarium is rather funky, kids enjoy seeing the famous Beluga whale family. There's also a re-creation of the Pacific coastline and an intriguing glimpse of the kinds of things that manage to live in the East River, plus the usual dolphin show and some truly awesome sharks. Watch the dolphins being fed daily at 11:30am and 3pm. Added bonus: Coney Island's Astroland is just a short stroll away.

Play spaces

Playspace
2473 Broadway at 92nd St (769-2300). Subway: 1, 2, 3, 9 to 96th St. Mon–Sat 9:30am–6pm, Sun 10am–6pm. $5.50. No credit cards. Children ages six and under build in the immense sandbox, ride on toy trucks, dress up and climb on the jungle gym, while parents look on from the café area. There are also drop-in art classes and storytimes.

Rain or Shine
115 E 29th St between Park Ave and Lexington Aves (741-9650). Subway: 6 to 28th St. Mon–Fri 9am–6pm; Sat, Sun 10am–6pm. Children $8.95, $1 discount for siblings; parents free. No credit cards. This is a parent-accompanied play space in a rainforest setting, filled with activity areas and toys that encourage imaginative play, including a giant sandbox and a tree house. Suitable for kids ages six months to six years.

Babysitting

Babysitters' Guild
682-0227. 9am–9pm daily. No credit cards. Long- or short-term babysitters cost $12–$20 an hour and speak 16 languages among them. If you tell the agency you'll need a sitter more than once during your stay, they'll do their best to book the same sitter for you each time.

Avalon Nurse Registry & Child Service
245-0250. Mon–Fri 8:30am–5:30pm; Sat, Sun 9am–8pm. No credit cards. Avalon arranges full- or part-time nannies and babysitting. A sitter (four-hour minimum) costs $10 an hour, plus $2 for each additional child and travel expenses.

Pinch Sitters
260-6005. Mon–Fri 7am–5pm. No credit cards. Pinch Sitters specializes in emergency child care, mainly by creative types moonlighting between engagements, and mainly for creative types with unpredictable schedules. The agency will try to get you a sitter within the hour. To be safe, call in the morning for an evening sitter or the previous afternoon for a daytime sitter. Charges are $12 an hour (four-hour minimum).

Clubs

Despite the city's new "quality of life" measures, New York's club life still presents lots of wild nocturnal options

Under crackdown-loving Mayor Rudolph Giuliani (dubbed "Mayor Rapknuckles" in *The New York Times*), Manhattan, an island of anarchy since colonial days, has become more regimented, and the clubs have consequently lost some of their wildness. But there's still plenty out there—you just have to look a little harder. Many of the more risqué events shun publicity (and hence may not be listed here), so if you're interested in events of a semi-legal nature, it's best to ask around. Also, because of the political climate, much of the scene revolves around lounges (*see* **This ain't no disco**).

New Yorkers are a cynical bunch and hard to impress. But despite the perennial "been there, done that" attitude, New York's club scene is proud of its history and traditions. Most post-twentysomething clubbers grew up on disco and old-school rap, and DJs program a fair number of "classics" in

their sets. While some clubs seem overly nostalgic for legendary, long-gone nightspots like Paradise Garage (a famed gay disco and the namesake of the British term for gospel-influenced vocal house music), classics give props to the past and connect the musical dots between then and now.

New York DJs are more eclectic than their counterparts elsewhere, often spinning everything from hip-hop, reggae and soul to house, disco, drum 'n' bass and Latin over the course of a night. The crowds, too, tend to be varied (though certain clubs are almost exclusively populated by white gay musclemen). A gay sensibility is common, and a "straight" night generally means "mixed."

Although glamour-oriented clubs do have door policies, economic and fashion trends have forced most places to accept the money of the sartorially challenged. You may want to dress the part,

*Café olé: Dancers groove to a Latin beat at **Kit Kat Klub**'s Café Con Leche.*

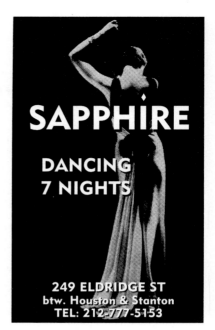

though, as this trend can change like the weather. Particularly straight venues often refuse entry to groups of men in order to maintain a desirable gender balance and to prevent testosterone overload.

In pre-Giuliani times, weapons were the only items verboten in clubs, but the current climate has forced some clubs to monitor drug use as well, so if getting high is your cup of E, be careful. And leave the guns and knives at home. Since we're on the subject, it should be said that while New York isn't nearly as dangerous as it used to be, this is still a city where anything can happen. If you visit a club in a nonresidential area, you might want to take a taxi or call a car service as you leave.

Alcohol is sold until 4 am, and some after-hours clubs are open late enough to reopen their bars at 8am (noon on Sunday), the earliest allowed by law. Wherever you go, most people won't arrive before midnight (some clubs don't fill up—or even open their doors—until well past 4am).

Though Friday and Saturday are of course the biggest nights to go out, many hipsters and locals stick to midweek clubbing in order to avoid the throngs of suburbanites (the "bridge and tunnel" crowd) that overwhelm Manhattan every weekend, and many of the more interesting and unusual events happen during the week.

The club scene is mercurial: Parties move weekly and clubs can differ wildly from night to night. For example, a primarily gay establishment may "go straight" one night a week because a promoter can fill the place. At press time, several reopenings were expected in the months ahead—chief among them being Limelight (made possible by owner Peter Gatien's acquittal on drug conspiracy charges, *see* **Tunnel**) and the next incarnation of the space that housed the legendary after-hours club Save the Robots. Calling ahead is a good idea, as is consulting *Time Out New York* or the monthly style magazine *Paper*. The gay listings magazine *HX* (Homo Xtra) is also good for club reviews, albeit with a gym-queen–oriented slant. Happy hunting.

Admission prices for the clubs listed below vary according to the night, but usually range from $5–$20. The term "club" is also used to describe live music venues and discos. For DJ bars (lounges), see **This ain't no disco**.

Clubs

Axis
17 W 19th St between Fifth and Sixth Aves (633-1717). Subway: F, N, R to 23rd St. Hours vary with event. The newish Axis has become a viable option on the club scene (partly due to the scarcity of midsize dance clubs). The first Tuesday of each month, promoter Rob Fernandez hosts Subliminal, a dance-music industry party sponsored by producer/DJ Erick Morillo's label of the same name, with Morillo joined by house and hip-hop spinners such as David Morales and "Little" Louie Vega.

Broadway II
2700 Queens Plaza, Long Island City, Queens (1-718-937-7111). Subway: N, R to Queensboro Plaza. Thu–Sat 9pm–4:30am. One of the city's premier Latin clubs, Broadway II is worth a journey on the N or R. The dancers are first-rate, but you shouldn't find any attitude if you're not as skilled. Most nights feature a band and a DJ (spinning everything from New York and Colombian salsa to tribal house). Jackets are required for men.

Cheetah
12 W 21st St between Fifth and Sixth Aves (206-7770). Subway: F, N, R to 23rd St. Hours vary with event. While drink prices are outrageous and the crowd can tend toward model-worshippers and Eurotrash, the cheetah-print booths and indoor waterfall are fun. Purr, a hip-hop/R&B/classics party on Monday, is popular for its attractive, racially mixed crowd of trendy downtown heteros on the make. Plenty of models and celebs, too. Other nights, resident DJ Nelson "That Boy" Diaz is worth checking out for his masterful blending of salsa, merengue, house, disco, hip-hop and more.

Coney Island High
15 St. Marks Pl between Second and Third Aves (674-7959). Subway: 6 to Astor Pl; N, R to 8th St. 11pm–4am alternate Sats. Most of the week, Coney Island High is a vortex of punky rock posing, in the old Max's Kansas City/CBGB vein. You'll see lots of guys with eyeliner, bondage trousers and

Dial-a-club

Let your fingers do the walking with these choice groovelines

Movable parties may change venues at a moment's notice, and keeping up can be a challenge. Calling the various hot lines can help put your finger on the pulse. These cover a wide range of events. Rave clothing and record store **Liquid Sky** has a popular phone line (226-0657), with details of rave-oriented parties. **Mello**'s line (631-1023) is also rave-oriented, but is geared more toward clubs and is less artsy.

Other rave lines include **Satellite Productions** (465-3299), **Digital Domain** (592-3676) and **Solar Luv** (629-2078). **Urban Works** (629-1786) cover a variety of events from hip-hop and rave to gay parties (such as Café Con Leche). **E-Man**'s line (330-8101) tracks a selection of underground house clubs, mostly—but by no means exclusively—of the mixed-to-gay variety. **Giant Step**'s line (714-8001) focuses on acid jazz, drum 'n' bass, trip-hop and the like. **Mixed Bag Productions** (604-4224) has a role in many events: In addition to running Konkrete Jungle, Mixed Bag helps promote various jungle, acid jazz and trip-hop parties, including larger-scale rave-like events.

This ain't no disco

To keep a lower profile and hear diverse music, get your lounge act together

Clubland's clever response to the difficulty of obtaining a city license to allow dancing is the lounge—a bar that features many of the trappings of a club (DJs, doormen, velvet ropes, expensive drinks) but doesn't (well, can't) allow dancing. With the dearth of smaller dance clubs, lounges have also become places to hear more left-field music. Laidback staff may look the other way if you start moving to the beat. Just don't plan to do any arabesques.

Beige
Bowery Bar, 40 E 4th St at the Bowery (475-2220). Subway: 6 to Bleecker St. Tue 11pm. DJs serve up a groovy, just-this-side-of-camp soundtrack that can include anything from gay show-tune standards to 1980s electro disco classics. Expect fashionistas, clubbies and off-duty drag queens. Hilarious and very visual.

bOb
235 Eldridge St between Houston and Stanton Sts (777-0588). Subway: F to Second Ave. 7pm–4am. bOb features everything from the standard hip-hop/reggae/classics to exotica and film noir soundtracks. The space doubles as an art gallery.

Idlewild
145 E Houston St between Eldridge and Forsyth Sts (477-5005). Subway: F to Second Ave. Sun–Wed 8pm–3am, Thu–Sat 8pm–4am. This space reopened in early 1998 as an impressively designed jet-themed bar. Idlewild (JFK International Airport's original name) looks just like a jet, with airplane seats, a curved, fuselage-shaped interior and a boarding-ramp entrance hall. Idlewild promises to be one of the year's hot spots.

Kush
183 Orchard St between Houston and Stanton Sts (677-7328). Subway: F to Second Ave. 8pm–4am. In a neighborhood overrun with pseudo-hip theme bars, Kush is hard to knock. Located on the main drag of the old Lower East Side bargain district, Kush is a beautifully designed bar that transports you to Morocco as soon as you enter. There are olives at the bar and cushions to sit on, and the music policy is commendably uncompromising. DJs spin mainly ethnic-influenced music—from rai and dub reggae to Arab-flavored dance music.

Lansky Lounge
104 Norfolk St at Delancey St (677-9489). Subway: F, J, M, Z to Delancey St. Hours vary with event. Only in New York would you find a speakeasy (complete with live swing bands) in the back of a legendary kosher Jewish restaurant. The restaurant is Ratner's, and though Lansky caters to a hipster crowd (mostly from the exploding swing scene), it serves rabbi-supervised kosher drinks and is closed on Jewish holidays. Its surreptitious entrance—through a basement alley between buildings and up into the back of the restaurant—adds novelty appeal.

Ludlow Bar
165 Ludlow St between Houston and Rivington Sts (353-0536). Subway: F to Second Ave. 6pm–4am. Ludlow is simply and tastefully appointed and features some of the more progressive music you'll hear on the Lower East Side—although, like many spots in the area, it's subject to suburban slummers. DJs spin every night, playing jazz, trip-hop, hip-hop, loungecore, drum 'n' bass, house, salsa, bossa nova and pretty much anything that's groovy.

Spy
101 Greene St between Prince and Spring Sts (343-9000). Subway: N, R to Prince St. Mon–Sun 5pm–4am. Totally trendy a couple of years ago, Spy is still a good bet for Soho people-watching. The former cabaret theater is laid out perfectly for it, with balconies and raised banquettes. DJs spin mostly mainstream lounge music. Good celebrity quotient, too.

Suzy Wong Room
E&O, 100 W Houston St between Thompson St and La Guardia Pl (254-7000). Subway: A, C, E, B, D, F, Q to W 4th St. Hours vary with event. Located in the basement of the hot pan-Asian eatery E&O, the cute little Suzy Wong Room lounge attracts trendoids itchin' to hear loungecore, salsa and more.

Void
16 Mercer St at Howard St (941-6492). Subway: J, M, N, R, Z, 6 to Canal St. Wed, Thu 8pm–2am; Fri, Sat 8pm–3am. Void, as you might expect from the name, is dark, stark and minimalist. A giant video screen engulfs one wall, and there are monitors embedded in the cocktail tables. Musically, you get DJs spinning armchair techno or live bands playing jazz.

*Ready for takeoff: The jet set chills at **Idlewild**.*

hair like Rod Stewart; they're probably the owners. Coney Island High hosts a variety of (mainly rock-oriented) club nights, such as Version City, a ska party held every other Saturday, and Trailer Park, a gay punk/glam rock night each Tuesday. Live bands are as common as DJs here.

Copacabana

617 W 57th St between Eleventh and Twelfth Aves (582-2672). Subway: A, C, B, D, 1, 9 to 59th St–Columbus Circle. Jun–Aug Tue 6pm–3am, Thu–Sat 6pm–4am; Sept–May Tue 6pm–3am, Fri 6pm–5am, Sat 10am–5pm. The famous Copa is a classy disco catering to a 25-plus, mainly black and Hispanic clientele. Although this isn't the same space Barry Manilow sang about, the look and feel have been preserved. A live band plays salsa and merengue every night and DJs fill the gaps with hip-hop, R&B and Latin sounds. You saw it looking its best in Martin Scorsese's *Goodfellas*. The dress code requires customers to look "casual but nice;" no jeans, sneakers or work boots, and gents must wear shirts with collars.

Don Hill's

511 Greenwich St at Spring St (334-1390). Subway 1, 9 to Houston Street. Tue–Sun 10pm–4am. Half dance club, half live music venue, its best night, Squeezebox, combines both: It's a gay rock party, with live bands and a drag queen DJ spinning glammy, punky, scummy rock for a mixed crowd (but queer in appearance and sensibility). All night, fashion and music celebrities drop by this festive alternative to house music.

Fahrenheit

349 Broadway at Leonard St (343-0957). Subway: A, C, E, 2, 3 to Chambers St. Hours vary with event. Most of the club caters to mature, middle- and middle-class Latino, African-American, Caribbean and African singles. The music generally ranges from hip-hop, R&B, house and classics to soca, reggae, African and Latin music.

Flamingo East

219 Second Ave between 13th and 14th Sts (533-2860). Subway: L to Third Ave; N, R, 4, 5, 6 to 14th St–Union Sq. Hours vary with event. Long ago, Flamingo East was some bon vivant's townhouse. Although the five-year-old party fittingly called Salon Wednesdays has a (largely deserved) reputation as a fashion-fag hangout, all are welcome. Besides the cruising and networking, the upstairs room features groovy disco and house, and you'll come across music industry types as well as fashionistas. Salon hosts some great drag shows, too. About a month, the promoters clear the tables and chairs downstairs, set up a DJ booth and turn the restaurant area into a pumping deep house dance floor, manned by DJ Emjay.

The Greatest Bar on Earth

1 World Trade Center, West St between Liberty and Vesey Sts, 107th floor (524-7000). Subway: C, E to World Trade Center; N, R to Cortlandt St. Hours vary with event. This restaurant and bar on top of the World Trade Center is the kind of place you'd take your cousins from Indiana, but in the past year or two, this bar has cleverly courted New York's trendies by adding lounge-core DJs to its lineup of middle-aged crooners and cover bands. Wednesday night's Mondo 107 night is the most popular, with a mix of vintage exotica and newer stuff in that vein (Pizzicato Five, Dimitri from Paris, etc.). While it's probably peaked as a hotspot—it's still fun, especially for the view on a clear night.

Kit Kat Klub

124 W 43rd St between Sixth Ave and Broadway (819-0377). Subway: B, D, F, Q to 42nd St. Fri–Sun 10pm–4am. Originally the Henry Miller Theater, the building was home to Xenon during the disco era. It's just been revamped, this time with a *Cabaret* theme; it also officially became a theater again.

ing a revival of the musical early in the evening. The place still looks rough around the edges, but there's charm in the chaos and decrepitude. Sunday's Café Con Leche party is an excellent, long-running night with Hispanic flavor for the gay, straight, undecided and impossible to tell. With pumping Latin hard house that's sometimes cheesy but always energetic, Café is as New York as you can get.

Krystal's

8925 Merrick Blvd, Jamaica, Queens (1-718-523-3662). Subway: E, J, Z to Jamaica Center. Mon, Tue, Fri, Sat 10pm–4am. If you fancy a trip out to the boroughs, you can get a slightly grittier taste of the city's musical life. Krystal's, in the Caribbean section of Jamaica, is where you'll hear a hot mix of hip-hop and reggae, played for a boisterous local audience.

Life/The Ki Club

158 Bleecker St at Thompson St (420-1999). Subway: A, C, E, B, D, F, Q to W 4th St–Washington Sq. Thu–Sun 10pm–4am. Life opened in 1996 in Greenwich Village on the former site of the legendary jazz club the Village Gate. In a neighborhood already teeming with bars (and, on weekends, drunken suburbanites), Life is attempting to keep the community happy by playing it safe musically and demographically. Thursdays are hip, with promoter Erich Conrad drawing a beautiful, gay but decadent downtown crowd, heavy on gay and fashion types. The music is a blend of underground vocal and instrumental house, while the VIP lounge (and on Thursdays, pretty much everyone is a VIP) features classics of all kinds—disco one week, new wave the next. Boy's Life on Sundays caters to gay gym bunnies. Wednesday night's Lust for Life is also very hot at the moment, drawing a fashionable mixed-to-queer crowd into glam rock, punk and posing. You may not get in unless you're dressed up or are looking particularly fashionable.

The Lounge

Lenox Lounge, 288 Lenox Ave between 124th and 125th Sts (617-4783). Subway: 2, 3 to 125th St. Tue, Thu 10pm. Go to the heart of Harlem for this twice-a-week gay hip-hop club—a phenomenon that's not nearly as unique as you might think. House, reggae, R&B and disco classics are thrown into the musical mix, and there's a more party-minded atmosphere than at other spots in the area, or, for that matter, at Chelsea gay clubs. It's a solidly black crowd, but new faces are welcome, regardless of their complexion. DJs include NFX, Cat and veteran spinner Andre Collins.

Mother

432 W 14th St at Washington St (366-5680). Subway: A, C, E to 14th St; L to Eighth Ave. Hours vary with event. Run by longtime club faces Chi Chi Valenti and Johnny Dynell (a popular DJ), Mother is home to a variety of highly imaginative events, ranging from gay techno parties to modern-dance recitals and spoken-word evenings. On Tuesdays, Jackie 60 (the club's long-running flagship) is a fascinating mix of gay, straight and everything in between. Johnny pumps out hard but funky New York style house, and all manner of performers do their thing on stage. Lots of artists, celebrities, freaks and club royalty are regulars, though the club's longevity and many press clippings bring in the tourist crowd, too. As for the rest of the week, Clit Club is a Friday night lesbian institution, and Saturday's Click and Drag is a brilliant crossbreeding of technological and sexual fetishism (featuring Internet chat and dominatrices, among other hot-wired things). A vague dress code exists on Tuesdays and Saturdays—according to that week's theme—but is selectively enforced.

NV

289 Spring St at Hudson St (929-NVNV). Subway: 1, 9 to Canal St. Wed–Fri 4:30pm–4am, Sat 8pm–4am. NV, located just west of Soho, caters to Eurotrash, yuppies and model-worshippers, but worthwhile parties do take place on occasion. The Sunday-night Passion event draws an upscale, good-looking mixed-to-black crowd, there to groove to the music (hip-hop, R&B, classics) and each other.

Nell's

246 W 14th St between Seventh and Eighth Aves (675-1567). Subway: A, C, E to 14th St; L to Eighth Ave. 10pm–4am. More than a decade old, Nell's is much the same as it's always been. Its formula: laid-back jazz and funky soul (often with live bands) upstairs, where there's a limited dining menu, and DJed hip-hop, R&B, reggae, house and classics below. The crowd is multi-racial (leaning to black), straight and ready to spend.

Night Strike

Bowlmor Lanes, 110 University Pl between 12th and 13th Sts (255-8158). Subway: L, N, R, 4, 5, 6 to 14th St–Union Sq. Mon 10pm. Scenesters exchange their platforms for bowling shoes, while DJs spin house and techno. There's something humanizing about a crowd of full-time night-crawlers, letting their hair down and hanging out the classic American white-trash way: drinking, bowling and shootin' the shit.

Organic Grooves

Various locations; call 439-1147 for details. Fri 10:30pm. The Go Global folks throw their parties at any old space, from Lower East Side antique shops to Brooklyn's decrepit waterfront. DJ Sasha spins soupy, trippy dub funk and acid jazz, while live musicians noodle the records. It's hippyish, but funky nonetheless. The crowd tends toward the sexually straight but racially mixed (and it's not a bad-looking bunch, either).

Planet 28

215 W 28th St between Seventh and Eighth Aves (726-8820). Subway: A, C, E to 34th St–Penn Station; 1, 9 to 28th St. Hours vary with event. Planet 28 features everything from gay black voguing balls (the fierce Clubhouse event on Wednesday is as close to *Paris Is Burning* as you're likely to get) to rave and hip-hop nights (the long-running Now & Later is currently here on Mondays, with rap DJ Stretch Armstrong).

Roxy

515 W 18th St between Tenth and Eleventh Aves (645-5156). Subway: A, C, E to 14th St; L to Eighth Ave. Hours vary with event. Until now, the Roxy was the front-runner in the Saturday night gay disco sweepstakes, and this warhorse of a club has come back to life with a steady Latin night on Fridays (featuring salsa, hip-hop, merengue, Latin house, etc.) The queens have returned on Saturdays (perhaps getting the jump on the early-'90s revival), packing the place as they used to do. The room is immense and impressive, and the sound system kicks ass. Worth a trip for first-timers.

Sapphire

249 Eldridge St between Houston and Stanton Sts (777-5153). Subway: F to Second Ave. 7pm–4am. Sapphire was one of the first trendy Lower East Side DJ bars. As such, the crowd has evolved from downtown hipsters to uptown slummers to outer-borough weekend warriors. Over the past year or so, Sapphire went to considerable lengths (and expense) to obtain a cabaret license, so it's now a legitimate (though still very small) dance club. The music is fairly typical: hip-hop, reggae, acid jazz, R&B, disco classics and the odd house tune.

XVI

16 First Ave between 1st and 2nd Sts (260-1549). Subway: F to Second Ave. Hours vary with event. The story goes that the incredibly funky basement used to be some sort of coke den

"I'm on the list": standing guard at **Life.**

and was accidentally discovered during renovation of the ground-floor storefront space. The lower level really is from a different time: all mirrored tiles, stone floors and gaudy brick arches. DJs play on both levels, though the music tends to be considerably more pedestrian than the decor. The Vampyros Lesbos party is a Thursday-night homage to the early-'70s soft-core porn/horror flicks of Spanish director Jesus Franco; DJ Franc O spins a selection of loungecore, exotica, strip-hop and other kitschy, groovy stuff from Franco films and their ilk. The crowd, meanwhile, does its best to be decadent, while slides of soft-core nudes and album sleeves illuminate the walls.

Sound Factory

618 W 46th St between Eleventh and Twelfth Aves (643-0728). Subway: A, C, E to 50th St. Hours vary with event. The long-awaited new incarnation of the legendary Sound Factory finally opened in January 1997. The space is different, but the sound system is allegedly the very same one. However, the club does not have DJ Junior Vasquez, and for many, that means it will never be the Sound Factory. The new model is more mainstream than underground. DJ Jonathan Peters spins an attack-oriented brand of hard house, with snare rolls and breakdowns seemingly every other minute. The enthusiastic Factory crowd is mixed genderwise and racially. Although closer to the politics of club promotion than its predecessor, the club is also keeping alive the long New York after-hours tradition of free munchies, offering a generous spread of fruit, cookies, potato chips, coffee and more. And it now has a full bar.

Speeed

20 W 39th St between Fifth and Sixth Aves (719-9867). Subway: B, D, F to 42nd St; 7 to Fifth Ave. Hours vary with event.

Speeed opened early in 1998 with much fanfare, and then, well… While it never achieved "in" status, it has a full line-up, mostly mainstream parties with hip-hop on the ground floor and house in the basement. The Wednesday-night event, rather regrettably called Sexy Suzy's Need for Speeed, aims to re-create the atmosphere of the old Lime-light, where an army of gender-bending club kids rubbed shoulders with yuppies, homeboys and suburbanites.

Studio 84

3534 Broadway at 145th St (234-8484). Subway: 1, 9 to 145th Street. Wed–Sun 9pm–4am. The frenzied brass of salsa and merengue can be heard throughout the city's many Spanish-speaking neighborhoods. Indulge in some Latin flavor at this energetic Dominican dance hall. DJs and live bands every night.

Tatou

151 E 50th St between Third and Lexington Aves (753-1144). Subway: 4, 5, 6 to 59th St; N, R to Lexington Ave. Mon–Sat 5pm–4am. A midtown supper-club cum-disco, Tatou is chiefly the domain of businessmen, Eurotrash and old-money types. The joint is pleasant enough in its own way. The upstairs lounge is comfy, and the DJs—who spin mostly well-known dance hits—are good at what they do. Downstairs, the dining room is turned over to dancing once the last table is cleared. Dressing up, or casually but neatly, is advised.

Thirteen

35 E 13th St at University Pl (979-6677). Subway: L, N, R, 4, 5, 6 to 14th St–Union Sq. Mon–Sun 10am–4am. In the 1980s, this postage-stamp–sized club was Peggy Sue's, a preppy hangout populated by New York University students. The club is more interesting in its new incarnation, and because the space has been a club for quite a few years, Thirteen enjoys the status of having the city's smallest legal dance floor. A variety of nights offer everything from the usual hip-hop/R&B/classics formula to rock and house music. Parties come and go, but one that has lasted is Sunday night's Shout!, which offers up Northern soul, freakbeat, 1960s psychedelic rock, garage punk and various other genres associated (rightly or wrongly) with mod.

Tunnel

220 Twelfth Ave at 27th St (695-4682). Subway: A, C, E to 23rd St. Fri 10pm–6am, Sat 11pm–noon, Sun 10–4pm. A stunningly massive place with equally impressive decor— there's a unisex bathroom complete with a bar and banquettes, a coffee house and the mind-blowingly psychedelic Cosmic Cavern, designed by pop artist Kenny Scharf (floor-to-ceiling fake fur, lava lamps, Internet terminals, black light paintings and a fountain). The 1996 police raid (and the subsequent arrest of owner Peter Gatien on drug conspiracy charges) dealt a blow to its spirit (not to mention its trendy cachet) from which the Tunnel hasn't fully recovered. However, Gatien was acquitted in January 1998, and top remixer/producer/DJ Danny Tenaglia packs the place on Saturday nights. Tenaglia is a highly regarded jock who can play anything from soulful vocal and deep house to minimal, funky techno. The main room isn't very conducive to disco epiphanies, and the crowd is mostly quite mainstream, but Tenaglia's crowd—gays, music industry types, old Garage heads—is here too. Head for one of the many smaller rooms, which usually feature more interesting music, decor and people.

Twilo

530 W 27th St between Tenth and Eleventh Aves(268-1600). Subway: C, E to 23rd St. Hours vary with event. With an immense sound system and dance floor, Twilo was designed to be a temple of music. Unfortunately, it also wants to be both underground and trendy, a difficult feat.

The result, sadly, is uneven music and crowds. Friday, the straight (i.e. mixed) night, draws lots of suburban ex-ravers who have graduated to disco shirts and club babe outfits. The music can be excellent, but the hype-driven booking policy yields uneven results; the upstairs lounge, on the other hand, has hosted everything from drum 'n' bass to loungecore. On Saturdays, Twilo attempts to re-store the magic of the old Sound Factory, with Junior Vasquez. But while the original Factory sound was hard, brutal and funky, Junior's music now is largely fluffy HiNRG, and his following has mutated from working-class, streetwise black and Latino gay kids to bourgeois white muscle clones zonked on Ketamine and more concerned with pecs and sex than dancing. Still, it's worth checking out who's playing on Fridays, and if you go on Saturday, you'll feel like you had a big night out.

205 Club

205 Chrystie St at Stanton St (473-5816). Subway: F to Second Ave. Hours vary with event. The 205 Club, like Sap-phire, is basically a nondescript bar that got hassled so much by the authorities for dancing that it went to the extraordinary step of obtaining a cabaret license. It's still a bit of a Bowery dive, but now you'll find everything from African music and reggae to hip-hop, drum 'n' bass and funk. On Fridays, Bang the Party (no relation to the U.K. house act) features solid, underground, New York–style house music by DJ E-Man and guests, including stars like David Morales and Ron Trent.

Vinyl

6 Hubert St at Hudson St (343-1379). Subway: A, C, E to Canal St; 1, 9 to Franklin St. Hours vary with event. Once home to the legendary mid-'80s disco Area and the Shelter. Vinyl echoes the Shelter's seminal NASA techno night on Fridays, hosting ravey events. Sunday afternoon's Body & Soul tea dance sees revered DJ/producer/remixer François K., along with Joe Claussell and Danny Krivit, spinning soulful house and Garage classics. It's similar to Shelter musically and conceptually, though the DJs' selections are somewhat more interesting. Ironically, Vinyl became a bit like the alcohol-free Garage when the club's liquor license was revoked in 1997.

The Warehouse

141 E 140th St between Grand Concourse and Walton Ave, Bronx (1-718-992-5974). Sat 10pm–6am. Most New York itineraries fail to include a visit to a gay black hip-hop and house club in the South Bronx. But adventurous and street-wise visitors will find the Warehouse a uniquely New York experience. Plummeting crime rates notwithstanding, the South Bronx is still probably one of the city's—hell, the nation's—worst areas. Once inside the club, though, you'll find a peaceful, friendly, attitude-free crowd. It's overwhelmingly black and queer, but all are welcome. The ground floor vibrates to the sounds of top-shelf hip-hop and R&B—neither too commercial nor too obscure. Meanwhile, on the surprisingly large main floor, it's New York–style urban house, ranging from tribal and funky sample tracks to vocal anthems.

Webster Hall

125 E 11th St between Third and Fourth Aves (353-1600). Subway: L, N, R, 4, 5, 6 to 14th St–Union Sq. Thu–Sat 10pm–4am. Webster Hall is an out-and-out commercial nightclub worth visiting in a fun-night-out-with-your-friends sort of way. There are four or five different main-stream musical zones, and though the crowd is essentially a suburban influx, there are a few New York freaks, special attractions (like the trapeze artists) and rampant hetero hormones to amuse newcomers.

Dance

**From Balanchine ballerinas to postmodern "Graham Crackers,"
terpsichorean New York is just tutu fabulous**

It's difficult to say exactly where and when modern dance was born, but one thing's for sure: It was raised and cultivated in New York, where it has flourished for nearly a century. Perhaps the most intriguing aspect of the contemporary dance scene in New York is that it's so varied; not only do the companies of late greats like Martha Graham and José Limón perform annually at City Center or the Joyce Theater, but a variety of emerging choreographers can be seen nearly every night of the week. Established modern choreographers such as Paul Taylor, Merce Cunningham, Trisha Brown, Bill T. Jones and Mark Morris present their companies fairly regularly at the Brooklyn Academy of Music, City Center and the Joyce, while experimental downtown venues like P.S. 122, Movement Research at the Judson Church, Danspace Project at St Mark's Church and Dance Theater Workshop

are excellent spaces to view the unexpected. These tickets are never more than $15—and though the choreographers are taken quite seriously, the crowds are, refreshingly, without airs.

Dance in New York has never been as well-funded as in Europe, and the ranks of choreographers have diminished since the '80s. Still, the scene is vital, and every year, choreographers such as Stephen Petronio, Doug Varone, Elisa Monte and Jennifer Muller make strides in their field. In fact, no other city in the world boasts such a high caliber of established companies and emerging choreographers. Of the two major seasons—from October to December and March to June—the spring stretch is decidedly the richer. Along with modern dance companies fighting for attention each weekend, both ballet troupes—New York City Ballet (NYCB), George Balanchine's neoclassical compa-

*Hi, Mom: The "Graham Crackers" spoof the mother of modern dance in **Martha at Mother**.*

ny, and American Ballet Theatre (ABT), which presents full-length classics—are in full swing.

The two ballet companies dazzle in different ways. At ABT, it's all romance, with captivating productions of classic ballets such as *Romeo and Juliet* and *The Sleeping Beauty*. It's the dancers who keep devoted fans in awe—and mainly, for that matter, it's the dashing men who do it: Angel Corella, Ethan Steifel, Vladimir Malakov and José Carreño. Pairings between young dancers like Corella and Paloma Herrera are stunning, but even better is the more mature partnering of older stars such as Carreño and Susan Jaffe. At NYCB, it's the stunning choreography that matters. Here, the dancers themselves aren't publicized (although as the cast lists printed inside the door of the New York State Theater each week attest, they do matter). The company is famously spontaneous: You're likely to see a star or two, but perhaps more exciting is to watch a corps dancer make a grand debut in a principal role.

Other classical companies include the Dance Theatre of Harlem. In 1968, motivated by news of Martin Luther King's assassination, former NYCB dancer Arthur Mitchell decided to devote himself to giving the children of Harlem the same opportunities he had enjoyed. After teaching out of a remodeled garage for a time, he founded the professional company and dance school with Karel Shook, his teacher and mentor. The troupe now makes more appearances at the Kennedy Center in Washington, D.C., than at the City Center, but offers informal performances at the school, as well as occasional stints at Harlem's Aaron Davis Hall. Another small but respected company is Eliot Feld's Ballet Tech, made up of his students, many of whom were plucked as children from auditions held in New York's public schools. Regional ballets perform at City Center or the Joyce; international companies, such as the Paris Opéra Ballet, usually grace the stage of the Metropolitan Opera House.

The Theater Development Fund's NYC/On Stage service (*see page 285*) offers information on all theater, dance and music events in town. For information on weekly performances, see *Time Out New York*, which covers everything from ballet to tap and modern dance, previews selected shows and lists dance classes. *The Village Voice* covers the downtown scene, and the Sunday *New York Times* includes a box of dance listings for the week. *Dance Magazine* ($3.95, monthly) is a good way to find out about a performance well ahead of time.

Ballet

Lincoln Center

Even if you don't have a ticket (or worse, it's not the right *season*), it's awfully satisfying to stand in the middle of all this dance history. Along with the ballets at the New York State Theater and the Metropolitan Opera House, there are a handful of dance performances held at the Clark Studio Theater, located in the David Rose Building, which is also home to the School of American Ballet (SAB), founded by Balanchine and Lincoln Kirstein. One of the most thrilling weekends for ballet addicts comes each June, when students from SAB present their annual workshop performances. As every dance fan knows, the next Darci Kistler might be waiting in the wings.

New York State Theater
Broadway at 63rd St (870-5570). Subway: 1, 9 to 66th St. $10–$82. AmEx, MC, V (telephone bookings only; $1 surcharge). Both the neoclassical New York City Ballet and

'Tis the season

Tchaikovsky secures a toehold and takes the town by twirl

In 1892, the great Marius Petipa and his assistant Lev Ivanov staged the original *Nutcracker*. Many versions of this Christmas tale give the city a lovely dash of Tchaikovsky each December, but George Balanchine's 1954 classic for the New York City Ballet is the most beloved—marzipan and all. Balanchine introduced Dewdrop, a leader for the "Waltz of the Flowers" and added new choreography for the Sugarplum Fairy's pas de deux with her Cavalier. Catch it at the State Theater from late November to early January—though it's a hot ticket, a trip to the box office will often turn up seats.

Other alternatives include Donald Byrd's *Harlem Nutcracker*. Set to Duke Ellington's spectacular arrangement of Tchaikovsky's *Nutcracker Suite,* it tells the poignant story of a widow, Clara, who grieves for her husband on Christmas Eve. In the second act, Byrd's company transports you to the Cotton Club. New York Theater Ballet presents a one-hour version geared toward children aged three to six. A group called Dances...Patrelle features Francis Patrelle's 19th-century *The Yorkville Nutcracker,* part of which is set in Central Park. And even the Rockettes get into the act at Radio City Music Hall (*see chapter* **Music**), doing their mighty kicks to excerpts from Tchaikovsky's great score.

New York City Opera hold court at this opulent garnet theater, which Philip Johnson designed to resemble a jewel box. NYCB hosts two seasons: Winter begins just before Thanksgiving, featuring more than a month of *Nutcracker* performances (*see* **'Tis the season**), and runs until the beginning of March; the spring season usually begins in April or May and lasts for eight weeks. Each season features plenty of repertory works by NYCB founder George Balanchine, founding choreographer Jerome Robbins and current ballet master-in-chief Peter Martins, as well as "Diamond Project" premieres—past choreographers include Angelin Preljocaj, Kevin O'Day and David Parsons. Even from the inexpensive fourth-ring seats, the view is unobstructed, but the best seats in the house are in the first ring, where the music is best appreciated, and one can enjoy the dazzling patterns of the lovely *corps de ballet*. The stage, 89 by 58 feet, was made to Balanchine's specifications.

Metropolitan Opera House

Broadway at 64th St (362-6000). Subway: 1, 9 to 66th St. $24–$145. AmEx, MC, V. Internet: www.metopera.org
During the autumn and winter, this institution is the land of the Metropolitan Opera; spring belongs to American Ballet Theatre. Founded in 1939 by Mikhail Mordkin as Ballet Theatre, the company offered classics and new works created by Mordkin in a traditional Russian style. The focus of ABT is still predominantly classical; along with ballet staples such as *La Bayadère, Giselle* and *Swan Lake*, artistic director Kevin McKenzie occasionally slips in an evening of Twyla Tharp or individual works by Anthony Tudor. Last year, Lar Lubovitch's full-length *Othello* was the most talked-about ballet of the season. ABT continues its two-week City Center fall season (Oct 26–Nov 8) with two world premieres and revivals of Antony Tudor's *Gala Performance* and *Pillar of Fire* and Anton Dolin's *Variations for Four*. Apart from ABT, the Met also hosts a range of top international companies. The acoustics are wonderful, but the theater is vast, so sit as close as you can afford.

Brooklyn Academy of Music

Opera House: 30 Lafayette Ave between Flatbush Ave and Fulton St (718-636-4100). $15–$60. Majestic Theater: 651 Fulton St between Ashland St and Rockwell Pl (718-636-4181). $10–40. Subway: B, D, Q, 2, 3, 4, 5, to Atlantic Ave; B, N, R to Pacific St. AmEx, MC, V. Internet: www.bam.org
Traveling to Brooklyn really isn't so difficult or so scary and BAM, as it's affectionately known, showcases many superb modern and out-of-town companies. BAM's Opera House, with its federal-style columns and carved marble, is one of the most beautiful stages for dance to be found in the city. (Mark Morris, always loyal to his roots, still performs here when he's in town.) The Majestic Theater, just around the corner, originally opened in 1904 and has played host to modern choreographers Ralph Lemon and David Roussève as well as a wealth of theater companies. The Next Wave Festival each autumn showcases both experimental and established dance and music groups, and during the spring, short festivals focus on ballet, tap, hip-hop and modern dance.

City Center Theater

131 W 55th St between Sixth and Seventh Aves (581-7907). Subway: B, D, E to Seventh Ave. $25–$50. AmEx, MC, V. Before the creation of Lincoln Center changed the cultural geography of New York, this was the home of the New York City Ballet (originally known as the Ballet Society), the Joffrey Ballet and American Ballet Theatre. The lavish decor is all golden; so are the established companies that pass through, including the Paul Taylor Dance Company (*see* **Alchemy on the hoof**), the Alvin Ailey American Dance Theater and the Martha Graham Dance Company. Les Ballets Russes de Monte Carlo is scheduled to perform in the spring (Apr 21–26).

Alchemy on the hoof

Modern master Paul Taylor puts together the pieces of a dream

Paul Taylor has performed with Pearl Lang, Merce Cunningham and Martha Graham, but his rich dance lineage isn't as impressive as his choreographic career, which has spanned more than 40 years. His offbeat, bittersweet work is full of mixed emotions—the seemingly funny pieces are the darkest. And like Balanchine before him, Taylor possesses the uncanny ability to allow you to see the music through the dance. Last season, Taylor premiered *The Word,* a haunting look at issues of conformity and morality, and *Piazzolla Caldera,* a steamy tango. His annual City Center engagement (Mar 9–21) is awaited anxiously by dance fans and critics alike. No one can really predict what he'll come up with next, but one thing's for sure: It'll be brilliant.

Taylor-made: Paul Taylor's Prime Numbers.

Joyce Theater

175 Eighth Ave at 19th St (242-0800). Subway: 1, 9 to 18th St; A, C, E to 23rd St. $7–$35. AmEx, DC, Disc, MC, V. Internet: www.joyce.org. The Joyce, once a vacant movie house, is one of the finest theaters in town. It's intimate, but not too small; of the 472 seats, there's not a bad one in the house. Choreographers ranging from Doug Elkins and David Dorfman to Bill T. Jones and Margie Gillis have performed recently. In residence is Eliot Feld's company, Ballet Tech. Feld, who began his performing career in Balanchine's *The Nutcracker* and Robbins's *West Side Story*, presents his company in two monthlong seasons (one in March, the other in July). The Joyce also plays host to a variety of out-of-town ensembles, along with a few staples, including the Pilobolus Dance Theatre in June and the Altogether Different Festival in January. During the summer, when many theaters are dark, the Joyce schedule often includes close to a dozen companies. The Joyce Soho offers rehearsal space for less-established choreographers and also showcases work.

Branch: Joyce Soho *155 Mercer St between Houston and Prince Sts (431-9233). Subway: B, D, F, Q to Broadway–Lafayette St; N, R to Prince St. $10–$15. No credit cards.*

Alternative venues

Aaron Davis Hall at City College

135th St at Convent Ave (650-7148). Subway: 1, 9 to 137th St. $15–$100. No credit cards. It's a trek, but worth it. Troupes here often celebrate African-American life and culture. Among the companies that have appeared at Davis: Donald Byrd/The Group and the Alvin Ailey Repertory Ensemble.

Merce Cunningham Studio

55 Bethune St between Washington and West Sts, 11th floor (691-9751). Subway: A, C, E to 14th St; 1, 9 to Christopher St. $5–$30. No credit cards. Located in the Westbeth complex on the edge of Greenwich Village (no matter which subway you take, be prepared for a good, wind-blown walk), the Cunningham Studio is rented by individual choreographers who don't feel like waiting to be asked to join DTW's lineup. As can be imagined, the quality of performances ranges from wonderful to horrid. Since the stage and the seating area are in Cunningham's large studio, be prepared to take off your shoes. Arrive early, too, or you'll have to sit on the floor. For more details, contact the Cunningham Dance Foundation (255-8240).

Dance Theater Workshop

Bessie Schönberg Theater, 219 W 19th St between Seventh and Eighth Aves (691-6500/box office 924-0077). Subway: 1, 9 to 18th St; C, E to 23rd St. $12–$15. AmEx, MC, V. Pointe shoes are generally looked down upon at this haven for experimental dance and theater. During popular shows, cushions are tossed on the floor for those without a seat (but reservations are taken). Drop by the intimate theater at any time for a schedule. It's one of the most user-friendly and best organized of the downtown venues, and a must-see if you're interested in exploring the full range of New York dance. You probably won't see performances by anyone now famous — but someday they might be. DTW has launched the careers of dozens of acclaimed artists, including Bill T. Jones, Mark Morris and Whoopi Goldberg.

Danspace Project

St Mark's Church in-the-Bowery, Second Ave at 10th St (674-8194). Subway: N, R, 4, 5, 6 to Union Sq; L to Third Ave. $12. No credit cards. A gorgeous, high-ceilinged sanctuary for downtown dance that is even more otherworldly when the music is live. Downtown choreographers are selected by the director, Laurie Uprichard, whose standards are, thankfully, high. Regular programs include: Global Exchange/Danza Libre, which features international artists and collabora-

Knight moves: **ABT** flirts with Don Quixote.

tions between choreographers; City/Dans, which focuses on New York choreographers; and Lone Stars, which showcases local artists.

The Kitchen

512 W 19th St between Tenth and Eleventh Aves (255-5793). Subway: A, C, E to 14th St; L to Eighth Ave. $8–$25. AmEx, MC, V. Best known as an avant-garde theater space, the Kitchen also features experimental choreographers from New York and elsewhere, occasionally including a multimedia element.

Martha at Mother

432 W 14th St at Washington St (642-5005). Subway: A, C, E to 14th St; L to Eighth Ave. 8, 10pm. $15. No credit cards. Richard Move and Janet Stapleton present their hilarious, award–winning series the first Wednesday of every month. Portraying Martha Graham, the mother of modern dance, Move hosts the evening; he's joined by an ensemble of "Graham Crackers" each month. As always, Martha introduces the evening's guest artists with short dance "herstory" lectures. Brilliant choreographers like Gus Solomons Jr, Keely Garfield and Jennifer Monson have presented their work in the past, but no one can top Move. Innovative, fresh and *highly* recommended (*see photo, page 232*).

Movement Research at Judson Church

55 Washington Sq South at Thompson St (477-6854). Subway: A, C, E, B, D, F, Q to W 4th St–Washington Sq. Free. Director Catherine Levine carries on the tradition of free Monday night performances at the Judson Church, a custom started in the 1960s by avant-garde choreographers Yvonne Rainer, Steve Paxton and Trisha Brown. At least two choreographers perform each night; the artists can be either established and emerging. The series runs from September to June. MR also offers a vast selection of classes and workshops, which are held at Context Studio and Danspace Project. Lectures are also held from time to time.

The New Jersey Performing Arts Center

1 Center St between Ronald H. Brown St and Park Pl, Newark, New Jersey (1-888-466-5722). Travel: PATH to Newark. $15–$60. AmEx, D, MC, V. The New Jersey Performing Arts

Center serves as home base for the New Jersey Symphony Orchestra and has hosted choreographers like Paulo Ribeiro and Donald Byrd. Large, open theaters make NJPAC a choice venue for dance.

P.S. 122

150 First Ave at 9th St (477-5288). Subway: 6 to Astor Pl, F to Second Ave, L to First Ave. $9-$15. AmEx, MC, V. Located in the heart of the East Village, P.S. 122 was once a public school (hence, the P.S.) and is now a performance space. It's dedicated to presenting emerging choreographers (as well as the occasional established talent) in new and unconventional works.

Playhouse 91

316 E 91st St between First and Second Aves (996-1100). Subway: 4, 5, 6 to 86th St; 6 to 96th St. $15. AmEx, MC, V. The annual monthlong 92nd Street Y Harkness Dance Project is presented uptown, at Playhouse 91. Last year's participants included Neil Greenberg, Neta Pulvermacher and Maia Claire Garrison. The festival is held each spring.

Symphony Space

2537 Broadway at 95th St (864-1414). Subway 1, 2, 3, 9 to 96th St. $10-$20. AmEx, MC, V. Located on an ungentrified stretch of upper Broadway, this is a center for all the performing arts. The World Music Institute produces many international dance troupes here.

Summer performances

Central Park SummerStage

Central Park, Rumsey Playfield at 72nd St (360-2777). Subway: B, C to 72nd St; 6 to 68th St. Free. This outdoor dance series runs on Fridays in July and the first couple of weeks in August. Temperatures can get steamy, but just think how the *dancers* must feel.

Dances for Wave Hill

W 249th St at Independence Ave, Riverdale, Bronx (989-6830). Subway: 1, 9 to 231st St, then Bx7, Bx10 or Bx24 bus to 252nd St. $4. No credit cards. This is a gorgeous setting for outdoor dance. The series, sponsored by Dancing in the Streets, runs in July.

Bargains

Theater Development Fund

1501 Broadway between 43rd and 44th Sts (221-0013). Subway: N, R, 1, 2, 3, 9, 7 to 42nd St–Times Sq. No credit cards. TDF offers a book of four vouchers for $28, which can be purchased at the TDF offices by visitors who bring their passport or out-of-state driver's license. Each voucher is good for one admission at Off-Off-Broadway music, theater and dance events, at venues such as the Joyce, the Kitchen, Dance Theater Workshop and P.S. 122. TDF also provides information by phone on all theater, dance and music events in town with its NYC/On Stage service (768-1818). *See also chapter* **Theater**.

Dance shopping

Both the New York City Ballet and American Ballet Theatre have gift shops, open during intermission, selling everything from autographed pointe shoes to ballet-themed T-shirts, nightlights and jewelry.

Capezio Dance-Theater Shop

1650 Broadway at 51st St (245-2130). Subway: C, E, 1, 9 to 50th St.; N, R to 49th St. Mon–Wed, Fri 9:30am–6:30pm;

Thu 9:30am–7pm, Sat 9:30am–6pm; Sun 11am–5pm. ● *136 E 61st St between Lexington and Park Aves (758-8833). Subway: N, R to Lexington Ave; 4, 5, 6 to 59th St. Mon, Fri 10am–6:30pm; Tue–Thu 10am–7pm; Sat 11am–6pm; Sun noon–5pm.* ● *1776 Broadway at 57th St (586-5140). Subway: A, C, B, D, 1, 9 to 59th St–Columbus Circle. Mon–Fri 10am–7pm, Sat 10am–6pm, Sun noon–5pm. AmEx, MC, V.* Capezio carries a good stock of professional-quality shoes, practice and performance gear, as well as dance duds that can be worn on the street.

KD Dance

339 Lafayette St at Bleecker St (533-1037). Subway: B, D, F, Q to Broadway–Lafayette St; 6 to Bleecker St. Mon–Sat noon–8pm. AmEx, MC, V. This shop, owned by Tricia Kaye, former principal dancer and ballet mistress of the Oakland Ballet, and dancer David Lee, features the softest, prettiest dance knits available.

Dance schools

Most major companies have their own schools. Amateurs are welcome at the following (classes for beginners start at $10 per session):

Alvin Ailey American Dance Center

211 W 61st St between Amsterdam and West End Aves, third floor (767-0940). Subway: A, C, B, D, 1, 9 to 59th St–Columbus Circle. Modern dance, tap, ballet.

American Ballet Theatre

890 Broadway at 19th St, third floor (477 3030). Subway: N, R to 23rd St; L to Sixth Ave. Classical ballet.

Ballet Hispanico School of Dance

167 W 89th St between Columbus and Amsterdam Aves (362-6710). Subway: 1, 9 to 86th St All styles of Latin and Spanish dance, including Flamenco.

Merce Cunningham Studio

55 Bethune St at Washington St (691-9751). Subway: A, C, E, 1, 2, 3, 9 to 14th St; L to Eighth Ave. Merce Cunningham technique.

Dance Space Inc.

622 Broadway between Bleecker and Houston Sts, sixth floor (777-8067). Subway: B, D, F, Q to Broadway–Lafayette St; 6 to Bleecker St. Simonson jazz, yoga, modern dance, ballet and stretch.

DanceSport

1845 Broadway at 60th St (307-1111). Subway A, C, B, D, 1, 9 to 59th St–Columbus Circle. Ballroom and Latin.

Martha Graham School

316 E 63rd St between First and Second Aves (838-5886). Subway: 4, 5, 6 to 59th St; N, R to Lexington Ave. Martha Graham technique.

Limón Institute

611 Broadway between Houston and Bleecker Sts, ninth floor (777-3353). Subway: B, D, F, Q to Broadway–Lafayette St; 6 to Bleecker St. José Limón and Doris Humphrey technique.

Paul Taylor School

552 Broadway between Prince and Spring Sts, second floor (431-5562). Subway: B, D, F, Q to Broadway–Lafayette St; 6 to Bleecker St. Daily modern technique class.

Film

If life is a movie, then New York City is the greatest set ever built

Visitors often feel as if they're in the middle of a movie as soon as they set foot on the mean streets of New York. It's not just the heightened intensity and quick-change pace of Manhattan life, it's the fact that many of the city's street corners have been the site of some cinematic drama, whether it's Lorraine Bracco taunting Ray Liotta in *Goodfellas* or Spike Lee tossing a trash can through a window in *Do the Right Thing.*

And the prospect of running into a movie being shot here—whether a Hollywood thriller or an angst-filled indie—is increasingly likely. With its recent rise in film projects, New York could be renamed Cin City: 213 movies were made in 1997, more than in any previous year. With better relations between production companies and local labor unions, and a mayor determined to boost film

and TV production, the film business is booming. Hollywood projects—especially savvy urban romances like *You've Got Mail* and megastar flicks like *The Out-of-Towners*—are back in force, while the indie community can often be found shooting on the Lower East Side and the East Village, making use of the areas' low-life atmosphere.

For viewing the finished product, there are hundreds of screens throughout the metropolis, from the deluxe 12-plex blockbuster mecca Sony Lincoln Square to one of the nation's premier homes for experimental film, the Anthology Film Archives. New Yorkers are famously knowledgeable about film; on opening nights of the latest blockbuster (or Scorsese picture), lines often wind around the corner and "Sold Out" signs are posted to ticket-sellers' windows. To guarantee seats for

Now playing: The Metro, on the Upper West Side, still bears its original Art Deco marquee.

the latest *Titanic* on its first weekend, call the automated 777-FILM ticket system well in advance.

New York is often used as a test market, so you can catch first-run films here long before they open in the rest of the country (and months or years before they get distributed in the U.K). It's also possible to be in on the birth of the filmmaking process; screenplay readings held at the Nuyorican Poets Cafe (*see chapter* **Books & Poetry**) have led to several production deals for local writers.

For those who want to bring home some cinematic goodies, check out the mammoth Warner Bros. Studio Store (*see chapter* **Shopping & Services**) for everything from Bugs Bunny memorabilia to

Casablanca swag. Anyone who wants to feel close to Mr. New York, Robert De Niro, must make a visit to his elegant Tribeca Grill (375 Greenwich Ave at Franklin St; 941-3900). De Niro's production offices are upstairs, and his late father's brilliantly hued paintings decorate the bistro's walls.

For the latest listings, including the whereabouts of your nearest first-run cinema, pick up the weekly *Time Out New York* or consult the film sections of *The Village Voice, New York* or *The New York Times*. And, if you stumble across a film set, remember that when they yell "Action!" it's time to hush up and watch.

For video rental stores, *see chapter* **Shopping & Services**.

The Goodfella's top ten

Legendary director Martin Scorsese lists his favorite New York films

The Musketeers of Pig Alley: "This D.W. Griffith short is astonishing. It's Lillian Gish's first film, and it's also the beginning of the gangster genre."

The Crowd: "King Vidor's film deals with a different side of New York life—middle-class desperation, the pressure of trying to make a decent living.… It mixes elements of expressionism with very sensitive location work."

Twentieth Century: "Only the beginning of Howard Hawks's film takes place in New York, but the insane energy between John Barrymore and Carole Lombard is pure Broadway throughout."

Midnight Cowboy: "A great, poignant film about the delusional side of New York."

Bad Lieutenant: "It's about the way the city can wear you down into nothing, and then when you've hit absolute rock bottom, you find grace."

The Seventh Victim: "It's about a cult of devil worshipers in Greenwich Village, and it uses the bohemian atmosphere in a delicately eerie way."

Shadows: "This John Cassavetes picture was a revelation for me, an almost unbearably truthful vision of people that seemed like it was grabbed off the streets."

Manhattan: "No list would be complete without mentioning Woody Allen. This is a great, bittersweet valentine to the city."

Escape From New York: "A very important film for anyone crazy enough to live here."

Rosemary's Baby: "Anything familiar about uptown Manhattan suddenly becomes strange, as if you're seeing it with new eyes."

Dark men: Dustin Hoffman in Midnight Cowboy *(left); John Cassavetes' Shadows.*

Popular cinemas

There are scores of first-run movie theaters throughout the city. New releases come and go relatively quickly; if a film does badly it might only show for a couple of weeks. Tickets usually cost $8.50–$9, with discounts for children and senior citizens (usually restricted to weekday afternoons). Friday is the opening night for most films, and the lines then can be staggeringly long. If you are lining up, check whether you're in the "ticket buyers' line" or the "ticket holders' line." The first showings on Saturday or Sunday (around noon or 1pm) are relatively free of crowds, even for brand-new releases.

Cineplex Odeon Encore Worldwide

340 W 50th St at Eighth Ave (246-1583). Subway: C, E, 1, 9 to 50th St. $3. AmEx, MC, V. Although you won't see the latest openings, you can check out recent Hollywood releases—for only three bucks a shot—at this six-screen theater.

Sony Lincoln Square

1998 Broadway at 68th St (336-5000/credit card reservations 228-7669). Subway: 1, 9 to 66th St. $9; $6.50 concessions. Imax tickets $9.50; $7.50 concessions. AmEx, MC, V. Across Broadway from the high culture of Lincoln Center, Sony has constructed a cinematic entertainment center that's more a theme park than a dull old multiplex. There are fiberglass decorations that conjure up classic movie sets; enough popcorn vendors to bloat entire armies; a gift shop selling movie memorabilia; and 12 fairly large screens (the one in the Loews Auditorium is the city's biggest for first-run features). The added attraction is the center's eight-story Imax screen, which apart from being truly enormous can also accommodate 3-D films (viewed through special headsets). Films screened here are the usual show-off-the-technology stuff (cities of the future and ultra-vivid underwater adventures) that last 35 to 45 minutes each. Services for the hearing-impaired are available.

The Ziegfeld

141 W 54th St between Sixth and Seventh Aves (765-7600). Subway: B, D, E to Seventh Ave. $9; $5.50 concessions. AmEx, MC, V. A place rich in history, once home to the Ziegfeld Follies, and still the grandest picture palace in town. It is often the venue for glitzy New York premieres.

Revival and art houses

The following cinemas specialize in showing art movies or old films.

Angelika Film Center

Houston and Mercer Sts (995-2000/box office 995-2570). Subway: 6 to Bleecker St; B, D, F, Q to Broadway–Lafayette St; N, R to Prince St. $8.50; $5 concessions. No credit cards. Popular with local NYU students, the Angelica is a six-screen cinema with diverse programming, featuring primarily new American independent and foreign films. There's an espresso-and-pastry bar to hang out in before or after the show.

Cinema Village

22 E 12th St between Fifth Ave and University Pl (924-3363/box office 924-3364). Subway: L, N, R, 4, 5, 6 to Union Square. $8; $4 concessions. No credit cards. Cinema Village specializes in small, American independent and foreign films that don't find their way into the more mainstream Angelica and Lincoln Plaza cinemas. The theater also hosts

Quiet on the set: Indie filmmakers grab a shot in Central Park, a popular location.

mini-festivals (Hong Kong action films are a popular attraction) and runs midnight horror shows on weekends.

A Different Light

151 W 19th St between Sixth and Seventh Ave South (989-4850). Subway: 1, 9 to 18th St. Free. A Different Light is a gay-themed bookstore that hosts Sunday-night screenings of screamers like *A Star Is Born, All About Eve* or anything starring queer icons Bette Davis, Joan Crawford or Tallulah Bankhead. Get ready for some major audience participation.

Film Forum

209 W Houston St between Sixth Ave and Varick St (727-8110/box office 727-8112). Subway: 1, 9 to Houston St. $8; $4.50 concessions. No credit cards. On Soho's edge, the three-screen Film Forum offers some of the best new films, documentaries and art movies around. Series or revivals, usually brilliantly curated, are also shown.

The Kitchen

See chapter **Dance** *for listings.* New York's oldest experimental arts center, the Kitchen presents innovative and alternative work by avant-garde video- and filmmakers.

Lincoln Plaza Cinemas

30 Lincoln Plaza, entrance on Broadway between 62nd and 63rd Sts (757-2280). Subway: A, C, B, D, 1, 9 to 59th St–Columbus Circle. $8.50; $5 concessions. No credit cards at box office. Commercially successful and worthy European art-house movies can be seen here alongside biggish American independent productions.

Quad Cinema

34 W 13th St between Fifth and Sixth Aves (255-8800/box office 255-2243). Subway: L, N, R, 4, 5, 6 to 14th St–Union Sq; F to 14th St. $8; $4 concessions. No credit cards. Four tiny screens show a broad selection of foreign films, American independents and documentaries, with a preponderance of those dealing with sexual and political issues. Often, these are movies you can't see anywhere else (or end up here after a short run elsewhere).

Sony Paris

4 W 58th St between Fifth and Sixth Aves (980-5656). Subway: N, R to Fifth Ave. $8.50; $5 concessions. No credit cards. Situated beside Bergdorf Goodman and across from the Plaza Hotel, the Paris has a stylish program of European art-house movies, alongside such eminently revivable films as Buñuel's *Belle de Jour.*

Museums and societies

Special film series and experimental films often appear in museums and galleries other than those listed here. Check *Time Out New York* or *The Village Voice* for details. *See also chapter* **Museums.**

American Museum of the Moving Image

See chapter **Museums** *for listings.* The first museum in the U.S. devoted to moving pictures is in Queens. More than 700 films and videos are shown each year, covering everything from Hollywood classics and series devoted to a single actor or director to industrial safety films. The schedule is inspired and entertaining.

Anthology Film Archives

32 Second Ave at 2nd St (505-5181). Subway: 6 to Bleecker Street; F to Second Ave. $7; $1–$5 concessions. No credit cards. Anthology is one of New York's treasures, housing the world's largest collection of written material documenting the history of independent film- and video-making. The Archives are sponsored by some of the biggest names in film and have a full program of movies, talks and lectures.

Film Society of Lincoln Center

Lincoln Center, 65th St between Broadway and Amsterdam Ave (875-5610). Subway: 1, 9 to 66th St. $8.50; $5 concessions. No credit cards. The Society was founded in 1969 to promote film and support filmmakers. It operates the Walter Reade Theater (built in 1991), a state-of-the-art showcase for contemporary film and video—with the most comfortable theater seats in New York. The program is usually organized in series built around a theme, often with a decidedly international perspective. Each autumn, the society hosts the **New York Film Festival** *(see page TK)*.

Imax Theater

American Museum of Natural History. See chapter **Museums** *for listings. Screenings every hour on the half-hour, Mon-Thur, Sun 10:30am-4:30pm; Fri, Sat 10:30am-7:30pm. Museum admission plus $12 or more (varies). AmEx, DC, V.* The Imax screen is four stories high and the daily programs concentrate on the natural world. On weekends, it is usually crowded with children and their parents.

International Center of Photography

See chapter **Museums** *for listings.* The ICP holds regular film screenings, mostly dealing with the history and technique of photography.

Metropolitan Museum of Art

See chapter **Museums** *for listings.* The Met shows a full program of documentary films on art (many of which relate to exhibitions on display) in the Uris Center Auditorium (near the 81st Street entrance). In addition, there are occasional themed series, with weekend showings.

Millennium Film Workshop

66 E 4th St between Second Ave and the Bowery (673-0090). Subway: F to Second Ave. $6 non-members, $4 members. No credit cards. This media-arts center conducts filmmaking classes and workshops, and screens avant-garde works, sometimes introduced by the films' directors.

Museum of Modern Art

See chapter **Museums** *for listings.* MoMA was one of the first museums to recognize film as an art form. Its first director, Alfred H. Barr, believed that film was "the only great art peculiar to the 20th century." The museum has massive archives of films, to which film scholars and researchers have access (appointments must be made in writ-

*A funny thing happened in the line for **Film Forum:** Cinema fanatics convene nightly.*

Screen test

Settle into the best seats in these great houses

We rate these New York cinemas best for...

Blockbusters: The Ziegfeld; Sony Lincoln Square; Cineplex Odeon Chelsea
Foreign films: Sony Paris; Angelika Film Center
Popcorn: Cineplex Odeon Waverly Twin
Romantic movies: The Ziegfeld
Cheap movies: Cineplex Odeon Encore Worldwide
Dinner dates: Screening Room
Midnight movies: Angelika Film Center
Classics: Film Forum
Campy revivals: A Different Light

---

ing). MoMA hosts about 25 screenings a week, often in series on the work of a particular director or other themes.

Museum of Television & Radio

See chapter **Museums** *for listings.* Television and radio works, rather than film, are archived here. The museum's collection includes more than 30,000 programs, which can be viewed at private consoles. In addition, there are two small screening rooms and a 63-seat video theater where a number of programs are shown daily. Screening theaters are open until 9pm on Fridays.

Whitney Museum of American Art

See chapter **Museums** *for listings.* In keeping with its portfolio of showing the best in contemporary American art, the Whitney has a busy and varied schedule of film and video works. Many of its exhibitions have a strong moving-image component, including the famous Biennial showcase of contemporary artworks; entry is free with museum admission.

Foreign-language films

Most or all of the above institutions will screen films in languages other than English, but the following show only foreign films.

Asia Society

See chapter **Museums** *for listings.* Shows films from India, China and many other Asian countries, as well as Asian-American films.

French Institute

55 E 59th St between Park and Madison Aves (355-6160). Subway: 4, 5, 6 to 59th St; N, R to Lexington Ave. Tue–Fri 11am–7pm; Sat, Sun 11am–3pm. $7 non-members; $5.50 concessions. Membership $65 per year. AmEx, MC, V. The Institute—also known as the Alliance Française—shows movies from back home. They're usually subtitled (and never dubbed).

Goethe-Institut/German Cultural Center

See chapter **Museums** *for listings.* A paragovernmental German cultural and educational organization, the Institut shows German films in various locations around the city, as well as in its own opulent auditorium.

Japan Society

333 E 47th St between First and Second Aves (832-1155/ recorded information 752-0824). Subway: 4, 5, 6, 7 to 42nd St–Grand Central Terminal. Call to confirm film schedule and special exhibition times. Prices vary. AmEx, MC, V. The Japan Society organizes a busy schedule of Japanese films, including two or three big series each year.

Libraries

Donnell Library Center

See chapter **Museums** *for listings.* A branch of the New York Public Library, the Donnell shows and circulates films (call to check screening times).

Library for the Performing Arts

See chapter **Museums** *for listings.* The library has an extensive collection of books, periodicals, clippings and posters on film, as well as a vast catalog of film memorabilia.

Film festivals

Every September and October for more than 25 years, the Lincoln Center Film Society has been running the prestigious **New York Film Festival**. More than two dozen American and foreign films are given New York, U.S. or world premieres, and the festival usually features several rarely seen classics. Opening- and closing-night screenings are held in the grand Avery Fisher Hall. Tickets for films by known directors are often hard to come by; tickets go on sale several weeks in advance. The Film Society, in collaboration with the Museum of Modern Art, also sponsors the **New Directors, New Films** festival each spring, where you will catch works from on-the-cusp filmmakers from around the world.

An annual **New York Gay and Lesbian Film Festival** is held each July (call 254-7228 for details). In August there's a month-long **Black Film Festival** (749-5298) as one of the attractions of the annual **Harlem Week**, with a blend of hard-hitting documentaries and features involving black music and culture. Screenings ($5) are at the Adam Clayton Powell Jr. State Office Building, 163 W 125th St. Car-less New Yorkers have their very own "drive-in" film festival in **Bryant Park** each year between June and September. The park (on Sixth Ave between 40th and 42nd Sts) has a series of free summer Monday-night showings (8:30pm) of classics like *Strangers on a Train* or *Casablanca* on a giant screen. See chapter **New York by Season** for details.

In addition, many of the art houses arrange their own, smaller festivals and series, often in conjunction with other institutions.

Gay & Lesbian New York

The vibrant world of queer New York is something to take pride in

From the offices of City Hall to the floor of the Stock Exchange, from the media and advertising conglomerates on Madison Avenue to the big business of design and fashion on Seventh Avenue, and from the bright lights of Broadway to the quiet white rooms of museums and art galleries—it is impossible to ignore that openly gay men and women are a powerful part of what makes New York one of the world's financial and cultural centers. As the site of the 1969 Stonewall riots and the birthplace of the American gay rights movement, New York City is a queer mecca and is home to more than 500 lesbian, gay, bisexual and transgender social and political organizations.

During Gay Pride, which takes place annually over the last weekend in June, the Empire State Building is lit up in glorious lavender (*see chapter* **New York by Season**). This amazing celebration draws hundreds of thousands of visitors (not to mention their tourist dollars) into the city. The Pride march, which takes place on the Sunday of Pride weekend, draws between 250,000 and 500,000 spectators, and a number of Manhattan businesses now fly the lesbian-and-gay–friendly rainbow flag in celebration. Pride is a great time to visit the Big Apple—you'll feel as though everyone here is queer. Arrive during the summer months and sample lesbian and gay resort culture on Fire Island, which is only a short trip from the center of

West end girls: The gay-and-lesbian–friendly **West Village** *is perfect for an afternoon stroll.*

Light-headed: *A Different Light is the world's largest gay-and-lesbian bookstore.*

town (*see page 244*); the stellar line-up of celluloid delights at the **New York Lesbian & Gay Film Festival** (254-7228) in June; and the cross-dressing extravaganza Wigstock (late summer, around Labor Day).

An essential stop for any lesbian or gay visitor to New York is the **Lesbian & Gay Community Center** (*see page 244*), a nexus of information and activity that serves as a meeting place for over 300 groups and organizations. There you can pick up copies of New York's free weekly gay and lesbian publications. And don't miss *Time Out New York*'s Gay & Lesbian listings for the latest happenings around town.

Though the sizable gay and lesbian population of New York is quite diverse, the lesbian and gay club and bar scenes don't really reflect this, since they are almost entirely gender-segregated and, like their straight counterparts, tend to attract the single, 35-and-under crowd. However, the social alternatives are plentiful, among them the burgeoning queer coffee-bar, bookstore and restaurant scenes and the dozens of gay and lesbian films and plays that are shown in mainstream venues (*see chapters* **Theater, Film** *and* **Cabaret & Comedy**).

There's no doubt about it: New York is a 24-hour nonstop city with a multitude of choices for queer entertainment. Enjoy!

Books and media

Publications

New York's gay weeklies are *HX* (Homo Xtra)—which includes expansive listings of bars, dance clubs, sex clubs, restaurants, cultural events and group meetings, and loads of funny personals—and *HX for Her*, New York's only lesbian weekly. The newspaper *LGNY* (Lesbian & Gay New York) offers political coverage and serious articles. *The New York Blade News*, a sister publication to *The Washington Blade*, also focuses on queer politics and news. All four are free at gay and lesbian venues and shops.

National publications include *Out* ($3.95) and *The Advocate* ($3.95), both of which are published monthly. *Girlfriends* ($4.95) and *Curve* ($3.95) are colorful, fun monthly magazines for lesbians. Also look for the rather tacky (and irregularly published) *Bad Attitude* ($3.95) and the far better sex quarterly *On Our Backs* ($5.95).

Fodor's Gay Guide to New York City ($12) is an excellent source of opinionated information about queer NYC and the surrounding areas. Daniel Hurewitz's *Stepping Out*, which details nine walking tours of gay and lesbian NYC, is another invaluable source. Both books—as well as the above-mentioned magazines—are available at A Different Light and the Oscar Wilde Memorial Bookshop (*see below*).

Television

There's an abundance of gay-related broadcasting, though nearly all of it is poorly produced and appears on public-access cable channels. There are confusing regional variations, and you may not be able to watch all these shows on a hotel TV. Some of the funniest programs are to be found on Channel 35 (in most of Manhattan), which is where the infamous Robin Byrd hosts her *Men for Men* soft-core strip show. Manhattan Neighborhood Network (channels 16, 34, 56 and 57 on all Manhattan cable systems) has plenty of gay shows, ranging from drag queens milking their 15 minutes of fame to serious discussion programs. You might also want to check out RuPaul's ongoing talk show on VH1. *HX* provides the most current TV listings.

Bookshops

Most New York bookshops have gay sections (*see chapter* **Shopping & Services**), but the following are exclusively lesbian and gay.

A Different Light Bookstore & Café

151 W 19th St between Sixth and Seventh Aves (989-4850). Subway: 1, 9 to 18th St. 10am–midnight. AmEx, Disc, MC, V. This is the biggest and best gay and lesbian bookshop in New York. It's great for browsing and has plenty of free readings, film screenings and art openings. There are also useful bulletin boards with local information, and a cute café.

Oscar Wilde Memorial Bookshop

15 Christopher St between Sixth and Seventh Aves (255-8097). Subway: 1, 9 to Christopher St–Sheridan Sq. Mon–Fri, Sun noon–8pm, Sat noon–9pm. AmEx, Disc, MC, V. New York's oldest gay and lesbian bookshop is stocked to the brim with books and magazines, and offers many discounts.

Centers and phone lines

For women's health care, *see page 250*.

Audre Lorde Project Center

85 S Oxford St at Lafayette Ave, Brooklyn (1-718-596-0342). Subway: C to Lafayette Ave. 10am–6pm. Actually known by the unwieldy moniker the Audre Lorde Project Center for Lesbian, Gay, Bisexual, Two-Spirit & Transgender People of

Color Communities, this community center provides a plethora of resources for queer people of color. Phone for information about events and group meetings.

Barnard Center for Research on Women

101 Barnard Hall, 3009 Broadway at 117th St (854-2067). Subway: 1, 9 to 116th St. Tue–Fri 9:30am–5pm, Mon 9:30am–9pm. An academic center with a distinctly off-putting name, this is where to explore scholarly feminism through a calendar of classes, lectures and film screenings. The library has an extensive archive of feminist journals and government reports.

Gay Men's Health Crisis

129 W 24th St between Sixth and Seventh Aves (367-1000; AIDS advice hotline 807-6655). Subway: 1, 9 to 23rd St. Advice hotline Mon–Fri 9am–9pm, Sat noon–3pm. Recorded information at other times. Office Mon–Fri 10am–6pm. This was the first organization in the world to take up the challenge of helping people with AIDS. It has a three-fold mission: to push the government to increase services, to help those who are sick by providing services and counselling to them and their families, and to educate the public and prevent the further spread of HIV. There are 250 staff members and 1,400 volunteers. Support groups usually meet in the evenings.

Gay & Lesbian Switchboard

777-1800. 10am–midnight. A phone information service only. Callers who need legal help can be referred to lawyers, and there's information on bars, restaurants and hotels. The switchboard is especially good at giving advice to people who have just come out or who may be considering suicide. There are also apartment and job listings and details on all sorts of other gay and lesbian organizations.

Lesbian & Gay Community Services Center

208 W 13th St between Seventh and Eighth Aves (620-7310). Subway: F, 1, 2, 3, 9 to 14th St; L to Eighth Ave. 9am–11pm. Internet: www.gaycenter.org. Founded in 1983, the center provides political, cultural, spiritual and emotional sustenance to the lesbian and gay community. While it principally offers programs and support for the city's residents, there's plenty to interest the visitor, including a free information packet for tourists and those new to the city. You'll be amazed at the diversity of groups (around 300) that meet here. It also houses the National Museum and Archive of Lesbian and Gay History and the Vito Russo lending library.

Lesbian Herstory Archive

P.O. Box 1258, New York, NY 10116 (1-718-768-3953; fax 1-718-768-4663). By appointment only. Newly founded in the Park Slope area of Brooklyn (becoming known as "Dyke Slope" for its large and growing lesbian population), the Herstory Archives, started by Joan Nestle and Deb Edel in 1974, includes more than 10,000 books (theory, fiction, poetry, plays), 1,400 periodicals and many items of personal memorabilia. You, too, can donate a treasured possession and become part of Herstory.

National Organization for Women

105 E 22nd St at Park Ave South (260-4422). Subway: 6 to 23rd St. Mon–Fri 10am–6pm. NOW is a political organization, not a community center, but you can stop by the Manhattan branch to pick up the bimonthly newsletter *NOW-NYC News* or the chapter calendar. NOW also runs various support groups for women, especially those who are divorced or separated.

NYC Gay & Lesbian Anti-Violence Project

647 Hudson St at Gansevoort St (807-0197). Subway: 1, 2, 3, 9 to 14th St. Mon–Thu 10am–8pm, Fri 10am–6pm; switchboard open 24 hours daily. The project provides support for the victims of anti-gay and anti-lesbian attacks. Working with the police department's bias unit, the project povides advice on seeking police help. Short- and long-term counseling is available.

Over the years, Fire Island— a long, thin strip of land off the southern coast of Long Island—has become the favorite summer habitat for New York's gay men and a growing number of lesbians. Two particular island locales have become synonymous with sun- and sea-worshiping fags and dykes, flamboyant parties and general seasonal extravagance: the Pines (snotty, affluent and mostly gay) and Cherry Grove (tacky, suburban and mostly lesbian). The majority of the accommodations in both the Pines and the Grove are in private houses, which are rented out as shares for the summer season. Make friends with the right person and you could land yourself an invite. Otherwise you might have to settle for a day trip, as there are very few hostel or hotel accommodations, and those there are tend to be expensive and far from luxurious. For details see *HX* or *HX for Her.*

GETTING THERE

By car or LIRR train from Penn Station to Sayville, then by passenger ferry. The station is about two miles from the ferry terminal and cabs are always around. There are between eight and 20 ferry departures a day, depending on the day and season. The ferry costs $10 round trip.

Long Island Railroad (LIRR)

1-718-217-5477 for schedules.

Sayville Ferry Company

1-516-589-0810 for schedules.

Boys' life

When *New York* magazine ran a cover story lamenting the new homogeneity of gay male culture, the focus of its critique was booming "fag chic" in Chelsea. While the West Village has quaint historical gay sites such as the Stonewall (*see page 247*), friendly show-tune piano cabarets and unpretentious stores full of rainbow knick-knacks and slogan T-shirts, the center of gay life has shifted slightly uptown. Chelsea also sports a new attitude that can be daunting.

The neighborhood's main drag is Eighth Avenue between 16th and 23rd Streets, which is lined with businesses catering to upwardly mobile gay men—gyms, sexy clothing and exotic home furnishing stores, tanning and grooming salons, galleries, cafés, bars and midrange restaurants for brunch, business lunches and late dinners. Perfectly toned, youngish (25–40), mostly Caucasian men who might describe themselves as "straight-acting

Come on and touch me, babe: Booze and schmooze at the East Village lounge **Wonder Bar.**

and appearing" are standard in Chelsea. If you're not one of them, be prepared to be snubbed or possibly ignored. Women, too, probably won't feel very welcome in Chelsea's luxurious surroundings–unless they look like supermodels.

Most of Manhattan's dance clubs are a hop, skip and jump from Chelsea, and feature a big gay house/techno night during the weekend, when you can spin and twirl with upwards of 500 half-naked men until the wee hours of the following day.

Somewhat in reaction to Chelsea, a counter-culture scene of rock-punk-glitter-fashion boys and theatrical drag queens thrives in the East Village, centered on a handful of small dive bars. The scene has an arty, bohemian vibe, and there are many equally lovely men to be found here, ranging from 1970s macho butches to Bowie-type androgynes. The scene tends to be even younger than the Chelsea version (although some men may appear to be younger than they are), and the crowd is more mixed, both racially and sexually. The bars also tend to feature terribly amusing live performances, which draw crowds in by midnight and spit them out by 4am.

Some habitués of Chelsea and the East Village do mix. Men of all ages, shapes and sizes frequent the leather/fetish bars and clubs, such as the Spike in Chelsea and the Lure in the West Village, an area known as the Meat Market (*see pages 246–247 for both*). If you're a devotee of the leather scene, you might want to plan your trip around either the New York Mr. Leather Contest, which takes place in the autumn, or the Black Party at Saint at Large—a special all-night

leather–and–S/M-themed circuit party which attracts thousands of people and is held every March (*see page 247*).

For open-air and open-market cruising, try the legendary old trucker piers located at the end of Christopher Street along the Hudson River, or the Ramble in Central Park, located below the 79th Street Transverse and the lake (but beware of police entrapments). And although the city has made every effort to clean up Times Square and turn it into an extension of Disney World, you can still find gay burlesque at the **Gaiety**, located right off Broadway on 46th Street (221-8868).

But if you're just an average T-shirt–and–jeans–type gay man, don't worry. Not only will you be fine in almost any gay space, you'll be surprised at how much cruising happens on the streets while you're walking around town, and how easy it is to turn a glance into a conversation.

Accommodations

Chelsea Mews Guest House

344 W 15th St between Eighth and Ninth Aves (255-9174). Subway: A, C, E to 14th St; L to Eighth Ave. Single $75, double $85–$150. No credit cards. Built in 1840, this guest house has accommodations primarily for gay men, but gay women are also welcome. The rooms are comfortable and well furnished. No smoking is allowed.

Chelsea Pines Inn

317 W 14th St between Eighth and Ninth Aves (929-1023; fax 620-5646). Subway: A, C, E to 14th St; L to Eighth Ave. Doubles and triples $79–$125. AmEx, DC, Disc, MC, V, Carte Blanche. This central location near the West Village and Chelsea welcomes gay male guests and lesbians as well.

Vintage movie posters set the mood, and the 23 rooms are clean and comfortable; some have private bathrooms and all have radio, television and air conditioning (essential in the summer months). Interestingly, heterosexuals are discouraged from booking.

Colonial House Inn

318 W 22nd St between Eighth and Ninth Aves (243-9669/ 1-800-689-3779). Subway: C, E to 23rd St. $80–$125. AmEx, MC, V. This beautifully renovated 1880s townhouse inn sits on a quiet street in the heart of Chelsea. It's run by, and primarily for, gay men. The Colonial House is a great place to stay, even if some of the cheaper rooms are small. Major bonuses: Free continental breakfast is served in the "Art Gallery Lounge" and a rooftop deck (nude sunbathing allowed!).

Incentra Village House

32 Eighth Ave between 12th and Jane Sts (206-0007). Subway: A, C, E to 14th St; L to Eighth Ave. $99–$179. AmEx, MC, V. Two cute 1841 historic townhouses perfectly situated in the West Village make up this guest house run by gay men; lesbians and gay men are welcome. The rooms (singles, doubles and suites) are spacious, with private bathrooms and kitchenettes; some have working fireplaces. There's also a 1939 Steinway baby grand piano for show-tune-spouting queens. While interestingly decorated, the rooms aren't always maintained at the height of cleanliness.

Bars

Most bars in New York offer themed nights, drink specials and happy hours, and the gay ones are no exception. Don't be shy, remember to tip the bartender and carry plenty of business cards. *See also* chapters **Cafés & Bars** *and* **Cabaret & Comedy.**

Chelsea

Axis

17 W 19th St between Fifth and Sixth Aves (633-1717). Subway: F, N, R to 23rd St. 5pm–4am. No credit cards. Thankfully, this midsize gay dance club (formerly known as Champs) has thrown in the towel on the tired sports-bar decor. Consistently crowded, Axis draws a cruisey crowd of youngish men interested in dancing or scoring, and not much else. The long-running party Milk on Monday nights draws a sexy Latino contingent.

Barracuda

275 W 22nd St at Eighth Ave (645-8613). Subway: C, E to 23rd St. 4pm–4am. No credit cards. This Chelsea bar—which actually feels more like the East Village—continues to draw hordes of boys. More comfy and friendly than its neighborhood competition, the space is split in two, with a traditional bar area up front and a frequently redecorated lounge in back, plus a pool table, pinball machine and nightly DJs. Theme nights include ferocious glamazon Mona Foot's Star Search on Thursdays. Boys on a budget, take note: There's never a cover.

g

223 W 19th St between Seventh and Eighth Aves (929-1085). Subway: 1, 2, 3, 9 to 18th St. 4pm–4am. No credit cards. This classy lounge is the latest Chelsea sensation, attracting an A-list crowd of hunky men who are also extremely friendly. Don't miss the trendy juice/power-drink bar. (Can an in-house pedicurist be far behind?) One word of warning: Late in the evening, the space is often filled to capacity, while outside there's an intimidating line of unfortunates waiting to get in. Go early and avoid the scene.

Main drag: Cha-cha at **La Nueva Escuelita.**

The Spike

120 Eleventh Ave at 20th St (243-9688). Subway: C, E to 23rd St. 9pm–4am. No credit cards. The Spike was once the quintessential late-1970s Levi's/leather gay bar. Today, however, it's pretty soft around the edges, since the new clones are all hanging out at the Lure (*see* **West Village**). Still, the Spike has taken on a newer and more varied generation of cruisers and pre-clubbers. Weekend evenings retain an easygoing and fairly traditional leather flavor.

East Village

Beige

Bowery Bar, 40 E 4th St at Bowery (475-2220). Subway: B, D, F, Q to Broadway–Lafayette St; 6 to Bleecker St. Tue 10pm. AmEx, DC, MC, V. Fashions may come and go, but here it's the fashionable who come and go, sashaying through these stylish rooms with designs on the good-looking crowd of boys and a few extremely stylish girls (some of them are even dykes). Dress to impress, or you'll feel out of place at this groovy fete.

Boiler Room

86 E 4th St between First and Second Aves (254-7536). Subway: F to Second Ave. 4pm–4am. No credit cards. For most self-respecting East Village boys, a stop here on the weekends isn't just an option—it's a moral imperative. Probably the most intensely cruisey of East Village bars, the unassuming haunt is busy on weeknights and absolutely mobbed on Friday and Saturday nights. The jukebox features a varied selection of new hits and classics, and there are video-game machines for the easily bored.

Wonder Bar

505 E 6th St at Ave B (777-9105). Subway: F to Second Ave. 6pm–4am. No credit cards. At its best, this lounge hosts an impossibly, appealingly diverse mix of people—most shockingly, men *and* women—making it an eclectic and ideal hangout. The only downside is that most nights the smoke is as thick as the crowd. DJs spin soul, trip-hop and classics.

West Village

hell

59 Gansevoort St between Ninth Ave and Washington St (727-1666). Subway: A, C, E to 14th St; L to Eighth Ave. 7pm–4am. AmEx, MC, V. Conveniently located near the club Mother and the late-night restaurant Florent, this newish bar sports the requisite red color scheme and celebrity photos with drawn-on devil horns. It's casual, chic and comfortable to boot.

The Lure

409 W 13th St at Ninth Ave (741-3919). Subway: A, C, E to 14th St; L to Eighth Ave. Mon–Sat 8pm–4am, Sun 5pm–4am. No credit cards. A newfangled fetish bar that attracts a broad, energetic, sometimes posey bunch. On Wednesdays it hosts Pork, a raunchy party for the younger set; you'll find men in uniforms, fetish performances and more mystery than most NYC bars offer. A strict (and very amusing) dress code is enforced; wear leather, rubber, uniforms, but don't dab on the cologne and don't even think about wearing tennis shoes (Wednesday night is less strict).

Stonewall

53 Christopher St at Seventh Ave (463-0950). Subway: 1, 9 to Christopher St–Sheridan Sq. 2:30pm–4am. No credit cards. A landmark bar, next door to the actual location of the 1969 gay rebellion against police harassment. If you don't already know it, ask the bartender to talk you through the story. There's a good pool table and friendly customers, but these days Stonewall is more a historical monument than an exciting destination.

Uptown

Cats

232 W 48th St between Seventh and Eighth Aves (unlisted). Subway: N, R to 49th St; 1, 9 to 50th St. Sun–Fri noon–4am, Sat 8am–4am. No credit cards. This great dive has nothing in common with the longest-running show on Broadway. Rather, it's the kind of place Andrew Lloyd Webber would go if he suddenly wanted to be pawed by mangy drag queens or wished to grope go-go boys boasting impressive record-breakers of their own. As one of the last bastions of seedy Times Square, this stop is for the adventurous only.

The Works

428 Columbus Ave between 80th and 81st Sts (799-7365). Subway: B, C to 81st St. 2pm–4am. No credit cards. The major hangout for young gay men on the Upper West Side attracts a decidedly yuppity thirtysomething crowd. On Sunday afternoons there's a popular beer blast: Between 6pm and 1am you pay $5 to drink all the brew you can manage. All contributions go to the Gay Men's Health Crisis.

Clubs

Almost all New York clubs have gay nights; many of those we list are one-nighters rather than permanent venues. There's also a large number of fund-raising parties and other events worth looking out for. For more clubs, the majority of which are gay-friendly, plus more information about some of those below, *see chapter* **Clubs**.

Dance Clubs

La Nueva Escuelita

301 W 39th St at Eighth Ave (631-0588). Subway: A, C, E to 42nd St. Thu–Sun 10pm–4am. V, MC. Extravagant, not-to-be-missed drag follies featuring a bevy of Latin talents are staged nightly here. There's also sweaty dancing to salsa, merengue and house. The predominantly Latin crowd is friendly.

Mother

432 W 14th St at Washington St (677-6060). Subway: A, C, E to 14th St; L to Eighth Ave. Tue–Sun 10:30pm. This is one of the only vestiges of truly twisted New York nightlife left. Queer (but not necessarily gay) revelers gather here every week for clever fetish, dress-up and performance-oriented theme nights such as Tuesday's legendary **Jackie 60**; Saturday's **Click & Drag**, a cyber-fetish costume parade (you must conform to the dress code, or at least wear all black—call for info); and Friday night's women's party **Clit Club** (see **Dyke Life**, below). Don't leave the city without checking out this incredible institution.

Saint at Large

Information: 674-8541. The now-mythical Saint, with its huge aluminum domed interior, was one of the first venues where New York's gay men enjoyed dance-floor freedom. The club closed, but the clientele keeps its memory alive with a series of four huge circuit parties each year. These parties—the S/M-tinged Black Party, the White Party (those names refer not to skin color but to the mood of the events), Halloween and New Year's Eve—attract legions of muscle-bound and image-conscious gay men from around the US.

Juniorverse

Twilo, 530 W 27th St between Tenth and Eleventh Aves (268-1600). Subway: C, E to 23rd St. Sat 10pm. Crowds of gay men flock to the this futuristic fete every Saturday night to worship at the shrine of super-DJ Junior Vasquez. Cavernous and always bursting at the seams, with a sound system that keeps you shivering for days, this is a sure bet for boogying boys.

Squeezebox

Don Hill's, 511 Greenwich St at Spring St (334-1390). Subway: 1, 9 to Houston St. Fri 10pm. Are you gay but sick and tired of disco? In the all-ages, pansexual, celebrity-studded crowd of twisted sisters and queer headbangers at this unique punk-glitter-glam-rock club. The crowd is about two-thirds gay, with a healthy smattering of women. Excellent live bands and rock & roll drag queens perform soul-shaking sets each week. Beware the mosh pit!

Roxy

515 W 18th St between Tenth and Eleventh Aves (645-5156). Subway: A, C, E to 14th St; L to Eighth Ave. 11pm. Promoters Marc Berkley and John Blair proved that you can go home again, as hordes of muscle boys and club crawlers have returned for Saturday nights at this venerable pleasure pit. The winning formula—the requisite go-go boys and carousing drag queens, and DJs spinning happy house music—guarantees a satisfying megaclub experience.

Sex Clubs

Despite the city's crackdown on adult businesses, a few active sex clubs for men continue to flourish. The most popular is the **Bijou** *(82 E 4th St between Second Ave and the Bowery, unlisted phone)*, followed by Chelsea's slightly spiffier **Unicorn** *(227 W 22nd St between Seventh and Eighth Aves, 924-2921)* and **J's Hangout** *(675*

Hudson St at 14th St, 242-9292), which is less blatantly sexual and more of an after-hours desperation cruise. For more details, consult *HX* magazine's "Getting Off" section.

Restaurants

Few New York restaurants would bat an eye at same-sex couples enjoying an intimate dinner. The neighborhoods mentioned above have hundreds of great eating places that are de facto gay restaurants, and many that are gay-owned and operated. Below are a few of the most obviously gay places in town. *See also chapter* **Restaurants.**

Candy Bar & Grill
131 Eighth Ave between 16th and 17th Sts (229-9702). Subway: A, C, E to 14th St; L to Eighth Ave; 1, 9 to 18th St. Dinner weekdays 6pm–midnight, weeknights noon–midnight. Average $25 or under. AmEx, Disc, DC, MC, V. The Candy is owned by a lesbian and gay partnership. Unique cocktails like the Thai and Pixie Stick martinis plus the Vampire's Kiss (a bloody mary with garlic-infused vodka) are the speciality of this trendy, mixed, see-and-be-seen restaurant and late-night hangout. The adequate cuisine is a mix of American and pan-Asian. Drinks are served until 1am.

Eighteenth & Eighth
159 Eighth Ave at 18th St (242-5000). Subway: A, C, E to 14th St; L to Eighth Ave; 1, 9 to 18th St. Meals Mon–Thu, Sun 9am–midnight; Fri, Sat 9am–12:30am. Average $10. MC, V, AmEx. Health-conscious, high-carbo food makes this small restaurant one of the great success stories of Chelsea. It's always full of cute, cruisey boys and girls, and the wait for a table is sometimes shockingly long.

Lips
2 Bank St at Greenwich Ave (675-7710). Subway: 1, 2, 3, 9 to 14th St. Brunch Sat, Sun noon–6pm. Dinner Mon–Thu, Sun 6–11:30pm; Fri, Sat 6pm–12:30am. Average $16. AmEx, DC, MC, V. The attraction at this drag-themed eatery is not the food, and it's certainly not the service. It's the novelty of having a dish named for a drag queen delivered to your table by a drag queen who at any moment will let loose in an old-fashioned lip-sync. It's about as mainstream as drag gets, but the loud showtunes and camp classics playing on video monitors will satisfy queens who relish the overblown.

La Nouvelle Justine
206 W 23rd St between Seventh and Eighth Aves (727-8642). Dinner Sun–Thu 6–11:30pm; Fri, Sat 6pm–1am. Bar open every night until 4am. Average $25. AmEx, MC, V, Disc. Expect all the (un)usual trappings at this S/M-themed restaurant and bar: a dark, Gothic dining room; leather-clad waiters; expert birthday spankings; verbal humiliation; and, oh yeah, some tasty French cuisine. It's less severe than it sounds, though; the owners have wisely retained a sense of humor and, like willing masochists, they seem quite content to be the butt of their own joke.

Townhouse Restaurant
206 E 58th St at Third Ave (826-6241). Subway: N, R to Lexington Ave; 4, 5, 6 to 59th St. Brunch Sun noon–4pm. Lunch Mon–Sat noon–3:30pm. Dinner Mon–Thu 5–11pm; Fri, Sat 5pm–midnight; Sun 6–11pm. Average brunch $12.50, dinner $16.50–$30. AmEx, DC, MC, V. A very elegant uptown haunt for true (read: more mature) gentlemen and their gentlemen friends (most of them in suits). Very gay, very upscale, but full of old-world discretion. The food is continental, decent and affordable.

Gyms

See chapter **Sports & Fitness** for more fitness facilities, including YMCAs.

American Fitness Center
128 Eighth Ave at 16th St (627-0065). Subway: A, C, E to 14th St; L to Eighth Ave; 1, 9 to 18th St. Membership $699 for 14 months, $156 per month, $15 per day. AmEx, MC, V, Disc. This fully equipped über-gym is barbell-bunny heaven. It's vast and spotless, with 15,000 square feet (1,400 square meters) of free-weight space, acres of cardiovascular machines and endless aerobics classes.

Chelsea Gym
267 W 17th St at Eighth Ave (255-1150). Subway: A, C, E to 14th St; L to Eighth Ave; 1, 9 to 18th St. Mon–Fri 6am–midnight; Sat, Sun 9am–9pm. Membership $494 per year, $104 per month, $35 per week, $12 per day. MC, V. There are hundreds of gyms in New York, but this modestly sized men-only facility is by far the gayest. It has three Nautilus machines, loads of free weights and a very active sauna, steam room and showers.

Dyke life

The most exciting aspect of lesbian life in Manhattan is that the women you'll see out and about in bars, clubs, restaurants, bookshops, community meetings and lesbian cabarets will truly defy all stereotypes. While lesbian culture is not as visible or as geographically concentrated as gay men's, it is also far less segregated (with some exceptions), either by age or race, and is far more friendly and welcoming.

If you're into community activism, you'll find plenty to spark your interest (although the glory days of outrageous civil disobedience have past): just check in at the Lesbian & Gay Community Services Center (*see page 244*). The center also offers a wide range of support groups and 12-step meetings for people in recovery. But if you're a dyke who's not into the activist or recovery scene, and just want to have some unbridled fun, New York City has plenty to offer.

Brooke Webster's full-time East Village lesbian bar Meow Mix (*see page 249*) has created a welcome gathering spot for alternadykes. And the unflappable promoter Caroline Clone continues to offer women large-scale dance parties like Her/SheBar and WOW Bar. The idea that lesbians want more for their money has also given old standard bars in the West Village a reason to try a little harder. Meanwhile, lesbian discos are getting progressively larger and are no longer held only in funky, out-of-the-way dives. Unfortunately, the rising popularity of these clubs doesn't guarantee they'll be around for long, so check the lesbian bar guide *HX for Her* or *Time Out New York* for the most current information. As a rule, your male friends, even if they are gay, will not be welcome in most women's bars

*Cats' meow: Catch Xena night at **Meow Mix**.*

and clubs unless the venue or the night is specifically advertised as mixed.

Outside Manhattan, Park Slope in Brooklyn remains a sort of lesbian residential hub, but beyond visiting the Lesbian Herstory Archives or the Audre Lorde Project (*see pages 243–244*), or just hanging out in the Prospect Park, there isn't much to see.

If you're staying with friends in Brooklyn and plan to travel into Manhattan to take advantage of dyke nightlife, take a taxi back home: Though stories of how dangerous New York is at night are greatly exaggerated, it's still not a good idea to ride the subway alone late at night (*see* **Safety**, *page 250*).

Accommodations

See also **Colonial House Inn** *and* **Incentra Village House**, *page 246*.

Allerton Hotel for Women
130 E 57th St at Lexington Ave (753-8841). Subway: N, R to Lexington Ave; 4, 5, 6 to 59th St. Singles from $55, $85 with bath. AmEx, MC, V. This clean, cheap and safe women-only hotel is located in a respectable but dull area. It's unfashionably decorated but good for those on a budget (or for cautious students).

East Village Bed & Breakfast
244 E 7th St at Ave C, apartment 6 (260-1865). Subway: F to Second Ave. Singles $50, doubles $75, breakfast included. No credit cards. A small, friendly, women-only B&B, run by women and located deep in the bowels of the East Village. There are only two rooms, so reservations are essential.

Markle Residence for Women
123 W 13th St between Sixth and Seventh Aves (242-2400). Subway: F, 1, 2, 3, 9 to 14th St; L to Sixth Ave. $123–$215 per week, including two meals (one-month minimum). MC, V. Offering women-only Salvation Army accommodation in a pleasant Greenwich Village location, the Markle has clean, comfortable rooms, all of which have telephones and private bathrooms.

Bars and lounges

See also **Beige** *and* **Wonder Bar** *page 246*.

Crazy Nanny's
21 Seventh Ave South at Leroy St (366-6312). Subway: 1, 9 to Christopher St–Sheridan Sq. 4pm–4am. An old faithful, Nanny's is a loud neon-decorated bar and disco with TV screens and a pool table downstairs; there's a DJ and a big-screen TV upstairs. Nanny's has also started staging theme nights; depending on who is DJing, the crowd might be predominantly black women or a mixed, trendy bunch of fags and dykes. It's a good place to hang out and have a frosty cold one, especially after a softball game on a weekend afternoon.

Henrietta Hudson
438 Hudson St at Morton St (243-9079). Subway: 1, 9 to Christopher St–Sheridan Sq. Mon–Fri 3pm–4am; Sat, Sun 1pm–4am. This is a watering hole for middle-class suburban girls with lots of hair. Women love it for cruising; it's laid out so you can eye everyone at once, then make your choice and make a move.

Julie's
204 E 53rd St between Second and Third Aves (688-1294). Subway: E, F to Lexington Ave; 6 to 51st St. 5pm. Julie's is an incredibly discreet, elegant bar for mature, professional, often closeted women in search of the same. Julie's stays open as late as 4am if business is good. Hors d'oeuvres are served from 5 to 8pm.

Meow Mix
269 Houston St at Suffolk St (254-1434). Subway: B, D, F, Q to Broadway–Lafayette St; 6 to Bleecker St. Tue–Sun 8pm–4am. Brooke Webster's alternative dyke bar appeals to youngish, edgy women and their men friends. There's a laid-back vibe even when the space plays host to raucous parties, go-go dancers, live bands (like Sexpod and the Lunachicks), readings and performances. Be on the lookout for slumming celebs.

Clubs

Great club nights are the holy grail of New York City—something that's fabulous one week sucks or is closed down the next, and so the search continues. These are the current lesbian hot spots, but don't panic if they're not around in a few months' time—there are bound to be new nights and venues blossoming in their places. Check *HX* for *Her* for current info.

Clit Club
Fridays at Mother (see page 247 for listings). Fri 10pm–5am The longest-running lesbian night (seven years and counting) is still going strong, with new weekly midnight performances ranging from sexy strip-teases to obscure performance art. Quality DJs and bodacious go-go girls are still standard here. New renovations have transformed this once-dark dive into a larger, more user-friendly space. Under the auspices of Mother, the club no longer has a restrictive

policy discouraging men, but the only males who come by are the Mother regulars—gays and cross-dressers, who hang out here other nights of the week. Similarly, dykes are welcome at Mother any night.

Squeezebox

See page 247 for listings. Squeezebox is New York's hippest, hottest drag/dyke rock & roll party. With great live bands and tattooed go-go boys and girls gyrating on the bar amid a super-mixed, celebrity-peppered crowd, you can count on seeing plenty of the hottest downtown dykes around.

Restaurants and cafés

See also **Candy Bar & Grill** *page 248.*

Big Cup

228 Eighth Ave at 21st St (206-0059). Subway: C, E to 23rd St. Mon–Thu, Sun 7am–2am; Fri, Sat 7am–3am. No credit cards. A big, colorful, bustling coffee joint with a modest selection of sweets and sandwiches, Big Cup's charm lies in its mismatched chairs, quippy staff and friendly, flirtatious clientele. You can hang out for hours during the day, but at night the throng can be overwhelming.

Cowgirl Hall of Fame

519 Hudson St at 10th St (633-1133). Subway: 1, 9 to Christopher St–Sheridan Sq. Lunch noon–4pm, dinner 5–11pm. Average $20. AmEx. In name and spirit, this is a great girl place. With its Tex-Mex food, country music on the jukebox and cowgirl memorabilia all over the walls, the place is pure country kitsch. Women with kids come again and again because their high-chair and entertainment needs are ably met by the sympathetic single-parent owner, Sherri. The pre-club scene revs up on frozen margaritas at the steer-horn-decorated bar; in the warmer months, the outdoor sidewalk tables are a people-watching plus.

Rubyfruit

531 Hudson St at Charles St (929-3343). Subway: 1, 9 to Christopher St–Sheridan Sq. Mon–Thu 3pm–2am; Fri, Sat 3pm–4am; Sun 11:30am–2am. Average $20. AmEx, DC, Disc, MC, V. A warm and energetic band of women patronizes Rubyfruit—the only lesbian bar and restaurant in town. Though the food is solidly good, it's not the main selling point. The congenial customers and a varied program of cabaret and music make this a good place for fun-loving old-school dykes.

Health

The public health-care system is practically non-existent in the United States and costs of private health care are exorbitant, so make sure you have comprehensive medical insurance when you travel to New York.

Michael Callen-Audre Lorde Community Health Center

356 W 18th St between Eighth and Ninth Aves (271-7200). Subway: A, C, E to 14th St; L to Eighth Ave. Mon–Thu 9am–8pm; Fri, Sat 9am–4pm. Internet: www.chp-health.org Formerly known as Community Health Project, this is the country's largest (and New York's only) health center primarily serving the gay, lesbian, bisexual and transgender community. The center offers an exhaustive list of services, including comprehensive primary care, HIV treatment, free adolescent services, STD screening and treatment, mental health services, peer counseling and education.

Planned Parenthood

Margaret Sanger Center, 26 Bleecker St at Mott St (274-7200). Subway: B, D, F, Q to Broadway–Lafayette Street; 6 to Bleecker St. Mon–Fri 8am–8pm, Sat 8am–4pm. No walk-ins. This is the main branch—newly relocated to a state-of-the-art facility—of the best-known, most reasonably priced network of family planning clinics in the US. Counseling and treatment are available for a full range of gynecological needs, including abortion, treatment of STDs, HIV testing and contraception. Phone for an appointment and more information about services.

Safety

New York women are used to the brazenness with which they are stared at by men and develop a hardened or dismissive attitude toward it. If your unwelcome admirers ever get verbal or start following you, ignoring them is better than responding—unless you are confident about your acid-tongued retorts. Walking into the nearest shop is your best bet to get rid of really persistent offenders.

As for more serious safety issues, with a minimum of awareness and common sense you can reduce the chances of anything happening to you to almost zero. Take the usual big-city precautions: Stay in areas where there are people, don't carry or wear anything that could catch a thief's eye and try not to look lost or vulnerable. Just act as if you know where you are going, and you will probably get there safely. Advice issued by the New York police department includes: never carry anything you'd fight for; don't carry a separate wad of "mugger's money" but simply hand over all your cash (if you're found to have kept money back, you'll be in worse trouble); and never resist when a weapon is involved. For further safety advice, *see chapter* **Essential Information.** For the NYC Gay & Lesbian Anti-Violence Project, see page 244.

Brooklyn Women's Martial Arts Center for Anti-Violence Education

421 Fifth Ave between 7th and 8th Sts, Brooklyn (1-718-788-1775). Subway: F, R to Fourth Ave–9th St. Mon–Fri 10am–7pm. No credit cards. A center dedicated to martial arts training for women and children. Its programs teach defensive techniques for real-life situations, including both physical and nonphysical methods of dealing with aggression or attack. Free child care is offered, and there are classes in the evenings and on weekends. Classes in karate and tai chi are offered.

Rape Hotline

Sex Crimes Report Line of the New York City Police Department (267-7273). Open 24 hours. Reports of sex crimes are handled by a female detective from the Police Department, who will inform the appropriate precinct, send an ambulance if requested and provide counseling and medical referrals. A detective from the Sex Crimes Squad will interview the victim.

Media

Home of the Times, the tabloids and even Howard Stern, New York is America's media capital

New York is awash in so many streams of information that you can get into town, check into your room and keep yourself entertained for a good week without wandering farther than the local newsstand. The city is saturated with mass communications: New Yorkers listen to "drive-time" news or talk radio on the ride to work or read the papers on the train, and the network television news is an evening ritual upon returning to the nest. The sabbath ritual of the city's intellectuals is the Sunday-morning reading of *The New York Times*, generally to the accompaniment of bagels and lox. On the subway, you can spot some people chipping away at the *Times* magazine's Sunday crossword puzzle all week long.

Newspapers and magazines

The Dailies

The New York Times, Olympian as ever after almost 150 years, remains the city's (and the nation's) paper of record. It has the broadest and deepest coverage of world and national events—as the masthead proclaims, it's "all the news that's fit to print." On local stories, it does get scooped periodically by its tabloid rivals. The mammoth Sunday *Times* weighs in at a full five pounds of newsprint, including magazine, book review, sports, arts, finance, real estate and other sections.

Until recently, change came slowly to this institution. In 1997, the erstwhile "Gray Lady" finally allowed the use of color on its front page and expanded its coverage of arts, business, sports, fashion and technology. The changes seemed overdue to some and heresy to others: The inauguration of "Public Lives," its version of a gossip column (however sedate), set tongues wagging, and the slightly updated language of recent years has provoked an outcry like the one that greeted the vernacular mass in the Catholic Church.

Two tabloids spar in the *Times*' wake, running much that may be less fit to print but is closer to the city's heart, stomach or, often enough, groin. The **Daily News**'s long tradition of sensational cover-

Extra, extra! Visit a newsstand when you want to read all about it—whatever it is.

age of crime, scandal and disaster has produced classic headlines, such as FORD TO CITY: DROP DEAD (when President Gerald Ford refused federal aid during the '70s fiscal crisis). The *News* has drifted politically from the Neanderthal right in the 1950s and 1960s to moderate but tough-minded under the ownership of real-estate mogul Mort Zuckerman. Pulitzer Prize–winning African-American

columnist E.R. Shipp and labor-friendly Latino pundit Juan Gonzalez have great street sense, and in 1997, the paper appointed its first female editor, Debby Krenek.

Competing tabloid the **New York Post** is the city's oldest surviving newspaper, founded in 1801 by Alexander Hamilton. After many decades as a standard-bearer for political liberalism, the

---

Don't believe everything you see

Just how realistic are the television shows set in New York City?

Imagine, if you can, living in the New York City depicted on television: affordable two-bedroom lofts in the Village for the unemployed, open-door policies with kooky but lovable neighbors, nearby cafés where everybody knows your name, a blessed lack of impossibly loud street noises coming through your bedroom window. TV's version of New York—it's a hell of a town.

In reality, though, television's New York is about as authentic as a six-pack of Lender's frozen bagels. If you believe the tube—and a lot of people who don't live here do—there's graffiti on every Big Apple building, steam is coming out of every Manhattan manhole cover and the easy-going East Village is the scariest place in the free world.

One possible explanation for this virtual reality is that Hollywood is completely out of touch with big-city life. Currently, there are 15 shows set in New York, and all but a handful of these are produced in Los Angeles. While NYC has always been the talk-show capital of the country, only a few locally shot prime-time series—such as *The Cosby Show* in the '80s—have popped up since the end of the New York production heyday of the 1960s (when programs such as *N.Y.P.D.* and *The Jackie Gleason Show* were filmed here). Perhaps absence has made the L.A.-based writer's heart grow fonder—or just more foolish.

Think of some of the scenarios Hollywood has drummed up in recent years. Is it really possible to get an American cab driver every time, as Paul and Jamie do on *Mad About You*? Could a cop dress better than a male model, à la Jimmy Smits on *NYPD Blue*? Would any respectable New Yorker ever let Kramer bust through his door as Jerry Seinfeld does? Was *Union Square*—a now thankfully defunct sitcom—ever funny? These questions can all be answered by one real New York saying: Fuhgeddaboudit.

Thanks to the success of the New York–filmed *Law & Order*, however, there's been a welcome trend of producing New York–set series right here in the big city. Since the crime show's debut in 1990, a number of high-profile prime-time series have opened offices in Manhattan. *Spin City, Soul Man, Cosby* and, on a part-time basis, *NYPD Blue* and *Brooklyn South* have all explored the benefits of shooting the real New York. By using stripped-from-tabloid storylines and actual street scenes, these shows present a broader and more accurate view of city life.

One problem even New York–based shows can't overcome, though, is how safe the city has become under Mayor Giuliani. Statistically, even Boise, Idaho, is a more dangerous place to live now, with homicides in New York at a 30-year low. This means that no matter how realistic gritty shows such as *Law & Order* and *NYPD Blue* appear to be, they've actually become more violent than reality. What is this city coming to?

Hey, nice suit: NYPD Blue's Dennis Franz, Jimmy Smits and Kim Delaney on the beat.

Post has swerved sharply to the right under current owner Rupert Murdoch. The *Post* has more column-inches of gossip than any other local paper, and its headlines are usually the ones to beat (although its best remains the '80s HEADLESS BODY IN TOPLESS BAR). The ardent and extensive coverage of local sports teams in the back of both tabloids reflects the deep partisanship of their readers. Many New Yorkers read the *News* and the *Post* from back to front.

New York Newsday is a Long Island–based daily with a tabloid format but a more sober news style. **USA Today**, also known as McPaper, specializes in polls and surveys, skin-deep capsules of news and a magazine-like treatment of world events. The **Amsterdam News** is one of the nation's oldest black newspapers, offering a left-of-center Afrocentric view. New York also supports two Spanish-language dailies, **El Diario** and **Noticias del Mundo**, and daily or weekly papers in every foreign tongue you can think of.

Weeklies

The New Yorker has served up fine wit, elegant prose and sophisticated cartoon art since the 1920s. In the postwar era it established itself as a venue for serious, long-form journalism. When Tina Brown joined as editor in 1992, the magazine ended its apparent ban on trend-spotting, and it now regularly runs aggressive and often exclusive coverage of the rich, famous and powerful. It usually makes for a lively, intelligent read.

The **New York Observer**, published on the Upper East Side, is a full-size weekly newspaper on salmon-colored paper. It focuses on the doings of "the overclass," its term for the upper echelons of business, finance, media and politics, and it contains some of the most knowing observations to be had on New York's power elite. It would certainly be F. Scott Fitzgerald's paper of choice. **New York** magazine is part newsweekly, part lifestyle report and part listings. Founded 30 years ago by Clay Felker, *New York* was a pioneer of New Journalism, showcasing such talents as Tom Wolfe, Gloria Steinem and Aaron Latham.

Downtown journalism is a battlefield pitting the neo-cons of the **New York Press** against the unreconstructed hippies of **The Village Voice**. The *Press* uses an all-column format; it has youth's energy and irreverence as well as its cynicism and self-absorption. The *Voice* is sometimes passionate and ironic, but just as often strident and predictable. Both papers are free. On the sidelines, found in a squadron of Manhattan street-corner newspaper bins, are **Our Town** and the **Manhattan Spirit**, two sister publications that feature neighborhood news and local political gossip.

And, of course, we think the best place to find out what's going on in town is **Time Out New**

*What's up: Check the **Times Square** ticker.*

York, launched in 1995. Based on the tried-and-trusted format of its London parent, *TONY* is an indispensable guide to the life of the city. In 1998, it was nominated for a National Magazine Award for General Excellence.

Monthlies

Andy Warhol's magazine, **Interview**, is still firmly New York–based, covering the world of fashion and entertainment with maximum style. **Paper** covers the city's trend-conscious set with plenty of insider buzz on bars, clubs, downtown boutiques and the people you'll find in them.

Television

A visit to New York often includes at least a small dose of cathode radiation and, particularly for British visitors, American TV can inflict culture shock. Each moment of network programming is constructed to instill fatal curiosity for the next, with commercial breaks coming thick and fast.

The TV day is scheduled down to the second, beginning with news and gossipy breakfast magazine programs (beware Kathie Lee Gifford), leading into a lobotomizing cycle of soap operas, vintage reruns and game shows—unbroken until around 3pm. Then talk shows such as *Oprah* and *Jerry Springer* take over, broadcasting peoples' not-so-private problems, with subjects along the lines of "I married my mother's lesbian lover" or "Mad Cow Disease ruined my family."

At 5pm, there's showbiz chat and local news, followed by national and international news at 6:30pm. Early evening is the domain of popular

So what's new?

Get the scoop whenever you want

The news never stops in these parts: Two electronic news tickers (the famous one in **Times Square** and a newer one at Rupert Murdoch's **News Corp.** building, Sixth Ave at 48th St) deliver the latest headlines to pedestrians in midtown. The city is also studded with newsstands: You can find huge periodical selections at **Eastern News** (687-1198) at the base of the Met-Life Building (above Grand Central Terminal) and **Hudson News**, 753 Broadway at 8th St (674-6655). Hudson News stands inside Grand Central, Penn Station and the Port Authority Bus Terminal stay open late. Shop for fanzines at **Tower Books**, 383 Lafayette St at 4th St (228-5100), and **Nikos**, Sixth Ave at 11th St (255-9175). The newsstands below are open 24 hours. All carry foreign papers; most have no phone.

Downtown

Amigo Mini-Mart *118 Delancey St at Essex St (777-3230). Subway: F to Delancey St; J, M, Z to Essex St.*
Gem Spa *131 Second Ave at St. Marks Pl (529-1146). Subway: 6 to Astor Pl.*
James Farrell Newsstand *Sheridan Square, Seventh Ave at Christopher St. Subway: 1, 9 to Christopher St–Sheridan Sq.*
S&S International News *Sixth Ave at 8th St. Subway: A, C, E, B, D, F, Q to W 4th St–Washington Sq.*

Midtown

Rose Bengal Newsstand *34th Street between Sixth Avenue and Broadway. Subway: B, D, F, Q to 34th St.*
Grand Hyatt *42nd St at Park Ave. Subway: S, 4, 5, 6, 7 to 42nd St–Grand Central.*

Uptown

Megdeed *Broadway at 72nd St. Subway: 1, 2, 3, 9 to 72nd St.*
Lucky Star *2660 Broadway at 101st St (749-6158). Subway: 1, 9 to 103rd St.*

reruns (*The Simpsons, Mad About You, Home Improvement*) and syndicated game shows such as *Jeopardy!* and *Wheel of Fortune*. Huge audiences tune in at prime time, when action series, sports, movies and sitcoms battle for ratings. Finally, as sedate viewers go to bed, out come the neon personalities of the various late-night talk shows.

The only broadcast alternative to consumerist programming is public television. These stations receive little money from the government and rely heavily on "membership" donations garnered dur-

ing on-air fund drives. Public television has its own nightly news and a few local productions; its *Frontline* and *P.O.V.* documentaries are often incisive.

And then there is cable—that is, the 50 or so channels of basic cable, plus "premium" channels offering uninterrupted movies and sports coverage. "Pay-per-view" channels provide a menu of recent films, exclusive concerts and sports events at around $5 a pop. Cable is also home of paid "infomercials" and the public-access channels, an array of weirdos and soft-core porn.

If you're feeling nostalgic, the Museum of Television & Radio has a huge collection of classic and hard-to-find TV shows. *See also chapter* **Museums**.

Time Out New York offers a rundown of weekly TV highlights. For full TV schedules, including broadcast and cable television, save the Sunday *New York Times* TV section or buy a daily paper; they all have 24-hour listings.

The networks

Six major networks broadcast nationwide. All offer ratings-led variations on a theme. **CBS** (Channel 2 in NYC) has the top investigative show, *60 Minutes,* on Sundays, and its programming overall is geared to a middle-age demographic (*Diagnosis Murder, Touched By an Angel*). But check out *Everybody Loves Raymond* (Mondays at 8:30pm) and *Late Show with David Letterman* (weeknights at 11:30pm) for some solid humor. The most popular network, **NBC** (Channel 4), is the home of the long-running sketch comedy series *Saturday Night Live* (Saturdays at 11:30pm) and some hugely popular sitcoms, such as *Friends, Frasier, Just Shoot Me* and *Mad About You.* **ABC** (Channel 7) is the king of daytime soaps and working-class sitcoms (*Home Improvement, The Drew Carey Show*), while **Fox** (Channel 5) is popular with younger audiences for hip shows such as *Ally McBeal, King of the Hill* and *The X-Files.* The other two networks, **UPN** (Channel 9) and the **WB** (Channel 11), don't attract huge audiences, but have some offbeat programming such as *Buffy, the Vampire Slayer, Dawson's Creek* and *Star Trek: Voyager.*

WWOR (Channel 9) is an affiliate of UPN and offers Mets baseball and popular reruns (*Baywatch, Married With Children, The Cosby Show*); **WPIX** (Channel 11) is now known for its 11pm repeats of *Seinfeld,* which often beat the other channels' nightly news in the ratings. There are also two Spanish channels, **WXTV** (Channel 41) and **WNJU** (Channel 47). As well as Mexican dramas and titillating game shows, these are your best bet for soccer.

Public TV

You'll find public TV on channels 13, 21 and 25. Documentaries, arts shows and science series alternate with *Masterpiece Theatre* and reruns of British shows like *Inspector Morse* and *Poirot* (in *Mystery!*). Channel 21 broadcasts *ITN World News* daily at 7pm and 11:30pm.

Cable

(Note: All channel numbers listed are for Time Warner Cable in Manhattan. In other locations or for other cable systems—such as RCN and Cablevision—check listings.) For music videos, there is the old-standby **MTV** (Channel 20) and its more conservative sibling **VH1** (19). The latter airs the popular *Pop-Up Video,* a show that offers funny, factual tidbits as a video plays. Sports fans have **ESPN** (8), **ESPN2** (48), **MSG** (Madison Square Garden, 32) and **Fox Sports New York** (26). **CNN** (10), **MSNBC** (43), **Fox News Channel** (46) and **NY-1** (1) offer news all day, the last with a local focus. **C-SPAN** (38) broadcasts the floor proceedings of the U.S. House of Representatives and an array of public affairs seminars.

Comedy Central (45) is your stop for 24-hour comedy, with hits like the raunchy cartoon *South Park* (Wednesdays at 10pm) and reruns of the British *Absolutely Fabulous*, plus a glut of stand-up and nightly reruns of classic *Saturday Night Live* shows starring the young Eddie Murphy, Chris Farley, et al. E! (Channel 24) is "Entertainment Television," a pop-culture mix of celebrities and movie news. This is where you'll find New York icon Howard Stern conducting hilariously intrusive interviews and such tabloid TV as *The Gossip Show* and the unmissable *Talk Soup*, where you can watch daily highlights from the best of America's talk shows.

Bravo (64) shows the kind of arts programs public TV would air if it could afford them, including *Inside the Actors Studio* and a good number of quality art-house films. A&E (14) airs the shallow but popular *Biography* documentary series, and Lifetime (12) is "television for women." The Discovery Channel (18) and the Learning Channel (52) feature science and nature programs, and show gruesome surgical operations, while Nickelodeon (6) offers programming more suitable for the kids. Court TV (51) scores big ratings with hot trials. The History Channel (17), the Weather Channel (36) and Sci-Fi Channel (44) are self-explanatory.

Public Access TV is on channels 16, 34, 56 and 57—surefire sources of bizarre camcorder amusement. Late-night Channel 35 is where you'll find the *Robin Byrd Show*, a forum for Times Square porn stars, riddled with ads for escort services and sex lines. Premium channels, often available for a fee in hotels, include HBO (Home Box Office), Showtime, Cinemax, The Movie Channel and Disney, all of which show uninterrupted feature films and exclusive "specials."

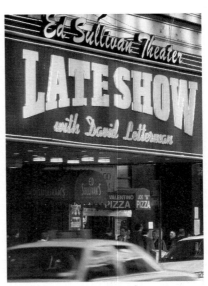

Stupid human tricks: David Letterman's lair.

Be the Audience

Tickets are available for all sorts of TV shows that are recorded in New York studios. Should you need more information, contact the New York Convention & Visitors Bureau.

The Daily Show

356 W 58th St between Eighth and Ninth Aves (560-3135). Subway: A, C, B, D, 1, 9, to 59th St–Columbus Circle. Mon–Thu 5:30pm. Reserve tickets three months ahead of time by phone, or call on the Friday before you'd like to attend to see if there are any canceled tickets. You must be at least 18 with photo ID.

Late Night With Conan O'Brien

NBC, 30 Rockefeller Plaza between Fifth and Sixth Aves (664-3056). Subway: B, D, F, Q to 47–50th Sts–Rockefeller Center. Tue–Fri 5:30pm. Send a postcard for tickets. A limited amount of same-day tickets are distributed at 9am. You must be at least 16.

Late Show With David Letterman

Ed Sullivan Theater, 1697 Broadway at 53rd St (975-1003). Subway: 1, 9 to 50th St. Mon–Thu 5:30pm, Thu 8pm. Send a postcard with your name, address and telephone number six to eight months in advance (zip code: 10019); standby tickets are available at 9am. You can also apply for tickets on the CBS Web page (www.cbs.com). You must be at least 16 with photo ID.

The Ricki Lake Show

2 E 37th St between Fifth and Madison Aves (889-6767). Subway: 6 to 33rd St. Wed–Thu 3:30, 5:30pm; Fri 2, 4pm. Send requests for tickets one month in advance by postcard to 401 Fifth Avenue, 7th Floor, New York, NY 10016. Standby tickets are available one hour before taping. You must be at least 18 with photo ID.

The Rosie O'Donnell Show

NBC, 30 Rockefeller Plaza between Fifth and Sixth Aves (664-3057). Subway: B, D, F, Q to 47–50th Sts–Rockefeller Center. Mon–Thu 10am. A ticket lottery for the whole season is held in April and May; only postcards received during those months are accepted for the shows (zip code: 10112). You will be notified one to two weeks in advance of taping if you have seats. A few same-day standby seats are available at 8am (but get there at around 5am if you really want to go) from the 49th Street entrance. You must be at least five.

Saturday Night Live

NBC, 30 Rockefeller Plaza between Fifth and Sixth Aves (664-3057). Subway: B, D, F, Q to 47–50th Sts–Rockefeller Center. Dress rehearsals at 7:30pm, live at 10pm. A ticket lottery for the whole season is held in August, and only postcards received in the month of August are accepted for the shows (zip code: 10112). You will be notified one to two weeks in advance of taping if you have seats. A few same-day standby tickets, for either the dress rehearsal or the live show, are distributed at 9:15am (but get there at around 5am if you really want to go). You must be at least 16.

Spin City

Chelsea Piers, Pier 62 (336-6993). Subway: C, E to 23rd St. Fri 7pm. Call for latest taping dates.

Radio

There are nearly 100 stations in the New York area, offering a huge range of sounds and styles. On the AM dial, you can find some intriguing talk radio and phone-in shows that attract everyone from priests to nutcases. There's plenty of news and sports as well. Although the Federal Communications Commission's recent deregulation of ownership rules has allowed such broadcast giants as Chancellor Media to buy up some of New York's most prominent commercial radio stations, many independent stations still thrive, offering everything from underground sounds to Celtic tunes. Radio highlights are printed weekly in *Time Out New York* and the Sunday *New York Times*, and daily in the *Daily News*.

News and talk

WINS-AM 1010, WABC-AM 770 and WCBS-AM 880 offer news throughout the day, plus traffic and weather reports. Commercial-free public radio stations WNYC-FM 93.9/-AM 820 and WBAI-FM 99.5 provide excellent news and current-affairs shows, including *All Things Considered* (weekdays AM: 4–6pm, 7:30–8pm; FM: 5–6pm, 6:30–8pm), and guest-driven talk shows, notably WNYC-AM's *New York and Company* (weekdays noon–2pm) and WNYC-FM's *Fresh Air* (weekdays 4–5pm). WNYC also airs Garrison Keillor's *A Prairie Home Companion* and Ira Glass's quirky *This American Life*. WBAI is one of the very few electronic media platforms for left-wing politics anywhere in the States.

The AM phone-in shows will take you from one extreme to the other. WLIB-AM 1190 provides the voice of militant black New York, with news and talk from an Afrocentric perspective, interspersed with Caribbean music. Neo-fascist Rush Limbaugh airs his scarily popular views on WABC, where you can also get a 45-minute late-morning dose of the barely suppressed self-righteousness of former mayor Edward Koch and, in the evening, the heavily street-accented demagoguery of Guardian Angels founder Curtis Sliwa.

Two classical stations, WQXR-FM 96.3 and WNYC-FM 93.9, serve a varied diet of music and opera, WNYC being slightly more progressive.

Jazz

WBGO-FM 88.3 "Jazz 88" plays phenomenal classic jazz. Here, Branford Marsalis broadcasts his weekly *JazzSet* program, which features many legendary artists. And there are special shows devoted to such categories as piano jazz and the blues. On Saturday mornings, you'll find Felix Hernandez playing classic R&B. WCWP-FM 88.1 and WQCD-FM 101.9 are also popular jazz stations in the city.

Dance and pop

American commercial radio is rigidly formatted, which makes most pop stations extremely tedious and repetitive during daylight hours. However, in the evenings and on weekends, you'll find more interesting programs. WQHT-FM 97.1 "Hot 97" is New York's commercial hip-hop station, with Lisa G and former *Yo! MTV Raps* hosts Dr. Dre and Ed Lover cooking up a breakfast show for the homies; there's rap and R&B throughout the day. The station also has some of the city's best house shows, with Tony Humphries very late on Fridays and Hex Hector and Johnny Vicious together late on Saturdays. WKTU-FM 103.5 is the city's premier dance music station; until recently, RuPaul was the morning-show host.

WBLS-FM 107.5 is an "urban (meaning black) adult" station, playing classic and contemporary funk, soul and R&B. Grandmaster Flash has a splendid mix show (weekdays at noon, Friday evening, Saturday night) and there's Chuck Mitchell's house and R&B mix overnight on Saturday, plus *Hal Jackson's Sunday Classics* (blues and soul). WWRL-AM 1600 switched from its gospel format to R&B in 1997.

WRKS-FM 98.7 "Kiss FM" has an "adult" contemporary format, which translates as unremarkable American pop. The only legacy of its more soulful days is the Sunday-morning gospel show (6–9am).

WCBS-FM 101.1 is strictly oldies, while WBIX-FM 105.1 "BIG 105" plays a mix of the '80s and '90s. WPLJ-FM 95.5 and WHTZ-FM 100.3 are Top 40 stations. WLTW-FM 106.7 "Lite FM" plays the kind of background music you hear in elevators.

Rock

WAXQ-FM 104.3, WNEW-FM 102.7 and WXRK-FM 92.3 "K-Rock" offer a digest of classic and alternative rock. K-Rock also attracts the city's largest group of morning listeners, thanks to Howard Stern's controversial 6–11am weekday show. WLIR-FM 92.7 offers "alternative" (indie and Gothic) sounds with a British bias. WSOU-FM 89.5 is a college station devoted to heavy metal. At WFMU-FM 91.1, the term "free-form radio" still has some meaning: An eclectic mix of music and oddities like Joe Frank's eerie stream-of-consciousness monologues (Thursdays at 7pm).

Other music

WQEW-AM 1560 plays American popular standards, WWXY-FM 107.1 plays country music. WEVD-AM 1050 broadcasts wacky talk shows, sports games and music. The Lower East Side's pirate radio station, WSTR-FM 88.7, presents an array of talk and music programming between 5pm and midnight throughout the week.

College radio

College radio is innovative and free of commercials. However, smaller transmitters mean that reception is often compromised by Manhattan's high-rise geography. Try New York University's WNYU-FM 89.1 and Columbia's WKCR-FM 89.9 for varied programming across the musical spectrum. Fordham University's WFUV-FM 90.7 is mostly a folk/Irish station, but also airs a variety of shows, including good old-fashioned radio drama on *Classic Radio* every Sunday evening.

Sports

WFAN-AM 660 covers games live. In the mornings, New York talk radio fixture, Don Imus, offers his take on sports and just about everything else going on in the world. WJWR-AM 620 has just started coverage of NY-NJ Metrostars soccer games; otherwise, it's a mostly sports-talk station.

Websites

Websites come and go with unpredictable frequency; check the Time Out Net (*below*) for the latest.

http://www.timeoutny.com/
Information on all the city has to offer.

http://www.ci.nyc.ny.us/
The "Official New York Web Site" is produced by the folks at City Hall.

http://www.citysearchnyc.com
Here's up-to-the minute information on events.

http://www.clubnyc.com
The latest news and grooves on the city's nocturnal scene.

http://www.echonyc.com
Arts reviews, events listings and a city guide.

http://www.nynetwork.com
This is a useful list of New York websites

http://www.sidewalk.com
Microsoft Network's NYC entertainment guide.

http://www.timeout.co.uk
The Time Out Net website includes a guide to NYC (among many other cities) with listings, features and free classified ads.

http://www.villagevoice.com
Listings and features from *The Village Voice*.

http://www.whitehouse.gov
Your connection to the high and mighty in U.S. government.

Music

Music lovers, welcome to paradise. Whatever your taste—
from rock to rap, symphonic to salsa—it gets top billing here.

The worlds of classical music and pop are moving closer together, with "crossover" quickly becoming the favorite word of music programmers all over the city. But whether your taste tends toward a postmodern, multigenre fusion of styles, basic stripped-down rock & roll or undiluted orchestral traditionalism, the city offers an endless array of choices. From chandelier-decorated concert halls to down and dirty dives where paint chips fall on your head as the decibels rise, New York is one giant stage, and folks come from the world over to perform on it.

TICKETS

You can buy tickets directly from most venues (though many of those listed under Rock, Pop & Soul will only take cash). If you want to book seats by credit card, you can call Ticketmaster, which sells tickets for the New York City Opera, performances at BAM, Broadway musicals and most bigtime rock concerts (but be prepared to pay a service fee). CarnegieCharge handles credit card sales for Carnegie Hall events, and Centercharge does the same for Alice Tully Hall and Avery Fisher Hall. The Ticket Buyers Club of the New York Philharmonic provides orchestral tickets at considerable discounts, and the Theater Development Fund offers good deals on Off-Off Broadway music, theater or dance events. TKTS offers 25 to 50 percent discounts (with a $2 service charge) for same-day tickets for most Lincoln Center events, including the New York Philharmonic, the Chamber Music Society, the Juilliard School and the New York City Opera (though not the Met).

*Stage dive: The down-and-dirty **Continental** is home to rock, punk and greasecore.*

CarnegieCharge
247-7800. 8am–8pm. AmEx, MC, V.

Centercharge
721-6500. Mon–Sat 10am–8pm, Sun noon–8pm. AmEx, Disc, MC, V.

**New York Philharmonic
Audience Services**
875-5656. Mon–Fri 10am–5:30pm. AmEx, DC, MC, V.

Ticketmaster
307-4100. Mon–Sat 9am–10pm, Sun 9am–9pm. AmEx, MC, V.

TKTS
Duffy Square, 47th St at Broadway (221-0013). Subway: N, R, S, 1, 2, 3, 9, 7 to 42nd St–Times Sq. Mon–Sat 3–8pm, Sun noon–8pm. No credit cards.
Branch: *2 World Trade Center, Mezzanine (221-0013).*

Popular music

It was touring musicians who christened New York the Big Apple because, of all their destinations, this was the place that promised the biggest payoff. While that's still true, it's far more likely that a hip sort of poverty awaits musicians seeking fame and fortune here. New York City is the home of the jazz diaspora and the birthplace of hip-hop. Lest you forget, the punk scene emerged here at CBGB a quarter of a century ago, emphasizing a do-it-yourself ethic at a time when corporate monoliths seemed to have squelched the possibilities for homegrown rock forever. Ever since, rock musicians have come here to tap into their muses' more aggressive qualities. The East Village is teeming with aspiring artistes, providing the local scene with all types of postpunk rock. Recently, there's been a resurgence in live funk and soul, driven by the breakbeat tastes of rap.

As you would expect in the center of world communications and culture, *everybody* from *everywhere* comes to play here; a constant barrage of big names and bright young things are all eager to add New York to the list on the back of their tour T-shirts. There are more live music venues here than ever before, from new large venues like the Hammerstein Ballroom and the Bowery Ballroom to small joints like Arlene Grocery and Baby Jupiter. Live hip-hop, apart from the shows at places like Wetlands and Tramps, is underpublicized, though live performances and open-mike shows often crop up. Jazz tends to be expensive, and happens mostly in venues where the food and drink minimums add plenty more to your bill. Latin music is also booming in New York. Many clubs host Latin nights, including the Copacabana and S.O.B.'s.

For more complete music listings, venues and information on upcoming shows, check *Time Out New York*. *The Village Voice* and *New York Press* also have listings; they're both free in Manhattan

and are available in stores, in sidewalk vending boxes and at some newsstands. For more live music venues, *see chapters* **Clubs, Cabaret & Comedy** *and* **Gay & Lesbian New York**.

If you want to drink alcohol at any of these venues, bring a photo ID that indicates your age. Even if you are obviously 21 or older, there's a good chance you'll be asked to prove it.

Major venues

See also chapter **Cabaret & Comedy**.

Apollo Theater
253 W 125th St between Malcolm X and Adam Clayton Powell Jr. Blvds (Lenox and Seventh Aves) (749-5838). Subway: A, C, B, D, 2, 3 to 125th St. $9–$30. AmEx, MC, V. At press time the Apollo's future seemed rather uncertain, with the physical space deteriorating, the number of gigs decreasing and its finances being investigated by the state. Still, in its heyday, there was no place as atmospheric as this classic Harlem spot to see a hip-hop or R&B gig, as well as Wednesday's Amateur Night—once a launching pad for stars such as Ella Fitzgerald and Michael Jackson, and now full of militant black comedians and soul singers hitting as many notes as they can before they reach the right one. Taped for TV's *Showtime at the Apollo*, this night is a fun way to see the Apollo audience in all its glory. There's an obvious police presence, especially for the rap gigs, which means there's no need to worry about venturing into Harlem at night.

Beacon Theatre
2124 Broadway at 74th St (496-7070). Subway: 1, 2, 3, 9 to 72nd St. $30–$80. No credit cards. Worth a visit just for the astonishing decor, the Beacon hosts an eclectic program of big acts and is the stage of choice for many established soul and R&B performers. Artists such as Bob Dylan, Ani DiFranco, Bryan Ferry, Ruben Blades and Garbage have performed here.

Irving Plaza
17 Irving Pl at 15th St (777-6800). Subway: L, N, R, 4, 5, 6, to 14th St–Union Square. $10–$30. No credit cards. A midlevel venue with a balcony and lovely decor, it's the only suitable venue for acts on the verge of bigger things (Tricky, Kula Shaker), longtime artists with substantial cults (Paul Westerberg, Laibach) or huge acts craving more intimacy (Bob Dylan, the Artist).

Hammerstein Ballroom
at the Manhattan Center
311 W 34th St between Eighth and Ninth Aves (564-4882). Subway: A, C, E to 34th St. $10–$20. No credit cards. Situated inside the Moonie-owned Manhattan Center, Hammerstein Ballroom is a cavernous space equipped with three balconies. In its first year of operation, Hammerstein has played host to rockers venerable (John Fogerty) and cutting edge (Radiohead), as well as visiting electronicists (Chemical Brothers, the Orb).

Madison Square Garden
Seventh Ave at 32nd St (465-6741). Subway: A, C, E, 1, 2, 3, 9 to 34th St–Penn Station. $22.50–$75. No credit cards. Awright, Noo Yawk! Are you ready to rock & roll? The acoustics may be more suited to the crunch of hockey and the slap of basketball, but MSG is the most famous rock venue the world over. It packs them in for massive events by folks such as Kiss, Puff Daddy and the Family, and the Stones.

Continental Airlines Arena

East Rutherford, NJ (1-201-935-3900). Travel: Bus from Port Authority Terminal (564-8484). From $22.50. No credit cards. New Jersey's answer to Madison Square Garden, in the Meadowlands Complex, is the place to see Jersey natives Bon Jovi or Bruce Springsteen, or perhaps a visiting Rage Against the Machine or Celine Dion.

Nassau Coliseum

1255 Hempstead Turnpike, Uniondale, NY (1-516-794-9303). Travel: LIRR to Hempstead, then N70, N71, N72 bus. From $22.50. No credit cards. Nassau Coliseum is Long Island's answer to Continental Airlines Arena. As such, it doesn't have a lot of character, but that quality isn't usually required for enormdomes, is it? Many of the same shows that run through MSG and the Continental Airlines Arena come here as well, although the Coliseum is probably the quintessential venue to view Billy Joel, who played a series of shows here in early '98, in all his splendor.

Radio City Music Hall

1260 Sixth Ave at 50th St (247-4777). Subway: B, D, F, Q to 47th–50th St–Rockefeller Center. From $25. No credit cards. The grandest Art Deco concert hall in the city, Radio City books huge acts, such as Tina Turner and Barry Manilow, only when the stage isn't the setting for *Riverdance* or the seasonal Rockette extravaganzas.

Roseland

239 W 52nd St between Broadway and Eighth Ave (245-5761/concert hot line 249-8870). Subway: B, D, E to Seventh Ave; C, 1, 9 to 50th St. From $15. No credit cards. If an act is not big enough for the Garden but too big for Irving Plaza, this ballroom does the trick. Pantera, Cheap Trick and the Foo Fighters played here in the last year. However, the average concertgoer is in for a most dehumanizing experience just by walking in—a pat-down from security goons is compulsory—and Roseland's acoustics leave a lot to be desired.

Roxy

515 W 18th St between Tenth and Eleventh Aves (645-5156). Subway: A, C, E to 14th St; L to Eighth Ave. $12–$20. No credit cards. This is mainly a dance club, with a history stretching back to when it was the epicenter of hip-hop. Live performances don't happen regularly, but the Chemical Brothers, Everything But the Girl and Sick of It All have all taken bows at this cavernous space.

The Theater at Madison Square Garden

Seventh Ave at 32nd St (465-6741). Subway: A, C, E, 1, 2, 3, 9 to 34th St–Penn Station. Prices vary. No credit cards. Underneath Madison Square Garden is this comfortable but sanitized modern venue, which hosts a broad selection of big-name pop artists (Sting, John Mellencamp) craving more intimacy than the Garden.

Town Hall

123 W 43rd St between Sixth and Seventh Aves (840-2824). Subway: B, D, F, Q to 42nd St; N, R, S, 1, 2, 3, 9, 7 to 42nd St–Times Sq. $15–$25 V, MC, AmEx. A venerable theater with ear-pleasing acoustics and seats for everyone hosts occasional medium to large concerts by such folks as Martha Wash and Fred Hersch, as well as its share of Celtic or worldbeat events.

Webster Hall

125 E 11th St between Third and Fourth Aves (353-1600). Subway: L, N, R, 4, 5, 6 to 14th St–Union Sq. $15–$20. No credit cards. Downtown's biggest room for live music has drawn the likes of the Mighty Mighty Bosstones and Morphine. After you've passed through security, you can look down on burgeoning glam bands from the spacious balcony or hang out at one of the many bars inside.

Rock, Pop & Soul

Acme Underground

9 Great Jones St at Lafayette St (420-1934). Subway: B, D, F, Q to Broadway–Lafayette St; 6 to Bleecker St. $6–$10. M, V, AmEx for food and drink only. The Acme Bar & Grill (*see chapter* **Eating & Drinking**) hides this small basement venue. After a few years of dodgy booking, the quality of acts here has soared, with everybody from drunk-core bard Mark Eitzel to rediscovered R&B legend Andre "Mr. Rhythm" Williams appearing.

Arlene Grocery

95 Stanton St between Ludlow and Orchard Sts (358-1633). Subway: F to Second Ave; J, M, Z to Essex St. Free. No credit cards. Irish-themed rock, hard-boiled folkies, indie fixtures and baby bands looking for a break abound at this crucial showcase venue, named for the actual Lower East Side market that it replaced. Unusual for a free venue, its sound system is top-notch.

Baby Jupiter

170 Orchard St at Stanton St (982-2229). Subway: F to Second Ave; J, M, Z to Essex St. Free–$3. MC, V. This pleasant, spacious Lower East Side venue not only has food, drink and theater events, but it's becoming an increasingly important spot for secret hipster shows (by the likes of Silver Jews and Will Oldham), as well as a decent spot for arty music by up-and-comers such as Ezster Balint. The sound system isn't great, but the comfy old couches and relaxed vibe more than make up for it.

Baggot Inn

82 W 3rd St between Thompson and Sullivan Sts (477-0622). Subway: A, C, E, B, D, F, Q to W 4th St–Washington Sq. $5. AmEx, MC, V. Formerly the Sun Mountain Café, the Baggot Inn refurbished its interior along with its booking policies: Good Irish rock can be heard, as well as typical horrid Bleecker Street fare.

Bitter End

147 Bleecker St at Thompson St (673-7030). Subway: A, C, E, B, D, F, Q to W 4th St–Washington Sq. $5. AmEx, Disc, MC, V. The ne plus ultra of Bleecker Street joints. Now free of the looming lease troubles that plagued it for years, the Bitter End will forever feature singer-songwriters who are quite jazzed to perform where Dylan played all those years ago.

Bottom Line

15 W 4th St at Mercer St (228-6300). Subway: N, R to 8th St. $15–$25. No credit cards. Word of warning: Catch the management on a bad night, or attend a particularly crowded evening, and you'll find yourself a prisoner at the Riker's Island of rock. That said, Allan Pepper's cabaret-style club has persisted for 25 years, longer than any similar venue. Roots music, singer-songwriter stylings, the occasional jazz or fusion gig and Buster-frigging-Poindexter and His Spanish Rocket Ship all find a home here.

Bowery Ballroom

Delancey St between the Bowery and Chrystie St (533-2111). Subway: 6 to Spring St; J, M to Bowery. $1–$20. V, MC bar only. This elegant new midsize venue (with a balcony and a downstairs lounge) was once home to a shoe store. It's run by the same folks who own Mercury Lounge—the Lounge Lizards, Bernard Butler and Girls Against Boys all played there within a month of its June 1998 opening.

Brownies

169 Ave A between 10th and 11th Sts (420-8392). Subway: L to First Ave. $6–$8. No credit cards. A loud, basic bar filled with loud, basic bands. Although its sound system doesn't exactly kick ass, in the last couple of years Brownies has been beating CBGB at its own game, booking the finest in upcoming rock, as well as hard-gigging local bands.

Back in black: After a long hiatus, punk icon Patti Smith has returned to NYC stages.

CBGB

315 Bowery at Bleecker St (982-4052). Subway: B, D, F, Q to Broadway–Lafayette St; 6 to Bleecker St. $3–$12. No credit cards. CBGB is beloved by every musician who's ever played there as much for the crystal-clear sound system as for the undeniable vibe of playing at the birthplace of punk rock. It's a little tougher for the fans, who must contend with horrid sightlines and a furnacelike atmosphere when it's crowded. CBGB has a spacious, newly renovated downstairs bar area and new bathrooms—which is quite a relief to anyone who experienced the old ones. The booking is hit or miss at best.

CB's 313 Gallery

313 Bowery at Bleecker St (677-0455). Subway: B, D, F, Q to Broadway–Lafayette St; 6 to Bleecker St. $6–$10. AmEx, MC, V. CBGB's more cultivated neighbor. It's just as long and narrow, but it's festooned with local artists' work instead of graffiti and layers of posters. The overall effect makes it seem that you're in a club in Toronto, not New York. Singer-songwriterly fare dominates.

Coney Island High

15 St. Marks Pl between Second and Third Aves (674-7959). Subway: N, R to 8th St; 6 to Astor Pl. $5–$10. No credit cards. Smack in the center of the East Village's most garish tourist strip is this three-floor glam/punk/metal stronghold, owned by D Generation's Jesse Malin. The downstairs main room hosts the big-name bills—the Fall, Hawkwind and Nashville Pussy have played there, and a multitude of heavy-metal and hardcore blowouts take place regularly—whereas the upstairs room features the gamut of small-fry outfits. CIH approaches CBGB levels of fetidness when it's packed, but it has shaped up as one of the best clubs around.

Continental

25 Third Ave at St. Marks Pl (529-6924). Subway: N, R to 8th St; 6 to Astor Pl. Free–$6. No credit cards. The skies will rain blood, the earth will belch fire, the day of reckoning will come and the celebrated dive bar Continental will still be there, booking local grease-a-billy, hard-rock, punk and garage bands for little or no cover.

The Cooler

416 W 14th St between Ninth Ave and Washington St (229-0785). Subway: A, C, E to 14th St; L to Eighth Ave. Free–$15. AmEx, MC, V. This spacious former meat locker isn't always climate-controlled—especially in the dead of winter or at a crowded summer show. Monday nights are free, and the bills are usually interesting, mixing indie rock with the more avant-garde. This club also hosts a local hip-hop showcase called Lyricist Lounge, as well as funk shows and lots of arty Sonic Youth–related side projects.

Don Hill's

511 Greenwich St at Spring St (334-1390). Subway: C, E to Spring St; 1, 9 to Houston St. $5–12. V, MC, AmEx, DC. Home of Squeezebox, the long-running punk-meets-drag summit, Don Hill's may be located in the upper reaches of Tribeca, but its heart is clearly in the East Village as host to weekly parties and special events that cater to the glam side of the rock spectrum. The decor has the inexplicably bizarre yet comforting feel of an airport lounge.

Downtime

251 W 30th St between Seventh and Eighth Aves (695-2747). Subway: 1, 9 to 28th St. $5–$12. AmEx, MC, V. During the week, run-of-the-mill rock bands play in this vertically spacious bar with an upstairs lounge and pool table. On Saturdays, retro-themed events for folks who can't get enough of the film *Swingers* take over.

Dumba

57 Jay St between Front and Water Sts, Brooklyn (726-2686). Subway: F to York St; A, C to High St. $5. No credit cards. This Brooklyn warehouse space is a safe haven for straight-edge punks and indie kids who are underage and who'd rather see their rock bands in a non-bar atmosphere. Sticking to bargain cover charge, all ages and no-alcohol policies, Dumba books such artists as God Is My Co-Pilot, Dub Narcotic Sound System and Red Monkey. There aren't shows here every night, so call for the schedule.

Fez

380 Lafayette St at Great Jones St (533-2680). Subway: B, D, F, Q to Broadway–Lafayette St; 6 to Bleecker St. $5–$18, plus two-drink minimum. AmEx, MC, V. With its gold lamé and red velvet curtains, Fez is one of the city's finest venues for that glittering lounge/cabaret atmosphere. It books a variety of local events including the popular Loser's Lounge series. Every Thursday night, the Mingus Big Band introduces a new generation of listeners to the robust, sanctified jazz of the late bassist-composer-bandleader Charles Mingus. There are also "alternative comedy" happenings. It's a sit-down, dinner-theater–style venue with little standing room.

Hotel Galvez

103 Ave B between 6th and 7th Sts (358-9683). Subway: F to Second Ave, 6 to Astor Pl. Free. AmEx, MC, V. After you've stuffed yourself with Galvez's fine Southern cooking, you can hear up-and-coming singer-songwriters in one of the smallest and coziest spaces in the East Village.

The Knitting Factory

74 Leonard St between Broadway and Church St (219-3055). Subway: A, C, E to Canal St; 1, 9 to Franklin St. $5–$20. AmEx, MC, V ($15 minimum). In addition to being the city's avant-indie music mall, the Knitting Factory features a variety of basic indie bands (Scrawl, Bedhead, Neutral Milk Hotel, Smog) in the main space, as well as smaller shows in the Alterknit Theater. *See also* **Jazz & Experimental** *and chapter* **Books & Poetry.**

Lakeside Lounge

162 Ave B between 10th and 11th Sts (529-8463). Subway: L to First Ave. Free. No credit cards. Not only does this two-year-old bar have an unmatchable country and blues jukebox, but appropriately roots-inflected local outfits throw it down regularly here for free.

Le Bar Bat

311 W 57th St between Eighth and Ninth Aves (307-7228). Subway: A, C, B, D, 1, 9 to 59th St–Columbus Circle. $10–$20; free before 9pm (8:30pm Sat). AmEx, MC, V. A bizarre bar venue set in an old cavelike recording studio. The bands here are usually happy party-time funk and soul providers and the crowd is a jolly bunch of after-workers.

Life/the Ki Club

158 Bleecker St at Thompson St (420-1999). Subway: A, C, E, B, D, F, Q to W 4th St–Washington Sq. $15–$20. AmEx, MC, V. One of Manhattan's hottest nightclubs is also host to an erratic music schedule. If you don't feel like dancing to typical DJ-mixed club fodder, come here for the "Lust for Life" parties on Wednesday nights, when punked-up bands such as the Donnas, the Upper Crust and the Toilet Boys take the place over.

Lion's Den

214 Sullivan St between Bleecker and 3rd Sts (477-2782). Subway: A, C, E, B, D, F, Q to W 4th St–Washington Sq. $5–$10. AmEx. This cavernous dive caters to the tastes of Bleecker Street regulars and NYU students. Lion's Den books plenty of Deadhead-friendly jam bands, reggae, funk and rock.

The Living Room

84 Stanton St at Allen St (533-7235). Subway: F to Second Ave; J, M, Z to Essex St. Free. No credit cards. The Living Room is another of the many young clubs popping up in the Ludlow/Lower East Side hipster mecca. It has been booking very small shows so far.

Luna Lounge

171 Ludlow St between Houston and Stanton Sts (260-2323). Subway: F to Second Ave. Free. No credit cards. A nice alternative to the often overcrowded Max Fish across the street, Luna Lounge offers free rock shows in a comfy environment—meaning old beat-up sofas and chairs in the band room and vinyl booths in the bar room.

Max's Kansas City

240 W 52nd St between Eighth Ave and Broadway (245-5656). Subway: B, D, E to Seventh Ave; C, 1, 9 to 50th St. Free–$10. AmEx, MC, V. The New York demimonde flocked to Max's Kansas City throughout the '70s when it was situated on Park Avenue South. Oddly, Max's has now reopened on Broadway (on the site of the old Lone Star Roadhouse) as a club-restaurant, and as of early '98 the vibe hadn't yet been recaptured, although the club's booking may kick in soon.

Maxwell's

1039 Washington St, Hoboken, NJ (1-201-798 4064). Travel: PATH train from 33rd, 23rd, 14th, 9th or Christopher St to Hoboken; bus #126 from Port Authority Terminal. $5–$12. AmEx, DC, MC, V. There are probably more bars per capita in Hoboken than anywhere in the U.S., and Maxwell's has recently become much like all the others along Washington Street. The days when it rivaled CBGB are gone, but 'Swells still manages to attract a great bill now and again.

Meow Mix

269 Houston St at Suffolk St (254-0688). Subway: F to Second Ave. $5. No credit cards. One of the hipper lesbian establishments (it was featured prominently in *Chasing Amy*), Meow Mix is also a mecca for homo-friendly downtown music that ranges from trashed-up glam to singer-songwriter fare. In terms of atmosphere, it's your typical brew-fueled neighborhood watering hole. Check out their popular tribute nights every last Sunday of the month, when a handful of downtown faves give it up for anybody from KISS to the Monkees.

Mercury Lounge

217 E Houston St at Ave A (260-4700). Subway: F to Second Ave. $6–$12. AmEx, Disc, MC, V. With a good ear for booking future faves like Bis and a knack for attracting bands seemingly above its station (like Wilco) combined with unassailable acoustics and sightlines, the Mercury Lounge is the small venue to beat in New York. If Band X doesn't sound good here, it's invariably because Band X does not have its shit together.

Nell's

246 W 14th St between Seventh and Eighth Aves (675-1567). Subway: A, C, E, 1, 2, 3, 9 to 14th St; L to Eighth Ave. $10–$15. AmEx, MC, V. With plush interiors modeled after a Victorian gentlemen's club, this lushly appointed room was the place to be seen in the late 1980s—if you could get in. The crowd has shifted from the international jet set to the upscale hip-hop set (the late Notorious B.I.G. shot a video here). On the ground floor they feature live jazz, blues and reggae. DJs pack the dance floor downstairs.

Nightingale Bar

213 Second Ave at 13th St (473-9398). Subway: L to First Ave. $5. No credit cards. The stage at this noisy bar is about six inches off the ground and the mirror behind the stage gives an illusion of space. But when seeing a band at Nightingale, there's no way to avoid feeling as though you're right up there with them. This is the place that gave the world Blues Traveler and the Spin Doctors.

Paddy Reilly's Music Bar

519 Second Ave at 29th St (686-1210). Subway: 6 to 28th St. $5–$10. AmEx. The premier local venue for Irish rock hosts the likes of Black 47, the Prodigals and a weekly *seisiun* (a traditional Irish jam session).

Rodeo Bar

375 Third Ave at 27th St (683-6500). Subway: 6 to 28th St. Free. AmEx, MC, V. It looks like any other Murray Hill joint—and half of it is, actually. But the sawdust-strewn

northern half books local roots outfits and the occasional nascent phenomenon.

Sidewalk

94 Ave A at 6th St (473-7373). Subway: F to Second Ave, 6 to Astor Pl. Free. AmEx, MC, V. Behind the front room at this neighborhood café, you'll find the world capital of "antifolk." In other words, low-maintenance acoustic music rules, whether it's irreverent and ingenious (which describes antifolk guru Lach or perennials the Humans) or self-important folkie swill.

Shine

380 Canal St at West Broadway (941-0900). Subway: A, C, E, 1, 9 to Canal St. $6–$15. V, MC, AmEx (for drinks only). Formerly known as the New Music Cafe, this Soho/Tribeca nightspot has been hosting new bands such as Mono, Bran Van 3000, the Getaway People and even last-gaspers like A Flock of Seagulls.

Spiral

244 Houston St between Aves A and B (353-1740). Subway: F to Second Ave, 6 to Astor Pl. $6. As long as you have a phone, you can play at the Spiral. Located kitty-corner from the hub of Ludlow Street, this club recently had its dank atmosphere overhauled, with white walls and local art now gracing the walls. The musical fare still consists of straight-ahead small-fry rock bands.

St. Ann's Church

157 Montague St between Clinton and Henry Sts, Brooklyn Heights (1-718-858-2424). Subway: N, R to Court St; 2, 3, 4

*Big band boom: The Mingus Big Band blows into **Fez** every Thursday night.*

to Borough Hall. $20–$25. AmEx, MC, V (by phone only). Music can and should be a spiritually fulfilling experience, and there's no more heavenly venue than this Brooklyn church; music events here tend toward soft, acoustic fare such as Katell Keineg, Syd Straw and Victoria Williams.

Supper Club

240 W 47th St between Eighth Ave and Broadway (921-1940). Subway: N, R, S, 1, 2, 3, 9, 7 to 42nd St–Times Sq. $12–$15. AmEx, MC, V. This gilded midsize venue in midtown is extremely festive and acoustically pleasant, hosting a variety of artists from Beck and Elvis Costello to David Bowie and hosting a party called Saturday Night Swing.

Tramps

51 W 21st St between Fifth and Sixth Aves (727-7788). Subway: F, N, R to 23rd St. $5–$20. No credit cards. God-damn those two columns about seven feet in front of tramps' stage! Otherwise, we haven't a bad word to say about this midsize venue, which serves up plenty of alternative and modern rock along with loads of funk, reggae, country, blues and more. It is the only Manhattan venue regularly willing to book hip-hop.

Westbeth Theater Center Music Hall

151 Bank St between West and Washington Sts (741-0391). Subway: A, C, E to 14th St; L to Eighth Ave. $8–$35. No credit cards. The Westbeth is a 500-capacity space with decent sound that has seen recent shows from Pavement, Mary Lou Lord and Mark Eitzel. It has a nice extra bar area outside in which to hang if you're not digging the opening act.

Wetlands

161 Hudson St at Laight St (966-4225). Subway: A, C, E, 1, 9 to Canal St. Free–$15. AmEx, MC, V (drinks only). Deadheads seeking to keep the vibe alive after Jerry Garcia's death flock here for the weekly events that feature either Dead cover bands or musicians peripherally connected to the band. More than that, this club regularly books ska, funk, reggae, jungle, hip-hop and hardcore marathons—making it a veritable haven for urban sounds of all types. You can brief yourself on a number of political causes by perusing the postings.

Windows on the World

1 World Trade Center, Liberty St between West and Church Sts (524-7000). Subway: C, E to World Trade Center; N, R, 1, 9 to Cortlandt St. $5. AmEx, MC, V (drinks only). There simply isn't a more romantic place to sip pricey drinks and watch live music than at this spot atop the World Trade Center—on the 107th floor, actually. There are often DJs spinning in a funk or lounge environment, but there are also live acts, from Combustible Edison and Beat Positive to jazz acts and near-electronica types.

Jazz & Experimental

92nd Street Y

1395 Lexington Ave at 92nd St (415-5450). Subway: 4, 5, 6 to 86th St; 6 to 96th St. $10–$35. AmEx, MC, V. The superstars who perform at this century-old bastion are generally established poets and other tweedy types, but the Y's music program is surprisingly variegated. In addition to contemporary classical music, the schedule extends to gospel, various indigenous folkloric styles and jazz of the mainstream variety. Jazz in July, the program's centerpiece, invites both young and old swingers into the comfy surroundings.

Avenue B Social Club

99 Ave B between 6th and 7th Sts (no phone). Subway: F to Second Ave, 6 to Astor Pl. Free. No credit cards. You could get a crash course in the coolest retro sounds at this hip Lower East Side bar. The live bands traffic in a rootsy mix of bop,

twangy lounge music and pub rock, and the jukebox has all those legendary blues, jazz, funk and country names you've been curious about.

Birdland

315 W 44th St between Eighth and Ninth Aves (581-3080). Subway: A, C, E to 42nd St. From $10, plus $10 minimum. AmEx, MC, V. The flagship venue for the recent jazz resurgence in midtown, Birdland presents many of jazz's biggest names in the neon splendor of Times Square. The dining area's three-tiered floor plan allows for maximum visibility, so patrons can enjoy everyone from Pat Metheny to Jon Faddis and Chico O'Farrill while also enjoying the fine cuisine. To compete with the rest of the Monday night big bands in residence, the club has enlisted the Toshiko Akiyoshi Jazz Orchestra featuring Lew Tabackin.

Blue Note

131 W 3rd St between MacDougal St and Sixth Ave (475-8592). Subway: A, C, E, B, D, F, Q to W 4th St–Washington Sq. $7.50–$47.50, plus $5 minimum. AmEx, DC, MC, V. "The jazz capital of the world" is how this famous club describes itself, and the reception that the big names who play here are given often suggests visiting heads of state. Recent acts have included Dave Brubeck, David Sanborn, Ray Charles, Lionel Hampton and Grover Washington Jr. All this comes at a price: Dinner will cost you upwards of $25 a head.

Iridium

48 W 63rd St at Columbus Ave (582-2121). Subway: 1, 9 to 66th St–Lincoln Ctr. $25–$40, plus $5 minimum. AmEx, DC, Disc, JCB, MC, V. This club's location—across the street from Lincoln Center—guarantees that its lineups are generally top-notch. With a decor that's a little bit Art Nouveau and a little bit Dr. Seuss, Iridium lures the upscale crowds by booking a mix that is equally split between household names and jazzhold ones. Monday nights belong to the legendary guitarist, inventor and icon Les Paul, who often ends up sharing the stage with one of the guitar heroes who swear by his prize invention, the Gibson solid-body electric guitar.

The Jazz Standard

116 E 27th St between Park and Lexington Aves (576-2232). Subway: 6 to 28th St. $10–$20. V, MC, AmEx, DC. The Jazz Standard's two-level floor plan makes it a club for all jazz tastes. Upstairs there's a restaurant/watering hole that pipes in the kind of cool sounds that enhance dinner and conversation. Downstairs, where the talented instrumentalists and singers hold sway in 130-plus–capacity music room, the fine acoustics and unobstructed sightlines will delight both the aficionado and the jazz rookie out for a little night music.

Knitting Factory/
AlterKnit Theater/Old Office

74 Leonard St between Broadway and Church St (219-3055). Subway: A, C, E to Canal St; 1, 9 to Franklin St. $5–$20. AmEx, MC, V ($15 minimum). The Knitting Factory is recommended for those who like their music a little off the rails. New York's avant-garde music mall, it features an up-to-the-minute blend of experimental jazz, rock, alternative cinema and poetry. The café and bar are open throughout the day, and the main room holds 250 people.

Roulette

228 West Broadway at White St (219-8242). Subway: C, E to Canal St; 1, 9 to Franklin St. $8. No credit cards. Ever thought you might want live music in your living room? Well, improvising trombonist/Roulette proprietor Jim Staley has saved you the trouble. His friends represent a who's who of world-renowned music experimentalists, so the atmosphere in his ten-year-old salon is relaxed and informal—until the music starts up. You're just as likely to run into computer music pioneers such as David Behrman, as you are to hear avant-jazzers like Dave Douglas.

Air guitars

Outdoor concerts provide hot fun in the summertime

In a city that in July can feel like Death Valley with large buildings, three outdoor music series are about the only thing that can make you glad you're not in the Hamptons. Well, almost. Central Park SummerStage has offered free music from around the globe for 13 years, and Celebrate Brooklyn at the Prospect Park Bandshell and Battery Park City's Castle Clinton have been around almost as long.

Summer is not traditionally a time for adventurous classical programming, but it is ripe for other genres. Most of the city's musical institutions move out into the parks and open spaces, and those that stay indoors, like Lincoln Center's popular Mostly Mozart festival, become air-conditioning for the soul. The **Lincoln Center Festival** (875-5108) is attempting to change all that. Combining an eclectic mix of music, opera, dance and theater, the festival aspires to rival the Edinburgh and Spoleto festivals, and it's gotten off to a good start. Recent programs have featured Shanghai Kunju Opera Company's production of *Peony Pavilion,* a 900th birthday tribute to composer Hildegard of Bingen and the U.S. premiere of a new oratorio by Polish composer Krzysztof Penderecki. Other summer (mostly open-air) events around town include:

The Anchorage
Cadman Plaza West between Hicks and Old Fulton Sts, Brooklyn. (206-6674). Subway: 2, 3 to Clark St; A, C to High St. $7–$20. No credit cards. There isn't a more evocative space to catch an avant-rock or DJ event (think John Zorn, Giant Step, Sonic Youth) than this art cavern inside the base of the Brooklyn Bridge; it's so roomy, you'll think you're outside.

Bryant Park
Sixth Ave at 42nd St (983-4142). Subway: B, D, F, Q to 42nd St; N, R, 1, 2, 3, 9. 7 to 42nd St–Times Sq. Free. Directly behind the 42nd Street branch of the New York Public Library, Bryant Park is a serene, attractive and distinctly European park with a substantial free concert series.

Castle Clinton
Battery Park, Battery Pl at State St (835-2789). Subway: C, E to World Trade Center; N, R, 1, 9 to Cortlandt St; 2, 3 to Park Pl. Free. Space is limited at this well-preserved fortress situated between the financial district and Ellis Island, but its seats offer lucky summer music hounds a comfortable, unobstructed view of everyone from Frank Sinatra Jr. to John Mayall's Bluesbreakers and John Zorn's Masada.

Central Park
See chapter Sightseeing *for listings.* This vast oasis takes on a magical air on summer nights when the New York Philharmonic and the Metropolitan Opera stage concerts (some with fireworks).

Central Park SummerStage
Rumsey Playfield, 830 Fifth Ave at 72nd St (360-2777). Subway: B, C to 72nd St; 6 to 68th St. Free; benefit concerts $15–$25. No credit cards. During a humid summer weekend, SummerStage is one of the great treasures available to New Yorkers. Although there are always two or three shows with a substantial ticket price, the majority of concerts at this amphitheater are free. Think of it: Solomon Burke or Stereolab, Junior or James Brown, under crystal-blue skies, for no charge, with beer!

Downing Stadium
Randalls Island (582-0228). Subway: 4, 5, 6 to 125th St, then M60 bus to Stadium. This former soccer stadium and adjoining field on an East River island is home to events such as Lollapalooza, the Vans Warped Tour, the Tibetan Freedom Concert and Reggae Sunsplash. It is by no means lovely; it is by all means convenient.

Giants Stadium
Rte 3, East Rutherford, New Jersey (1-201-935-3900). Travel: Port Authority bus to Meadowlands. $20–$75. V,

*Sun city: Gilberto Gil at **SummerStage**.*

Splendor on the grass: **Central Park** *and the* **Metropolitan Opera** *make a perfect match.*

MC, AmEx. Here's where you catch biggies like U2 and the Stones while jet airliners heading to and from Newark Airport crowd the sky. The band members look like ants holding instruments, and you'll have to wait a long, long time for beer. But the hot dogs aren't that bad, and because it's outdoors, it's the last venue in the Meadowlands where you can actually smoke.

Jones Beach
Long Island (1-516-221-1000). Travel: LIRR from Penn Station to Freeport, then bus to the beach. $18-$45. No credit cards. From July to September, a diverse group of performers—Diana Ross, Oasis, Barry White and PJ Harvey—have all performed under the setting sun at this beachside amphitheater.

Lincoln Center Plaza
10 Lincoln Center Plaza at W 62nd St (875-5400). Subway: 1, 9 to 66th St–Lincoln Ctr. Free. Lincoln Center's summer Out-of-Doors and Midsummer Night Swing festivals, Lincoln Center Plaza plays host to as many of New York's sundry cultural communities as does Central Park SummerStage. Over the course of a week, it's possible to hear charmed interpretations of Mozart, the world's hottest Latino and African bands and a concert by tenor-saxophone god Sonny Rollins. It all takes place in the splendor of the city's key center for the performing arts.

Museum of Modern Art Summergarden
See chapter **Museums** *for listings.* Twentieth-century works are performed in the MoMA sculpture garden. You'll quite likely think you're in a Woody Allen movie. Bring your own neuroses.

Prospect Park Bandshell
9th St at Prospect Park West, Park Slope, Brooklyn (1-718 965 8969). Subway: F to Seventh Ave; 2, 3 to Grand Army Plaza. Free. Prospect Park Bandshell is to Brooklynites what Central Park SummerStage is to Manhattan residents: the place to hear great music in the great outdoors, at no cost. The shows, produced by Celebrate Brooklyn, mirror the borough's great melting pot, so you're just as likely to hear Afropop or Caribbean music as jazz and blues. Past acts have included Philip Glass, Randy Weston, and King David Rudder & Charlie's Roots.

Washington Square Music Festival
4th St and La Guardia Pl (431-1088). Subway: A,C, E, B, D, F, Q to W 4th St–Washington Sq. Free. This concert series, held in the heart of Greenwich Village, features chamber orchestra and ensemble works every Tuesday night in June and July.

Smalls

183 W 10th St at Seventh Ave (929-7565). Subway: 1, 9 to Christopher St–Sheridan Sq. $10. No credit cards. The spot where jazz new jacks rub elbows with their college-student counterparts and Beat-era nostalgists, Smalls books both high-profile up-and-comers and established stars such as Lee Konitz. There's no liquor license, but you can bring your own or sample some of the juices at the bar.

Sweet Basil

88 Seventh Ave South between Bleecker and Grove Sts (242-1785). Subway: 1, 9 to Christopher St–Sheridan Sq. $17.50, plus $10 minimum. AmEx, MC, V. Past players here have included Art Blakey and Abdullah Ibrahim; the club now showcases young players as well as veterans. There's a jazz brunch on Saturdays and Sundays.

Village Vanguard

178 Seventh Ave South at Perry St (255-4037). Subway: A, C, E, 1, 2, 3, 9 to 14th St; L to Eighth Ave. $15, plus $10 minimum. No credit cards. This basement club is still going strong after 60 years. Its stage—a small but mighty step-up that has seen the likes of John Coltrane, Bill Evans and Miles Davis—still hosts the crème de la crème of mainstream jazz talent. The Monday-night regular is the 17-piece Vanguard Jazz Orchestra, which has now held the same slot (originally as the Thad Jones/Mel Lewis Jazz Orchestra) for more than 30 years.

Zinno

126 W 13th St between Sixth and Seventh Aves (924-5182). Subway: F, 1, 2, 3, 9 to 14th St; L to Sixth Ave. $10, plus $15 minimum. AmEx, MC, V. A supper club for those who want more than mere polite background noise with their dinner, Zinno is where some of the mainstream's most accomplished jazzers (Hilton Ruiz, Michael Moore, Bucky Pizzarelli) get to perform in relaxed, intimate duos and trios. The cuisine isn't hard on the palate, either.

Reggae, World & Latin

Copacabana

617 W 57th St between Eleventh and Twelfth Aves (582-2672). Subway: A, C, B, D, 1, 9 to 59th St–Columbus Circle. $3–$40. AmEx, MC, V (for table reservations only). It's not for nothing that the Copacabana's reputation precedes it. For decades it has been the venue that introduced the superstars of Latin music to the tourist masses. The Copa can get pricey at times, but after an ecstatic night of dancing, you're not likely to leave disappointed.

Gonzalez y Gonzalez

625 Broadway between Bleecker and Houston Sts (473-8787). Subway: B, D, F, Q to Broadway–Lafayette St; 6 to Bleecker St. Free. AmEx, MC, V. From the front window Gonzalez may seem like merely a tourist Tex-Mex restaurant, but walk past the big sombreros and the bar and you'll find a Latino music lover's paradise complete with stage and cozy makeshift dance floor. Once there, you'll be compelled to find a partner and squeeze yourself in—especially on Wednesdays, when Johnny Almendra & Los Jovenes del Barrio hit you with a blast of flute- and violin-flavored Cuban *charanga*.

Latin Quarter

2551 Broadway at 96th St (864-7600). Subway: 1, 2, 3, 9 to 96th St. $15–$20. AmEx, MC, V. On the Latin music scale, the Latin Quarter is to the cognoscenti what the Copacabana is to everybody else. Connoisseurs by the hundreds mob the place during the weekend, making the Quarter's cavernous dance floor seem like a cozy corner. What the dancers come for is salsa, merengue and hot Latin freestyle.

S.O.B.'s

200 Varick St at Houston St (243-4940). Subway: 1, 9 to Houston St. $10–$25. AmEx, DC, Disc, JCB, MC, V. S.O.B.'s stands for Sounds of Brazil, but that's not the only kind of music you'll hear at the city's premier spot for musicians from south of the border. There's samba but also reggae and even Afropop. Mondays belong to La Tropica Nights, an evening devoted to the biggest names in salsa. Looking like the safari-style burger joint at Disneyland, S.O.B.'s will cure your thirst for all things percussive and exotic.

Symphony Space

2537 Broadway at 95th St (864-1414). Subway: 1, 2, 3, 9 to 96th St. $10–$25. AmEx, MC, V. Although Symphony Space plays host to a plethora of music from pop to classical, the 1,000-seat hall is probably best known as the stronghold for the multiculti concerts presented by the World Music Institute. The crowds register as much enthusiasm for Malian soulstress Oumou Sangare and Gypsy revelers Haidouks, as they do for the Cuban song-and-dance troupe Los Muñequitos de Matanzas. Almost without fail, the many local homesick nationals end up dancing on stage with the visiting stars by concert's end.

Zinc Bar

90 Houston St between La Guardia Pl and Thompson St (477-8337). Subway: A, C, E, B, D, F, Q to W 4th St–Washington Sq. $15, $5 minimum. No credit cards. A cozy—and we mean cozy—subnook situated where Noho meets Soho, Zinc Bar is the place to catch up with the most die-hard night owls. It's got an after-hours feel that actually starts well before daybreak, and the atmosphere is enhanced by the astonishingly cool mix of jazz, Latino, Brazilian and flamenco bands that gig there nightly.

Blues, Folk & Country

Chicago B.L.U.E.S.

73 Eighth Ave between 13th and 14th Sts (924-9755). Subway: A, C, E to 14th St; L to Eighth Ave. Free–$20. AmEx, MC, V. When Otis Rush or some other titan of the blues comes to town, he often settles in at this cozy West Village club. The opening acts can be startlingly bad, but the chance of seeing the likes of Johnnie Johnson at close range makes this a must-visit club. The open jams are also of note.

Fast Folk Café

41 North Moore St between Varick and Hudson Sts (274-1636). Subway: A, C, E to Canal St; 1, 9 to Franklin St. Free–$15. No credit cards. No local venue wants much to be known as a folk venue, save for this tiny Tribeca bastion of intimate acousticism.

Louisiana Bar & Grill

622 Broadway between Bleecker and Houston Sts (460-9633). Subway: B, D, F, Q to Broadway–Lafayette St; 6 to Bleecker St. Free. AmEx, MC, V. Apart from the fine Cajun cuisine available here, the Louisiana is known for booking top-shelf rockabilly, country and blues acts, including local legends the Harlem All-Stars.

Manny's Car Wash

1558 Third Ave between 87th and 88th Sts (369-2583). Subway: 4, 5, 6 to 86th St. Free–$15. AmEx, MC, V. Every evening, nationally prominent and popular local blues acts blare from the tiny stage of this elongated nightspot on the city's Upper East Side. Patrons are generally locals and can be serious blues lovers or junior Wall Streeters ogling the single women (women get in free on Monday nights). A blues jam occurs on Sunday nights, when there's mostly standing room only.

Terra Blues

149 Bleecker St at Thompson St (777-7776). Subway: A, C, E, B, D, F, Q to W 4th St–Washington Sq. Free–$15. AmEx, MC, V. Gracing the stage at this otherwise typical Bleecker Street bar are a wide range of blues-based artists, both local and imported, ranging from authentic Chicago guitar pickers to the local blues duo Satan and Adam.

Classical music

A glance through the listings of a typical week will reveal more than a dozen classical-music events occuring in a single evening, probably more than anywhere except London. Carnegie Hall is still the place to play for visiting orchestras and soloists, and Lincoln Center on a busy night might simultaneously host two operas, an orchestral concert and a piano recital. The number of performances in the city's churches, schools, cultural centers and other venues is also quite staggering.

For information on concerts, times and venues, see *Time Out New York*'s classical-music listings or the Sunday *New York Times*. The Theater Development Fund (*see chapter* **Dance**) also provides information on all music events via its NYC/On Stage service.

BACKSTAGE PASS

It's possible to go behind the scenes at several of the city's major concert venues. **Lincoln Center's Guided Tours** (875-5350) escort you inside all three of the center's major halls; **Backstage at the Met** (769-7000) takes you around the famous opera house; **Carnegie Hall** (247-7800) runs several tours, including some connected with exhibitions at the hall's Rose Museum. It's also possible to sit in on rehearsals of the New York Philharmonic, usually held on the Thursday before a concert.

Concert halls

For the New York State Theater, Avery Fisher Hall, Metropolitan Opera House and Alice Tully Hall, see **Houses of high culture**, page 270.

Brooklyn Academy of Music

30 Lafayette Ave between Flatbush Ave and Fulton St, Brooklyn (1-718-636-4100). Subway: B, D, Q, 2, 3, 4, 5 to Atlantic Ave. $20–$75. AmEx, MC, V. Internet: *www.bam.org.* BAM stages music and dance in a beautiful house that is America's oldest academy for the performing arts (though a recent refurbishing has converted the Leperq Recital Hall into a snazzy jazz café). The programming is more East Village than Upper West Side: BAM helped launch the likes of Philip Glass and John Zorn. Its resident Brooklyn Philharmonic Orchestra became a home for American composers under conductor Dennis Russell Davies, and current music director Robert Spano has made the orchestra actually play together and sound good. Every fall and winter, the Next Wave Festival of theater and music provides an overview of the more established avant-garde, while the spring BAM Opera season brings innovative European productions to downtown Brooklyn. *See also chapters* **Dance** *and* **Theater**.

Carnegie Hall

154 W 57th St at Seventh Ave (247-7800). Subway: A, C, B, D, 1, 9 to 59th St–Columbus Circle; N, R to 57th St. $20–$70. AmEx, MC, V. Tchaikovsky conducted the opening concert here in 1891, and despite being earmarked for demolition in the 1960s, Carnegie Hall remains the crème de la crème of the city's visiting-artist concert venues. A varied roster of American and international stars regularly appears. There are two auditoriums: Carnegie Hall itself and the smaller Weill Recital Hall. The heavy hitters are well represented: from violinist Anne-Sophie Mutter and pianist Maurizio Pollini to the Berlin Philharmonic and the London Symphony.

Colden Center for the Performing Arts

Queens College, 65-30 Kissena Blvd, Flushing, Queens (1-718-793-8080). Subway: F, R to Parsons Blvd, then Q25 or Q25–34 bus. $8–$25. AmEx, Disc, MC, V. The home of the Queens Philharmonic, this multipurpose hall also stages concerts by international artists who are in town for Manhattan performances. Due to the Colden Center's remote location, tickets are often half the Manhattan price.

Florence Gould Hall at the Alliance Française

55 E 59th St between Park and Madison Aves (355-6160). Subway: N, R to Fifth Ave; 4, 5, 6 to 59th St. $15–$35. AmEx, MC, V. Recitals and chamber works are performed in this intimate space. Programming has a decidedly French accent, in terms of both artists and repertoire.

Kaufmann Concert Hall at the 92nd Street Y

1395 Lexington Ave at 92nd St (415-5440). Subway: 4, 5, 6 to 86th St; 6 to 96th St. $20–$40. AmEx, MC, V. Back in the 1970s, the Y began to exercise the ears as well as the body by developing an extensive and imaginative series for its acoustically excellent Kaufmann Concert Hall. The programming got very adventurous a few years ago (evenings devoted to Luciano Berio; Peter Sellars's stagings of Bach cantatas with costumes by Isaac Mizrahi), but nowadays, the emphasis is on more traditional orchestral, solo and chamber masterworks.

Merkin Concert Hall

Abraham Goodman House, 129 W 67th St between Broadway and Amsterdam Ave (501-3330). Subway: 1, 9 to 66th St–Lincoln Ctr. $10–$25. AmEx, MC, V. This unattractive theater with rather dry acoustics is shamefacedly tucked away on a side street in the shadow of Lincoln Center, but its mix of early music and avant-garde programming—heavy on recitals and chamber concerts—can make it a rewarding stop.

New Jersey Performing Arts Center

1 Center St at the waterfront, Newark, NJ (1-973-642-8989). Travel: PATH train to Newark, then Loop shuttle bus two stops to the Center. $10–$66. AmEx, MC, V, DC. Designed by Los Angeles–based architect Barton Myers, NJPAC is the first major concert hall to have been built on the East Coast in more than 30 years. The complex is impressive, boasting the oval-shaped, wooden 2,750-seat Prudential Hall and the more institutional-looking 514-seat Victoria Theater. It may sound far away, but in fact it takes only about 15 minutes to get to NJPAC from mid-Manhattan. It's a good place to catch big-name acts that may be sold out at stodgy Manhattan venues. The 1998–99 season includes visits by the Philadelphia Orchestra, the London Symphony, the Los Angeles Philharmonic and the Cleveland Orchestra.

Town Hall

123 W 43rd St between Sixth and Seventh Aves (840-2824). Subway: B, D, F, Q to 42nd St; N, R, S, 1, 2, 3, 9, 7 to 42nd St–Times Sq. Prices vary. AmEx, MC, V. This recently renovated hall has a wonderful, intimate stage and excellent acoustics. Classical music often shares the programming lineup with New Age speakers, pop concerts and movie screenings.

Other venues

These are some of the more notable spaces. In addition, many other museums, libraries and galleries offer chamber music.

Bargemusic
Fulton Ferry Landing, Brooklyn (1-718-624-4061). Subway: A, C to High St. $15–$23. No credit cards. Two concerts a week (Thursday and Sunday) are held year-round on this barge, moored by the Brooklyn Navy Yard. It's a magical experience, with gorgeous views of the Manhattan skyline—but dress warmly in winter.

CAMI Hall
165 W 57th St between Sixth and Seventh Aves (397-6900). Subway: N, R to 57th St. Prices vary. No credit cards. Located across the street from Carnegie Hall, this 200-seat recital hall is rented out for individual events, mostly by classical artists.

Continental Center
180 Maiden Lane at Front St (799-5000, ext 313). Subway: 2, 3 to Wall St. Free. The Juilliard Artists in Concert series offers free lunchtime student recitals once a week, more frequently during the summer.

Hotel Wales
1295 Madison Ave at 92nd St (876-6000). Subway: 6 to 96th St. Free. Along with the Mansfield Hotel, the Wales offers free chamber-music concerts one night each week.

The Kitchen
512 W 19th St between Tenth and Eleventh Aves (255-5793). Subway: C, E to 23rd St. $10–$20. AmEx, MC, V. Occupying a 19th-century building that was once an icehouse, the Kitchen has been a meeting place of the avant-garde in music, dance and theater for more than 25 years.

Kosciuszko Foundation House
15 E 65th St at Fifth Ave (734-2130). Subway: N, R to Fifth Ave; 6 to 68th St. $10–$15. MC, V. This renovated East Side townhouse accommodates a fine chamber-music series with a twist: Each program must feature at least one work by a Polish composer.

The Mansfield Hotel
12 W 44th St between Fifth and Sixth Aves (944-6050). Subway: B, D, F, Q to 42nd St. Free. See Hotel Wales, above.

Metropolitan Museum of Art
*See chapter **Museums** for listings.* Concerts are held in the Grace Rainey Rogers Auditorium, near the Egyptian galleries,

Houses of high culture
From Beethoven to Bang on a Can, music at Lincoln Center is world-class

In the 1950s, the tenements and playgrounds that were the setting for Leonard Bernstein's *West Side Story* were demolished. The land, an area near the southwest corner of Central Park, was developed into Lincoln Center, a four-block complex of buildings and public spaces housing many of the city's most important musical institutions. The striking concrete-pillared 1960s architecture of Avery Fisher Hall, the New York State Theater and the Metropolitan Opera House surrounds a black marble fountain by Philip Johnson. There's also the Lincoln Center Theater building, containing the Vivian Beaumont and Mitzi E. Newhouse theaters, as well as Damrosch Park's Guggenheim Bandshell and the New York Public Library for the Performing Arts (*see pages 267 and 271*). Restaurants at Lincoln Center include the overpriced but convenient Café Vienna, the **Panevino Ristorante** in Avery Fisher Hall (874-7000) and the **Grand Tier** at the Met (799-3400).

Lincoln Center has tended to rely on the tried and true: The **Great Performers** series (Oct–June) attracts the likes of Jessye Norman, Yo-Yo Ma and Daniel Barenboim (call 721-6500 for tickets). But recent additions like the Bang on a Can Festival and the Bard Music Festival are a welcome change. More adventurous still is the Lincoln Center Festival (*see page 266*), the polar opposite of the center's long-running Mostly Mozart series.

Lincoln Center *65th St at Columbus Ave (875-5400/programs and information LIN-COLN). Subway: 1, 9 to 66th St–Lincoln Ctr. AmEx, MC, V.*

Alice Tully Hall
875-5050. $25–$40. Built to house the Chamber Music Society of Lincoln Center (875-5788), Alice Tully Hall somehow makes its 1,000 seats feel intimate. It has no central aisle; the rows have extra leg room to compensate. The hall accommodates both music and spoken text well; its vocal recital series is one of the most extensive in town.

Avery Fisher Hall
875-5030. $10–$70. Originally called Philharmonic Hall, this 2,700-seat auditorium used to have unbearable acoustics. It took the largess of electronics millionaire Avery Fisher, and several major renovations, to improve the sound quality. The venue is now both handsome and comfortable. It's home to the New York Philharmonic (875-5656), now under the direction of Kurt Masur, which is the country's oldest orchestra (founded in 1842) and one of the world's finest. Its evangelical philosophy has given rise to free concerts and regular open rehearsals. The hall also hosts performances by top international ensembles as part of the Great Performers series. Every summer, the famous Mostly Mozart series is held here.

Metropolitan Opera House
362-6000. $24–$200. With enormous mystical paintings by Marc Chagall hanging inside its five geometric arches, the Met is the grandest of the Lincoln Center buildings and a spectacular place to see and hear opera. It's home to the Metropolitan Opera, and it's also where major visiting companies are most likely to appear. Met productions are lavish (though not necessarily tasteful) and casts are an interna-

or occasionally beside the Temple of Dendur. Since this is one of the city's best chamber-music venues, the concerts usually sell out quickly.

Miller Theater at Columbia University
Broadway at 116th St (854-7799). Subway: 1, 9 to 116th St. $15. Don't come expecting only student recitals. Columbia's acoustically excellent space attracts some big international names and innovative, multidisciplinary programming. (When was the last time you saw a staged version of Jacques Offenbach's *A Trip to the Moon*?)

New York Public Library for the Performing Arts
40 Lincoln Center Plaza (870-1630). Subway: 1, 9 to 66th St–Lincoln Ctr. Free. Recitals, solo performances and lectures are held in the Bruno Walter Auditorium. On the library's ground floor, you can listen to recordings from the collection at private turntables; on the third floor is a wonderful archive, including programs, press books and photographs.

Roulette
228 West Broadway at White St (219-8242). Subway: A, C, E to Canal St; 1, 9 to Franklin St. $8. No credit cards. Roulette is *the* place to go for a range of experimental music in a Tribeca loft—very downtown.

Sylvia & Danny Kaye Playhouse
Hunter College, 68th St at Lexington Ave (772-4448). Subway: 6 to 68th St. $20-$45. MC, V. Across town from Lincoln Center, this refurbished theater has an eclectic program of professional music and dance.

Symphony Space
2537 Broadway at 95th St (864-5400). Subway: 1, 9 to 96th St. $10-$20. AmEx, MC, V. The programming here is eclectic; best bets are the annual Wall to Wall marathons, which offer a full day of music featuring a given composer or theme.

John L. Tishman Auditorium
The New School, 66 W 12th St at Sixth Ave (229-5689). Subway: F, 1, 2, 3, 9 to 14th St. $8. AmEx, MC, V. The New School offers a modestly priced chamber-music series that runs from April to October and features up-and-coming young musicians, as well as more established artists who play here for a fraction of the price.

World Financial Center
West St between Liberty and Vesey Sts (945-0505). Subway: N, R, 1, 9 to Cortlandt St. Free. Logan's Run meets *Blade Runner* at the glassed-in Winter Garden (palm trees spring straight from the marble floor, and you can see the bright lights of the World Financial Center and the World Trade

tional Who's Who of current stars. Under the baton of artistic director James Levine, the orchestra has become a true symphonic force. Audiences at the Met are knowledgeable and fiercely partisan—subscriptions stay in families for generations. Tickets are expensive, and unless you can afford good seats, the view won't be great. Still, standing-room tickets are available for less than $15, though you have to wait in line on Saturday mornings to buy them. English-language subtitles that now appear on the backs of seats allow the audiences to laugh in all the right places. While over-the-top Franco Zeffirelli productions still tend to be the norm, the Met has started commissioning productions by the likes of Robert Wilson—to mixed reception from conservative Met audiences (Wilson was booed at the premiere of his production of *Lohengrin* last year). Upcoming productions include Met premieres of Schoenberg's *Moses und Aron* and Carlisle Floyd's *Susannah*.

New York State Theater
870-5570. $20-$85. Philip Johnson's jewel box of chandeliers and glass is home to the New York City Opera, which has tried to upgrade its second-best reputation by being defiantly popular and defiantly ambitious. This means hiring only American singers, performing many works in English, bringing American musicals into opera houses, giving a more theatrical spin to old favorites and developing supertitles for foreign-language productions. City Opera has championed modern opera, mixing Tan Dun's *Ghost Opera* with *Madama Butterfly*, with a few great successes and other noble failures. It's ultimately much cooler than its stodgier neighbor. Tickets are about half the price of the Met, and the theater is a gem.

Walter Reade Theater
875-5601. $15-$30. Lincoln Center's newest concert hall is a glorified movie house: It's home to the Film Society of Lincoln Center, and its acoustics are the driest in the complex. Yet the uniformly perfect sightlines make up for it. The Chamber Music Society uses the space for its Music of Our Time series, and the post-Minimalist Bang on a Can festival houses its resident ensemble here. A Sunday-morning concert series features pastries and hot drinks in the lobby.

Met life: A giant Chagall greets opera fans.

*Body language: Kurt Masur conducts the New York Philharmonic at **Avery Fisher Hall**.*

Center). The free concerts (timed to fit the schedule of the working day and usually amplified) range from chamber and choral music to Eno-esque installations for public spaces.

Churches

An enticing variety of music, both sacred and secular, is performed in New York's churches. Many of the resident choirs are excellent, while superb acoustics and serene surroundings make the churches particularly attractive venues. A bonus, some concerts are free or very cheap. **The Gotham Early Music Foundation** sponsors a terrific annual early-music series at churches around the city. For tickets and information, call 1-516-329-6166.

Cathedral of St. John the Divine

1047 Amsterdam Ave at 112th St (662-2133). Subway: 1, 9 to 110th St. The 3,000-seat interior is an acoustical cavern, but the stunning Gothic surroundings provide a comfortable

home to such groups as the Ensemble for Early Music and the church's own heavenly choir.

Christ and St. Stephen's Church

120 W 69th St at Broadway (787-2755). Subway: 1, 2, 3, 9 to 72nd St. This West Side church offers one of the most diverse concert rosters in the city.

Church of the Heavenly Rest

2 E 90th St at Fifth Ave (289-3400). Subway: 4, 5, 6 to 86th St. Heavenly Rest is home to the Canterbury Choral Society and the New York Pro Arte Chamber Orchestra.

Church of St. Ignatius Loyola

980 Park Ave at 84th St (288-2520). Subway: 4, 5, 6 to 86th St. This church's Sacred Music in a Sacred Space is a high point of Upper East Side musical life.

Corpus Christi Church

529 W 121st Street between Broadway and Amsterdam Ave (666-9350). Subway: 1, 9 to 125th St. New York's early-music fans get their fix from Music Before 1800 (666-9266), a resident ensemble that has also presented the U.S. debuts of many prominent European groups.

Good Shepherd Presbyterian Church
152 W 66th St between Broadway and Amsterdam Ave (799-1259). Subway: 1, 9 to 66th St. Musically, Good Shepherd is best known for the twice-weekly recitals of the Jupiter Symphony, under music director Jens Nygaard. Other classical music events are presented here as well.

Riverside Church
490 Riverside Dr at 122nd St (870-6700). Subway: 1, 9 to 125th St. With its active internal musical life (fine choir, fine organ) and visiting guests (the Orpheus Chamber Orchestra, among others), Riverside plays a large part in local musical life.

St. Bartholomew's Church
109 E 50th St between Park and Lexington Aves (378-0248). Subway: E, F to Lexington Ave; 6 to 51st St. Large-scale choral music and occasional chapel recitals fill the magnificent dome behind the church's facade, designed by Stanford White.

St. Paul's Chapel
Broadway at Fulton St (602-0747). Subway: J, M, 4, 5 to Fulton St; N, R, 1, 9 to Cortlandt St; 2, 3 to Park Pl. This historic church in the financial district hosts the Noonday Concerts series with nearby Trinity Church.

St. Thomas Church Fifth Avenue
1 W 53rd St at Fifth Ave (757-7013). Subway: B, D, F, Q to 47th–50th Sts–Rockefeller Center. Some of the finest choral music in the city, with the only fully accredited choir school for boys in the country, can be heard here. The church's annual *Messiah* is a must.

Trinity Church
Broadway at Wall St (602-0747). Subway: A, C, J to Broadway–Nassau St; N, R, 1, 9 to Rector St; 2, 3, 4, 5 to Wall St. See **St. Paul's Chapel.**

Schools

Juilliard, Mannes and the Manhattan School of Music are all renowned for their students, their faculty and their artists-in-residence, all of whom regularly perform for free or for minimal admission fees. Noteworthy music and innovative programming can be found at several other colleges and schools in the city.

Brooklyn Center for the Performing Arts at Brooklyn College
Campus Rd at Hillel Pl off Nostrand Ave, Brooklyn (1-718-951-4543). Subway: 2, 5 to Flatbush Ave–Brooklyn College. $25–$40. AmEx, MC, V. While it mostly hosts concerts by mass-appeal pop performers, this hall smack in the middle of Flatbush also serves as a destination for traveling opera troupes and soloists of international caliber.

Greenwich House Music School
46 Barrow St between Bedford St and Seventh Ave South (242-4770). Subway: 1, 9 to Christopher St–Sheridan Sq. Prices vary. MC, V. Greenwich House's Renee Weiler Concert Hall puts on a wide variety of chamber concerts by students, faculty and visiting guests. Student recitals are free.

Juilliard School of Music
Juilliard Theater, Morse Hall, Paul Recital Hall, 60 Lincoln Center Plaza (769-7406). Subway: 1, 9 to 66th St. Mostly free. New York's premier conservatory stages weekly concerts by student soloists, orchestras and chamber ensembles, as well as excellent student opera productions.

Manhattan School of Music
120 Claremont Ave at 122nd St (749-2802). Subway: 1, 9 to 125th St. Mostly free. Now directed by Marta Istomen, once of Washington's Kennedy Center, this school offers master classes, recitals and off-site concerts by its students, faculty and visiting pros. The opera program is one of the most adventurous in town.

Mannes College of Music
150 W 85th St between Columbus and Amsterdam Aves (496-8524). Subway: B, C, 1, 9 to 86th St. Free. Long considered a distant third in the city's conservatory triumvirate, Mannes has recently been raising its profile. Concerts are by a mix of student, faculty and professional ensembles-in-residence. See the Orion String Quartet at Lincoln Center for big bucks, or here for free.

Opera

The Metropolitan Opera and the New York City Opera may be the big guys (*see* **Houses of high culture,** *page 270*), but they're hardly the only ones in town. The following companies perform a varied repertory—both warhorses and works-in-progress—from Verdi's *Aida* to Wargo's *Chekhov Trilogy.* Phone the individual organizations for ticket prices, schedules and venue details.

Amato Opera Theater
319 Bowery at 2nd St (228-8200). Subway: 6 to Bleecker St. With a theater only 20 feet wide, Anthony and Sally Amato's charming, fully-staged productions are like watching opera in someone's living room. Lots of well-known singers have sung here, but multiple casting breeds inconsistency.

American Opera Projects
463 Broome St between Greene and Mercer Sts (431-8102). Subway: 6 to Canal St. Not so much an opera company as a living, breathing workshop for the art form. Productions are often a way to follow a work-in-progress.

Dicapo Opera Theater
184 E 76th St between Third and Lexington Aves (228-9438). Subway: 6 to 77th St. This top-notch chamber-opera troupe benefits from City Opera–quality singers performing in intelligently designed small-scale sets. A real treat.

New York Gilbert & Sullivan Players
302 W 91st St between West End Ave and Riverside Dr (769-1000). Subway: 1, 9 to 96th St. Every January at Symphony Space, this troupe presents one of the Big Three (*HMS Pinafore, The Mikado* or *The Pirates of Penzance*) alongside another G&S work.

Opera Orchestra of New York
154 W 57th St at Seventh Ave (799-1982). Subway: A, C, B, D, 1, 9 to 59th St–Columbus Circle; N, R to 57th St. The program organizers have an uncanny ability to find and showcase great new talent and to unearth forgotten operatic gems, in these semi-staged concert performances at Carnegie Hall.

Regina Opera Company
Regina Hall, 65th St and Twelfth Ave, Brooklyn (1-718-232-3555). Subway: B to 62nd St, N to Ft. Hamilton Pkwy. The only year-round opera company in Brooklyn, Regina offers full orchestras and fully staged productions.

Sports & Fitness

***Whether you're a would-be pro or a professional fan,
New York's got a court, field—or bar—for you***

New York is a great sports town. When it comes to spectator sports, particularly the big four (baseball, basketball, football and hockey), New Yorkers believe they hold a special monopoly on wisdom. This is a place where every third person you meet is convinced that given enough time and money, he or she could run at least one local team better than whoever is running it now. New Yorkers read the tabloids back to front, and arguments over half-remembered sports trivia can be far more heated than any disputes about politics, sex or religion.

The New York metropolitan area has more professional teams than any other city in America—two basketball, three hockey, two baseball and two football. New Yorkers are passionately devoted to their local heroes—they may grouse about the players and condemn the owners, but when the home team is in contention for a championship, the city practically grinds to a halt during games. If the team wins, it's ticker-tape parades and pandemonium in the streets.

Baseball is very much a product of the five boroughs. The basic rules of the game were drawn up by a New York team in 1846, and the first professional leagues originated in the city during the 1870s. Babe Ruth and the Yankees' "Murderers' Row" of the 1920s cemented the game's hold on the popular imagination. Joe DiMaggio reinforced it in the 1930s. During the 1950s, three of New York's boroughs had great teams; there were endless debates on the relative merits of the Bronx-based Yankees' Mickey Mantle, the Manhattan-based Giants' Willie Mays and the Brooklyn Dodgers' Duke Snider.

For a time, when "Broadway" Joe Namath stood at the helm of the New York Jets, it seemed as though the football gridiron might supplant the baseball diamond in the hearts of New Yorkers. But it is basketball that grips the city now, with the Knicks as perennial contenders for a championship (and perennial losers) and the up-and-coming New Jersey Nets exciting fans across the river.

New York also offers plenty for those who define "sports" as something a bit more active than watching television and drinking beer. Central Park is an oasis for everybody from skaters to hurlers. Gyms have practically replaced bars as hip pick-up spots, and massive complexes such as Chelsea Piers have brought suburban space and convenience to the big city.

Spectator sports

Information

All the daily papers carry massive amounts of sports analysis and give listings of the day's events and TV coverage—concentrating on the NBA, NHL, NFL and Major League Baseball. *The New York Times* may have the most literate coverage, but the tabloids—*The Daily News* and *The New York Post*—provide both in-depth news and blunt, often heated opinions. For news of special events, contact the **New York Convention & Visitors Bureau** (397-8222).

Tickets

Your first call for tickets should be to the team itself. You may be referred to **Ticketmaster** (307-7171), which sells the same tickets, with a service charge added. For many events, however—especially football and basketball—demand for tickets far outstrips supply. If you are certain that neither the team nor Ticketmaster can help, you have two options: scalpers or ticket brokers. If you're staying in a hotel, it's worth having a word with the concierge, as they often have excellent connections.

Scalpers

If you buy from scalpers, you won't be able to get your money back if you're tricked—but if you're careful, this can be a reliable way of buying seats. Before you part with any cash, check that the ticket has the correct details, and make sure you know where your seats will be. Diagrams of stadium seating arrangements are printed in the front of the Yellow Pages. Sometimes scalpers will overestimate demand and, as game time nears, try to unload their tickets at bargain prices. The police have been cracking down on scalpers in recent years—particularly outside Madison Square Garden, home of the Knicks and Rangers—so be discreet.

Ticket brokers

Ticket brokers offer much the same service as scalpers, although their activities are more regulated. It's illegal in New York State to sell a ticket for more than its face value plus a service charge, so these companies operate from other states by phone. They can almost guarantee tickets for sold-

Star in stripes: Pitching great Mariano Rivera has helped make the **Yankees** a power again.

out events, and tend to deal in the better seats. Not surprisingly, this is a service you pay for. Good seats for the basketball playoffs run close to $1,000, and tickets for most Giants football games start at $100. Look under "Ticket Sales" in the Yellow Pages for brokers. Three of the more established are **Prestige Entertainment** (1-800-2-GET-TIX), **Ticket Window** (1-800-SOLD-OUT) and **Union Tickets** (1-800-CITY-TIX).

Baseball

The 1995 players' strike turned off many fans nationwide, and Yankee owner George Steinbrenner's meddling ways and frequent threats to leave the Bronx have not exactly endeared him to the locals, but New Yorkers have not stopped loving baseball. Tickets are available at the stadiums for most games from April to early October, but almost impossible to get for the post-season championship games—which in recent years have been a likely destination for the Yankees but not the Mets.

New York Mets
Shea Stadium, 123-01 Roosevelt Ave at 126th St, Flushing, Queens (information 1-718-507-8499). Subway: 7 to Willets

Point–Shea Stadium. Open for information Mon–Fri 9am–5:30pm. $9–$24. AmEx, MC, V, Disc.

New York Yankees
Yankee Stadium, River Ave at 161st St, Bronx (information 1-718-293-4300/ticket office 1-718-293-6000). Subway: C, D, 4 to 161st St–Yankee Stadium. Open for information Mon–Fri 9am–5pm, Sat and during games 10am–3pm. $12–$23. AmEx, Disc, MC, V.

Basketball

The basketball scene is dominated by the two professional NBA teams, the New York Knicks and the New Jersey Nets, with the Knicks reigning supreme in most New Yorkers' hearts. Tickets for most games, however, range from expensive to unobtainable. If you miss out or can't afford it, exciting basketball action can be had at the local colleges, or for free by watching the hustlers play pick-up games on street courts (*see* **Hoops—there it is,** *page 276*).

New York Knickerbockers (Knicks)
Madison Square Garden, Seventh Ave at 32nd St (information 465-6741). Subway: A, C, E, 1, 2, 3, 9 to 34th St–Penn Station. Ticket office open Mon–Fri 9am–6pm, Sat 10am–3pm. Official prices are fairly meaningless—ticket information is usually restricted to "This game is sold out."

Continental Airlines Arena, East Rutherford, New Jersey (information 1-201-935- 8888/tickets 1-201-935-3900). Travel: Bus from Port Authority Bus Terminal, 42nd St and Eighth Ave, $3.25 each way (information 564-8484). Ticket office open Mon–Fri 9am–6pm, Sat 10am–6pm, Sun noon– 5pm. $16–$50. AmEx, MC, V.

Boxing

Madison Square Garden

Seventh Ave at 32rd St (information 465-6741). Subway: A, C, E, 1, 2, 3, 9 to 34th St–Penn Station. After several decades in which the biggest bouts were fought in Atlantic City or Las Vegas, boxing has been returning to the Garden, once considered a mecca for fans of the sport. There are usually a few major fights in the course of a year.

Golden Gloves Boxing Championships

The Theater at Madison Square Garden. The Golden Gloves, a long-running New York tradition and amateur boxing's most prestigious competition, takes place every April.

Cricket

The comedy of hearing an American attempt to explain cricket is rivaled only by a European doing

---

Hoops—there it is

From Coney Island's rough-and-tumble playgrounds to the Garden's superstar celebrity glitz, basketball rules in New York City

They don't call basketball "the city game" for nothing. It may be the invention of a New England WASP, Dr. James Naismith, but it was black inner-city youths who perfected the sport. Basketball's minimal demands on space and equipment make it ideal for an urban environment, and the level of play on the street courts of the city today is good enough to draw in the pros during their off-season. If you have the skills to ball with the best—or just want to see some high-quality hoops, check out any of the public courts below.

The hottest ticket in town today is courtside for New York Knicks games at Madison Square Garden, where scene-makers, corporate types and hardcore fans rub shoulders with celebrity fixtures like Spike Lee and Woody Allen. What draws them is a mix of pure athleticism, intuition, improvisation and individual expression not seen in any other sport—and the perpetual hope of a championship. If you can't find (or afford) tickets, get down to a good sports bar and drink in the atmosphere.

The current Knicks team, which has had the misfortune to play in the same era as the sublime Michael Jordan and his Chicago Bulls, seems doomed to eternal bridesmaidhood. New York's also-ran status is a bitter pill for a town that not-so-secretly believes itself the navel of the world. The team today is like the city—richly talented and neurotically insecure. Both are slightly unsettling and incredibly exciting to watch. Meanwhile, across the river in New Jersey, the Nets are a rapidly maturing team that may be poised to eclipse the Knicks before long.

Hottest street games

Asphalt Green
90th St at East End Ave. Subway: 4, 5, 6 to 86th St.

The Battlegrounds
151st St at Amsterdam Ave. Subway: 1, 9 to 145th St.

Goat Park
99th St at Amsterdam Ave. Subway: 1, 2, 3, 9 to 96th St.

Marcus Garvey Park
121st St at Madison Ave. Subway: 4, 5, 6 to 125th St.

West 4th Street Courts (the Cage)
Sixth Ave at 4th St. Subway: A, C, E, B, D, F, Q to W 4th St–Washington Sq.

*He got game: shootin' rock at **the Cage**.*

the same for baseball. Nonetheless, New York—with its large populations of Indians, Pakistanis and West Indians, not to mention Brits—has more than 50 teams and at least two parks where the sound of leather on willow can be heard. The season runs from April to October.

Van Cortlandt Park
Van Cortlandt Park South and Bailey Ave, Bronx. Subway: 1, 9 to 242nd St. There are six or seven pitches here. The Commonwealth Cricket League, the largest league in the nation, plays on Sundays, May–September. The New York Cricket League (1-201-343-4544) also arranges Sunday matches.

Walker Park
50 Bard Ave at Delafield Court, Staten Island. Travel: Ferry to Staten Island, then S61 or S74 bus to Bard Ave. The Staten Island Cricket Club (1-718-447-5442) plays here most weekends during the season.

Football

The combination of beer and machismo known as football culture may be more indigenous to the American heartland than to this sophisticated metropolis, but New York is one of the few cities capable of supporting two professional teams. Of course, they both play in Giants Stadium, which is in New Jersey, but that's just a technicality. From August to December every year—and longer if the playoffs are involved, which they often are—New York is as fanatical a football town as any.

Giants Stadium
Meadowlands Sports Complex, East Rutherford, New Jersey (1-201-935-3900). Travel: Bus from Port Authority Bus Terminal, 42nd St at Eighth Ave, $3.25 each way (information 564-8484).
The Giants have a 20-year waiting list for season tickets, so the only way to see a game is to know someone with a season ticket or pay blood money to a broker. The Jets are slightly more accessible. They have a waiting list of 11,000 but sell scattered single seats for $25 on a first-come, first-served, cash-only basis from the New York Jets office (1000 Fulton Ave, Hempstead, NY) and via Ticketmaster. Even this limited opportunity may soon disappear if the Jets continue to improve as they have in recent years.

New York Giants
Information 1-201-935-8222.

New York Jets
Information 1-516-560-8100/tickets 1-516-560-8200.

Horse racing

There are four major race tracks just outside New York—Belmont, Aqueduct, the Meadowlands and Yonkers. If you don't want to trek out to Long Island or Jersey, head for an Off-Track Betting (OTB) shop and catch the action and atmosphere there instead.

Aqueduct Racetrack
110th St at Rockaway Blvd, Ozone Park, Queens (1-718-641-4700). Subway: A to Aqueduct Racetrack. Nov–May. Clubhouse $3, grandstand $1. No credit cards. Thoroughbred flat races are held here five days a week (Wed–Sun) during the season.

I like to watch

Rather drink than play? Catch all the action at a mega sports bar.

New York may or may not be the sports capital of the world, but it's almost certainly the sports-*bar* capital. Hundreds of New York bars provide TV sports as a drinking companion, but some go to extremes to take you to big-screen sports heaven—and to provide an audience for your illuminating (if not always sober) insights into the big game.

The All-Star Cafe, 1540 Broadway at 45th St (840-TEAM), is the prototype for these spaceship-like spaces overflowing with TV sets, electronic score tickers and overpriced fried food. This theme restaurant also features plenty of cool memorabilia from sports celebrities hanging on the walls, à la the Hard Rock Cafe. **Mickey Mantle's**, 42 Central Park South near Sixth Ave (688-7777), has ten huge screens. **The Sporting Club**, 99 Hudson St at Franklin St (219-0900), has "only" nine, but throws in trivia betting machines at the bar.

If you're feeling the urge to actually participate in a sport, check out **Hackers Hitters & Hoops**, 123 W 18th St between Sixth and Seventh Aves (929-7482), a bar with a sporting club attached. It boasts one basketball court, two baseball batting cages, a golf simulator, a mini-golf game and two giant screens, for the lazy members in your group.

If you get tired of the televisual glitz of American sports, there's always **McCormack's**, 365 Third Ave at 27th St (683-0911) or **British Open**, 320 59th St between First and Second Aves (355-8467), the best places to watch British football in the company of some expatriate hooligans.

Belmont Park
Hempstead Turnpike at Plainfield Ave, Elmont, Long Island (1-718-641-4700). Travel: Pony Express from Penn Station to Belmont Park. May–Oct. Clubhouse $4, grandstand $2. No credit cards. Thoroughbred flat racing five days a week (Wed–Sun) in season. The Belmont Stakes, the third leg of the Triple Crown, is usually held on the second Saturday in June.

Meadowlands Racetrack
East Rutherford, New Jersey (1-201-935-8500). Travel: Bus from Port Authority Bus Terminal, 42nd St at Eighth Ave, $3.25 each way (information 564-8484). Jan–Aug harness racing, Sept–Dec Thoroughbred. Clubhouse $3, grandstand $1. No credit cards. Wed–Sun, Feb–Apr; Tue–Sat, May–Aug; Wed–Sat, Sept–Dec.

Fit to be tried

Need a gym fix? Single-day passes can help you sweat it out.

For some, the idea of going to a gym while on vacation is about as alluring as doing your taxes while having sex. Other travelers, though, find that they just don't feel right without their regular workout. For them, the following mega-gyms offer single-day memberships (some form of photo ID is usually required). Most have more than one branch: phone for more details, as well as information about opening times, classes and facilities. Towel and locker rental is usually available.

Asphalt Green

555 E 90th St at York Ave (369-8890). Subway: 4, 5, 6 to 86th St. Day membership $15. The fee gets you access to either the pool, the gym or the aerobics classes. An additional $15 is required for each additional facility; sauna and steam rooms are free.

New York Health & Fitness Club

39 Whitehall St at Water St (269-9800). Subway: N, R to Whitehall St. Day membership $50, $20 if you're a member's guest. This six-story facility has two swimming pools, two separate floors for weights and cardio equipment, a climbing wall, a boxing gym, basketball courts, a sauna, a steam room and indoor golf greens and simulators. Racquetball and squash costs extra.

New York Sports Club

151 E 86th St between Lexington and Third Aves (860-8630). Subway: 4, 5, 6 to 86th St. Day membership $25. Daily membership at New York Sports Club includes weight room, aerobics classes, squash courts, cardio machines and studios, steam room and sauna. For a little extra, you can also get a massage.

Sports Center at Chelsea Piers

Pier 60, 23rd St at the Hudson River (336-6000). Subway: C, E to 23rd St. Day membership $31 ($50 on weekends). Part of the sprawling, 1.7-million-square-foot Chelsea Piers (the largest public sports complex in the U.S.), the Sports Center contains a quarter-mile indoor track, Olympic swimming pool, basketball courts, hard and sand volleyball courts, weight room and cardio machines, two studios of fitness classes, steam room, sauna and an indoor climbing wall.

World Gym of Greenwich Village

232 Mercer St between Bleecker and 3rd Sts (780-7407). Subway: B, D, F, Q to Broadway–Lafayette St; 6 to Bleecker St. Day membership $18. All the amenities of regular membership (except personal training) are available, including a weight room, aerobics classes and machines, a boxing gym, and steam rooms in both the men's and women's locker rooms.

*Pump it up: getting in tone at **World Gym**.*

*FORE! After teeing off at the **Chelsea Piers**' year-round driving range, take a few cuts in the batting cage, or head to the indoor soccer field, ice rinks and in-line skating rinks.*

Yonkers Raceway

Central Park Ave, Yonkers, New York (1-914-968-4200). Subway: 4 to Woodlawn, then #20 bus to the track. Mon, Tue, Thu, Fri, Sat 7:40pm. All year. Clubhouse $4.25; main level $2.75 evenings, free in the daytime. No credit cards. Harness racing isn't as glamorous as Thoroughbred racing, but you can still lose your money here all the same.

Ice hockey

A game of speed and skill with the perpetual threat of spectacular violence, hockey is popular in New York, but not prohibitively so. While hard to get, tickets are available; they go on sale at the beginning of the season, which runs from October to April.

New Jersey Devils

Continental Airlines Arena, East Rutherford, New Jersey (Devils information 1-201-935-6050). Travel: Bus from Port Authority Bus Terminal, 42nd St at Eighth Ave, $3.25 each way (information 564-8484). Daily 9am–6pm and during games. $20–$65. AmEx, MC, V.

New York Islanders

Nassau Memorial Coliseum, Hempstead Turnpike, Uniondale, Long Island (Islanders information 1-516-794-4100). Travel: Long Island Railroad (1-718-217-5477) from Penn Station, Seventh Ave at 32nd St, to Westbury Station. 10:45am–5:45pm and during games. $19–$60. AmEx, MC, V.

New York Rangers

Madison Square Garden, Seventh Ave at 32nd St (465-6741). Subway: A, C, E, 1, 2, 3, 9 to 34th St–Penn Station. $22–$55. AmEx, Disc, MC, V, DC.

Soccer

Soccer is very popular in New York, especially in the outer boroughs, where you can catch matches every summer weekend in parks in the Polish, Italian and Latin American neighborhoods. A higher standard of play can be seen in the games of the New York/New Jersey MetroStars, part of the professional Major League Soccer that was established after America hosted the World Cup in 1994. The team plays in Giants Stadium in New Jersey, and the season runs from March to September. The MetroStars draw an international crowd and have already attracted a devoted following.

New York/New Jersey MetroStars

Giants Stadium, East Rutherford, New Jersey (information 1-201-935-3900). Travel: Bus from Port Authority Terminal, 42nd St at Eighth Ave, $3.25 each way (information 564-8484). Mon–Fri 9am–6pm, Sat 10am–5pm, Sun noon–5pm. Apr–Aug $11–$22. AmEx, MC, V.

Tennis

U.S. Open

USTA Tennis Center, Flushing, Queens (information 1-718-760-6200/tickets 1-888-673-6849). Subway: 7 to Willets Point–Shea Stadium. Late Aug–early Sept. $30–$65 day tickets. AmEx, DC, Disc, MC, V. Tickets go on sale May 31, though seating tends to be snapped up by corporate sponsors.

Chase Championships

Madison Square Garden, Seventh Avenue at 32nd St (465-6500). Subway: A, C, E, 1, 2, 3, 9 to 34th St–Penn Station. Second and third weeks of Nov. $15–$45. AmEx, MC, V. The top 16 women's singles players and top 32 doubles teams compete for megabucks in this premier indoor tournament. Tickets go on sale at the end of April.

Oddball sports

New York's omnivorous appetite for spectator sports has led to plenty of outlandish variations. Cockfights, dog matches and professional foosball tournaments are held in the five boroughs, but some of the more mainstream events, though sanitized for mass consumption, are just as bizarre.

Professional Wrestling

Madison Square Garden (465-6741), Nassau Memorial Coliseum, Uniondale, Long Island (1-516-794-9303), and Continental Airlines Arena (1-201-935-3900). Call for dates and ticket information. The Greco-Roman athletes of old would be dismayed to see what goes by the name "wrestling" these days. On the other hand, they might have a lot of fun. Professional wrestling is more entertainment than sport, featuring cartoonish violence, "secret holds" and themed characters, such as the Undertaker and the Honky Tonk Man. The great part is, nobody gets hurt—not very often, anyway.

General Information

Department of Parks & Recreation

Information 360-3456.

Women's Sports Foundation

Information and referral service: 1-800-227-3988. 9am–5pm. Mon–Fri. The staff here is happy to answer any queries you may have about women's events, facilities and sporting history.

Bowling

Bowlmor Lanes

110 University Pl at 12th St (255-8188). Subway: L, N, R, 4, 5, 6 to 14th St–Union Sq. Tue–Thu, Sun 10am–1am; Mon, Fri, Sat 10am–4am. $3.50 per person per game before 5pm, $4.50 after, $4.95 on weekends; $3 shoe rental. AmEx, MC, V. A recent renovation of this historic Greenwich Village alley (Richard Nixon bowled here!) has made it the bowling equivalent of a hip downtown nightclub.

Leisure Time Recreation

625 Eighth Ave at 40th St, in the Port Authority Bus Terminal (268-6909). Subway: A, C, E to 42nd St; N, R, S, 1, 2, 3, 9, 7 to 42nd St–Times Sq. Sun–Thu 10am–11pm; Fri, Sat 10am–4am. $4.25 per person per game; $2.50 shoe rental. MC, V. Let fly a few strikes down one of 30 lanes while you're waiting for your bus. Or sink some shots at the bar.

AMF Chelsea Bowl

Chelsea Piers, 23rd St at the Hudson River (835-BOWL). Subway: C, E to 23rd St, then M23 bus or walk west to river. Sun–Thu 9am–2am, Fri–Sat 9am–4am. $6 per person per game; $4 ball and shoe rental. Amex, MC, V, Disc. This mega-complex features 40 lanes, a huge arcade and bar, and glow-in-the-dark "disco" bowling every night.

Karma chameleons

Yoga is in vogue, so stash your cell phone in the locker and strike a pose

Achieving nirvana and a supple spine has never been easier, now that yoga has replaced spinning as the latest fitness craze. For years it was mostly a West Coast fad, but yoga centers are now popping up all over Manhattan, offering a kind of mind-body rejuvenation for the city's overheated lifestyle. Why, even corporate types have become unlikely regulars at local yoga centers—just hope their cell phones don't ring during the breathing segment.

Equinox

2465 Broadway at 92nd St (799-1818). Subway: 1, 2, 3, 9 to 96th St. ● 897 Broadway at 19th St (780-9300). Subway: N, R, to 14th St. Some Equinox fitness clubs offer yoga classes to nonmembers using the club's $26 day pass. Classes are taught by some of the better-known yoga-fitness gurus, including Molly Fox and Michael Lechonczak; variations include Power Yoga, Gentle Yoga, Pre-natal Yoga—there's even a class combining yoga and aerobics. Call for class schedules.

Integral Yoga Institute

227 W 13th St between Seventh and Greenwich Aves (929-0585). Subway: A, C, E to 14th St; L to Eighth Ave; 1, 2, 3, 9 to 14th St. Mon–Fri 10am–8:30pm, Sat 8am–6pm, Sun 10am–2pm. Hatha III classes are $11; all others are $9. ● 200 W 72nd St at Broadway, fourth floor (721-4000). Subway: 1, 2, 3, 9 to 72nd St. Integral Yoga Institute offers classes for beginners as well as more advanced students. Their schedule is flexible, so there's no need to book ahead.

Jivamukti Yoga Center

404 Lafayette St between 4th St and Astor Pl, third floor (353-0214 / 800-295-6814). Subway: N, R to 8th St; 6 to Astor Pl. Mon–Fri 6:45am–10:00pm, Sat 9am–5pm, Sun 6:45am–7:30pm; $15 per class for non-members. Jivamukti Yoga Center, 9,000 square feet of celebrity-packed chanting, is currently the hottest yoga center in the city. Jivamukti's founders, Sharon Gannon and David Life, combine spiritual teachings with Hatha yoga. They recently moved to a new space on the East Village border, replete with an indoor waterfall, asana rooms for practice, smaller rooms for private classes and massage, a meditation temple and a boutique. Open, basic and Astanga classes are available, each lasting about 95 minutes.

92nd Street Y

1395 Lexington Ave at 92nd St. (996-1100). Subway: 4, 5, 6 to 96th St. The 92nd Street Y offers yoga classes to non-members (prices are according to each student's level). Class times vary, so call for schedules.

Yoga Zone

138 Fifth Ave between 18th and 19th Sts, fourth floor (647-YOGA). Subway: N, R, 4, 5, 6 to 14th St. Mon–Thu 7:30am–9pm, Fri 7:30am–7:30pm, Sat 9am–5:45pm, Sun 9am–6:30pm. Introductory offer: three classes for $20; $15 per class, or $10 for early morning/lunchtime classes. ● 160 E 56th St between Lexington and Third Aves, 12th floor (935-YOGA). Subway: E, F to Lexington Ave; 4, 5, 6 to 59th St. Hours vary. You'll practically trip over all the models and actors, but that's beside the point. Classes here emphasize the less strenuous side of yoga and last at least an hour. Ample time is devoted to breathing, postures and stretching. Yoga Zone also offers Pilates classes.

*Twist but don't shout: Students get balanced at the **Jivamukti Yoga Center**.*

Biking

Bike New York

Hosteling International, New York, 891 Amsterdam Ave at 103rd Street (932-2300). Subway: 1, 9 to 103rd St. Advice and classes on all aspects of cycling, from risking death in the busy Manhattan streets to scenic mountain biking outside the city limits. The club also arranges the excellent Five-Borough Bike Tour every May.

Time's Up Club

Information 802-8222. This alternative transportation advocacy group sponsors rides throughout the year, including the monthly "Critical Mass," in which hundreds of cyclists and skaters go tearing through Greenwich Village.

Bike rental

You can rent bikes in and around Central Park (at the Loeb Boathouse), where the 7.2-mile road loop is closed to traffic on weekends. *See chapter* **Sightseeing**.

Metro Bicycles

1311 Lexington Ave at 88th St (427-4450). Subway: 4, 5, 6 to 86th St. Mon, Tue, Fri–Sun 9:30am–6:30pm; Wed, Thu 9:30am–7:30pm. $6 per hour, $25 per eight-hour day. AmEx, Disc, MC, V. Driver's license or credit card required as security.

Golf

See also **Chelsea Piers**, *page 278.*

Kissena Park Golf Course

164-15 Booth Memorial Ave at 164th St, Queens (1-718-939-4594). Subway: 7 to Main St, Flushing, then Q65 bus. Daily dawn–dusk. Green fees $18 Mon–Fri before 3pm; $20 Sat, Sun; $10 after 3pm Mon–Sun. Club rental $10 per round. No credit cards. There's a short "executive" course with great views of the Manhattan skyline. Pro lessons cost $35 for 30 minutes. Book six and get one free. Par 64.

Richard Metz Golf Studio

425 Madison Ave at 49th St, third floor (759-6940). Subway: E, F to Lexington Ave; 6 to 51st St. Mon–Fri 9am–7pm, Sat 10am–6pm, Sun 11am–5pm. One lesson $60, five lessons $250, ten lessons $350. AmEx, DC, Disc, JCB, MC, V. Practice your swing into a teaching net and then analyze the movement on video. Lessons last 30 minutes and cater to all levels. There are three nets, several putting areas and a golf shop.

Silver Lake Park

915 Victory Blvd at Clove Rd, Staten Island (1-718-447-5686). Travel: Ferry to Staten Island, then S67 bus. Daily dawn–dusk. Green fees $18 Mon–Fri; $20 Sat, Sun; $2 booking fee. AmEx, MC, V. The course is difficult, with narrow fairways and hills to negotiate. Console yourself with nature when your golf ball ends in the woods once again—it's a very picturesque setting. Par 69.

Van Cortlandt Golf Course

Van Cortlandt Park South at Bailey Ave, Bronx (1-718-543-4595). Subway: 1, 9 to 242nd St. Daily 30 minutes before sunrise to 30 minutes after sunset. Green fees $26. Club rental from $25 per round. AmEx, V. The oldest public course in the country, rich in history and easily the most "New York" of the city's 13 public courses. It's quite short but challenging—narrow with lots of trees and hilly in places. Lessons cost $35 for 30 minutes. Par 70.

Horseback riding

Claremont Riding Academy

175 W 89th St at Amsterdam Ave (724-5100). Subway: 1, 9 to 86th St. Mon–Fri 6:30am–10pm; Sat, Sun 6:30am–5pm. Rental $33 per hour. Lessons $40 per 30 minutes.. No credit cards. The academy teaches English-style (as opposed to Western-style) riding. Beginners use an indoor arena; experienced riders can also clomp along the six miles (9.6km) of trails in Central Park.

Jamaica Bay Riding Academy

7000 Shore Pkwy, Brooklyn (1-718-531-8949). Travel: By car via Belt Parkway. Rides leave hourly Mon–Fri noon–5pm; Sat, Sun 10am–5pm. Guided trail ride $23. Lessons $50 per hour by appointment, Mon–Sun. No credit cards. The trail ride, through the 300-acre Jamaica Bay Wildlife Refuge in Brooklyn, lasts 45 minutes. English and Western riding.

Kensington Stables

51 Caton Pl, Brooklyn (1-718-972-4588). Subway: F to Fort Hamilton Parkway. 10am–sundown. Guided trail ride $20 per hour. Lessons $40 per hour. AmEx, V, MC. The ring here is small, but there are miles of trails in lovely nearby Prospect Park (Brooklyn's answer to Central Park).

Pool

Chelsea Billiards

54 W 21st St between Fifth and Sixth Aves (989-0096). Subway: F, N, R to 23rd St. 24 hours. 9am–5pm $4 per hour for first player, $8 for two or more players; Mon–Thu, Sun 5pm–9am $5 per hour for first player, $10 for two or more players; Fri, Sat 5pm–9am $6 per hour for first player, $14 for two or more players. AmEx, MC, V. Cue up in this comfortable and welcoming pool hall (with full-size snooker tables, too). Hot dogs and snacks are available.

Racquetball

Manhattan Plaza Racquet Club

450 W 43rd St between Ninth and Tenth Aves (594-0554). Subway: A, C, E to 42nd Street. 6am–midnight. $13–$28 per court per hour, plus $10 guest fee. AmEx, MC, V. Rates vary according to the time of day. The club also has five hard-surface tennis courts ($28–$38 per court per hour, plus $20 guest fee).

In-line skating

A familiar sound on New York streets is the quiet "skish-skish" of in-line skaters. It's not unusual to see the more insane skaters hurtling toward oncoming traffic at 30 miles per hour. A slightly more tame version can be found whirling around Central Park, either on the Park Drive loop (closed to traffic on weekends) or near the bandshell at 72nd Street. The "coneheads," or slalomers, strut their stuff at Central Park West and 67th Street, across from the Tavern on the Green.

To give it a try yourself, visit Wollman Memorial Rink (*see chapter* **Sightseeing**). If you don't want to be restricted to the rink, you can rent skates from one of many shops close to the park. Try **Blades**, 160 E 86th St (996-1644) and 120 W 72nd St (787- 3911). Your safest bet is to stick with the pack and follow the flow of traffic. On weekends there are plenty of people around to rescue you if you wipe out—there's even a volunteer force of skate patrollers (in red T-shirts with white crosses) who run free stopping clinics for beginners. You'll find them on Saturdays and Sundays from 12:30pm to 5:30pm at the 72nd Street entrance near the Rumsey Playfield. If you'd prefer to be indoors, head for the new Chelsea Piers complex (*see* **Fit to be tried**, *page 278*).

Running

Join the joggers in Central Park, Riverside Park or around Washington Square in the early morning or early evening. It's best, for women especially, to avoid jogging alone. And don't carry anything that's obviously valuable. For the New York City Marathon, *see chapter* **New York by Season.**

New York Road Runners Club

9 E 89th St between Madison and Fifth Aves (860-4455). Subway: 4, 5, 6 to 86th Street. Mon–Fri 10am–8pm, Sat 10am–5pm, Sun 10am–3pm. Membership from $30. AmEx, Disc, MC, V. Hardly a weekend goes by without some sort of run or race sponsored by the NYRRC, the largest running club in the world. Most take place in Central Park and are open to the public. The club also offers safety and training tips.

Ice skating

For Central Park's Wollman Memorial Rink, see chapter **Sightseeing.**

Rockefeller Center Ice Rink

1 Rockefeller Plaza, Fifth Ave between 49th and 50th Sts (recorded information 332–7654). Subway: B, D, F, Q to 47th–50th St–Rockefeller Center. Oct–Apr Mon–Thu 9am–1pm, 1:30–5:30pm, 6–10:30pm; Fri, Sat 8:30–11am, 11:30am–2pm, 2:30–5pm, 5:30–8pm, 8:30pm–midnight; Sun 8:30–11am, 11:30am–2pm, 2:30–5pm, 5:30–10pm. Mon–Thu adults $7.50, children under 12 $6; Fri–Sun adults $9, cildren under 12 $6.75. Skate rental $4. No credit cards. The famous outdoor rink, under the giant statue of Prometheus, is perfect for atmosphere but a little small. It's unmissable, however, when the giant Christmas tree is lit.

Squash

The **West Side YMCA** *(see below)* has some courts and offers a day rate for membership. Court use is free for members. There are few other places where you can play squash cheaply.

Swimming

Municipal Pools

Parks Department hotline: 1-800-201-7275. An annual membership fee of $25, payable by money order only at any of the pools, entitles you to use all New York's municipal pools, both indoor and outdoor, for a year. Outdoor pools are free to all, and open from June to September. You need proof of your name, an address in the New York City area and a passport-size photograph to register. Some of the best and most beautifully-maintained city-run pools are: **Asser Levy Pool**, 23rd St at FDR Drive (447-2020); **Carmine Street Recreation Center**, Clarkson St and Seventh Ave South (242-5228); **East 54th Street Pool**, 348 E 54th St at First Ave (397-3154); **West 59th Street Pool**, 59th St between Tenth and Eleventh Aves (397-3159).

Sheraton Manhattan Hotel

790 Seventh Ave at 51st St (581-3300). Subway: B, D, E to Seventh Ave; N, R to 49th St. Open to non-residents Mon–Fri 6am–10pm; Sat, Sun 8am–8pm. $20 for non-residents. AmEx, DC, Disc, MC, V. Pricier than the municipal pools but much less crowded, this is the place to come if you want to swim in peace.

Tennis

The city maintains excellent municipal courts throughout the city. Permits are available from the Department of Parks (360-8133), cost $50 ($20 for senior citizens, $10 for those under) and are valid for the season (April to November). *See also* **Manhattan Plaza Racquet Club**, *page 281.*

HRC Tennis

East River at Wall and South Sts (422-9300). Subway: 2, 3 to Wall St. Open to non-members. Daily 6am–midnight. Court fees $50–$120 per hour. AmEx, MC, V. This is part of the New York Health & Racquet Club. There are eight green clay courts, under bubbles on twin piers by the river. Five tennis pros are on hand to give lessons ($28 per hour plus court fees).

Midtown Tennis Club

341 Eighth Ave at 27th St (989-8572). Subway: 1, 9 to 28th St. Mon–Thu 7am–11pm; Fri 7am–8pm; Sat, Sun 8am–8pm. Court fees $35–$70 per hour. AmEx, MC, V. This club offers eight indoor hard courts, four are uncovered in the summer.

YMCAs

There are Ys throughout the five boroughs, all with a wide range of facilities. Three of the Manhattan sites offer day rates for visitors. Y membership in another country may get you discounts; and if you're already paying for accommodation, the sports facilities are free.

Harlem YMCA

180 W 135th St at Seventh Ave (281-4100). Subway: B, C to 135th St. Mon–Fri 6am–10pm, Sat 6am–6pm. Membership $10 per day; $75 per month; $500 per year. MC, V. The main attractions here are four-lane swimming pool, basketball court, full gym and sauna.

Vanderbilt YMCA

224 E 47th St between Second and Third Aves (756-9600). Subway: 6 to 51st St. Mon–Fri 5am–11pm; Sat, Sun 7am–7pm. Membership $20 per day; $67 per month; $804 per year. MC, V. Members can use the two swimming pools, a running track, a sauna and a gym with basketball, handball and volleyball—plus yoga and aerobics classes.

West Side Branch YMCA

5 W 63rd St between Broadway and Central Park West (787-4400). Subway: A, C, B, D, 1, 9 to 59th St–Columbus Circle. Mon–Fri 6:30am–10pm, Sat 9am–6pm, Sun 9am–6pm. Membership $15 per day, $60 per week, $100 per month. MC, V. Two pools and three gyms with all the equipment you could imagine, plus an indoor track, squash courts and facilities for basketball, volleyball, handball, racquetball, boxing, aerobics and yoga are available here. There is also a full range of classes. Day rate includes access to everything.

Theater

Thanks to a vast choice of venues and a thrilling array of talent, New York is a great place to get stagestruck

The Big Apple is the big cheese when it comes to live theater. There are myriad venues throughout Manhattan—and more in the outer boroughs. New York's long tradition as an artist's proving ground is still accurate: This is the only city in the States where superstars regularly tread the boards eight times a week. Big-name players who have recently stuck their necks out on the sometimes unforgiving NYC stages include Marisa Tomei, Liam Neeson, Liza Minnelli, Natasha Richardson—even filmmaker and stage novice Quentin Tarantino and singer-songwriter Paul Simon, both of whom were crucified by local critics. The stakes are high, but the gamble remains ever alluring.

Audiences eager to experience this ephemeral art form continue to pack the city's performance spaces, which range from the landmark palaces of the glittering (and recently sanitized) "Great White Way" of Broadway to more intimate houses along 42nd Street's Theater Row (technically Off Broadway) and the nooks and crannies of Off-Off Broadway. Unlike in Hollywood, the performer-fan relationship is up-close-and-personal in the New York theater world. Not only can you watch your favorite actors with only a bit of air separating you, but you can also grab autographs at the stage door, and maybe even head for the same restaurant afterward. Whatever your dramatic wishes may be, New York theater can and undoubtedly *will* satisfy you.

INFORMATION

The Sunday Arts and Leisure and Friday Weekend sections of *The New York Times* are reliable sources

Give 'em the old razzle-dazzle: Sexy Chicago, *which opened in 1996, still packs the house.*

LEGENDARY MUSICAL THEATRE

The PHANTOM of the OPERA

Ⓢ Majestic Theatre 247 West 44th St.

Miss Saigon

Ⓢ Broadway Theatre 53rd Street & Broadway

Les Misérables

Ⓢ Imperial Theatre 249 W. 45th St.

of information, as are the listings in *Time Out New York*, *In Theater*, *New York* magazine, *The New Yorker* and the free *Village Voice*. In addition, there are several phone lines offering everything from plot synopses and show times to an agent ready to sell tickets (you'll need a touch-tone phone). The best is **NYC/On Stage** (768-1818), a service of the Theater Development Fund (*see chapter* **Dance**), which will tell you about performances on Broadway, Off Broadway and Off-Off Broadway, as well as classical music, dance and opera events. The **Broadway Line** (302-4111, outside New York 1-888-411-BWAY) gives similar information, but is restricted to Broadway and Off Broadway shows, and you must know which show you are interested in before using it.

BUYING TICKETS

Provided you have one of the major credit cards, buying Broadway tickets requires little more effort than picking up a telephone. Almost all Broadway and Off Broadway shows are served by one of the city's 24-hour booking agencies. The information lines (above) will refer you to ticket agents, often on the same call. **Telecharge** (239-6200) and **Ticketmaster** (307-4100) carve up the bulk of the shows between them, with the smaller **Ticket Central** (279-4200) specializing in Off Broadway and Off-Off Broadway shows. You'll have to pay a service charge to the agency, but since most theaters don't take telephone orders, you don't have much choice, unless you opt to buy tickets in person at the theater box office.

The cheapest full-price tickets on Broadway are for standing room and cost about $15, though not all theaters offer these. If a show is sold out, it's worth trying for standby tickets just before show time. Tickets are slightly cheaper for matinees and previews, and for students or groups of 20 or more. Keep an eye out for "two-fers"—vouchers that allow you to buy two tickets for slightly more than the price of one. These generally promote long-running Broadway shows and occasionally the larger Off Broadway ones. Some sell-out shows offer good seats at reduced rates (usually $20) after 6pm on the day of performance; those in the know start lining up hours beforehand. The best way to obtain discounted tickets, however, is to go to **TKTS** (*see chapter* **Music**) where you can get as much as 75 percent off the face value of some tickets. Arrive early to avoid the line, or come at around 7pm, when most shows are about to start. You can also buy tickets to matinees the day before at the TKTS booth in the World Trade Center. (One caveat: Avoid scam artists selling tickets to those waiting in line. Often the tickets are fake.)

NEW YORK SHAKESPEARE FESTIVAL

The Delacorte Theater in Central Park is the fair-weather sister to the Public Theater (*see page 289*). When not producing Shakespeare under its roof

Bare tracks

Broadway embraces the sex that once titillated Times Square

Despite Mayor Rudolph Giuliani's efforts to expel adult businesses from the Broadway district, sex continues to be a major draw. And you won't find it only in peep shows and strip clubs; it's right smack-dab in the hot spotlights on Broadway's stages.

Of course, explicit carnality onstage is nothing new. *Hair* (1967) and *Oh, Calcutta!* (1969) gave undressing a free-love hipness and led to such landmark displays of male nudity as *Equus* (1973) and *Love! Valour! Compassion!* (1994).

These days, sex is quite overtly selling the hit musical *Cabaret*, and even serious dramas like David Hare's *The Judas Kiss* and Peter Whelan's *The Herbal Bed* treated audiences to a few bare bods. The unstoppable revival of *Chicago* owes much to the sensuality and well-toned flesh of its slinky ensemble.

While many of these plays have married ass with class, Off and Off-Off Broadway's aspirations are often less lofty. Downtown theaters have lately employed a variety of nudie gimmicks (actual porn-star actors baring all, strip poker as a key plot device) aimed primarily at eager gay audiences.

But in Times Square, the only safe sex may soon be inside Broadway theaters. And with ticket prices near $75, it's only a matter of time before audiences start asking for a complimentary after-show cigarette.

Cabaret *queen: Natasha Richardson.*

for a price (recently, *Macbeth* got the all-star treatment from Alec Baldwin and Angela Bassett), the Public offers the Bard outdoors for free in the New York Shakespeare Festival (June to September). If you're in the city during the summer, you won't want to miss these innovative, alfresco productions. The 1998 summer schedule includes Thornton Wilder's *The Skin of Our Teeth* (starring John Goodman, Frances Conroy and Kristen Johnston) and Andrei Serban's interpretation of Shakespeare's *Cymbeline*. Tickets are free and are distributed at 1pm on the day of the performance, at both the Delacorte and the Public. Normally, 11:30am is a safe time to get there, but when shows feature box-office giants, the line starts as early as 7am. Two tickets are allotted per person.

Delacorte Theater
A few minutes' walk inside Central Park. Enter the park from either Central Park West at 81st St or Fifth Ave at 79th St (539-8750). Subway B, C to 81st St; 6 to 77th St. Then follow the signs in the park.

Broadway

Broadway is booming. In recent years, box-office receipts for newly opened shows have repeatedly broken records and, by putting big-name movie stars in leading roles, Broadway now competes directly with Hollywood for its audiences. It hasn't hurt matters that the formerly seedy and sex-oriented Times Square has been the target of an extensive cleanup. (Disney is a major investor in area real estate, and the neighborhood is becoming more and more like one of its theme parks.)

"Broadway," in theatrical terms, is the district around Times Square on either side of Broadway (the street), generally between 41st and 53rd Streets. This is where the grand theaters are clustered, most built in the first 30 years of this century, several newly renovated. Officially, 37 of them are designated as being on Broadway, for which full-price tickets cost up to $75. The big shows are hard to ignore; newer blockbusters like *The Lion King, Chicago, Ragtime* and *Cabaret* join long-running shows such as *Cats, Phantom of the Opera, Les Misérables, Miss Saigon* and *Rent*, all of which declare themselves on vast billboards. Still, there's more to Broadway than cartoon-based musicals and flashy Andrew Lloyd Webber spectacles. In recent years, provocative new dramas by such playwrights as Tony Kushner, Terrence McNally, Horton Foote and Wendy Wasserstein have been resounding successes, as have many revived classics and British imports.

Look out for the irrepressible **Roundabout Theater** (1530 Broadway at 45th St, 719-1300), the critically acclaimed home of classics played by all-star casts (and the force behind *Cabaret*'s latest incarnation). The Roundabout houses both a large

Paws for emphasis: All hail The Lion King.

theater (considered Broadway) and a more intimate space (considered Off Broadway).

Broadway District
Subways: A, C, E, N, R, 1, 2, 3, 9, 7 to 42nd St–Times Sq; B, D, F, Q to 42nd St; N, R to 49th St; 1, 9, to 50th St.

Off Broadway

Off Broadway theaters usually have fewer than 500 seats; earlier in the century, most were located in Greenwich Village. These days, Off Broadway theaters can be found on the Upper West Side, the Upper East Side and in midtown.

As Broadway increasingly becomes a place of spectacle *sans* substance, playwrights who would once have been granted a Broadway production now find themselves in the more audacious (and less financially demanding) Off Broadway houses, where they find audiences who want plays that have something to say.

So if it's brain food and adventure you're after, dine Off or Off-Off Broadway—but be prepared for considerable variations in quality. Listed below are some of the most reliable theaters and repertory companies. Tickets cost about $10 to $45.

Atlantic Theater Company
336 W 20th St between Eighth and Ninth Aves (645-1242). Subway: C, E, 1, 9 to 23rd St. Created 15 years ago as an off-shoot of acting workshops taught by David Mamet and William H. Macy, this dynamic little theater (in a former church sanctuary on a lovely Chelsea street) has presented more than 80 plays. Productions have included Mamet's *Edmond*, the premieres of Howard Korder's *Boys' Life* and Craig Lucas's *Missing Persons*, and the American premiere of Martin McDonagh's *The Beauty Queen of Leenane*.

Brooklyn Academy of Music
30 Lafayette Ave between Flatbush Ave and Fulton St, Brooklyn (1-718-636-4100). Subway: B, D, Q, 2, 3, 4, 5 to Atlantic Ave; B, N, R to Pacific St. Internet: www.bam.org. Brooklyn's grand old opera house—as well as the Majestic Theater, one block away at 651 Fulton St—stages the famous Next Wave Festival during the last three months of each year. The festival is a program of theatrical, musical and dance pieces by American and international artists. Recent ventures included a much acclaimed all-male Cheek by Jowl production of *As You Like It* and the Robert Wilson-Lou Reed collaboration *Time Rocker. See also chapter* **Dance**.

Lincoln Center
62nd to 65th Sts between Columbus and Amsterdam Aves (239-6200/information 362-7600). Subway: 1 9 to 66th St. The Lincoln Center complex houses two amphitheater-shaped drama venues: the 1,040-seat Vivian Beaumont Theater (considered a Broadway house) and the 290-seat Mitzi E. Newhouse Theater (considered Off Broadway). Expect polished productions of new and classic plays, with many a big-name actor.

La MaMa E.T.C.
74A E 4th St between the Bowery and Second Ave (475-7710). Subway: 6 to Astor Pl. This little gem is where Off Broadway began. When acclaimed producer Ellen Stewart opened La MaMa ("Mama" is her nickname) in 1962, it was New York's best-kept theater secret (Did you know, for example, that Harvey Fierstein's *Torch Song Trilogy* started at La MaMa?) Now, with more than 50 Obie (Off Broadway) Awards to its name, it's a fixture in the city's dramatic life. If you're looking for traditional theater, skip La MaMa. New ground is routinely broken here, and some of it is rather muddy.

Manhattan Theater Club
City Center, 131 W 55th St between Sixth and Seventh Aves (box office 581-1212). Subway: D, E to Seventh Ave. Manhattan Theater Club has a reputation for sending young playwrights on to Broadway. The club's two theaters, in the basement of City Center, are the 299-seat Mainstage Theater, which offers four plays each year by both new and established playwrights, and the more flexible Stage II Theater, an outlet for works in progress, workshops and staged readings. One of the Club's highlights is its Writers in Performance series. Guest speakers have included Isabel Allende, Eric Bogosian and Toni Morrison.

New York Theatre Workshop
79 E 4th St between Second Ave and the Bowery (460-5475). Subway: 6 to Astor Pl. Founded in 1979, this Off Broadway company produces new plays using young directors who are eager to harness challenging works. Besides initiating plays by such authors as David Rabe (*A Question of Mercy*), Caryl Churchill (*Mad Forest*) and Tony Kushner (*Slavs!*), it is most noted for premiering *Rent*, Jonathan Larson's Pulitzer Prize–winning musical. The Workshop also offers a home to upstart performance artists through its O Solo Mio festival.

Playwrights Horizons
416 W 42nd St between Ninth and Tenth Aves (564-1235). Subway: A, C, E to 42nd St. This power-packed company boasts more than 300 premieres of important contemporary plays, including dramatic offerings like *The Substance of Fire*, *Driving Miss Daisy* and *The Heidi Chronicles*, and musicals such as *March of the Falsettos* and *Sunday in the Park with George*. More recently, the works of newcomers Adam Guettel (*Floyd Collins*) and Brian Crawkey (*Violet*) have been staged.

The Public Theater
425 Lafayette St between Astor Pl and E 4th St (539-8500). Subway: 6 to Astor Pl; N, R to 8th St. This Astor Place landmark is one of the most consistently interesting theaters in the city. Founded by Joseph Papp and dedicated to the production of New American playwrights and performers, the Public also presents new explorations of Shakespeare and the classics; there's a constant influx of short-run goodies. The building houses five stages and a cabaret space, plus a new coffee bar. The Public is now under the aegis of George C. Wolfe, responsible for *Bring in 'da Noise, Bring in 'da Funk* and the first New York production of Tony Kushner's *Angels in America. See also* **New York Shakespeare Festival**, *page 284*.

The Vineyard Theater
108 E 15th St at Union Sq East (353-3874). Subway: L, N, R, 4, 5, 6 to 14th St–Union Sq. Internet: www.vineyard.org. This subscription theater in Union Square produces new plays and musicals, and also attempts to revitalize works that have failed in other arenas. The Vineyard has recently been on a streak of successes, including Paula Vogel's *How I Learned to Drive* and Edward Albee's *Three Tall Women*. This consistently excellent theater is also home to such playwrights as Craig Lucas and caustic wit Nicky Silver.

Off-Off Broadway

The technical definition of Off-Off Broadway is a show at a theater with fewer than 100 seats created by artists who may not be card-carrying pros. It's here that the most innovative and daring writers and performers get the opportunity to experiment. Pieces often meld various media, including music, dance, mime, film, video and performance monologue—sometimes resulting in an all-too-indulgent combo of theater and psychotherapy.

But Off-Off Broadway is not restricted to experimental work. You can also see classical works and more traditional contemporary plays by companies such as the Jean Cocteau Repertory Company and at venues like the Theater for the New City. Tickets at Off-Off Broadway venues cost roughly $10 to $25. *See also chapters* **Dance** *and* **Cabaret & Comedy**.

Adobe Theater Company
453 W 16th St between Ninth and Tenth Aves (352-0441). Subway: A, C, E to 14th St; L to Eighth Ave. Keep your eyes peeled for new work by this spry nonprofit company, which has mounted 22 shows in the past seven years. Their wacky works appeal to young, hip audiences that can appreciate a theatrical stew filled with pop-culture references. Recent productions have included *Notions in Motion*, a juicy update of Pirandello; *The Handless Maiden*, a modern fable; and *Duet!*, a romance for cynics.

Bouwerie Lane Theatre

330 Bowery at Bond St (677-0060). Subway: F to Second Ave, 6 to Bleecker St. Housed in the old cast-iron German Exchange Bank, this is the resident theater of the Jean Cocteau Repertory Company, which is devoted to producing the classics in rep. Recent works include Orton's *What the Butler Saw*, Tom Stoppard's *Rough Crossing* and Seamus Heaney's *The Cure at Troy*.

En Garde Arts

(279-1461). This company presents site-specific theater throughout the city. En Garde produced *Stonewall 25* on the scene of the original riots; *J.P. Morgan Saves the Nation*, smack in the middle of Wall Street; *The Trojan Women*, at a graffiti-laden abandoned amphitheater on the East River; Tyne Daly in *Mystery School*, in a cavernous synagogue; and Fiona Shaw's startling rendition of T.S. Eliot's *The Wasteland* at the Liberty Theater, while the venue was undergoing renovation.

Drama Dept.

(541-8299). This newish company leaped onto the scene with a couple of high-profile critical hits, including Douglas Carter Beane's *As Bees In Honey Drown* and a revival of Lardner and Kaufman's *June Moon*. Fueled by Hollywood money and a large company of heavy-hitting actors, writers and directors, Drama Dept. mounts lively and ambitious productions that are worth checking out.

Irish Repertory Theatre

132 W 22nd St between Sixth and Seventh Aves (727-2737). Subway: 1, 9 to 23rd St. Dedicated to performing works from both veteran and contemporary Irish playwrights, this company in Chelsea has produced some interesting sell-out shows. Notable are the productions of Frank McCourt's *The Irish and How They Got That Way* and Hugh Leonard's *Da*. There's no blarney here.

The Kitchen

512 W 19th St between Tenth and Eleventh Aves (255-5793). Subway: A, C, E to 14th St. This small, experimental theater—with a season running from September to May—recently celebrated its 25th anniversary. It presents an eclectic repertoire of theater, music, dance, video and performance art. The Kitchen is a reputable place to see edgy New York experimentation. Artists such as Laurie Anderson, David Byrne and Cindy Sherman began their careers here.

Pearl Theatre Company

80 St. Marks Pl between First and Second Aves (505-3401). Subway: 6 to Astor Pl; N, R to 8th St. Housed on the punk promenade of the East Village, this troupe of resident players relies primarily on its actors' ability to present the classics clearly. Besides Shakespeare and the Greeks, Pearl has successfully produced the works of Ionesco, Sheridan, Molière and Shaw, plus lesser-known authors like Ostrofsky and Otway—all on a minimally dressed small stage, with actors in the simplest of costumes.

Performance Space 122

150 First Ave at E 9th St (477-5288). Subway: 6 to Astor Pl; N, R to 8th St. One of New York's most exciting venues, P.S. 122 (as it's casually known) is housed in an abandoned school in the East Village. It's a nonprofit arts center for experimental performance, with two theaters presenting dance, performance, music, film and video. Artists develop, practice and present their work here; P.S. 122 has provided a platform for Eric Bogosian, Whoopi Goldberg, John Leguizamo and Philip Glass.

The Performing Garage

33 Wooster St between Broome and Grand Sts (966-3651). Subway: 1, 2, 3, 9 to Houston St; C, E, to Spring St. The Performing Garage features the works of the Wooster Group, whose members include Richard Foreman, Willem Dafoe, Elizabeth LeCompte and Spalding Gray. Gray developed his well-known monologues here, among them *Swimming to Cambodia;* Dafoe once played the lead in Eugene O'Neill's *The Hairy Ape* and appeared in a daring blackface version of *The Emperor Jones.* In addition to presenting deconstructed versions of theater classics, the company hosts a visiting artists series, dance performances and monthly readings.

Second Stage Theatre

2162 Broadway at 76th St (787-3392). Subway: 1, 2, 3, 9 to 72nd St. Created as a venue for American plays that didn't get the critical reception it was thought they deserved, Second Stage now also produces the works of new American playwrights. It staged the premiere of Lanford Wilson's *Sympathetic Magic* and the revival of his *Lemon Sky*, as well as the premieres of Tina Howe's *Painting Churches* and *Coastal Disturbances*, David Mamet's *The Woods*, and *Ricky Jay and His 52 Assistants*, directed by Mamet.

Signature Theatre Company

555 W 42nd St between Tenth and Eleventh Aves (244-7529). Subway A, C, E to 42nd St. Each season this unique award-winning company focuses on the works of a single playwright in residence (the '97 scribe was Arthur Miller). Signature has in the past delved into the oeuvres of Edward Albee, Sam Shepard and Horton Foote, whose *The Young Man from Atlanta* originated here and went on to win the Pulitzer Prize.

Theater for the New City

155 First Ave between 9th and 10th Sts (254-1109). Subway: L to First Ave, 6 to Astor Pl. Hard-hitting political dramas are often performed by the Living Theater group in one of the building's four theaters. Recent productions have included *Caprichos*, as well as *Already Seen, Rite of Passage* and *My Name Is* (as part of the Out on the Edge Festival of Lesbian and Gay Theater).

Watts up: Kate Valk of the Wooster Group in House/Lights *at the **Performing Garage**.*

All aboard! When you really must flee, trains leave from Penn Station and Grand Central.

Trips Out of Town

Trips Out of Town

If New York isn't enough for you, there are beaches, mountains and more, not too far beyond the city limits

Sometimes it seems as if the residents of New York City only live here so they can earn enough money to leave town once in a while. The astonishing weekend congestion at all points of exit suggests that as much as New Yorkers may love it here, they also love to get away.

GENERAL INFORMATION

Some large magazine stores carry a number of periodicals specific to resort towns (there are lots of these, especially for the more affluent vacation communities). *The New York Times* is always worth consulting for articles on nearby attractions; its Sunday travel section is crammed with getaway suggestions and advertising for resorts and guest houses. Each week, *Time Out New York*'s Get Out section covers one or more destinations and provides listings for other major cities as well.

GETTING THERE

For all the places listed below, we've included information on how to get there from New York City. See chapter **Getting Around** for a list of suggested car rental companies. New York rates are exorbitant—you can save up to 50 percent by renting a car from somewhere outside the city, even if it's from the same company.

Metro-North (532-4900) and the **Long Island Rail Road**, or LIRR (1-718-217-5477), are the two main commuter rail systems. Both offer themed tours in the summer. **Amtrak** (582-6875, 1-800-USA-RAIL) is the national rail service for intercity travel. Call the **Port Authority Bus Terminal** (564-8484) for information on all bus transportation from the city. For airport, train and bus information, see chapter **Getting Around.**

*Send 'em to the big house: There's plenty of grass to frolic on at 430-acre **Montgomery Place**.*

Beach life

You can get sand between your toes for a minimum cash outlay ($1.50) by visiting the three beach areas accessible on the subway. These are **Coney Island** (*see chapter* **New York by Neighborhood: The Outer Boroughs**), **Rockaway Beach** (Subway: A to Rockaway Park) and **Orchard Beach** (Subway: 6 to Pelham Bay Park). These are usually noisy and crowded, and for a slightly larger investment, you can find yourself on some less cluttered stretches of oceanfront.

Long Island

Escaping to the small towns and vast beaches of Long Island, the finger of land to the east of Manhattan Island, is relatively quick and easy. The beaches get more impressive the farther you travel from Manhattan, and some, like those in the Hamptons, are among the most unspoiled in the USA. You can reach sea and sand by hopping on an LIRR train, which will leave from Penn Station. In the summer, there are shuttle buses from the Long Island train stations to various beaches.

If you want an easy beach experience, take the LIRR to **Long Beach**. The Atlantic, which is warm enough to swim in from July to September, is a few short blocks from the station. The beach can be absolutely packed in the summer.

If frying underneath the sun all day is not your idea of a good time, head farther east to **Jones Beach**. Here, you can play pitch-and-putt golf, shoot hoops, fly a kite, or join in one of the numerous beach-volleyball games. The west end of the beach is usually packed with families; the farther east you hike, the more it thins out. The far east side attracts gay and lesbian sun worshipers; unofficial nude sunbathing is tolerated on the easternmost edge of the beach. Jones Beach is also where some of the biggest summer concerts are staged.

Next up is the **Robert Moses State Park**. While the beach here is the farthest of these three, it's recommended for its white sand and the boardwalks that wind through the endless shrubby dunes.

In the summer season between Memorial Day (late May) and Labor Day (early September), harried New Yorkers scramble to get out to their beachside rental homes in the Hamptons, **Fire Island** (*see chapter* **Gay & Lesbian New York**), **Sag Harbor, Bridgehampton, Shelter Island** and **Montauk**.

The **Hamptons** (West, East and South) are the perfect backdrop for the socialites, artists and celebrities who drift from benefit bash to benefit bash throughout the summer. Their homes, wonderful as some are, can't help being upstaged by the spectacular beaches. (Each year at Memorial Day, *Time Out New York* previews the Hamptons'

upcoming season; afterward, look for details on the Internet (www.timeoutny.com).

Montauk Point is Long Island's farthest tip, remote and not too crowded; it is probably the least commercialized spot in the Hamptons. It's too far for a day trip but has many rental cottages and motels. These can be fairly expensive at the height of the season, but pre- and post-season deals abound.

Try **Fort Pond Lodge**, 515 Second-House Rd, Montauk (1-516-668-2042), a quiet, old-style motel set on a lake, minutes from the ocean (from $60 a night). Rent a bike and you're all set. Although Montauk is unpretentious, it attracts its share of celebrities.

East Hampton Chamber of Commerce
79A Main St, East Hampton, NY 11937 (1-516-324-0362).

Montauk Chamber of Commerce
P.O. Box 5029, Montauk, NY 11954 (1-516-668-2428).

Southampton Chamber of Commerce
76 Main St, Southampton, NY 11968 (1-516-283-0402).

Shelter Island

This tiny, uncommercialized island can only be reached by ferry from Long Island, which keeps it free from crowds. There are a few gift shops and an ice cream parlor but little else to distract you from sailing, cycling, fishing or just relaxing on the beach. About a third of its area, **Mashomack Preserve**, is unpopulated except for birds.

The first house was built here in 1652, and the island gained a reputation as a refuge for pirates. Quakers who were driven out of Boston also took shelter; you can visit the **Quaker Cemetery** on the outer boundary of **Sylvester Manor**. Other historic destinations are the **Shelter Island Historical Society Museum, Manhasset Chapel Museum** and **Haven House**.

If you have time, take the short ferry ride to **Sag Harbor**. The information center on Main Street will tell you what you can do. Try to see the **Sag Harbor Whaling Museum** (1-516-725-0770).

There aren't many hotels on Shelter Island, but the following are worth a try. The **Chequit Inn** (23 Grand Ave, Shelter Island Heights; 1-516-749-0018) costs $72–$195 a night. The **Pridwin Hotel and Cottages** at Crescent Beach (81 Shore Rd, Shelter Island; 1-516-749-0476) is $124–$164 a night for rooms, $184 for a cottage, (rates higher on weekends) but is only open from April to November. The **Ram's Head Inn** (1-516-749-0811) is open all year 'round. It costs $110–$230 a night (including breakfast).

Shelter Island Chamber of Commerce
P.O. Box 598, Shelter Island, NY 11964 (1-516-749-0399).

GETTING THERE
Sunrise Express Bus Service from New York City (departs from 44th St between Lexington and Third Aves) to Green-

port (1-516-477-1200; $29 round trip) or Long Island Rail Road (see page 292) from Penn Station to Greenport; then take the ferry ($1).

The Jersey Shore

New Jersey, along with its residents, is a prime target for many New Yorkers' scathing wit. But the state's hundred miles of Atlantic seafront include some splendid beaches (though erosion has taken its toll) and other places worth a visit for an insight into American oceanside culture. The best beaches are often private (**Long Beach** and **Ocean Beach**); the public ones are usually choked with noisy crowds from northern Jersey's industrial cities. If you're a Bruce Springsteen fan, you might want to make the pilgrimage to his beloved **Asbury Park**, but there are more beautiful stretches of coastline in New Jersey.

Cape May (*see below*), on the southernmost tip of New Jersey, is the country's oldest seaside resort and has a delicate 19th-century feel to it. Just north is **Wildwood**, home to enormous beaches and a monstrous boardwalk that dwarfs Coney Island's; the wooden promenade is packed with fairground rides, sideshows and food stands. Try some saltwater taffy, frozen custard, a pork roll or an elephant ear—all local delicacies. Ride on the roller coasters

or the huge Ferris wheel, have an old-time photo taken, or just stroll along the boardwalk.

The beaches north of Wildwood, at **Avalon**, **Sea Isle City** and **Strathmere**, are very pleasant and less commercialized. The area just inland is a mass of tiny islands, bays and inlets. These connect the different beaches and provide the perfect setting for sailing, fishing, windsurfing and Jet Skiing.

Atlantic City has little in the way of attractive coastline. What draws people here is gambling—and lots of it (*see* **Gambling**, *page 299*). Farther up the coast, however, are some beautiful spots, such as **Island Beach**, which is a state park. The comparatively limited access here means unspoiled beaches, and the natural scenery is quite beautiful.

New Jersey Department of Parks
501 E State St, Trenton, NJ 08625 (1-609-292-2797).

New Jersey Division of Tourism
20 State St, CN 826, Trenton, NJ 08625 (1-609-292-2470, 1-888-239-1288).

Cape May

Cape May, in southern New Jersey, 170 miles from New York City, is the nation's oldest seaside resort. Its hundreds of Victorian gingerbread homes make

*Rock, rock, **Rockaway Beach**: You can hitch a ride to the Ramones' favorite spot.*

the entire town a national landmark. The best time to go is early September, when the crowds have thinned but the water is still warm enough to swim in. Rent a bike and visit **Cape May Point**, where the Atlantic meets **Delaware Bay** and visitors sift through the sand for pieces of polished quartz known as Cape May diamonds. **Cape May Point State Park** has a lovely bird sanctuary and one of the country's oldest lighthouses, built in 1823.

If you want to stay, note that in the summer and during October's Victorian Week, most hotels require a two- to four-night minimum stay. The **Chalfonte Hotel** at 301 Howard St (1-609-884-8409) includes breakfast and dinner in its $103–$188 room rate.

Greater Cape May Chamber of Commerce
P.O. Box 556, Cape May, NJ 08204 (1-609-884-5508).

Mid-Atlantic Center for the Arts
1048 Washington St, Cape May, NJ 08204 (1-609-884-5404).

GETTING THERE
NJ Transit bus from Port Authority Terminal (*see page 292*). By car, take the Garden State Parkway (from the Lincoln or Holland tunnel) south to the last exit.

Mountain ranges

Nearly half the population of New York State is crammed into the five boroughs of New York City. This leaves the other 47,000 square miles (122,000 square kilometers) relatively unpopulated. Hikers and skiers will be pleased to hear that this area includes some of the most dramatic mountain scenery in the United States.

Bear Mountain
For a fine day-trip alternative to the beaches, Manhattan's closest wilderness is to be found at **Bear Mountain State Park**, Palisades Pkwy and Rte 9W (1-914-786-2701). It's only an hour by bus (**Short Line Buses**, 736-4700; $19.20 round trip from Port Authority Terminal).

The bus will drop you at an appalling visitors' center with fast food and hundreds of families picnicking in the parking lot, but a ten-minute walk along one of the many trails will take you away from it all.

If you have a car, head to the area around **Cranberry Lake**, where there's a campsite and a trail lodge and things are organized less for the day-tripping hordes and more for the serious hiker.

The Catskills
The Catskills mountain range, an offshoot of the **Appalachian Mountains** just 90 miles from the city, is New York's nearest major forest and park area. The landscape is magnificent. There are hiking and cycling trails, trout-filled streams, white-

24-hour pass
These day trips will give you a natural break from the concrete

Robert Moses State Park This long stretch of white sand fronts the grassy dunes of Fire Island. If you walk far enough toward the lighthouse, you can strip down on a little-known nude beach (*see* **Beach life** *page 293*).

Delaware Water Gap Only 90 minutes from the city (west on I- 80) lies a beautiful section of the Appalachian Trail for you to hike. Don't forget the trail mix.

Hunter Mountain Here's where New Yorkers come to schuss when the snow falls (*see* **Skiing and snowboarding** *page 298*).

The Cloisters In Fort Tryon Park near the northern edge of Manhattan, this peaceful, medievaly setting for a romantic picnic (*see chapter* **Museums**).

Brighton Beach Immerse yourself in Brooklyn's Little Odessa with a chilled vodka, a stroll on the seaside boardwalk and some genuine Russian cabaret at **Rasputin** (2670 Coney Island Ave at Ave X, 1-718-332-8111).

water rapids for canoeing, golf courses, tennis courts, campsites, ski resorts and lakes.

In addition to the Catskills' natural beauty, there are other attractions. You can explore mountain caverns at **Ice Caves Mountain** in Ellenville (1-914-647-7989) and go on organized canoe trips on the Delaware and other rivers running through the park.

A taste of local history can be found at the **Hurley Patentee Manor** (1-914-331-5414; open June–Labor Day) in Hurley, the **Tulthilltown Grist Mill** (1-914-255-5695) in Gardiner, and the **Fort Delaware Museum of Colonial History** (1-914-252-6660; closed in winter) in Narrowsburgh.

Kingston, the largest town in the Catskills, is home to the **Hudson River Maritime Museum** (1-914-338-0071) and a well-stocked **Trolley Museum** (1-914-331-3399; closed in winter). The **Rhinebeck Aerodrome** (1-914-758-8610), in Rhinebeck, has several vintage World War I airplanes on display.

There are several ski resorts in the Catskills. The most popular is **Hunter Mountain**, where the 48 trails are usually packed with New Yorkers during the season. As it is on most of the area mountains, the snow at **Ski Windham**, another large resort, is 100-percent machine-made. (*For more information, see* **Skiing and snowboarding**, *page 298*.)

The Catskills have a good range of accommodations. The **Mohonk Mountain House Hotel**

(1-914-255-1000, 1-800-772-6646) is a lavish castle on a secluded lake where rooms cost $280–$505 a night (including full board for two people). A more economical option is **Jingle Bells Farms** (1-914-255-6588), an intimate bed and breakfast costing $115–130 a night.

There are also some great wineries in the area, including **Benmarl Winery** (1-914-236-4265) and **Brotherhood Winery** (1-914-496-9101).

The only thing you can't escape in this wilderness is New Yorkers: From Friday night to Sunday evening the Catskills is packed with them. On weekends, the road between the Catskills and New York City is backed up for miles. If possible, plan your trip to avoid the traffic jams.

Delaware County Chamber of Commerce
114 Main St, Delhi, NY 13753 (1-607-746-2281, 1-800-642-4443).

Greene County Promotion Department
Box 527, Catskill, NY 12414 (1-518-943-3223).

National Park Service, Upper Delaware National Scenic & Recreational River
P.O. Box C, Narrowsburg, NY 12764 (1-914-252-3947).

Sullivan County Office of Public Information
1-914-794-3000.

Ulster County Public Information Office
County Office Building, Box 1800, Kingston, NY 12401 (1-914-340-3566, 1-800-342-5826).

Ulster County Chamber of Commerce
7 Albany Ave, suite 93, Kingston, NY 12401-2998 (1-914-338-5100).

The Adirondacks

In the northeastern part of New York lies **Adirondack Park**, the largest area of untouched beauty in the state. At least 40 percent of the park is officially classified as wilderness. Route 87, which runs north through the eastern side of the park, is the best road from the city (the trip takes about five hours). The park is suitable for all the usual outdoor activities and, despite some nine million annual visitors, remains relatively unspoiled.

Lake George—a long, thin lake, dotted with tiny islands and surrounded by mountains—runs along the southeastern side of the park. **Glens Falls**, at the south end, is a booming tourist town. North of Lake George is **Lake Champlain**. Straddling the Vermont/New York border and continuing north beyond the Canadian border into Quebec, it is the largest lake in Adirondack Park and a popular vacation spot. For people who enjoy feeling terrified, **Ausable Chasm** (1-518-834-7454, 1-800-537-1211) is a narrow (20 feet/6 meters) gorge in Lake Champlain where you can ride the roaring rapids, *Deliverance*-style. This hair-raising excursion runs daily from mid-May until mid-Oc-

tober ($19 for adults, $17 for children under 12, free for the under-fives).

Saranac Lake (1-518-891-1990, 1-800-347-1992) and **Tupper Lake** (1-518-359-3328) are two gorgeous spots, with a full complement of hotels, campsites and other outdoor facilities. Robert Louis Stevenson rented a house on Saranac Lake; he called the area "Little Switzerland" and wrote *The Master of Ballantrae* there.

The three highest mountains in the park are Whiteface, Marcy and Jo. Marcy, at 5,344 feet (1,036m) above sea level, is the highest in New York. Whiteface, an alpine glacier, has some of the most challenging ski slopes in the east, as well as gentler runs for the novice, and high-speed lifts. For more information, call 1-518-946-2223.

The nearby town of **Lake Placid** was host to the 1932 and 1980 Winter Olympics. The architecture of its chalet-style shops, bars, clubs, restaurants and hotels is very European, and the town has a long tradition of hospitality toward visitors. In the summer, golfing, boating, fishing, camping and hiking are all available. Call 1-800-462-6236 for more information.

Other big ski resorts in the Adirondacks include **Gore Mountain** (1-518-251-2411, 1-800-342-1234) and **Big Tupper** (1-518-359-3651). These raw and beautiful peaks can be dangerous, however: Winds can gust up to 60 miles (96km) per hour, and temperatures can plummet to –60°F (–15°C).

Central Adirondack Association & Tourist Information Center
P.O. Box 68, Old Forge, NY 13420 (1-315-369-6983).

Lake Placid Chamber of Commerce & Visitor Center
216 Main St, Lake Placid, NY 12946 (1-518-523-2445).

Outdoor pursuits

If you're the windswept and outdoorsy type, you needn't leave your adventuresome pastimes behind just because you're in New York. There are few activities that aren't possible in the region. For others, see chapter **Sports & Fitness**.

Boating

Boating, canoeing and white-water rafting are popular sports in the many rivers, waterways, lakes, sounds, bays and ocean within reach of New York. The network of canals that was so instrumental in the industrialization of America is a prime leisure resource, with access free to everyone. The Erie Barge Canal links east with west by joining the Atlantic Ocean and the Hudson River to the St. Lawrence River and the Great Lakes. The Champlain Canal connects the 110-mile (176km) Lake Champlain with the Hudson River.

Batenkill Sports Quarters
937 State Rte 313, Cambridge, NY 12816 (1-518-677-8868). This company offers canoe, kayak and tubing trips.

McDonnell's Adirondack Challenges
R.R. 1 Box 262, Lake Clear, NY 12945 (1-518-891-1176). McDonnell's arranges canoeing and kayaking, as well as hiking, fishing and camping for individuals and groups.

Middle Earth Expeditions
H.C.R.O. 1 Box 37, Lake Placid, NY 12946 (1-518-523-9572). Outdoor pursuits for groups and individuals.

NYS Passenger Vessel Association
P.O. Box 95, Rifton, NY 12471 (1-800-852-0095). Offers information on the many boating operators throughout New York State.

Port Jervis Tri-State Chamber of Commerce
10 Sussex St, P.O. Box 121, Port Jervis, NY 12771 (1-914-856-6694). Information on trips down the Delaware River, including white-water rafting.

Rivett's Marine
P.O. Box 601, Lake Trail, Old Forge Lake, Old Forge, NY 13420 (1-315-369-3123). Boat rental, sale and service.

Wild & Scenic River Tours
166 Rte 97, Burryville, NY 12719 (1-914-557-8783, 1-800-836-0366). Canoeing, kayaking and white-water rafting.

Camping

There are 500 public and privately owned campsites throughout New York State. Some are deep in the wilderness and only accessible by boat; others are relatively close to a town or city. Reservations are recommended, but not always necessary. For more information, contact:

New York State Office of Parks, Recreation & Historic Preservation
Empire State Plaza, Albany, NY 12238 (1-518-474-0458). Information on all parks and park activities within the state.

New York State Campgrounds
1-800-456-CAMP. Call to make campsite reservations.

Climbing

The Shawangunks, or "Gunks," in the Catskills offer some of the best climbing in the country, with sheer stone cliffs, many of which are more than 300 feet (95m) high. You need to buy a day pass ($5, weekends and holidays $7) from the **Mohonk Preserve**, 1000 Mountain Rest Rd, Mohonk Lake, New Paltz, NY (1-914-255-0919). The local equipment store, **Rock and Snow**, at 44 Main St, New Paltz (1-914-255-1311), will be happy to give advice.

*Rip it, dude: Nearby **Hunter Mountain** attracts weekend 'boarders and skiers.*

Tents & Trails

21 Park Pl between Church St and Broadway (227-1760). Subway: A, C to Chambers St. Mon–Wed, Sat 9:30am–6pm; Thu, Fri 9:30am–7pm; Sun noon–6pm. AmEx, MC, V. Apart from the supermarket-style chain Eastern Mountain Sports, this is the only specialist climbing equipment store in Manhattan. Full of colorful ropes and friendly advice.

Cycling

A choice of landscapes in the area surrounding New York City means there's something for all cyclists, from recreational to racing. For information on cycling in a particular area, contact the local Chamber of Commerce, the New York State Office of Parks, Recreation & Historic Preservation (*see* **Camping** *above*), or the **League of American Bicyclists**, 1612 K Street, suite 401, Washington, D.C. 20006 (1-202-822-1333).

Fishing

With a license, you can fish in New York State's 70,000 miles (112,000 kilometers) of streams and rivers and 4,000 lakes and ponds. The first day of the fishing season (generally April 1, check the dates with the Department of Environmental Conservation, listed below) is a big day on the New York social/sporting calendar.

For freshwater fishing, you must get a license ($14 resident, $35 non-resident for the season, three- and five-day passes available) if you are between the ages of 16 and 69; they can be purchased at most fishing tackle stores. For information on licenses for New York call 1-518-457-3521; for New Jersey,1-609-292-2965; for Connecticut, 1-860-424-3105. To get a license by mail, or for other fishing information, contact the DEC (*see below*).

The favorite fishing spots in New York State are Lakes Erie and Ontario (two of the Great Lakes), Chautauqua Lake, the Finger Lakes, Oneida Lake, Lake Champlain and Lake George and the St. Lawrence, Delaware, Hudson and Allegheny rivers. Caleb Smith and Connetqout River State Parks, both in Long Island, are also favored spots for freshwater fishing, as are Burr Pond and Kent Fall State Parks, both of which are in Connecticut.

There are plenty of coastal areas where sea fishing is permitted. The resorts on Long Island and the Jersey shore have companies that charter boats and equipment. These operators can usually also take care of licensing requirements (sea fishing requires a different license than freshwater fishing).

Capitol Fishing

218 W 23rd St between Seventh and Eighth Aves (929-6132). Subway: A, C, E, 1, 9 to 23rd St. Mon–Wed, Fri 9am–6pm; Thu 9am–7pm; Sat 9am–5pm. AmEx, Disc, MC, V. Both saltwater and freshwater equipment are sold here. It's also possible to rent equipment.

Department of Environmental Conservation (DEC)

50 Wolf Rd, Albany, NY 12233 (1-518-457-5420).

Urban Angler

118 E 25th St between Lexington and Park Aves, third floor (979-7600). Subway: 6 to 28th St. Mon, Tue, Thu, Fri 10am–6pm; Wed 10am–7pm; Sat 10am–5pm. AmEx, MC, V. This is the best fly-fishing store in New York. Stop by for licenses, equipment and friendly information on the top places to fish in the region, both surf-casting (saltwater) and freshwater.

Hiking

Some of the most spectacular and challenging trails in the country can be found in New York State. The most famous, and popular, is the **Appalachian Trail**. Stretching from Maine to Georgia, this 2,159-mile (3,450km) trek is tackled by four million hikers annually. For more information about hiking in the region, contact:

Adirondack Mountain Club

814 Goggins Rd, Lake George, NY 12845 (1-518-668-4117; fax 1-518-668-3746).

Appalachian Mountain Club

New York–North Jersey Chapter, 5 Tudor City Pl at E 41st St, New York, NY 10016 (986-1430). Wed–Thu 2–5pm.

Finger Lakes Trail Conference

P.O. Box 18048, Rochester, NY 14618-0048 (1-716-288-7191).

Long Island Greenbelt Trail Conference

102 New Mill Rd, Smithtown, NY 11787 (1-516-360-0753).

Horseback riding

New York's splendid countryside contains miles of trails and special facilities for riders and horses as well as parks, campsites and stables where you can ride for a daily fee. For information on these, contact the local Chamber of Commerce. Check whether or not you will be covered by the stable's insurance; some only insure experienced riders and only if they go no faster than a walk.

Forty-one of New York State's counties have county fairs, almost all with equestrian events. They are usually held during the summer. For information on these, contact the **Department of Agriculture and Markets**, Winners Circle, Albany, NY 12235 (1-518-457-0127).

The following address is useful for all equestrian inquiries:

American Horse Show Association in New York State

Suite 409, 220 E 42nd St between Second and Third Aves, New York, NY 10017 (972-2472). Subway: S, 4, 5, 6, 7 to 42nd St–Grand Central.

Skiing and snowboarding

For information on the excellent skiing in the area, consult the travel section of Sunday's *New York Times*. In addition to the **Catskills** and **Adirondacks** (*see pages 295–296*), there are challenging ski resorts in the **Berkshires**, on the Massachusetts border, 110 miles (177km) from New York City.

*Sand dollars: Separate yourself from your money at **Atlantic City**'s Taj Mahal casino.*

Some of the larger sports stores arrange all-inclusive day trips by bus during the season, usually to Hunter Mountain, for both skiing and snowboarding, including equipment rentals and lessons, if necessary. Day trips cost $60–$70. Some of the best-organized excursions are run by Blades, Paragon and Scandinavian.

Blades
659 Broadway at Bleecker St (477-7350). Subway: B, D, F, Q to Broadway–Lafayette St; 6 to Bleecker St. Mon–Sat 11am–9pm, Sun 11am–7pm. AmEx, MC, V. Blades emphasizes snowboarding; its trips usually consist of noisy busloads of young "shredders."

New York Ski Club
Hostelling International–New York, 891 Amsterdam Ave at 103rd St (932-2300). Subway: 1, 9 to 103rd St. This organization runs trips and offers advice for anyone skiing on a budget.

Paragon Sports
867 Broadway at 18th St (255-8036). Subway: L, N, R, 4, 5, 6 to 14th St–Union Sq. Mon–Sat 10am–8pm, Sun 11am–6:30pm. AmEx, Disc, MC, V. Paragon's trips are slightly more adult than Blades, with an even blend of skiers and boarders.

Scandinavian
40 W 57th St between Fifth and Sixth Aves (757-8524). Subway: B, Q to 57th St. Mon, Tue 10am–6pm; Wed–Sat 10am–6:30am; Sun 11am–5pm. AmEx, MC, V. In addition to stocking a wide range of equipment, Scandinavian also has informative leaflets and offers helpful advice.

Snow Conditions & Information
Adirondacks Whiteface (1-518-946-2223, recorded message 1-518-946-7171); Lake Placid (1-800-462-6236); Gore Mountain (1-518-251-2411, 1-800-342-1234); Big Tupper (1-518-359-7902). **Berkshires** Catamount (1-518-325-3200, 1-413-528-1262). **Catskills** Hunter Mountain (1-518-263-4223, 1-800-FOR-SNOW). **Ski Windham** (1-518-734-4300, 1-800-729-4SNO).

Whale watching

Riverhead Foundation for Marine Research & Preservation
431 E Main St, Riverhead, NY (1-516-369-9840). MC, V. Whale-watching trips run between May 1 and Labor Day; excursions last between four and six hours.

Gambling

Casino gambling is illegal in most states. If you're not content with New York's various city and state lotteries, and the heavily promoted Off Track Betting fails to turn you on, you'd better leave town. Las Vegas is almost a full continent away, but you can hop on a bus and be hemorrhaging money on the blackjack tables in **Atlantic City** or **Verona** within a couple of hours.

Atlantic City
New Jersey. Travel: Greyhound bus from Port Authority Terminal to various casinos; return bus picks you up at the Atlantic City Bus Terminal, two blocks from Boardwalk. $24

Milking it: Guides at the 17th-century Dutch house **Phillipsburg Manor** *don period costumes.*

round trip. The trip to Atlantic City takes about two and a half hours. While many New Yorkers disparage the place, anyone who's never encountered organized casino gambling before will find it amazing. The most famous of its many casinos are **Trump Plaza**, **Caesar's Palace** and Donald Trump's latest, the **Taj Mahal**. Once you're inside one casino, you can get to the others by way of the **Boardwalk**, which runs along the edge of the Atlantic Ocean, or take the Pacific Avenue bus. Bring your own spending money, or just watch the crazed antics of the frenzied crowd. Besides bars, restaurants and gift shops, there are floor shows and, at some casinos, concerts. The annual Miss America Pageant is held in September at the **Atlantic City Convention Center** at 2001 Kirkman Blvd. Shoppers should head for Ocean One, a vast shopping mall set right on the water. Call the **Atlantic City Convention & Visitors Authority** (1-609-348-7130) for more information.

Foxwoods Resort Casino

Ledyard, CT (1-860-885-3000, 1-800-PLAY-BIG). Travel: By car take I-95 north to exit 92, then eight miles (13km) on Rte 2 west. By bus, Greyhound (1-800-231-2222). By train, Metro-North from Grand Central Terminal to New Haven, then connecting bus (one trip daily). Amtrak offers Foxwoods vacation packages (1-800-321-8684). The various Indian nations, not bound to state gambling laws, are free to make their own rules for—and revenues from—games of chance. The Mashantucket-Pequot tribe turns a very nice profit at this immense resort casino located 145 miles north of New York in bucolic Connecticut. With 4,000 slot machines, a 3,200-seat bingo hall, hundreds of games tables and a 75-table poker room, visitors have plenty of opportunities to squander their life savings. For the more cautious, Foxwoods offers concerts by such stars as Ray Charles, Willie Nelson and Smokey Robinson.

Theme parks

Mountain Creek

Vernon, NJ, on Rte 94, 47 miles (72km) from Manhattan (1-973-827-2000). Travel: By car take Rte 80 west, then Rte 15 north and Rte 94 north. By bus, NJ Transit (1-201-762-5100). Jun 15–Sept 1 10am–7pm. Adults $28, children 48–54 inches tall $26, children under four feet tall $20, small children free. Group discounts available. AmEx, MC, V. An immense water park in the summer, Mountain Creek (formerly Action Park) caters to fun-loving families looking to splash away the summer heat. Now under new ownership, the area has been revamped (de-cheesed!) to better fit its beautiful mountain setting—200 acres of woods and hills. Bring your swimming gear and enjoy high-action rides like "Wild River," or more kid-friendly diversions like "Lost Island." The area is also in the process of expanding its winter facilities.

Playland

Rye, NY (amusement park 1-914-967-5230/ice-skating rinks 1-914-967-2040). Travel: Metro-North from Grand Central Terminal to Rye, then connecting bus. Summer Tue–Thu, Sun noon–11pm; Fri, Sat noon–midnight; call for details of winter hours. Admission to park free, rides "cost" 3–5 tickets ($18 for 36 tickets, $14 for 24). MC, V. An old-fashioned amusement and theme park set on the banks of the Long Island Sound, this 70-year-old facility is popular for both its historic and new rides and attractions, including the Derby Racer and the Dragon Coaster, as well as the new "Chaos." There's a separate Kiddie Land for children. There are also picnic grounds, a pool and, of course, the beautiful beach. A fireworks display is held on Wednesday and Friday nights during July and August.

Six Flags Great Adventure & Safari Park

Jackson, NJ, on Rte 537, 50 miles (80km) from Manhattan (1-732-928-1821). Travel: By car take exit 7A off the New Jersey Tpke or exit 98 off the Garden State Pkwy to Interstate 195, exit 16. By bus, NJ Transit (201-762-5100) from Port Authority Terminal ($39 round trip, incl. admission). May–Sept 10am–10pm (closing time sometimes later), limited opening times in Oct. Adults $35–38, children under 54 inches tall $25–28, senior citizens $18–21. AmEx, Disc, MC, V. "Bigger than Disneyland and a whole lot closer" is the slogan with which this theme park entices Manhattanites. There's a huge drive-through safari park with 1,305 land animals, a massive collection of top-of-the-range rides and the obligatory fast food and souvenirs. Not to be missed are the Great American Scream Machine and the "Batman and Robin: The Chiller" ride, where you can experience 0–70 mph acceleration forwards and backwards.

Historical tours

If you're keen on history or just enjoy scenery, you'll get both with a trip up the **Hudson Valley**. Beautiful summer residences of famous New Yorkers line the river. Most are open from March until the end of the year. You can get information from **Historic Hudson Valley**, 150 White Plains Rd, Tarrytown, NY 10591 (1-914-631-8200/reservations 1-800-533-3779), which, in conjunction with the **New York Waterway** (1-800-53FERRY), offers boat trips from Manhattan or New Jersey to several of the historic houses. Also, the Historic Hudson Valley office and any of the sites listed below can provide you with detailed driving instructions.

Metro-North, the commuter railway that leaves Manhattan's Grand Central Terminal, is a fast, easy and scenic way to get to towns near these sights, and tours are often available. Or you can take an Amtrak train from Penn Station. See chapter **Getting Around** for more information.

Cold Spring

Travel: Metro-North Hudson Line to Cold Spring, NY. $14. Any time of the year, Cold Spring offers spectacular close-up views of the Hudson River. It's only 50 miles (80km) from Manhattan, but light years away culturally. If you arrive by train, walk through the underpass to get to Main Street, where a number of narrow-frame houses with porches and shutters sit alongside the four-story commercial buildings. The tiny town has plenty of shops. For nearly a century, life centered on the **Cold Spring Foundry**, ironworks that opened in 1817 and made gun tubes and steam engines. Head down to the water, where you'll find a gazebo, the town dock and a small beach. You'll get a great view of the lush, green **Hudson Highlands** across the way. The **Main Street Café** (129 Main) sells fresh-baked buns for breakfast, good sandwiches and homemade fruit pies. **Hudson House** (2 Main), a landmark 1832 inn, serves American food; **Dockside Harbor** (2 North St), which is on a grassy point by the water, has a seafood menu and a play area for kids.

Kykuit

North Tarrytown, NY (1-914-631-9491). Travel: By car take New York State Thruway (I-87) north to exit 9, Tarrytown. By train, Metro-North to Tarrytown, then five-mile (eight-km) cab ride to Phillipsburg Manor Visitor's Center. May–Nov 9:30am–4:45pm. $18 adults, $17 seniors. Call in advance for tour reservations. John D. Rockefeller Jr. was given the task of building this beautiful estate by his oil tycoon dad John Sr. Completed in 1913, Kykuit was home to four generations of Rockefellers—including former New York Governor Nelson, who lived here in the '60s and '70s. The Beaux Arts mansion contains extraordinary art, fine furniture and ceramics, while the terraced garden is dotted with both classical and 20th-century sculpture. The grounds offer spectacular views of the Hudson River, and the collection of antique cars and horse-drawn vehicles is not to be missed.

Montgomery Place

River Rd, Annandale-on-Hudson, NY (1-914-758-5461). Travel: Amtrak to Rhinecliff Station, then call the Blue Coach cab service when you arrive (1-914-876-2900). Apr–Oct Mon, Wed–Sun 10am–5pm; call for off-season hours. $6, children over six $3. AmEx, V. This fabulous mansion is about 100 miles (160km) from Manhattan. Built in 1804 for Janet Livingston Montgomery, the widow of a Revolutionary War patriot, it is set on 434 lush acres along the Hudson. There are formal gardens, woodlands, views of the Catskill Mountains and a lawn where games are played and lemonade is served. Visitors can pick their own raspberries in July and peaches in August.

Old Westbury Gardens

Old Westbury, NY 11568 (1-516-333-0048). Travel: By car take the Long Island Expwy east to exit 39S, Glen Cove Rd; follow service road east for 1.2 miles (1.9 km) to Old Westbury Rd. By train, LIRR to Old Westbury, then cab. Apr–Dec Mon, Wed–Sun 10am–5pm. $6 gardens; $10 house and garden. No credit cards. Carnegie loot was behind this eclectic pile created by the English designer George Crawley for the Phipps family in 1906. The house is built in Restoration style and includes pieces by Chippendale and Reynolds. The wonderful grounds are huge and contain examples of just about everything from formal alleys to Japanese gardens and sweeping parkland.

Phillipsburg Manor

Upper Hills, Tarrytown, NY (1-914-631-8200). Travel: By car, north on New York State Thruway (I-87), take exit 9 for Tarrytown; the sign is two miles (three km) on the left. By train, Metro-North to Tarrytown, then five-mile (eight-km) cab ride. Mar–Dec Mon, Wed–Sun 10am–5pm. AmEx, MC, V. The manor was once the home of Frederick Flypse (later called Flypsen, then Philipse), who came to the New World in the early 1650s as Governor Peter Stuyvesant's carpenter. Through business acumen and some shrewd marriages, Frederick managed to elevate his land-holding of about 52,500 acres to the status of "Lordship or Mannour of Philpsborough." At the Upper Mills, which was just a small portion of his holding, Frederick constructed a dam, grist mill and manor house, with a Dutch church adjacent to the property. The grist mill still works and the Dutch barn is filled with animals. Guides wear period costumes.

Sunnyside

Tarrytown, NY (1-914-631-8200). Travel: By car, north on New York State Thruway (I-87), take exit 9 for Tarrytown and go one mile south on Rte 9, then right. By train, Metro-North to Irvington, NY, then a 20-minute walk, or call for a cab (1-914-631-0031). Mar–Dec Mon, Wed–Sun 10am–5pm. Guided tours 10:30am–4pm. $8, $4–$7 concessions. AmEx, MC, V. This delightful building was the home of Washington Irving, author of *Rip Van Winkle* and *The Legend of Sleepy Hollow.* Sunnyside was built on the banks of the Hudson in 1835. Chatty guides in period costume lead you through the home; you can escape them by strolling through the lovely grounds.

Van Cortlandt Manor

Croton-on-Hudson, NY (1-914-631-8200). Travel: By car, north on New York State Thruway (I-87); take exit 9 for Tarrytown, then go nine miles (15km) north. By train, Metro-North to Croton-Harmon, then ten-minute walk. Mar–Oct

Mon, Wed–Sun 10am–5pm; Nov–Dec Sat, Sun 10am–5pm. $8, $4–$7 concessions. AmEx, Disc, MC, V. Set into a hillside overlooking the Croton and Hudson Rivers, the mansion was once home to Pierre Van Cortlandt, the state's first Lieutenant Governor, and his son Phillip, who served as both an officer under General Washington and a U.S. Congressman. Now there's a gift shop and picnic area on his estate.

Upstate destinations

Beyond the cast-iron and concrete expanse of the city, New York State offers scenery of stupendous natural beauty. The best time to admire its grandeur is in the autumn, when the trees turn deep scarlet, flaming orange and soft gold.

In addition to the regions covered below and elsewhere in this chapter, there are a number of other places that should be seen if you're driving through the state. Wonders can be found in the most unlikely places.

The **Thousand Islands Region** on the St. Lawrence Seaway is a favorite vacation spot for New Yorkers and Canadians. Boating and fishing are the main pastimes. Glaciers carved gouges right through the middle of the state and left long bony indentations called the **Finger Lakes**. This area has become popular for lots of outdoor activities, for its vineyards and wineries, and for **Watkins Glen** gorge and raceway.

Rochester and **Syracuse** are the biggest local cities. One highlight in Rochester is the Kodak Factory tour and museum. **Allegheny State Park** and **Chautauqua Lake** are huge natural refuges in the very southwestern corner of the state near Jamestown.

Elmira, near the southern border of New York, is where Mark Twain summered and wrote much of his best work, or visit **Corning**, where you can go on the Corning Glass Factory Tours.

Hostelling International–New York

891 Amsterdam Ave at 103rd St, New York, NY 10025 (932-1860). The American Youth Hostels organization is an excellent source of information on all outdoor activities, statewide and nationwide.

New York State Tourist & Travel Information Center

1-518-474-4116, 1-800-225-5697.

Albany

Although overshadowed by New York City, **Albany** is the capital of the Empire State, and the nation's oldest chartered city (1686). The **Empire State Plaza**, overlooking the city, is where many of the state government buildings are located. The imposing **Corning Tower** is open from 9am until 4pm every day, and there are daily tours of the State Capitol building. The **Albany Institute of History and Art** (1-518-463-4478) is the elegant home of a wonderful collection of locally made silver and furniture. Other places near Albany

worth a visit include **Schenectady, Saratoga** and **Cooperstown**.

Just 70 miles (112km) west of Albany, in Cooperstown, is the diamond where Abner Doubleday is said to have invented baseball in 1839 and the **Baseball Hall of Fame** (1-607-547-7200), filled with memorabilia of the national pastime.

For more information about the greater Albany area, contact the **Albany County Convention & Visitors Bureau** at 52 S Pearl St, Albany, NY 12207 (1-518-434-1217, 1-800-258-3582).

Niagara Falls

It may be a long way from New York City, but good things are worth traveling for and Niagara Falls is one of the best. No matter what is done to make a buck off this natural wonder (and plenty is), its beauty and power remain undiminished. The falls, which are part of the Niagara River, separate the United States from Canada and Lake Erie from Lake Ontario. The **American** and **Bridal Veil Falls** are in the United States, and the **Horseshoe Falls** are on the Canadian side.

The 185-foot-high (55m) falls span 3,260 feet (953m) and throw three quarters of a million gallons of water over the edge per second. A bridge out to **Goat Island**, which separates the two countries' waterfalls, provides an impressive view of the cascades. You can hear the roar of the falls and see the mist and rainbows they produce especially well from there. The **Cave of the Winds** is where raincoats are an absolute must. Visitors go down in an elevator to the bottom of the American falls, travel a short distance and look out through the falls while standing under and behind them. The water acts as a prism when there is sufficient light, so it can be like standing in a rainbow.

Other attractions on the American side are the observation tower on **Prospect Point**, which provides a panoramic view of the falls, and the **Maid of the Mist** boat trips, which get close enough to the falls for all to be tossed around and get thoroughly drenched. Farther down the gorge are the infamous whirlpools, the **Schoellkopf Geological Center**, the **Robert Moses Niagara Power Plant** (which supplies much of the East Coast with electricity) and **Old Fort Niagara**. The Canadian side of the falls (accessible by bus from Buffalo) has the best views of the water, and some incredibly kitschy honeymoon hotels. The biggest attraction, apart from the water, is the **Native American Center**, a fascinating collection of artifacts housed in a turtle-shaped building.

The area has more to offer than the falls. **Buffalo**, New York State's second largest city, is one of the most attractively renovated old industrial cities of America. Other sights worth visiting are the Erie Canal, Lakes Erie and Ontario, and the fabulous Albright-Knox Art Gallery.

*Rock 'feller: A daredevil scales the "**Gunks**," one of America's best climbing spots.*

Escape to the city

Still haven't satisfied your urban thirst? Try these nearby alternatives.

New York is hardly representative of American cities—or East Coast cities, for that matter. If you're itching to get a taste of another kind of American urban life, it's easy to take a short jaunt to three of the country's most important cities—each with a very distinctive, very different vibe.

Boston

Slower-paced and with a more civilized feel than New York, Boston was the birthplace of the United States as an independent nation. The biggest city in America until 1755, Boston remained the busiest foreign port in the British Empire throughout the colonial period. The buildings that remain from this early growth in the 17th and 18th centuries give the city its refreshingly human scale.

Walking the **Freedom Trail**, marked by red bricks set in the street, is the easiest way to take in the city's history and flavor. A number of excellent museums dot the waterfront, including the **Boston Tea Party Ship and Museum**. Shop to your heart's content in downtown's **Quincy Market** and **Faneuil Hall**. Home to many colleges and universities, Boston has an active, young social scene. Cross the river to Cambridge to see the cloisters of Ivy League academia that is **Harvard**. For information on travel, lodging and other attractions, call the **Greater Boston Chamber of Commerce** (1-617-227-4500, 1-888-733-2678) or the **Greater Boston Convention and Visitors Center** (1-617-536-4100).

Philadelphia

When Charles II rid himself of a troublesome nonconformist, William Penn, by giving him a chunk of the New World, Pennsylvania was founded. The capital was built in 1682 on a grid system of Penn's devising, which became the norm for American cities. He called his city Philadelphia, meaning "city of brotherly love"; Penn even signed a treaty ensuring peaceful coexistence with the local American Indians.

Much of Philadelphia's history is tied to the events of the American Revolution. It was here that the **Declaration of Independence** was first read, and also where the **U.S. Constitution** was drawn up. **Independence Hall**, **Congress Hall** and **Old City Hall**, the original governmental buildings of the young U.S., are here, as are a smattering of sites where America's founding fathers slept, worked and worshiped. Not to be missed is the **Liberty Bell**, the famous cracked bell which rang out for each Patriot victory and was later adopted as an antislavery symbol.

Philly has lots of bars catering to its large and influential student population, while more upscale eating establishments are located on **South Street**. For information on travel, accommodations and attractions, call the **Philadelphia Convention & Visitors Bureau** (1-215-636-3300) or the city's **Visitor Center** (1-215-636-1666).

Washington, D.C.

Once swampland, now the nation's capital, Washington, D.C. is full of gracious avenues, imposing buildings, powerful politicians and smart-looking wannabes. Beyond the formal grandeur, however, are neighborhoods racked by extreme poverty and violence. Washington was the first American city to have a black majority, but its wealth is largely divided along racial lines.

Take a free tour around the **U.S. Capitol**, the white-domed home of the Senate and the House of Representatives. Other government attractions include the **U.S. Supreme Court**, and the **White House**, home and office of the President. The largest library in the world, the **Library of Congress**, grew from Thomas Jefferson's private collection and now contains more than 100 million books. Take a trip to **The Mall**, a large formal park graced by the **Washington Monument** and the **Lincoln Memorial**; to the north are the **National Archives, Museum of Natural History** and **Museum of American History**, to the south the **Air & Space Museum**.

Many of the city's galleries and museums are part of the **Smithsonian Institution**. The visitor center for the Smithsonian is at the Castle, halfway down the Mall; guides there will provide details on all the various attractions in the area.

Excellent food, drink and live entertainment abound in the lively **Adams Morgan** neighborhood, as well as in the areas surrounding Washington's universities, such as **Georgetown**. For more information on travel, lodging and attractions, call the **Washington, D. C. Convention & Visitors Association** (1-202-789-7000).

**Greater Buffalo Convention
& Visitors Bureau**
617 Main St, Buffalo, NY 14203 (1-800-283-3256).

**Niagara County Convention
& Visitors Bureau**
139 Niagara St, Lockport, NY 14094 (1-800-338-7890).

**Niagara County Tourism
& Fishing Office**
139 Niagara St, Lockport 14094 (1-716-439-7300).

Saratoga

Located about 175 miles (282km) north of Manhattan, **Saratoga** gained fame for its mineral-water baths and racetrack. Its heyday was in the late 19th century, but it's still a deservedly popular tourist destination. From July to September, the **Saratoga Race Course** (1-518-584-6200), the country's oldest and loveliest, is in season.

From June to early September the **Saratoga Performing Arts Center (SPAC)**, formed in 1966, attracts lovers of classical and pop music as well as jazz, ballet and opera fans. In July, the New York City Ballet takes up residence here for three weeks, followed by a jazz festival and opera series. The Philadelphia Orchestra makes its annual visit at this time.

The wealthy built beautiful homes in Saratoga; most are located along Union Avenue, North Broadway and Caroline Street. There is also the **National Museum of Racing**, Union Ave and Ludlow St (1-518-584-0400), and the **National Museum of Dance** (1-518-584-9330).

You should also get a massage at the **Lincoln Mineral Baths** in Saratoga Spa State Park (1-518-584-2011). View the area, plus the Green Mountains of Vermont, from a hot-air balloon, on a tour with Adirondack Balloon Flights (*see below*).

While the cost of a stay at the **Adelphi Hotel** on Broadway (1-518-587-4688) may be steep for the average tourist (rooms start at $130), you should at least take a look at its lobby. Built in 1877, it's the only authentic grand hotel in town. Most of the fine restaurants and bars are clustered on Broadway. For nightlife, make a reservation at **Caffe Lena** on Phila Street (1-518-583-0022): Everybody has played here, including Bob Dylan back in 1962. For more information about Saratoga, contact the Chamber of Commerce.

Adirondack Balloon Flights
P.O. Box 65, Glens Falls, NY 12801 (1-518-793-6342). $175 per person. AmEx, Disc, MC, V. Internet: www. adkballoonflights.com The one-hour balloon ride is especially beautiful during the autumn. Flights are scheduled around

*Diamond life: Explore the national pastime at the **Baseball Hall of Fame** in Cooperstown.*

*A-a-a-nd they're off: Play the ponies at **Saratoga Race Course**, the nation's oldest track.*

sunrise and three hours before sunset and may be canceled if the weather is bad.

Saratoga County Chamber of Commerce
28 Clinton St, Saratoga Springs, NY 12866 (1-518-584-3255).

Saratoga County Tourism Department
County Municipal Center, Ballston Spa, NY 12020 (1-800-526-8970).

Saratoga Performing Arts Center (SPAC)
Saratoga Springs, NY 12866 (1-518-584-9330/credit card reservations 518-587-3330). Jun–Sept. Call for event schedules. AmEx, MC, V. Tickets for jazz events range from $27.50 for a lawn seat purchased in advance to $45 for an orchestra seat. Tickets for the New York City Ballet or the Philadelphia Orchestra cost $15–$45, and you will pay up to $75 for the Ballet's season-ending gala performance in July.

GETTING THERE
By Amtrak (*see page 292*), the journey takes roughly three hours and costs $65 round trip; by **Greyhound** bus (1-800-231-2222), it takes approximately four hours and costs $50 round trip.

General information

For more information on areas worth visiting within New York State, contact:

Allegheny State Park, Recreation & Historic Preservation Region
2373 Route 1, Salamanca, NY 14779 (1-716-354-9121).

Allegheny Historical Society County Museum
Court St, Belmont, NY 14813 (1-716-268-9293).

Central New York State Park Region
6105 E Seneca Turnpike, Jamesville, NY 13078 (1-315-492-1756).

Economic Development & Tourist Information
1-716-268-922.

Finger Lakes Association
309 Lake St, Penn Yan, NY 14527 (1-315-536-7488).

Greater Rochester Visitors' Association
126 Andrew St, Rochester, NY 14604 (1-716-546-3070).

Northern Chautauqua County Chamber of Commerce
212 Lakeshore Drive West, Dunkirk, NY 14048 (1-716-366-6200).

Syracuse Convention & Visitors Bureau
572 S Salina St, Syracuse, NY 13202 (1-315-470-1800).

Thousand Islands State Park & Recreation Region
P.O. Box 247, Alexandria Bay, NY 13607 (1-315-482-2593, 1-800-537-7676).

Directory assistance: The Statue of Liberty lets visitors know they've arrived.

Directory

Directory

These indispensable tips will help you conquer the Naked City

Essential information

For information about the abbreviations used in this guide, see **About the Guide**, page vi.

If you're calling from outside Manhattan, dial 1, then area code 212 before the numbers listed in this guide (unless otherwise stated). All 800, 888 and 877 numbers (dial 1 first) are free, although many hotels add a surcharge for the use of their phones, no matter what number you call (*see also* **Telephones**, *page 310*).

Visas

Under the Visa Waiver Program, citizens of the U.K., Japan, Australia, New Zealand and all Western European countries (except for Portugal, Greece and Vatican City) do not need a visa for stays shorter than 90 days (business or pleasure), as long as they have a passport that is valid for the full 90-day period and a return ticket. An open standby ticket is acceptable.

Canadians and Mexicans don't need visas but must have legal proof of their residency. All other travelers must have visas. Full information and visa application forms can be obtained from your nearest U.S. embassy or consulate. In general, send in your application at least three weeks before you plan to travel. To apply for a visa on shorter notice, contact the travel agent booking your ticket.

For information on student visas, *see page 317*.

U.S. Embassy Visa Information
In the U.S. 1-202-663-1225. In the U.K. 0891-200-290.

Immigration and customs

Standard immigration regulations apply to all visitors, which means you may have to wait (up to an hour) when you arrive. During your flight, you will be handed an Immigration form and a Customs declaration form to be presented to an official when you land.

You may be expected to explain your visit, so be polite and be prepared. You will usually be granted an entry permit to cover the length of your stay. Work permits are hard to get, and you are not permitted to work without one (*see* **Students**, *page 317*).

U.S. Customs allows returning Americans to bring in $100 worth of gifts ($400 for foreigners)

before paying duty. One carton of 200 cigarettes (or 100 cigars) and one liter of liquor (spirits) is allowed. No plants, fruit, meat or fresh produce can be taken through customs. If you carry more than $10,000 worth of currency, you will have to fill out a report.

If you must bring prescription drugs to the U.S., make sure the container is clearly marked and that you bring your doctor's statement or a prescription. Of course, marijuana, cocaine and most opiate derivatives and other chemicals are not permitted, and possession of them is punishable by stiff fines and/or imprisonment. Check with the **U.S. Customs Service** (1-800-697-3662) before you arrive if you have any questions about what you can bring. If you lose or need to renew your passport once in the U.S., contact your country's embassy (*see* **Foreign consulates**, *page 315*).

Insurance

If you live in the U.K., it's advisable to take out comprehensive insurance before arriving: It's almost impossible to arrange in the U.S. Make sure that you have adequate health coverage, since medical expenses can be high. *See* **Emergency rooms**, *page 316*, for a list of New York urgent-care facilities.

Money

The U.S. dollar ($) is 100 cents (¢). A cent is copper and more likely to be called a "penny." Nickels (5¢), dimes (10¢) and quarters (25¢) are silver. Paper money is all the same size and color, so make sure you fork over the right denomination. Small shops will rarely break a $50 or $100 bill. Occasionally you might get a silver dollar, a Susan B. Anthony dollar (about the size of a quarter) or a $2 note in change. These are rare and worth keeping.

If you run out of "greenbacks," don't expect your embassy or consulate to lend you money—they won't, although they may be persuaded to repatriate you. In an emergency, you can have money wired to **Western Union**; call 1-800-325-6000 for the location of the nearest office. Another service is **MoneyGram**, which has 1,300 locations in Manhattan (call 1-800-926-9400 for information).

Banks and currency exchange

Banks are open from 9am to 3pm Monday to Friday. You need photo identification, such as a passport, to change traveler's checks. Many banks will not exchange foreign currency, and the *bureaux de changes*, limited to tourist-trap areas, close around 6 or 7pm. It's best to arrive with some dollars in cash but to pay mostly with traveler's checks (possible in most restaurants and larger stores—but ask first and be prepared to show ID). In an emergency, most big hotels offer 24-hour exchange facilities but charge high commissions and give atrocious rates.

ATMs

New York City is full of Automated Teller Machines (ATMs). Most accept Visa, MasterCard or American Express, among other cards, if they have an affiliated PIN number. There is often a usage fee, although the convenience (and the superior exchange rate) often makes it worth the extra charge.

Call the following for ATM locations: **Cirrus** (1-800-424-7787); **Wells Fargo** (1-800-869-3557); **Plus Systems** (1-800-843-7587). If you've lost your number or have somehow demagnetized your card, most banks will give cash to card holders.

Credit cards

Bring plastic if you have it, or be prepared for a logistical nightmare. It's essential for things like renting cars and booking hotels and handy for buying tickets over the phone. The five major credit cards accepted in the U.S. are **Visa, MasterCard, Discover, Diners Club** and **American Express**.

Lost or stolen credit cards

American Express *1-800-992-6377*

Diners Club *1-800-234-6377*

Discover *1-800-347-2683*

MasterCard *1-800-826-2181*

JCB *1-800-366-4522*

Visa *1-800-336-8472*

Lost or stolen traveler's checks

American Express *1-800-221-7282*

Visa *1-800-336-8472*

Exchange offices

American Express Travel Service

65 Broadway between Rector St and Exchange Pl (493-6500). Subway: N, R, 1 to Rector St. Mon–Fri 8:30am–5:30pm. AmEx will change money and traveler's checks and offer other services such as poste restante. Phone for the location of other branches.

Chequepoint USA

22 Central Park South between Fifth and Sixth Aves (750-2400). Subway: N, R to 59th St. 8am–9:30pm. Foreign currency, traveler's checks and bank drafts are available here.
Branch: *1568 Broadway at 47th St (869–6281).*

People's Foreign Exchange

19 W 44th St between Fifth and Sixth Aves, suite 306 (944-6780). Subway: B, D, F, Q to 42nd St. Mon–Fri 9am–6pm; Sat, Sun 10am–3pm. Free foreign exchange on banknotes and travelers' checks.

Thomas Cook Currency Services

29 Broadway at Morris St (1-800-287-7362). Subway: 4, 5 to Bowling Green. Mon–Fri 9am–5pm. Complete foreign exchange service is offered. There are seven branches in JFK Airport, all open 7:30am–10:30pm daily (1-718-656-8444), in addition to those listed below.
Branches: *1590 Broadway at 48th St; 511 Madison Ave at 53rd St (all branches 1-800-287-7362).*

Time and date

New York is on Eastern Standard Time, which extends from the Atlantic coast to the eastern side of Lake Michigan and south to the Gulf of Mexico: This is five hours behind Greenwich Mean Time. Clocks are set forward one hour in early April and back one hour at the end of October. Going from east to west, Eastern Standard Time is one hour ahead of Central Time, two hours ahead of Mountain Time and three hours ahead of Pacific Time.

In the U.S., dates are written in the order of month, day, year; so 2/5/98 is the fifth of February, not the second of May.

Electricity

The U.S. uses a 110–120V, 60-cycle AC voltage, rather than the 220–240V, 50-cycle AC used in Europe and elsewhere. Except for dual-voltage, flat-pin plug shavers, you will need to run any foriegn-bought appliances via an adaptor, available at airport shops, pharmacies and department stores.

Postal services

For information on overnight delivery, *see* **Air couriers**, *page 319*.

General Post Office

421 Eighth Ave at 33rd St (967-8585/24-hour postal information 1-800-725-2161). Subway: A, C, E to 34th St–Penn Station. Open 24 hours; midnight–6pm for money orders and registered mail. This is the city's main post office; call for the local branch nearest to you. There are 59 full-service post offices in New York; lines are long, but stamps are also available from self-service vending machines. Branches are usually open 9am to 5pm, Monday through Friday; Saturday hours vary from office to office. The 24-hour line provides extensive postal information.

Express Mail

Information: 967-8585. You need to use special envelopes and fill out a form, which can be done either at a post office or by arranging a pickup. You are guaranteed 24-hour mail delivery to major U.S. cities. Letters—both domestic and international—must be sent before 5pm.

General Delivery

390 Ninth Ave at 30th St. Visitors without a local address can have their mail sent here; mail should be addressed to recipient's name, General Delivery, New York, NY, 10199. You will need to show some form of identification—a passport or ID card—when picking up letters. Call 330-3099 for more information.

Stamps

Stamps are available at all post offices and from vending machines in most drugstores (where they cost more). Airmail letters to anywhere overseas cost 60¢ for the first 0.5oz (14g) and 40¢ each additional 0.5oz. It costs 32¢ to send a letter within the U.S., and 50¢ to send a postcard anywhere in the world.

Western Union Telegrams

1-800-325-6000. Open 24 hours. Telegrams to addresses worldwide are taken over the phone at any time of day or night, and charges are added to your phone bill. Service is not available from pay phones.

Disabled access

New York is one of the most challenging cities for a disabled visitor, but there is support and guidance close by. The **Society for the Advancement of Travel for the Handicapped**, which promotes travel for the disabled worldwide, is based in New York City. This nonprofit group was founded in 1976 to educate people about travel facilities for the disabled. Membership is $45 a year ($30 for students and senior citizens) and includes access to an information service and a quarterly newsletter. Write or call SATH, 347 Fifth Ave, suite 610, New York, NY 10016 (447-7284, fax 725-8253).

Another useful resource is the **Hospital Audiences, Inc.** (HAI) guide to New York's cultural institutions, *Access for All* ($5). The book lets you know how accessible each place really is, and includes information on the height of telephones and water fountains, hearing and visual aids, passenger loading zones and alternative entrances.

HAI also has a service for the visually impaired that provides audio descriptions of theater performances. The program, called Describe! consists of prerecorded audiocassettes with a description of the theater, the sets, characters, costumes and special effects. It also offers live service during performances: Call 575-7660 for more information.

All Broadway theaters are equipped with devices for the hearing impaired; call **Sound Associates** (239-6200) for more information. There are a number of other stage-related resources for the disabled. Call **Telecharge** (239-6200) to reserve tickets for wheelchair seating in Broadway and Off Broadway venues. **Theater Development Fund's Theater Access Program** (TAP) arranges sign language interpretation for Broadway shows. Call 221-1103 or 719-4537. **Hands On** (627-4898) does the same for Off-Broadway performances. For more information on facilities for the disabled, *see page 314*.

Safety

Statistics on New York's crime rate, particularly violent crime, have nose-dived in the past few years, though bad things still happen to good people. More than ever, most of it stays within specific ethnic groups, happening late at night in low-income neighborhoods. Don't arrive thinking you need an armed guard to accompany you wherever you go; it is highly unlikely that you will ever be bothered.

Still, a bit of common sense won't hurt. Do not flaunt your money and valuables. Avoid lonely and poorly lit streets, and if necessary walk facing the traffic so no one can drive up alongside you. On deserted sidewalks, walk close to the street; muggers prefer to hang back in doorways and shadows. If the worst happens and you find yourself threatened, hand over your wallet or camera at once (your attacker will be as anxious to get it over with as you are), then call the police as soon as you can (dial 911 from any pay phone).

Beware of pickpockets and street hustlers—especially in busy tourist areas like Times Square —and don't be seduced by card sharks or other tricksters you may come across. A shrink-wrapped camcorder for 50 bucks could turn out to be a load of bricks or magazines when you open the box.

As a rule, if you look comfortable rather than lost, you should deter troublemakers.

Smoking

New Yorkers are the target of some of the strictest antismoking laws on the planet (*see* **About the Guide**). Now could be the time to quit.

Telephones

Public pay phones are easy to find. Most of them work, but the Bell Atlantic ones are the best: Those from other phone companies tend to be poorly maintained. If someone's left the receiver dangling, it's a sign that something's wrong. Phones take any combination of silver coins: Local calls usually cost 25¢ for three minutes. If you're used to British phones, know that the ringing tone is long; the "engaged" tone, or busy signal, is short and higher pitched.

The Manhattan area codes are 212 and, beginning in fall 1998, 646 (*see also* **About the Guide** for more information about dialing New York City numbers). In this guide, all seven-digit numbers are Manhattan numbers. You must dial 1 plus the area code for all other numbers. The area codes for New Jersey are 201, 732, 973, 609, and 908.

If you want to call long distance or make an international call from a pay phone, you need to use one of the long-distance companies. In New York, most pay phones automatically use AT&T, but there are other options. Look in the Yellow Pages under

Telephone Companies. Sprint and MCI are respected brand names, and beware of imposters. Some renegade firms charge unannounced and outlandish rates—until they get caught.

Make the call either by dialing 0 for an operator or by dialing direct (cheaper). To find out how much a call will cost, dial the number and a voice will tell you how much money to deposit.

You can pay for calls with your credit card. The best way of making calls, however, is with a phone card, available in various denominations from any post office branch or from large chain stores such as Duane Reade or Rite Aid.

Operator assistance dial 0
Directory assistance (local) dial 411 (free from pay phones)
International calls dial 011 + country code (U.K. 44; New Zealand 64; Australia 61)
Long-distance directory assistance dial 1 + area code + 555-1212 (long-distance charges apply)
Toll-free directory dial 1 +800 + 555-1212 (no charge).
Collect calls (reverse charges) dial 0 followed by the area code and number, or dial AT&T's 1-800-CALLATT, MCI's 1-800-COLLECT, Sprint's 1-800-ONE-DIME; for calls to the U.K., dial 1-800-445-5667.

Tax and tipping

You'd be hard pressed to find anything more expensive in New York than in most Western-world capitals, but you will have to account for a few extras. Sales tax (8.25 percent) is added to the price of most purchases, but is not marked on price tags. In addition, there's a lot of tipping to do. Wait staff get 15–20 percent (as a rough guide, double the sales tax on your bill) and cabbies 15 percent. But don't forget to tip bartenders ($1 a round), hairdressers (10–15 percent), hotel doormen ($1 for hailing a cab) porters ($1 per bag) and maid service ($2 per day on departure). Remember that the person who delivers your Chinese food probably receives no salary at all ($2 is considered a good tip).

Tourist information

Hotels are usually full of maps, leaflets and free tourist magazines that give advice about entertainment and events. Be aware that advice from hotels is not always impartial. Plenty of other magazines (including the weekly *Time Out New York*) offer entertainment and practical information (*see chapter* **Media**).

New York Convention & Visitors Bureau

2 Columbus Circle, Broadway at W 59th St (397-8222). Subway: A, C, B, D, 1, 9 to 59th St–Columbus Circle. Mon–Fri 9am–6pm; Sat, Sun 10am–3pm. Leaflets on all manner of things; plus free, helpful advice about accommodations and entertainment, coupons for discounts and free maps are available here. The phone number gives you access to either a multilingual human or a huge menu of recorded information. In addition to the main office, there are booths at JFK Airport International Arrivals Building, Grand Central Terminal, Penn Station and 2 World Trade Center.

Are you holding?

Don't be a dope about possession of controlled substances

"Psst. Psst. Sens, sens. Coke, coke…" Ah, the good old days, when a stroll down any East Village street virtually guaranteed an encounter with someone offering to make your day more pleasant. Drug trafficking and consumption in public spaces was a given and enforcement was lax. That was then. A resurgence of America's puritan streak, coupled with Mayor Giuliani's vaunted "quality of life" reforms, have turned off—or certainly dimmed—the party lights.

As a result, dealers have gone underground, or more accurately, over the air: Most now use pagers and cell phones to fill their orders to a network of regular clients. Pills and powders are still proffered in a good number of clubs, but the purity is unreliable and police busts common. Nickel bags and loose joints are sold in the downtown parks, but such transactions require keen street sense, especially in Washington Square Park, where cameras have been added. Official NYPD policy targets upper-level drug dealers; still, some 150 busts for simple possession occur every day, and New York State's drug laws are severe. Possession of even trace amounts of illegal substances can put a big damper on your visit.

Jail time for simple possession, as stated in the legal code, ranges from three months to one year for marijuana (not a "controlled substance," legally speaking) to up to 15 years for more than an ounce of hashish—not that you're likely to find any in this town, or this country, for that matter. Up to 1,000 micrograms of LSD can get you a year—and with the quality of acid on the street these days, you'll be lucky if 10 hits adds up to that much (there's no telling what other active ingredients are soaked in that blotter). Any more than that puts you in felony country, which is a very nasty place indeed. As for coke (which is apparently making a comeback), heroin and ecstasy—don't even think about it. Decadence just ain't what it used to be.

Getting around

Information on subways and buses is available by calling the **Metropolitan Transport Authority's helpline** at 1-718-330-1234 (1-718-330-4847 for non-English speakers). The phone line is staffed from 6am to 9pm daily and offers recorded information at other times. Alternatively, you can call the New York Convention & Visitors Bureau Information Center (397-8222) for instructions on the best way to get between any two places in the city.

To and from the airport

"If the Martians land, they'd better not use JFK or they'll be two hours late getting into the city." The same joke could be applied to Newark and La Guardia, metro New York's other two airports.

Though public transportation is the cheapest method, the routes are indirect and frustrating to use. Private bus services are usually the best budget option. **Gray Line** runs a minibus service from each of the three airports to any address in midtown (between 23rd and 63rd Streets) from 7am to midnight; the wait at the airport is never more than 20 minutes. On the outbound journey, Gray Line picks up at several hotels (you must book in advance). Call 757-6840 or 1-800-622-3427 for details. Or take a **Carey Bus**, operating between 6am and midnight, with stops at Grand Central Terminal, the Port Authority terminal (both on 42nd Street, *see page 314*) and a host of midtown hotels. Call 1-718-632-0500 for recorded details. For a full list of these and other transportation services between New York City and its three airports call **1-800-AIR-RIDE**, a touch-tone menu of recorded information provided by the Port Authority.

A **yellow cab** is the most effortless method to get from plane to hotel, though by no means the cheapest: The trip to Manhattan is now a flat-rate $30, plus tip and bridge tolls. It's actually cheaper to book a private car service or limousine to meet you (arrange it before you fly, or call from the airport). This will cost around $25 plus tolls and tip. **Tel Aviv** (777-7777) aims to pick you up from any airport three minutes after you call. For a little more you can order a "stretch" limo and arrive in truly glamorous style.

John F. Kennedy Airport

1-718-244-4444. There's a subway link from JFK (extremely cheap at $1.50), but this involves waiting for a shuttle bus to the Howard Beach station and then more than an hour's ride into Manhattan. Other options: **Gray Line** minibus $16; **Carey Bus** $13; **yellow cab** $30.

La Guardia Airport

1-718-476-5000. Seasoned New Yorkers take a 20-minute ride on the **M60 bus** ($1.50) which runs between the airport and 106th Street at Broadway. The route crosses Manhattan at 125th Street in Harlem (not a good place to be at night), where

you can get off at the Lexington Avenue subway station for the 4, 5 and 6 trains or at Lenox Avenue for the 2 and 3. You can also disembark on Broadway at the 116th Street–Columbia University subway station, where you can take the 1 and 9 trains. Other options: **Gray Line** $13; **Carey Bus** $10; **yellow cab** $25–$35.

Newark Airport

The **New Jersey Transit** bus company goes to the Port Authority bus terminal (Eighth Ave between 40th and 42nd Sts). The fare is $7 and buses leave every 10–15 minutes (information 1-973-762-5100). **Olympia Trails** (964-6233) leaves from Penn Station, Grand Central Terminal, Port Authority and World Trade Center; the fare is $10 and buses leave every 15–20 minutes. Various hotels also offer shuttles. **Yellow cab** $45.

Subways

Much maligned but actually clean, efficient, heated, air-conditioned and far safer than its reputation would suggest, the subway is easily the fastest way to get around during daylight hours. It runs all night, but with sparse service and fewer riders it's advisable (and usually quicker) to take a cab after 9 or 10pm. Entry to the system requires a MetroCard or a token costing $1.50. You can buy both from a booth inside the entrance to a station and can use both on buses as well. Staff are not required to accept bills bigger than $20.

Once through the turnstile you can travel anywhere on the network. If you're planning to use the subway a lot, it's worth buying a magnetic-strip MetroCard. These can be used by any number of passengers, start at $3 for two trips, and run as high as $80. A $15 card offers 11 trips for the price of 10. They can be bought in selected stores as well as subway stations. With a MetroCard, you can transfer free from subways to buses and from buses to subways.

Trains are known by letters and numbers and are color-coded according to which line they run on. "Express" trains run between major stops; "local" trains stop at every station. Check on the map (available free at the token booth in all stations) before you board; for a subway map of Manhattan, *see page 345*. Stations are usually named after the street they're on, so they're easy to find. Entrances are marked with a green globe (a red globe marks an entrance that is not always open). Some stations don't have connecting walkways, so there are separate entrances to the uptown and downtown platforms.

To ensure safety, don't wear flashy jewelry, hold your bag with the opening facing you and board the train from the off-peak waiting area marked at the center of every platform. This is monitored by cameras and is where a conductor's car will stop.

Buses

Buses are fine if you aren't in a hurry. If your feet hurt from walking around, a bus is a good way of continuing your street-level sightseeing. They're white and blue with a route number and a digital destination sign. The fare is $1.50, payable either with a token or MetroCard (the same ones that you buy for the subway) or in change (no bills are accepted). Express buses operate on some routes; these cost $3. If you're traveling on a bus going up- or downtown and want to continue your journey crosstown (or vice versa) ask the driver for a "transfer" when you get on—you'll be given a ticket for use on the second stage. (MetroCards allow ticketless, automatic transfers from bus to bus and from buses to subways.) You can rely on other passengers for advice, but bus maps are available from all subway stations. Almost all buses are now equipped with wheelchair lifts.

Taxis

Once you start using cabs in New York, you'll begin to wish there were these cheap everywhere in the world. Yellow cabs are hardly ever in short supply, except in the rain and at around 4 or 5pm, when rush hour gets going and when many cabbies—inexplicably—change shifts. If the center light on top of the cab is lit, it means the cab is available and will stop if you stick your arm out. Jump in first and then tell the driver where you're going. Cabs carry up to four people for the same price: $2 plus 30¢ per fifth of a mile, with an extra 50¢ charge after 8pm. This makes an average fare for a three-mile (4.5km) ride about $5 to $7, depending on the traffic and time of day. Unfortunately, some cabbies know the city as poorly as you do, so it helps if you know where you're going—and don't be afraid to speak up. Tip 10–15 percent or round the fare up to the nearest dollar plus one. The cab number and driver's number are posted on the dashboard if you have a problem. There's also a meter number on the receipt. If you want to complain or trace lost property, phone the **Taxi and Limousine Commission** at 302-8294 (Mon–Fri 9am–5pm). Late at night, cabbies stick to fast-flowing routes and reliably lucrative areas. Try the Avenues and the key east/west streets (Canal, Houston, 14th, 23rd, 42nd, 59th, 86th). Bridge and tunnel exits are also good for a steady flow from the airports, and passengerless cabbies will usually head for nightclubs and big hotels. Otherwise, try one of the following:

Chinatown: Chatham Square, where Mott Street meets the Bowery, is an unofficial taxi stand; or try the Bowery at Canal Street, where you can hail one exiting the Manhattan Bridge.
Financial District: Not the most nocturnal of neighborhoods; try the Marriott World Trade Center or 1 World Trade Center. There may be a line but there'll certainly be a cab.
Lincoln Center: The crowd heads toward Columbus Circle for a cab; those in the know go west to Amsterdam Avenue.

Lower East Side: Katz's Deli (Houston St at Ludlow St) is a cabbies' hangout; otherwise try Delancey Street, where cabs come in over the Williamsburg Bridge.
Midtown: Penn Station and Grand Central Terminal attract cabs through the night, as does the Port Authority (Eighth Ave between 40th and 42nd Sts) and Times Square.
Soho: If you're west, try Sixth Avenue; east, the gas station on Houston St at Broadway.
Tribeca: Cabs here (many arriving from the Holland Tunnel) head up Hudson Street. Canal Street is also a good bet.

Car service companies

The following companies will pick you up anywhere in the city, at any time of day or night: **All City Taxis** (1-718-402-2323); **Bell Radio Taxi** (691-9191); **Sabra** (777-7171); **Tel Aviv** (777-7777).

Driving

A car is often useless in Manhattan. Drivers are fearless, and taking it to the streets (not to mention finding a place to park) is not for the faint-hearted. Don't bother renting a car unless you are planning a trip out of town; if you do, restrict your driving to evening hours, when traffic is less heavy and on-street parking plentiful. Even then, keep your eyes on the road and be prepared for anything.

Car rental is much cheaper on the city's outskirts and in New Jersey and Connecticut. Reserve ahead for weekends, and note that street parking is very restricted, especially in the summer. Don't ever park within 15 feet (5m) of a fire hydrant, and make sure you read the parking signs. Unless there are meters, most streets have "alternate side parking"—i.e., each side is off limits for certain hours on alternate days. The **New York City Department of Transportation** (442-7080) provides information on daily changes to parking regulations.

If you're coming from the U.K., most New York authorities will let you drive on a U.K. license for a limited time, though an international one (available in the U.K. from the AA or RAC) is better. All car rental companies listed below add sales tax. They also offer a "loss damage waiver" (LDW). This is expensive—almost as much as the rental itself—but without it you are responsible for the cost of repairing even the slightest damage. If you pay with an AmEx card or a gold Visa or MasterCard, the LDW may be covered by the credit card company; it might also be covered by a reciprocal agreement with an automotive organization. Personal liability insurance is optional but recommended (but check whether your vacation or home insurance covers it already). You will need a credit card (or a *large* cash deposit) to rent a car and usually have to be over 25 years of age. If you know you want to rent a car before you travel, ask your travel agent or airline if they can offer any good deals.

Avis

1-800-331-1212. 24 hours. Rates from $50 a day, unlimited mileage; special weekend rates. AmEx, DC, Disc, MC, V.

Enterprise

1-800-325-8007. Mon–Fri 7am–7pm, Sat 8am–2pm, Sun 9am–9pm. Rates from $35 a day outside Manhattan; around $60 a day on the island; unlimited mileage restricted to New York, New Jersey and Connecticut. AmEx, DC, Disc, MC, V. We highly recommend this cheap and reliable service. The most accessible branches outside Manhattan are Hoboken (PATH train from 34th Street) and Greenwich (Metro-North from Grand Central). Agents will collect you from the station.

Trains

All long-distance **Amtrak** trains (1-800-872-7245) depart from Penn Station. Commuter rail services that operate within the immediate metropolitan area include **Metro-North** (532-4900, 1-800-638-7646); the **Long Island Rail Road** (1-718 217-5477); and **NJ Transit** (1-973-762-5100, 1-800-772-2222). *See chapter* **Trips Out of Town** *for more information.*

Grand Central Terminal

42nd–44th Sts between Vanderbilt and Lexington Aves. Subway: S, 4, 5, 6, 7 to 42nd St–Grand Central. Grand Central is home to Metro-North, which runs trains to more than 100 stations throughout New York State and Connecticut.

PATH Trains

PATH (Port Authority Trans Hudson) trains run from six stations in Manhattan to various places across the river in New Jersey (including Hoboken, Jersey City and Newark). The system is fully automated and costs $1 for each trip. You need change or a crisp dollar bill to put in the machines. Trains run 24 hours a day, but you can face a very long wait outside rush hours. Manhattan PATH stations are marked on the subway map. For more information call 1-800-234-PATH.

Penn Station

31st–33rd Sts between Seventh and Eighth Aves. Subway: A, C, E to 34th St–Penn Station. Long Island Rail Road, New Jersey Transit and Amtrak (long-distance) trains depart from this terminal.

Greyhound Trailways

1-800-231-2222. 24 hours. AmEx, Disc, MC, V. Call this company about long-distance bus travel.

Port Authority Bus Terminal

40th–42nd Sts between Eighth and Ninth Aves (564-8484). Subway: A, C, E to 42nd St. The number listed above gives information and times for almost all bus transportation out of New York. Be warned that the area around the terminal is notoriously seedy.

Resources

Auto services

Breakdowns/car towing

Towing prices are regulated by the city and everyone charges the same—that is, the maximum.

Citywide Towing

522 W 38th St between Tenth and Eleventh Aves (924-8104). 24 hours. No credit cards. All types of repairs are done on foreign and domestic autos. Free towing is offered if the firm gets the repair job.

Car wash

Carzapoppin'

610 Broadway at Houston St (673-5115). 24 hours. No credit cards. It's still only $5 to give the exterior of your car a shampoo. Interior cleaning costs extra.

24-hour gas stations

Downtown

Amoco *610 Broadway at Houston St (473-5924). AmEx, DC, Disc, JCB, MC, V. No repairs.*

Midtown

Gulf *FDR Drive at 23rd St (686-4784). AmEx, Disc, Gulf, MC, V. Some repairs.*
Hess *Tenth Ave at 45th St (245-6594). AmEx, Disc, MC, V. No Repairs.*

Uptown

Shell *Amsterdam Ave at 181st St (928-3100). AmEx, Disc, MC, V. Repairs.*

Communications

For information about postal services and telephones, *see* **Essential information** *page 308.*

Disabled

For more information *see* **Disabled access,** *page 310, and* **About the Guide.**

Mayor's Office for People with Disabilities

52 Chambers St at Broadway, room 206 (788-2830). Subway: A, C, 1, 2, 3 to Chambers St. Mon–Fri 9am–5pm. The office organizes services for disabled people and offers help and advice.

Lighthouse Incorporated

111 E 59th St between Park and Lexington Aves (821-9200, 1-800-334-5497). Subway: 4, 5, 6 to 59th St; N, R to Lexington Ave. Mon–Fri 9am–5pm. In addition to running a store selling handy items for sight-impaired people, this organization provides help and information for the blind dealing with life—or a holiday—in New York City.

New York Society for the Deaf

817 Broadway at 12th St (777-3900). Subway: L, N, R, 4, 5, 6, to 14th St–Union Sq. Mon–Thu 9am–5pm, Fri 9am–4pm. Advice and information on facilities for the deaf.

Emergencies

Ambulances

In an emergency, dial **911** for an ambulance or call the operator (dial 0). To complain about slow service or poor treatment, call the **Department of Health: Emergency Medical Service** (1-718-416-7000).

Fire

In an emergency, dial **911**.

Police

In an emergency, dial **911**. For the location of the nearest police precinct or for general information about police services, call **374-5000**.

Foreign consulates

Check the Yellow Pages for a complete list of consulates and embassies.

Australia *408-8400*
Canada *596-1700*
Great Britain *745-0200*
Ireland *319-2555*
New Zealand *832-4038*

General information

The Yellow Pages and White Pages have a wealth of useful information at the front, including theater-seating diagrams and maps. Hotels will have copies; otherwise, try libraries or Bell Atlantic (the phone company) payment centers.

Recorded information phone lines

These 24-hour information lines add extra costs to your phone bill. An opening message should tell you how much per minute you are paying.

Sports scores *1-900-976-1313*
Stock market quotations *1-900-976-4141*
Time *1-900-976-1616*
Weather forecast *1-900-976-1212*

Health advice

For advice on AIDS and HIV, *see chapter* **Gay & Lesbian New York**.

Alcoholics Anonymous

647-1680. 24 hours.

Cocaine Anonymous

262-2463. 24-hour recorded info.

Drug Abuse Information Line

1-800-522-5353. 24 hours. This state-run program refers callers to statewide recovery programs.

NYC Department of Health Bureau of Maternity Services & Family Planning

2 Lafayette St at Reade St, 18th floor (442-1740). Subway: N, R to City Hall. Mon–Fri 8am–5pm. Pick up leaflets and advice; call for an appointment. Contact the **Women's Health Line** (230-1111) on the 21st floor of the same building for contraceptive advice.

NYC Department of Health VD Information Hotline

427-5120. Mon–Fri 8am–4pm. Call for information or referral for treatment and counseling.

Pills Anonymous

874-0700. 24-hour answering service. Here, you'll find information on drug-recovery programs for users of marijuana, cocaine, alcohol and other addictive substances, as well as referrals to Narcotics Anonymous meetings.

Help lines and agencies

Consumer help

Better Business Bureau

533-6200. Mon–Fri 9am–5pm. The BBB offers advice on consumer-related complaints: shopping, services, etc. Each inquiry costs $4.30 including New York City tax.

New York City Department of Consumer Affairs

487-4444. Mon–Fri 9:30am–4:30pm. Report complaints on consumer-related affairs.

Con Ed Emergency Line

Gas emergency 683-8830, electrical or steam emergency 683-0862. 24 hours. Call these numbers if you smell gas or spot a steam leak, or if your electricity fails. Gas leaks are dealt with quickly. Other problems tend not to be.

Department of Health: Professional Medical Conduct Division

613-2650. Mon–Fri 9am–5pm Call if you want to complain about medical misconduct or excessive charges.

Crisis hotlines

Center for Inner Resource Development

734-5876. 24 hours. Trained therapists will talk to you day or night, and deal with all kinds of emotional problems, including the consequences of rape.

Childhelp's National Child Abuse Hotline

1-800-422-4453. 24 hours. Trained psychologists provide general crisis counseling and can help in an emergency. Callers include abused children, parents having problems with children and runaways.

Help Line

532-2400. 9am–10pm. Trained volunteers will talk to anyone contemplating suicide, and can also help with other personal problems.

St. Luke's/Roosevelt Hospital Rape Crisis Center

523-4728. Mon–Fri 9am–5pm, recorded referral message at other times. The Rape Crisis Center provides a trained volunteer who will accompany you through all aspects of reporting a rape and getting emergency treatment.

The Samaritans

673-3000. 24 hours. People thinking of committing suicide or suffering from depression, grief, sexual anxiety or alcoholism can call this organization for advice.

Sex Crimes Report Line of the New York Police Department (NYPD)

267-7273. 24 hours. Reports of sex crimes are handled by a female detective. She will inform the appropriate precinct, send an ambulance if requested and provide counseling and medical referrals. The detectives will make house calls. Other issues handled: violence against gays and lesbians, child victimization and referrals for the family and friends of victims.

Victim Services Agency

577-7777. 24 hours. VSA offers telephone and one-to-one counseling for any victim of domestic violence, personal crime or rape, as well as practical help with court processes, compensation and legal aid.

Legal assistance

Legal Services for New York City
431-7200. Mon–Fri 9am–5pm. This is a government-funded referral service that offers assistance to people with any kind of legal problem.

Legal Aid Society
577-3300. Mon–Fri 9am–5pm. Legal Aid gives free advice and referral on legal matters.

Sandback, Birnbaum & Michelen Criminal Law
517-3200, 1-800-766-5800. 24 hours. This is the number to have in your head when the cops read you your rights in the middle of the night.

Lost property

For property lost in the street, contact the police. For lost credit cards or traveler's checks, *see page 309.*

Buses and subways
New York City Transit Authority, Eighth Ave–34th St subway station, near the A train platform (1-718-625-6200). Mon–Wed, Fri 8am–noon; Thu 11am–6:45pm.

Grand Central Terminal
532-4900. Call for items left on Metro-North trains.

JFK
Contact the airline on which you traveled, or call 1-718-244-4444 for further information.

La Guardia
Contact your airline or call 1-718-476-5115.

Newark
Contact your airline or call 1-973-961-6000.

Penn Station
630-7389. For items left on Amtrak, New Jersey Transit and the Long Island Rail Road.

Taxis
221-8294. Call this number if you leave anything in a taxi. (It worked for Wallace and Gromit!)

Luggage lockers

Luggage lockers appear to be a thing of the past, for security reasons. However, there are baggage rooms at Penn Station, Grand Central Terminal and the Port Authority Bus Terminal.

Medical treatment

Clinics

Walk-in clinics offer treatment for minor ailments. Most require immediate payment, although some will send their bill directly to your insurance company. You will have to file a claim to recover the cost of prescription medicines.

Eastern Women's Center
44 E 30th St between Park and Madison Aves (686-6066). Subway: 6 to 33rd St. Tue–Sat 9am–5pm. AmEx, MC, V.

Pregnancy tests cost $20; counseling and gynecological tests are also available.

Doctors Walk-in
57 E 34th St between Madison and Park Aves (252-6000). Subway: 6 to 33rd St. Mon–Fri 8am–5:30pm; Sat 10am–1:30pm. Basic fee $75. AmEx, MC, V. If you need X rays or lab tests, go as early as possible—no later than 4pm Monday through Friday. No lab work is done on Saturday.

Dentists

Emergency Dental Associates
1-800-439-9299. 24 hours.

NYU College of Dentistry
998-9800. Mon–Thu 8:30am–8pm, Fri 9am–6pm. MC, V. If you need your teeth fixed on a budget, you can become a guinea pig for final-year students. They're slow but proficient, and an experienced dentist is always on hand to supervise. The basic fee is $65.

Doctors: house calls

BLT Answering Service
1-718-238-2100. Basic fee: private address from $75, hotel from $125. Cash only. Doctors will make house calls from 8am to midnight. Expect to wait about two hours.

Drugstores

See also chapter **Shopping & Services.**

Duane Reade
224 57th St at Broadway (541-9708) ●*2465 Broadway at 91st St (799-3172)* ●*1279 Third Ave at 74th St (744-2668)* ●*378 Sixth Ave at Waverly Pl (674-5357). 24 hours. AmEx, MC, V.* This chain operates all over the city, but not all stores maintain 24-hour service. Check phone book for other locations.

Love Drug
209 E 86th St between Second and Third Aves (427-0954) Subway: 4, 5, 6 to 86th St. Mon–Sat 8am–midnight, Sun 9am–midnight. ●*2330 Broadway between 84th and 85th Sts (362-6558). Subway: 1, 9 to 86th St. Mon–Fri 10am–6:45pm, Sat 10am–5:45pm.* ●*661 Broadway at Bleecker St (475-5683). Mon–Thu 7am–12:30am; Fri, Sat 8am–2am. No pharmacy.* This chain has pharmacies in its uptown locations but also runs health and beauty supply stores throughout the city. Check the phone book for other locations.

Emergency rooms

You will have to pay for emergency treatment. If you can, contact the emergency number on your travel insurance before seeking treatment to find out which hospitals accept your insurance. Emergency rooms are always open at:

Cabrini Medical Center
227 E 19th St between Second and Third Aves (995-6120). Subway: L, N, R, 4, 5, 6 to 14th St–Union Sq.

Mount Sinai Hospital
Madison Ave at 100th St (241-7171). Subway: 4, 5, 6 to 96th St.

Roosevelt Hospital
428 W 59th St at Ninth Ave (523-4000). Subway: A, C, B, D, 1, 9, to 59th St–Columbus Circle.

St. Luke's Hospital
1111 Amsterdam Ave at 113th St (523-3335). Subway: 1, 9 to 116th St.

St. Vincent's Hospital
153 W 11th St at Seventh Ave (604-7998). Subway: 1, 2, 3, 9 to 14th St; L to Sixth Ave.

Restrooms

See **Sweet relief** *in chapter* **Sightseeing.**

Security

The following emergency locksmiths are open 24 hours. Both require proof of residency or car ownership plus ID.

Champion Locksmiths
16 locations in Manhattan (362-7000). $15 service charge day or night plus minimum of $35 to fit a lock. AmEx, MC, V.

Elite Locksmiths
470 Third Ave between 32nd and 33rd Sts (685-1472). $35 during the day; $75–$90 at night. No credit cards.

Transportation

For information on travel to and from the three major airports and general transport information, *see* **Getting Around**, *page 312*. For a complete list of airlines, consult the Yellow Pages.

U.S. Airlines

The Satellite Companies Airlines Ticket Office
125 Park Ave at 42nd St. 8am–7pm. ● *1 E 59th St at Fifth Ave. 8:30am–6pm.* ● *166 W 32nd St between Sixth and Seventh Aves. 8am–7pm. Call 986-0888 for more information.* This is an umbrella service which issues tickets for Delta, Northwestern, Continental, Virgin Atlantic, American and Scandinavian airlines.

Alaska Airlines *1-800-426-0333*
America West *1-800-235-9292*
American *1-800-433-7300*
Continental *319-9494, 1-800-231-0856*
Delta *239-0700*
Kiwi International Airlines *1-800-538-5494*
Northwest *Domestic 1-800-225-2525, international 1-800-447-4747*
Tower Air *1-718-553-8500*
United *1-800-241-6522*
U.S. Air *1-800-428-4322*

Students

Immigration

Upon entering the U.S. as a student, you will need to show a passport, a special visa (see below) and proof of your plans to leave (a return airline ticket). Even if you have a student visa, you may be asked to show means of support during your stay (cash, credit cards, traveler's checks, etc.).

Visas

Before they can apply for a visa, non-nationals who want to study in New York (or anywhere else in the U.S.) must obtain an I-20 Certificate of Eligibility from the school or university they plan to attend. If you are enrolling in an authorized exchange-visitor program—including a summer course or program such as BUNAC (*see* **Work**, *below*), wait until you have been accepted by the course or program before worrying about immigration. You will be guided through the process by the school.

You are admitted as a student for the length of your course, plus a limited period of any associated (and approved) practical training, plus a 60-day grace period. After this you must leave the country or apply to change or extend your immigration status. Requests to extend a visa must be submitted 15 to 60 days before the initial departure date. The rules are strict, and you risk deportation if you break them.

Information on these and all other immigration matters is available from the **U.S. Immigration and Naturalization Service** (INS). Its New York office is in the Jacob Javits Federal Building, 26 Federal Plaza, New York, NY 10278. The "Ask Immigration" hotline (206-6500) is a vast menu of recorded information in English and Spanish. It is available 24 hours and is clear and helpful. Advisors are available at 1-800-375-5283 from 8am to 5:30pm Mon–Fri. If you already know which forms you need, you can order them by calling 870-3676. You can visit the INS between 7:30am and 3:30pm Mon–Fri.

The **U.S. Embassy Visa Information** line (in the U.S. 202-663-1225; in the U.K. 0891-200-290) provides more information on obtaining student visas. Alternatively, you can write to the Visa Branch of the Embassy of the United States of America, 5 Upper Grosvenor Street, London W1A 2JB.

Work

When you apply for your student visa, you will be expected to prove your ability to support yourself financially (including the payment of school fees), without working, for at least the first nine months of your course. After the first nine months, you may be eligible to work part-time, though you must have specific permission to do so.

If you are a British student who wants to spend a summer vacation working in the States, contact **BUNAC** at 16 Bowling Green Lane, London EC1R 0BD (0171-251-3472), which can help arrange a temporary job and the requisite visa.

Student identification

Foreign students should get themselves an **International Student Identity Card** (ISIC) as proof of student status and to secure discounts. These can be bought from your local student travel agent (ask at your students' union). If you buy the card in New York, you will also get basic accident insurance—a bargain. The New York branch of the **Council on International Educational Exchange** can supply one on the spot. It's at 205 East 42nd Street between Second and Third Avenues, (822-2700) and is open from 9am–6:45pm Mon–Fri. Note that a student identity card may not always be accepted as proof of age for drinking (you must be 21).

Accommodations

Medium- to long-term accommodation is expensive and hard to find in Manhattan. However, if you're studying as part of a U.S. college or university program, the institution will help you out. Large colleges have many residential properties and usually provide residence-hall accommodation for foreign students. If lodging is unavailable, or you'd prefer to share an apartment, many institutions also run an apartment or roommate-finder operation.

If you'd like to live with a U.S. family, the IIE (*see* **Go to the head of the class**, *below*) publishes the Homestay Information Sheet, listing places where you can live with an American host and thereby get authentic exposure to U.S. culture. Call or write to them for details.

Several of the hostels listed in chapter **Accommodations** offer special rates for long-term residents.

Travel

Most agents offer discount fares for those under 26; U.K. specialists in student deals include **Council Travel**, 28A Poland Street, London W1V 3DB (0171-287-3337) and 205 East 42nd Street, New York, NY 10017 (822-2700); and **STA Travel**, based in the U.K. but with more than 100 offices worldwide. In London, contact them at 86 Old Brompton Road, London SW7 3LQ (0171-937-9971); in the U.S., call 1-800-777-0122 for the nearest office.

Go to the head of the class

Here in the university of NYC, the whole metropolis is your campus

New York would miss them if they weren't here, but students don't figure very largely in the life of the city. There is little of the student-only entertainment culture familiar on European campuses. One reason is that American scholars tend to be too busy working to pay for their education to have much fun—in addition to their studies, most are compelled to hold down jobs to support themselves. But a better explanation is simply that there is such a vast range of accessible entertainment possibilities throughout the city that there is no need for students here to segregate themselves.

The *Time Out New York Student Guide* is a good source of information, covering details of where to get work, where to entertain the folks, and what to do if you get arrested, locked out or robbed, as well as where to shop, eat, drink and generally paint the town red. Published annually in the autumn, it's available free from colleges and some stores.

There are few more exciting places to study than New York, and its colleges and universities attract people from all over the world. Most vocational courses here have strong links with the city's businesses and are thus able to help find work for their graduates. Interning (working for free) at a major company is an essential part of many students' time in the city.

The admissions offices of most U.S. educational institutions accept applications directly from international students and can also supply details about visas, fees, student housing (on or off campus) and other information. The Institute of International Education (IIE) has an information center and publishes a directory of U.S. educational institutions and course catalogs, as well as information on financial aid. It's at 809 United Nations Plaza, New York, NY 10017 (883-8200). You can also check the bookstores for one of the many college guides that are updated every year. U.K. students can contact the Educational Advisory service of the Fulbright Commission, 62 Doughty Street, WC1N 2LS (0171-404-6994) or the U.S. International Commission Agency at any U.S. embassy for information on study in the U.S. The Council on International Educational Exchange (CIEE), 52 Poland Street, London W1V 4JQ (0171-478-2000), can arrange admissions to and help obtain visas for summer courses at a clutch of colleges and can navigate the bureaucracy for summer-course students looking for internships.

Medical and dental care

If you're enrolled in a course of study with a U.S. college or university, you are usually eligible for treatment at the campus clinic. It may still be advisable to obtain medical insurance; ask your college advisor for guidance. If you need dental treatment, the NYU Dental Center, 345 East 24th Street at First Avenue (998-9800), gives 25-percent student discounts on top of its already low fees (about half commercial rates). Your treatment will be provided by about-to-graduate students, under supervision. For more health-care information, *see* **Medical treatment**, *page 316.*

Business

Information

The business world's bible, *The Wall Street Journal* (75¢), contains all the up-to-date facts and figures on U.S. and worldwide commerce. In-depth business profiles are published in *Fortune* ($4.50) and *Forbes* ($5) magazines; *Inc.* ($3) is a glossy, monthly mag that makes business seem like fun. You'll find many more business mags at newsstands.

Dow Jones Report
24-hour recorded information 976-4141.

New York Partnership & Chamber of Commerce
Battery Park Plaza between State and Whitehall Sts (493-7500). Subway: 1, 9 to South Ferry; 4, 5 to Bowling Green. Mon–Fri 8:30am–5:30pm. The Chamber gives advice on local needs and provides market information. The NYC Partnership organizes training programs.

NYC Department of Business Services
110 William St near Fulton St (696-2442). Subway: J, M, 2, 3, 4, 5 to Fulton St. Mon–Fri 9am–5pm. Get free advice on starting and running a business, plus information about grants or loans the city may be able to offer.

Stock exchanges

See chapters **Sightseeing** *and* **New York by Neighborhood: Downtown** *for information.*

Libraries

See also chapter **Museums.**

Brooklyn Public Library (Business Branch)
280 Cadman Plaza West at Tillary St (1-718-722-3333). Subway: 2, 3, 4, 5 to Borough Hall. Mon 10am–8pm; Tue 1–8pm; Wed, Fri 10am–6pm; Thu 1–6pm; Sat 10am–5pm. Free. This library, which is separate from the New York Public Library (see below), is a great resource for all sorts of U.S. business information.

New York Public Library Science, Industry & Business Library
188 Madison Ave at 34th St (592-7000). Subway: 6 to 33rd St. Mon, Fri, Sat 10am–6pm; Tue–Thu 11am–7pm. Free. The NYPL's state-of-the-art business library opened in May 1996 at a cost of $100 million, and contains a vast range of business and industry resources. Many of these are accessible online either at terminals within the building or by dialing in.

Importing and exporting

U.S. Customs Service (New York Region)
6 World Trade Center, Vesey St between West and Church Sts (customs information 466-4547/recorded information 1-800-697-3662). Subway: N, R, 1, 9 to Cortlandt St. Mon–Fri 8am–4:30pm. The staff deals with inquiries on import duty, licenses and restricted goods. There's also a useful magazine, *Importing into the US* ($6.50).

U.S. Department of Commerce
6 World Trade Center, Vesey St between West and Church Sts, suite 635 (466-5222). Subway: N, R, 1, 9 to Cortlandt St. Mon–Fri 9am–5pm. The department regulates and encourages exports from the U.S.

Governor's Office of Regulatory Reform
Alfred E. Smith Building, P.O. Box 7027, 17th floor, Albany, NY 12225 (1-518-486-3292, 1-800-342-3464). Mon–Fri 9am–5pm. Here, you'll find free information on which, if any, New York State permits are necessary for starting up a particular business. Topics include incorporation, employment, taxes and business standards.

Services

Air couriers

DHL Worldwide Express
2 World Trade Center, Liberty St between West and Church Sts (1-800-225-5345). Subway: E to World Trade Ctr. 8:30am–8:30pm. AmEx, DC, Disc, MC, V. DHL will send a courier to pick up at any address in New York City, or you can deliver packages to its offices and drop-off points in person. No cash transactions are allowed. Along with its international services, DHL also operates a messenger service within New York.

Federal Express
Various locations throughout the city; call and give your zip code to find out the nearest office or get free pickup at your door (1-800-247-4747). 24 hours. AmEx, DC, Disc, MC, V. Federal Express rates (like those of its competitor United Parcel Service) are based on the distance shipped rather than a flat fee. An overnight letter to London costs about $25.50. You save $3 per package on the cost if you bring it to a Federal Express office. Packages headed overseas should be dropped off by 3pm, packages for most destinations in the U.S. by 8pm (some locations have a later time; call to check).

Cellular phones/pagers

InTouch USA
(391-8323, 1-800-872-7626). Mon–Fri 9am–5pm. AmEx, Disc, MC, V. The city's largest cellular phone rental company, InTouch rents out equipment by the day, week or

month. It also offers (and can deliver) satellite pagers (with nationwide coverage), portable faxes and walkie-talkies.

Computers

There are hundreds of computer dealers in Manhattan. If you are considering a purchase, you might want to buy out of state to avoid the hefty sales tax. Many out-of-state dealers advertise in New York papers and magazines.

Kinko's

24 E 12th St between University Pl and Fifth Ave (924-0802). Subway: L, N, R, 4, 5, 6 to 14th St–Union Sq. 24 hours daily. AmEx, Disc, MC, V. This is a very efficient and friendly place to use computers and copiers. Most branches have several workstations and design stations, including IBM and Macintosh, plus all the major programs. Color output is available. Check the phone book for other locations.

User-Friendly

139 W 72nd St between Columbus and Amsterdam Aves (580-4433). Subway: 1, 2, 3, 9 to 72nd Street. Mon–Thu 9am–10pm; Fri 9am–6pm; Sat 11am–7pm; Sun noon–8pm. ●*1065 Sixth Ave at 40th St (call 575-3536 for hours).* AmEx, MC, V. Rent Macs and PCs loaded with all the big programs at User-Friendly's two locations.

USPC

360 W 31st St between Eighth and Ninth Aves (594-2222). Subway: A, C, E to 34th St–Penn Station. 9am–5pm Mon–Fri. AmEx, MC, V. Rent by the day, week, month or year from a range of computers, systems and networks from IBM, Compaq, Macintosh and Hewlett-Packard. Delivery within one hour is possible.

Desktop publishing

Fitch Graphics

130 Cedar St at Liberty St (619-3800). Subway: N, R, 1, 9 to Cortlandt St. Mon–Fri 8am–11pm (until 5pm only). ●*5 W 45th St (call 840-3091 for hours).* AmEx, MC, V. A full-service desktop publishing firm, with color laser output and all pre-press facilities. Fitch works with both Apple Mac and IBM platforms and has a bulletin board so customers can reach them online.

Mailbox rental

Mail Boxes Etc. USA

1173A Second Ave between 61st and 62nd Sts (832-1390). Subway: N, R to Lexington Ave; 4, 5, 6 to 59th St. Mon–Fri 9am–7pm; Sat 10am–5pm. AmEx, MC, V. Mailbox rental, mail forwarding, overnight delivery, packaging and shipping are available. There's also a phone-message service, photocopying and faxing, telexing, typing and business printing. There are more than 30 branches in Manhattan, many offering 24-hour access to mailboxes; check phone book for locations.

Messenger services

A to Z Couriers

65 W 36th St at Sixth Ave (633-2410). Cheerful couriers deliver to all neighborhoods, including the Bronx, Brooklyn, Queens and Long Island.

Breakaway

43 Walker St at Church St (219-8500). Subway: A, C, E to Canal St. Mon–Fri 7am–9pm; by arrangement Sat, Sun. AmEx, Disc, MC, V. Breakaway is a highly recommended citywide messenger service with 25 messengers who promise to pick up within 15 minutes of a request and deliver within the hour.

Jefron Messenger Service

141 Duane St between West Broadway and Church St (964-8441). Subway: 1, 2, 3, 9 to Chambers St. Mon–Fri 7am–6pm. No credit cards. Jefron specializes in transporting import/export documents.

Office rental

Bauer Business Communications Center

New York Hilton, 1335 Sixth Ave at 54th St (262-1329). Subway: B, D, F, Q to 47th–50th Sts–Rockefeller Ctr. Mon–Fri 7am–5pm. AmEx, Disc, MC, V. Rent fully equipped desk space here, with full support services. Workstations have a PC or Mac, printer and a selection of useful software. Office services include word processing, faxing, photocopying, transcription, office equipment rental and a reference library.

World-Wide Business Centers

575 Madison Ave between 56th and 57th Sts (605-0200). Subway: N, R to Lexington Ave; 4, 5, 6 to 59th St. Mon–Fri 9am–5:30pm. AmEx, MC, V. The company provides furnished, staffed offices, from half a day to long term, equipped with fax, computers and phones. Fax and secretarial services are available without rental of office space.

Photocopying

Servco

130 Cedar St at Liberty St (285-9245). Subway: N, R, 1, 9 to Cortlandt St. 8:30am–5:30pm. ●*56 W 45th St (call 575-0991 for hours). No credit cards.* Photocopying, offset printing, blueprints and binding services.

Kinko's Copy Center

24 E 12th St between Fifth Ave and University Pl (924-0802). Subway: L, N, R, 4, 5, 6 to 14th St–Union Sq. 24 hours. AmEx, Disc, MC, V. Copying, faxing and passport photos, plus on-site use of Apple Macs ($12 per hour, $24 for big graphics machines, charged by the minute). Check the phone book for your nearest branch.

Printing

Dependable Printing

Flatiron Building, 175 Fifth Ave at 32rd St (533-7560). Subway: N, R to 23rd St. Mon–Fri 8:30am–6pm, Sat 10am–4pm. ●*257 Park Ave South between 20th and 21st Sts (call 982-0353 for hours).* MC, V. Dependable provides offset and color printing, large-size Xerox copies, color laser printing, binding, rubber stamps, typing, forms, labels, brochures, flyers, newsletters, manuscripts, fax service, transparencies and more.

Directional Printing Services

280 Madison Ave between 39th and 40th Sts (213-6700). Subway: S, 4, 5, 6, 7 to 42nd St–Grand Central. Mon–Fri 9:30am–5:30pm. No credit cards. This company specializes in assisting international firms and offers foreign-language typesetting and printing, as well as graphic design, brochures and reports, and more.

Telegrams

Western Union

1-800-325-6000. 24 hours. Disc, MC, V. Arrange telegrams at any time of day or night; the service is charged to your credit card. If you want to write the message in person, or don't have a card, go to one of the branches (call to find the nearest). Western Union can also organize international money transfers.

Telephone-answering service

Messages Plus
1317 Third Ave between 75th and 76th Sts (879-4144). Subway: 6 to 77th St. 24 hours. AmEx, MC, V. Messages Plus provides telephone-answering services, with specialized (medical, bilingual, etc.) receptionists if required, and plenty of ways of delivering your messages. It also offers pay or toll-free incoming call services, which can include options such as call forwarding, periodic generation of database reports tracking the user's telephone activity and pager rental. Faxes and telexes can be sent and delivered.

Translation

All Language Services
545 Fifth Ave at 45th St (986-1688; fax 986-3396). Subway: S, 4, 5, 6, 7 to 42nd St–Grand Central. 24 hours. MC, V. Will type or translate documents in any of 59 languages and provide interpreters.

Writers

Dial-A-Writer
1501 Broadway between 43rd and 44th Sts, suite 302 (24-hour answering service 398-1934). No credit cards. A referral service for professional writers, researchers, editors and publicists.

Trade conventions

For further information, get in touch with the **New York Convention & Visitors Bureau** (397-8222). New York's two principal convention centers are:

Jacob K. Javits Convention Center
Eleventh Ave between 34th and 39th Sts, main entrance at 36th St and Eleventh Ave (216-2000). Subway: A, C, E, 1, 2, 3, 9 to 34th St–Penn Station, then take the M34 crosstown bus to the Center.

New York Passenger Ship Terminal
711 Twelfth Ave at 55th St (246-5451). Subway: C, E to 50th St.

Size conversion chart for clothes

Women's clothes									
British	8	10	12	14	16	•	•	•	•
American	6	8	10	12	14	•	•	•	•
French	36	38	40	42	44	•	•	•	•
Italian	38	40	42	44	46	•	•	•	•
Women's shoes									
British	3	4	5	6	7	8	9	•	•
American	5	6	7	8	9	10	11	•	•
Continental	36	37	38	39	40	41	42	•	•
Men's suits/overcoats									
British	38	40	42	44	46	•	•	•	•
American	38	40	42	44	46	•	•	•	•
Continental	48	50/52	54	56	58/60	•	•	•	•
Men's shirts									
British	14	14.5	15	15.5	16	16.5	17	•	•
American	14	14.5	15	15.5	16	16.5	17	•	•
Continental	35	36/37	38	39/40	41	42/43	44	•	•
Men's shoes									
British	8	9	10	11	12	•	•	•	•
American	9	10	11	12	13	•	•	•	•
Continental	42	43	44	45	46	•	•	•	•
Children's shoes									
British	7	8	9	10	11	12	13	1	2
American	7.5	8.5	9.5	10.5	11.5	12.5	13.5	1.5	2.5
Continental	24	25.5	27	28	29	30	32	33	34

Children's clothes
In all countries, size descriptions vary by manufacturer but are usually based on age or height.

Further Reading

History

Allen, Irving Lewis: *The City in Slang*. How New York living has spawned hundreds of new words and phrases.
Federal Writers' Project: *The WPA Guide to New York City*. A wonderful snapshot of 1930s New York, by the writers employed under FDR's New Deal.
Fitch, Robert: *The Assassination of New York*. Essay on the economic death of New York in the 1980s.
Hood, Clifton: *722 Miles*. History of the subway.
Koolhaas, Rem: *Delirious New York*. New York as a terminal city. Urbanism and the culture of congestion.
Lewis, David Levering: *When Harlem Was in Vogue*. A study of the 1920s Harlem renaissance.
O'Connell, Shaun: *Remarkable, Unspeakable New York*. History of New York as literary inspiration.
Riis, Jacob: *How the Other Half Lives*. Pioneering photojournalistic record of gruesome tenement life.
Rosenzweig, Roy, & Blackmar, Elizabeth: *The Park and the People*. A lengthy history of Central Park.
Sante, Luc: *Low Life*. Opium dens, brothels, tenements and suicide salons in 1840-1920s New York.
Schwartzman, Paul, & Polner, Rob: *New York Notorious*. New York's most infamous crime scenes.
Stern, Robert A.M.: *New York 1930*. A massive coffee-table slab with stunning pictures.
Stern, Robert A.M.: *New York 1960*. Another.
Stilm, Bayrd: *Mirror for Gotham*. New York as seen by its inhabitants, from Dutch days to the present.
Wallace, Mike: *Gotham: A History of New York City to 1898*. The first volume of a mammoth history of NYC.

Culture and recollections

Chauncey, George: *Gay New York*. New York gay life from the 1890s on.
Cole, William (ed): *Quotable New York*. Hundreds of hilarious quotes about the city.
Cooper, Martha, & Chalfant, Henry: *Subway Art*.
Donaldson, Greg: *The Ville: Cops and Kids in Urban America*. Gripping sociology of Brownsville, Brooklyn.
Friedman, Josh Alan: *Tales From Times Square*. Sleaze, scum, filth and depredation in Times Square.
Kinkead, Gwen: *Chinatown: A Portrait of a Closed Society*.
Liebling, A.J.: *Back Where I Came From*. Personal recollections from the famous *New Yorker* columnist.
Toop, David: *Rap Attack 2; African Rap to Global Hip Hop*. The best cultural history of hip-hop.
Torres, Andrés: *Between Melting Pot and Mosaic*. African Americans' and Puerto Ricans' role in the city's life from 1945 to 1995.
Trebay, Guy: *In the Place To Be*. Wonderfully observed essays by a leading *Village Voice* writer.
Wyatt Sexton, Andrea (ed): *The Brooklyn Reader*. Thirty writers celebrate America's favorite borough.

Architecture

Gayle, Margot: *Cast Iron Architecture in New York*.
Goldberger, Paul: *The City Observed*. A noted architecture critic leads you round the city.
Klotz, Heinrich: *New York Architecture 1970-90*. A vast and beautiful full-color volume.

Sabbagh, Karl: *Skyscraper*. How a skyscraper is built.
Willensky, Elliot, & White, Norval : *American Institute of Architects Guide to New York City*. A comprehensive directory of important buildings.
Wolfe, Gerard R.: *A Guide to the Metropolis*. Historical and architectural walking tours.

In-depth guides

Bell, Trudy: *Bicycling Around New York City*.
Berman, Eleanor: *Away for the Weekend: New York*. Trips within a 250-mile radius of New York.
Brown, Arthur S., & Holmes, Barbara: *Vegetarian Dining in New York City*. Includes vegan places.
Freudenheim, Ellen: *Brooklyn: Where to Go, What to Do, How to Get There*. The subtitle says it all.
Leon, Ruth: *Applause: New York's Guide to the Performing Arts*. Astonishingly detailed directory of performance venues.
Marden, William: *Marden's Guide to New York Booksellers*. Some 500 dealers and stores.
Michel, John & Barbara: *Antiquing New York*. More than 1,000 antique dealers, markets and fairs listed.
Miller, Bryan: *New York Times Guide to Restaurants in New York City*. By the famous food critic.
Pollan, Corky: *Shopping Manhattan: the Discriminating Buyer's Guide to Finding Almost Anything*. If you can't find what you're looking for here, then it probably doesn't exist.
Rovere, Vicki: *Worn Again, Hallelujah!* Guide to NYC's thrift stores and treasure troves.
Sandvick, Victoria, & Bergman, Michael Ian: *Single in New York*.
Steinbicker, Earl: *Daytrips From New York*.
Zagat: *New York City Restaurants*. The leading, and bewildering, comprehensive guide.

Fiction

Auster, Paul: *The New York Trilogy*. Walking the Manhattan grid in search of the madness behind its method.
Baldwin, James: *Another Country*. Racism under the bohemian veneer of the 1960s.
Barnhardt, Wilton: *Emma Who Saved My Life*. Big ambitions set against colorful 1970s NYC.
Carr, Caleb *The Alienist*. Hunting a serial killer in New York's turn-of-the-century demimonde.
Ellison, Ralph: *Invisible Man*. Coming of age as a black man in 1950s New York.
Friedman, Kinky: *Kinky Friedman Crime Club*. Cigar-chomping cowboy 'tec wisecracks through '90s NYC.
Janowitz, Tama: *Slaves of New York*. Satirical stories of 1980s NYC bohemia.
Kramer, Larry: *Faggots*. Hilarious gay New York.
Miller, Henry: *Crazy Cock*. Most of Miller's novels are set in Brooklyn; this is 1920s Greenwich Village.
Price, Richard: *Clockers*. Cops, kids and crack in urban Jersey City, but just as easily the South Bronx.
Selby, Hubert Jr: *Last Exit to Brooklyn*. Depicts 1960s Brooklyn dockland degradation.
Smith, Betty: *A Tree Grows in Brooklyn*. An Irish girl in 1930s Brooklyn.
Wharton, Edith: *Old New York*. Four novellas of 19th-century New York, by the author of *The Age of Innocence*.
Wolfe, Tom: *Bonfire of the Vanities*. Rich/poor, black/white. An unmatched slice of 1980s New York.

Index

New York is Book Country
Festival 212
Puerto Rican Day parade 28
puppets 221–222

q

Queens **105, 108**
Queensboro Bridge 105
Queens College 269
Queens Council on the Arts 108
Queens County Farm Museum 108
Queens Museum of Art **66**, 108

r

race tracks *see* gambling
racquetball 281
radio **255–256**
    museum **71**, 241
Radio City Music Hall 33, 57, 90, 233,
    261
Rainbow & Stars *215,* **216**
Rainbow Room *37,* 89, **136**
Raoul's 138
rape crisis center 315
Ratner's 80, 155
    Lansky Lounge 162
readings **212–214**
    screenplays 238
recording industry 88
repairs 197
Restaurant Row *86,* 88
Restaurant Week 135
restaurants 88, 106–107, **133–157**
    American 136–138, 140–144
    bars in 162
    brunch 139
    budget 139–140
    Chinese 80, 144–145
    fast food 76, 157
    French 145–146
    gay 248, 250
    Indian 82, 147–149
    international **144–156**
    Italian 81, 135, 149–154
    Japanese 154
    kosher 155
    Mexican 155
    seafood 76, 109, 136, 142–143
    vegetarian 156–157
rest rooms **45**
Richmond Town, Historic 32, **43**, 110
Riis, Jacob 12
River Café, The 138
Riverside Church 102, 273
Rockefeller, John D. 13, 57
Rockefeller Center **41**, 57, 89–90
    Christmas tree lighting 33
    GE Building *84,* 89
    Ice Rink 282
    see also Rainbow Room
Rockefeller University 94
Rollerblading *see* skating
Roosevelt, Franklin D. 16
Roosevelt, Theodore 13–14
    birthplace 85, **86**
Roosevelt Island **94–95**
Rosa Mexicano 155
Round Table *see* Algonquin Hotel
Royalton hotel 119
running 33, 282
Russian Orthodox Cathedral of St.
    Nicholas 92

s

safety 83, 227, 249, **250, 310**
Sag Harbor 293
St. Mark's Church in-the-Bowery **83**
    Poetry Project 214
    Danspace Project 235
St. Marks Place 82
St. Patrick's Cathedral *35,* 90
St. Patrick's Day Parade 28
St. Paul's Chapel 53, 273
Saks Fifth Avenue 90, 170
sales, discount 169
Salmagundi Club **81**
Sammy's Roumanian 80, 155
sample sales 169
S&B Report 169
Saratoga 305–306
Saturday Night Live 255
Schomburg Center for Research in
    Black Culture **72**, 98, **101**, *101*
science
    hands-on lab 91, 221
    library 72
    museums 71–72, 221
Scorsese, Martin 238
sculpture, public 74, 82, 91, 110
    Isamu Noguchi Garden **66**,
        68, 108
    Sculpture Center 95
    Socrates Sculpture Park 108, 221
Sea, Air and Space Museum *65,*
    71, 89
    Fleet Week 28
Seagram Building 57, 91
Second Avenue Deli 140
Seinfeld 142, 157, 252
    Kramer's Reality Tour 50
Seton, Elizabeth Ann, Shrine of 74
Seventh Regiment Armory 92, 94
    events in 33
Seventh Street 169
sex 87–88, 285
    clubs 247–248
Shakespeare Festival, New York 30,
    82, **285–287**
Shea Stadium **43**, 108, 275
Sheep Meadow *48,* 48
Shelter Island 293
shoes 197–198
    repairs 197
shopping **167–200**
    antiques 33, 179, 191
    department stores 169–170
    districts 76, 77, 79, 81, 83, 90, 92,
        95–96, 98, 106–107, 167–169,
        172–173
    fashion *see* clothing stores
    food and drink 81, 105, 109,
        187–188
    records/CDs/tapes 107, 195–197
    shoes 197–198
    specialty 188–190, 191–194,
        198–199
Silicon Alley 23
69th Regiment Armory 85
skating
    ice 49, 282
    in-line 49, 224, 281
skiing 295, 298–299
    snow conditions info line 299
slang 26
smoking
    laws *vi,* 310

shops 199
Sniffen Court 91
Snug Harbor Cultural Center 110
soccer 279
Society of Illustrators 92, 94
Soho **79**, 167
    art galleries 207–208
    SoHo Grand Hotel 119
Sony Building 58, 91
    Sony Wonder Technology Lab
        91, **221**
South-Asian Americans 21, 82
South Street Seaport 30, **38**, 76
    museum **70**
spas **192–193**
Spin City 252, 255
spoken word performances 212,
    213–214
sporting goods 199
sports **274–282**
    bars 277
    collectibles 198
    radio 256
    scores info 315
    see also individual sports
squash 282
stand-up *see* comedy
Staten Island 32, 43, **110**
    Ferry **47**, 74, 110
Statue of Liberty 11, **37–38**, *38,*
    70, 74
steak houses 143–144
steam, sidewalk 22
Stock Exchange 74, **76**, *77*
stock market boom 23
Strand Book Store *170,* 171
Strawberry Fields 48
street fairs *see* festivals
street plan 25
students **318**
Studio Museum in Harlem **66**, 98
Stuyvesant, Peter 7
subways **312**
    history 13, 14–15
    architecture 96
swimming 282
Sylvia's 98, **142**
Symphony Space 96, 236
synagogues 79

t

Tammany Hall 14, 78
tapas 156
tattooing 199–200
Tavern on the Green 136
taxes
    hotel 113
    sales 169, 311
taxis 313
Taylor, Paul **234**
    school 236
TDF *see* Theater Development Fund
Tea & Sympathy *158,* 159
Telecharge 285
telegrams 310, 320
telephones *vi,* 310–311
    answering service 321
television **253–255**
    gay 243
    museum 71
    networks 254
    New York as seen on 252
    programming 253–254

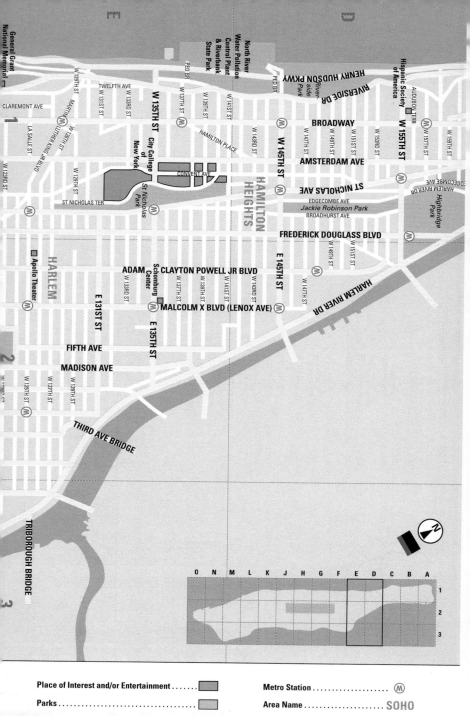

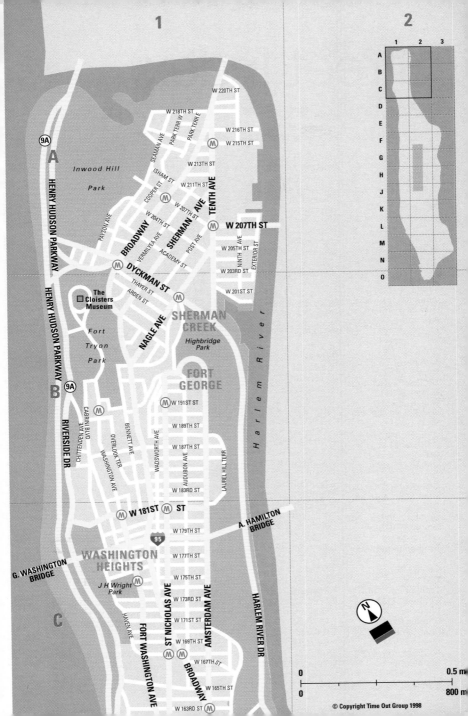

Street Index

65th St Transverse Rd - H2
79th St Transverse Rd - H2
86th St Transverse Rd - G2
97th St Transverse Rd - G2

Academy St - A1
Adam Clayton Powell Jr Blvd - D2, F2
Albany St - N2
Allen St - M3
Amsterdam Ave - C1-G1
Ann St - N2
Arden St - B1
Audubon Ave - B1
Audubon Terr - D1
Ave of the Americas - L2

Bank St - L1
Barclay St - N2
Barrow St - L1
Battery Pl - N2
Baxter St - M2
Beach St - M2
Bedford St - L2
Beekman St - N2
Bennett Ave - B1
Bethune St - L1
Bleecker St - L2
Bridge St - N2
Broad St - N2
Broadhurst Ave - D1
Broadway - A1-H1
Broadway - K2-M2
Brooklyn Bridge - N3
Brooklyn-Battery Tunnel - O2
Broome St - M2, 3

Cabrini Blvd - B1
Canal St - M2
Catherine St - M3
Centre St - M2
Chambers St - M2
Charles St - L1
Charlton St - M2
Cherry St - M3
Chittenden Ave - B1
Christopher St - L1

Chrystie St - M3
Church St - M2
Claremont Ave - E1, F1
Clarkson St - M2
Clinton St - M3
Columbus Ave - F1
Convent Ave - E1
Cooper St - A1
Crosby St - M2

Delancey St - M3
Desbrosses St - M2
Dominick St - M2
Duane St - M2
Dyckman St - A1, B1

E 2nd St - L2, 3
E 4th St - L2, 3
E 6th St - L2, 3
E 8th St - L2, 3
E 8th St - L3
E 10th St - L2, 3
E 12th St - L2, 3
E 14th St - L2, 3
E 16th St - L2
E 18th St - L2
E 20th St - L2
E 22nd St - K2
E 23rd St - K2, 3
E 26th St - K2
E 28th St - K2
E 30th St - K2, 3
E 32nd St - K2
E 34th St - K2, 3
E 36th St - K2, 3
E 38th St - K2, 3
E 40th St - K2
E 42nd St - J2, 3
E 44th St - J2, 3
E 46th St - J2, 3
E 48th St - J2, 3
E 50th St - J2, 3
E 52nd St - J2, 3
E 54th St - J2, 3
E 56th St - J2, 3
E 58th St - J2, 3
E 60th St - J2, 3
E 62nd St - J2, 3
E 64th St - H2, 3
E 66th St - H2, 3
E 68th St - H2, 3
E 70th St - H2, 3

E 72nd St - H2, 3
E 74th St - H2, 3
E 76th St - H2, 3
E 78th St - H2, 3
E 79th St - H2, 3
E 80th St - H2, 3
E 82nd St - H2, 3
E 84th St - G2, 3
E 86th St - G2, 3
E 88th St - G2, 3
E 90th St - G2, 3
E 92nd St - G2, 3
E 94th St - G2
E 96th St - G2
E 98th St - G2
E 100th St - G2, 3
E 102nd St - G2, 3
E 103rd St - F2
E 105th St - F2
E 107th St - F2
E 109th St - F2
E 111th St - F2
E 113th St - F2
E 115th St - F2, 3
E 117th St - F2, 3
E 119th St - F2, 3
E 121st St - F2
E 131st St - E2
E 135th St - E2
E 145th St - D2
East Broadway - M3
East Drive - G2, H2
East End Ave - G3
East Houston St - L3
Edgecombe Ave - D1
Eighth Ave - J1, K1
Eldridge St - M3
Eleventh Ave - J1, K1
Elizabeth St - M2
Entrance St - M2
Essex St - M3
Exchange Pl - N2
Exterior St - A1

Fifth Ave - E2-L2
First Ave - F3-K3
First Pl - N2
Forsyth St - M3
Fort Washington Ave - C1
Frankfort St - N2
Franklin D Roosevelt Dr - G3, K3, L3, N2, 3

Franklin St - M2
Frederick Douglas Blvd - D1, E1
Freedom Pl - H1
Front St - N2
Fulton St - N2

Gold St - N2
Grand St - M2, 3
Greene St - M2
Greenwich Ave - L2
Greenwich St - L1, M2, N2

Hamilton Place - E1
Harlem River Dr - C1, D1, 2
Haven Ave - C1
Henry Hudson Pkwy - D1-H1
Henry St - M3
Hester St - M2
Horatio St - L1
Howard St - M2
Hubert St - M2
Hudson St - L1, 2, M2

Isham St - A1

Jackson St - M3
Jane St - L1
John St - N2

Kenmare St - M2
King St - M2

Lafayette St - L2, M2
Laight St - M2
La Salle St - E1
Laurel Hill Ter - B1
Lenox Ave - D2, F2
Leonard St - M2
Lexington Ave - F2-K2
Liberty St - N2
Lincoln Tunnel - K1
Lispenard St - M2
Little W 12th St - L1
Ludlow St - M3

Madison Ave - E2-J2
Madison St - M3
Maiden Lane - N2

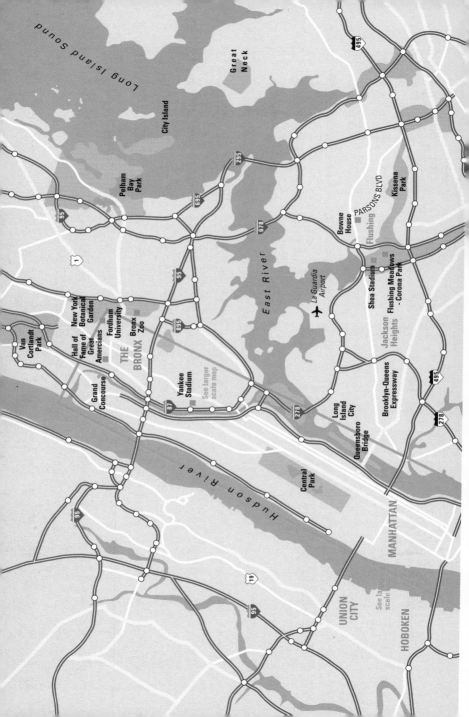

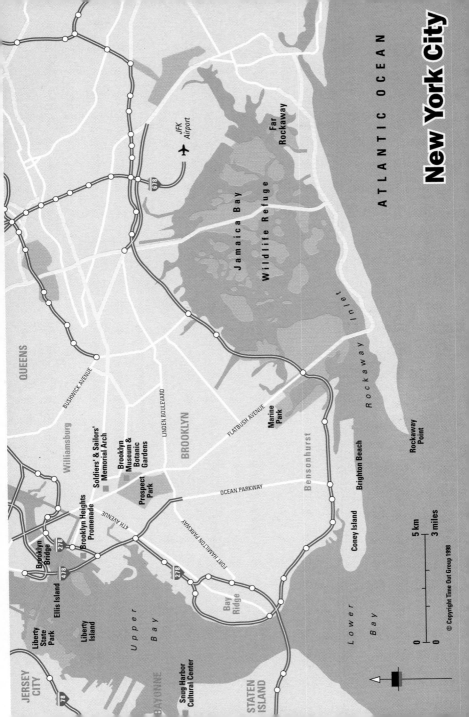

Trips Out of Town

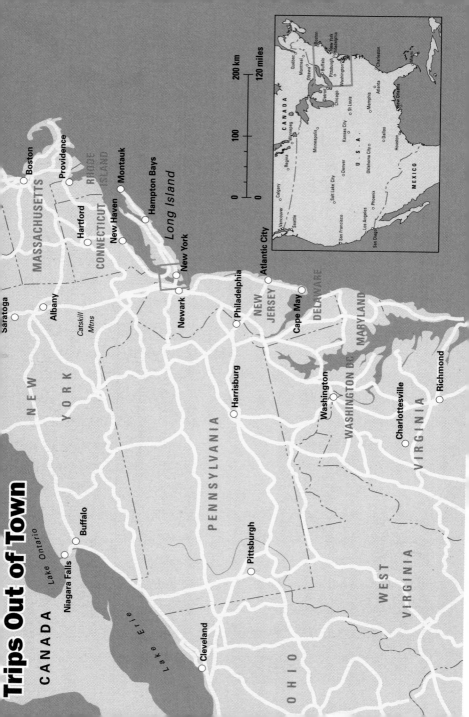

The Wright stuff: Take a trip to the Smithsonian's National Air and Space Museum in Washington, D.C., to view the brothers' original flyer, which took off on December 17, 1903.

(may I cut in?)

©1998 AT&T

Reservations at seven. Sitter's got strep. Use AT&T Wireless to tell Dad, "Hold a cozy table for three."

It's all within your reach.

1 800 IMAGINE® or www.att.com

Manhattan
Subway Map

MTA New York City Transit

June 1998
©1998 New York City Transit Authority Unauthorized duplication prohibited

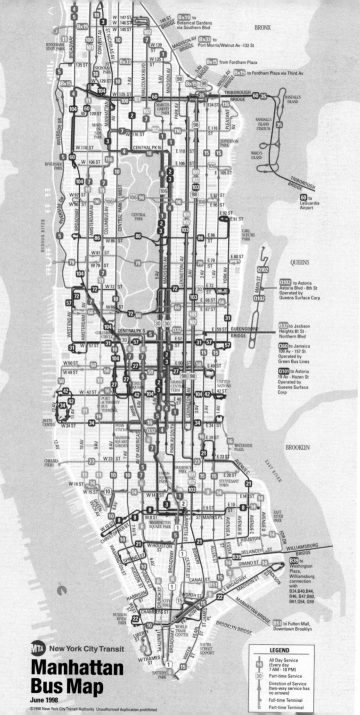

New York City Transit

Manhattan
Bus Map

June 1998

©1998 New York City Transit Authority. Unauthorized duplication prohibited.

TimeOut New York Guide Please let us know what you think.

About this guide...

1. How useful did you find the following sections?

	Very	Fairly	Not very
In Context	☐	☐	☐
Sightseeing	☐	☐	☐
NY By Neighborhood	☐	☐	☐
Accommodations	☐	☐	☐
Eating & Drinking	☐	☐	☐
Shopping & Services	☐	☐	☐
Arts & Entertainment	☐	☐	☐
Trips Out of Town	☐	☐	☐
Directory	☐	☐	☐

2. Did you travel to New York:

Alone? ☐   With partner? ☐
As part of a group? ☐   With children? ☐

3. How long was your trip to New York?

Less than three days ☐
Three days to one week ☐
One to two weeks ☐
Over two weeks ☐

4. Did you visit any other destinations?
If so, which?

_____
_____
_____
_____

5. Is there anything you'd like us to cover in greater depth?

_____
_____
_____
_____
_____
_____
_____
_____

Florence & Tuscany Guide	☐
Las Vegas Guide	☐
Lisbon Guide	☐
London Guide	☐
Los Angeles Guide	☐
Madrid Guide	☐
Miami Guide	☐
Moscow Guide	☐
New Orleans Guide	☐
Paris Guide	☐
Prague Guide	☐
Rome Guide	☐
San Francisco Guide	☐
Sydney Guide	☐
Film Guide	☐
Kids Out magazine	☐
London Eating & Drinking Guide	☐
London Pubs & Bars Guide	☐
London Visitors' Guide	☐
ici Londres	☐
Paris Eating & Drinking Guide	☐
Paris Free Guide	☐
London Shopping Guide	☐
Student Guide	☐
Book of Country Walks	☐
Book of London Walks	☐
Book of New York Short Stories	☐
Time Out New York magazine	☐
Time Out Roma	☐
Time Out Diary	☐
www.timeout.co.uk	☐

About other Time Out publications...

6. Have you bought/used other Time Out publications? If so, which ones?

Time Out magazine ☐

City Guides:
Amsterdam Guide	☐
Barcelona Guide	☐
Berlin Guide	☐
Brussels Guide	☐
Budapest Guide	☐
Dublin Guide	☐
Edinburgh Guide	☐

About you...

(BLOCK CAPITALS PLEASE)

7. Title (Mrs, Miss etc)

First name: _____

Surname: _____

Address: _____

_____

Postcode: _____

8. Year of birth:

_____

9. Sex: Male ☐   Female ☐

10. Are you:

employed full-time ☐   employed part-time ☐
self-employed ☐   unemployed ☐
student ☐   home-maker ☐

11. At the moment do you earn:

under £10,000	☐
over £10,000 and up to £14,999	☐
over £15,000 and up to £19,999	☐
over £20,000 and up to £24,999	☐
over £25,000 and up to £39,999	☐
over £40,000 and up to £49,999	☐
over £50,000	☐

☐ Please tick here if you do not want to receive information on other Time Out products.
If you prefer to return this in an envelope, please use the FREEPOST address overleaf.

Time Out Guides

FREEPOST 20 (WC3187)
LONDON
W1E 0DQ